CURRICULUM-BASED ASSESSMENT *AND* PROGRAMMING

THIRD EDITION

JOYCE S. CHOATE
Northeast Louisiana University

BRIAN E. ENRIGHT
University of North Carolina at Charlotte

LAMOINE J. MILLER
Northeast Louisiana University

JAMES A. POTEET
Ball State University

THOMAS A. RAKES
University of Memphis

ALLYN AND BACON
Boston   London   Toronto   Sydney   Tokyo   Singapore

Series Editor: Ray Short
Editorial Assistant: Christine M. Shaw
Marketing Manager: Ellen Mann
Editorial-Production Administrator: Annette Joseph
Editorial-Production Service: Colophon Production Service
Composition Buyer: Linda Cox
Cover Administrator: Linda Knowles
Cover Designer: Suzanne Harbison

Copyright © 1995, 1992 by Allyn & Bacon
A Simon & Schuster Company
Needham Heights, MA 02194

The first edition, by Joyce S. Choate, Toni Z. Bennett, Brian E. Enright, Lamoine J. Miller, James A. Poteet, and Thomas A. Rakes, was published under the title *Assessing and Programming Basic Curriculum Skills,* © 1987 by Allyn and Bacon, Inc.

 This book is printed on recycled, acid-free paper.

Library of Congress Cataloging-in-Publication Data

Curriculum-based assessment and programming / Joyce S. Choate . . . [et al.]. — 3rd ed.
     p.   cm.
    Includes bibliographical references and indexes.
    ISBN 0–205–16174–X
    1. Curriculum planning—Case studies.   2. Curriculum-based assessment.   3. Individualized instruction.   4. Language arts—Ability testing.   5. Mathematical ability—Testing.   I. Choate, Joyce S.
LB1570.A795   1995
375′.001–dc20   94–28845
                                             CIP

PRINTED IN THE UNITED STATES OF AMERICA

10 9 8 7 6 5 4 3 2 1   99 98 97 96 95 94

CONTENTS

PREFACE

PURPOSE

Curriculum-Based Assessment and Programming, Third Edition, is designed for teachers, prospective teachers, and educational diagnosticians who are concerned with assessing the skills and performances of students at risk and students with disabilities in the basic academic areas *and* improving the quality of instruction. Although the approach presented focuses primarily on the assessment and programming of students with learning problems, it is equally appropriate for students whose achievement is average or even above average. Utilizing the general education curriculum as the axis of all assessment and programming activities, step-by-step procedures are introduced to identify curricular components, to assess individual students' needs, and to deliver a personalized educational program based on the assessed needs. The intent is to enable the reader to translate sound assessment and instructional theory into effective classroom practices.

THE NEW EDITION

Much has been written about curricula, assessment, and instruction since the publication of previous editions of this book. Various curriculum-based assessment models have emerged and been categorized to explain their differences. Based upon our conviction that useful assessment is so interwoven with instruction that it defies separation, our assessment model is distinguished again by its inclusion of what most others only imply—the direct link to programming with specific suggestions for application. Thus, the central thesis of the book remains the same, but with added clarity. Also retained are the basic organization, the major topics, and much of the content.

This third edition is intended to present practical assessment and programming procedures appropriate for personalized instruction that will empower students to function effectively in the twenty-first century. All topics have been updated to reflect current research and affairs. Inclusive education, increased holistic and integrative learning, adaptations for diverse learners, and authentic instruction are among the curricular changes addressed. Incorporated in discussions throughout the book are subtle shifts among the interrelationships of curricular components: integrating skills, topics, and literature across the curriculum; applying subject-area skills as strategies for accomplishing grander and more authentic goals; and using technology effectively as a powerful study strategy across the curriculum. The supportive roles of social skills and study strategies in academic curricula are again emphasized and expanded. Authentic, alternative, and performance assessment techniques are presented, discussed, and then specifically applied to each subject area. Collaboration among professionals, parents, and students, as well as application-level tasks reflecting real-world demands, are advocated for both assessment and programming. The resequencing of chapters reflects a more holistic approach. However, a skill-based approach predominates because it permits the targeted assessment and programming needed by special students. Based on the experiences and suggestions of teachers who follow the model, additional problems and some solutions are identified, thereby strengthening the practicality of the curriculum-based assessment and programming process and the book itself.

Organization

The book is divided into two main parts: foundations and implementation. The first three chapters provide the foundation for the curriculum-based assessment and programming approach. Chapter 1 introduces the basic skills of curricula for elementary achievement levels. It also includes an overview of the roles formal and informal assessment play in making instructional decisions and introduces the rationale for using curriculum-based assessment. Some important principles of assessment conclude the discussions. Chapter 2 establishes the basis for the curricular focus of the book. The major functions of the general education curriculum and the development of curricula are discussed and some important programming principles are presented. Chapter 3 presents the curriculum-based assessment/programming model for planning and providing cyclical instruction based on ongoing diagnosis. Included are explanations for the three levels of assessment tasks and programming incorporated into the model: developmental, corrective, and maintenance.

Chapters 4 through 10 focus on implementation. Chapter 4 addresses teacher expectations, students' learning style, school adjustment behaviors, and observational assessment. The role of social skills in the support curriculum is emphasized with a few suggestions offered for improving students' social behaviors. Chapters 5 through 10 constitute the subject-specific chapters: Reading Word Recognition, Reading Comprehension, Written Expression, Spelling and Handwriting, Basic Mathematics, and Content and Study Strategies. With the exception of study strategies, these are all subjects in which students are typically graded or evaluated. Each content chapter presents a similar format. First, a detailed analysis of the typical curriculum and the role of each skill and task is presented. Second, suggestions for indirect and direct assessment of each task are given. Finally, strategies for teaching and programming each described task are recommended.

Chapter 11 offers a synthesis of the assessment and programming procedures and some practical suggestions for implementation. Included in the appendices are skill objectives and sample tests for every described task in each subject area, and the references are provided in a complete, indexed listing.

Features

This book emphasizes the bond between curriculum-based assessment *and* curriculum-based programming. Each chapter begins with objectives for the reader and ends with a brief summary, model case study, practice cases, topics for discussion, and enrichment activities. In addition to incorporating the curriculum-based assessment/programming model throughout, each content chapter is written by someone who specializes in that particular subject area. Included are methods and instruments useful for determining teacher and curricular expectations as well as surveys for rating students' learning styles and academic adjustment. Provided for each subject area—reading word recognition, reading comprehension, written expression, spelling, handwriting, basic mathematics, science, social studies, and study strategies (levels kindergarten through grade six)—are six major resources:

— Detailed and sequenced curriculum charts based upon typical textbook levels
— Specific suggestions for constructing tests to assess every described task
— Precise strategies for teaching every itemized task
— Teaching suggestions for learners at three different stages of learning: developmental, corrective, and maintenance
— Sample test items for every listed task
— Objectives for assessing and programming each task

Available in an instructor's manual are additional activities to supplement educators' learning and implementation. Summaries of the major points of each chapter are included as well as copy-ready charts that illustrate key concepts.

The model supporting the recommended assessment and programming activities within the context of the general education curriculum is comprehensive but concise. The suggested strategies are grounded in research and shaped by more than a decade of field testing. The included resources extend the practicality of the approach and of the book itself. In summary, this book contains the elements and resources to teach, learn, and implement curriculum-based assessment *and* programming.

ACKNOWLEDGMENTS

The content of this book reflects the inspiration and suggestions of several thousand teachers, students, and educational diagnosticians. To all who field-tested and helped to shape the final product, we are indeed grateful. We are similarly indebted to our field reviewers whose professional recommendations are incorporated in the revisions: Virginia Bauhof (Western Michigan University), and Judith S. Finkel (West Chester University). We again acknowledge the contributions of Toni Z. Bennett (Northwestern State University) in helping to launch the first edition and sharing her practical wisdom in Chapter 4. And for expert assistance, advice, and support, we thank our very special editor at Allyn and Bacon—Ray Short.

In addition, we sincerely appreciate the sustained patience, encouragement, and support of our colleagues and families. And, once again, we acknowledge the Council for Educational Diagnostic Services (CEDS), a division of the Council for Exceptional Children, the organization within which the authors met and continue to realize our sense of unity and professional purpose.

CHAPTER 1

EDUCATIONAL ASSESSMENT

JAMES A. POTEET

CHAPTER OBJECTIVES

This chapter is designed to enable the reader to:

1. List the subject content of the core, collateral, and support curricula and explain the interrelationships.
2. Define educational "assessment" and describe a model of assessment appropriate for use in both general and special education.
3. Specify the three major purposes of assessment and the assessment tools and techniques appropriate for each purpose.
4. Discuss several factors to consider in test selection, including the criteria of a good test.
5. Define curriculum-based assessment and justify five reasons for its use.

Although the twenty-first century is approaching, the basic curriculum in most schools is still the same as mentioned in the popular song by Cobb and Edwards written in 1907:

> *School days, school days, dear old golden*
> *rule days,*
> *Readin' and 'ritin' and 'rithmetic,*
> *Taught to the tune of a hickry stick,*
> *You were my queen in calico,*
> *I was your bashful barefoot beau,*
> *And you wrote on my slate,*
> *I love you Joe,*
> *When we were a couple of kids.*

Students still write "love notes," the three Rs remain as important today as they did then, and humane instructional strategies have replaced the "hickry stick." There are many students in today's schools, however, who have not acquired basic academic skills in "readin', 'ritin', and 'rithmetic." Consequently, many professional educators and parents are asking that teachers emphasize skills essential for successful living upon completion of schooling.

Students in today's schools range in ability from those who are gifted and talented to those with mental retardation. The movement for inclusion of all types of learners in general education classrooms grew from federal requirements that all students with disabilities be educated alongside students without disabilities as much as is appropriate and possible. Such placement is called the Least Restrictive Environment (LRE). *Inclusion* is a concept of education wherein all students are provided an appropriate education in the neighborhood school. Such an approach to education requires the restructuring of buildings, programs, and personal attitudes. Many professional organizations (e.g., Council for Exceptional Children, National Association of School Psychologists, National Joint Committee on Learning Disabilities, Council for Learning Disabilities, Learning Disability Association) have written policies detailing their stance on the topic of inclusion. With this national movement well under way, it is obvious that today's students represent a variety of cultures, languages, races, and ranges of learning characteristics, giving us classrooms best described as pluralistic in nature. Because of this wide range of characteristics, on any given day in any classroom, students will be achieving at different levels in the curriculum. Coordinately, the instructional needs of the students cover as wide a range as their ability and achievement levels. *The purpose of this book is to teach you how to determine which skills in your curriculum to teach your students.*

Students requiring your special attention are those not learning at the level expected by parents and teachers. These underachievers are found in general education classrooms, in remedial and tutorial classes, and in special education programs. *The approach presented in this text for identifying skills to teach is appropriate for all students, including those with special instructional needs, regardless of their school placement.*

This first chapter introduces you to the contents of the curriculum as used throughout this book, and presents a viewpoint of assessment. Chapter 2 teaches you about curriculum development and how to personalize the curriculum for each student. In Chapters 2, 3, and 4, you will learn how to personalize your assessment of the basic curriculum skills and plan for personalized programming for each student. Chapters 5 through 10 present personalized assessment and programming techniques for the core curriculum

of reading, written expression, and arithmetic; for the collateral curriculum of social studies and science; and for the support curriculum of spelling, handwriting, and study skills. Chapter 11 teaches you to assimilate your newly learned skills of assessment and programming to serve students with special instructional needs.

Let's begin by looking more closely at the different subjects (or content areas) in the curriculum.

THE CURRICULUM

The curriculum is that set of courses and instructional experiences offered to students. Each school system has its own curriculum usually developed by a team of teachers, school administrators, parents, and other community people. The curriculum differs from school system to school system. Often, it can differ from district to district or even from school to school within a school system. Each state has requirements and guidelines to help establish the curriculum for each school system. Some states even have a list of approved textbooks by content areas of the curriculum.

Dempster (1993) notes that the usual curriculum is "dangerously overstuffed," and that we would be wise to reduce the size of the curriculum so that effective teaching principles can take place, for example, building frequent distributed practice into instructional time. However, we must not remove those subject areas necessary to prepare students for successful employment. While knowledge of basic school subjects is expected by employers, it is the *use* of this knowledge to solve problems and communicate with others that is being demanded on the job (White, 1992). For those students with severe disabilities, a functional curriculum has been developed wherein age-appropriate and useful skills are taught; also, an ecological curriculum has been designed that emphasizes the relationship between the environment and the skills necessary to be successful within that environment (Rainforth, York, & Macdonald, 1992).

The Core Curriculum

Today's curriculum specialists are likely to express the three Rs (readin', 'ritin', and 'rithmetic) as reading (word recognition and comprehension), written expression, and arithmetic (computation and problem solving). These three areas constitute the *core* of the curriculum, since all other skills and subject matter are built upon them (see Figure 1.1).

Language Development and the Core Curriculum

Two of the core curriculum skills, reading and written expression, are acquired as language develops. Language development begins at birth and continues throughout one's life. Therefore, genetic endowment, sensory and physical conditions, environmental factors, and schooling all affect the quality and extent of language development. Language development, in turn, affects achievement of curriculum skills. Figure 1.2 illustrates the components of language development.

Language permits communication with each other and with ourselves. Initially, we develop an inner language of concepts and ideas before learning to communicate with others. As maturity develops, so does listening and understanding and then speaking. Later, in school, the student learns to read and understand what others have written and to write for others to read. Language development, then, is both receptive (getting from others) and expressive (giving to others). This getting and giving is the interchange of the communication process.

FIGURE 1.1   The Core Curriculum

READING
      Word Recognition
      Comprehension
WRITTEN EXPRESSION
ARITHMETIC
      Computation
      Problem Solving

FIGURE 1.2   Components of Language Development

[RECEPTIVE]	[EXPRESSIVE]
(4) Reading	(5) Written Expression
(2) Listening	(3) Oral Expression
(1) Inner Language	

Because of the importance of language in daily living, it is easy to understand why reading and written expression are two of the core curriculum skills. Mastery of these two skills is necessary for both understanding and expressing knowledge in other subjects within the curriculum and for purposeful communication in and out of school. Reading and written expression along with spelling are often called the language arts. Skills in listening and speaking are often added to the language arts curriculum.

Contemporary instruction in language arts teaches the separate components of language as a related and integrated whole (see Figure 1.3). This *whole language* approach serves to unify the components instead of fragmenting their development into unrelated bits and pieces of achievement. The term *construction of meaning* is related to how children learn the language arts. As children construct their own meaning, they comprehend what they read more easily. According to Hennings (1992), children actively construct meaning by using their prior knowledge about the reading topic, anticipating and predicting, questioning and answering, visualizing, inferring, generalizing, comparing and contrasting, using related examples, organizing facts and concepts, feeling, thinking critically and creatively, and self-monitoring their understanding and reactions. She further points out that the reader uses prior knowledge, knowledge of language structure, knowledge of text structure and organization, and metacognition to aid in the interpretation of text.

Walmsley and Adams (1993) interviewed teachers currently using the whole-language ap-

FIGURE 1.3   Components of Whole Language Instruction

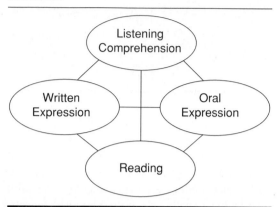

proach to teach literacy. The teachers noted that whole language instruction (a) is more demanding than traditional basal reading instruction, since it generally emphasizes child-centered rather than teacher-dominated instruction, opposes direct teaching of isolated skills, and replaces the basal reader with trade books; (b) is difficult to manage in terms of organizing the day, because there are no prepackaged sets of materials and books (like some basal programs), instruction is not teacher dominated, and covering the list of isolated skills for each grade level in the school curriculum may not be possible; and (c) is not compatible with traditional assessment, because what is taught in the whole-language classroom is not what is tested on the usual standardized test. The grapheme/phoneme relationship (phonics) should be part of the whole-language curriculum because, along with semantics and syntax, it is one of the cues used to understand text. Since these three cues are available in authentic reading settings, they should be taught so they can be used (Mills, O'Keefe, & Stephens, 1992).

When students with mild disabilities are in whole-language programs, direct instruction must be provided to them in all components of the program. Oral and written language, as well as thinking skills, should be part of their instructional program according to Westby (1992). She lists names of children's books appropriate for each topic of instruction in a whole-language program. A variety of instructional techniques, appropriate explicit instruction, direct instruction in the alphabetic code, and direct teaching of basic reading skills are required for learning-disabled students and those with severe reading disabilities who are in whole-language programs (Lerner, Cousin, & Richek, 1992; Mather, 1992).

Arithmetic and the Core Curriculum

Although the third core curriculum skill, arithmetic, is not part of the communication language development scheme, it is part of a larger body of information known as mathematics. Success in arithmetic requires skill in reasoning. To the extent that reasoning relies on language skills, success in language is related to success in arithmetic and mathematics. Obviously, the three core curriculum skills do not develop in isolation from each other.

The basic arithmetic skills of computation and problem solving are necessities for appropriate adaptive behaviors in everyday life. They are also prerequisite to advanced mathematical study required for the development of technology highly valued by our society. Knowledge of basic arithmetic skills, then, is an important part of the core curriculum.

The Collateral Curriculum

Although reading, written expression, and arithmetic are considered the most important basic curriculum skills, other subjects are also deemed valuable by curriculum experts, teachers, and parents. These subjects constitute the collateral curriculum of science and social studies.

With the launch of Sputnik in 1957, schools began to focus on the development of scientific knowledge for all students. That thrust to develop a command of technology has not abated. Science, then, has acquired a place in the *collateral* curriculum because of the demands of society.

Information is a highly valued commodity (Naisbitt & Aburdene, 1990). The knowledge base doubles so frequently that much current data are soon outdated. However, as the knowledge base expands, no one has yet learned how to organize, file, retrieve, or control the knowledge so that it can be used in the most efficient way. As technology increases, so does society's need for human contact. According to Naisbitt (1982), the more "high tech" available, the more "high touch" needed; "humanness" must not be forgotten. The decade of the 1990s will be the turning point toward a society of partnerships, especially between men and women (Aburdene & Naisbitt, 1992). We would like to add to that partnership teachers, parents, and students. To teach the value of collaboration for the future partnerships and to maintain the balance of humanities and science, social studies is included in the collateral curriculum with science. The collateral curriculum of science and social studies supplements the core curriculum of the three Rs.

The Support Curriculum

To be successful in the basic curriculum skills, one must have certain support skills. Classroom learning is supported by skillful social functioning. Recognizing and conforming to expected behaviors, monitoring and controlling one's own behavior, and interacting positively with peers and teachers facilitate learning and performance across subjects and curricula. Because of their important role in supporting academics, social skills are considered in this book as an integral part of the academic curriculum.

Written expression characterized by misspelled words does not effectively communicate its message. Many people view correct spelling as the mark of an educated person. Spelling is taught from the time the student first begins to print words. Spelling, too, has become a vital support skill as part of the school curriculum.

Similarly, in order to communicate effectively in writing, one must have legible handwriting.

Handwriting (or possibly other communication systems such as braille, typing, or computers) is an important support skill to written expression. The writing of a scholar may reflect profound thoughts that can change the course of human life, but if the writing cannot be read, it will be of no value because the information has not been communicated.

Also, educators have investigated the processes required to learn the basic curriculum skills and have identified certain study strategies beneficial to the student. Consequently, study strategies are an important part of the support curriculum. The use of these study strategies makes learning more efficient and content more easily remembered. Computer literacy and word-processing skills have become important strategies to prepare students for the next century.

The Enrichment Curriculum

The academics are important to foster intellectual and cognitive growth. However, our society values the whole person. Educators offer additional studies through the enrichment curriculum which enhance the lifestyle of students. These skills help develop appropriate leisure-time activities. The creative arts and physical education comprise this enrichment curriculum.

The Basic Curriculum Skills

Educators have determined the skills required for students to become self-sufficient, productive, and contributing members of society. These curriculum skills are, in fact, *basic* to a well-rounded education that prepares the student to take his or her place in adult society. These *basic curriculum skills* (illustrated in Figure 1.4) are taught in the four curricula. However, because of their academic nature, the first three curricula—core, collateral, and support—are the focus of this book.

Your job is to determine which skills from the basic curriculum should be taught to each student.

FIGURE 1.4   Function of the Basic Skills in the School Curriculum

CORE CURRICULUM	COLLATERAL CURRICULUM	SUPPORT CURRICULUM	ENRICHMENT CURRICULUM
Reading	Social Studies	Social Skills	Creative Arts (Music, Art, Theatre)
Written Expression	Science	Spelling	
			Physical Education
Arithmetic		Handwriting Study Strategies	
FOUNDATION SUBJECTS	EXPANSION SUBJECTS	ENABLING SUBJECTS	ENHANCING SUBJECTS

To do this you will need to know which skills the student has and has not mastered. Getting this information is called assessment. ***Assessment means the process of gathering information. For teachers, assessment is conducted for the purpose of deciding which skills to teach.***

Assessment can be conducted for three major educational purposes: screening, placement, and instruction. *This text focuses primarily on assessment for the purpose of instruction.* However, it is important that you also know how assessment is used for screening and for placement since, as a teacher, you will be required to conduct assessments for all three purposes. In the remaining part of this chapter you will learn about several issues relating to assessment so that you can use the process correctly and make good decisions about teaching your students.

ASSESSMENT

This section presents a general approach to assessment. It discusses tools and techniques used for screening, determining eligibility for special education, and instruction. It presents the different types of tests and what characteristics they should have. The federal rules and regulations guiding assessment practices for students suspected of being disabled are briefly presented so that you will know the correct steps and procedures to follow. The major emphasis of this section is on assessment for the purposes of

instruction, using the curriculum as the main focus for the assessment. This section prepares you for Chapters 5 through 10, which teach curriculum-based assessment procedures for eight subject areas in the basic curriculum.

An Individualized Approach to Assessment

"*Assessment* is the process of gathering information, using appropriate tools and techniques" (Hargrove & Poteet, 1984, p. 5). When assessing, you must always remember that you are dealing with a whole human being who is more important than the skills you are trying to assess. Give consideration to the many different aspects of the student's life that influence behaviors and functioning in the classroom. Knowledge of the student's home situation, family expectations, racial and cultural mores, personal interests, and numerous other factors all contribute to your ability to make sense of the total person. A *life-skills* orientation to both curriculum and assessment focuses on the needs of adolescents as they approach maturity. Current skill needs and future life demands are valuable components to consider for students who have had learning difficulties in school for more than ten years (Polloway, Patton, Epstein, & Smith, 1993).

With all these points in mind, consider some assessment strategies that enable you to pinpoint the learning needs of your students. The approach to assessment that relies on three basic

CHAPTER ONE   EDUCATIONAL ASSESSMENT   **7**

diagnostic skills is taken from Hargrove and Poteet (1984).

Assessment strategies use the skills of diagnostic looking, diagnostic asking, and diagnostic listening. The word *diagnostic* means a process to try to explain the *cause* of whatever is being *diagnosed*. *Diagnostic looking* is the observation of a student's behavior and an attempt to explain why a particular behavior occurs. It involves the critical investigation of anything that can be analyzed visually, such as worksheets, written responses, etc. *Diagnostic asking* is the use of questioning to reveal possible reasons for error patterns or to pinpoint answers to the teacher's diagnostic questions. The teacher may develop a hypothesis about the cause of the student's lack of achievement or observed error patterns. In some instances, the causes relate to factors not immediately seen, such as prerequisite skills or possibly a delay in language development. As information is acquired, the hypothesis may be either accepted or rejected and other hypotheses developed. *Diagnostic listening* is the careful evaluation of what the student actually says compared to what the student may imply by his or her responses. The teacher or diagnostician uses these three assessment skills to determine as many learning characteristics about the student as possible. Some of these characteristics you should identify through your assessment are given in Figure 1.5.

FIGURE 1.5 Learning Characteristics to Determine Through Assessment

1. Curriculum skills known and unknown
2. Preferred environment for learning (large/small group, one-to-one, formal/informal setting)
3. Preferred Instructional personnel (teacher, peer/cross-age tutor, paraprofessional, parent)
4. Modality preferences for learning, responding, and practice (see Keefe, 1979)
5. Thinking style (approach to the task, learning and memory strategies used)
6. Effect, if any, of emotions on learning

Attention must be given to your awareness of the cultural diversity of your students, especially during assessment. Many traditional standardized, norm-referenced tests have been labeled as biased against minority cultures and races. For example, to avoid bias with gifted and talented African American learners, Patton (1992) gives a list of appropriate assessment tools and techniques. A list of assessment instruments for Spanish and Chinese students is provided by O'Connor and Rotatori (1987).

For those students with limited English proficiency (LEP) who are being assessed to determine eligibility for special education, Ortiz and Wilkinson (1991) recommend the use of curriculum-based assessment of the students' English-as-a-second-language (ESL) program *and* native-language skills to validate test results from norm-referenced tests, which are usually administered in standard American English. Low performance on the English standardized test is not sufficient to declare a student with LEP eligible for special education. Jacobs (1991) discusses the difficulties in the assessment of students from diverse cultures. (Her ethnographic research focuses on the assessment of four Hmong students.)

Harry (1992) points out that there have been several court cases dealing with inappropriate assessment of students from non-English-speaking backgrounds, specifically Hispanics and Native Americans. Tests were in English, and no measure of adaptive behavior was conducted. She discusses assessment problems with second-language and culturally diverse students, particularly Hispanic, Asian Pacific, Native American, and African American students. Garcia (1994) suggests that we examine our own fundamental values, attitudes, dispositions, and belief systems as we interact with diverse students. Such introspection is especially important to help ensure that our assessment strategies remain professional, unbiased, and appropriate for the purpose.

When you conduct an assessment, you use different types of assessment tools and techniques. (See Figure 1.6.) Specific instruments and their evaluations can be found in *The Eleventh Mental*

FIGURE 1.6   Assessment Tools and Techniques

1. TESTS
   - ▬ Formal (Standardized, Norm-referenced)
   - ▬ Informal (Teacher-made; Published inventories, checklists, etc.)
   - ▬ Criterion-referenced (Mastery of skill determined by attaining a criterion usually established by the teacher [Hofmeister & Preston, 1981; Kuhs, et al., 1983; Linn, et al., 1984]. Percentage of the reference group getting correct answers is given as a p value for each item.) Some tests considered as criterion-referenced:
     - ▪ KeyMath Revised (Connolly, 1988)
     - ▪ Stanford Diagnostic Reading Test (Karlsen & Gardner, 1984)
     - ▪ Stanford Diagnostic Mathematics Test (Beatty et al., 1984)
     - ▪ Fountain Valley Teacher Support System (1975)

2. RATING SCALES
   - ▬ Rater marks descriptive words, sentences, phrases to describe the student
   - ▬ Quick, clear, and easy to understand and offer valuable adjunct information to other tools and techniques (Kerlinger, 1986) Some examples:
     - ▪ Checklist of Written Expression (Poteet, 1980)
     - ▪ Behavior Rating Profile-2 (Brown & Hammill, 1990)
     - ▪ Mooney Problem Check List (Mooney, 1950)
     - ▪ Pupil Rating Scale Revised (Myklebust, 1981)
     - ▪ Academic Adjustment (in Chapter 4)

3. INTERVIEWS
   - ▬ Published or teacher made; may be structured or open
   - ▬ Suggestions for interviewing teachers (presented later in this book)
     - ▪ Vineland Adaptive Behavior Scales—Interview Edition (Sparrow, Balla, & Cicchetti, 1985)
     - ▪ AAMR Adaptive Behavior Scales—School Edition (Nihira, Lambert, & Leland, 1993)

4. OBSERVATION
   - ▬ The target behavior is observed and recorded in some manner
   - ▬ Following systematic observation, specific approaches to deal with behavior given by Sparzo and Poteet (1989)
   - ▬ Examples of charting (*Journal of Applied Behavior Analysis*)
   - ▬ Instruction for charting (Cooper, 1981; Hall, 1983; Kerr, & Nelson, 1983; Wolery, Bailey Jr., & Sugai, 1988)

5. CLINICAL JUDGMENT
   - ▬ An informed professional opinion based on training, experience, and knowledge about similar situations (Hargrove & Poteet, 1984)
   - ▬ Useful with very young or mentally retarded children
   - ▬ Recommended by the Learning Disabilities Association in their 1990 position paper; clinical judgment to be based on information from several sources and used in the diagnosis of specific learning disabilities.

Measurements Yearbook (Kramer & Conoley, 1992) as well as in earlier editions. By being familiar with several assessment tools and techniques you can select those that best suit the purposes of your assessment.

To be a professional educator, it is important that you have certain knowledge and skills relating to the assessment process. As outlined in Figures 1.7 and 1.8, the Council for Educational Diagnostic Services (CEDS) recommends specific assessment knowledge and skills as being essential for teachers at two levels: beginning teachers and master teachers. Based on a nationwide validation survey by Walker and Bruno (1992), the standards for beginning teachers also have been incorporated into the Council for

FIGURE 1.7   Knowledge and Skills Needed by Beginning Teachers in the Area of Assessment: Recommendations by the Council for Educational Diagnostic Services

1. Knowledge of Basic Terminology
   (fundamental terms and concepts used in assessment)

2. Knowledge of Required Credentials for Competent Assessment
   (necessary training and qualifications to administer instruments in a professionally competent manner)

3. Knowledge of the Multidisciplinary Approach to Decision Making
   (role of assessment in multidisciplinary decision making requires performing required tasks with competence, professional responsibility, and integrity)

4. Knowledge of the Proper Handling of Confidential Information
   (understanding of federal and state guidelines regarding confidential records and assessment information)

5. Knowledge and Skills in the Use of Assessment Tools and Techniques
   (use of rating scales and questionnaires, interviews, direct observations, tests—informal and criterion-referenced—work samples, anecdotal records, and clinical judgment for making data-based evaluations of instruction and for program planning and modifications)

6. Knowledge and Skills in Specific Areas of Assessment
   (skilled in assessing general achievement and basic specific academic areas such as reading, written expression, and arithmetic, as well as learning styles)

7. Skills in Establishing Positive Personal Relations
   (good student/examiner rapport and professional collaboration are vital skills for beginning teachers)

8. Skills in Interpreting and Using Test Results
   (while not required to be an expert in using formal standardized assessment instruments, the beginning teacher must be able to interpret their results and implications for instructional planning)

Source: CEDS Communiqué, 19 (3), 1–2, Spring 1992. Adapted and reprinted by permission.

Exceptional Children's core competencies for beginning special education teachers (Swan & Sirvis, 1992).

The Use of Tests

All professionals who use tests, including classroom teachers, must consider principles of ethics and competency. The American Psychological Association (APA) has several publications concerning the ethics and competency of people who use tests in their profession. Generally, the test user must be well trained in the administration, scoring, and interpretation of the tests used. Some individually administered tests require specialized training. Group administered tests are usually designed so that teachers who have had a course in tests and measurements can administer, score, and interpret them with minimal preparation. To use a test for which you are not trained is clearly unprofessional and a breach of ethics. Some popular standardized norm-referenced tests are listed in Figure 1.9.

Factors in Test Selection

When choosing a test, it is first necessary to know what characteristics make a test acceptable. Many professionals consider the use of unacceptable or inappropriate tests unethical. The most respected source for acceptable test characteristics is the *Standards for Educational and Psychological Testing* (American Psychological Association, 1985). This booklet is the product of many people belonging to three professional organizations concerned with testing: The American Educational Research Association, The American

FIGURE 1.8   Knowledge and Skills Needed by Master Teachers in the Area of Assessment: Recommendations of the Council for Educational Diagnostic Services

1. Knowledge of Basic Terminology
   (fundamental terms and concepts used in assessment)

2. Knowledge of Legal Issues and Professional Standards
   (clear understanding of legal guidelines, ethical issues, professional responsibility and standards, and current assessment issues)

3. Knowledge of the Multidisciplinary Approach to Decision Making
   (role of assessment in multidisciplinary decision making requires performing required tasks with competence, professional responsibility, and integrity)

4. Knowledge and Skills in Using Proper Procedures
   (understanding of and skills in appropriate procedures for referral, assessment, and classification of students)

5. Knowledge and Skills in the Selection and Use of Assessment Tools and Techniques
   (understanding of and skills in appropriate use of assessment approaches and procedures, selection of appropriate instruments to answer assessment questions, use of assessment information to develop diagnostic hypotheses and select procedures to test those hypotheses, and selection and effective use of rating scales and questionnaires, interviews, direct observations, tests—norm-referenced and curriculum-based—work samples, anecdotal records, and clinical judgment)

6. Knowledge and Skills in Specific Areas of Assessment
   (understanding of and skills in assessing general achievement and basic foundation subjects, such as reading, oral language, written expression, and arithmetic, as well as learning styles for instructional planning)

7. Skills in Establishing Positive Personal Relations
   (ability to establish good student/examiner rapport and effectively collaborate with other professionals to ensure appropriate placement and services for students)

8. Skills in Interpreting and Using Assessment Results
   (skills in organizing assessment information for effective IEPs, synthesizing data for appropriate adjustments, maintaining records, and collecting data to monitor, evaluate, and modify programs)

Source: CEDS Communiqué, 20 (3), 3, Spring 1993. Adapted and reprinted by permission.

Psychological Association, and the National Council on Measurement in Education. Anyone who uses tests should be familiar with the content of this booklet.

There are numerous sources that can be consulted which describe published tests, give the technical and psychometric properties of the tests, cite research studies on the tests, and provide an opinion about their value. Figure 1.10 lists some of these. Taylor (1993) presents a summary and review of research findings for many tests used in education. Useful critiques of many tests are given by Luftig (1989). His text can serve as an excellent resource for the practicing teacher and

diagnostician. Lists of tests that are appropriate for a variety of educational purposes are given by McLoughlin and Lewis (1994) and by Salvia and Ysseldyke (1995).

Potential cultural biases and linguistic distortions in standardized tests are also important factors to consider when selecting tests. Lupi and Woo (1989) offer suggestions for modifying and eliminating these problems when assessing limited English proficient students of East Asian origin. Similar concerns are expressed by Figueroa (1989) when testing Hispanic and other linguistic-minority or bilingual students. Clearly, when selecting a test, factors related to its pur-

FIGURE 1.9   Popular Standardized, Norm-Referenced Tests

Intelligence

Individually Administered:

Wechsler Intelligence Scale for Children III (Wisc-III)

Stanford Binét Intelligence Scale (4th Edition)

Slosson Intelligence Test (Revised)

Achievement

Individually Administered:

Brigance Comprehensive Inventory of Basic Skills

Enright Inventory of Basic Arithmetic Skills

Kaufman Test of Educational Achievement

KeyMath (Revised)

Peabody Individual Achievement Test (Revised)

Wechsler Individual Achievement Test

Wide Range Achievement Test (Revised)

Wookcock Reading Mastery Test (Revised)

Group Administered:

California Achievement Tests

Iowa Tests of Basic Skills

Metropolitan Achievement Tests

Stanford Achievement Tests

Intelligence and achievement

Individually Administered:

Kaufman Assessment Battery for Children

Woodcock-Johnson Psycho-Educational Battery (Revised)

pose and use and the characteristics of students who will be given the test must be given careful consideration.

Criteria of a Good Test

A good test is one that best meets the purpose of the assessment. While there are different opinions about what constitutes a good test, most professionals would agree that it should have the following five characteristics:

1. Acceptable technical characteristics
   a. Validity
   b. Reliability
2. Easy to administer
3. Easy to score
4. Not too time-consuming
5. Pleasant for the student
   a. Interesting format
   b. Variety of types of items

A few comments about validity and reliability are appropriate here because they are such important variables to consider in selecting a test.

Validity.   Test validity is the most important characteristic for any test to have according to the 1985 *Standards for Educational and Psychological Testing.* Obviously, if a test does not measure what it is supposed to measure, it should not be used for that purpose. For instance, one would

FIGURE 1.10   Some Sources of Information about Tests

- *CEDS Communiqué* (Council for Educational Diagnostic Services Newsletter, serial editions)
- *A Consumer's Guide to Tests in Print* (Hammill, Brown, & Bryant, 1992)
- *Directory of Psychological Tests in the Sport and Exercise Sciences* (Ostrow, 1992)
- *The Eleventh Mental Measurements Yearbook* (Kramer & Conoley, 1992; also earlier editions)
- *The ETS Test Collection Catalog* (Test Collection, Educational Testing Service)
  Vol. 1 (1986) Achievement Tests & Measurement Devices
  Vol. 2 (1988) Vocational Tests and Measurement Devices
  Vol. 3 (1989) Tests for Special Populations
  Vol. 4 (1990) Cognitive, Aptitude, and Intelligence Tests
  Vol. 5 (1991) Aptitude Tests
  Vol. 6 (1992) Affective Measures and Personality Tests
- *Test Critiques* (Keyser & Sweetland, 1993, serial editions)

not use the Peabody Picture Vocabulary Test—Revised (Dunn & Dunn, 1981), which asks a student to point to one of four pictures to represent the stimulus word spoken by the examiner, to measure general intelligence. This test, however, could be used to measure comprehension of a list of words (vocabulary) spoken by an examiner.

Hofmeister and Preston (1981) note that tests are only valid for certain purposes such as screening, placement, program planning and evaluation, and progress reporting. These purposes should be kept in mind when selecting a test.

There are three basic types of validity: construct validity, criterion validity, and content validity. Figure 1.11 illustrates the questions answered by these types of validity.

You will want to select a test that will give a consistent indication of skill mastery. In other words, you want the test to be reliable, another important characteristic to consider when selecting a test.

Reliability. Test reliability is determined by correlating two sets of responses. The statistical relationships of these two sets of responses is expressed as a correlation coefficient. The coefficient is a number that can range from -1.00 through +1.00. A reliability coefficient of +.93 is very high while a coefficient of +.26 is rather low. The coefficient is an indication of the degree of relationship between the two sets of measures. For example, if scores are *consistently* high (or

low) on one set of responses *and* high (or low) on the second set of responses, the relationship (and the correlation coefficient) will be high and positive. Likewise, if scores are *sometimes* high on one set of responses and low on the other, the relationship (and the correlation coefficient) will be low.

When responses from one half of a test are correlated with responses from the other half, *split-half* reliability is measured. This type of reliability indicates the relation of a student's performance on the beginning of the test with performance on the ending of the test. Split-half reliability can also be obtained by correlating the odd versus the even items.

With *test re-test* reliability, scores from the first administration of a test are correlated with scores from the same test administered about two weeks later. A high correlation indicates that the student's responses are reliable (consistent) over this period of time. A test that is highly reliable has less "error"; therefore, we can be reasonably sure that the student's obtained score is a true measure of the student's skills. However, when a test is repeatedly given to the same student, the score will reflect a "practice effect" in which the student remembers the test item (and the answer given previously) on the repeat administrations of the test. Under these conditions, the score will be higher than what it normally would be.

Professionals differ on what they consider to be high or acceptable levels of reliability. Nunnally (1967) notes that when making decisions about individuals, the reliability coefficient should be at least +.95 and unacceptable if below +.90. Many tests used to make decisions about individual students do not have a reliability level this high. The choice should be to use tests with reliabilities that are as close to these recommended levels as possible (+.90 or above) or to use some other equally appropriate assessment tool or technique such as informal or teacher-made tests. In general, select those assessment tools and techniques that are valid and reliable and are best suited for specific assessment purposes.

FIGURE 1.11   Types of Validity

1. CONSTRUCT VALIDITY

   How accurately does the test measure the underlying theoretical assumptions? (Does the intelligence test really measure intelligence?)

2. CRITERION (PREDICTIVE) VALIDITY

   How accurately does the test predict a score on another test?

3. CONTENT VALIDITY

   How accurately does the test measure what was taught (the content of instruction)?

THREE PURPOSES OF ASSESSMENT

There are three primary educational purposes or levels of assessment: screening, determining eligibility for special education, and instruction (Hargrove & Poteet, 1984). These levels serve distinct purposes, and each level suggests the type of assessment tools and techniques to use.

Level I—Screening

Screening activities, Level I, are those procedures used for the purpose of distinguishing target students from others. The primary assessment tool used at this level is the formal, standardized, often group-administered test. Someone must decide the cut-off score that distinguishes the target students from the others. When the target students are those at high risk, they are typically given additional tests to pinpoint the areas of suspected problems.

In addition to tests, rating scales are often used as part of the screening process. The teacher's or parent's opinions about the student's behaviors are noted on the scale. As with tests, a cut-off point must be decided to determine which students are to receive further assessment. In addition to tests and rating scales, observation is sometimes used. With observation, a certain frequency of behaviors might be used to decide if additional assessment should be conducted.

The results of screening can be used in building-based teams established to solve teacher concerns prior to referring a student to the multidisciplinary team for a comprehensive evaluation. These *prereferral teams* have many names: teacher-assistance teams, teacher-support teams, student-support teams, general education intervention procedures, child-study teams, and so on. Their purpose is to review concerns reported by a teacher or parent, plan an intervention strategy, implement the plan, and evaluate its outcome. These teams have been very successful in solving problems at the building level. They save the school system time and money by not requiring the comprehensive services of other costly professionals.

Level II—Determining Eligibility for Special Education

Level II activities are those procedures conducted for the purpose of determining if a student does or does not have a disability, and, therefore, is or is not eligible for special-education programming. Activities at this level are usually inappropriate for determining instructional needs. All assessment tools and techniques are appropriate for use at this level.

Determining if a student can be categorized as having disabilities requires comparing the referred student's performance with the average performance of other students of similar age or grade level. For such comparisons, the standard score from standardized, norm-referenced tests must be used. A test is standardized when administration and scoring procedures are identical for all who use it; directions for these procedures are stated in a manual for easy reference. The test is administered to many students (usually thousands, representing all regions of the United States; both genders; and different cultural and economic levels, ages, and grades). The average scores (called "norms") for these students is determined for different age and grade groups. The raw score indicating the number of correct responses earned by a referred student is entered in a norms table to obtain a standard score; this score indicates how the student compared to the average score of the norm group for his or her age or grade. The standard scores for most tests used today have an average of 100 and a standard deviation of 15 points. These standard scores have been called "Sped" (special education) scores by Hargrove and Poteet (1984) to differentiate them from other standard scores with different means and standard deviations. Standard scores are used in statistical formulas to determine discrepancies (e.g., between scores on intelligence and achievement tests) and to determine if a discrepancy is reliable (statistically significant). Some test companies are providing computer scoring software. These programs are highly recommended, because the scoring of some of the newer tests is highly complex and conducive to many errors. Since each test has its own rules for determining the first item to administer and its own basal and ceiling scores, the examiner must take care to ensure that the raw score is correctly computed.

The most useful way to interpret results from norm-referenced tests is the percentile score, which indicates the percent of students in the norm group who scored lower than the score obtained by your student. Scores that should not be used are grade or age equivalents, because they usually give misleading information and suggest false levels of attainment (see Hargrove and Poteet, 1984, for ten "myths" concerning grade and age equivalents). Some newer tests are using appropriate procedures to establish age and grade equivalents, however. The test manual must always be consulted to determine if standardization procedures were appropriate and if these scores should or should not be used. Results from standardized, norm-referenced tests are minimally useful in determining what to teach, because the test will not reflect all that has been taught in the classroom. (Figure 1.8 lists popular standardized, norm-referenced tests.) The protocols for some newer norm-referenced tests are designed to show error analyses of test items or to illustrate certain characteristics of the items (for example, to determine if a word illustrates the CVC phonic generalization). While these approaches do provide a breakdown of item characteristics, only a curriculum-based assessment can tell whether those items actually *in the classroom curriculum* have been learned or not. Consequently, curriculum-based assessment is the best approach to determine instructional objectives.

The performance of a student with disabilities would be significantly below the average performance of nondisabled students. For example, a referred student might be considered mildly disabled if the obtained score on an IQ test is two standard deviations below the mean of the test (at the second percentile or below), and if other criteria are met.

Rating scales and/or interviews may also be used to obtain judgments of the targeted student's behaviors from parents, teachers, and other people whose opinions are valued. Interviews may be conducted with people who are familiar with the student. Parents are typically interviewed to obtain information about the student's developmental patterns and other data that may contribute to an understanding of the suspected disability. Observations are conducted in order to compare the student's behavior in the classroom and in other social settings with information obtained from other forms of assessment. Clinical judgment may be required when no valid or otherwise logical assessment tool or technique is available. In particular, in the assessment of very young children, clinical judgment may be the most appropriate technique to use.

Deciding whether a student does or does not have a disability is very serious business. There are federal and state laws and guidelines that must be used to make those decisions.

The Individuals with Disabilities Education Act (IDEA)

The *Individuals with Disabilities Education Act* (Congressional Federal Register, 1992) sets forth evaluation standards that guide all assessment practices. Everyone involved in assessment must be familiar with these standards and procedures. Of particular interest to diagnosticians are the new age-ranges covered (birth to three years, three to five years), the new categories of disabilities (autism, traumatic brain injury), and transition planning. Educators involved in assessment may need to develop new skills to cover these areas. Major points of IDEA are given in Figure 1.12.

IDEA is formerly the Education of the Handicapped Act; as of September 29, 1992, it includes Public Law (PL) 94–142, PL 99–457, PL 101–476, PL 102–173, and PL 102–119. The wording of these public laws was changed to reflect the emphasis on the individual and to replace the term "handicapped" with "disability."

FIGURE 1.12   Major Points of IDEA

1. To assure that a free, appropriate public education (FAPE) that emphasizes special education and related services designated to meet the child's unique needs is available to all children with disabilities.

2. To assure that the rights of children with disabilities and their parents or guardians are protected.

3. To assist states and localities to provide for the education of all children with disabilities.

4. To assess and ensure the effectiveness of efforts to educate children with disabilities.

5. To authorize grants to underwrite a variety of costs to states and local agencies.

6. To authorize training, research, instructional media, and early intervention services.

7. Requires an Individualized Family Services Plan for developmentally delayed infants and toddlers which includes present levels of development (physical, cognitive, speech/language, psychosocial, motor, and self-help).

8. Requires a statement of transition services needed by students 16 years or over (14 years where appropriate) to be included in the IEP.

9. Adds "autism" and "traumatic brain injury" as two new categories of disabilities.

10. Replaces the term "handicapped" with the term "disability."

Assessment activities certainly contribute to successful transition planning required by IDEA. Classroom curriculum-based assessment, vocational assessment, and ecological assessment are especially appropriate for this purpose. Curriculum-based assessment in the classroom (discussed later in this chapter) provides a record of academic skills the student has accomplished. *Vocational* assessment, on the other hand, is aimed toward understanding the student's potential and preferences for employment (NICHCY, 1993). This approach to assessment has traditionally been provided by commercial agencies that specialize in matching an individual to a job. However, a newer approach, curriculum-based

vocational assessment, focuses on the continuous performance of students within a program of study. This approach is discussed by Gajar, Goodman, and McAfee (1993). Ecological assessment studies the relationship of the student to the environment. A student is given a task, such as riding a bus to work, and is then observed to determine which parts of the task are performed successfully (NICHCY, 1993). Along a similar line is the concept of assessing the *functional* skills of individuals with severe disabilities, such as daily-living skills required in any environment. The interested reader is referred to Browder (1991), Clark and Kolstoe (1990), and to Downing and Perino (1992). Assessing *risk factors* (e.g., nature of disability, severity, temperament, social relationships, frustration tolerance, attention deficit, poverty, unemployment, family dysfunction, and divorce) and *protective* factors (e.g., communication skills, personal control, proactive approach, understanding of self, interpersonal skills, goal setting, task orientation, problem solving, perseverance, family/community support systems, networking, and use of resources) is related to functional assessment and has been advocated by Spekman, Herman, and Vogel (1993), especially as applied to learning disabilities. It seems that such an orientation could easily relate to any assessment situation.

Level III—Instruction

Level III activities determine instructional strategies to use with the targeted student. Informal inventories, teacher-made tests, and criterion-referenced tests are primarily used at this level.

It is quite likely that you will be contributing to the development of individual education programs (IEPs) for students with disabilities in either the general or the special education classroom. Because IDEA specifies that such students must be placed in the "least restrictive environment," general classroom teachers will find that these students are "mainstreamed" into their classes. As the concept of *inclusion* gains acceptance, both general and special education teachers will work together with all students in the general education classrooms for a greater portion of the school day. Special education teachers will find that the mainstreamed students will need special instruction on skills that are taught in the general curriculum. General classroom teachers must also adjust instruction to meet the needs of the low-achieving students who do not qualify for special education programs. Consequently, both general and special education teachers need a Level III assessment approach to determine the best instructional practices to use with these students.

TRADITIONAL ASSESSMENT AND ALTERNATIVE APPROACHES

Dissatisfaction with the content and use of traditional multiple-choice, norm-referenced tests has led to social, educational, and political demands that alternative approaches be developed. According to Poteet, Choate, and Stewart (1993), criticisms of traditional testing point out the limited view of student learning reflected in the test items, the unfairness to some minorities and students with disabilities, and the use of test scores to reward high achievement while distracting attention from seriously needed remedies for low-achieving schools. Other criticisms address the lack of quality control, time and expense, and the message to students that only one answer is the correct answer, even for complex situations such as the Civil War. However, probably the greatest criticism is aimed at using test results as gatekeepers, not allowing equal opportunity for all. Scores on many standardized tests are used to turn people away from employment, education, and other opportunities. When test results are used in education to determine which district, school, or teacher is "better" than others, and when the results are published in the local newspaper, the content of the test becomes the curriculum taught to the students. Instructional time is then spent memorizing lists of facts for easy recall. Time is spent taking practice tests similar to

the ones on which such decisions are made. This narrowing of the curriculum is a central point of criticism.

Educators demanded a different type of assessment that allowed students to display what they had learned in a manner teachers could use to make instructional decisions, and that reflected knowledge of real-life, real-world situations. This approach to assessment has been given many names, but *alternative assessment* is a good umbrella term.

Along with curriculum-based assessment, *performance assessment* is one of the most popular alternative-assessment terms in use today. Performance assessment has been around for several years in the vocational-education field and is beginning to be required at many local and state levels; it has replaced the traditional norm-referenced testing in some locations, notably Kentucky. There are differing definitions of a performance test, but they all imply that the person *demonstrate* knowledge and skill; the word *performance* refers to the type of response required by the task (Meyer, 1992).

The term *portfolio assessment* is actually a *system* of assessment rather than a particular type. In portfolio assessment, student work is gathered over a period of time and evaluated to indicate changes in and current levels of skill. Vermont has a statewide portfolio-assessment strategy. *Authentic* assessment focuses on real-life, real-world demands as seen in on-the job or simulated settings. Some approaches to authentic tasks are presented in Figure 1.13.

Along with the recognition of alternatives to traditional assessment is the growing awareness of a need for different responses to all forms of assessment, the alternative as well as the traditional. The three basic response levels are *selection, production,* and *application.* The traditional multiple-choice test requires a student to select the response from several available choices, one of which is correct. Tests that require short answers, fill-in-the-blanks, playing a musical instrument, giving a speech, or writing an essay are

FIGURE 1.13   Some Approaches to Authentic Performance Assessment

1. Give a speech supporting a worthy cause.
2. Give an introduction to a guest speaker.
3. Formally debate some controversial issue.
4. Give directions to some location to a stranger.
5. Give step-by-step instructions to build a model or to assemble something.
6. Tell an interesting story to children describing a trip.
7. Actively participate in a group discussion.
8. Respond orally to taped questions.
9. Write an essay on the value of art in contemporary society.
10. Write a business letter.
11. Write a piece for a local newspaper or for a newsletter.
12. Write a short story for a newsletter or magazine.
13. Write a critique of a work of art, a piece of music, a lecture, or a written work.
14. Write an interpretation of an essay by a famous writer.
15. Document the steps used in solving a problem.
16. Prepare a portfolio representing one's accomplishments and abilities.
17. Conduct an experiment using the scientific method and write the research in a formal report.

examples of a *production* response. When an assessment task requires performance or generalization of knowledge in a real-life, real-world setting or simulation, the response level is an *application* one. (Examples of these response levels are given in later chapters in this book.)

The alternative viewpoints to assessment (performance, portfolio, and authentic) and the performance levels of responses (selection, production, and application) dovetail with *curriculum-based assessment,* the major focus of this text, which is discussed in the next section.

CURRICULUM-BASED ASSESSMENT

Curriculum-based assessment (CBA) is the process of determining students' *instructional needs* within a curriculum by directly assessing specific curriculum skills. CBA originated when the first teacher decided to determine if the student learned what was taught. Since CBA is concerned with instructional needs, the assessment tools and techniques appropriate for Level III, assessment for instruction, are appropriate for use in CBA. As you recall, these techniques are primarily informal and teacher-made tests. The teacher is at the center of the assessment process by making and giving tests.

The use of standardized, norm-referenced achievement tests to determine mastery of *specific* skills in *your* curriculum is inappropriate, because many skills in your curriculum simply are not assessed by these tests. Shapiro and Derr (1990) discuss their earlier research using hypothetical data which showed that there was very little overlap between scores on four popular individual achievement tests and words taught in five popular basal reading programs.

Because of the concerns with standardized, norm-referenced tests, the appropriate procedure to determine the instructional needs of your students is *direct* assessment of the basic skills in your curriculum. For example, if your curriculum indicates that the student should be able to read at sight the 220 Dolch basic words, then you would present each of the words on a flash card and ask the student to read them. Since direct assessment leads to direct instruction, the student's instructional needs would be the unknown words on the Dolch list.

Different Approaches to Curriculum-Based Assessment

Just as there are "different ways to skin a cat," there are different ways to use curriculum-based assessment. Several of the more popular ways are presented in Figure 1.14.

FIGURE 1.14   Different Approaches to
Curriculum-Based Assessment

1985 Blankenship • Test the curriculum objectives, teach, then re-test.

1985 Deno • "Curriculum-Based Measurement" with emphasis on fluency (rate). Use short assessment tasks (probes) of 1–3 minutes for number of words read or written, words spelled correctly, problems solved.

1985 Gickling & Thompson • Measure curriculum achievement by observing academic learning time—ALT (percent of time student engages in task-related behaviors, number of items attempted, and task comprehension).

1986 Idol, Nevin, & Paolucci-Whitcomb • Classroom teachers obtain or create three test items for each curriculum skill. Use them to establish reliability of achievement.

1987 Howell & Morehead • "Curriculum-Based Evaluation." Use task analysis of academic and social skills to integrate teaching, curriculum, and evaluation (functional assessment).

1990 Salvia & Hughes • Use decision-making by analyzing the display of data collected from assessing curriculum objectives.

1990 Shapiro & Derr • Not designed to evaluate curriculum content problems. Use CBA in combination with a general behavioral consultation approach for service delivery.

1990 Tindal & Marston • Use CBA across a range of educational decisions. Recommend use of local norms. A Kindergarten Assessment pilot instrument is given.

1992 Ysseldyke, Thurlow, & Shriner • Outcome-Based Education.

1992 Choate, Enright, Miller, Poteet, & Rakes • Use the critical parts of the general education curriculum for students who are "at risk" or have mild disabilities as a basis for CBA to guide skills chosen for effective teaching practices.

The approach taken in this book is termed *Curriculum-Based Assessment and Programming (CBA/P)*. Chapter 3 provides an explanation and discussion of this model. The general characteristics of the model, which incorporate the strengths

and avoid the weaknesses of teacher-made tests mentioned by Fuchs and Fuchs (1990), are presented in Figure 1.15.

With these characteristics of CBA/P, concerns about the usefulness and meaningfulness of teacher-made tests are abated. In fact, most teachers are more likely to use CBA when the assessment reflects instruction more completely than simply counting words read or written.

CBA is generally considered a type of criterion-referenced test wherein a standard (criterion) is designated within a set of items (domain) to indicate mastery of what is being assessed. An excellent article for teachers' use of criterion-referenced testing in the classroom was written several years ago by Airasian and Madaus (1972). Swezey (1981) addresses the psychometric characteristics of validity and reliability with

FIGURE 1.15   Some Characteristics of the CBA/P Model

---

1. Use CBA/P in different settings at different times of the school day to avoid any consistently "down" time and place the student might be experiencing.

2. Assess frequently during a unit of instruction so you can make instructional changes if necessary.

3. Use a variety of student responses (selection, production, and varied responses to authentic, performance assessment tasks).

4. Use mostly BRIEF tasks (but have three alternate forms) to avoid too much time spent in creating test items.

5. Assess each skill frequently (including during the maintenance stage) to insure reliability.

6. Assess the skills actually taught to insure curriculum content validity.

7. Check on generalization of learning by using real-world assessment tasks in the real world whenever possible (checking to see if correct change was received at a fast food restaurant).

8. Show changes in student growth by frequently displaying assessment results in some form.

criterion-referenced tests and how they can be measured.

Why Use CBA?

The major reasons for using CBA are outlined in Figure 1.16. Each reason is then discussed briefly.

1. **Curriculum-based assessment helps you determine what to teach.**   In many school systems, the curriculum has been developed by school personnel and parents to represent necessary and desirable skills for students to learn. Some curricula are highly specific with instructional objectives while others are quite general and often presented as curriculum guides. The curriculum may be what is presented in an adopted textbook. Your job is to see that your students learn the curricular content. To do this, you will have to determine, through assessment, which curriculum skills, at the appropriate level for the student's age and grade, have and have not been mastered. Those skills that have *not* been mastered will receive priority for instruction.

Teachers have found that the IEP is not useful for planning day to day instruction for special education students (Dudley-Marling, 1985). Similarly, Deno (1985) noted that teachers do not use standardized tests for making decisions about daily instruction and that grade equivalent scores are unreliable and cannot be used to

show achievement growth over the period of an academic year. Assessing the basic curriculum skills seems to be the best alternative for determining what to teach. It allows the strengths and weaknesses of students to be emphasized rather than categories or labels assigned to the student (Will, 1986). To make these instructional decisions, you will have to monitor achievement frequently as part of your instructional program. This requirement leads to the next reason for using CBA.

2. **Curriculum-based assessment is efficient.** Brief samples of curriculum skills obtained frequently, even daily, may be charted to illustrate the student's progress. Some teachers use a mastery learning approach, setting a certain percentage of correct skills as the criterion of mastery. The use of frequent assessment and charting allows progress toward mastery and attainment of short-term instructional objectives specified in the student's IEP to be exhibited. Charting also is an appealing method of presenting achievement progress to parents.

3. **Curriculum-based assessment facilitates evaluation of student progress, program effectiveness, and educational research.** Intermittent monitoring of a student's knowledge of basic curriculum skills allows you to evaluate his or her progress. Administrators and parents find this approach to evaluation easy to understand, especially if the results are graphed to show progress over a period of time, such as a marking period.

A teacher may wish to know the effectiveness of a particular instructional method being used. For instance, when teaching basic vocabulary, a teacher may decide to compare "programmed" workbooks with "language experience" workbooks. CBA gives precise information for determining which approach facilitates better achievement.

A teacher may want to determine if students with a particular learning style profit more from one method of teaching than another, if a particular instructional grouping provides better achieve-

FIGURE 1.16   Reasons for Using Curriculum-Based Assessment

1. CBA helps you determine what to teach.
2. CBA is efficient.
3. CBA facilitates evaluation of student progress, program effectiveness, and educational research.
4. CBA is both valid and reliable.
5. CBA increases student achievement.
6. CBA can be used to help make referral decisions.
7. CBA complies with the requirements of IDEA.

ment than another, or if achievement improves when students are given a certain amount of time-on-task. There are many research ideas to aid instructional decision making that the classroom teacher can investigate using CBA.

Some teachers are involved in special programs and projects. Often, the success of these projects hinges on the students showing increased achievement from pre- to post-testing. Other teachers are required by their directors or supervisors to conduct beginning and/or end-of-year evaluations for all students in the classroom. IDEA requires that all students in special education programs be reevaluated at a minimum of every three years and that progress be evaluated at least annually. Teachers can easily accomplish these evaluations by using CBA as part of their instructional program.

4. Curriculum-based assessment is both valid and reliable.   Some group tests lack necessary validity and reliability characteristics (Salvia & Ysseldyke, 1995). However, Shinn and Marston (1985) note that since curriculum-based assessment uses material from the student's own curriculum, content validity is assured. They also point out that since the measurements are brief, repeated samplings are easily obtained, thus giving increased reliability to estimates of the student's performance. Curriculum-based assessment clearly is superior in validity and reliability to most other measures.

5. Curriculum-based assessment increases student achievement.   In his discussion of the minimum-competency testing programs in Texas, Detroit, South Carolina, and Maryland, Popham (1985) notes that the testing program can be a major force in improving the instructional program. He points out that "if the assessment devices used are criterion-related tests that have been deliberately constructed to illuminate instructional decision making and if there are significant instructional consequences tied to pupils' test performances, then the testing program will drive the instructional program" (p. 629). Similarly, when curriculum-based assessment is used to develop controlled instruction matched to the curriculum, it is effective in promoting achievement with mainstreamed, low-achieving, and attention deficit disorder students in time-on-task, task completion, and task comprehension (Gickling & Thompson, 1985). *Obviously, when what is taught becomes what is assessed, student achievement increases.*

6. Curriculum-based assessment can be used to help make referral decisions.   Students with learning disabilities and mild mental disabilities achieve lower than Chapter I and general education students on curriculum-based assessments in reading, spelling, math, and written expression. These findings by Shinn and Marston (1985) led them to suggest that CBA could be a valid and reliable way to define low achievement and to select students for referral for special education evaluation. Gickling and Thompson (1985) point out that since 1983 the state of Louisiana has required a curriculum-based assessment prior to referring a student. The purpose of the assessment is to determine if the problems are curricular and/or teaching related or if the student does, in fact, learn differently from his or her peers who are achieving normally.

Curriculum-based assessment prior to referral is a logical assessment strategy for the referring general classroom teacher. If a targeted student is suspected of being learning disabled, the general classroom teacher must be a member of the multidisciplinary evaluation team to determine if the student has a disability. Data provided from curriculum-based assessment to the team by the teacher would be valid and reliable information to consider.

7. Curriculum-based assessment complies with the requirements of IDEA for assessing students suspected as having a disability.   Direct curriculum-based assessment specifies the present level of educational performance at the time of assessment; it is an objective procedure for evaluating the degree to which instructional objectives are being attained. Since these are required procedures within IDEA, the use of curriculum-based assessment insures that teachers are legally compliant with the assessment regulations. Other relationships between CBA and IDEA are shown in Figure 1.17.

PRINCIPLES OF ASSESSMENT

There are two very important points to keep in mind about the assessment process. These two points permeate all ten principles of assessment detailed later. The first point is that the entire assessment process must be a positive one. The diagnostician or teacher who conducts the

FIGURE 1.17   Curriculum-Based Assessment and IDEA

- CBA assists in properly writing IEP objectives (Fuchs & Shinn, 1989).
- CBA can be used to evaluate IEP goals and objectives (Fuchs & Fuchs, 1984a).
- CBA can be used to make decisions about annual reviews of achievement for students in special education (Allen, 1989).
- CBA is "legally imperative" because of validation problems with many norm-referenced tests (Galagan (1985).
- CBA is not racially or culturally biased (Galagan, 1985).
- CBA renders the assessment valid for its intended purpose. CBA is both valid and reliable (Deno, 1985).
- CBA can be used to screen and decide eligibility for special education (Deno, 1989; Shinn, 1989a, 1989b).
- CBA can be used to help evaluate the overall special education program (Tindal, 1989).
- Some states have adopted the use of CBA during the assessment process (Mercer, King-Sears, & Mercer, 1990).
- Assessment must be in the student's native language. Most teachers using CBA also teach in the student's native language, be it standard American English, Braille, American Sign Language, etc.).

assessment must do so in a frame of mind that searches for strengths as well as for areas of remediation. This approach is called "success analysis" and is advocated throughout this book. Appropriate programming can also be planned if the teacher knows the skills a student has mastered as well as the skills in need of remediation. "Success analysis," then, is equally as important as "error analysis."

The second point is the relationship of time spent in testing to time spent in teaching. Although testing is part of the instructional process, the main responsibility of the teacher is to teach, not to test. Granted, testing provides valuable information for the teaching process, but it must never become more important than instruction. If a teacher finds that assessment procedures are taking valuable time from teaching or that the results of the assessment do not have direct application to instruction, then the assessment activities need to be reexamined. Assessment should never be abandoned; it must be kept in proper perspective. The basic principles of assessment are presented in Figure 1.18.

You have learned about the curriculum, the assessment process, and how the two can be combined to determine instructional needs of the student. Now it is time for you to learn how to *begin* the assessment process for instructional purposes.

IMPLEMENTING THE ASSESSMENT PROCESS FOR INSTRUCTION

The five basic steps necessary to determine the most appropriate instructional needs of your students are presented in Figure 1.19. Each step is briefly discussed here.

Step 1: Know the curriculum.   For each basic curriculum content area (reading, arithmetic, spelling, etc.) list the skills in the sequence in which they are to be taught. Skill sequences are presented later in this text. Some teachers find it profitable to write performance objectives for each skill in the

FIGURE 1.18   Ten Basic Principles of Assessment

1. Manage the assessment process so that it is efficient and purposeful.
   - CBA is most useful to determine which academic skills are known and unknown.
   - With this information, you know explicit skills to introduce, review, and practice.
2. Relate assessment to the requirements of the curriculum.
   - Choose only the critical skills from the curriculum for "at-risk" students.
   - Assess only those skills actually taught.
3. Set priorities for assessment.
   - Set as *first* priority the core curriculum skills being failed and new skills introduced.
   - Set as *second* priority the skills prerequisite for later skills.
   - Set as *third* priority the skills allowing student pleasure and fun, in and out of school.
4. Use only those tools and techniques that are appropriate.
   - The PURPOSE of assessment determines what tools and techniques to use.
   - Review "Protection in Evaluation" section of IDEA.
5. Proceed from broad, general areas to specific skills.
   - A survey test can help determine placement within a hierarchy of skills.
   - If skill is known within a hierarchy, test next most difficult skill.
   - Use modified assessment techniques to alter response requirements if necessary.
   - See Hargrove and Poteet (1984) for discussion on modified assessment techniques.
6. Analyze all errors.
   - If a pattern of errors occurs frequently, remediate to avoid future errors.
   - See Gable and Hendrickson (1990a) for a sourcebook of error analysis and correction.
7. Determine strategies the student uses to do tasks.
   - Ask the student how he or she accomplishes tasks.
   - Have the student talk aloud while working on the tasks.
8. Substantiate assessment findings.
   - Assess the same skill several times within a few days to provide evidence of mastery or nonmastery of the skill (Fuchs, Deno, & Marston, 1983).
   - Balance the number of items used to assess a skill with the time required to do so (Stowitschek, Stowitschek, Henderson, & Day, 1984).
   - To determine mastery of one skill, use 3 to 4 items:
     - If 3 to 5 items are used, *all* must be correct to determine mastery,
     - If 6 to 15 items are used, 1 error is permitted,
     - If 16 to 20 items are used, 2 errors are permitted. (Stowitschek, Gable, & Hendrickson, 1980).
   - Intermittent assessment of the same skills is necessary to determine if a skill is being maintained (using the skill in real life situations helps maintain it).
9. Record and report results of assessment.
   - Chart records of assessment to show progress and to pinpoint skills to be introduced, reviewed, or practiced.
   - Use a checklist of skills to show progress and current instruction tasks.
10. Continually improve assessment practices.
    - Study and learn new assessment instruments and approaches.
    - Study and learn new instructional strategies to use with results of your assessment.

FIGURE 1.19   Five Steps to Determine
Instructional Needs of Students

___

Step 1: Know the curriculum.

Step 2: Establish the beginning point of assessment.

Step 3: Analyze the responses.

Step 4: Select appropriate instructional strategies.

Step 5: Schedule the instructional sessions and use effective teaching skills.

___

curriculum. Each objective states the *conditions* under which the skill is to be displayed ("Given a pencil and a worksheet with 20 addition problems, sums to ten . . ."); the observed *behavior* the student is to display (". . . the student will *write* the answers on the worksheet . . ."); and the *criterion* for skill attainment (". . . at a rate of 100 percent correct for two consecutive school days") (Mager, 1962). The relationship between the performance objective and the test to measure the objective is obvious.

Step 2: Establish the beginning point of assessment.   Observe the student's performance on tasks in the classroom to obtain an idea of where to begin assessment. The assessment should move from the general to the specific. For instance, a student may be asked to write a short story about an interesting picture. The student's response is analyzed, and it is determined that capitalization is a problem throughout the story. The teacher would then select or make a test that assesses the various places for proper capitalization. The results indicate which specific skills in the use of capital letters should be taught. The Enright Diagnostic Inventory of Basic Arithmetic Skills (Enright, 1983) uses this approach to focus gradually on the precise arithmetic skill to teach.

Step 3: Analyze the responses.   Errors are of primary interest because they often indicate if the student is making inefficient use of the process required for the task or if the student simply does not understand the task. This error analysis approach guides the instructional decisions.

Also conduct a success analysis, looking for those skills that are performed successfully. When the assessment is directly tied to the curriculum, the teacher often finds that the student has learned some skills out of sequence. This is perfectly acceptable. The teacher should first consider teaching the unknown skills which lie between known skills in the sequence. Then, the remaining skills can be taught in order.

Step 4: Select appropriate instructional strategies.   Establish groups in which each student needs to learn the same skill. The number of students in the group can vary from one to several. Then select appropriate instructional strategies to use with each group. The teacher must be familiar with a variety of instructional materials and know their characteristics.

By being atuned to each student's unique learning characteristics, the teacher can select *appropriate* instructional materials for use with each student. When used with disabled students, this combination of assessment and teaching meets the legal requirement that instruction be appropriate for these students.

Good teaching requires more than just the selecting of appropriate materials; it requires knowledge and practice using techniques of effective instruction. Instruction is considered "effective" if it results in appropriate student achievement. Techniques for using effective instruction strategies have been detailed by Archer and her associates (1989). Their approach states that the teacher must gain the student's *attention, review* what is already known, establish the *goal* of the lesson, *model* what is to be taught, *prompt* student responses, *check* student work, *review* what was taught, *preview* the next lesson, then assign *independent work*. Specific skills can be found in Archer and Gleason (1989, 1990).

Those who have the responsibility of providing preservice or inservice training for other teachers will find helpful articles on teaching others how to use instructional strategies in Thousand and McNeil (1990).

Step 5: Schedule the instructional sessions and use effective teaching skills. Once the assessment has taken place, the skill groups determined, and the appropriate materials obtained, begin the actual instruction and use effective teaching skills. Assign independent work and other activities for practice and maintenance of skills only after you are certain that the required tasks in the independent work can be performed correctly by the student. Independent work, rather than playing games, must be used when students are not receiving direct instruction.

Consider not only curriculum skills, but also the whole child with his or her various familial, cultural, and personal interests and expectations that impact school behavior and learning. Include performance assessment tasks to help decide if the student can generalize those skills for success in the real world.

From this point, assessment should become integrated with instruction, and the cycle of teaching and testing should become routine.

SUMMARY

In this chapter you learned that the *core* curriculum consists of reading (word recognition and comprehension), written expression, and arithmetic (computation and problem solving); that the *collateral* curriculum consists of social studies and science; that the *support* curriculum includes social skills, spelling, handwriting, and study strategies; and that the enrichment curriculum includes the creative arts and physical education. All these curricula constitute the basic curriculum skills, but the first three are considered the academic curricula and are the major focus of this book.

You learned about an approach to assessment that defines the major assessment tools and techniques as tests (formal, informal, and criterion-referenced), rating scales, interviews, observations, and clinical judgment. Then you learned how to make good use of tests and what factors to consider in their selection. You remember that two factors were validity and reliability.

One of the most important things you read was that the *purpose* of assessment determines the tools and techniques to use. The three major educational purposes of assessment are screening, determining eligibility for special education, and instruction.

Curriculum-based assessment was presented as the most appropriate approach for instruction. At the end of the chapter you read about principles of assessment. You must keep these principles in mind as you read the other chapters in the text because they apply to all curriculum areas you assess and teach. The end of this chapter presented you with the five basic steps to begin your assessment of the basic curriculum skills.

You have learned a great deal in this chapter. It establishes the foundation on which all other chapters build. It would be a good idea to review it before going on to Chapter 2. In Chapter 2 you will read about curriculum development and how it can be individualized for each student. Building from a knowledge base of the individualized curriculum, you will learn the basic principles of personalized assessment and programming, that is, how to select the important part of your curriculum to fit the needs of each student. The case studies will illustrate how the curriculum can be both individualized and personalized. The enrich- ment activities that conclude this chapter will allow you to apply ideas and skills you have learned.

ENRICHMENT ACTIVITIES

Discussion

1. Discuss why the three Rs have continued to be the core curriculum for so many years. Will this trend continue into the future?

2. Discuss possible future changes in the basic curriculum areas. What part does computer literacy play in these changes?

3. Discuss the role of the federal government in schooling. Identify contemporary issues about the relationship of local schools and federal control. Specifically, what are the pros and cons of continued, federally mandated policies and procedures in special education?

4. Discuss student rights in the assessment process. How should they be monitored to insure they are not violated?

5. Discuss the pros and cons of norm-referenced and criterion-referenced assessment.

Special Projects

1. Interview a special education resource room teacher. Determine what assessment tools and techniques the teacher uses. Classify them as either formal or informal. Which category has the most tests in it? Why?

2. Obtain a copy of a norm-referenced test, a criterion-referenced test, and a published informal inventory. Compare the three in terms of content, ease of administration and scoring, and usefulness for instructional purposes. Which type do you view most favorably? Why?

3. Ask a special-education teacher to select a student for you to test. Use the instrument you viewed most favorably in activity 2. Write a one-page report of your findings and give it to the student's teacher. Solicit the teacher's opinion as to the validity of your test findings. Explain any discrepancies.

4. Conduct a survey. Phone ten special-education teachers. Ask them to name the tests they use most frequently and record their responses. Make a chart, listing the tests in order, beginning with the most frequently used test and ending with the least frequently used. Explain your chart to your class.

5. Visit an "inclusionary" school and a grade level where a special education teacher is team-teaching with the general education teacher. Observe how the special education teacher interacts with the general education students and how the general education teacher interacts with the special education students. Is there a

difference? If so, how might you explain it? Notice the role that informal assessment plays throughout the day in this classroom. Is it any different than what might be seen in a noninclusive school? Why or why not? Discuss your impressions with both teachers at the end of the school day. Note their reactions and report both your reactions and their reactions back to your college class.

CHAPTER 2

UNDERSTANDING CURRICULUM

JOYCE S. CHOATE

CHAPTER OBJECTIVES

This chapter is designed to enable the reader to:

1. Explain the role of the regular education curriculum in the educational process for all students.
2. Describe the factors that shape the curriculum of a school system and of an individual teacher.
3. Explain the variables that determine the degree of personalized instruction practical and possible.
4. Describe guidelines for personalizing instruction.
5. Modify curricular units, lessons, and tasks to meet the needs of selected teachers and students.

The role of the curriculum in the educational process is a powerful one. The curriculum functions in a variety of ways; however, in a discussion of assessment and programming, the most important functions are as the determinant of the educational program presented students and as the criterion for students' academic success. That is, the curriculum is the logical source for both assessment data and programming data. Before examining the ways in which a curriculum can be adjusted to accommodate the learning needs of individual students, this chapter addresses several issues. These include a definition of curriculum, a discussion of how systemwide and specific curricula are developed and imple-

mented, and an analysis of the specific functions of a curriculum.

CURRICULUM DEFINED

Not unlike many areas in education, each professional who writes about curriculum and instruction has developed a personal definition. However, the importance of curricula is widely acknowledged. In speaking of curricula in general, Oliva (1992) notes that definitions vary because of differences in philosophical beliefs. The interpretations he cites range from curriculum as a set of materials, or sequence of courses, to curriculum as content, or everything planned by school personnel. Doll (1992) refers to a curriculum as the content, or actual subjects and specific subject matter taught, as well as the process by which the content is expected to be learned. Jackson (1992) interprets the various definitions as arguments to support particular curricular theories. For purposes of this book, the curriculum is viewed as the educational program. This includes the subjects, specific subject matter, *and* the processes that are both planned and used to implement instruction of the content.

CURRICULUM DEVELOPMENT

The development of a formal curriculum requires considerable time, effort, and expertise on the part of a number of professionals. Depending upon the number of persons involved and their relative efficiency, the process for developing an initial design often extends over one or more years. Periodic revisions are then undertaken to update the original plan. Many factors, often unrecognized, influence the design and content of the curriculum.

The Mechanics of Development

The mechanics of developing a formal, systemwide curriculum typically begin with the formation of a curriculum planning committee. Members of the committee are usually drawn from the unit for which the plan is being developed. Occasionally outside consultants are called upon to participate. The committee may include among its members a variety of professionals such as classroom teachers, reading and math specialists, supervisors, principals, assistant superintendent, and even knowledgeable parents.

The model that Tyler recommended in 1949 still provides the basic structure for preparing most curricula today (Doll, 1992). The major elements of this model include the development of objectives and activities, the organization of activities, and the plans for evaluation. The actions required to plan a curriculum usually begin with a statement of philosophy, the ordering of priori-

ties, and the formulation of objectives. The specificity of plans for evaluation and for instruction depends upon the depth and breadth of the envisioned plan. This process may involve originating or borrowing ideas. As noted by Doll, schools commonly copy portions of curricula from other schools. Effective use of technology facilitates collaboration and communication, the writing process, and publication of the formal document.

Content Influences

The selection of the actual content of the formal curriculum is influenced by several forces in addition to the professional biases of individual curriculum committee members. These shaping forces include status quo tendencies, national government, state and regional government, influential groups, and textbooks (Cuban, 1992).

Status Quo

A tendency to maintain the status quo influences the development of many curricula. The tendency of curricula to remain static may be reinforced by the safety of the status quo and the reduced time, energy, and commitment to maintain it. Cuban (1992) lists the agents contributing to curricular stability as public expectations, accrediting and testing agencies, textbooks, historical curricula, students, teachers, principals, and physical structures.

National Government

In describing policy changes in curricular development and governance, Elmore and Fuhrman (1994) assert that the United States is increasingly favoring a more performance-based and national curricular policy. The influence of the national government on curriculum is imparted through court decisions, legislation that mandates programs, and financial appropriations. In most cases, receipt of federal monies by state and local agencies is contingent upon meeting specific federal guidelines or complying with the litigation, and/or legislation. In the United States, Public Law 94–142, reauthorized as the Individuals with

Disabilities Education Act (IDEA), which mandates not only a free and appropriate education for all children but also the individualized education program (IEP), is a classic example of the impact of government on curricular content and practice. The IEP is, by definition, the nucleus of curriculum development in special education. A more recent major legislative initiative, Goals 2000: Educate America Act, is designed to develop national goals and raise standards for *all* students, revise assessment programs to evaluate progress, and reeducate teachers (A. Lewis, 1993). This legislation is viewed by many as formalizing the development of a national curriculum.

State and Regional Government

The influence of states or regions upon the curriculum varies. The regulations and designated funding imposed by boards of education and legislative acts help shape local curricula. Factors such as graduation requirements, school accreditation, required subjects, time allotments, programs, and priorities are subject to state and regional control. Occasionally, subjects are emphasized in response to various political pressures (Doll, 1992).

Influential Groups

Teachers, administrators, and special groups, including the general public, also shape curricula. The degree of influence by teacher unions, specialists, and professional interest and reform groups depends upon their visibility and activity level. Standards developed by professional organizations, or learned societies, are important sources for identifying curricular scope and sequence in the various disciplines. A number of professional organizations have sponsored comprehensive projects, many federally funded, to develop national standards in their particular areas of interest and expertise. The success of these projects is reflected in national standards, in various stages of completion, for such subjects as mathematics, physical education, science, the arts, English-language arts, and at least four areas

of social studies (O'Neil, 1993). In most cases, the standards are intended for mastery by *all* students (Shriner, Ysseldyke, & Thurlow, 1994) and thus provide the framework for content and change of curricula, teacher education, and textbook publishers. Such standards are expected to become part of an evolving national curriculum. Widely held views of the general public (i.e., parents, taxpayers, businesses) concerning curricula are eventually translated into local, regional, state, and/or national legislation.

Pressures from special groups are evident in their periodic demand for school reform. For example, during the 1980s school-reform efforts increased state involvement and also site-based restructuring. Site-based management resulted in schools assuming greatly increased responsibility for curricula, improvements, and governance, an approach relatively popular with teachers, but one which has, thus far, failed to impact teaching and learning significantly (Fullan, 1993).

Special interest groups also help limit curricular boundaries. For example, conservative groups periodically condemn particular teaching methods and/or materials as being unpatriotic, anti-Christian, or generally objectionable. Recent targets of criticism include elements of outcome-based education, whole-language approaches, problem-solving and thinking curricula, collaborative learning, integrated content (McCarthy, 1993), and textbook content. As a result, some programs and textbooks have been revised or discontinued.

Textbooks

Numerous authors note the power of textbooks to influence curricula (e.g., Apple, 1985, 1990; Doll, 1992; Venezky, 1992). Venezky describes textbooks as the *surrogate curriculum* containing a *manifest curriculum* (the actual topics and difficulty level) and a *latent curriculum* (the secondary messages as influenced by author and publisher). He cites the two major influences on textbook content as being market-driven publishers, and society. Apple (1988) expresses the degree of influence effected by textbooks as well as professional concerns in his statement, "Whether we like it or not, the curriculum in most American schools is not defined by courses of study or suggested programs, but by one particular artifact, the standardized, grade-level-specific text in mathematics, reading, social studies, science (when it is even taught), and so on" (p. 225). He warns that much of the content of textbooks may be selected according to marketability rather than according to sound academic principles. Apple concludes that because of the parallel reliance of curricula upon texts and of texts upon the market, much curricular content is defined by the market. Apple (1990) further asserts that the United States does indeed have a national curriculum—one that is determined by the market for textbooks (p. 528).

Curriculum Models

The curriculum plan is eventually recorded as a curriculum guide. These guides, formal statements of the curriculum, bear various titles according to the preference of the developers. Some areas offer separate curriculum guides for special education, usually modified and less demanding than the guides for regular education.

Formats

Most state or regional departments of education publish a curriculum for each school grade and subject area. Many local school systems use these publications as a guide to develop their own, frequently more stringent, curricula.

The specificity of curriculum guides varies from broad and general to detailed volumes. A comprehensive guide may contain statements of philosophy, objectives, scope and sequence of each subject area, suggestions for instruction of each task, including student activities and materials, general policies, and resource information. A course of study, more specific but less comprehensive than the curriculum guide, may recommend detailed teaching strategies in each subject area.

Supplementary curriculum guides are often developed to be used alone or in conjunction with more general guides. The supplements contain such aids as resource units, resource listings, and scattered teaching suggestions. A brief segment of such a resource unit, used to supplement the course of study for fourth-grade social studies, is presented with Case Study B at the end of this chapter. Teaching ideas are sometimes disseminated regularly as bulletins or compiled as a unit to describe teaching practices that relate to the curriculum content.

General Education Curricula

Prominent curricular approaches of the 1990s include basics, individualized education plans, literacy, whole language, and cooperative learning (Schubert, 1993), outcome-based education and interdisciplinary instruction, team and collaborative learning, higher-order thinking skills, authentic instruction, and inclusive education (Darling-Hammond, 1993). The influence of constructivism on curricula is evident in such emphases as relevant problems and thematic presentations (Brooks & Brooks, 1993). Each approach may be adopted in part or as a whole to impact what does or does not go on in classrooms.

The most familiar curriculum design is subject-centered. The content is selected according to decisions about the specific subject and the scope and sequence of appropriate skills. This model is typically highly structured and well organized into orderly divisions. The larger divisions relate the specific subject to school levels or grades, and the component subskills comprise the subdivisions. Some plans are also organized according to logical teaching units.

Competency-Based Design. The competency-based curricular model is a more limited design. This design directly relates learning objectives, stated in behavioral terms, to learning activities and to student performance of the objectives. The learner's successful performance of each objective allows forward movement through the curriculum. This model is often combined with subject-centered models and is popular with prospective employers.

Spiral Design. The spiral curriculum plan calls for similar concepts and skills to be presented to each grade. The student's understanding is gradually broadened and deepened as his or her degree of sophistication increases with each level. Social studies curricula are particularly suited to this type of organization. The diagram in Figure 2.1 represents the strands of a spiral social studies curriculum.

Process Design.   A process design emphasizes learning strategies and the skills to solve school and real-life problems. Especially appropriate for a science curriculum, this plan is defined by the instructional methodology around which it is organized. It is intended to teach specific thinking skills as well as the content of the curriculum. Process designs are most often incorporated as a central portion of another design rather than as

a total curriculum model and are supported by advocates for lifelong learning.

Problems Design.   The problems design focuses on solving community and societal problems (Doll, 1992). The content usually centers around real-life needs, wants, and activities. This design is appropriate for social reform curricula and is useful as a major element of other designs.

Interdisciplinary Design.   The interdisciplinary curriculum focuses on integrating instruction across subject boundaries. The interdisciplinary model is particularly suited for the thematic unit approach. Using Jacobs' spoked wheel as the graphic organizer (1989), an interdisciplinary unit for the circus is depicted in Figure 2.2. As can be seen, interdisciplinary designs, like process models, may be better suited as key components of other designs instead of a total curriculum model.

Individual Need Design.   Individual need models emphasize both the needs and interests of the students. Such curricula are the basis of special programs which utilize ability and homogeneous groupings. Programs for special groups of students with disabilities, gifted youngsters, cultural groups, and alternative schools typically follow this model. Plans are characterized by their flexibility and options for students, and the individual need model incorporates diagnostic and corrective teaching into the overall plan. The mastery-learning-model, espoused by Bloom (1976), adheres to this plan as does this book.

Special Education Curricula

Unlike general education curricula, which often share common content because of reliance on textbooks and national assessment measures, most special education curricula share only two common characteristics: The structure is often somewhat arbitrary and a portion of the content is shaped by the Individualized Education Programs (IEPs) of target students. Some curricular plans frequently used in special education programs are IEPs, specific special education cur-

FIGURE 2.1   Sample Spiral Curriculum

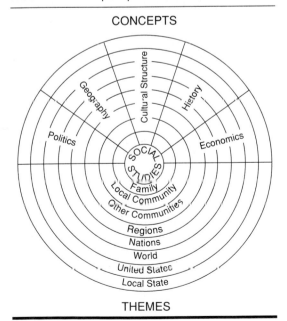

CONCEPTS

THEMES

FIGURE 2.2   Interdisciplinary Circus Unit

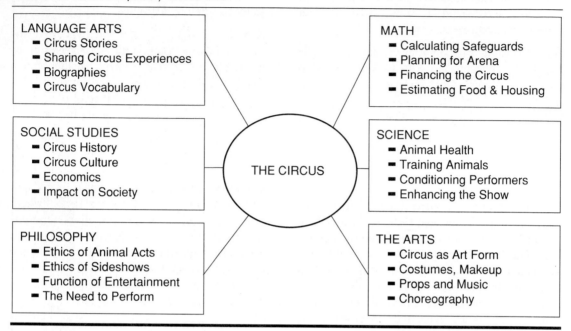

ricula, remedial and tutorial curricula, and correlated curricula.

Individual Curricula.   Separate curriculum
guides for students with disabilities are not
widely used. Instead, the mandated IEP, intended
to specify the adaptations of the general education curriculum that are required to meet the
individual student's needs, is usually the curriculum for students with disabilities. Included in the
IEP for older students, usually ages 14 through
16, must be plans for transition services, or the
individual transition plan (ITP). For these older
students, curricular elements must be selected to
meet their individual life goals. Unfortunately,
many special education teachers all but ignore
the general classroom and its curriculum and define and teach their own curricula. Thus, the content of special education curricula is often
fragmented, limited to low-level basic skills and
low-level texts, includes few constructivist elements, and offers few subjects (Pugach &
Warger, 1993).

Specific Curricula.   A few very specific curricula for special education are available. Direct instruction in social skills is incorporated into a
variety of special education programs (see discussion in Chapter 4). The *Skillstreaming Program*
(McGinnis, Goldstein, Sprafkin, & Gershaw,
1984) presents a flexible curriculum for social-
skills training. Brolin (1989) details a career education curriculum and Clark and Kolstoe (1990)
describe several plans for career development.
Functional curricula, with more emphasis on social goals than academic goals, are appropriate
for students with moderate to severe disabilities.
Originally designed for adolescents, some methods of the Learning Strategies Model (Alley &
Deshler, 1979) may be adapted for younger students. As discussed later in Chapter 10, teaching
students the strategies to learn across subject
areas is rapidly gaining favor in both general and
special education programs.

Remedial and Tutorial Models.   Two common
special education curricula are the remedial basic

skill model and the tutorial model. Remediation in basic skills provides intensive instruction in the core curriculum while tutorial assistance aims for support instruction to supplement and maintain the student in the general education curriculum. A modification of the general education curriculum is a common curricular model applied in special education. There may be no appreciable difference in the content and implementation of the general and special education curricula, since they are both based on similar principles. Curricular content is affected by a specific student's abilities and the special techniques required to teach him or her. It is the severity of the disability that determines the degree to which the content differs from the classroom curriculum. The content of the general elementary curriculum is suitable for most students with mild disabilities, although the pacing and emphasis may differ. The methods used to teach the content may also differ according to the nature and degree of disability. Because the instructional setting influences the way in which the curriculum is implemented, the selection of placement according to degree of restrictiveness is one way to try to match the learner's needs with the curriculum.

Correlated Curricula.   Many educators contend that the general education curriculum is appropriate for most students with mild disabilities but with some program modifications and also with supports, such as consulting teachers and instruction in study strategies (Lovitt, 1993). The correlation of the special education curriculum with the general education curriculum is crucial to the success of students with mild disabilities. Insofar as possible, the special education curriculum should be the same, but like the curriculum for students without disabilities, also varied for individual needs (Reynolds, 1990). The goal of such a procedure is to equip students with special needs to function with their age peers.

Cooperative and Inclusive Curricula

Both mainstreaming and the Regular Education Initiative of the late 1980s represent notable cooperative efforts of general and special educators. A third major cooperative effort that emphasizes and nurtures collaboration—inclusive education—is gaining momentum.

Inclusion refers to education in the general classroom with one's chronological peers to the maximum extent appropriate, with individual learning objectives, and with whatever support is needed from special education and related services (York, Doyle, & Kronberg, 1992). The philosophy of inclusive education addresses not only the needs of students with disabilities but also accommodates cultural diversity (Garcia, 1994) and may help solve problems of other students who are at-risk of school failure.

In their discussion of the problems associated with traditional lockstep curricula, Pugach and Warger (1993) call for special and general educators to collaborate in restructuring curricula to facilitate inclusive education. Schulz and Carpenter (1995) recommend adapting the general curricular content by supplementing, simplifying, or changing levels. Other strategies recommended to facilitate and support inclusion are direct instruction, cooperative learning, peer-mediated learning, reciprocal teaching, collaborative teaching, and curriculum adaptations (Shrag & Burnette, 1994). Giangreco, Cloninger, and Iverson (1992) describe four options for inclusive curricular adaptations, each progressively more restrictive: (1) follow the general classroom curriculum; (2) use a multilevel curriculum with the same lessons as the general curriculum but at different levels; (3) offer an overlapping curriculum with the same activities as the general curriculum but with different objectives in different areas; and (4) provide an alternative curriculum with activities and objectives that differ from the general curriculum.

Certain features of authentic, outcome-based, and nongraded curricula are highly compatible with the goals of inclusive education. *All* students need an authentic and meaningful curriculum that prepares them to function effectively in the classroom, community, and workplace. However, students with disabilities need specific instruction in the basic skills, but within the context of a thinking, problem-solving, integrated curriculum that emphasizes authentic, real-world demands (Poteet, Choate, & Stewart, 1993). This approach combines specific skills instruction with Brophy's holistic skills instruction (1992), which views skills as strategies and teaches when, why, and how to apply them. Outcome-based education, similar to mastery learning but updated and expanded to include and focus on significant outcomes, is in concert with national standards calling for meaningful performance outcomes. The outcomes model is amenable to inclusive education because it accommodates individual needs and learning rates (Ysseldyke, Thurlow, & Shriner, 1992). The nongraded curriculum is especially hospitable for students with disabilities because of its structure, integrated content, and recognition and accommodations for individual differences (Anderson & Pavan, 1993). The highlights of these approaches—authentic content and skills, significant outcomes, accommodations for individual needs, and nongraded structure—constitute important considerations for inclusive curricula.

Shrag and Burnette (1994) insist that flexible curricula and instruction are essential. Thus, general and special educators should collaborate as they restructure curricula to incorporate adaptations that are more fluid, flexible, authentic, and generally more appropriate for inclusive general education.

CURRICULUM IMPLEMENTATION

The extent to which curriculum guides are enforced varies from system to system, and even from school to school. Some teachers are advised to use the guide(s) as a respectful suggestion, while others are cautioned to adhere to every detail. The more specific the guide, the more likely the insistence to observe it. The supervisory practices within a school are also responsible for each teacher's degree of compliance with the guide. Obviously, the practical and useful guides are

more likely to be voluntarily followed, regardless of enforcement practices.

The Teacher's Curriculum

Although the degree of autonomy enjoyed by individual teachers varies across and within systems and schools, every teacher exerts a pronounced influence on the classroom curriculum. According to Berliner (1984): "The final arbiter of what it is that gets taught is the classroom teacher" (p. 53). Teachers develop curricula in their classrooms daily when they add and delete topics or use supplementary materials. Doyle (1992) asserts that teachers select and use textbooks as resources to match their *own* curricula. Even in school systems that demand teachers follow curriculum guides, the personal and professional biases of teachers exert a strong influence on the curriculum. The classroom teacher makes the decisions concerning the exact content of each lesson, the time allotment for each concept and task, and the instructional pacing of each skill area. Therefore, a teacher's practices and priorities establish the true classroom curriculum—a curriculum that remains fairly static (Cuban, 1992). However, the resources available to a teacher may modify the classroom curriculum.

Instructional Resources

Stated curricula and the teacher's practiced curriculum provide clues to what students are expected to accomplish. However, it is the delivery of the instruction and the evaluation procedures in the skill areas which facilitate or impede student success. How instruction is delivered depends upon several factors: the resources available to the teacher, the teacher's reliance on and/or use of resources, and the methods the teacher prefers.

Textbooks

The major resource available to teachers is textbooks. The influence of the market in determining the content of textbooks was discussed in an earlier section. Textbooks are often selected according to the degree their scope and sequence mesh with the formal curriculum, although the reverse is sometimes true. Textbooks may, in the final analysis, structure the content, sequence, and learning activities of the classroom curriculum. It has even been suggested that one way to determine the types and quality of learning experiences presented in any classroom is to examine the textbooks used.

Other Resources

Availability and judicious use by the teacher of additional resources also shape the classroom curriculum. Such support as supplementary paraprofessionals, sophisticated media and supplies, as well as adjunct programs broaden both the teacher's instructional options and the students' learning options. Utilization of computers, telecommunication networks, and multimedia directly impacts curricula. The physical structure of the classroom limits or expands instructional opportunities, thus further influencing the classroom curriculum.

Evaluation Procedures

The procedures used to evaluate the progress of students are important contributors to the classroom curriculum. What is taught and how it is taught are partially determined by the evaluation procedures used on a daily basis by the teacher, and by those regularly used by the school system to determine success and failure (Doll, 1992). The adage quoted by Lemlech (1990) illustrates the significance of these techniques: "Let me prepare your tests, and I will have designed your curriculum" (p. 16).

Curriculum Functions

The curriculum operates as a measuring device for educators and students. It also serves important, but different purposes for the school system, the teacher, and the students. In the planning of individualized instruction, the curriculum is the foundation of the assessment and programming process.

School Systems

For a school system, the formal curriculum functions as a philosophical statement of purpose. In addition, it serves to delineate instructional policy and procedures and set academic standards. Depending on the depth and breadth of the curriculum guide, minimum or baseline standards or maximum goals toward which to strive may be stated. Student success is partially defined by the formal curriculum. Some systems measure teacher success by the progress of their students through the curriculum.

Teachers

For teachers, a curriculum guide functions as a definition of teaching content or as a point of departure, depending upon the degree of enforcement of the curriculum within the system and a teacher's individual initiative. Many teachers use the guide as a source of instructional strategies, while others deliver the content using their own strategies. This is true even in cases where the textbook is used as the curriculum guide. In the same manner that some systems measure teacher success by the curriculum, teachers use a curriculum, either their own, the school system's, or an amalgamation of both, as a standard by which to measure their students' progress and success. The teacher's curriculum provides the initial content for individualizing or personalizing an instructional program for a specific student.

Students

The student's academic life is controlled by the curriculum, whether it is the formal one published as a guide or the teacher's own rendition. The curriculum is the what and how of instruction provided to the student. Gickling and Thompson (1985) stress that most curricula require the same performance of all students. They highlight the properties of curricula that are normative in nature.

Assessment and Programming

The related functions of the curriculum for system, teacher, and student are, in turn, reflected in its influence on the assessment and programming process. The scope and sequence, or breadth and order, define the boundaries of a curriculum. Specification of skill sequence is essential to establishing what was, is, and will be required of a student. As will be discussed in the next chapters, the specific tasks demanded by a student's curriculum provide the baseline data with which to interpret assessment results and compare his or her skills for programming purposes.

CURRICULUM INDIVIDUALIZATION

The translation of a specific student's assessment findings into instructional content and strategies results in an individualized curriculum. The process through which the individualized curriculum is formulated is synonymous with programming in this text; the plan and the actual implementation are also referred to as the individualized or personalized program, or simply the program. The relationship between assessment and the individualized curriculum or program is a reciprocal one. Assessment is only as worthy as the programming to which it leads, and, conversely, programming is only as valuable as the assessment upon which it is based. Throughout this and the following chapters, the symbiotic nature of the assessment/programming relationship is stressed.

The purpose of individualized programming is to produce a systematic scheme for delivering instruction appropriate to the needs of the learner(s). This purpose applies to plans developed for students in programs in general education, special education, alternative education, or combination programs. To implement a personalized program, a variety of delivery systems and instructional approaches are available.

Program Delivery Systems

Section 121a. 550 (b) of Public Law 94–142 mandates the least restrictive environment be provided for the education of exceptional stu-

dents. This section specifies that separate schooling of students with disabilities must only occur when the nature or severity of the disability prohibits regular schooling. It does not require all exceptional children to be placed or mainstreamed into the general classroom, but does mean that students must not be denied participation in the general classroom any more than is necessary to meet their instructional needs (Mercer & Mercer, 1993). To comply with the law, a continuum of placements must be offered, ranging from the least to the most restrictive. Although several models have been used to describe this service continuum (e.g., Polloway & Patton 1993), they generally describe variations of services in three settings: the general education classroom, the resource room, and the special class or school.

The General Education Classroom

The classroom teacher bears the major responsibility for the success of the students with and without disabilities and the gifted students placed in the least restrictive of the setting options, the general classroom. Sometimes the teacher is aided by a special consulting teacher who may suggest ways of meeting the special needs of particular students, obtain special materials, or otherwise collaborate and assist the classroom teacher.

Students with special needs assigned to a general classroom on a full-time basis may also be assigned to a resource room for one to five periods per week. The resource setting is considered a pull-out plan, since the student is usually pulled out of the classroom and taught in a separate classroom by a special educator. Other pull-out plans include remedial reading and math programs as well as a number of other special supplementary plans available to both general and special education students.

The Resource Class

As noted, some students are taught in a special education resource room for one period per day or two to three periods per week, depending on the student's needs. These students continue to be enrolled as full-time, general education students. A more restrictive placement involves having students attend a partial-day resource program for two to three periods per day, and then return to the classroom for the remainder of the school day. Remedial and supplementary instruction are typically provided through the resource program. The teacher of the resource program may also function as a consultant to the classroom teacher, recommending strategies for teaching target students in the general class and requesting suggestions for special help with specific content skills in the resource program.

The Special Class

Special class settings range from classes in a mainstream school or in a separate school to ones in a hospital or residential setting. Within the regular school, students usually receive their academic instruction from the special education teacher, but may have lunch, art, and physical education and attend assemblies with general education students. Separate school placement is generally reserved for those with severe or multiple disabilities, but the students return home at the end of the school day. Hospital and residential settings are for those with more severe disabilities; these students may only return home occasionally, if at all.

This book is primarily concerned with students who are provided services within the settings of general or special education resource classes. These settings directly influence the curriculum offered, and their selection is an attempt to match the learner's needs with the curriculum. Instructional options available to a student can vary according to the teacher and the instructional setting. Polloway and Patton (1993) suggest four criteria for determining the optimum placement for a student: the severity of the problem, the general education class situation, the availability of school supportive personnel, and the availability of outside resources.

Programming Elements

The three vital elements of any educational program are content, instruction, and organization. Although the content of a student's program is derived from the scope and sequence of the formal and teacher's curricula, the way in which the content is presented depends upon several factors. Both the organization and the nature of the instruction which are possible and practical are contingent to a large degree upon the instructional setting. Individualization is facilitated by active teaching, availability of assistant teachers, method modifications, adjustments to materials, classroom routines, and class management plans. Adapted methods and materials are discussed in further detail in Chapter 3, and incorporated in the instructional strategies for each subject area in Chapters 5 through 10; specific techniques for organizing and managing both assessment and programming are suggested in Chapter 11. However, each element is briefly described here to provide the framework for key principles of programming presented in the final section of this chapter.

Instructional Approach

Regardless of program delivery, instructional design should center around direct and active teaching in which students are actively involved in learning. Activities, led and paced by the teacher, tend to increase student engagement more than activities that are paced by the students (Doyle, 1986). A consistent finding from studies of effective teaching is efficient use of allocated learning time to maximize student engagement, a key axiom for planning and implementing effective instruction (Brophy & Good, 1986).

The teacher-pupil ratio is a major determinant of the degree of instructional flexibility within a class. In the general classroom the teacher may be responsible for teaching as many as 20–30 students at a time. Without substantial accommodation, this number of students does not leave much time for individual attention to the special needs of two or three students with disabilities. In the resource class, the teacher may teach from 20–25 students per day but only have five to eight students during any one period. In the special education, self-contained class, teachers are generally responsible for the education of the same eight to ten students during the instructional day. Thus, the resource and special education, self-contained models allow more opportunity for the teacher to provide individual instruction for each student.

Paraprofessionals, volunteer aides, parents, or student teachers can greatly increase opportunities for providing individual instruction. Use of student tutors is another means for decreasing the teacher-student ratio, increasing opportunities for individualized instruction. Carefully constructed and supervised cooperative learning groups also provide avenues for active engagement of learners.

Method Adaptation. Choosing one method or adjustment over another depends not only on a student's demonstrated response to a particular approach, but also on a teacher's preference. The target student's learning characteristics should be a primary factor used to determine the particular method chosen, adjustments made to materials, and the manner in which instruction and the setting are organized.

Instructional methods can be adjusted in a variety of ways, many of which are discussed in later chapters. According to the learners' diagnosed needs, instruction may be directed toward developing the learner's aptitudes or circumventing his or her inaptitudes; adaptations may consist of a minor procedural alteration or a major shift in instructional goals. Corrective strategies, such as those discussed in Chapters 5–10, present likely instructional alternatives; they, too, can be further modified to meet the needs of individual students. Sometimes changes in methods necessitate modifying instructional materials.

Evidence suggests that cognitive training approaches, which directly teach students how to learn, may increase instructional effectiveness for many students with mild disabilities (MacMillan, Keogh, & Jones, 1986). In addition, several specialized teaching approaches are appropriate for

the student whose academic performance is significantly below the expected level. When the usual developmental and corrective strategies have not produced success, more intense strategies are useful. These are discussed according to subject area in Chapters 5–10. Sufficient maintenance or practice activities to ensure long-term task mastery are vital components of any sound educational program; they are particularly important to low-achieving students.

Adjustments to Materials. Adjustments to learning materials can further individualize the personalized program, and be accomplished by altering materials and/or changing assignments. Adapting materials can save time and effort for both teacher and student. When alterations are not practical, using different materials or adding supplementary learning aids may enhance the program.

Organization

In addition to ample and competent personnel available to deliver direct instruction and appropriate modifications of methods and materials, several adjustments to the classroom routine also expand the capabilities for individualizing instruction. The way instruction is organized and managed can either facilitate or impede student achievement and the individualization process.

Instructional Arrangements. Certain classroom organization plans are more amenable to adjustment for individualization than others. The arrangement of the physical setting, seating and work space in particular, should be designed to maximize teaching and learning opportunities. Designated areas for both large and small group interaction are key components for meeting instructional needs as they emerge. Learning centers greatly expand instructional options, particularly if the centers offer a range of activities at various levels, and if the students are assigned to specific centers on the basis of their unique needs and interests. One way to provide particular instruction to target students is to form relatively homogeneous student groups by specific skill needs. Group size, as well as the members of the group, should be varied according to student need. Cooperative learning groups are appropriate to use in combination with other grouping plans. With sufficient resources teaching a student on a one-to-one basis is always an option. The instructional setting, the available resources, and the nature of student needs must be taken into consideration in selecting grouping plans.

Classroom Management.   Individualization as well as effective teaching and learning may be increased by using a variety of management techniques. Efficient classroom management, positively related to achievement gains is the orchestration of instruction. According to Evertson and colleagues (1994), in addition to arranging the physical layout of the classroom to promote learning, important procedures to construct and maintain an orderly learning environment include establishing rules, routines, and smooth traffic patterns. Transitions between learning activities should be fluid and used to prepare students for the next task. Standards should be set, made known, and enforced. Specific management techniques for facilitating the assessment/programming process appear in Chapter 11. A thorough, concise resource for additional suggestions is *Instructional Management: Detecting and Correcting Special Problems* (Evans, Evans, Gable, & Schmid, 1991).

Contrasts in Programming Practices

Many combinations of classroom accommodations are possible. By combining some type of integrated assessment/programming plan with sound management, even the teacher with a class of 30 students can orchestrate considerable individualization. Conversely, the teacher of only six students can totally avoid individualizing instruction by teaching the text and the curriculum instead of the students. Contrasts in adjustments made to learner needs are presented in the four

descriptions which follow; they illustrate how a teacher's influence can promote a student's progress or almost force a student to fail.

Ms. Alison's Inclusive Third-Grade Class

Ms. Alison teaches a third-grade class of 24 students. Three of the students have been identified as gifted, two have mild disabilities, one has moderate disabilities, one is awaiting evaluation, four are low achievers, and the remaining 13 are average achievers with varying degrees of ability across subject areas. Of the students with special needs, only one attends a special program for two hours per day. A consulting teacher works with Ms. Alison for 45 minutes per week in planning programs and monitoring the progress of the other exceptional students.

An IEP has been developed for all six students, emphasizing their needs in the inclusive classroom. To permit individualized and small group instruction, four learning centers have been organized adjacent to the small skill-group instruction station. In a listening center in the front of the room, tapes of all content texts as well as of specific tasks are filed for student use. Two additional stations are available for tutorial work or teacher/student conferences.

Ms. Alison charts each student's progress on a minimum-competency skill listing and on the skill listings that accompany the reading and math programs. She makes special notations of needs in language, social studies, and science. Often, when a student completes an assignment, he or she checks off mastered tasks. Once or twice a week Ms. Alison arranges a brief conference with each student, involving him or her in future assignment planning, particularly for the activities in the learning centers.

As students arrive each morning, they retrieve their individualized assignments for the day from the pocket chart by the door. Although large group instruction occurs at the beginning of each lesson, students follow their assignment cards for their small, skill-group schedule, independent practice, and reinforcement. While most students are completing their scheduled activities in the learning centers, Ms. Alison provides direct instruction to three to five students at the small skill-group station. Students are grouped according to similar skill needs for small group instruction in reading, math, and language. The assignments for the gifted students are primarily enrichment and expansion activities, while those for the students with special needs are mostly remedial in nature. The other students frequently have skill needs similar to those of the students with identified disabilities and are grouped accordingly. Skill groups are not static but change as the individual students progress. When small skill-group instruction is not enough to meet a student's needs, peer tutors reteach. Two students from the eighth grade function as cross-age tutors on Tuesdays and Thursdays during their study hall period.

Ms. Alison admits that she takes considerable work home at night in order to stay abreast of the students' progress and needs. She estimates that she has spent approximately one-hundred dollars of her personal money for instructional materials each school year, thus adding to her stock of materials over the past five years. She tapes the students' texts and learning activity packets during her planning period, and occasionally at home. She plans to ask two parents to work three days a week as teaching aids to assist with the record keeping.

Mr. Leo's Third-Grade Class

When Ms. Alison's plan is compared to that of Mr. Leo, the teacher of the adjacent third-grade classroom, her efforts to individualize instruction can be better appreciated. Mr. Leo's classroom includes a table of books for the students to read when they have finished their assignments, a science center, and a small skill-group instructional station. He uses the small group station to instruct three reading groups; when students are not involved in reading group, they are expected to complete the written assignments noted on the chalkboard. When written work is completed, students may go to the reading table or science center. Unfortunately, only the fastest workers ever

have the opportunity to use the reading and science centers. No special grouping is used for instruction in other subject areas. All students are expected to accomplish the same tasks with the same instruction. It is not surprising that Mr. Leo has six students awaiting evaluation to determine their eligibility for special education!

When these two teachers are observed, the supervisor notes that both are industrious, conscientious, and very involved in their teaching. However, Ms. Alison is effective with many students while Mr. Leo is effective with only some students. Much the same situation exists when two special educators are observed.

Mrs. McKinnon's Resource Class

Mrs. McKinnon teaches special education resource classes. Most of her students have mild disabilities and are scheduled into the resource class one period per day. She teaches from six to eight students in class each period. Since Mrs. McKinnon's resource class is a new one for which no instructional materials have arrived, she is using discarded texts and workbooks from the school's supply room. On the basis of the original diagnoses, Mrs. McKinnon has "placed" each student in a text in the subject area in which his or her skills are most deficient. As the students enter class each day, she hands them their own text and workbook with the place marked where they stopped work the day before. All direct instruction is provided on a one-to-one basis because each student is working in a different text. As a result, the teacher must rotate frequently among the students, providing sporadic instruction limited to a total of five to six minutes to each pupil. During the last few minutes of each period she grades the students' work and marks the place where they will begin the next day. Some students may respond positively to Mrs. McKinnon's program; however, far more could progress in Sister Teresa's program.

Sister Teresa's Resource Class

In a nearby school, Sister Teresa teaches similar resource classes of six to eight students with mild disabilities each period. She also uses discarded texts while awaiting the arrival of more appropriate instructional materials. Unlike Mrs. McKinnon, Sister Teresa conducts her own assessment to identify the exact tasks on which each student should begin. She then restructures her texts and workbooks according to each student's diagnosed needs. With scissors, paste, stapler, plastic sheet protectors, and a wide-tipped black felt marker, she deletes the tasks that are inappropriate, adds simplified directions and extra practice activities, and changes terminology. Whole pages are removed, and others added. The modified pages are stapled together or placed individually into clear plastic folders and filed in a box.

Sister Teresa has effectively designed a learning activity packet that addresses each student's specific academic needs. Methods of instruction are planned to complement each student's learning style. When appropriate, two or three students are grouped for similar skill instruction. Often, all students are taught as a single group, but only for part of a period. Appropriate, small and large group teaching increases the amount of direct instructional time which she is able to offer each student. Lessons are scheduled and charted weekly in a file folder for each student, and the teacher and student collaborate to plan and evaluate the lessons daily. Sister Teresa's students not only progress, but also begin to assume some responsibility for their own achievement.

Comparisons

Mr. Leo's students will "finish all their texts" by the end of the school year; some of Ms. Alison's students will not. Mrs. McKinnon provides more one to one instruction to her students than does Sister Teresa. Yet, few would question the more effective teaching of Ms. Alison and Sister Teresa. Both Ms. Alison and Sister Teresa have structured their teaching so that they are able to expand both the quality and quantity of direct instruction. Their teaching is designed to meet many personal learning needs of individual students. These two professionals are teaching the students, not the texts and curricula.

The four classrooms are hypothetical and provided to briefly illustrate the value of making adjustments in organization, methods, and materials. The differences in these classrooms reflect basic differences in the principles that guide each teacher's instructional program.

PRINCIPLES OF PERSONALIZED PROGRAMMING

For programming to be so individualized that it becomes personalized, it must be carefully and systematically planned. Several principles are useful for systematizing and guiding philosophically the programming process. These principles, outlined in Figure 2.3, address the three major components of programming: content, instructional approach, and organization.

1. **Teach personalized content**
— *Follow the scope and sequence of the general education curriculum.*

FIGURE 2.3   Principles of Programming

Teach personalized content
  — Follow the scope and sequence of the general curriculum
  — Set content priorities according to their value to student success
  — Pace teaching according to student learning rate

Personalize the instructional approach
  — Teach the way the student learns best
  — Teach the strategies for accomplishing tasks
  — Actively teach involved learners
  — Adjust methods and materials according to success and errors of student
  — Teach for task mastery

Organize for ongoing personalized instruction
  — Base plans on personalized assessment and assess as you program
  — Efficiently manage the instructional process
  — Maximize individualization opportunities through efficient use of resources
  — Plan an integrated and coordinated program

The curriculum of the general education program is the measure of a student's academic success (or failure). Teaching content, from the point on the curricular continuum, that a student is capable of mastering, is too logical to ignore.

— *Set content priorities according to their value to student success.*

Rank subject areas and the tasks within them in terms of their contribution to the student's total academic and real-life functioning, then teach them in their order of importance. Difficulties in the core curriculum areas should be considered first.

— *Pace teaching according to student learning rate.*

The number and complexity of new tasks which a learner can master in one lesson can vary among students; this is also true of an individual student across subject areas and task types. Teaching that outpaces the learner is a futile gesture.

2. Personalize the instructional approach

— *Teach the way the student learns best.*

Learning style is a very personal concept. If we all learned in the same manner and at the same rate when exposed to the same teaching, there would be few individual differences. "Just tell me how to do it" or "Show me what you want" are statements heard daily in classrooms. These are clear-cut statements of, at least, a temporary learning preference by the students who make such requests. Although not all elements of learning style are readily amenable to teacher control, use those that are vehicles for efficient and effective instruction.

— *Teach the strategies for accomplishing tasks.*

Offer instruction in how to learn. Teach skills as strategies and incorporate effective learning and study strategies into each area of the curriculum. Rather than assuming students know how to think through tasks, directly teach the procedures for accomplishing each task.

— *Actively teach involved learners.*

Increase explicit teaching and student engagement. Conduct brisk lessons that entice students to actively participate, think, and achieve. Maximize cooperative and collaborative learning opportunities to increase interest and interaction. Remember: Teaching only occurs when learning results, and neither is a passive process.

— *Adjust methods and materials according to the success and errors of a student.*

Accentuate those methods that produce student success; eliminate or modify those that produce student errors or slow the rate of progress. This applies equally to methods, materials, and learning conditions. Effective programming requires constant revision to adjust to student needs.

— *Teach for task mastery.*

Assume that the student can accomplish each important task, communicate high expectations, and adjust instruction as needed, teaching until each student masters target tasks. Remember that momentary mastery of a task does not guarantee long-term retention. For an accomplishment to become usable and transferable to other learning, it must be mastered at more than a surface level. Maintain each gain the student makes through review, reinforcement, and practice in an authentic context. Plan maintenance activities as an integral part of the program.

3. Organize for ongoing personalized instruction

— *Base plans on personalized assessment and assess as you program.*

There are innumerable tasks within a curriculum; select the ones that you know the student needs rather than guess at the ones which are probably needed. This practice provides the specifics for an initial program; for an ongoing plan, diagnose while teaching so that you always know what to teach tomorrow.

— *Efficiently manage the instructional process.*

To produce and nurture interactive learning, carefully structure the classroom and establish facilitative rules and routines. Then remain on guard to anticipate student needs before they occur. The combination of a structured environment and an alert leader stacks the deck in favor of both student and teacher success.

— *Maximize individualization opportunities through efficient use of resources.*

Become an acquisition and requisition expert. Capitalize on the parent who says, "Let me know if there is anything I can do to help." Take the time to train, monitor, and then utilize teaching assistants. Be the first teacher in the school to study the manual for the new media equipment and then "adopt" it.

— *Plan an integrated and coordinated program.*

Integrate instruction in several skill areas when feasible. Coordinate your program with all others in which a target student participates. Collaborate with not only other professionals, but also the parents and particularly the student in the development, monitoring, and revisions of the program. An involved student is more likely to become a committed student who progresses.

Although these principles are not all inclusive, they address many important issues involved in planning and providing a personalized program of instruction. In the next chapter, both these and the assessment principles, previously discussed, are placed in the context of an assessment and programming model.

SUMMARY

Curriculum is defined as the educational program, including subject matter and instructional procedures. The curriculum guide sets system standards, suggests teaching content and methods, and together with the teacher's curriculum, provides the foundation for assessment and programming of individualized instruction. Content selection of the curriculum guide is influenced by many factors. These guides vary from detailed to general. Subject-centered and competency-based curricula are the most common plans for general education. Special education curricula are either specialized, IEP-based, or modifications of the general education program. A curriculum, including the IEP, which is related to the general education curriculum increases the likelihood of success for special education students. General and special educators should collaborate as they restructure curricula to incorporate adaptations for individual learners that are more fluid, flexible, authentic, and generally more appropriate for inclusive general education. The teacher, guided by personal and professional biases, determines the classroom curriculum by the selection of lesson content, time allotments, and pacing.

The individualization of a curriculum to a specific student's needs depends upon the instructional delivery system, the teacher's resources, organization, and adjustments to methods and materials. The three crucial elements of programming are the content, instructional approach, and organization. To systemize and guide the personalized programming process, this book suggests 12 basic programming principles. (See Figure 2.3.)

CASE STUDIES

Case A

Liz, a student with mild disabilities, is currently in second grade. Her attention span is very brief.

She is reading at a preprimer level with limited comprehension. Her knowledge of phonics is confined to the initial sounds of "t," "s," and "m"; she recognizes at sight these words: "and, the, is, boy, run, see, Liz, fun, red, blue, Juan." Based on what you have read and what little you now know about Liz, adjust the worksheet in Figure 2.4 to meet her instructional needs, then describe how you would present the page to her.

Case B

You are a beginning teacher of a fourth-grade class. Social studies is your first lesson to teach tomorrow, your first day of school. The textbooks have not yet arrived. From the appropriate section of the abbreviated curriculum guide in Figure 2.5, indicate the additions, deletions, or modifications you feel are needed to construct a meaningful 40-minute lesson. (You may use textbooks and other curriculum guides as well as any additional references that are helpful to recommend changes.)

ENRICHMENT ACTIVITIES

Discussion

1. Describe the school and classroom circumstances that may cause a student to succeed in one third-grade class and fail in another; discuss the conditions that may accelerate a student's progress in a special education class.

2. Discuss the role of the general education curriculum in the education of students with and without disabilities.

3. How much does an elementary teacher need to know about the curricula of adjacent grades? How much does a special education teacher need to know about the kindergarten through sixth grade curricula? Justify your answers.

4. Consider the three instructional elements that facilitate programming to meet the individual learners' needs: content, instructional approach, and organization. Which is probably the most important in a general education classroom? Why?

FIGURE 2.4   Worksheet for Adaptations

Read the Sentence.
Circle **YES** or **NO.**

1. Juan is a boy.	YES	NO
2. Tom is a girl.	YES	NO
3. Jane is a boy.	YES	NO
4. Mary is a girl.	YES	NO
5. Mother can run fast.	YES	NO
6. Boys don't like surprises.	YES	NO
7. Tom's ball is red.	YES	NO
8. Juan can run fast.	YES	NO
9. Jane and Tom walk.	YES	NO
10. Mary likes surprises.	YES	NO

FIGURE 2.5   Abbreviated Curriculum Guide

Unit: Climate

Concept: Climate varies by location

Objective: The student will describe and explain the differences in the climates of mountain regions, desert regions, coastal regions, and tropical regions.

Activity A: Have students review the physical features of the different regions.

Activity B: Have students chart the physical features of each region.

Activity C: Ask students to write a paragraph contrasting the climate of two of the regions.

Activity D: Have students make a chart listing annual rainfall for a major city in each of the regions.

Evaluation: Essay test

Which is least important? What about their relative importance in special classes? Justify your position.

5. Review the 12 principles of programming and then rank them in terms of their importance to providing individualized instruction. Reconsider your rankings with two different specific students in mind. Is there a difference? Discuss and compare your rankings with peers.

Special Projects

1. Analyze the teacher's edition of a primary-grade math text. Compare and contrast the text with a curriculum guide in terms of specificity and usefulness to teacher and student. Which of these resources would be the most helpful to a beginning teacher and why? Which would be the most helpful to an experienced teacher and why?

2. Interview a veteran elementary teacher to determine the changes in formal curricula that have occurred during the past five years. Research and identify at least seven factors that influenced the changes. Repeat the process by interviewing a veteran special educator. Are the curricular influences the same? Why or why not?

3. Discuss with two special education and two general education teachers the advantages and disadvantages of complete teacher autonomy in implementing the classroom curriculum. From their opinions, develop your own list. Formulate a policy for the school that your firstborn child will (or did) attend.

4. Consider and then list the advantages and disadvantages of general education, assuming greater responsibility for the education of students with special needs from each of the following perspectives:

   General classroom teachers
   Special education teachers
   Students with special needs
   Parents of students with special needs
   Classroom methodology
   Programmatic costs

   Interview a general education teacher, a special education teacher, and/or a school principal, and contrast their viewpoints with yours.

5. Observe in a general and a special classroom to compare instructional content, approach, and classroom organization. Itemize differences in terms of those that are slight and substantial, and estimate the reason and effectiveness of differences.

CHAPTER 3

CURRICULAR ASSESSMENT AND PROGRAMMING

JOYCE S. CHOATE
LAMOINE J. MILLER

CHAPTER OBJECTIVES

This chapter is designed to enable the reader to:

1. Explain the importance to personalized programming of curriculum assessment and student mastery of curricular tasks.
2. Describe the steps in the assessment/programming cycle.
3. Describe the different stages of assessment and programming and explain their roles in personalizing the assessment/programming process.
4. Differentiate and critique the formats for assessment procedures.
5. Differentiate the stimulus presentations and response requirements of commercial programs for selected subject areas.
6. Plan the step-by-step implementation of the assessment/programming cycle for a specific student.

Academic success or failure is contingent upon the relationship of a student's skills with the demands of the school curriculum. The student whose skill development coincides with the regular curricular content and sequence enjoys academic success. In fact, the degree of fit is perhaps equally as important to academic success as the amount of progress. Gickling and Thompson (1985) describe those students whose skill development does not match the curriculum as "curriculum casualties." Typically, failure, regardless of the label applied by the school, is the fate awaiting those students whose performance falls behind the schedule set by the classroom curriculum. "Official" failure means that students are retained in a grade, a practice that generally worsens future achievement (Shepard & Smith, 1990), to await the magical moment when their skills will match the curricular agenda. Sometimes, this sad fate is delayed by promoting students and continuing the scheduled instruction despite the gaps in their skills. Some students experience the "learned helplessness" syndrome; that is, they overreact to negative feedback and become apathetic from repeated failure (Lerner, 1993).

Following failure, many students are referred to special education services for eligibility testing (Will, 1986). Of those referred, over half are subsequently placed in a special education program (Salvia & Ysseldyke, 1995). Here, students often confront a curriculum which differs so dramatically from the one taught in regular education that they only learn to function as model special education students. That is, students who are taught the special education curriculum can probably function better in the special class, but not necessarily in a regular class. In addition, the inflexible grade or subject curriculum may present the more able student a different type of failure experience, because it impedes individual progress. Rather than perpetuating student failure, why not adjust the curriculum to meet the student's learning needs and pace? Would not such adjustment improve the quantity and rate of a student's mastery of basic skills?

A RATIONALE AND MODEL

The basic tenets of assessment and programming in this text may be illustrated by answering these questions:

What is expected of the student by the curriculum?

What is the position of the student's skills on the curricular continuum?

What is the best plan to adjust the curriculum to meet the student's needs?

These same questions form the theoretical foundation of the various curriculum-based assessment (CBA) models described in Chapter 1. The remainder of this book describes our CBA model, reflecting our professional bias and experience both in terminology and procedures. "Personalized" is used to emphasize the highly individualized nature of the process. Assessment and programming are most often discussed together to stress the value of CBA as formative assessment, to emphasize the importance of programming, or instruction, to the process, and to highlight their strong cyclical interrelationship. Thus, using Marston's analysis of CBA models (1989), ours is a criterion-referenced CBA model that values the answers to the three questions for their instructional implications. This chapter, and those following, refer to these basic questions, suggest procedures for obtaining answers, and illustrate how to use the answers to personalize assessment and programming for a student.

To individualize instruction effectively, informed decisions must be made about what to teach and how to teach it. In recommending how to determine what to teach, Howell, Fox, and Morehead (1993) suggest that teachers decide whether the task needs additional instruction or no instruction; if additional instruction is indicated, then the decision is whether to build accuracy, fluency, or automaticity. This decision is simplified by identifying the specific criteria (curricula) used to gauge the student's academic progress and those performances that do or do not meet the criteria (curricula).

Deciding What to Teach

To discover what to teach, or the task level, one must compare the relative position of the student's skills on the curricular continuum with the curricular expectations. A student's probable success point in the general education program can be predicted by comparing his or her learning needs and pace with the prevailing curriculum. This procedure also provides the substance of required curricular adjustments. Expectations about levels of curriculum mastery may need to be differentiated for many students, especially those with special needs. For example, the appropriate point within the elementary curriculum for a ten-year-old boy with a disability may be at the third-grade level in math and at the second-grade level in reading; additional curricular adjustments may even include many first-grade phonics tasks. Other examples of curricular level adjustments are cited in Figure 3.1.

FIGURE 3.1   Curricular-Level Adjustments

Examples	*Adjustments*
Lottie, a sixth-grade student identified as learning disabled, is performing at mid-third-grade level in reading and spelling. She is mainstreamed into social studies and science. The teacher reports she is verbal and participates in class discussions, but has difficulty reading the science and social studies texts. The classroom teacher made curriculum adjustments by tape recording the texts and administering her tests orally. Lottie is able to perform successfully with these minor adjustments.	Third-grade word recognition skills and fourth-grade comprehension — Teachers or peers tape record texts in science and social studies — Teacher administers test orally
Jeff, a highly distractable third grader, has excellent reading and spelling skills, but is performing at mid-first grade in arithmetic. He counts on his fingers when flashed basic addition facts. His third-grade teacher realizes he is not ready for third-grade math and adjusts his curriculum accordingly. Jeff is permitted to use manipulatives. Assignments have been adjusted to his level and shortened in accordance with his attention span.	Third-grade reading Third-grade social studies First-grade arithmetic — Reteach basic addition facts (2 digit plus 2 digit, no reg.) — Reteach basic subtraction facts (2 digit minus 1 digit, no reg.) — Use manipulatives — Shorten assignments
Jenell, a fourth-grade student, is failing because of her slow rate of responding, and her inability to complete assignments. Mrs. Green, her fourth-grade teacher, reports she reads at grade level and appears to have little difficulty understanding concepts presented in class, but she is unable to give Jenell a grade because she does not complete or turn tasks in to be graded. After consultation with the resource teacher, Mrs. Green adapted the curriculum by extending the time for Jenell to complete tests and shortened Jenell's assignments.	Fourth-grade level curriculum — Cut workbook pages into strips, time her, and have her compete against herself — Emphasize concept mastery, not quantity — Extend time for test taking — Implement Premack principle into her curriculum

Tests that do not follow the content of the general curriculum may provide placement information, but seldom generate specific prescriptive data. These tests reveal little about student strategies in problem solution. Gable and Hendrickson (1990b) note the difficulty of identifying the "patterns of strategies students employ to execute skills and solve problems without multiple trials on a level/skill" (p. 6). It is also important to identify which strategies the student is or is not using effectively to learn and perform target tasks. It is imperative that the student's needs be identified in relation to the true measure, the classroom curriculum (Ysseldyke & Algozzine, 1995). Then you can determine what to teach so the curriculum conforms to the student's learning needs.

Deciding How to Teach

Once the student's instructional needs have been identified, thus determining what to teach, decisions must be made about how to teach. Analysis of a student's task performance under varying conditions helps you to decide how to teach. By carefully observing the student's response, you can isolate variables that promote task mastery.

Factors for scrutiny include the learning situation, methods, materials, presentation mode, response demand, and learner preference. Through systematic modification of these factors, the best plan for how and where to teach can be developed.

The selection of the best methods, materials, and strategies to use in an instructional program depends upon how the student learns best. According to Mercer and Mercer (1993), knowing how to assess the best way to teach a student is a very critical skill, one that has received too little emphasis in teacher training programs. The decision about how to teach is usually based on what was generally successful in the past with similar students. The student might also be assessed directly in an effort to find out how best to teach. When this is the case, the instructional environment should be analyzed as well. Analysis of the teaching environment, or ecological assessment, examines learning preferences (objective vs. essay tests, visual vs. auditory presentation, reading vs. listening, inductive vs. deductive, easy vs. difficult, and primary vs. social rewards) and preferences in the physical setting (bright vs. dim lights, silence vs. sound, warm vs. cool, front or middle vs. rear of classroom, plus the type of classroom organization and degree of structure).

One system for assessing the instructional environment is The Instructional Environment System II (TIES-II) (Ysseldyke & Christenson, 1993). Through observation and interviews with the student and teachers, TIES is designed to describe the extent to which a student's academic or behavior problems are a function of factors in the instructional environment, and identify starting points in designing appropriate instructional interventions for individual students. The Learning Style Inventory (Dunn, Dunn, & Price, 1989) is used to assess an individual's preferences in each of five areas: (1) immediate environment (sound, light, temperature, design); (2) emotionality (motivation, persistence, responsibility, need for structure); (3) sociological preferences (learning alone, in pairs, teams, small groups, or with adult, and patterns, routine, and variety); (4) physiological characteristics (auditory, visual, tactual,

kinesthetic perceptual preferences, food intake, time of day, energy levels, and mobility needs); and (5) processing inclinations (global/analytic, right/left, impulsive/reflective). Mercer and Mercer (1993) have developed a rating scale that also measures the student's behavior in many of these same areas. Additional discussions of the learning ecology are presented in publications by Evans, Evans, and Schmid (1989), Evans, Evans, Gable, and Schmid (1991), Hammill and Bartel (1995), and Taylor (1993). In addition to evaluating the instructional environment, observing how well the student is progressing in the current instructional program requires evaluating how much the student's behavior is changing over time. This necessitates observing the student's performance in the current instructional program several days and initiating monitoring procedures such as those described by Howell, Fox, and Morehead (1993). Information from all sources should be considered in determining how to teach. As the teacher becomes more experienced with the student, decisions about how and where to teach should be based on data derived from the ongoing monitoring and evaluation of student progress.

The Curriculum-Based Assessment/ Programming Model

The model in Figure 3.2 is a guide for how to develop and implement the best plan to meet the needs of an individual student. In many respects, the model is a version of the test-teach-test-reteach cycle expanded to incorporate the basic elements of CBA, yet emphasize instruction. Our professional biases are reflected in the use of the term *programming* to highlight the active and targeted nature of the planning and teaching process.

The curriculum-based assessment/programming (CBA/P) cycle presented in Figure 3.2 is an attempt to refine further the process of developing individualized instructional programs. The skill-based model values skills as strategies to accomplish grander and more authentic goals. The cycle contains procedures to assess and program for the

FIGURE 3.2   The Curriculum-Based Assessment/Programming Model

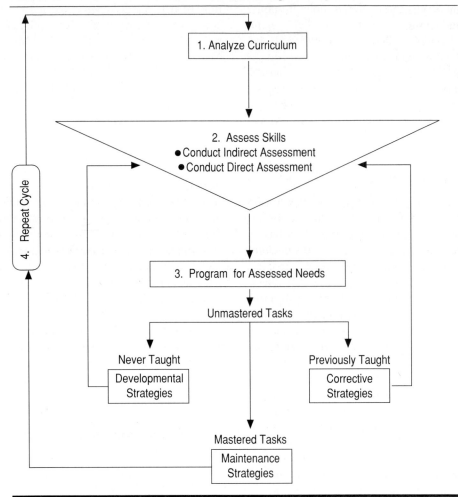

student's needed skills, as well as to ensure that target tasks are mastered on both short- and long-term bases. These four steps include:

Step 1: Analyze curricula to identify the skills, subskills, and tasks expected of the student.

Step 2: Assess the student's mastery of skills, subskills, and tasks in the content areas required by the current curriculum; use indirect and direct measures that generate prescriptive data specific to a student's curricular content.

Step 3: Program for instruction to meet the student's assessed needs; provide three stages of instruction: developmental, corrective, and maintenance, according to student's needs. Reassess (Step 2) until mastery is confirmed.

Step 4: Reenter and repeat the cycle, comparing the student's performance with the curriculum analysis in Step 1, and then either add new tasks or shift program emphasis. Collaborate and communicate progress and needs with all who are involved in the student's education.

This cycle helps to identify expectations, skill position, and the best plan. Throughout this chapter, each related step is described in greater detail as factors involved in defining a student's academic needs and providing an instructional program are discussed. An expanded treatment of the CBA/P cycle in Figure 3.15 then summarizes the process. The intent is to go one step beyond individualizing to personalizing the assessment and programming process.

THE PERSONALIZED ASSESSMENT PROCESS

Personalized assessment involves four major components: analysis of the curriculum, selection of assessment techniques, indirect student assessment, and direct student assessment. Each function increases cumulatively the information base for developing a personalized educational program. In harmony with the principles discussed in Chapter 1, the approach is purposeful and classroom-related.

Analysis of the Curriculum

If academic success or failure hinges upon the interrelationships of the learner's skills with the curriculum, then the assessment process most logically begins with the general education curriculum. The objective is to determine the true nature of the academic tasks confronting a student. To accomplish this requires identifying the actual subjects, specific subject matter taught, and the process by which the content is expected to be learned (Doll, 1992). Thus, analyzing the curriculum is the first step in the curriculum-based assessment and programming process. As outlined in Figure 3.3, this analysis involves a search for skill listings, interviews for clarification, observations for confirmation, and charts for referencing.

The purpose of the search is to locate formal statements of curricula. The object of the search is an itemized and sequenced listing of the academic requirements for each subject area. The logical sources for subject and skill explanations are curriculum guides published by state departments

FIGURE 3.3   Step 1: Analyze Curricula

- Locate formal listings of curricula or formulate by modifying similar listings
- Interview teacher
  Confirm and/or modify content
  Verify scope and sequence
  Identify performance levels and criteria
  Identify teaching/learning processes
- Mark expectations of student on curricular listings

of education and local school systems. Copies of these guides are usually available through the offices of the state or system educational agencies, educational media centers, the principal's office of local schools, and/or the library of local universities. Specifications of minimum standards for each grade and subject, if formalized, may be available from the same sources. Ideally, these guides also include a brief and concise scope and sequence listing, summarizing all included tasks for preschool through at least grade six. If, however, the curriculum guides are not organized in this way, several options remain:

1. Scan the pages and highlight with a felt marker the specific tasks;
2. Copy the specific tasks to formulate a listing;
3. Locate scope and sequence charts of each text in use; or
4. Obtain an alternate, but similar listing, and modify it to conform to each subject area requirement.

Since it is possible that the listings may need changes to reflect the actual classroom curriculum, the primary task is to obtain short, manageable lists that are reasonably similar to the formal curricula. Abbreviated skill listings simplify assessment of the curriculum.

As has been noted, the individual teacher is the one who ultimately determines the classroom curriculum (Berliner, 1984). Interviews aid in clarifying the specific components of an individual teacher's classroom curriculum. An informal interview with, or quick phone call to, a school principal, secretary, or teacher can usually serve to identify exactly which subjects are typically included in the grade-level curriculum. For each of these subject areas, the abbreviated skill listings serve as the focus for the teacher interviews. Whether the diagnostician is the responding teacher or an outside agent, the questions are the same:

What are the specific tasks that the student must master to succeed in this classroom?

What is the sequence in which these tasks are presented?

What are the minimum skills required for success in the system?

Which subskills and tasks has the teacher added and/or subtracted from the listings?

The answers to these questions can be recorded on the listings as an aid in beginning the tentative curriculum chart for the target student. Additional information, which only the teacher can provide, includes the classroom subject and subskill emphasis, evaluation procedures, performance standards, methods of instruction, supplementary learning experiences, plus available resources and options. (Specific formats for teacher interviews are presented in Chapter 4.)

The importance of developing an accurate listing of the student's curriculum cannot be overemphasized. The teacher's curricular modifications, noted on the listing or chart, portray the measure by which the student's progress is gauged. This curriculum chart will guide the ongoing assessment and programming of the student within his or her curricular context.

Assessment of Student Performance

Several important questions must be answered before deciding just how to go about assessing students' mastery of identified skills. What level of performance should be tapped? Which particular assessment format is best suited for eliciting the target performances? Which assessment procedures should exclude (i.e., indirect assessment), or include (i.e., direct assessment) the student's physical presence? How should assessment results be documented? Since these questions have no set answers, informed decisions must be made after considering all variables.

Curriculum-Referenced Assessment Techniques

In order to decide how to assess student performance in any area, the target behaviors first must be identified. As mentioned in the discussion of curricular analysis, this entails describing the desired outcome behaviors for each curricular component. Available assessment options can then be considered according to their potential for evaluating the desired behaviors in the most efficient, effective, and appealing manner.

Specifying Performances. Before selecting the assessment content and format, the desired performances must be specified, including the exact nature of the tasks and the targeted level of proficiency. A table of specifications for each curricular task greatly simplifies the process of both specifying performance and developing appropriate measures to assess that performance.

Task Content. When deciding what to assess, the first question that occurs is what skills are needed? The actual skills expected of the student are the ones listed or charted as a result of analyzing the curriculum. These are typically stated in language that most teachers readily understand. For example, few teachers would wonder about the intent of "adds two single-digit numbers with no regrouping." They might wonder about the level of proficiency expected of their students, an issue discussed in the next section. However, for the moment, consider this issue: What process are the students expected to use to find their answers? How are they expected to go about adding those numbers?

The way that students go about answering and performing is equally or more important than their performance, itself, because their strategies can be applied beyond the task at hand. That is, the strategies used to facilitate performance enable the student to perform other tasks independently. Thus, strategy assessment is an important component of assessment in any subject area. Tests should ask *how* the answer is found in addition to *what* the answer is.

Performance Level.   The manner in which students are required to demonstrate knowledge or perform tasks determines the level of their performance. That is, certain types of performance demand less skill proficiency than others. In this book we speak of three levels of performance that correspond to the most typical classroom task formats: (1) Selection, (2) Production, and (3) Application. These three levels not only describe the response expected of students but they also parallel the typical instructional sequence.

SELECTION.   This performance level requires the respondent to select answers from among choices. Multiple choice and true/false formats are examples of this level. Other selection formats might require the student to circle, point to, or underline, for example, the word that means the opposite of a stimulus word. Or a student might be asked to cross out or read the three words that do not mean the same as a stimulus word. The key component of this level is the provision of choices from which to select, making this the easiest assessment level for students to accomplish. It also is easier for teachers to grade than the others because the possible answers are restricted.

PRODUCTION.   The response for this level must be produced by the student. Although the quality and quantity of clues and prompts may vary, the student is expected to generate responses which can also vary in quality and quantity. Thus, this format might require a one-word response, as in fill-in-the-blank with the word that means the opposite, or a multiword response, as in explain why this word means the opposite of that one (or fill in-the-BIG-blank). Production level tasks are typically more difficult for students to accomplish and for teachers to grade than selection tasks, but less demanding than ones at the application level.

APPLICATION.   The application level requires students to apply skills in context and also to generalize them to other situations. For example, a student might be asked to use his or her knowledge of antonyms to state or write a convincing argument for shorter or longer school hours. Using addition skills to solve arithmetic word problems also requires application. Thus, application demands responses at the production level as well.

When skills are *applied* to real-life situations, then *authentic performance assessment* results. According to the Office of Technology Assessment (1992), performance assessment (PA) is characterized by real-world tasks requiring students to construct responses that may be interpreted according to thinking patterns as well as correctness. Thus, PA presupposes an authentic curriculum from which are drawn the authentic performance tasks—practices that now occur occasionally in many classrooms but dominate few. Aside from vocational assessment and instruction programs that have historically emphasized authenticity, the effects of implementing authentic curricula and PA with students with disabilities are mostly speculative (Choate & Evans, 1992; Poteet, Choate, & Stewart, 1993). However, investigations of such issues as appropriateness for students with special needs, theoretical bases, technical qualities, efficiency, and effectiveness continue (Coutinho & Malouf, 1993). Meanwhile, suggestions for increasing the authenticity of application-level assessment as well as corrective instruction are interspersed throughout the chapters that follow.

The graduated difficulty of the three performance levels—selection, production, and application—is apparent in classroom instruction when teachers first guide students to select correct answers, next produce them, and finally, apply the skills in context. The nature of the skill, the time and level of its introduction, the ages and abilities of the students, as well as the standards of the particular teacher and school are determinants of the level of performance that will be taught and, thus, expected of students. In designing assessment tasks, the level of performance to measure is the level demanded by the individual student's curriculum. A table of specifications is a useful device for making both content and level decisions, and then formulating appropriate assessment tasks.

Matching Test to Task. A table of specifications is a matrix listing curricular content by task and level of performance. Whether derived from the curriculum, or constructed before or during its formulation (the better practice), the utility is the same: the table serves as a blueprint for instruction and for developing assessment items. With table in hand, one needs only to locate the task and level of performance required by the curriculum; to refer to a listing of behavioral objectives or write a description of the behavior that signals mastery; then to design a task to elicit and measure that behavior. For example, if the target task is phonics, initial *m,* and the desired level is production, then the mission is to design a measure of the behavior "produces the sound of *m.*" This behavior could be measured in several ways, one of which might be to display the word milk, then ask the student to voice the beginning sound. At the application level, assessment might consist of evaluating the student's pronunciation of the beginning *m* in at least five difficult words in the context of a reading passage. As illustrated by the table of specifications for adding whole numbers in Figure 3.4, the assessment task becomes obvious when behavior is indicated in a cell along

with the number of items to include on a test to weight it and draw a fair sample of performance. For the first task listed, you simply attach the itemization of the task to the description under performance level to gain an explanation of the assessment task at the selection level: Adds 2, one-digit numbers with sums < 10 . . . and selects answer from four choices (in at least five samples). To measure the second task at the application level, the assessment task would be: Adds 2, one-digit numbers with sums < 20 and applies to solving 5 word problems (in at least five samples). Although a table of specifications is not essential for constructing curriculum-based tests, the itemizations facilitate both teaching and test construction (Gronlund & Linn, 1990). Simply stated, the use of the table is a means to ensure that the test design matches the task demanded by the prevailing curriculum.

Performance Criteria. In addition to the actual task that is to be demonstrated, the degree of accuracy which signals mastery must be established. Performance criteria are apparent for those tasks described by behavioral objective statements. However, standards often vary across tasks and among individuals. For the most essential skills, such as high-frequency sight words or basic number facts, absolute mastery and also a specified rate of fluency may be required (e.g.,

FIGURE 3.4 Sample Table of Specifications

TASK	SELECTION LEVEL	PRODUCTION LEVEL	APPLICATION LEVEL
Whole Number Computation Adds:			
2 one-digit numbers sums < 10	and selects answer from 4 choices (5 samples)	and tells or writes correct answers (5 samples)	and applies to solve word problems (5 samples)
2 one-digit numbers sums < 20	and selects answer from 4 choices (5 samples)	and tells or writes correct answers (5 samples)	and applies to solve word problems (5 samples)
3 one-digit numbers sums < 20	and selects answer from 4 choices (5 samples)	and tells or writes correct answers (5 samples)	and applies to solve word problems (5 samples)

adds 2, one-digit numbers with sums less than 10 and tells *correct* answers at a rate of 2/second). For higher order skills, standards may be lower (e.g., adds 2, one-digit numbers with sums less than 10 and applies to solve word problems with 80% accuracy). Furthermore, the accuracy expected of individual students may vary according to their learning stages and perceived capabilities (e.g., 80% accuracy in first grade but 100% in second grade, or 70% accuracy for a student with disabilities but 100% for a gifted student). Thus, it is the school and the particular teacher (i.e., the specific curriculum) that determine the accuracy and fluency standards for each target task and for each individual student. These standards, then, serve as the criteria for judging whether and when a task is unmastered or mastered.

Choosing Assessment Procedures.   After deciding upon the task content and level of performance that match the curricular demands, the next decision is which assessment technique to use. Growing recognition of the importance of teaching and testing application and generalization of skills, as well as the systematic use of study and learning strategies, has increased interest in alternative assessment procedures to measure those behaviors. Application of both skills and strategies can be assessed by restructuring traditional procedures to incorporate the application tasks into selection and production testing formats, or by using more novel assessment techniques.

Selection Formats.   Several strategies to assess application of skills and strategies can be incorporated into the traditional selection format by restructuring directions and/or question stems to include application and strategy questions, illustrated in these examples:

— Choose the best answer: The best strategy to use in finding the main idea is . . .
— Mark each question as true or false, then justify each answer and write (or tell) how you found it.
— Underline the best answer, then tell how you can use this information.

— Select the correct answer, then demonstrate its utility by describing and/or developing a special project.

Several states have incorporated these elements into their statewide assessment programs. Production formats can be similarly restructured to include target content.

Production Formats.   Whether conducted during the course of daily instruction or inserted into a formal assessment routine, opportunities abound to assess application of skills and strategies using production formats. For each response produced, one simply asks, "How do you know? How will you use that? Demonstrate." Or the production tasks can be restructured to include target content as illustrated in a few examples:

— Fill the blank with the correct word, then describe how you will use this concept.
— Complete each statement, then tell (or write) how and why you chose your answer.
— List the steps you would follow to accomplish these three tasks.
— Cite three examples of the use of . . .
— Write (or tell) the name of the strategy that should be used to accomplish each task.
— Use the listed strategies to locate the answers to these questions.

The feasibility of incorporating application tasks into production-level assessment routines is partially contingent upon time constraints. In the typical classroom testing situation, teachers call "time" when they observe that most of their students have finished. That is, most classroom tests are basically untimed as are many informal assessment procedures. The flexible timelines permit the extension of production-level testing to include the additional elements.

BASAL SERIES TESTS.   Most tests that accompany basal textbook series are untimed. These tests typically involve production-level tasks (although some follow a selection format) tied to the instructional objectives of the texts, and are designed to either place students in an appropriate level of the series, or to measure achievement at the end of units of study within the specific books. After completion of the tests, strategy questions can readily be posed or application tasks assigned to individual students.

FLUENCY MEASURES. The most stringent time-lines apply when administering standardized tests or using probes. *Probes,* the typical format for precision teaching (Lindsley, 1964, 1990) and fluency-based measurement models (Shinn, 1989c), time the rate at which students respond. Measures of rate are suggested for quantifying students' performance changes (West, Young, & Spooner, 1990). This technique is used as an integrated teaching/learning approach, and is recommended in this book for assessing fluency and rate of performance of the most basic skills (e.g., instant recognition of letters and sight words or number facts) that students need to know automatically. Because of the time constraints, assessment of application and strategies cannot easily be directly infused. However, students may be questioned about application and strategies immediately following the timed probes.

Application Formats. Assessing skills in context and using some of the more novel measurement techniques are clearly application-level activities. When the use of strategies is also incorporated into these techniques, they tap higher order elements such as conceptual understanding and problem solving. In addition to the traditional skills-in-context tasks, several formats can be used to assess performance at the application level and also to render the tasks more authentic.

PORTFOLIO ASSESSMENT. The observable evidence of application or performance tasks can be readily organized in portfolios (Poteet, Choate, & Stewart, 1993). Analysis of samples of student's classwork is an assessment strategy recommended throughout this text. Portfolio assessment is a fresh title for systematizing and expanding this vintage and valuable assessment procedure. Perhaps the most familiar portfolio is the student

work-folder, a collection of students' classroom work filed in a folder, the central element of a time-honored teacher routine. Traditionally these work-folders have been used in the classroom for three purposes: to keep parents and students informed of school performance; as a resource for teachers to consult when assigning term grades; and as documentation for the grades assigned, should they be questioned by parents or students. In addition, many special educators utilize a work-folder format to organize individualized assignments before and after completion, and some maintain the folders for use as part of the re-evaluation process. However, enhancing their value as a formalized assessment technique requires restructuring and expanding the basic purposes of the work-folders and the ways in which they are developed and utilized to include: preselecting content and spacing assignments to display progress; selecting tasks to include all three levels of performance; conducting a qualitative as well as quantitative analysis of the performance; analyzing both error and success patterns; evaluating performance of the folder contents with each student; and then, of course, planning subsequent instruction and assignments on the basis of the assessed performance.

Several variations of portfolio assessment are emerging, each including critical analyses of collections of student work by student and/or teacher. Creative writing projects are particularly adaptable to portfolio assessment since collections of written expression are often organized as logs, journals, or compilations in book form. Samples to evaluate from a reading portfolio might include written assignments, results of a variety of tests, records of observations, a list of books read, and perhaps audio and video tapes as well. Portfolios also present opportunities for teachers to guide students toward self-assessment and independent learning. Except for complaints about the extra time required, classroom teachers report that portfolio assessment has a highly positive impact on most classroom activities (Viechnicki et al., 1993–1994).

LONG-TERM PROJECTS.   Student performance on long-term projects offers another format for application-level assessment. Individual and group projects in the arts, social studies, science, or written expression, especially projects that attempt to solve authentic problems, are likely candidates for assessment. Exhibitions and performances that require skill demonstration as well as long-term planning, development, and practice are examples of application, but their relevance may be greater for the arts and content areas than for the most basic skills. Research projects test the basic skills as well as higher order thinking and strategies.

SIMULATIONS.   Whether written or acted-out, simulations are popular for their interest and instructional value, particularly in the field of gifted education, but their assessment value has received little attention. For example, mock trials and debates might be likely targets for assessment in social studies. Solving simulated problems that approximate real-world problems increases the authenticity of the tasks.

Multi-Level Formats.   Several assessment techniques are inherently suitable for evaluating student performance at any one or all of the three levels. These include observations, student-developed tasks, and computerized tasks.

OBSERVATIONS.   Student performance of a variety of tasks can be directly observed, measured and interpreted by watching students as they go about completing assignments in their class settings. When in-class observation is not practical or an outside observer would be intrusive, recording target performances on videotape is an appealing alternative. In fact, because the videotapes permit closeup viewing, pausing, and replaying to scrutinize target behaviors at the convenience of the observer, they may be the preferred alternative in some cases. Both direct observation and work-sample analysis, or observation of permanent products, are discussed further in Chapter 4 and recommended as integral

components of the assessment process in Chapters 5–10.

CHECKLISTS AND RATING SCALES.   Regardless of the particular assessment technique used or the performance level involved, both checklists and rating scales facilitate the targeting, recording, and analyzing of student performance. They can be used to structure observations and interviews, record the results of those or other assessment formats, and summarize performances. Checklists and rating scales also present a convenient format for monitoring student progress (Choate, 1990a).

STUDENT-DEVELOPED EVALUATION. Brown (1989) endorses student-generated assessment for testing "thoughtfulness," noting the concomitant instructional value of such activities. He also mentions peer-evaluations of performance and evaluation by jury as innovative assessment techniques. Each of these approaches could be implemented for selection, production, and/or application level tasks.

AUDIOTUTORIAL ASSESSMENT.   As described by Gable and Hendrickson (1990b), audiotutorial assessment utilizes the medium of audio equipment to deliver assessment tasks. That is, students respond to pretaped stimuli by either writing or tape-recording answers. Described as a convenient technique for diagnosticians and appealing to some students, this format provides opportunities to include assessment of all task levels if the taped instructions so specify.

COMPUTER ASSESSMENT.   Recent advances in computer hardware and software hold great promise for increasing the effectiveness and individualization of both assessment and programming, regardless of task level (Desberg, 1994). Carnine (1989) comments on the convenience and efficiency that technology adds to the assessment and instructional process. Haney and Madaus (1989) cite the theoretical advantages of computerized adaptive testing programs that branch in difficulty according to student performance. Hasselbring and Moore (1990) note that expert computer systems for educational diagnosis, in the early stages of development, will become increasingly powerful and useful within this decade. However, as with their predecessors, the capacities of the evolving programs will be limited by the educational soundness of their design and the wisdom of the educators who select and direct them.

After specifying the performances to be measured, the assessment format and technique can be chosen. The next decision involves choosing which performances to measure indirectly and which ones to measure directly.

Indirect Student Assessment

Before directly interacting with a student, one can partially assess his or her performance through indirect means. Indirect assessment methods often produce valuable diagnostic information that may not become obvious during testing sessions. The specific procedures we recommend include teacher interviews, questionnaires, rating scales, and analysis of school records and work-samples. Even when the diagnostician *is* the teacher, such procedures systemize the collection and interpretation of vital assessment data.

Teacher Interview. The teacher to interview is the one most familiar with the target student. As portrayed in the sample formats in Chapter 4, the interview with a student's teacher serves several purposes. After assessing the curriculum, the second purpose of the interview is to learn the teacher's perceptions of the student's skill mastery in each subject area. The teacher's estimate of the student's relative performance across subjects identifies broad areas for concern. His or her ranking of the student's achievement in each sub-skill area within subjects of concern and descriptions of tasks particularly difficult for the student, narrows the assessment focus. A review of the student's cumulative folder offers a wealth of valuable information. Of special note is evidence suggesting reasons for skill gaps or poor performance. Comparison of grades and test scores in

past years with current data, the number of grades repeated, absences, the number of schools attended, and any medical or health problems may offer explanations as well as additional questions.

The third purpose of the teacher interview is to ascertain his or her impression of the student's learning patterns. The importance of determining the student's learning style cannot be overlooked if a truly personalized instructional program is to be developed. As noted previously, numerous factors must be considered in determining the student's learning style.

When identifying a student's learning style, "identify the conditions under which the student is 'easier to teach' and therefore more likely to learn, and the conditions under which the student is 'harder to teach' and therefore less likely to profit from instruction" (Zigmond, Vallecorsa, & Silverman, 1983, p. 281). The variables most amenable to teacher manipulation include learning rate, stimulus/response mode, and learning environment. Information about the learner's preferences provides data for maximizing learning conditions throughout the instructional program.

The fourth purpose of the interview is to obtain the teacher's rating of the student's adjustment to the school environment. The suggestion by Good and Brophy (1994) to focus on behaviors most directly related to school is practical. To examine the degree a student has adjusted to what these authors refer to as the school role, concentrate on those behaviors that most directly impede or facilitate academic performance. In this context, the school role is defined as the student's demonstration of those behaviors expected by teachers. The student's proficiency in playing the school role appears to be a practical concept. Among the task-related behaviors appropriate for discussion are those that have been correlated with academic performance. Does the student work independently? Are assignments usually completed on time? Does the student follow instructions? What is the attention span of the student? These and many other concerns can be categorized as the student's attitude, independence, organization, self-control, and social skills. Some behaviors that disrupt learning disappear through direct instruction and proper programming (Kauffman, 1993). It is not the intent of this text to treat serious behavioral difficulties. Evans, Evans, and Schmid (1989), Kauffman (1993), Rosenberg, Wilson, Maheady, and Sindelar (1992), Sparzo and Poteet (1989), and Walker and Shea (1991) present strategies for teaching and managing students who require more specialized treatment.

Work-Sample Analysis.   Although analyzing the student's permanent products or classroom work samples is a type of observation, we consider it an indirect assessment because it can be accomplished without the physical presence of the student. Work samples, or the student's written performance on daily classroom activities, offer valuable clues for making needed changes in his or her instructional program (Gable & Hendrickson, 1990a; Salvia & Hughes, 1990; Taylor, 1993). The diagnostician analyzes the student's performance for consistent success and error patterns. Partially correct responses are examined further to identify the exact point and nature of error. If Dean reverses the digits in the sum of two numbers, the correct answers are there but not in order. Since Dean evidences partial skill mastery, instruction should be planned at the point of error; the entire process should not be retaught. The exact point of error is identified through error analysis. There are some cases in which error analysis does not lead to direct intervention. When the student gives no response or answers "I don't know," little direction for intervention has been provided. The student also may use a unique strategy that appears inconsistent or make mistakes that are the result of random errors that defy analysis (Salvia & Hughes, 1990).

Having collected all available data from indirect sources (teacher interview, questionnaires, rating scales, school records, and work samples), the data are analyzed and interpreted. These integrated data are then used to identify learning patterns and critical behaviors needing intervention

and to establish the initial hypotheses that determine the focus for direct assessment.

Direct Student Assessment

Direct student assessment describes direct contact and/or face-to-face interaction between diagnostician and student. The focus of the process is established by the data collected through indirect means. The synthesized information leads to diagnostic hypotheses, priorities, and assessment plans. (See Figure 3.5 for the procedural steps in the diagnostic hypotheses.) The three major approaches for directly assessing the student's skill mastery are directly observing the student in the classroom, interviewing the student, and testing the student.

Preliminary Procedures.   Organizing for direct assessment involves the interpretation of all information gathered from curriculum guides, teachers, school records, and analyses of the student's work. Findings from these sources give reasonably sound answers to the following questions about a student's academic functioning:

> Which specific curriculum tasks are expected to be mastered?
> What is the student's general level of academic functioning?
> Which subject and subskill areas are primary and secondary concerns?
> What is the suspected learning style?

FIGURE 3.5   Diagnostic Hypothesizing

1. Analyze and synthesize available data
   a. school records
   b. recent test results
   c. teacher survey
   d. observations
   e. work sample analysis
2. Formulate statements of diagnostic hypotheses
3. Prioritize, plan, and conduct direct assessment
4. Validate or reject hypotheses

Which desirable, school adjustment behaviors are exhibited?

What are some specific success and error patterns?

Are there disparities in performances across subject and teaching approaches?

Are there any interfering physical problems?

Seeking possible explanations for a student's performance, assumed causes, or "diagnostic asking," often results in one or more diagnostic hypotheses. Reviewing the data to trial test the hypotheses assists in the establishment of assessment priorities, as can be seen in the case of Angela in Figure 3.6. In this case, the first priority is probably the diagnosis of reading comprehension performance, that is, watching for differences among literal, interpretive, and critical subskills. The second priority is to analyze and compare performance of word meaning tasks

and to other word recognition tasks. The third priority is to assess understanding of social-studies terminology. Even if these hypotheses and priorities should be disproven or modified through direct assessment, a logical and purposeful assessment scheme has been formulated.

Observation. Observations are an important component in the overall assessment of the student. They confirm the classroom curriculum and also yield important assessment information about the student's functioning within the curriculum. Additional insights into the instructional time, methods, and evaluation procedures can best be documented by direct observation. Many student behaviors that influence classroom success do not result in permanent products and can only be measured through direct observation. Observations may be systematic or nonsystematic.

FIGURE 3.6 Angela, A Case in Progress

Indirect Assessment Results
- Curricular expectations: Read and understand texts at Fifth-Grade Level
- General Academic Functioning: Fourth-Grade Level
- Primary Areas of Concern
  Reading: Approximately Third-Grade Level
     Comprehension = Second- or Third-Grade Level
     Word meaning = Second-Grade Level
  Social Studies: Approximately Third-Grade Level

Tentative Hypothesis:
Reading and word meaning difficulties interfere in both subjects; but why aren't other subjects affected? Contrast stimulus/response patterns and work samples in two areas with those in other subjects.

Additional Indirect Assessment Results
In reading and social studies, Angela must formulate oral and written answers based upon what is read; in other subjects she selects responses based on oral discussion. She succeeds at recall of details, particularly when given a choice of answers, but has difficulty interpreting and synthesizing; work habits and independence are problematic.

Working Hypotheses:
- *The primary area of concern is probably reading comprehension.*
- *Detail comprehension may be superior to interpretive/critical subskills.*
- *Word meaning problems may interfere with interpretive/critical comprehension.*
- *Organizational/independent habits may interfere with total academic performance.*

Systematic observation requires repeated measures of a specifically defined behavior that is both observable and measurable. Repeated measures are critical for students whose behavior is inconsistent, since they provide a more accurate measure of the student's typical performance patterns (Brown and Snell, 1993; Luftig, 1989; McLoughlin & Lewis, 1994). They supply baseline data of the student's current performance on a specified behavior and are much more reliable than nonsystematic observations. Selecting the appropriate measurement technique is essential to the collection of accurate observation data. For example, frequency or event recording may be used when the behavior is well defined and discrete, such as the number of words correctly pronounced. If the major concern is the length of time required to complete a given task, then a more accurate measurement technique would be duration recording. Although systematic observation is briefly discussed in Chapter 4, more in-depth discussions can be found in publications by Alberto and Troutman (1994), Kazdin (1994), and Taylor (1993).

Nonsystematic observation does not require repeated measures but notes behaviors exhibited by students while performing daily tasks. For example, a student may be observed pronouncing the first sound of an unknown word and wildly guessing at the rest of the word. Another student may be noticed performing on-task with a copy of directions in hand but off task when given oral directions. This type of information can be invaluable in planning additional assessment strategies.

Informal Student Interview.   An informal interview with the student often clarifies the assessment priorities and may reveal information not otherwise obtainable. The purpose of the interview is twofold: to establish rapport with the student and to collect diagnostic information. It is appropriate to conduct this interview as a prelude to the first direct testing session. The diagnostic hypotheses serve as the logical source for probing explanations from the student. Since this inter-

view should establish a friendly relationship, it is important to maintain an informal tone. Therefore, accent the positive before approaching the negative. Questions such as "What do you like and/or do best in school and why?" and "What happens in the classroom to help you in this area?" should precede similar questions about the student's weaknesses and dislikes. (See sample student interview form in Chapter 4). The student's perspective of his or her performance and of the conditions facilitating learning are often quite illuminating. Many opinions voiced by the teacher, particularly those about methods and interaction, may be viewed differently by the student. In reviewing research on classroom dynamics, Good and Brophy (1994) emphasize the disparities between what teachers think they do and what they actually do. Therefore, the student's perceptions of the ways in which instruction is presented and reinforced are vital. If, in the previous example of Angela, the student explains that it is only during reading and social studies lessons that she sits next to her best friend, the working hypotheses may require substantial alteration. When this occurs, synthesizing all data should suggest assessment priorities.

Personalized Curricular Tests.   Accurate assessment of the student's academic skills is essential to entering the student within the curriculum at the appropriate level. Although it may be a time consuming process, you are *strongly encouraged* to develop original tests based upon the student's current curriculum. These curriculum tests will provide more accurate assessment information than most published tests and greatly enhance the student's chances of making progress.

Suggestions for Constructing Personalized Tests. Copies of the system's adopted curriculum texts and other resource materials used for instruction in the classroom provide the most appropriate sources for constructing personalized tests (Nolet, 1992; Shapiro & Derr, 1990; Ysseldyke & Algozzine, 1995). Once these materials have been secured, the diagnostician is ready to begin developing the tests. It is critical to select tasks that match the ones identified by the teacher and that are listed on the curriculum chart as important for student success. Administration of the test items must parallel the presentation mode and response demands required of the student in the classroom. That is, if the teacher's presentation of spelling words is through sentence dictation, the presentation mode is an auditory one and the response demand is a written one. Many written tests may be administered in a group setting. However, for tasks that typically require oral responses or when the process by which written responses are derived is an issue, the tests should be administered individually.

Using Other Tests. For those who lack the time or sophistication to develop original, personalized assessment measures, Appendices A–F provide sample test items. The items included in the tests are representative of typical text-level skills. Use these test items selectively, comparing the scope and sequence charts of currently used texts, the student's subject area chart, and the stimulus/response format of each subtest to verify each sample's congruence with the curriculum. This strategy ensures that any subtest selected may be legitimately included in the personalized assessment procedures. The sample items may also be used as a model for developing original tests. Additional sources for sample tasks include *Curriculum-Based Evaluation: Teaching and Decision Making* (Howell, Fox, & Morehead, 1993), *Models of Curriculum-Based Assessment* (Idol, Nevin, & Paolucci-Whitcomb, 1986), and *A Guide to Educating Mainstreamed Students* (Mann, Suiter, & McClung, 1992).

If you suspect the student's rate of response is partially responsible for poor performance, then include precision measurement in the assessment process. Precision measurement is a system of monitoring, charting, analyzing, and evaluating behavioral acceleration and deceleration rates. Lindsley (1964, 1990) and Lovitt, Fister, Freston, Kemp, Shroeder, and Bauernschmidt (1990) con-

tend that it is a set of procedures to be used with any method of teaching. This technique involves pinpointing target behavior, recording frequency or movement cycles per minute, computing performance rate, charting performance, and changing rate. The basic measure in precision teaching is rate, or the number of movement cycles divided by the number of minutes the teacher observed. For example, a student who writes fifty letters in five minutes would have a write-letter rate of 10 letters per minute (50 divided by 5). Developing and implementing strategies for increasing the student's response rate may significantly improve his/her academic performance.

Those comfortable with particular commercial criterion-referenced instruments may elect to use these in tandem with other curricular measures. Selected portions of published inventories such as ENRIGHT Diagnostic Inventory of Basic Arithmetic Skills (Enright, 1983) may be used to identify computation skills and errors. Certain subtests of the Hudson Education Skills Inventory (Hudson, Colson, Welch, Banikowski, & Mehring, 1989) and the Brigance Diagnostic Comprehensive Inventory of Basic Skills (Brigance, 1983) may provide needed data in several content areas. In any case, the diagnostician must always carefully check the scope and sequence chart of the current curriculum to determine which skills should be assessed and at what point in the continuum they are introduced.

Test Administration. Given ideal conditions, only the actual curriculum materials that the student is, was, or will be expected to use in class should be used to construct the testing materials. Assessment, using these materials, usually provides more reliable, accurate and useful information about the student's academic performance than the information obtained from commercially prepared instruments (Fuchs & Fuchs, 1990; Gable & Hendrickson, 1990a; Marston, 1989). However, choosing certain subtests from other sources for their similarity to both content and format of curricular tasks may condense the testing without negating the integrity of the diagnosis. In some instances these sources provide, in one format, more examples of target tasks than are typically presented in text materials. It is important to remember concise assessment is pragmatic assessment. When time constraints and other professional responsibilities are too great to allow the diagnostician the perfect circumstances for a thorough assessment, certain compromises are appropriate.

In addition to the general principles of assessment discussed in Chapter 1, several practical suggestions for direct assessment should be considered. These suggestions are presented in Figure 3.7 and are designed to limit the amount of time consumed by testing. Testing in subject areas not indicated as problematic can await the additional assessment provided through the CBA/P cycle. There are, however, certain procedures that are unique to particular content areas. The content specific suggestions for administering tests are presented in Chapters 5–10.

Documenting Student Needs

Administered tests must be scored and tabulated to determine areas of strengths and weaknesses. Error analysis should be conducted on targeted skill areas to verify and substantiate skill needs. Charting identified strengths and needs on the student's curriculum chart provides direction for the instructional program that follows.

Substantiating Needs.   You are obligated to use all available information to substantiate the skill needs of the student. Compare existing standardized test data, criterion-referenced test data, and data from other prescriptive measures with the student's performance in the classroom. Note and investigate any discrepancies. Additional assessment is indicated in any area where conflicting data cannot be easily justified or explained.

Occasionally, you may need to conduct or refer the student for further testing. The student's performance should dictate the necessity of additional evaluation. For instance, you may observe that Jerry periodically holds reading materials very close to his face, even though he has passed the vision screening test. Thus, Jerry may need further vision assessment. As reported by Marston (1989) and Salvia and Hughes (1990), repeated measures of a task through daily work samples aid in identifying those tasks that are mastered and any needing additional instruction. Consider the skill mastered when the student retains task proficiency throughout three CBA/P cycles. In cases where the diagnostician is not the classroom teacher, this individual should discuss the assessment results with the classroom teacher. Compare these results with the student's classroom performance.

Interpreting Assessment Results.   Error analysis involves a detailed inspection of a student's incorrect responses on work samples to ascertain if a pattern of errors exists that contributes to the wrong answers. Gable and Hendrickson (1990b) provide a series of activities to complete in con-

FIGURE 3.7   Practical Suggestions for Direct Assessment

1. Begin direct testing with the subject area(s) indicated by the teacher and student as most problematic.
2. Within the subskill area(s) of the subjects identified, administer a survey test of specific tasks. Analyze survey results to pinpoint those tasks requiring additional testing.
3. Select the testing procedure that matches the curriculum in both content and format and requires the least time and effort to complete by the diagnostician and student; use the student's text or workbook pages or criterion-referenced test items that present the task to be assessed.
4. If the student evidences mastery of the most difficult task, assume that the prerequisite tasks are also mastered, and present the next task in this skill sequence.
5. If the student cannot perform presented tasks, test his or her performance on lesser tasks in sequence.

ducting error analysis. These activities require the diagnostician to score the student's assignments, categorize student errors, determine if there is a discernible pattern, tabulate the types of errors, and hypothesize why the errors were made. You can specify more accurately where the learning is impeded if you analyze the student's performance throughout the learning task. One particularly effective procedure for facilitating this process is to have students work slowly through the task as they verbalize each step. To detect excessive or infrequent types of performance, incorporate success and error analysis into the assessment process. Evaluating the student's correct and incorrect responses in terms of the specific task required, the stimulus, and the response demand is essential.

Questions one might ask include:

How was the stimulus presented to the student (orally, written)?

What kind of response was required (verbal, matching, written, etc.)?

How consistent were the students' responses?

Were there significant differences in stimulus presentations and response modes between correct and incorrect responses?

Obtaining answers to these questions will assist you in identifying what in the instructional environment may be contributing to the student's learning difficulties. Combining this information with the error analysis data will increase your chances of developing an effective instructional program for the student.

Charting Skill Needs.   An important component of the assessment/programming cycle is charting the student's skill needs. Each student must have his or her own chart. Use the charts accompanying the basal texts, the ones provided in Chapters 5–10 of this text, or develop your own for each individual student. At the conclusion of the initial assessment, refer to the student's curriculum chart and check off those skills mastered and identify those in need of instruction. With

each successive assessment, update the student's chart.

Two Stages of Assessment

Built into Step 2 of the CBA/P Model are two stages of assessment. Stage 1 is the initial assessment of a student entering the cycle. Stage 2 is the assessment of the student's performance after he or she has been taught within the context of the CBA/P cycle.

Assessment at Stage 1 moves from general to specific, starting with the entire skill continuum and progressing to assessment of specific tasks within skill and subskill areas. As outlined in Figure 3.8, once the curriculum has been analyzed and you have identified exactly what the curriculum demands, you are ready to initiate indirect assessment. Data from teacher interviews, questionnaires, rating scales, school records, and work samples are collected, analyzed, and interpreted for possible contributions to or causes for the learning performance. During this stage of assessment, a concerted effort is made to identify patterns of strengths and weaknesses. From the

FIGURE 3.8   Stage 1 Assessment

Conduct indirect assessment
- Collect available data
    Teacher interview
    Questionnaires
    Rating scales
    School records
    Work samples
- Analyze and interpret
- Identify success and error patterns
- Formulate diagnostic hypothesis

Conduct direct assessment
- Develop plan for direct assessment
- Observe student in critical areas
- Develop test items
- Administer test
- Analyze responses
- Synthesize indirect and direct data
- Record on student's curriculum chart

identified areas of weakness, select the two to three behaviors that are most critical to the student's academic progress. Formulate diagnostic hypotheses and develop a plan for direct assessment. Direct assessment requires observing the target student in the classroom during lessons that involve the critical areas of concern. Since test item formats should reflect how each task is taught and evaluated in the classroom setting, identify curricular performance criteria and analyze the teacher's presentation style, the student's approach to learning tasks, and the nature of the instructional environment. Administer test items, analyze responses, and note success and error patterns. Synthesize information obtained from both indirect and direct assessment and record on the student's curriculum chart the mastered and unmastered tasks according to curricular performance standards.

Assessment in Stage 2, outlined in Figure 3.9, determines the student's mastery of specific tasks that were identified for teaching in Stage 1, then taught within the CBA/P cycle. Although limited, indirect assessment may occur here in the form of analyses of work samples produced during personalized instruction and perhaps specific questions of a teacher for clarification, direct assessment is the primary activity. Assessment, at this stage, conforms to the traditional classroom procedure of testing to determine how much a student has learned from instruction and to evaluate the success of the instructional program. In

FIGURE 3.9   Stage 2 Assessment

- Assess unmastered tasks taught in CBA/P cycle
- Analyze and note error patterns
- Categorize tasks
  mastered
  tentatively mastered
  unmastered
- Design program accordingly
- Record and chart tasks retained for 3 CBA/P cycles
- Recycle unmastered tasks

Stage 2, the initially unmastered tasks which have been taught in the CBA/P cycle must be reassessed using a format that parallels instruction. Responses are then analyzed and patterns of errors noted. Tasks are categorized as mastered, tentatively mastered, and unmastered according to curricular criteria, and a personalized program is designed accordingly. Mastered tasks are recorded on the curriculum chart when they have been retained through three CBA/P cycles. Unmastered tasks are further grouped by whether or not they have previously been taught. This type of specific task assessment evaluates the effectiveness of the instructional program for the student and provides continued direction for program design.

PERSONALIZED PROGRAMMING PROCEDURES

Assessment results provide the data base to make informed, instructional decisions. Obviously, an educational program developed for an individual student should provide a specific set of learning experiences that will allow progress through the curriculum at the student's optimum level and pace. That is, the content, methods, and materials should be planned in order to ensure a high probability of skill mastery. Methods and materials, with which a student has previously experienced success, may be considered in developing the prescriptive program. Without modification, no methods and materials, which have produced failure, should be included. It is the combination of the particular skill content, methods selected and materials chosen that produces an educational program specific to a student's needs.

Content Selection

Assessment results dictate program content. The content areas in which a student's skills are found to be minimal provide the core content for his or her individual program. As noted by Walberg (1990), "Teaching students what they already know and teaching them what they are yet incapable of learning are equally wasteful practices and may even be harmful to motivation" (p. 475). However, mastered tasks related to deficit areas must also be included in the program to avoid overwhelming the student (Gickling & Thompson, 1985; Ysseldyke & Algozzine 1995). Because the constant bombardment of a student with difficult tasks is likely to produce frustration and failure, only 20 to 30 percent of the program should be unfamiliar material. The remainder of the content should provide opportunities for review and reinforcement and the context for application.

Content emphasis is determined by ranking the relative importance to a student's progress of identified target skill areas. Within each area, rank specific subskills according to orderly sequence as well as relative importance. Several sources provide the data for this ranking, including objective evaluation of assessment results, teacher and system policy and priorities, and their relative significance to student and parent. Consider four students with similar performance profiles: third-grade social studies and science skills, second-grade reading and written-expression skills, first-grade math and social skills. Math and social skills are obvious priorities for Jermaine, who is in third grade receiving supportive instruction; since Ali's age (15) and low performance are the critical elements in targeting transition skills (Gajar, Goodman, & McAfee, 1993), the basic math and social skills required for employment will receive primary emphasis; cultural and language differences make integrated instruction in reading and written expression using a thematic approach a top priority (Garcia, 1994) for Angel; and improvements in Jorenda's social skills are the most critical variable in helping to reorient her to the inclusive classroom. It is also important to identify the learning strategies related to the highest priority task and the degree to which the target student is or is not applying these strategies. A practical ranking of skills, subskills, tasks and strategies by priority should emerge from a composite consideration of assessment results, teacher and system policy, as well as student and parent concerns.

Method Selection

Principles of effective teaching should be included in the individualized program to maximize the students' opportunities for success. Several of these principles indicate that effective teachers set high expectations, keep students actively engaged in learning, reward appropriate work and effort, provide corrective instruction, ensure high levels of success, and establish a positive classroom climate (Kindsvatter, Wilen, & Ishler, 1988; Wang, Haertel, & Walberg, 1993–1994). *Inspiring Active Learning* (Harmin, 1994) is a resource book that offers good ideas to increase student involvement. Many of the suggested instructional activities easily can be adapted to meet individual learner needs.

The specific instructional methods chosen to implement a student's education program must meet the needs of *both* student and teacher. Selecting methods that will most likely promote a student's academic success depends upon several factors such as the student's level of task mastery, his or her learning style, specific skill areas involved, instructional resources, learning environment, along with teacher preference and expertise. The combination of these variables dictates the most appropriate methods for developing the initial program.

Mastery Learning

The mastery-learning strategies formulated by Bloom (1976) hold particular promise for increasing not only instructional individualization, but also the achievement of many types of learners (Vergason & Anderegg, 1991). Although a popular, general education strategy, mastery learning represents the basic tenet of special education. As noted by Guskey (1985), "Theory of mastery learning stresses that all students can learn very well when appropriate instructional conditions are provided" (p. 140). This approach features programming for success or mastery, constant teacher feedback, and corrections on a prescriptive basis. Good and Brophy (1994) cite research which documents that the approach successfully increases the number of students who master basic skills. Outcome-based education is basically an updated version of mastery learning (Ysseldyke, Thurlow, & Shriner, 1992). According to Bloom (1985), some form of teaching for mastery learning is probably used by most effective teachers. Bloom suggests that learning can be substantially increased by combining mastery learning with improved curricula.

Level of Intensity

A student's relative mastery of each target task must also be considered in selecting the intensity of instruction. Throughout this text, instructional strategies are categorized as developmental, corrective, or maintenance. Developmental strategies refer to the student's first exposures to a task or concept. Corrective strategies refer to the methods used to reteach a task as well as to those designed to suit an individual student's learning needs. These procedures are usually more specific and intense and may include specialized remedial methods such as the Gillingham and Stillman (1977) and the Fernald (1943, 1988). It is highly probable that you will modify and adapt some developmental strategies for use as corrective strategies. Maintenance strategies are appropriate when a student has partially mastered a skill and needs additional practice, drill, and reinforcement for mastery, fluency, and generalization to occur.

Learning Patterns

To confirm the types of approaches from which the learner will most likely profit, refer to the student's typical learning pattern (Dunn & Dunn, 1993; Lerner, 1993; Wood, 1992). Although specific cultures demonstrate distinctive learning patterns, variation within groups results in individual learners developing their own unique learning styles (Guild, 1994). Selecting a method

according to a student's learning style may result in highly individualized instruction. Dunn & Dunn (1992, 1993) cite numerous studies documenting the efficacy of tailoring instruction to a student's learning preference. They conclude that teaching in terms of a student's learning style significantly increases academic achievement of both underachievers and gifted students. The model, developed by Kenneth and Rita Dunn (1978), focuses not only on the student's strongest modality, but also on environmental, emotional, and sociological factors, and physical variables. Whether a visual or an auditory approach or a directive or a nondirective strategy is selected depends upon the student's learning preference and those methods with which the student has previously experienced success or failure. Suggestions for teaching in terms of a student's learning style are interspersed throughout the remainder of this text. A review of research on learning styles in general education (Curry, 1990) and special education (Snider, 1992) would suggest critically examining the learning style literature before widespread implementation of this approach. However, considering learning style when teaching students experiencing academic difficulties is rapidly gaining acceptance in both general and special education.

Strategy Usage

Each specific skill area further limits the types of methods to be selected. Along with content, methods should focus on teaching students *how* to learn. Research on learning strategies indicates that teaching students to effectively apply learning strategies improves their performance (e.g., Vergason & Anderegg, 1991). Pressley and his associates (1990) have identified numerous empirically supported strategies that may be used in various subject areas. According to Weinstein and Mayer (1986), learning strategies can be categorized into three groups, rehearsal strategies, elaboration strategies, and organizational strategies, each of which may be simple or complex, and two additional groups, comprehension monitoring and motivational.

Resources

The availability of human resources to the teacher helps to determine which methods are practical in that class. Paraprofessionals, volunteers, and peer tutors may provide supplementary instruction in the content areas as well as perform clerical chores. With appropriate training and supervision and effective collaboration, these assistants may function as individual tutors or as the teachers of small skill groups. They greatly expand the teacher's capabilities (Wood, 1993). Similarly, the teacher who has a large room, a small class, and a planning period is likely to employ more creative instructional strategies than one operating under adverse conditions. The frequency of large group, small group, and one-to-one instruction occurring in a classroom is also contingent upon teaching resources. Using student tutors increases the opportunity for providing one-to-one instruction. Student tutors may be peers of the target student or older students from the same school. Evidence suggests that both tutor and tutee benefit from such an arrangement (Vergason & Anderegg, 1991). Beyond the few minutes the teacher has to spend structuring and monitoring the tutoring sessions, this practice requires little of his or her time. A variation of this concept is the cooperative learning model in which students of varying abilities are grouped together as a learning team with a common goal. The members of the heterogeneous groups then teach each other according to specific guidelines provided by the teacher. Research results indicate an increase in achievement for participating students, particularly those of low abilities (Anderson, 1985; Pugach & Wesson, 1990; and Slavin, 1991).

Technology is a powerful resource that multiplies instructional options. Computer-assisted instruction, telecommunications, and multimedia environments can be used effectively to personalize assessment and instruction, present interactive group or one-to-one lessons, offer a variety of creative teaching strategies, expand students' ex-

periential knowledge, enhance classroom research capabilities, conduct meaningful dialogue with remote experts, provide reinforcement, and also to perform clerical chores (Desberg, 1994; Kanning, 1994; Male, 1994). These examples are but a few of the almost endless possibilities for greatly expanding teaching and learning opportunities.

The learning situation in which the student is most comfortable may influence which methods are most appropriate. Thus, the student's preferences for working in study carrels or small group instruction and/or with peer tutoring, taped programs, and computer-assisted instruction should be considered in choosing the ideal methods. Classroom resources and structure are major determinants of which methods are practical.

Teacher Preference

Although most teachers are familiar with several methods in each skill area, they tend to favor those with which they have previously experienced success. Convenience and simplicity are also factors in determining preferred methods. When the teacher's preference matches the student's skill and learning needs, the methods of choice are obvious. However, when a mismatch occurs, the teacher may need to consult additional professional resources to determine alternate strategies for meeting the student's needs.

Materials Selection

Like the selection of methods, the choice of materials is influenced by the student's learning style, specific skill area involved, other instructional resources, learning environment, as well as teacher preference and expertise. The materials chosen must be compatible with the methods selected. Mercer and Mercer (1993) present major factors involved in material evaluation while Evans, Evans, Gable, and Schmid (1991) offer guidelines and a useful checklist. Schloss, Smith, and Schloss (1990) present numerous suggestions for selecting materials for secondary students that may be adapted for elementary students as well.

The material content, format, and amenability to modification influence their workability for both teacher and student, and ultimately the resulting performance of the student.

Availability

Several sources may be consulted for appropriate instructional materials. Ask supervisors, principals, and your colleagues about available technology and where to find software, surplus texts, and related activities. Examine the school storeroom, central office depository, library, and local resource center for additional materials which can be requisitioned. Investigate the possibility of borrowing selected materials from other regular and special education teachers for students whose performance is above or below grade placement. Consult supervisors to determine if funds are available to order specialized materials. The industrious teacher may want to develop original, supplementary materials to meet the program needs of a specific student. The teacher who enjoys attending rummage sales may accidentally discover appropriate program supplements. Not to be overlooked are the occasional complimentary copies of materials supplied by publisher representatives. With persistence and ingenuity, materials can be acquired.

Content

Instructional materials should be critically analyzed to establish if they include specific skills needed by a student. Compare the skill sequence of the texts with that of the student's curriculum to verify agreement. These texts must include not only target skills and similar skill sequencing, but also terminology not markedly different from that typically used in implementing the current curriculum. One way to ensure continuity is to select a different level of the same text series the student is expected to master in the regular curriculum; however, it is important to use only those activities that address target skills. Finding instructional materials whose level of difficulty matches the student's present skill level is crucial. Most concepts can be presented at several levels of dif-

ficulty. The determinants of textual complexity include readability, the number of concepts per lesson, the number of details included, the degree of abstraction, and the amount of repetition and clarification activities provided. Although some publishers offer parallel versions of texts at two or more levels of difficulty, in most instances a thorough search is necessary to locate instructional materials that match the skill needs of a specific student.

Format

The format of instructional materials also affects student achievement. The overall structure of traditional texts, workbooks, worksheets, and audio/video tapes produces different student reactions and partially determines teacher presentation and use. The student's motivation and the quality and quantity of his or her learning may depend upon the number of activities on the page and the inclusion of illustrations, self-correcting strategies, manipulative supplements, primary stimulus mode and types of questions. Some formats are obviously designed for independent practice; others require direct teacher instruction or are appropriate for either purpose. For initial instruction in any skill area, choose formats offering both independent and direct instructional activities.

Modifications

The probability and rate of a student's progress may be increased by modifying the content and format of selected materials. Designate only those skill activities that match a student's needs by correlating the student's curriculum chart with the text. Wood (1992) suggests using indexing strategies such as separate testing, circling certain page numbers, highlighting, or marking tables of contents. The modifications that can be made to render instructional materials more appropriate to the needs of an individual student are almost limitless, but a few modifications are listed in Figure 3.10. For comprehensive treatments of material selection, management, and adaptation, refer to *Designing Instructional Strategies* (Kameenui &

FIGURE 3.10   Sample Modifications of Instructional Materials

Select and mark only the activities that match student's needs
- Use indexing strategies
- Restructure directions
- Number activities for best order of presentation
- Add prompts, cues, and examples
- Substitute terminology to improve relevance
- Supplement materials with concept previews and reviews
- Supplement with study guides
- Cross index, integrate, and use lesson fragments from several sources
- Change response demands
- Change or supplement presentation method (e.g., A/V tape)
- Adjust activity length
  Cross out items
  Mark target items with highlighter
  Section off pages
  Insert additional activities
- Supply answer keys for independent practice activities

Simmons, 1990), and *Instructional Methods for Adolescents with Learning and Behavior Problems* (Schloss, Smith, & Schloss, 1990).

Three Stages of Programming

The assessment data collected in Step 2 of the CBA/P cycle provides the content and a portion of the methodology for programming in Step 3. To plan a balanced instructional program, select 2 to 3 of the most critical unmastered tasks and 10 to 12 adjacent mastered tasks (i.e., 3 unknown addition facts and 10 to 12 known facts). Program development should take into consideration the student's learning characteristics and the methods, materials, and strategies that match these characteristics. The student's learning stages must also be accommodated.

As indicated in Figure 3.11, Step 3 of the CBA/P model includes three stages of program-

ming: developmental, corrective, and maintenance instruction. Developmental strategies are teaching procedures and activities that provide guidance during the acquisition of a task. Corrective strategies are appropriate for unmastered tasks for which instruction has been unsuccessful and must be modified. Tasks which appear to be mastered but require additional practice and reinforcement are assigned maintenance strategies. The particular stage chosen depends upon the curricular performance criteria for judging mastery and the student's learning stage and the instructional history.

Developmental Instruction

Developmental strategies are those teaching procedures and activities that teachers typically use to introduce a new skill or concept to students. Suggestions for developmental instruction accompany many basal text programs. These strategies provide step-by-step guidance during acquisition of lesson content and should be pre-

FIGURE 3.11   Program for Assessed Needs

- Select critical tasks
  2 to 3 unmastered tasks
  10 to 12 mastered tasks
- Determine stage of programming for each task
  Developmental—new task; never been taught
  Corrective—old task; needs reteaching
  Maintenance—partial mastery; reinforce and practice
- Develop 3 stage instructional program and teach
- Reassess performance and reprogram
  Use corrective strategies for unmastered tasks
  a. Modify methods, reassess, reprogram
  b. Modify materials, reassess, reprogram
  c. Modify methods and materials, reassess, reprogram
  d. Modify task level, reassess, reprogram
  Provide maintenance strategies for tentatively mastered skills
- Repeat CBA/P cycle

sented in sequential steps from lower to higher difficulty levels in terms of content presentation and task assignments (Wood, 1993). Developmental strategies should also require active student involvement. Less structured and time-consuming than corrective strategies and much more direct than maintenance strategies, developmental strategies should be chosen for tasks that are new and have not previously been taught to the student. Then, based on reassessment in Step 2, maintenance strategies are appropriate for tasks the student tentatively masters and corrective strategies are indicated for unmastered tasks.

Corrective Instruction

Corrective strategies are appropriate for reteaching an unmastered task. These strategies are introduced into programming when needed tasks have been taught but are easily forgotten, confused, or remain unmastered. When compared to developmental strategies, corrective strategies are more structured and systematic, require direct, one-to-one or small group instruction, and often take longer to implement. As depicted in Figure 3.7, four types of modifications are recommended for corrective instruction: methods, materials, methods and materials, and task level.

Modify Methods. Modifying the methods of instruction may mean bringing in an additional sensory mode, using peer tutoring, instructing one-to-one, using study carrels, and the like. After modification of the methods and reteaching, the tasks are recycled through Step 2 for reassessment. If tentative mastery is not achieved, a modification of materials is recommended.

Modify Materials. Material modifications may include highlighting key points, shortening assignments, taping directions, changing to a totally different format, or any of the variables discussed in an earlier section. Following instruction using the modified materials, the task is recycled through Stage 2 assessment once again. If the task remains unmastered, a modification in both methods and materials is suggested.

Modify Methods and Materials. The third type of alteration combines the modifications suggested for methods and for materials. Pairing the methods and the materials to which the student appeared to respond best is the logical starting point. Another possibility is the introduction of a new method combined with old materials or vice versa. After instruction, the task is again recycled through Step 2 for reassessment. If, after this third modification, the student does not achieve accuracy, then the task level should be changed.

Modify Task Level. Modifying the task level may include breaking the task into smaller steps, selecting a matching instead of an essay type task, or moving to an easier and prerequisite task. The assumption is: the task is too difficult for the student who continues to experience problems after the three prior instructional adjustments. Following instruction, the task at the new level is reassessed through Stage 2 assessment.

At any point in the sequence of modifications, when tentative mastery is indicated, corrective instruction ceases and maintenance instruction begins.

Maintenance Instruction

Maintenance strategies are appropriate for tasks that have been tentatively or partially mastered. For most tasks, an accuracy rate of 80 percent suggests the need for additional practice and reinforcement to achieve mastery and fluency (Ysseldyke & Algozzine, 1995). Students with learning difficulties have special problems generalizing learned skills (Mercer, 1992; Lerner, 1993). That is, they may have difficulty transferring skills and concepts across subjects, settings, people, behaviors, or time without the same events that were present in the teaching session. Thus, in addition to focusing on mastery and fluency, maintenance instruction must target generalization. Among the guidelines that have been suggested to assist students in generalizing information are these: teach responses likely to be maintained in the student's natural environment; use different teachers and different stimuli; vary instruction, stimuli, and reinforcers; use peers as tutors; and teach students to self-record and self-reinforce (Mercer, 1992). Wood (1993) adds these suggestions: use initial examples that represent the concept; present a variety of examples to cover the full range of divergence; include both examples and nonexamples; and clarify the distinctive features of the concept.

Some independent activities that require minimal teacher direction may be suitable for maintenance instruction. However, to enable students to achieve mastery, fluency, and generalization, teachers must provide feedback to reinforce acceptable responses and correct misconceptions and errors, and continuously monitor students' performance. Accuracy and fluency at the criterion levels, designated by the curriculum as signaling mastery, must be maintained and demonstrated throughout at least three CBA/P cycles for a task to be considered mastered.

Throughout the CBA/P cycle, the student's performance and the instructional variables should be analyzed and documented. As tasks are mastered in the CBA/P cycle, new tasks will replace them and be taught using developmental, corrective, and/or maintenance strategies according to assessed needs. To repeat the cycle, chart and record all data, reviewing Steps 2 and 3 to identify implications for subsequent assessment

and programming. At this point, the results of the process should be communicated with the student and all persons involved in his or her educational program.

Once the instructional program has been implemented, decisions must be made to determine its effectiveness. A simple graph is one means for quickly charting and recording a student's progress in an effort to measure program effectiveness. For example, Lashona, a fourth-grader in Mr. Garcia's resource room, has difficulty completing math assignments because she hasn't learned her multiplication facts. Mr. Garcia administers daily a 3-minute, 50-item fact test to improve Lashona's scores. Her progress is charted on a changing criterion design. The first week Lashona worked 25 to 28 facts correctly, establishing the base from which Mr. Garcia determined his first criterion: 30 correct responses. When she worked 30 facts correctly within 3 minutes, she earned 5 minutes of "free time." As shown in Figure 3.12, Lashona reached criterion in 2 days, remained at that level 3 additional days, and was raised to 40 facts. Five days later, she reached the second criterion. Mr. Garcia continued to raise the criterion until Lashona performed 50 facts correctly.

Charting the student's performance on a daily or weekly basis provides the teacher information

FIGURE 3.12   Math Progress: Lashona

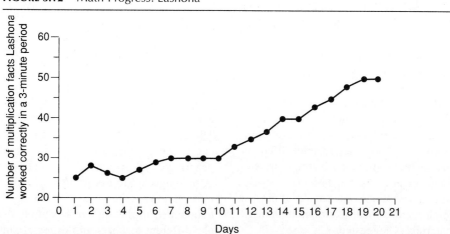

concerning the effectiveness of the instructional program. If the data indicate no progress is being made, then a change in the instructional program is warranted. Howell, Fox, & Morehead (1993) have devised more specific and sensitive charting procedures for determining a student's growth. Just how long one should wait before changing a program is a matter of professional judgement. Howell and colleagues recommend changing a program when it is not working, and the more quickly the change takes place the more student time will be saved. Fuchs, Deno, and Mirkin (1984) allow seven to ten days of inadequate student performance before initiating changes. The present authors recommend a program change when the student demonstrates three data points of inadequate performance. Simple charting of a student's performance may be completed on any academic behavior and quickly alerts the teacher to areas requiring a change in instruction.

Communicating Student Needs and Progress

The active involvement of supervisors, various specialists, general education teachers, parents, and, indeed, the child in the assessment and programming process greatly increases the probability of the student's academic success. The rate of student progress is improved when these individuals collaborate to form an educational team. Through continuous collaboration among the team members, the separate efforts of each can be coordinated to focus on similar objectives. Although the needs of team members differ somewhat, their goals are the same; each wants the target student to succeed. Frequent conferences and periodic written reports that address the individual needs of the student, the professionals, and the family members facilitate successful program coordination and student progress.

The Educational Team

The student's progress in a specialized academic program should be reported on a regular basis to several educational team members: supervisors, special teachers, general education teachers, other specialists as appropriate, the parents, and, of course, the student. The specific needs of each team member differ according to concern, responsibility, and expertise as indicated in Figure 3.13.

Students need both daily reports and periodic summative evaluations if they are to assume the responsibility for their own academic progress. Such reporting encourages the involvement of a student in program planning and reinforces student learning.

FIGURE 3.13   Functions of Progress Reports for Team Members

EDUCATIONAL TEAM MEMBER	FUNCTION OF REPORT
Supervisors	Evaluate program effectiveness; make placement decisions; plan alternate programs; order appropriate materials
Special Teachers (Special educator, speech therapist, remedial teachers, enrichment teachers, etc.)	Develop and coordinate appropriate individual and small group instruction
Regular Class Teachers	Update large- and small-group instruction to complement special programs
Other Specialists (e.g., Medical doctors)	Assist in interpreting treatment effectiveness
Parents	Provide support and assistance to school programs
Student	Reinforce learning, assume responsibility for own academic progress

Conferences

Regardless of the number of participants, conferences involve an important exchange of information and provide a forum for collaborative problem solving. Regular conferences, whether in person or by phone, with members of the educational team are vital to successful program coordination. As an active participant in evaluating his or her program, the student should be included in appropriate conferences. Since work samples of the student's performance on a day-to-day basis realistically indicate his or her current accomplishments, these may be sent home in advance of a phone conference or displayed during a personal conference. The student's annotated curriculum chart should be the focal point for discussing progress and unmastered skills. Productive topics of discussion include analyzing student success or failure with specific methods, materials, and content; providing positive learning environments; reordering program priorities; restructuring the student's core or supplementary programs; or any appropriate theme that will strengthen the student's coordinated educational program. Alper, Schloss, and Schloss (1994), Morsink, Thomas, and Correa (1991), and Shea and Bauer (1991) address the vital role of parents in the educational process and offer guidelines for effective collaboration.

Written Reports

Written reports present a permanent record of the student's program and a vehicle for communicating with team members who are not available for a conference. They provide the data required to evaluate student status objectively in order to plan appropriate program adjustments and also serve to structure conferences. It is a good practice to include a photocopy of the student's curricular chart with the report, recording his or her currently mastered tasks and explaining the correlation between charted performance and the local grading system.

All members of the educational team need a formal written report detailing annual progress and major changes in the student's performance or program, including the student's annotated curricular chart. This formal report should thoroughly review the student's performance in relation to all program components and major content areas and make recommendations for future planning of his or her entire educational program. Primary use of these formal reports is to document the placement and the program emphasis that are most appropriate for the specific student.

Brief and informal written reports are appropriate for communicating student needs and progress on a daily, weekly, or monthly basis. These reports either present information, request assistance, or both. They are typically concerned with the student's performance of specific tasks. For example, an informal note is sent home advising parents that the student has correctly pronounced all primer words; the classroom teacher sends to the speech therapist a request for supplementary instruction in three specific consonant blends; or attached to a progress chart is a note commending the student on current progress. The primary use of these informal reports is to notify the educational team members of immediate and short-term program concerns.

Grading

The best procedure for *grading* and then *reporting grades* for students with disabilities remains a controversial issue. Traditional letter grades are assigned to students by comparing performances among classmates—a "norm-referenced practice" (Willis, 1993a) that may unjustly penalize students with special needs. Grading will become a more significant issue as inclusionary practices increase. Numerous alternative grading systems have been identified. Research by Michael and Trippi (1987) indicated the Individually Written Report (IWR) and the Individual Education Plan (IEP) to be favored by administrators, special education teachers, and general education teachers. These and other alternative grading systems are outlined in Figure 3.14.

Consistent two-way communication is essential to the curriculum-based assessment/ programming process. All members of the educational team, particularly the student, should be

FIGURE 3.14   Alternative Grading Systems

1. IEP	The criterion of each objective for a student's Individual Education Plan is used as the baseline grade, with the student's actual mastery prorated in comparison (e.g., a student who masters an objective to 80% accuracy earns a grade of B) (Schulz & Carpenter, 1995).
2. IWR	The Individually Written Report, a narrative report written by the special education teacher, serves as the student's report card (Michael & Trippi, 1987).
3. Contract Grading	Teacher and student agree on the quantity and quality of work to complete for specific grades (Salend, 1994).
4. Pass/Fail Systems	Minimum competencies are established. Students pass who meet the minimum. Students who don't fail.
5. Mastery Level/Criterion Systems	Pretest is administered to determine skill needs. Needed skills are taught. Posttest is administered to demonstrate mastery and move to next higher skill.
6. Multiple Grading	The student receives a grade for each subject in three areas: ability, effort and achievement. The student may receive three grades or an average of all three (Michael & Trippi, 1987)
7. Level Grading	A subscript is attached to the grade to indicate the level of difficulty on which the student's grade is based.
8. Shared Grading	The general and special education teachers collaboratively assign grades for students they are instructing (Salend, 1994).
9. Descriptive Grading	Teacher comments with a listings of skills mastered are added to assigned grades on the report card (Polloway & Patton, 1993).
10. Student Self-Comparison	Teacher and student collaboratively determine instructional goals within the curriculum. Student measures progress by gains made relative to the curriculum. Teacher and student monitor progress and report on student's report card (Wood, 1992).
11. Point System	The grade is determined by points assigned to activities and assignments which are totaled for the final grade.
12. Portfolio Evaluation	In each specific content area a portfolio is maintained to demonstrate achievement throughout the year (Wood, 1992).

aware of progress and plans at all times. Collaboration is the logical activity to conclude and begin each curriculum-based assessment/programming cycle.

IMPLEMENTING THE MODEL

The model for implementing the curriculum-based assessment/programming cycle (CBA/P cycle) was presented in Figure 3.2. Each step of the model was then individually displayed and described in detail. Figure 3.15 once again places the four steps in sequence to depict the step-by-step approach for personalizing and implementing the CBA/P process. These steps enable you to continuously assess and adjust the instructional program to meet the learner's needs as they are determined by the student's response to each instructional activity. The results of each CBA/P step present a diagnostic map that leads to refinement of the individualization process.

Step 1: Analyze Curricula

Locate or formulate with school personnel an itemized scope and sequence chart for each sub-

FIGURE 3.15   Implementing the Curriculum-Based Assessment/Programming Model

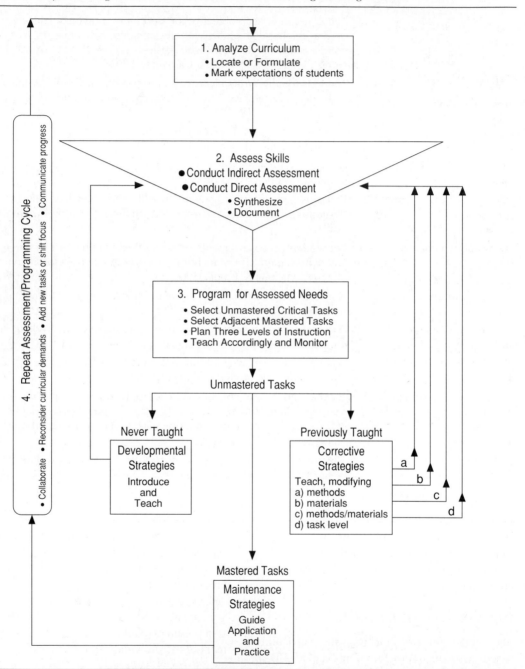

ject area. Within each area, identify the subskills and specific tasks for each subject. Mark on the curriculum charts the current expectations of the student.

Step 2: Assess Skills

Assess the student's performance of subskills and tasks, using the content of the curriculum as the assessment content. Begin by selecting assessment techniques to match available data and curricular tasks. Next, initiate indirect assessment, collecting available data from teacher interviews, school records, and samples of the target student's classwork. Analyze and interpret the data to identify performance patterns and critical behaviors. Then proceed to direct assessment, formulating diagnostic hypotheses and directly observing the student in the classroom, followed by interviewing the student. Using materials, performance levels, and assessment formats congruent with the student's curricula, develop appropriate assessment tasks. Administer the test items and analyze responses for error and success patterns. Synthesize indirect and direct data and record the student's accomplishments on the curriculum chart. Reassess performance of the tasks for which personalized instruction has been provided in Step 3, and plan subsequent programming accordingly. As additional tasks are demonstrated, note the date of the "short-term mastery" on a list such as the one provided in Figure 3.16. Consider tasks mastered if the student demonstrates skill retention through three CBA/P cycles. Then record mastery on the student's curriculum chart by checking the appropriate tasks.

Step 3: Program for Tasks

Using the assessment data collected in Step 2 as a base, develop a tentative educational program of methods, materials, and conditions that reflect the student's subskill needs in terms of priorities. From within the subskill area judged to be most important to the student's progress, choose a few

of the most elementary and critical tasks. Use these unmastered tasks as the focus of instruction and form the balance (70 to 80%) of instructional activities from adjacent mastered tasks. Initially select methods and materials according to the student's learning strengths, most efficient stimulus/response mode, teacher and curricular demands, and instructional resources. Plan a personalized program containing three stages: developmental strategies for unmastered tasks never taught; corrective strategies for tasks taught but unmastered; and maintenance strategies for tentatively mastered tasks.

DEVELOPMENTAL INSTRUCTION. To introduce and teach new tasks, use developmental strategies; then reassess performance in Step 2. If the tasks remain unmastered, use corrective strategies. When tentative mastery is achieved, provide maintenance instruction.

CORRECTIVE INSTRUCTION. Use corrective strategies to teach unmastered tasks for which prior instruction was ineffective; recycle the unmastered tasks through Step 2, skill assessment, and Step 3, modifying instruction, until the student demonstrates tentative mastery. As depicted in Figure 3.15, first change the methods, next the materials, then methods and materials, and finally the task level, proceeding through this sequence of change only so far as necessary to elicit accuracy. As tasks are tentatively mastered, implement maintenance strategies.

MAINTENANCE INSTRUCTION. Use maintenance strategies to promote permanent retention of tentatively mastered tasks. These review and reinforcement strategies are particularly important, at this point, to preserve the student's temporary competence, thereby increasing the efficiency of the teaching/learning process.

As you teach the tasks, carefully note the rate of presentation, methods, materials, and conditions that appear to be effective. A format such as the one in Figure 3.17 provides the structure to organize and document instruction. Record each task as tentatively mastered and check it off on

FIGURE 3.16   Personalized Assessment Plan

(Student's Name)   _(Academic Subjects)_   _(Teacher)_

Subject	Task#	Task	Test Source	Success	Error	Assessment/Programming Implications	Dates Checked			Charted

NOTES:

FIGURE 3.17   Personalized Programming Plan

(Student's Name)				(Academic Subjects)	(Teacher)
CONTENT Subject Task	STRATEGIES/DATES			DESCRIPTION OF STRATEGIES/MATERIALS	RESULTS
	Dev.	Corr.	Main		

NOTES:

the curriculum chart as mastered upon the student's skill retention through three CBA/P cycles.

Step 4: Repeat the Cycle

Reenter the CBA/P cycle for review or reapplication. Review Steps 2 and 3 to determine which tasks should be added to the cycle as replacements for those that are mastered and maintained or to identify the need to shift the program focus. This may involve changing the skill area, subskill or task emphasis through a periodic reordering of instructional priorities. In order to design and present specific instruction that will meet a student's ongoing learning needs, continually repeat the assessment/programming process. Throughout the process, collaborate and communicate the student's progress with both the student and the other professionals involved before the cycle is reentered. Continue the CBA/P cycle until the student has achieved long-term mastery of those subskills and tasks that must be learned for successful functioning within his or her curriculum.

The philosophy of the curriculum-based assessment/programming model parallels what Howell (1991) calls "curriculum-based thought." His suggestions for focusing the curriculum-based process summarize a final reminder for implementing the CBA/P model: *Think* about the essential elements of the curriculum—what *can* be taught, what *is* taught, and *how* it is taught. Then decide how it *should* be taught and then make it happen!

SUMMARY

The three basic questions guiding the personalized assessment and programming process concern the curricular expectations of a student, the student's relative skill position, and the best plan for adjusting the curriculum to meet the student's skill needs. The approaches for answering the questions include assessment of the curriculum, selection of assessment techniques, and indirect and direct student assessment. Sources of valuable indirect assessment data include the classroom teacher's estimates of the student's relative skill mastery, the student's learning style and school adjustment, analysis of work samples and school records, and observations. Synthesizing the information from these sources leads to diagnostic hypotheses, priorities, and plans for focusing direct assessment. Direct assessment involves observing, interviewing, and testing the student. The student's curricular materials should form the content of the tests. Items from other tests may be used if they match the curriculum. The student's mastery of skills, subskills, and tasks should be recorded on a curriculum chart.

The purpose of the personalized assessment process is to establish the best plan for developing an educational program for an individual student. The recommended model views skills as strategies to accomplish authentic goals. To develop a personalized educational program, content, methods, and materials must be selected that match both student and teacher needs. To implement the program, the assessment/programming cycle includes several steps: develop a tentative program based on assessment of the student's curricular mastery; assess task mastery for tasks within priority subskills; according to assessment results, plan a personalized program that includes developmental strategies for new tasks never taught, corrective strategies for tasks taught but not mastered, and maintenance strategies for tentatively mastered tasks. Repeat the CBA/P cycle until the student achieves mastery of the tasks necessary for successful functioning within the curriculum. School personnel, specialists, parents, and student are encouraged to participate throughout the curriculum-based assessment/programming process.

CASE STUDIES

Missy

You are a fourth-grade teacher in a regular classroom. Six weeks ago Missy transferred from another state into your class. Her former teacher sent a report indicating that Missy was "barely" passing all subjects. Describe the procedures you would use to obtain the information to complete the four steps of the assessment/programming cycle (see Figure 3.2).

Ron

You remember Ron from last year as the terror of the class next door. Now he is repeating first grade in your class. Describe the assessment information of the most immediate interest, how you plan to obtain it, and its importance to the CBA/P plan.

ENRICHMENT ACTIVITIES

Discussion

1. In response to parental concerns, Jorenda, a fifth-grade student, has been assessed. Results reveal that most of her skills are below the level presented in her assigned textbooks. However, her teacher reports that her skill level is as high or higher than the majority of her classmates. What actions should be taken by the teacher, parents, and student?

2. What are the advantages and disadvantages to both student and teacher of requiring a student whose skills are below grade level to repeat the grade a second year under the same teacher? How would repeating under a different teacher in the same school change program effectiveness? What other instructional placements and options should be considered and what are their relative merits?

3. Describe the personalized assessment and programming procedures appropriate and/or inappropriate for a severely disabled student. Justify your answers.

4. After reviewing the discussion of assessment techniques, describe the manner in which you would prefer to have your performances assessed and tell why.

5. Consider the advantages and disadvantages of personalized assessment and programming from the perspective of each of the following:
    Mainstreamed exceptional student
    Nonexceptional student
    Special education teacher
    General classroom teacher

Special Projects

1. Locate the stated curricula operating in your local school system; record your personal and professional bias by ranking the subjects according to your priorities; compare your rankings with those of peers.

2. Again using the local curricula, select one subject area. Within that particular curriculum, rank the subskills according to your priorities and then use your profes-

sional judgment to sequence the tasks within each subskill. Compare and discuss your rankings and sequence with one or more peers.

3. Compare two commercial materials from the same content area according to stimulus presentation and the responses required of the student. Then identify the one most amenable to possible alterations for accommodating students' needs.

4. From the teacher's edition of an elementary textbook, choose a brief lesson. After reviewing the discussion of the three stages of programming, restructure the lesson for corrective instruction and then for maintenance instruction.

5. Today, Henri will take home a note from the teacher stating: Henri is still failing math; please do something. Evaluate the potential impact of this note on Henri, his parents, and the teacher. Then rewrite the note to improve its communicative and educational value.

CHAPTER 4

GETTING STARTED

JAMES A. POTEET
JOYCE S. CHOATE
TONI Z. BENNETT

CHAPTER OBJECTIVES

This chapter is designed to enable the reader to:

1. Evaluate the contributions to the assessment/programming process of curriculum analysis, the student's reported performances, and analysis of school records.
2. Describe the role of learning patterns and school adjustment in the assessment/programming process.
3. Observe, record, and interpret a student's classroom behaviors.
4. Plan a personalized program to improve a student's self control and social interaction skills.
5. Explain the importance to assessment and programming of the student interview.

The assessment process must be focused and efficient. Its purpose is to determine specific skills in the curriculum to introduce to the student, to review, and to maintain. To obtain this information you will have to develop an organized and sensible sequential approach. This chapter is aimed at getting you started with such an approach—from notification that a teacher is concerned about a target student, to collection of information about those concerns, through to your actual assessment activities, and on to initial consideration of programming that will address the student's specific needs.

ASSESSMENT

The assessment process progresses logically from indirect to direct assessment to post-assessment procedures. Before discussing these procedures, we consider a few activities that will be useful for your general preparation.

General Preparation

Prior to encountering a target student or concerned teacher, there are certain steps you can take to organize and mobilize yourself for implementing the assessment and programming process. The first step is to either obtain or create a concise listing of the curricula for your school district. Next, locate, create, and duplicate the forms you will use on a regular basis for both indirect and direct assessment. Then, develop your own "test kit" that matches the system's curricula and is ready for modifications to match specific teachers' curricula and students' individual needs. (Some specific suggestions for accomplishing these general organizational tasks are presented in Chapter 11; component tasks for each of the steps involved as well as for indirect and direct assessment are outlined later in Figure 4.11.)

Indirect Assessment: The General Teacher Survey

Before directly approaching the target student, you need to know curricular expectations and an estimate of his or her current performance. The most logical source to consult first for this information is the teacher who is most familiar with the target student. To do this, we recommend the General Teacher Survey.

The general teacher survey is presented in Figures 4.1 through 4.4. It consists of four different parts and provides the structure for a face-to-face interview with the teacher. However, the questions may be completed independently. The survey serves as a model for *indirectly* assessing general academic needs and performances. Sometimes it may be necessary to modify the survey by adding, rephrasing, deleting, or substituting certain items. In some instances the interviewer also is the responding teacher; then the survey functions to help that one person consolidate background data. Each part of the general teacher survey is discussed in the next sections.

Part I: Assessment of Curricula

The purpose of the first portion of the survey in Figure 4.1 is to begin analysis of the student's curriculum, especially those subjects that carry the most weight in making promotion and retention decisions, and the resources available within

the school. The effectiveness of any special program in which the student has participated is also noted. Viable options for future programming are suggested by teacher responses. Identification of successful strategies provides insights into problems and suggests methods for programming.

Part II: Estimate of Achievement

Indirect assessment saves time by organizing judgments of those who have observed and taught the student in the past, and who are presently doing so. While adding to information about the curriculum, indirect assessment focuses on reports about the student's performance, learning patterns, and academic adjustment.

Indirect assessment of a student's school performance begins with teacher estimates. As outlined in Figure 4.2, the first section of Part II of the General Teacher Survey seeks information from the teacher about a student's current and past performance in each subject.

Description.   Much like the information obtained in the analysis of curricula, reports of the student's performances also directly influence assessment plans. That is, the description of past and existing conditions help to narrow the assessment focus. This is an important part of survey assessment and also the Level I Screening activities described in Chapter 1. These data permit the diagnostician to aim for the source of difficulty instead of attempting the impossible task of ascertaining exactly what the student can and cannot do in all academic areas.

Teacher Estimates.   The first item on this part of the survey asks the teacher to estimate the student's grade-level functioning in each subject of the curriculum. When possible, further specification of a student's current achievement within a grade level as beginning, middle, or end is helpful (e.g., a notation of "M3" for the student who is performing at the mid-third-grade level). This estimate serves several important purposes: One or more subject areas of greatest concern are identified; relative strengths and weaknesses are noted; and the levels are identified at which direct

FIGURE 4.1   General Teacher Survey

PART I: ASSESSMENT OF CURRICULUM

Student_____ Date_____

Teacher_____ Interviewer_____

ADDITIONAL COMMENTS

1. Check the subject areas that are a major part of this student's present curriculum:
   __Word Recognition   __Spelling
   __Reading Comprehension   __Handwriting
   __Arithmetic Computation   __Science
   __Arithmetic Problem Solving __Social Studies
   __Written Expression   __Other _____

Star (*) the ones that are the primary determinants of promotion or retention.

2. Mark support programs available in your school:
   __Remedial Reading Lab   __Teacher Aides
   __Remedial Math Lab   __Volunteer Aides
   __Inter-class Grouping   __Cross-age Tutors
   __Intra-class Grouping   __Other _____

Star (*) the ones in which the student has participated this or last school year.

3. Estimate the duration of the student's participation in each special program above:
   Program_____ ____ weeks ____ months
   Program_____ ____ weeks ____ months
   Program_____ ____ weeks ____ months
   Program_____ ____ weeks ____ months

Frequency of student involvement in each:
__hrs./day   __days/wk.
__hrs./day   __days/wk.
__hrs./day   __days/wk.
__hrs./day   __days/wk.

4. Indicate to what degree these programs have been successful with this student:
   ____ Student accomplished goals of the program
   ____ Student performs satisfactorily in proper instructional level and appropriate text
   ____ Student performs in a tutoring situation
   ____ Student cannot perform successfully

Possible reasons for success or lack of success:

5. Indicate in-class modifications that you have attempted with this student:
   ___Increased instructional time from _____ to _____
   ___Provided a Tutor__ Aide__ Peer__ Other _____
   ___Changed instructional group from _____ to _____
   ___Changed instructional material. Describe _____
   _____
   ___Other _____

Subjects in which they were attempted:

6. These modifications were successful enough for the student to perform:
   ___In class with the lowest instructional group
   ___In class with an adult tutor
   ___In class with a peer tutor
   ___In another grade level class
   ___In an undetermined arrangement and level

Possible reasons for success or lack of success:

7. Check how long you estimate it will take to eliminate the major problems with appropriate instruction:
   ___One grading period
   ___One semester
   ___One school year
   ___If longer how much longer? _____

FIGURE 4.2 General Teacher Survey

PART II: ESTIMATE OF ACHIEVEMENT

Student's Name _____

ADDITIONAL COMMENTS

1. TEACHER ESTIMATES:
   A. Plot your estimate of this student's grade-level functioning in each area below. Connect the plotted points. Draw a vertical line down the entire graph to represent the student's grade placement. Star (*) the major areas of concern.

Attach and date any pertinent samples of student's class work.

ACADEMIC AREA	PK	K	1	2	3	4	5	6	7	8	8+
Word Recognition											
Reading Comprehension											
Arithmetic Computation											
Arithmetic Problem Solving											
Written Expression											
Spelling											
Handwriting											
Science											
Social Studies											
Study Strategies											
Other:											
Oral Language											

   B. In order to be successful in your classroom and in comparison to the remainder of your class, this student will need to improve in the major areas of concern:
   __At least one-half grade level　__More than a grade level
   __At least one grade level　　　__Classroom behavior

List academic areas:

Describe behaviors:

2. SCHOOL RECORDS:
   A. In each grade level block, specify P (Pass), F (Fail), or S (Social Promotion). There may be more than one letter in a block.

K	1	2	3	4	5	6	7	8

   B. List the scores of the most recent achievement test.
   Test Title: _____　Date: _____

	Percentile	Stanine
Total Reading		
Total Math		
Total Language		
Science		
Social Studies		
Other:		

List report card grades for last year (final avg.) and this year's grades to date:

Subject	Past	Present
Reading		
Math		
Language		
Spelling		
Handwriting		
Science		
Social Studies		
Conduct		

Results of other pertinent tests

   C. Check items that apply to the student and explain:
   ___Recurring health problems _____
   ___Known medical problems _____
   ___Chronic illness _____
   ___Takes medication regularly _____
   ___Physical handicap _____
   ___Receives special counseling _____

Influence of each on academic performance:

assessment should begin. (*Direct assessment should begin with the skills in most need of remediation,* usually those that are estimated at the lowest grade level). The resulting graph is a useful stimulus for discussions about the student's performances. Clarification at this point focuses the investigation and eliminates needless assessment later.

School Records. The second section of Part II deals with information from school records. Probing questions about these records may initiate discussions that reveal possible explanations for the student's achievement fluctuations, including important information the teacher hesitates to put in writing.

Implications. The primary impact of reports of student performance is on the plans made for direct student assessment. The data collected from Part II are typically general, but they point to the major areas of present concern and place those areas in an historical perspective. The assessment implications depend upon the student's general performance profile. A profile of marked peaks and valleys may suggest targeting the valleys for direct assessment, while an even, low profile, or low plateau, may suggest focusing first on the basic skills of the core curriculum, then later on the support and collateral subjects. When teacher estimates and school records do not coincide, consistently low performance areas, indicated by the teacher on Part I: Assessment of Curriculum as primary determinants of promotion and retention, should be initially assessed. Inasmuch as programming is driven by assessment, reported student performances target broad areas for both assessment and subsequent programming.

Part III: Learning Patterns

The teacher's estimate of a student's learning patterns provides information that influences not only assessment, but also programming. The information in Part III: Learning Patterns (Figure 4.3) provides an overview of some important elements of learning patterns. For more in-depth assessment measures, one of the published inventories of learning style and environmental preferences should be consulted (e.g., Canfield, 1988, or Ysseldyke & Christenson, 1993).

Description. Part III: Learning Patterns of the General Teacher Survey (Figure 4.3) requests the teacher to analyze the effect of specific learning conditions on the student's academic performance. This form may also be used to note direct observations of the student at work in the classroom or rephrased as multiple-choice questions to ask the student in a direct interview.

The amount of time the student can best attend to task and his or her stimulus/response preference provide insights into the type of direct assessment that will elicit the most accurate test performances from the student. These patterns also provide the methodological base for the personalized educational program to be planned upon completion of initial assessment activities. It is a relatively simple task to alter the stimulus and response demand of an assessment task. It is equally painless to adjust instructional input and/or output requirements in accord with the learner's needs.

Implications. A student's learning style is a major consideration in developing an efficient assessment plan and an effective educational program. When planning assessment tasks and subsequent programming, the student's attention span should be accommodated. To ensure accurate performance, brief and varied tasks and frequent breaks should be planned for the student with a brief attention span; to economize on time, longer tasks with fewer breaks should be planned for students who can tolerate the format. Distractions should be minimized regardless of attention span. The student's stimulus/response preferences suggest the format for assessment and instruction and also may indicate the level of performance (i.e., selection, production, or application) expected by the teacher. In addition, the student's educational environmental preferences should be explored and then accommodated throughout assessment and programming. Although the learning patterns, initially described

FIGURE 4.3   General Teacher Survey

PART III: LEARNING PATTERNS

Student's Name _____   ADDITIONAL COMMENTS

1. **Time on Task** Estimate the amount of time this student can best attend to an   Describe student's behavior
   academic task.   when not attending to task:
   __Same as most in class   __5 to 10 minutes
   __10 to 20 minutes   __Less than 5 minutes
   __Time varies by task (explain) _____
   __Time varies by other factors (explain)_____

2. **Learning Rate** Estimate how quickly the student masters new concepts in   Describe behavior when stu-
   the subjects where his or her performance is strongest and weakest.   dent does not comprehend:
               Strongest: Weakest:
   _____   Faster than most of the class   _____
   _____   Same as most of the class   _____
   _____   Same as most in lowest group   _____
   _____   Slower than lowest group   _____

3. **Stimulus** The student learns and remembers best what he or she: Example lessons:
   __Sees   __Reads   __Hears   __Does   __Writes
   __Combination_____

4. **Stimulus** The student learns fastest by these methods of instruction: Example lessons:
   __Demonstration   __Discussion   __Guided Reading
   __Discovery   __Other _____

5. **Response** This student answers most items correctly when responding by: Example lessons:
   __Saying   __Choosing   __Filling in blank   __Writing
   __Showing   __Other _____

6. **Stimulus/Response** The student performs best when the lessons include   Examples:
   these materials:
   __Worksheets   __Computer Games   __Tape Recordings
   __Workbooks   __Computer Drill   __Active Games
   __Flash Cards   __Board Work   __Passive Games
   __Other_____

7. **Study Strategies** The student effectively applies study strategies to accom-   Describe:
   plish tasks in these areas:
   Specify_____

8. **Settings** The student learns and performs best when the setting is: Describe:
   __One-to-one with teacher   __One-to-one with peer
   __Large Group   __Small Group   __Other _____

9. **Structure** The structure that seems to promote the student's learning and   Describe:
   performance is:
   __Rigorous   __Formal   __Informal   __Permissive

10. **Effective Lesson** Describe a recent lesson in which the student mastered a
    new concept at a rate that equaled or exceeded your expectations accord-
    ing to learning factors.
    Subject: _____   Concept: _____
    Stimulus: _____   Response: _____
    Setting: _____   Structure: _____

by the teacher, may require alterations or may not be substantiated later in the assessment and programming cycle, they present preliminary data to verify through assessment.

Part IV: Academic Adjustment

The Teacher Rating Scale of Academic Adjustment (TRSAA) in Part IV of the General Teacher Survey (Figure 4.4) suggests behaviors to anticipate during testing and throughout classroom observations. In the broadest sense, these behaviors constitute the classroom *social skills,* a vital component of the support curriculum. Five groups of behaviors, each containing from seven to ten descriptors, are considered: attitude, independence, organization, self-control, and social interaction skills. Presented in the present context as a tool for quickly obtaining the teacher's rating of the student's typical classroom behaviors, the TRSAA is also useful for assessing and monitoring adjustment behaviors throughout the curriculum-based assessment/programming process.

Description.   The TRSAA represents the compilation of behaviors cited by approximately 600 veteran teachers and confirmed by the professional literature as being important indices of a student's adjustment to classroom settings. Preliminary studies indicate that the TRSAA differentiates between kindergarten students of different developmental ages (Dunham, Baker, Minder, McGuire, & McCormick, 1989); analyses indicate five factors roughly corresponding with the five categories of the survey, although some self-control and independence items appear to overlap (McCormick, Baker, & Dunham, 1991).

The adjustment indicators of the TRSAA may be viewed as the student's operational assets and liabilities in terms of their effect upon academic performance. The ratings indicate the degree to which the student is conforming to the behaviors that most teachers expect and, thus, yield an overall measure of the student's social functioning. Many of these statements describe behaviors that ingratiate the student in the eyes of the teacher,

encouraging the teacher to strive harder to assist the student. If a student, who is proficient at "playing the school game," is experiencing academic difficulty, it is likely that his or her needs are very real ones requiring substantial programming. The reverse may be true of the student who receives an abundance of negative ratings. When facing a student who doesn't appear to try or even care, it is a rare teacher who exerts maximum efforts to personalize instruction.

Implications.   The negative indicators of a student's school adjustment, as indicated on the Teacher Rating Scale of Academic Adjustment (Figure 4.4) should be targeted for verification during assessment and for modification throughout programming. It is important to remember that behaviors noted as problematic represent disparities between teacher expectations and student performance (Schulz & Carpenter, 1995). Certainly, positive behaviors should be reinforced and intensified during both assessment and programming.

Because negative school behaviors tend to alienate teachers and compound a student's academic difficulties, correcting the behaviors may be as important as improving the skill content of a program. Correcting academic difficulties may even concomitantly correct classroom behaviors (Krupski, 1985). Due to the pivotal role of these behaviors, a few programming suggestions to improve academic adjustment and social skills are presented later in this chapter.

The General Teacher Survey, then, serves as a vehicle for collecting a wealth of data useful for generating hypotheses about the student's skills in continuing diagnosis or for helping the building-based team make prereferral decisions. More specific information about the student's performance in the areas of concern is needed, however, before direct assessment can even be considered. This may be accomplished as an extension of the general survey or at a later date. In the chapters on content that follow, a one-page teacher survey for each subject is presented to meet this need.

FIGURE 4.4   General Teacher Survey

PART IV: ACADEMIC ADJUSTMENT
The Teacher Rating Scale of Academic Adjustment

Student's Name _____

Check the column that best describes the student's typical performance.

1 = Never   3 = Often
2 = Sometimes 4 = Always

A. **Attitude** At school, this student typically:

	1	2	3	4
1) Is polite				
2) Seems to enjoy class				
3) Cooperates with teachers and peers				
4) Appears interested				
5) Displays effort				
6) Seems eager to learn				
7) Participates in discussions				
8) Volunteers for tasks				

B. **Independence** At school, this student typically:

	1	2	3	4
1) Requires little teacher supervision				
2) Needs only occasional praise or encouragement				
3) Completes several tasks in succession on own				
4) Displays a moderate degree of self-motivation				
5) Makes good use of leisure time				
6) Works independently when task is understood				
7) Asks appropriate questions				

C. **Organization** At school, this student typically:

	1	2	3	4
1) Brings paper to class				
2) Has pen or sharpened pencil				
3) Has other necessary school supplies				
4) Organizes supplies to begin tasks on cue				
5) Remembers to bring homework assignments				
6) Keeps an orderly desk				
7) Finishes work on time to best of ability				
8) Follows correct format for written assignments				
9) Checks work for accuracy before turning in				

D. **Self-control** At school, this student typically:

	1	2	3	4
1) Follows classroom rules				
2) Talks only at appropriate times				
3) Sits quietly in desk when necessary				
4) Seldom distracts or annoys peers or teacher				
5) Ignores most distractions				
6) Pays attention				
7) Begins work immediately				
8) Follows directions to best of ability				
9) Exhibits on-task behavior most of the time				
10) Tolerates mild frustration				

E. **Social Interaction** At school, this student typically:

	1	2	3	4
1) Exhibits a positive attitude towards self and others				
2) Is accepted by the majority of peers				
3) Interacts positively with peers most of the time				
4) Displays even temperment				
5) Tolerates mild teasing				
6) Exhibits a sense of humor				
7) Functions effectively with small peer groups				
8) Displays age appropriate maturity				

For each category rated above, indicate how often the student's
academic adjustment interferes with grades and progress:

	1	2	3	4
A. **Attitude**				
B. **Independence**				
C. **Organization**				
D. **Self-control**				
E. **Social Interaction**				

Observation: Indirect and Direct Assessment

Observation is appropriate for both indirectly and directly assessing student performances. Checklists and rating scales offer convenient formats to structure and record observations. Their use for indirect assessment of learning patterns and academic adjustment (Figures 4.3–4.4) was already suggested. These same formats can also be used to structure direct assessment by assigning and observing the performance of specific tasks that evaluate listed behaviors. Sometimes indirect and direct assessment information from the same checklist or rating scale is desirable to compare judgments.

Whether observation is used as an indirect assessment technique, a direct assessment measure, or a combination of both depends upon the nature of the target behavior, time constraints, resource availability, and the inclinations of the observer and student. Regardless of the approach, observations can yield invaluable assessment and programming data.

Description. Teachers continuously observe students in an informal manner. However, when it is necessary to define a specific problem, systematic observations provide valuable information that cannot be obtained from casual observations or from other sources. Thus, observation becomes an assessment technique for the purpose of identifying a specific problem. Observations also provide important information for evaluating ongoing educational programs. Through systematic observation, data about academic skills, social skills, and other adjustment behaviors can be collected.

There are numerous observation techniques and recording formats available. For the purposes of this text, the observation form in Figure 4.5 is described and discussed to explain the observation process and to provide a sample format for recording observation data.

Defining Behavior. After recording the identifying information at the top of the form, Section A

is to be completed. First, determine the specific target behavior to be observed. In 1973, Poteet defined target behavior as "the behavior which is labeled, specifically defined, and is the target for observation, recording and, consequently, for modification" (p. 8).

Target behaviors must be described in specific, observable, and measurable terms. All such behaviors must have a beginning point and an ending point in order to be counted. Some target behaviors are easier to define than others. For instance, it is difficult to define "paying attention" because it is not a specific behavior, it cannot be seen, and it does not have an obvious beginning and ending point. However, McKenzie and others in 1970 defined "attending" as "facing instructional materials, teachers, blackboard, instructional devices, or a reciting pupil, whichever is appropriate." Their definition makes "paying attention" more measurable.

Ideas for target behaviors requiring observation can be gleaned from responses on the teacher survey. When the target behavior is determined, write the definition on the form beside "Target Behavior #1." Space is available for entering the definition of a second target behavior if needed. Once this information is written in Section A, then the type of observation and the setting are noted.

Types of Observations. The nature of the defined target behaviors determines the type of observation needed to obtain accurate data. Within this chapter, only two types of observations are considered: permanent product and classroom observation.

Permanent products include responses on math worksheets and test papers, models constructed, designs created, or any type of written or taped assignment. Counting and recording the number of misspelled words on a weekly test is an example of product recording. Product recording allows decisions to be made about a student without the student being present or without being present when the behavior occurred. We know something about the way Plato thought, because he left us

FIGURE 4.5 Report of Observations

Student's Name _____ Grade _____ Date _____
School _____ Teacher _____ Observer _____

SECTION A

Target Behavior #1 _____
Target Behavior #2 _____

TYPE OF OBSERVATION:

__Permanent Product   __Classroom Observation

Setting for Observation:
__Large group, total class   __Individual instruction
__Small group, direct instruction   __Individual seat work

SECTION B

PERMANENT PRODUCT ANALYSIS:
Academic Area _____
Work Reviewed _____ Number of items completed _____
_____ Percentage correct _____
_____ Time to complete _____
Analysis of Work Sample _____
_____
_____
_____
_____
_____
_____

SECTION C

CLASSROOM OBSERVATION

Interval-Time Recording   Frequency _____ seconds/minutes
Time of Observation _____ Length of Observation _____

TARGET STUDENT   **CONTROL STUDENT**

Analysis of Observation Data _____
_____
_____
_____
_____

SECTION D
Performances to Check Through Direct Assessment _____
_____
Need for Further Observation _____
_____
_____

his *Republic,* a product written over two thousand years ago (Sparzo & Poteet, 1989).

Some classroom behaviors do not leave permanent products for observation or analysis (e.g., discussions, fights, or lectures). When equipment is not available to record these behaviors for later analysis, the behaviors must be observed and recorded by using direct observation within the classroom setting.

Direct observation is better suited for measuring the student's reactions and adjustment to the academic environment. Such behaviors as preparation for class, on-task behavior, work completion, and other performances listed on the adjustment survey can be verified through direct observation.

Ideally the target behaviors should be observed in a variety of settings, over a period of time, and when possible by more than one observer. Likewise, it is advisable to observe target behaviors at least three or more times to establish the reliability of the observations. If two or more observers are used, it is necessary to inspect the degree with which they agree in their observations and recordings. To complete Section A, check which type of observation is to be used for the target behavior written above it, and check the setting for the observation. Once this is finished, proceed to complete Section B if the type of observation is permanent product, or Section C if it is classroom observation. These procedures are discussed next.

Section B of Figure 4.5 is designed to help the observer gather and analyze *permanent product* data. The academic area(s) of concern must be identified. These areas have probably been specified during the teacher interview. The actual work which is reviewed (test papers, essays, etc.) should also be noted on the form. Various types of student work need to be included in the observations. Three basic methods for collecting permanent product measures are noted on the form: number of items completed, percentage correct, and the time necessary to complete the task (Gable & Hendrickson, 1990a; Kazdin, 1994). A completed form is shown in Figure 4.6 that illustrates the analysis of a student's written math work.

When analyzing work samples, one should review all points of success and error. It is most important to search for any commonalities or patterns among the errors. There is space in Section B to write a brief description of the type of errors made, any patterns discovered, and the prerequisite skills mastered. When using indirect assessment it is important to focus on diagnostic hypotheses by asking which factors might be contributing to the behavior of concern. Your working hypothesis can be checked out by activities conducted during direct assessment discussed next.

Section C of the Report of Observations form is designed for analyzing *direct classroom observations.* If the target behaviors do not yield per-

FIGURE 4.6 Permanent Product Analysis

SECTION B

PERMANENT PRODUCT ANALYSIS:
Academic Area MATH – Subtraction of 2 - digit numbers
Work Reviewed Math Workbook   Number of items completed 13/30 – 54/100 – 6/12
        Test Papers   Percentage correct Average of 43 – 54%
        Homework   Time to complete Test – 1 hour
Analysis of Work Sample: 80% of the problems marked incorrect, involved subtraction with zero. All errors were consistent in that the skill needed to regroup when the zero was in the minuend, has not been mastered. Regrouping with other numbers appears to be in place. The time given to complete seatwork and test is adequate as all items are completed within time limit.

manent products, but indicate concerns in academic adjustment or learning patterns, classroom observations are the method of choice. There are several possible ways to gather these data. Two techniques, interval-time recording and frequency recording, are reviewed here and others may be found in a number of references, including those by Evans, Evans, and Schmid (1989), Kauffman (1993), Kazdin (1994), McLoughlin and Lewis (1994), and Taylor (1993).

Interval-time recording is a method of measuring whether or not a behavior occurs within the specific time period. After the target behavior has been determined, a decision must be made as to the designated interval of time to observe. A number is recorded on the form in Figure 4.7, Section C, beside the word "frequency" to indicate the time span of each interval. The words "seconds" or "minutes" should be circled to designate the frequency of each time span. The time of day that the observation was made is noted on the form beside "Time of Observation." The number of minutes spent observing is noted beside "Length of Observation."

An independent observer may easily observe behaviors in thirty-second time spans. A teacher with classroom responsibilities may prefer to use more convenient time spans, such as three minutes, five minutes, or ten minutes. Observations may be conducted before, during, or after direct instruction. For comparative purposes one other student in addition to the target child can serve as a control comparison and should be observed. The control student should be one identified by the teacher as average in all areas. Using a watch or clock with a second hand, begin the thirty-second observation interval by first observing the target student. (The classroom teacher may prefer a timer that rings at the end of the longer time period so that clock-watching will not interfere with teaching.) At the end of the interval, record a plus sign in the box if the behavior occurred anytime during that time span. If it did not, make a minus sign. Note that only one observation is recorded within each time span. After recording the behavior of the target student, begin the next thirty-second interval observing the control student. Repeat the recording procedure. Continue the entire process for the specified length of the observation alternating between the target and the control student. Interpret the frequencies of the behavior in terms of events that occurred immediately before and immediately after the target behavior. Figure 4.8 is an example of the recording and analysis of one classroom observation.

Frequency recording can easily be accomplished by classroom teachers or independent observers. The observer simply marks on a piece of

---

FIGURE 4.7   Defining Behavior and Establishing Intervals

SECTION A

Target Behavior #1 _____ *Off - task behavior — out of desk, talking to others* _____
Target Behavior #2 _____

TYPE OF OBSERVATION:
___ Permanent Product ✔ Classroom Observation

Setting for Observation:
✔ Large group, total class   ___ Individual instruction
___ Small group, direct instruction   ✔ Individual seat work

SECTION C

CLASSROOM OBSERVATION:

Interval-Time Recording   Frequency _____ *every 30* _____ (seconds)/minutes
                                     Time of Observation *9:00 AM* Length of Observation *10 min*.

FIGURE 4.8   Analysis of Classroom Observation

SECTION C

CLASSROOM OBSERVATION:

Target Student

+	+	−	−	−	+	−	−	+	+

Control Student

−	+	+	+	+	−	+	+	+	+

Analysis of Observation Data ___Off − task 50% off total time as compared to 20% off −___
___task behavior for the control student. Off − task behaviors include searching___
___through desk, walking to pencil sharpener, and stopping to talk with other___
___students.___

paper the actual number of times the target behavior is performed by the student for a given length of time. The bottom half of Section C could be used for this purpose by simply writing "Frequency Recording" beside "Classroom Observation" and using the space for your tabulation. One teacher, in an effort not to be obvious in her recording, wrapped two inches of masking tape around her wrist. Every time she saw the student at the pencil sharpener, she subtly made a mark on the masking tape with a pencil. Other teachers have simply made marks on a piece of paper placed in the book from which they are teaching.

Frequency recording is convenient and appropriate to use for behaviors that occur repeatedly. But what about the student who exhibits only one behavior, and does so for a long time, such as staring out the window? In that situation, interval-time recording would be the appropriate method to use because it would tell *how long* (as opposed to how many times) the target behavior occurred.

Systematic classroom observation often indicates the need for further investigation. Analysis of permanent products and work samples may necessitate direct assessment of some performances. For example, in Figure 4.6, assessment of the student's math skills is indicated; it would be important to use the approach taken with the Fundamental Processes in Arithmetic (Buswell &

John, 1925) wherein the student explains aloud his or her thinking process while working the arithmetic problems. In Figure 4.7, additional observations are needed to determine if the off-task behavior occurs in all instructional settings, and the extent to which this behavior interferes with achievement. Section D of the observation form is reserved for these comments.

Implications.   Systematic observation is a particularly appropriate technique for assessing performance and monitoring a student's progress throughout an educational program and, at the conclusion of a program phase, for evaluating the program's effectiveness. Individualized programming does not cease with the careful planning of an initial program. For the program to remain personalized it must be continuously monitored to ensure a match with the student's evolving needs. Both permanent product analysis and classroom observations are useful means of monitoring a student's performance under specified conditions. If, for example, a student's accuracy rate decreases as a result of a particular stimulus/response pattern, observations will reflect the decrease. Additional observations following instructional modifications will detect changes in the target behavior. Observational data provide the basis for making informed decisions about both assessment and programming.

Direct Assessment

Direct assessment requires the physical presence of the target student. Procedures for directly assessing a student's performance include direct observation, interviewing the student, and a variety of formats that each entail assigning the student a task and evaluating his or her performance.

Direct Observation

Unlike indirect observations (i.e., analysis of permanent products), direct observation of the student during learning activities permits analysis of the factors that impinge on student performances. Such observation has been termed *clinical observation* by Hargrove and Poteet (1984). Clinical observation is regarded as an important assessment technique. Essentially it is diagnostic looking, that is, looking with a purpose. One of the main purposes of clinical observation is to completely describe the behaviors and condition of the target student, noting what occurs before and after an event of interest. Such observation is necessary to estimate correlates and possible causes of the problem behavior under consideration, or to explain the behavior. Clinical observation is often performed in a one-to-one setting when complete attention can be directed to the student.

These clinical settings for observation can occur in a variety of locations (e.g., the classroom, at recess, or in learning circles). The observer should note details regarding the student's appearance and motor, affective, social, and cognitive behaviors. Hargrove and Poteet (1984) provide a list of "checkpoints" to facilitate the observations of these specific areas. Of particular importance is the student's use of speech and level of language development. Diagnostic listening comes into play along with diagnostic looking and diagnostic asking whenever clinical observation is being conducted.

As an extension of the preceding discussions of systematic classroom observations, a few cautions should be noted. To preserve validity, the student should not be aware of the observer's scrutiny, particularly during initial classroom observations. The observer's discretion should continue throughout all assessment and programming activities so as not to intrude upon performance, although, as rapport is established, most students expect their teachers to be alert observers. In some instances performances should be measured under deliberately varied conditions for comparative purposes. Smith (1994) gives additional pointers for using observation as a part of the assessment process.

Student Interview

A personal interview with the target student is recommended in all cases. In addition to the diagnostic data that can be obtained, interviews also provide a forum for becoming initially or better acquainted with the student.

Description.   Students sometimes show remarkable insight into the nature and source of their academic successes and difficulties. Interviewing the student to discuss the information obtained from the teacher, as well as any additional points of concern or interest, is a useful procedure with which to continue the direct assessment process. An interview can be conducted as an introductory activity for direct testing or as a separate activity prior to direct testing. The purpose of interviewing the student is to gain his or her perspective on the same issues addressed by the teacher. Figure 4.9, Student Interview, presents some suggested questions to use in structuring the interview. To the right of the number of each question and in parentheses are numerals and letters coded to related items on the four parts of the General Teacher Survey. For example, the first question on the Student Interview is coded to Part I: Assessment of Curriculum, item 1, Figure 4.1. By using this cross reference, discrepancies between teacher and student responses can be detailed. Questions should be paraphrased rather than read to the student. Some answers may lead to other questions. A casual and informal interview offers an excellent opportunity to establish

FIGURE 4.9   Student Interview

These questions are designed for structuring a face-to-face interview with a student for whom a teacher survey has been completed. The letters and numbers in parentheses refer to similar items on the General Teacher Survey (Parts I through IV). Questions should be paraphrased, not read.

1.(I.1) What does your teacher think is the most important subject? _____
How do you know? _____

2.(I.1) Which subject does your teacher think is the least important? _____
How do you know? _____

3.(II.1) Which school subject is the easiest for you? _____
Why? _____

4.(II.1) Which school subject is hardest for you? _____
Why? _____

5.(III.4) What does the teacher do that helps you learn the fastest? _____
Describe: _____

6.(III.5) What kind of answers are easiest for you? _____
(tell, choose, fill-blank, write, show)

Describe: _____

7.(III.6) What kind of work is easiest for you? _____
(worksheet, workbook, flash cards, computer, board work, tapes, games)

Describe: _____

8.(III.8) When do you learn best: when the teacher teaches the whole class? your small group? only you? or when another student helps you? _____
Why? _____

9.(III) What else helps you learn? _____
Why? _____

10.(IV.A) How do you feel about school? Your teacher? _____
Why? _____

11.(IV.B) When the teacher is busy, what is the hardest thing about doing your schoolwork? _____
Why? _____

12.(IV.C) How do you remember what your homework is? _____
How do you remember what to bring to school? _____

13.(IV.D) Tell me about the last three times you got in trouble with your teacher. _____
_____

14.(IV.E) Name your three best friends; which one(s) are in your class? _____
_____

15.(General) What do you most want to learn at school? _____
Why? _____

Other questions or comments: _____
_____

rapport with the student. The use of this form has been found to glean valuable diagnostic information in a short amount of time.

Implications.   The student's opinions of the extent and causes of his or her academic successes and problems provide valuable diagnostic hypotheses to explore through assessment. They also offer clues to the type of programming that may be productive. The very act of interviewing the student communicates the message that his or her opinions are important. The interview can also be used as a beginning point for involving the student in the assessment/programming process.

Academic Skills

Once the four parts of the General Teacher Survey have been completed and the direct assessment has begun with classroom observations and the student interview, preparation for assessing the student's performance in specific subject areas should begin. For help in deciding which academic area(s) to select for *initial* assessment, review the completed General Teacher Survey. Based on the teacher estimates (Part II), begin assessing in the academic area cited as *lowest* achievement. If the profile has peaks and valleys, begin with the *lowest* areas; if the profile is even and low, begin with basic skills in the core curriculum. If the teacher estimate does not match test data from school records, begin assessing starred items (determinants of promotion or retention) in Part I.

Checklists like the one presented in Figure 4.10 and the more detailed one in Figure 4.11 are useful for planning, scheduling, and monitoring assessment activities. (These checklists also offer a preview of the assessment procedures that are recommended throughout the remainder of this book.) The subjects are to be selected according to major teacher concerns, student concerns, and diagnostic hypotheses.

Post-Assessment Activities

As indicated in Figure 4.11, immediately following assessment the data must be interpreted and

recorded, and a brief report must be prepared for the major teacher. This is the point at which to begin organizing for programming.

PROGRAMMING

The curriculum-based assessment/programming cycle presented in Chapter 3 is advocated as a guide for integrating assessment and programming activities. Because it is related to all subject areas and intertwined with academic progress, academic adjustment is one of the first considerations in planning programs for most students. Thus, programming to improve academic adjustment is presented here before discussing how to improve performance in each of the academic areas.

Academic Adjustment

The academic adjustment behaviors outlined in Figure 4.4, particularly the social skills, permeate all academic areas. Of these five groups of behavior—attitude, independence, organization, self-control, and social interaction—the last two receive the most emphasis in many special programs. Because programming in any one of these five areas often affects behaviors in the other groups, several strategies are appropriate for improving behaviors in more than one area. These strategies are briefly discussed prior to considering strategies specific to a single area.

General Behaviors

A well-organized and managed classroom is essential for developing a constructive learning environment. Wang, Haertel, and Walberg (1993–1994) depict classroom management as a major influence on all types of learning. Thus, effective classroom management strategies as described by Evertson, Emmer, Clements, and Worsham (1994) are clearly useful for encouraging many desirable behaviors.

In addition, three time-honored behavioral strategies are particularly appropriate for improving many adjustment behaviors: reinforcement,

FIGURE 4.10 Assessment Planning Checksheet for _____

DATES BEGUN/COMPLETED		

_____/_____   1.   CURRICULUM ANALYSIS

_____/_____   2.   INDIRECT ASSESSMENT

_____/_____   — General Teacher Survey; Teacher: _____

_____/_____   •Assessment of Curriculum, Part I

_____/_____   •Estimate of Achievement, Part II

_____/_____   •Learning Patterns, Part III

_____/_____   •Academic Adjustment Survey, Part IV

_____/_____   — Specific Subject Teacher Survey; Teacher(s) & Subject(s):_____

_____

_____/_____   — Work Samples Analysis; Subjects: _____

_____/_____   — Other Available Data: _____

_____

_____/_____   — Curriculum Chart Marked

_____/_____   3.   DIRECT ASSESSMENT

> _Target Skills for Direct Assessment:_ _____
>
>
> _Diagnostic Hypotheses:_____
>
>

_____/_____   — Observation in Classroom

_____/_____   — Student Interview

_____/_____   — Personalized Test Items

_____/_____   •To Use; Source:_____

_____/_____   •To Adapt; Source: _____

_____/_____   •To Develop; Materials Needed: _____

_____/_____   — Testing Scheduled; Date: _____

NOTES:

FIGURE 4.11 A Checklist for Managing the Assessment Process

ASSESSMENT CHECKLIST
Organization and Sequence of Activities

I. General Preparation for Implementing the Curriculum-Based Assessment Process

_____A. Obtain or create a concise list of skills (curriculum chart) for each academic area you will consider.

____1. Make sure the skills cover kindergarten through at least 6th grade.

____2. List skills hierarchically and by major sub-areas.

____3. Consider writing learning objectives for each skill.

____4. Make the curriculum chart user-friendly with provisions to indicate

___ a. which skills are appropriate for assessment,

___ b. if *selection, production,* or *application* tasks have been given,

___ c. if *developmental, corrective,* or *maintenance* strategies have been used.

_____B. Duplicate necessary forms you will often use for both indirect and direct assessment.

____1. Place at least 10 copies of each form in clearly marked files for quick accessibility.

____2. Use your own color-coding system for ease of identification.

_____C. Prepare test items for *selection, production,* or *application* levels of responses.

____1. Make your own personal "test kit" to match your local curriculum.

___ a. Use a 3-ring notebook as a flip-chart; for each test item, place the stimulus on one side for student view and a copy of student item, directions, and answer on opposing side for your view.

___ b. For reading comprehension, photocopy passages, put each page in a plastic cover, put pages in a 3-hole notebook, and separate grade levels with divider tabs; use this notebook as the student copy. Follow a similar format for the teacher copy, but include pockets for teacher forms for each grade level.

____2. Prepare a generic kit with a curriculum chart for each academic area in which you might assess.

____3. Use color-coded tabs for quick identification of specific sections.

II. Indirect Assessment Activities (Target student is *not* face-to-face with diagnostician)

_____A. Carefully review referral information.

____1. Informally talk with teacher(s) as needed to clarify concerns.

____2. Determine if assessment is appropriate at this time.

_____B. Organize for assessment of target student.

____1. Schedule teacher interview.

____2. Compile forms and materials as needed for target student; fill in demographic data and place forms in student's assessment folder.

_____C. Complete the General Teacher Survey (Figures 4.1–4.4),

____1. Part I: Assessment of Curriculum,

____2. Part II: Estimate of Achievement,

____3. Part III: Learning Patterns,

____4. Part IV: Academic Adjustment.

_____D. Conduct teacher interview/survey(s) in academic area(s) selected for direct assessment.

_____E. Schedule direct assessment dates, times, and places.

III. Direct Assessment Activities (Target student *is* face-to-face with diagnostician)

_____A. Conduct classroom observation.

_____B. Conduct student interview (Figure 4.9).

_____C. Conduct a student interview specifically concerning academic area(s) being directly assessed (optional).

_____D. Administer appropriate items from your personal test kit, modifying tasks as needed.

____1. Use your curriculum chart to notate performance for items administered.

____2. Begin testing on an item of probable success for the student.

____3. Continue testing on more difficult items until 3 consecutive items are passed.

____4. If appropriate, continue testing on easier items until 5 consecutive items are passed.

____5. Determine if additional testing is required to cover *selection, production,* and *application* items; if so, continue with those items or schedule for another time.

IV. Post-Assessment Activities

_____A. Annotate curriculum chart to accurately reflect student's performance.

_____B. Prepare a brief report for referring teacher.

____1. List skills known and designate strategies for *maintenance.*

____2. List skills unknown and designate strategies as either *corrective* or *developmental.*

_____C. Determine if a recycle is necessary for this initial assessment; if so, schedule and if not begin programming.

contracts, and modeling. Most teachers use these techniques, but not all apply them deliberately and systematically.

A behavioral orientation toward teaching and changing behaviors of students has been available for several years (e.g., Poteet, 1973; Sulzer & Mayer, 1972; Vargas, 1977). The popularity of the approach is evidenced by the continuing publications on the topic (e.g., Alberto & Troutman, 1994; Kameenui & Darch, 1995; Sparzo & Poteet, 1989).

Reinforcement.   Verbal and/or nonverbal reinforcement of positive behaviors can be a powerful behavior change and behavior management technique. All students come to the classroom with a well-established set of responses to particular environmental stimuli in the typical classroom. For example, when the teacher speaks, most students listen and do what was asked. However, some students apparently have learned to respond in unusual ways to these typical stimuli. It is for those students who respond in atypical ways that teachers need to plan specific instructional programs so that the newly learned responses contribute toward scholastic achievement, improved self-esteem, and improved social skills.

A comprehensive treatment of the approaches to behavior modification, applied behavioral analysis, or behaviorology is beyond the scope of this chapter; there are many excellent publications which cover this topic, some of which were just listed. Briefly mentioned, here, are some aspects of a behavioral approach to classroom situations that have been shown to result in positive directions for classroom teaching, classroom management, and student behaviors.

The teacher can use the principles of reinforcement to assist in changing student behaviors and in managing a classroom. Briefly stated, the teacher must remember: *Behavior which is positively reinforced will be repeated.* The trick is to determine just what that reinforcer actually is. What the teacher views as a reinforcer might not be what the student thinks a reinforcer is. For some students, a visit to the principal's office might be a reinforcer, while for others a punishment.

Probably the most powerful reinforcer classroom teachers can use is their attention. Realizing this, the problem now becomes deciding just when to "give" that reinforcer to the student. The teacher must first determine what behaviors he or she wants the target student to do in a consistent manner, over and over again (e.g., get started on a task as soon as it is verbally assigned instead of roaming around the room). If teacher attention is a positive reinforcer for the target student, then the teacher should attend, even if briefly, to the student as soon as desired behavior is shown. This attention can be verbal and specific: "I like the way you got right down to work, Juan; you'll get your work done sooner that way." With more mature students, all that is necessary is a brief comment: "Nice going!" For some students, nonverbal indications such as a smile or a "thumbs up" sign is all that is needed. For use in situations where quick answers are needed, Sparzo and Poteet (1989) describe how to select and use reinforcers and apply them to increase or decrease a variety of classroom behaviors. Sequenced steps are explicitly presented that proceed from the least punitive and intrusive (talking with the student) to the most punitive (response cost, time out, etc.).

One problem arises in the use of reinforcers when the student does not do the behavior that the teacher wants to reinforce. How can you reinforce getting down to work when the student is actually roaming around the room? Several procedures might work in such a situation. Begin with reminding the group of the task to be done. Be sure that the target student has the skill to actually do the work. Most of us do not want to do things that we cannot do, and it is the same with students. The teacher must be certain that the student can perform the skill at a high rate of correct responses *before* the task is practiced as independent work (Archer, et al., 1989). In situations where the student can do the work, but won't, the use of successive approximations often works. The teacher attends to behaviors that are aimed toward the goal of getting down to work. For instance, the teacher might acknowledge that the student has the workbook and a pencil on top of her desk, ready to get down to work.

Another problem with reinforcers is using them when they should not be used. In other words, the teacher attends to a student when the student is doing what should not be done. If teachers attend to maladaptive behavior, it will happen again and again. The uninformed teacher will wonder why the students never do the "right" thing.

A problem with not attending to "incorrect" behaviors is that they may be maintained because they are reinforced, not by the teacher, but by other events in the environment. For example, when a student "clowns around" and other students laugh, chances are that the student will clown around again. For more serious behaviors that can cause harm and injury to others, direct and immediate intervention by the teacher is required. The student must be removed from the situation for the health and safety of all. This procedure, termed "time out," involves time out from positive reinforcement. Remember that "positive" has nothing to do with being good or right; it simply means that the reinforcer increases the probability that the behavior which occurred before, will occur again. The National Crisis Prevention Institute (1989) produces a set of three videotapes designed to teach educators how to use a safe, nonharmful behavior management system for agitated or out of control students. This training package is directed toward teachers at the secondary level, but can be adapted for younger students.

The teacher can try to ignore milder forms of "incorrect" behavior (e.g., going to the pencil sharpener and other actions that are not harmful), instead of saying things such as "Betty Sue, sit down! I've told you a thousand times that you must have my permission to go to the pencil sharpener when we are supposed to be reading!" The problem with this procedure is that teachers have not learned how to ignore inappropriate behaviors. The best way to develop this skill is to attend to those behaviors that are productive, oriented toward school success, and appropriate social interactions.

Contracts.   A second general behavioral strategy that can make a significant contribution toward improved classroom behaviors is the use of contracts. A simple written agreement between two or more people that specifies a relationship between behavior and consequences, usually in "if/then" terms, is a contract. The participants, the student and the teacher, for example, both must be involved in establishing the terms of the agreement and sign the dated, written document. Contracts serve as records of agreed-to terms of responsibilities and consequences of performing specific tasks. They have been used in a wide range of problem areas, from truancy to drug abuse (Sparzo & Poteet, 1989).

A good contract is stated in positive terms and gives the standard or criterion to judge the attainment of the contract terms. For example, "To receive a grade of B in American History, you will (1) pass three of four tests in American History with a grade of B or better, (2) write a two-page report on a book read from the approved reading list, and (3) make a five-minute oral presentation on a current event and explain how it is related to some similar historical event." It is important that the terms of a contract be clear to all parties involved.

Contingency contracts are useful when both teacher and students follow through on the agreements. Although Adamson, Matthews, and Schuller (1990) specifically recommend that the regular and special education teachers collaborate, using "daily check-outs" for monitoring behavior contracts, the regular recording, charting, and display of progress toward contract fulfillment is applicable in most any classroom setting and essential for the success of the strategy.

Modeling.   The third behavioral strategy is modeling. Modeling can be used to change students' behavior and is used in two different ways—as an example of appropriate behavior and as an instructional strategy. An admired student can serve as a model for specified behavior for a student wanting to behave like the model. Such behaviors are easily imitated when the target student is rewarded for attending and actually imitating the model's behavior. The target student is also more likely to imitate the model's behavior when a similarity is noted by the target student between the model and his or her own self and when the model's behaviors are perceived as leading to a positive reinforcement or the avoidance of punishment (Sparzo & Poteet, 1989). When selecting a model, the model's competence also should be considered; students are more likely to imitate models who have been successful in what they chose to do.

The second approach to modeling is using it as a teaching technique. Effective teaching studies have pointed out that academic achievement is more likely when the teacher models the behavior to be learned and when modeling is used as part of a specified sequence of instruction. For example Archer and others (1989) have incorporated modeling as one step in a nine-step procedure for effective instruction. In their model, an effective lesson consists of three parts: an opening, the body, and the closing. Each of these major parts of a lesson has three sections. The opening consists of gaining the student's attention, reviewing what information the student can bring to the lesson that applies to what is to be learned, and establishing the purpose and goal of the current lesson. The body of the lesson begins with the teacher modeling the behavior the student is expected to perform. For example, if the lesson is on handwriting, the teacher would model the behavior in a slow and exaggerated manner while verbalizing the actions being shown. This procedure is especially appropriate for motor skills. The student then proceeds to practice the new skill under the supervision of the teacher as prompts are given to avoid practicing errors. The teacher provides corrective feedback during this "prompt" stage. The body of the lesson is closed by having the student perform the behaviors on his or her own while the teacher monitors the accuracy of the responses. If a high error rate is observed, the instructional process is recycled back to the Model stage at the beginning of the body of the lesson. The lesson is closed out with a review of what was learned, a preview of the next lesson, and/or the assignment of independent work (if the student demonstrates a high rate of correct responses).

The target student can better understand exactly what is expected when a task is explained and modeled by the teacher or a peer. Modeling is easy to do, requires no special equipment, and can be implemented at a moment's notice in about any lesson, skill, or behavior that is appropriate for a student to learn.

Self-Monitoring.   In addition to the three generic techniques, self-monitoring strategies are particularly appropriate for helping the student who is experiencing mild to moderate difficulty in working independently, organizing self and supplies, or in maintaining self-control. (See discussion in Chapter 3 for references dealing with major difficulties with self-control.) When a student's academic adjustment in any of these three categories interferes with grades and progress, then self-monitoring strategies should immediately be planned as an integral part of the personalized program. Figure 4.12 gives one such strategy. General guidelines for implementing the outlined activity and other self-monitoring strategies are: (1) define target behaviors and identify reinforcers; (2) design the self-monitoring strategy and then coach students in its use; and (3) fade the use of the strategy (Dunlap, Dunlap, Koegel, & Koegel, 1991). A decided advantage to implementing self-monitoring strategies is the student's heightened awareness of and responsibility for his or her own behavior (Lewis & Doorlag, 1991).

Lovitt (1984) describes in detail 50 strategies for teaching students independent and management skills. One strategy is particularly suitable for teaching students self-monitoring techniques. "Getting It All Together: Organization Cards," requires the student to consult a brief checklist before, during, and after a task. The list may follow a number of formats; for example, it can be

FIGURE 4.12   Stop, Look, Listen, Act: A Strategy to Teach Self-Monitoring

Student uses driving a car as an analogy for this strategy. When approaching a stop sign or railroad crossing, the driver stops, looks, and listens, then acts by driving on if the way is clear. The student uses some signal in the environment that is causing trouble as the "Stop" sign. This strategy is useful for impulsive students who interrupt without thinking in social and academic situations (Sparzo & Poteet, 1989).

STOP:
- Stop talking or doing something. Get yourself together. Calm down.

LOOK:
- Watch what is going on right now. What is the other person doing?

LISTEN:
- Listen carefully to what is being said. What is the other person saying? Wait until a stopping place occurs, then say or do something.

ACT:
- Do what is appropriate and responsible.

placed in a notebook or written on an index card and taped to the desk. The student checks off each reminder as it is accomplished. Rewards are given for meeting the requirements of the student's personal list. The content of the checklist varies according to student needs. The list may include school supplies, time on task, or any of the statements categorized as independence, organization, and self-control on the teacher survey. Archer and Gleason (1989) suggest a similar procedure for monitoring the format of specific lessons, completing assignments, and proofing assignments. Aside from providing an external reward for a satisfactory checklist, the act of checking off each step as it is completed is a reward in itself and reinforces the behavior. (Those who make "things to do" lists understand all too well the satisfactions in checking off each task as "finally done.")

Teaching students to monitor their own behaviors enables them to assume part of the responsibility for their own learning and performance. Although the teacher could stand over the student with constant reminders to collect supplies and

follow the rules, self-monitoring is a much more powerful technique. Such skills may also be generalized to other settings (Frith & Armstrong, 1986). The value of self-monitoring may be compared to the adage: "Give me a fish and I eat for a day; teach me to fish and I eat for a lifetime."

Attitude

Evidence suggests that positive behaviors share a reciprocal relationship with academic progress. Attitudes toward the school and the teacher are certain to improve as the student gains small academic successes. Adapting the curriculum to the needs of the student is a major means for influencing attitude. Some ideas for doing this are presented in Figure 4.13. The ten-step system suggested by Canfield (1990) to increase students' self-esteem can also be readily adapted for use with special students.

The more positive the self-concept of the student, the more positively he or she is likely to view peers and, conversely, the better the peers acceptance the more positive the student's attitude toward all facets of school. Therefore, deliberate attempts to improve social interactions should be viewed as a specific strategy for improving the student's attitude.

Since gains in academic performance and improvements in independence, organization, self-control, and social interaction exert positive effects on attitude, the prominent display of each step of progress is important. Whether progress is graphed, charted, or depicted in other ways, it should be regularly acknowledged and rewarded as well as discussed and reviewed with the student.

Independence

The relationship between independence in the classroom and successful academic performance is also reciprocal. That is, for most students, the more capable they become in performing tasks, the more capable they become in performing those tasks independently, and the reverse is also true. Adjusting the curriculum to students' learning needs often builds and increases classroom

FIGURE 4.13   Curriculum Adaptations to Improve Attitudes

1. ***Library Books.*** Choose those dealing with good self-concept, school problems, or other special problems similar to those of the student. Books about the triumph over these issues are useful.

2. ***Listening Tapes.*** Choose (or make) taped books as mentioned in item 1 above. Use tapes when a students has difficulty in reading these books.

3. ***Sharing Time.*** Set aside time each week for students to share their personal triumphs.

4. ***"Good News/Bad News" Journals.*** Have students write incidents during the week in their personal journals that could be described as "good news" and those that could be viewed as "bad news." The weekly page for recording these incidents could be divided vertically and one side designated as "Good News" and the other side as "Bad News." The student could be asked to volunteer one from each side in a sharing time mentioned in item 3 above.

5. ***Special Interest Notes.*** Teacher writes a brief note to selected students stating some area or behavior the teacher expects the student to do for the week. This is a personal and very positive approach to behavior change. Teacher must be sure to positively reinforce incidences of the change in private. Students can keep the notes in their personal folders.

6. ***Independent Projects.*** Assign projects that can be accomplished first when working in a small group, then when working independently. The student learns that he or she can be successful when working independently.

7. ***Organization.*** Help students organize their responsibilities. Teach them how to keep an appointment calendar which shows the dates due for assignments and other responsibilities. The teacher will have to monitor this closely until the students become accustomed to the procedure.

---

independence. The desired behaviors can also be directly taught along with maintenance instruction for target academic tasks. However, some students require additional assistance in acquiring habits of independence.

A major avenue for building independence is direct and explicit instruction in how to learn. Such learning strategies are discussed in Chapter 3 and throughout Chapters 5–10. Many of the study strategies discussed in Chapter 10 contribute to independent learning and performance. For the strategies to be useful, however, students must be provided appropriate opportunities to apply them and guidance to do so. Beckman and Weller (1990) suggest the Consolidated Method for Independent Learning (CMIL), a three-phase model.

Also, teaching students to pace themselves and manage their time efficiently may increase their capacity for working independently. However, they must be informed of the amount of time available for each activity and have easy access to a watch or clock. Explicit instruction for adhering to timelines and for cued practice activities are given in Figure 4.14. As students begin to respond to practice activities, coach them to schedule their time prior to beginning larger and more complex tasks.

Certain teacher behaviors also promote independent performances. Prior to independent activities, the teacher must give good, comprehensible instructions. Asking a student to rephrase the directions for a peer or to describe what he or she will be doing is a way to ensure that the instructions are clear and understood. Demonstrating the task, then asking the student to orally perform a sample task, is a good practice. A specific routine must be established and followed for requesting teacher or peer assistance during independent work sessions. Sometimes just the reassurance that assistance is available is enough to motivate students to try to work independently. Classroom routines should also be established for what students should do when they complete their work. When students are involved in for-

FIGURE 4.14   Self-Pacing Reminders and Cues for Time Management

---

- You have 10 minutes to complete the 10 items in this exercise; that gives you 1 minute per item; begin now.

- You now have 8 minutes; you should have finished the first 2 items.

- With 4 minutes to go, you should be on at least number 6—remember, find the question mark, read the question, and then go to the beginning and read the entire problem.

- You have 2 more minutes.

- Time is up; turn your papers face down on your desk.

---

mulating the classroom routines, they are more likely to remember them, then need only brief and periodic reviews and rephrasings to remind them.

Organization

Organizational skills, a prerequisite or corequisite to many of the study strategies discussed in Chapter 10, may also need to be directly taught to some students. They tend to improve in structured situations. Inasmuch as the organized student is mobilized to learn, organization as a readiness skill is useful for every lesson.

Since organization involves several mechanical behaviors, self-monitoring and contracting are particularly applicable. Many of the behaviors are easily quantified in checklist form for students to follow, check off, and then confirm with the teacher for charting. Figure 4.15 lists several hints to help the teacher organize the physical facilities of the classroom and classroom routines.

Certain types of school supplies can be used for helping students organize. Require a three-ring binder with pocket dividers for all students, even young ones. Then teach them how to use and organize their assignments in the binders. Have students keep pens, pencils, crayons, and miscel-

laneous supplies in personal school boxes marked with their names. Insist that notebooks and school boxes be kept neat and orderly and regularly monitor their status. Gall, Gall, Jacobsen, and Bullock (1990) suggest using a checklist for students to evaluate their own or peers' organization of supplies, binders, and desks. Some type of reward (e.g., praise, tokens, or tangible reinforcers) should be awarded students whose organization passes inspection.

Teachers usually keep extra pencils, crayons, and paper for the student who occasionally needs them. Since it is important that the accommodation not become an excuse for students to avoid the responsibility for maintaining proper supplies, it should not be too readily offered or appealing or reinforcing (i.e., lend fat, dull crayons and short scruffy pencils, or insist that the student lend the teacher something in return). A specific behavior modification program may be required for the student who consistently forgets or loses materials.

To encourage the completion of homework assignments and their submission on time, reinforcement and corrective feedback should be provided in a timely manner for every assignment. This practice sends a clear message to students that the assignments are important and valued. Other homework procedures are suggested by Sparzo and Poteet (1989) and are used in the ideas given in Figure 4.16.

Self-Control

Self-control, or self-regulation, is the process of controlling and managing one's own behavior (Reynolds, 1990). With self-control, the responsibility for behavior management and change lies with the student. Such behaviors are highly valued, but the educational system has only recently begun to teach students these skills on a limited basis, even though it espouses the value of independence. Self-regulated strategies are often contrasted with teacher-directed instruction which typically includes verbal direction, modeling, physical assistance, and feedback. Techniques to

FIGURE 4.15   Hints for Organization

PHYSICAL FACILITIES

— Have a special place for *each* student's books and supplies.

— Clearly mark all Learning Centers.

— Have all bookcases and desks arranged in some meaningful order and keep it that way as much as possible. Assign students to straighten them up as a reinforcement activity.

— Have a special big box or place for "things" that are used frequently and need a place to be kept to avoid cluttering the room; name it the *Thing Box.*

— Have a specified procedure and place for turning in all assignments; shoe organizers or boxes for each student work well as a *mail box.*

— Provide a good model of an organized teacher.

CLASSROOM ROUTINES

— Establish a procedure and place for turning in all assignments.

— Establish a ritual for cleaning out and organizing desks every Friday afternoon.

— Develop procedures for when and how to sharpen pencils.

— Establish and post time limits for doing assignments.

— Display a sample lesson format; keep it posted for all to see.

— Display written instructions for where, when, and how to submit written assignments.

— Establish procedures for self-checking assignments (use of peer partners, teacher aides, etc.).

— Consistently review homework assignments. 15 minutes prior to dismissal, teacher explains assignment, writes it on board for students to copy in their assignment notebook, models any required skills, monitors students practice, and provides corrective feedback to students.

— Establish routines for beginning the school day (organize supplies needed for the day).

— Establish routines for ending the school day: record homework assignments, take home supplies needed to accomplish the assignments, identify supplies which need to be replaced, list needed supplies, organize desk for the next school day.

teach these skills involve teaching the student specific verbalizations or teaching by modeling and transfer of the verbalizations to student control (Whitman, 1987). A cognitive-behavioral treatment program can be effective in reducing aggressive behaviors and increasing self-controlled behavior (Etscheidt, 1991).

The technique of teaching via modeling is based on the concept of cognitive behavior modification advocated by Meichenbaum (1986). His model for self-talk as a means of self-direction includes cognitive modeling, direct guidance, self-talk, faded self-talk, and self-instruction. The student should be directly involved in selecting and then applying the strategy.

Alberto and Troutman (1994) note that the procedures for self-control are the same as for any other behavior management system. They point out that self management procedures consist of self-data recording, evaluation of self-behavior, and providing self-consequences via rewards and punishment. Self-instruction is useful for manipulating behavioral antecedents. These writers give a comprehensive approach for teaching and using self-instructional and self-management techniques.

FIGURE 4.16   Homework Procedures

- Determine if there is a school-wide policy regarding homework.
- Establish a policy for homework and inform students and parents about it.
- Assign homework *only* after student can perform the task correctly during guided practice time when teacher monitors the work and provides corrective feedback.
- Establish classroom procedures for writing assignments and seeing that students take home necessary supplies to complete the assignment.
- Establish a classroom procedure for turning in assignments and for checking them.
- Make sure that the amount of homework and the required time for completion are reasonable.
- Consider individualizing homework assignments.
- Assign as homework *only* meaningful activities that directly relate to a curriculum task and avoid busywork.
- Make sure assignments have a stated purposes and are understood by *all* students.
- Provide feedback on *all* homework assignments using grades or written comments.
- Have parents record the amount of on-task time required to do the homework; this procedure lets the teacher monitor the quality of work assigned.
- Establish a Homework Folder for each student in which assignments are placed and recorded.

Kauffman (1993) notes the many cognitive behavior modification techniques incorporated in the procedure advocated by Fagen and Long (1979). He lists their requirements as the ability to perceive incoming information accurately, retain the information, organize actions logically, relate actions to outcomes, cope with obstacles, postpone impulses to do other things, and to reduce internal tension.

Student inattention is a frequent and troublesome problem for many special students and their teachers. The teacher's task is to catch the student's attention, focus attention, and directly teach attending behaviors. Among the suggestions for managing attention are actively involving students in lessons, improving their organization skills, and helping them use self-monitoring strategies. George (1986) suggests several verbal strategies for teachers to use: increase lesson pace, request multiple answers to numerous drill questions, cue responses, have students repeat correct responses, and verbally reinforce responses. Additional specific and detailed suggestions for handling attention problems are described by Fouse and Brians (1993), Goldstein and Goldstein (1990), and Parker (1992).

A more broad-based orientation to self-control is presented as a teaching model by Joyce and Weil (1992). Their self-control model includes the following phases: introduction to behavioral principles, establishing the baseline, setting up the program, and monitoring and modification. They note that this model has been successfully used in improving study habits. The length of the study periods should be gradually increased and reinforced. They recommend taking a break between intervals of study.

It seems clear that one of the goals of education should be to transfer the control of learning from the teacher to the student. The techniques of self-control, self-instruction, and self-management all contribute toward this goal. While this process is typically not found in the curriculum, it can become a vital part of a written curriculum, or it can be taught as the need arises. In any case, the teacher should be atuned to its importance and strive to actively implement a planned program to teach this vital set of skills.

Social Interaction

Social interaction skills are those behaviors approved by our society. In the schools, they are often taught as part of the Support Curriculum as discussed in Chapter 1. Social skills, along with academic and physical skills, comprise a broader sense of personal competence (Greenspan, 1981). Experienced classroom teachers can testify that a sense of personal competence is developed through a reciprocal relationship among skills in academic tasks and self-esteem and relationships with others. In many cases, it appears that success in academic tasks provides direct contributions to social successes. School is probably the most important socializing influence on students, other than the family; success or failure in school contributes to perceptions of one's self as being either a success or a failure (Kauffman, 1993). Smith (1994) points out the importance of having students with learning disabilities practice acceptable social behaviors because they often have less chances to interact with their nondisabled peers. When the teacher provides learning situations where academic success results, often, social and behavioral problems tend to lessen to a significant degree. Providing instructional tasks at a level designed for success can be an important step toward increasing social skills.

Some students have well-developed social interaction skills which allow them to become popular, sought-after friends, and leaders in school settings. Other students however, require the direct intervention of the teacher to facilitate development of a positive self-esteem and appropriate interaction with peers. Teachers often do not have a structured social skills curriculum and must adopt either one that is part of a published program to teach social skills or attempt to develop appropriate social behaviors as the need arises. A brief social skills curriculum is given by Mercer and Mercer (1993) covering skills in conversation, friendship, difficult situations, and problem-solving. In their overview of packaged curricula for teaching prosocial behaviors, Sabornie and Beard (1990) cite several effective behavioral interventions. These include token reinforcement

and teacher reinforcement of appropriate social behaviors and selective use of time-out techniques to reduce negative behaviors. They also recommend social behavior instruction within cooperative groups.

Fox and Weaver (1989) believe that social skills training can best be done if it is infused into the regular curriculum. They describe a clever strategy that can be used in English class when studying the concept of "adjective." They suggest having students name adjectives that are positive descriptions of themselves and of their peers rather than describing some concrete object. They suggest that this procedure allows the students to evaluate themselves in a positive light, promoting self-esteem, and gives positive views of each other. It also informs less socially adept students about the traits viewed as positive by peers. These writers provide a table listing names and addresses for 20 different social skills training programs and curricula for elementary and secondary students.

To increase self-esteem and improve social interaction skills, Sparzo and Poteet (1989) offer these suggestions: Focus on providing as much success for the student as possible; teach the student to make positive self-statements; use a program to establish friendships; and carefully structure a buddy system, peer tutoring, and cooperative learning activities. Many of the excellent activities to improve self-concept suggested by Canfield and his associates (Canfield & Siccone, 1993; Canfield & Wells, 1994; Siccone & Canfield, 1993) also are appropriate or can be adapted for use with special students of various ages.

Planning classroom activities that include a deliberate pairing of the student with peers who are popular, congenial, or exhibit appropriate behavior may be helpful. The teacher must be careful to ensure that the differences between students are not too great. Johnson and Johnson (1986) advocate using the cooperative learning model to maximize the social development of students with and without disabilities, and Slavin (1991) cites evidence to support the practice. When the cooperative learning activities are highly structured, the positive peer interactions between disabled and nondisabled increase, and when the students also receive instruction for collaborative skills, the social interactions are even better (Putnam, Rynders, Johnson, & Johnson, 1989).

Role playing is an approach than can be used to help students study social behavior and social values. Role playing can be used to begin a systematic program of training social interaction skills, or it might be used to deal with an immediate interpersonal problem that has arisen in the classroom according to Joyce and Weil (1992). According to those writers, social interaction problems amenable to change through role playing include: interpersonal conflicts, intergroup relations, individual dilemma, and historical or contemporary problems.

Because inadequate social interaction skills may be accentuated in unstructured situations, students may need preparatory training. The Structured Recess Program described by Adamson, Matthews, and Schuller (1990) involves phased learning and practice sessions that are carefully structured before entering unstructured play at recess, a troublesome setting for students with inadequate social interaction skills.

Recognition of the need for formal instruction in conflict resolution is a relatively recent development resulting from concern about increasing school violence. Interest in teaching students with and without disabilities systematic strategies for constructive problem solving, negotiation, and mediation appears to be growing quickly (Van Acker, 1993; Willis, 1993b).

The "skills streaming" approach to teaching a variety of social skills has been advocated for adolescents by Goldstein, Sprafkin, Gershaw, and Klein (1980) and for elementary school students by McGinnis and Goldstein (1984). Their methods are based on a psychoeducational, behavioral approach for providing instruction in prosocial skills. The model is termed "Structured Learning" and consists of modeling,

role playing, performance feedback, and transfer of training.

Specific activities for improving peer interactions are presented by Lovitt (1984) and Polloway and Patton (1993). Additional suggestions are scattered throughout the text by Good and Brophy (1994). A comprehensive treatment of social and motivational characteristics of students with learning disabilities is given by Gresham (1988). Forness and Kavale (1991), in noting the expanding research on social competence of learning disabled students, caution that assessment and programming for social skills are both very complex. Schumaker and Hazel (1984a, 1984b) note that the careful arrangement of antecedent and consequent events as well as self-control procedures appear to useful instructional strategies. They further note that the instructional procedures can be categorized as descriptive (telling and explaining how to act), modeling (showing how to act), rehearsal (self-instruction and role-play), and feedback (evaluation of rehearsal strategies). These strategies are equally appropriate for students with and without disabilities. Bos and Vaughn (1994) summarize their descriptions of social-skills programs appropriate for use with special students with some basic and generic principles. In addition to the use of cooperative learning activities, they offer these recommendations: follow the principles of effective teaching, teach needed strategies and skills, use student strengths, and help the target student develop close friendships.

Traditional academic skills are considered in the content chapters (Chapters 5–10). For each academic subject, developmental, corrective and maintenance strategies are offered for inclusion in a personalized program. Each chapter follows a similar format. Remember that assessment should be focused on the area of greatest concern at any given time and that a student would never have all assessment strategies in every subject applied to him or her. Instead, performance in only one or two school subjects should be assessed for the purpose of developing an appropriate personalized program in the subject(s). As the student progresses in the chosen subjects, he or she can then be assessed for programming in other subjects. As information is obtained through assessment procedures in the subject areas, it should be synthesized with that from the teacher survey for all areas, from the observations, and from the student interview. Such a synthesis increases the probability of developing an effective educational program for an individual student.

SUMMARY

An interview with the teacher of a target student is the first step in initiating the curriculum-based assessment/programming process. This interview serves several purposes for indirect assessment of the student's performance; it identifies the academic subjects for which the student is responsible, makes known the available instructional resources, and detects strategies that have, and have not been effective. The teacher estimates the student's grade-level performance in each subject area, his or her learning patterns, and academic adjustment, or school social skills, all important variables that hold implications for both assessment and programming. Analysis of the student's class work and observations in the classroom are additional strategies for focusing the assessment process. Direct assessment continues by interviewing the student to gain his or her overall perspective of the academic environment. More specific assessment is then conducted in the appropriate subject area(s).

The academic adjustment behaviors grouped as attitude, organization, independence, self-control, and social interaction are central to school success. When planning instruction for students who exhibit particular problems in these areas, improving academic adjustment skills should be a programming priority.

CASE STUDY

You are a resource teacher in an elementary school. This morning a new student, Dane, age eight, transferred to your school. Dane's records indicate that he has been in an ungraded primary setting, attending resource class one hour per day. An attached note advises that the special education records will be forwarded shortly. The principal asks you (because you're the expert on special education students) to "work with him till noon and decide in which regular class we'll place him after lunch." Remembering that the teacher is unavailable to you, use each section of the general teacher survey as a guide for describing the information you can collect, the methods and source of collection, and the importance of the data:

General Teacher Survey
 I. Assessment of the Curriculum
 II. Estimate of Achievement
 III. Learning Patterns
 IV. Academic Adjustment

ENRICHMENT ACTIVITIES

Discussion

1. What are the conditions that might render the information collected through the teacher survey invalid? Assuming that you are not both interviewer and respondent, should the information seem invalid, what must you do?

2. Debate the relative importance of each of the statements on the academic adjustment survey: to the teacher, to the class as a total unit, and to the student who is experiencing academic difficulty.

3. Angel's first grade teacher describes the child as functioning at a preschool level in all academic areas, with undetermined learning patterns and almost entirely negative adjustment. What will be the major focus of your classroom observations of Angel? Defend your answers.

4. Consider the effects of an outside observer on the behavior of a target student. Then discuss the advantages and disadvantages of asking the student's regular teacher to conduct the observations.

5. Evaluate the sample questions for interviewing a student in Figure 4.9. Which ones are likely to yield the most important assessment information? Programming information? What additions, deletions, and modifications do you suggest?

Special Projects

1. With a peer, practice the teacher interview. The individual who plays the teacher must have a student in mind when answering the questions. Jot in the margin under "Additional Comments" extra questions you feel the need to ask and the extra comments that the peer feels a need to offer.

2. Using the General Teacher Survey, Part III, answer the questions about your own learning patterns. Then write a brief synopsis of the factors likely to increase your learning. The next time you are in a learning situation validate your conclusions.

3. Systematically observe the classroom behavior of a student, peer, or instructor. Using a form such as the one in Figure 4.5, define the target behavior(s), observe, record, and interpret the data. (Remember that target behaviors can be positive ones!)

4. Obtain a copy of a second- or third-grade student's spelling or math paper that contains many errors. Using the observation form (Figure 4.5), systematically analyze and record the student's performance, identifying success and error patterns. What are the implications for additional assessment? For programming?

5. Evaluate a student's school social skills using the Teacher Rating Scale of Academic Adjustment (Figure 4.4); then plan a personalized program to improve that student's school adjustment behaviors, particularly in the areas of self-control and social interaction.

CHAPTER 5

READING WORD RECOGNITION

JOYCE S. CHOATE

CHAPTER OBJECTIVES

This chapter is designed to enable the reader to:

1. Explain the relative importance of word recognition and each subskill to a student's academic success.
2. Describe the indirect assessment procedures and resulting data that are the most relevant to a student's word recognition and general academic progress.
3. Develop appropriate plans for the direct assessment of the word recognition performance of specific students, then justify the plans.
4. Select and justify developmental, corrective, and maintenance strategies according to the assessed word recognition skills of specific students.
5. Plan a tentative word recognition program that is personalized for specific students.

Reading is the most essential basic skill of any school curriculum. Although the ultimate goal of reading instruction is text comprehension, identification of words and word meanings is a skill area that must be mastered to facilitate comprehension (Collins, 1991; Rubin, 1994). Separation of comprehension from word recognition, a component of the comprehension process, is admittedly an artificial division. However, this procedure is partially justified by the traditional separation of skills by standard curricula.

Word recognition skills are important to a student's academic success for three reasons: (1) in order for a person to appear to be literate, correct pronunciation and knowledge of the meaning of certain words is necessary; (2) the word recognitions skills are *strategies* for comprehending; and (3) skilled word recognition is required by school curricula. The first reason primarily satisfies a social need; mispronunciation of those words considered to be "at a student's level" results in embarrassment to the student and to his or her teacher. Specialists have debated the exact level and degree of word recognition skills that must precede comprehension. However, most experts agree with Samuels (1976) that knowledge of a large percentage of the words in a passage frees the reader from much of the decoding struggle so he or she can attend to comprehension. It is further assumed that as strategies for comprehending, mastery of word recognition skills will contribute to understanding the meaning of the passage. The third reason for stressing these skills rests upon the second; one reasons that if word recognition skills are prerequisite to reading comprehension, then the curriculum must stress such tasks. And, indeed, heavy emphasis is placed upon such skills by most reading curricula.

WORD RECOGNITION SKILLS

Word recognition skills may be divided into four subskill areas: (1) basic sight vocabulary, (2) phonics, (3) structural analysis, and (4) word meaning. In each of the four subskill areas, certain tasks traditionally have been designated as *reading readiness* tasks. However, proponents of the whole language philosophy of reading instruction speak of emergent literacy instead (Rubin, 1994). Regardless of approach or terminology, early instruction that leads to recognition of words is designated, herein, as part of the kindergarten curriculum. Attaching meaning to words is the obvious goal of word meaning, the fourth subskill area. Pronunciation is the goal of the first three subskill areas, known collectively as word analysis skills. It is assumed that once a word is pronounced that it is within the reader's speaking and listening vocabulary. The word analysis skills require related but different tasks of the learner and are usually taught differently. Frequently, instruction in sight words, phonics, and structural analysis does not include word meaning activities. Although sound learning theory dictates that pronunciation and word meaning skills should be considered concomitantly, this is not always a common instructional practice (Durkin, 1993). Therefore, for assessment purposes, the four areas are considered separately. For programming purposes, however, suggestions are offered for pairing word meaning activities with all word analysis activities.

Sight Vocabulary

Words that the reader understands and pronounces at first sight are said to be within that reader's sight vocabulary. As shown in Figure 5.1, sight vocabulary may be basic words or high frequency words or letters. Visual discrimination is a prerequisite task. Basic vocabulary refers to the words that occur most often within a given text or reading materials. High-frequency vocabulary, the words that occur most often within our language, necessarily appears with equal frequency in reading materials. Prompt recognition of such connecting words as *the, what, but,* and *with* is required for fluent reading. Sight words are typically taught using the look-say or whole-word approach. For a youngster to become a fluent reader, the frequency of these words dictates that he or she must recognize them with little or no effort in order to direct the larger portion of the decoding effort toward the words of lower frequency. Rapid acquisition of sight words depends heavily upon a student's visual memory skills. Mature readers recognize most words as sight vocabulary, even though the words may have originally been decoded using phonics, structural analysis, and/or context.

Phonetic Analysis

Phonics, the second of the pronunciation subskills, deals with the specific sound/symbol associations of the most regular elements of the language. Primarily an auditory task, phonics requires the student to discriminate, remember, and pronounce the sounds associated with specific letters and groups of letters. As depicted in Figure 5.1, the specific sound/symbol relationships generally studied include single consonants; consonant blends, in which two or three adjacent letters retain their separate sounds but are blended when spoken; and consonant digraphs, in which adjacent consonants form spoken sound patterns that differ from the component letter sounds. Instruction in the sound/symbol relationships of vowels includes long- and short-vowel patterns as

FIGURE 5.1   Sample Word Recognition Curriculum Chart

Student's Name_____Grade_____Teacher_____School_____Date_____

Directions: Circle the specific tasks required for success at this student's current level; in the space provided list any other tasks appropriate to the existing curriculum.

Typical Text Level for Tasks

WORD RECOGNITION SUBSKILLS	K	1	2	3	4	5	6	
I SIGHT VOCABULARY	I	I	I	I	I	I		
A Basic Vocabulary	A.1 Name .2 Colors .3 Numbers	A.4 Basal PP/P/1	A.5 Basal 2.1/2.2	A.6 Basal 3.1/3.2	A.7 Basal 4th Rdr.	A.8 Basal 5th Rdr.	A.9 Basal 6th Rdr.	
B High-Frequency Vocabulary		B.1 Upper Letters .2 Lower Letters	B.3 Common Nouns .4 PP/P/1	B.5 2nd	B.6 3rd			
C Visual Discrimination		C.1 Shapes .2 Letters .3 Words						
	K	1	2	3	4	5	6	
II PHONETIC ANALYSIS	II	II	II	II				
A Single Consonants		A.1 Aud. Discr. Initial .2 Aud. Discr. Final	A.3 Initial .4 Final	A.5 Medial				
B Consonant Blends			B.1 Initial Two Letter	B.2 Final nd,nt,st .3 Three Letter				
C Consonant Digraphs			C.1 Initial ch,ph, sh,th,wh	C.2 Final ck,ng				
D Variant Consonants			D.1 kn,wr,gn .2 c,g	D.3 s,qu,x, gh	D.4 Silent mb,p,t,s .5 Multi.Sds.			
E Vowels		E.1 Aud. Discr. Rhymes	E.2 Long .3 Short .4 ai,ay,ea ee,oa .5 r-Control.	E.6 l-Control .7 oi,oy,ou, ow .8 oo .9 schwa				
F Phonic Generalizations			F.1 CVC	F.2 CVCe .3 CV				
	K	1	2	3	4	5	6	
III STRUCTURAL ANALYSIS	III	III	III	III	III	III	III	III
A Root Words		A.1 Basal, PP/P/1	A.2 Basal 2.1/2.2	A.3 Basal 3.1/3.2	A.4 Basal 4th Rdr.	A.5 Basal 5th Rdr.	A.6 Basal 6th Rdr.	
B Suffixes		B.1 s,ed,d, t,ing .2 er,est	B.3 ly,ful	B.4 less, ness	B.5 able,ment, ty,th,al, ist,ive, ize,or,ion tion,age,y		B.6 ish,ant,ent, ance,ence,ten, eous,our,ious ation,ible,re	
C Prefixes			C.1 a,be,un, re	C.2 dis	C.3 pre,ex,in, mis,sub	C.4 non,com,con, post,tri,de, trans,bi, inter,per, super,pro	C.5 on,im,ad, ab,an,tele, contra	
D Compound Words		D.1 Basal PP/P/1	D.2 Basal 2.1/2.2					
E Contractions			E.1 Omit One Letter	E.2 Omit Two+ Letters				

continued to next page

FIGURE 5.1   *(continued)*

Typical Text Level for Tasks

WORD RECOGNITION SUBSKILLS							
	K	1	2	3	4	5	6
III STRUCTURAL ANALYSIS (con't)		III	III	III	III	III	III
F Syllabication	F.1 Aud. Disc. One & Two Syll.			F.2 Two Consnt. .3 Affixes .4 (c)le .5 Dbl. Letter .6 Blends, Diagraphs .7 CV .8 Primary Accent	Accent: F.9 Two Syll .10 Affixes .11 Long Vowel .12 Secondary		
	K	1	2	3	4	5	6
IV WORD MEANING	IV	IV	IV	IV	IV	IV	IV
A Basic Vocabulary	A.1 Direction Words	A.2 Basal PP/P/1	A.3 Basal 2.1/2.2	A.4 Basal 3.1/3.2	A.5 Basal 4th Rdr.	A.6 Basal 5th Rdr.	A.7 Basal 6th Rdr.
B Classification	B.1 Pictures .2 Nouns	B.3 Basal PP/P/1	B.4 Basal 2.1/2.2	B.5 Basal 3.1/3.2	B.6 Basal 4th Rdr.	B.7 Basal 5th Rdr.	B.8 Basal 6th Rdr.
C Pronoun References			C.1 they,it she,he	C.2 them,we, him,her			
D Affixes		D.1 Basal PP/P/1	D.2 Basal 2.1/2.2	D.3 Basal 3.1/3.2	D.4 Basal 4th Rdr.	D.5 Basal 5th Rdr.	D.6 Basal 6th Rdr.
E Vocabulary Relationships	E.1 Descriptions: home and school		E.2 Synonyms .3 Antonyms .4 Homonyms	E.5 Homographs .6 Multiple Meanings .7 Descriptives		E.8 Abstracts .9 Colloquials	E.10 Neologisms .11 Euphemisms .12 Pejoratives .13 Etymology
	K	1	2	3	4	5	6
V ADDITIONAL SKILLS							

COMMENTS

NOTE: Check subskills and tasks as mastery is demonstrated, circling additional tasks required for student advancement.

well as several variant and special vowel or vowel/consonant combinations. The specific curriculum dictates whether major phonic rules for spelling patterns are taught directly or are inferred or generalized. Direct instruction in phonics is included in the overwhelming majority of the general reading curricula and is even taught as a separate subject in some lower grade curricula. The study of phonics also is a valuable supplement to whole language programs (Hull, 1994). Some students experience extreme difficulty mastering the phonetic intricacies and may not benefit from such instruction beyond the initial sounds. Nevertheless, phonics is generally considered to be an integral part of the primary grade curriculum, receiving decreasing emphasis as students progress beyond the fourth-grade reading level.

Structural Analysis

Structural analysis involves using the meaningful parts of words as an aid to pronunciation. Instruction in the subskills, listed in Figure 5.1, primarily focuses on word roots and affixes. The student is encouraged to quickly recognize, at sight, these word parts as a total unit. Thus, instruction in this subskill may combine a look-say approach to unit recognition with an analytical approach to discerning the meaningful word parts. The word parts are usually categorized as root or base words, prefixes attached to the beginning of a root word, and suffixes at the end of root words. Identification of the component root words within compound words and contractions is presented in a similar manner. The division of words into syllables, with the appropriate syllable(s) accented, is also included in the typical structural analysis curriculum. Although instruction in structural analysis begins in the first grade, the emphasis continues and may increase through high school. However, at the upper grades, the emphasis generally shifts from that of pronunciation to that of determining word meaning.

Word Meaning

Student knowledge of the meaning of words is perhaps the most important of the word recognition subskills. Instruction in the word analysis subskills is predicated upon a student's understanding of the meaning of the words that are decoded. A student's comprehension of passages, the major goal of reading instruction, is facilitated or impeded by skills in word meaning (Heilman, Blair, & Rupley, 1994). Proficiency in this area often reflects an enriched language background. However, significant gains in vocabulary knowledge may be obtained through direct instruction. In the typical classroom, word meaning is given at least cursory attention in the introduction of the basic vocabulary words that recur throughout a text. Additional activities listed in Figure 5.1 that expand a student's word knowledge include the classification of words and concepts into broad categories; the study of the relationships among synonyms, antonyms, homonyms, and homographs; direct instruction in descriptive terms and words with multiple, abstract, and colloquial meanings; and the formulation, change in meanings, and history of words and word parts. Word meaning instruction begins at the preschool level and extends throughout the grades into higher education.

PERSONALIZED ASSESSMENT PROCEDURES

Assessment for program planning must necessarily include examination of the student's word recognition curriculum as well as the evaluation of the student's specific word recognition skills, subskills, and tasks. The results of such assessment provide the basis for planning a word recognition program that will likely foster student achievement gains. However, both assessment and programming for word recognition skills must be analyzed in relation to the student's reading comprehension skills and to the specific reading comprehension curriculum (see Chapter 6). Although treated separately in this chapter, in accord with traditional curricula, word recognition

FIGURE 5.2   Assessment Planning Checksheet for Jorenda

DATES BEGUN/COMPLETED	Jorenda
4/16 / (4/23)	1. CURRICULUM ANALYSIS
4/16 / (4/23)	2. INDIRECT ASSESSMENT
4/16 / 4/18	—General Teacher Survey; Teacher: ___Mrs. Mason___
4/16 / 4/16	•Assessment of Curriculum, Part I
4/16 / 4/17	•Indirect Student Assessment, Part II
4/16 / 4/18	•Learning Patterns, Part III
4/16 / 4/18	•Academic Adjustment Survey, Part IV *note — easily distracted*
4/16 / 4/18	—Specific Subject Teacher Survey; Teacher(s) & Subject(s) ___Mason —___
	3rd grade — all
4/16 / 4/23	—Work Samples Analysis; Subjects: ___Reading, Social Studies___
4/18 / 4/20	—Other Available Data: ___Report cards 92 – 95, Basic Skills___
	Tests 93 – 94, private tutor summary
4/18 / 4/23	—Curriculum Chart Marked
4/25 /	3. DIRECT ASSESSMENT

> *Target Skills for Direct Assessment:* ___Sight vocabulary and___
>   word meaning
>
> *Diagnostic Hypotheses:* ___1) Overemphasis on pronunciation___
>   vs. meaning   2) Probably not using context —
>   check to see

4/25 /4/25-26	—Observation in Classroom
4/26 / 4/26	—Student Interview
4/26 /	—Personalized Test Items
4/26 / 4/26	•To Use; Source: ___Cloze Plus, pp. 13 – 15; CBA/P IV E 2 – 4___
4/27 / 4/27	•To Adapt; Source: ___HBJ Workbook, 23, 35 – 36___
4/27 / 4/30	•To Develop; Materials Needed: ___HBJ, pp. 42 – 43, 76 – 77___
4/30 /	—Testing Scheduled; Data: ___5/3 – 4___

NOTES: Compare oral vs. silent comprehension and word
recognition in isolation vs. in context; can she use context
silently? What about word usage in written expression?

and comprehension skills are so interrelated that they defy total separation. Thus, to interpret accurately a student's curricular status in reading, results of comprehension assessment must be synthesized with those in word recognition skills.

In word recognition, as in other subjects, to personalize assessment procedures you must first establish the content and sequence of the word recognition curriculum within which the student is expected to function. As illustrated in the sample checksheet in Figure 5.2, carefully planned indirect and direct assessment of student performance further ensures that the assessment procedures are indeed personalized.

Curriculum Analysis

Although most word recognition curricula include similar elements, the degree of emphasis may differ, and there may be a slight variance in the levels at which specific tasks are introduced. The first five items of the teacher survey on word recognition skills (Figure 5.3) present the structure for assessing a student's word recognition curriculum. Using this survey, the student's teacher is asked to designate the word recognition subskills and tasks that the student must master at specific levels on a curriculum chart. The curriculum chart may be the school's published word recognition curriculum, the scope and sequence chart of a main reading text used for word recognition instruction, or the chart in Figure 5.1. The listing of word recognition tasks by objectives in Appendix A presents an alternate format.

It may be helpful to complete both the word recognition and comprehension surveys at one sitting to allow for comparison of teacher priorities and student skills in these two, interrelated areas. Careful note of the teacher's perceptions in both these areas will provide substantial data for program priorities and planning.

Teacher designation of required word recognition tasks on the chosen curriculum chart provides the skill content for assessment. Circled items on the chart, which represent the content of the curriculum, serve as a list of the specific word recognition tasks for which assessment techniques must be developed. As in other subject areas, the charting of the word recognition curriculum does not end with the survey but continues throughout the assessment/programming cycle.

Indirect Student Assessment

Before presenting the student with actual test items, one can partially assess the student's word recognition skills through indirect assessment procedures. These indirect methods include a continuation of the survey on word recognition skills to determine the teacher's estimate of specific word recognition needs and an analysis of available data from other sources. Indirect assessment in word recognition, as in other skill areas, generates, and may even confirm, diagnostic hypotheses, improving the precision of the assessment process.

Teacher Perceptions

The second portion of the teacher survey on word recognition skills (Figure 5.3) requires the teacher to indicate his or her perception of the student's skills. Identifying specific tasks that are difficult for the target student to perform helps narrow the assessment focus. Word recognition is an integral part of all subject areas, increasing in importance as the student advances in school. If interference in other subject areas is suspected, plan to directly assess the student's mastery of the vocabulary specific to each questionable subject. Collect representative samples of the student's class work for the tasks cited in Item 6.

Available Data

Analyzing available data refines assessment of word recognition skills. Relevant information can be obtained from the completed general teacher survey (Figures 4.1–4.4) and from reports of observations, school records, any recently administered tests, and samples of the student's daily work. Carefully review these data, specifically relating each bit of information to word recognition skills.

FIGURE 5.3   Teacher Survey: Word Recognition Skills

Student_____ Date_____

Teacher_____ Interviewer_____

ADDITIONAL COMMENTS

A. ASSESSMENT OF CURRICULUM:

1. Indicate appropriate skills, subskills, and tasks on an attached word recognition curriculum chart.

    List available text titles/levels you would consider as options:

2. List current text titles and levels in which student is expected to master word recognition:

    _____
    _____
    _____

3. Check the primary source(s) of student's report grades in word recognition:

    __Reading Workbook   __Vocabulary Workbook
    __Teacher Tests   __Board Work
    __Combination _____
    __Other _____

    Describe grade sources:

4. Indicate the relative importance of each subskill to student's grades in word recognition using *1* as the most important:

    __Sight Vocabulary   __Structural Analysis
    __Phonetic Analysis   __Word Meaning

    Indicate time devoted to each by current curriculum and texts:

5. Describe modifications in word recognition that you have attempted with this student:

    _____
    _____

    Degree of success:

B. INDIRECT STUDENT ASSESSMENT:

6. Rank order this student's word recognition subskills using *1* as the strongest:

    __Sight Vocabulary   __Structural Analysis
    __Phonetic Analysis   __Word Meaning

    In weakest area(s) identify the most difficult tasks for this student:

7. Check the best description of the student's emotional reaction to his or her word recognition performance:

    __Over concern   __No concern
    __Some concern   __Other reaction

    Describe student's emotional reaction:

8. Check any other subject areas in which student's word recognition skill interferes with performance:

    __Reading Comprehension   __Spelling
    __Math   __Social Studies
    __English   __Science
    __Other _____

    Indicate why and to what extent:

9. List specifically what you want to know about this student's word recognition performance:_____

    _____
    _____

    Attach representative samples of the student's work

10. Interviewer Summary: _____

    _____
    _____

When reviewing the student's performance on any tests administered within the preceding five or six weeks, watch for error and success patterns. If possible, analyze test items to identify additional tasks requiring attention or to determine the impact of the student's word recognition performance on his or her reading comprehension and other subjects as well.

Samples of a student's written responses to reading (e.g., reactions, workbook activities, and worksheets) are usually readily available. For a quick skill itemization, check the workbook for the student's chapter and/or unit word recognition tests. Analyze the task portions that are accurately and inaccurately performed to identify the entry task for direct assessment and the specific point where instruction should probably begin. Also note the effective use of word attack strategies and the stimulus/response formats that seem to facilitate or impede student performance. For example, a student's performance on a fill-in-the-blank exercise may be significantly less accurate than one on a matching exercise, although both activities include the same subskill content. Many students can pronounce and understand the meaning of target words but do not attend to the detail required of worktext activities.

The indirect assessment process serves the primary purpose of formulating diagnostic hypotheses to be tested through direct assessment. Abbreviation of the direct assessment procedures is a secondary purpose, if sufficient information is gathered to justify omitting a few of the direct assessment tasks. Summarize indirect data and record assessment questions and hypotheses to begin a diagnostic map that will guide the initial procedures in the direct assessment of the student's word recognition performance.

Direct Student Assessment

Direct assessment of the student's word recognition performance entails observing the student in the classroom, interviewing the student, and administering and interpreting personalized tests. Several procedures should precede the direct interview and testing. These include (1) interpreting the indirect assessment data, (2) formulating diagnostic hypotheses, (3) establishing assessment priorities, and (4) developing streamlined direct assessment plans.

Preliminary Procedures

Synthesizing the information relevant to the student's word recognition performance helps to generate tentative diagnostic hypotheses. Suppose the teacher has noted sight vocabulary as Marie's greatest problem and phonetic analysis as the next weakest subskill. Through work-sample analysis, you note that Marie is not using a systematic approach to decoding unknown words. If her teacher has also expressed concern about Marie's memory of new words, then you might hypothesize that deficient phonic skills are causing her to approach each new word as a totally new task without the benefit of at least rudimentary sound/symbol clues. In establishing assessment priorities, the initial and final consonant sounds might become the primary tasks to be evaluated, with high frequency words and basic vocabulary as secondary concerns. Even if this hypothesis should be confirmed through direct assessment, you have a defensible reason for the focus and beginning point of testing and can approach the assessment process by systematically confirming or rejecting hypotheses.

Planning for direct assessment involves not only making full use of the indirect assessment data to develop diagnostic hypotheses and priorities, but also deciding how to use teacher and student time and effort most efficiently. Schedule the classroom observations for a time when the target student will be called upon to demonstrate key word recognition skills; plan the student interview for a time that will not conflict with classroom reading lessons. In addition to the general recommendations for streamlining assessment presented in Chapter 3, three strategies are specific to assessment of word recognition performance: (1) use the sight vocabulary tests as survey tests; (2) if indicated by diagnostic concerns, begin testing phonetic and structural analysis subskills within the student's instructional level established by the survey test; and (3) if word meaning subskills are an area of concern, begin testing at the student's current grade placement level.

Plan to use the basic and high frequency vocabulary lists for each grade level to determine not only the student's mastery of sight vocabulary, but also the level at which to begin the testing of phonetic and structural analysis subskills. If a student pronounces more than 85 percent of the words on a list, proceed to the basic and high frequency vocabulary lists at the next higher level. If less than 70 percent of the words are pronounced correctly, decrease levels until you find the one at which the student's pronunciation is within the 70 to 80 percent range. The rationale for this procedure rests upon the supposition that effective application of phonetic and structural analysis subskills enables the student to pronounce the majority of words on a sight word list. The beginning point of phonetic and structural analysis assessment is at the level in which the student pronounces most sight words. Diagnostic hypotheses govern priorities, and student performance determines whether the assessment proceeds above or below the beginning level. Begin assessment of word meaning subskills at the current grade placement, even if the student is not performing on level. Some students comprehend words that they are unable to pronounce on sight. For this reason, the most efficient and accurate assessment of the student's abilities may involve stretching performance by presenting tasks at or above grade level and then decreasing the difficulty level as needed.

Classroom Observations

Ideally, the target student should be observed in the classroom during formal reading instruction and also during at least one content lesson such as social studies. However, this may not be possible since reading is typically taught in the morning and social studies in the afternoon. Regardless of the lessons observed, target behaviors should include those cited by the teacher as problematic,

word pronunciation and oral reading patterns, questions asked by the student, and evidence of the extent to which word recognition performance impedes or facilitates achievement in various subjects. The conditions under which the student is expected to perform and variance in behavior across conditions should also be noted. Some of the remaining uncertainties often can be incorporated in the student interview for clarification.

Informal Student Interview

A direct and informal interview with a student can provide valuable insight into the factors that facilitate and interfere with performance in word recognition. Many students may say they are bored with the workbooks or do not perform well because they cannot spell the words. Some students may say they are simply sleepy in the mornings during the period of reading instruction. Through the interviewing process, you can also determine the student's preference for instructional methods and activities. Consider rephrasing the questions on Part B of the teacher survey on word recognition skills (Figure 5.3) for the content of this interview. For example, rephrase Question 6 so that you ask the student, "In remembering words, which is easiest (or hardest) for you: memorizing, sounding out, knowing the meaning, or figuring out the word parts?" Then, to encourage elaboration, "Why do you think that _____ is easiest (or hardest)?" The sample interview in Figure 5.4 is shorter and contains slightly different questions, but the intent is the same. Regardless of the exact questions asked, the information gained provides additional data for generating diagnostic hypotheses to be tested.

Personalized Word Recognition Tests

Several tools and techniques are appropriate for direct testing of a student's word recognition skills. Tests developed from the classroom reading materials are the most likely means of collecting relevant data. Certain sample items for tests of word recognition included in Appendix A and subtests from other published assessment in-

FIGURE 5.4   Sample Student Interview for Word Recognition

1. When your teacher give you a new word to learn, how do you remember it?

2. When you read by yourself and come to a word you don't know, how do you figure it out?

3. Which task is easiest for you?
   - Memorize how words look?
   - Sound out words?
   - Figure out word parts?
   - Understand the word meanings?
   - Which task is hardest for you?

4. Which lessons in your classroom have the hardest words in them?
   - Reading, Mathematics, Science, Social Studies?

5. Describe the word-reading activities that you enjoy doing in your class.

6. Name five new words that you would like to learn to read. Why are those words special to you?

7. Name five new words that you would like to learn to write. Why?

struments may correlate with the classroom curriculum. The key factor in selecting a specific task is its direct relationship with the word recognition tasks that the student is required to master in the classroom.

Suggestions for Constructing Tests.   The instructional materials and expectations in whole language programs vary widely; request the teacher's assistance in selecting materials representative of curricular expectations. For structured programs using primarily a basal approach, the student's text, teacher's guide, accompanying workbook and skills activities, plus any supplementary reading aids provide the materials for personalized assessment of word recognition skills. The particular student text from which you select test tasks depends upon the flexibility of the curriculum. If the school permits cross-grade text usage, then initially draw assessment materials from the student's grade-level text. Use content from higher or lower level texts within the same series until the level at which the student achieves 80 percent accuracy on the majority of word recognition tasks is determined. Even in systems where cross-grade texts are not available

or the practice is not permitted, measure the student's performance of adjacent level tasks in order to plan an effective program.

When appropriate, use actual workbook pages as the stimulus for assessing word recognition skills. Select pages for the target task that represent the specific workbook's typical, or most frequently occurring, format. If the student is usually required to write the letters with which the names of pictures begin or end, then such an exercise is appropriate for assessment purposes. Often vocabulary or other tests appear at the end of a unit in the workbook; these offer obvious sources for assessment and analysis of word recognition performance. Although published workbooks may not be used in whole language reading programs, virtually all reading curricula include some form of written skill assignments appropriate for adaptation as assessment materials.

The following suggestions are for designing assessment tasks that present words or word-parts in isolation primarily at the production level; however, application and use of strategies can be assessed with followup questions or tasks described in Chapter 3. The suggested procedures are numbered according to the word recognition curriculum chart (Figure 5.1) and the correlated skill objectives in Appendix A. The scoring criteria are presented as guides and should fluctuate with each student's curriculum. The interpretive remarks are intended as an aid in weighting the student's performance of each task.

Sight Vocabulary

Basic Vocabulary: Name, Colors, Numbers, (IA.1–.3). *Materials:* Student's whole name, eight primary color names, and/or number words (1–10); print or type words in list form or use flashcards or a tachistoscope (tach-x). *Strategy:* Ask student to read words aloud; record error patterns. *Interpretation:* 100% accuracy for Name, 75% Colors, 80% Numbers; the first task is an important index of reading readiness; recognition of color and number words provides the initial core vocabulary and concepts around which to build beginning stories.

Vocabulary: Basal R–6, (IA.4–.9). *Materials:* Word list in back of student reading text; randomly select twenty words to highlight in book. Write or type in list form, on flashcards, or use tach-x. *Strategy:* Ask student to read aloud twenty words; note specific error patterns. *Interpretation:* 80% accuracy; if student correctly pronounces less than criterion level, follow same procedure at decreasingly lower levels of same text series until 80% level is found. This is the level at which he or she can probably benefit from instruction in pronunciation of words in isolation. Because the vocabulary is the most basic skill to the mastery of other word and comprehension skills, it is essential that the appropriate instructional level be determined for the student.

High Frequency Vocabulary: Upper/Lower Case Letters, (IB.1–.2). *Materials:* 26 letters, printed in upper case and in lower case; write or type in random order on list, flashcards, or for tach-x. *Strategy:* Ask student to name letters; record error patterns. *Interpretation:* 100% accuracy; recognition of letters is an essential reading readiness task that provides the student with needed security when first approached with formal reading instruction.

High Frequency Vocabulary: Nouns and PP– 3, (IB.3–.6). *Materials:* List of high frequency words, such as the ones by Dolch (1942) and Fry (1980), at the level student is currently required to read; compile all words at required level as well as at the levels a grade above and a grade below. Write or type in list form, on flashcards, or for tach-x. *Strategy:* Ask student to pronounce words; record error patterns. *Interpretation:* 90–95% accuracy; if student correctly pronounces less than criterion level, decrease level until criterion level is found. This is the level at which student will probably benefit from instruction. Because high-frequency words are so often encountered in reading texts, less than 90–95% accuracy may pose serious problems to the student's reading growth; this subskill may be considered one of the MOST basic reading skills as mastery of the other word attack skills may depend upon mastery of these words.

Visual Discrimination: Shapes, Letters, Words, (IC.1–.3). *Materials:* Two sets of flashcards, each consisting of ten pictures or drawings of basic shapes, 26 upper and lower case letters, and/or ten random words of three to five letters. *Strategy:* Ask student to select same or different pictures from cards of similar figures; present five sets of three to five cards for each task. *Interpretation:* 100% accuracy; the tasks progress in order of difficulty and importance. The visual discrimination between letters and words is prerequisite to beginning reading. However, the young student who confuses letters that are visually similar may later be taught to compensate with context clues; if letter/word confusion significantly impedes reading progress, special intervention techniques may be required.

Phonetic Analysis

Single Consonants: Initial and Final Auditory Discrimination, (IIA.1–.2). *Materials:* Student reading text, vocabulary list, workbook; for readiness, use vocabulary from texts, PP1–3 Levels. Prepare two lists of 20 pairs of words that differ by (1) beginning sound and by (2) ending sound. Also include five pairs that do not differ.

Strategy: Say the words aloud in pairs to student; ask him or her to say "yes" if the words are the same and "no" if they differ. *Interpretation:* 100% Consonants, 80% Vowels; these tasks are vital to the student's use of phonics as a decoding strategy. The student who does not hear the sound differences will experience extreme difficulty in a phonetic reading program. Be sure student understands directions; give several practice items.

Single Consonants: Initial, Final, Medial, (IIA.3–.5). *Materials:* Student reading text, vocabulary list, workbook; from word lists select words that begin, end, or have single consonants in medial position. Compile a separate list for each category. *Strategy:* Dictate each word, asking student to name the letter which is heard in the target position. *Interpretation:* Varies according to specific sounds student is expected to master at given levels. If student experiences difficulty, give him or her three letters from which to select each letter; allow student to point, say, circle, or write the answer.

Consonant Blends: Initial, Medial, Final, (IIB.1–.3). *Materials:* Student reading text, vocabulary lists, workbook; from text words, select those containing consonant blends in three positions to list for examiner use. *Strategy:* (1) Tell student the target blend; read words with the blends in three positions and ask student to tell where target sounds occur or (2) read words to student; give choices of blends and ask student to indicate which one occurs in each word. *Interpretation:* Varies according to specific blends student is expected to master at given levels. If student's reading program is phonetically based, these tasks and the preceding one are vital; if phonics instruction is peripheral to the reading program, then these tasks are among the basic ones.

Consonant Digraphs: Initial and Final, (IIC.1–.2). *Materials:* Student reading vocabulary list; select ten words that begin with digraphs, ten that end with digraphs, and list for examiner use. *Strategy:* Read list aloud, asking student to say or write the digraph contained in each word. *Interpretation:* Varies according to digraphs student is expected to master at given levels. This is a difficult task for some students; they may tend to pronounce the single consonant sounds when decoding and make random errors when encoding; if performance is unsatisfactory, give student three choices from which to select digraphs occurring in dictated words.

Variant Consonants, (IID.1–.5). *Materials:* Student reading text, vocabulary list; select two words containing each of the variant sounds of *c, g, kn, wr, gn, s, qu, x, gh, silent mb, p, t, s* and use only those indicated as basic for the specific curriculum. List the variations of each sound together *Strategy:* Ask student to read each pair of words orally or silently and say another word that represents each variant consonant. *Interpretation:* Varies according to specific variant consonants expected at given levels. Some variant consonants which have not been presented for mastery may be present in sight or high-frequency vocabulary; the student's teacher will determine those that should be mastered. Some students may actually perform above level on this task because of incidental learning.

Vowels: Auditory Discrimination in Rhymes, (IIE.1). *Materials:* Vocabulary list from reading texts, PP1–3 Levels. From the word lists select 20 pairs of words which rhyme and 10 pairs that do not rhyme; write or type in list form for teacher use (random order). *Strategy:* Dictate word pairs, asking student to say "yes" if words rhyme and "no" if they don't. *Interpretation:* 100% mastery; give several practice items because student may confuse the concept of rhyming with that of "same" and "different" as presented in previous test of auditory discrimination. This is a key task in the acquisition of phonetic analysis subskills.

Vowels: Long and Short, (IIE.2–.3). *Materials:* Student reading text, workbook; select five words that contain the long sound of each vowel (total of 30 words) and five for each short vowel. Prepare the two lists in random order along with the vowel letters. *Strategy:* (1) Ask student to pronounce each word, naming the long vowel (or short vowel) in each, or (2) dictate words to student and ask for the target vowel heard in each. *Interpretation:* 90% accuracy; the first assessment task is obviously easier than the second, but both should be used if student is expected to apply knowledge of vowels. The long vowels are the easiest sounds for most students to hear and identify because they are the names of the letters. The short vowels, although more difficult, are typically taught before long vowels. If student has auditory discrimination problems, this may be a difficult task; however, it is a vital part of phonetic analysis.

Vowels: Combinations, (IIE.4). Materials: Student reading text; select three words representing each of the CVVC vowel combinations (*ai; ae; ay; ea; ee; oa*) and list randomly. *Strategy:* Ask student to name or underline the vowel heard when the word is pronounced and to cross out or name any silent letters. *Interpretation:* Varies according to curricular demands; although these vowel combinations represent the phonic generalization CVVC, many students may have mastered combinations without generalizing the principle to others. Unmastered combinations should be included in intervention plans if student has mastered at least two of the combinations.

Vowels: R–Controlled and L–Controlled, (IIE .5–.6). Materials: Student reading texts, vocabulary list; select ten words with r-controlled vowels and ten with l-controlled vowels and randomly list the syllables containing target vowels. *Strategy:* Ask student to pronounce the syllables. *Interpretation:* 90% mastery; syllables are presented instead of the total word to discriminate between student application of phonetic analysis and acquired sight vocabulary. Because these syllables occur frequently in student texts, these are basic tasks.

Vowels: Diphthongs, (IIE.7–.8). Materials: Student vocabulary lists; select five words containing each diphthong: *oi, ow, oy, ou, oo.* Randomly list syllables containing these diphthongs. *Strategy:* Ask student to pronounce the

syllables. *Interpretation:* Varies according to specific skills of student's curriculum. Syllables are presented for reasons listed in preceding test; this task is not as important as some because student can correct pronunciation by context or, in some cases, give the separate sound of each letter and approximate the correct sound.

Vowels: Schwa, (IIE.9). Materials: Student vocabulary lists; select ten words that contain the schwa sound and list. *Strategy:* Ask student to pronounce the words. *Interpretation:* 80% accuracy; even if an alternate pronunciation is given in isolation, most students will correct according to context. Observe contextual pronunciation before planning intervention.

Phonic Generalizations: CVCe; CV; CVC, (IIF.1–.3). Materials: Student vocabulary lists; select ten words representing each of the three phonic generalizations. Randomly list only syllables containing target patterns. *Strategy:* Ask student to pronounce the syllables. *Interpretation:* Varies according to curriculum. Many students master these principles without receiving direct instruction on the principles themselves; of those presented, the CVCe and CVC patterns are perhaps the most important to word recognition progress.

Structural Analysis

Root Words, (IIIA.1–.6). Materials: Student reading text, workbook, teacher guide; select 15 words with suffixes and 15 with prefixes and list randomly. *Strategy:* Ask student to say only the root words. *Interpretation:* 80% mastery, decreasing list level until 80% achieved. These tasks are basic not only to word analysis skills but also to unlocking word meanings; unsatisfactory performance calls for direct intervention.

Suffixes and Prefixes, (IIIB.1–.6; IIIC.1–.5). Materials: Student reading text, workbook, teacher guide; select ten root words and all suffixes attached to words on list, and/or ten root words and their prefixes. Make two lists, listing on each the root words in one column and affixes in another; make an answer key listing all possible meaningful combinations. *Strategy:* Ask student to form and pronounce as many "real" words as he or she can, combining affixes with each root word. *Interpretation:* 80% accuracy; these tasks increase in importance from grade-level three upward. Mastery of affixes not only increases word-pronunciation performance, but also greatly expands knowledge of word meanings.

Compound Words, (IIID.1–.2). Materials: Student reading text, workbook, teacher guide; select all compound words included in appropriate level(s) list. Present to student in tabular form. *Strategy:* Ask student to pronounce all words, citing the two words that form each compound. *Interpretation:* 100% mastery; compound words are typically formed with words from lower level vocabulary than target level. This task is typically presented at the first- and second-grade level, with little direct instruction provided thereafter.

Contractions, (IIIE.1–.2). Materials: Student reading text, workbook, teacher guide; select all contractions included in appropriate level(s) list. Present in tabular form. *Strategy:* Ask student to pronounce each contraction and tell which two words are represented or to name omitted letter(s). *Interpretation:* 80% accuracy; this task is mastered by most students in oral language but requires translation into written language. If student has difficulty with task, ask him or her to combine two words to form target contractions.

Syllabication: Auditory Discrimination, (IIIF.1). Materials: Vocabulary list from PP1–3 and P texts; select ten, one-syllable and ten, two-syllable words. Orally present to student in random order. *Strategy:* Ask how many syllables are heard in each word. *Interpretation:* 100% accuracy; this auditory readiness task prepares the student specifically for syllabication skills and generally for attending to the distinctive auditory features of words.

Syllabication: General, (IIIF.2–.7). Materials: Student reading text, workbook, teacher guide; select words representative of the syllabication principles governing words with affixes, two consonants, blends and digraphs, and double letters. Prepare a list of 20 to 25 words. *Strategy:* Ask student to point or draw a vertical line to the point(s) of syllable division. *Interpretation:* Varies according to curricular emphasis; if student can pronounce the word, he or she has effectively divided it into syllables! Student's need to hyphenate at syllabic division in formal writing can be satisfied by referring to a dictionary. Ask the teacher to specify student's need for this task.

Syllabication: Accent, (IIIF.8–.12). Materials: Student reading text, workbook, teacher guide; select ten words with one primary accented syllable and ten with secondary accented syllables to present in list form. *Strategy:* Ask student to tell which syllable(s) should be accented or to mark the words as they should be accented. *Interpretation:* Varies according to curricular emphasis; the task presented is similar to the one usually required as a classroom assignment. A more useful task would be to mark the words for the student and ask for the correct pronunciation. The student who can place correct accent marks on words knows how to pronounce them, thereby negating the necessity for marking them. However, the skill of pronouncing words according to diacritical markings is important to a student's independent acquisition of new vocabulary. Verify with teacher the importance of task.

Word Meaning

Basic Vocabulary: Direction Words, (IVA.1). Materials: Direction words (top, bottom, up, etc.) from teacher's edition of readiness and PP Levels of reading text; list words randomly for teacher use. *Strategy:* Ask student to point to or place a pencil in the position indicated by each word. *Interpretation:* 80% accuracy; these concepts are essential to adequate classroom functioning at every level but are particularly important as readiness tasks. If difficulty is noted with "left" and "right" (concepts frequently not mastered until late first grade), specific intervention should be offered.

Basic Vocabulary: PP–6 (IVA.2–.7). Materials: Reading vocabulary list in student reading text; randomly select 20 words. Locate a sentence using each word in text and copy onto worksheet or flashcards. *Strategy:* (1) Give student three choices from which to select the meaning of the word in the sentence, or (2) ask what the word means in the sentence. *Interpretation:* 80% accuracy; some students understand the meanings of words but have difficulty expressing them. Consider comparing student performance on both options (using different words) to identify problems. These word meanings are among the most basic reading tasks.

Classification: Pictures, Nouns, PP–6, (IVB .1–.9). Materials: Twenty pictures cut from readiness text, or 20 nouns belonging to 3 to 5 categories from PP–P Levels of text, or 20 to 25 words belonging to 3 to 5 categories from PP–6 text list. Mount pictures on index cards, list nouns in random order, or list words in random order. *Strategy:* (1) Ask student to classify pictures or words according to categories supplied by examiner (people, pets, etc.) or (2) ask student to group pictures or words according to similarities and then develop classification labels. *Interpretation:* 80% accuracy; task 1 is considerably less demanding than task 2. The student who accomplishes task 2 not only understands the word meanings but does so at a much higher cognitive level. This is a very important task for promoting retention of word meanings.

Pronoun Referents, (IVC.1–.2). Materials: Student reading text; randomly select 10 to 20 sentences containing names or objects for which pronoun referents can be substituted; present sentences on board, worksheet, or cards with words to be replaced, underlined. *Strategy:* Ask student to substitute a pronoun for the underlined word(s). *Interpretation:* 70% accuracy; most students have mastered this in oral language but must translate to reading to avoid needless rereading.

Affixes: PP–6 (IVD.1–.6). Materials: Student vocabulary list; select the prefixes and suffixes which appear most frequently in the words. Then list ten root words, recording the affixes sepa-

rately. *Strategy:* (1) Ask for the meaning of each affix, or (2) ask student to form new words by using the root words and affixes and then tell how the meanings change. *Interpretation:* Knowledge of affix meaning assumes increasingly greater importance from grade three and up; this task is vital to independent discovery of word meanings.

Vocabulary Relationships: Description, (IVE .1). Materials: Pictures of several views, inside and out, of homes and schools. *Strategy:* Ask student to describe at least five things about each picture; then ask student to tell at least five things about his or her home and classroom. *Interpretation:* 100% quality descriptors; if student has difficulty, ask him or her to describe specified objects in the classroom and/or to bring pictures of home and perform a similar task; this is a readiness task for building the expressive vocabulary in preparation for reading.

Vocabulary Relationships: Synonyms and Antonyms, (IVE.2–.3). Materials: Student reading text and word list; randomly select 10 to 20 words. Prepare in list form (1), or locate sentences in text that contain target words and copy, underlining each target word (2). *Strategy:* (1) Ask student to name a word that means the same or opposite of the stimulus word, or (2) ask for a word that means the same or opposite of the underlined word in each sentence. *Interpretation:* 80% accuracy; this is an important task to overall language development as well as to word recognition growth. However, the older student may be introduced to a thesaurus if a specific weakness is evidenced. Task 1 is more difficult than task 2 because of the context clues available in the second option. Comparison of student performance on both tasks may reveal information about utilization of context clues.

Vocabulary Relationships: Homonyms, (IVE .4). Materials: Student reading text and word list; select from list pairs of words that are spelled differently, are pronounced the same, and have different meanings. Locate these words in sentences in text and copy 10 to 20 sentences leaving blanks for homonyms. *Strategy:* For each blank, ask student to select the correct word and pronounce it. *Interpretation:* 70% accuracy; this is more important to spelling than to word recognition. The key question here is whether the student can say and understand the meaning of the word in the sentence.

Vocabulary Relationships: Homographs, (IVE.5). *Materials:* Student reading text and word list; select from list pairs of words that are spelled the same, are pronounced differently, and have different meanings. Locate the words in sentences in text and copy 10 to 20 sentences, leaving blanks for homographs. *Strategy:* Ask student to read each sentence and pronounce the word as it should be said in the specific sentence. *Interpretation:* 70% accuracy; demonstration of proficiency not only indicates application of word meaning subskills but also confirms the student's effective use of context.

Vocabulary Relationships: Multiple Meanings, (IVE.6). *Materials:* 10 to 20 words that have several meanings, selected from reading vocabulary list; prepare in list form, indicating beside each word the number of possible meanings. *Strategy:* Ask student to formulate the indicated number of oral or written sentences to demonstrate the different possible meanings of each word. *Interpretation:* 60% accuracy; the criterion level is indicative of the wide variety of possible meanings, some of which are obscure. Many students will discover alternate meanings as they occur in context. However, if the curriculum requires it or if deficient performance is interfering with overall reading performance, then direct instruction is indicated.

Vocabulary Relationships: Descriptive Words, (IVE.7). *Materials:* Student reading vocabulary list; select 10 to 20 descriptive words to list on cards or worksheet. *Strategy:* Ask student to say each word and name five appropriate objects or situations that could be appropriately described by each word. *Interpretation:* 70% accuracy; students who evidence a high degree of verbal fluency will probably excel at this task. If task appears too difficult, ask student to give the meaning of each descriptor or select from three choices the correct meaning.

Vocabulary Relationships: Abstract Terms, (IVE.8). *Materials:* Student reading text and word list; select from list five to ten words with abstract meanings (e.g., justice, freedom). Copy from text a sentence containing each word, underlining target words. *Strategy:* Ask student to read each sentence and tell the meaning of underlined words. *Interpretation:* 70% accuracy; this is an extremely difficult task. If student performs below level, ask him or her to give three examples of each concept.

Vocabulary Relationships: Colloquial Terms, (IVE.9). *Materials:* Student reading text; locate in text examples of colloquial terms. Copy a sentence containing each term and the sentence preceding and following target term. *Strategy:* Ask student to explain the meaning of each colloquial term or state another sentence using the term. *Interpretation:* 70% accuracy; terms may differ according to time period of story text, region, culture, etc. Examine student errors to determine if student should understand terms without direct instruction.

Vocabulary Relationships: Neologisms, (IVE.10). *Materials:* Student reading text; locate in text examples of neologisms. Copy a sentence containing each term, underlining target words or phrases. *Strategy:* Ask student to read each sentence and define the underlined neologisms. *Interpretation:* Varies according to curricular emphasis. Very few neologisms are found in reading texts; those which do appear are often presented as colloquialisms, slang, or may not be so obviously new. If student text contains appropriate examples, student mastery of those specific terms is important.

Vocabulary Relationships: Euphemisms, (IVE.11). *Materials:* Student reading text, vocabulary list; select 20 words that are euphemistic and list on cards or worksheet. *Strategy:* (1) Ask student to pronounce words and tell the REAL meaning, or (2) give student the more derogatory words as stimuli and ask for the euphemisms.

Interpretation: 70% accuracy; knowledge of euphemisms is an important social skill. The use of such terms should be included in communication instruction. Since such terms are not often highlighted in reading textbooks, this is not a vital reading task unless deemed so in the curriculum.

Vocabulary Relationships: Pejoratives, (IVE .12). *Materials:* Student reading text, vocabulary list; select 5 pejoratives and 15 other words to list on cards or worksheet. *Strategy:* Ask student to locate the five pejoratives and give their negative meanings. *Interpretation:* 70% mastery; this task, much like the preceding three tasks, is only as important as the particular curriculum dictates. Many would consider these tasks enrichment activities. Interpret performance in view of curricular demands and text content.

Vocabulary Relationships: Etymology, (IVE .13). *Materials:* Student vocabulary list; select 20 words that have interesting and popular histories. Prepare in list form. *Strategy:* Ask student to choose any five words and describe the word origin. *Interpretation:* 80% mastery; student cannot be expected to evidence mastery of the specific words unless he or she has been provided direct instruction in their history. Even though many curricula cite this as a basic task at the intermediate levels, it is seldom taught or included in texts. If student does not achieve criterion, direct instruction in the history of the 20 words selected for this assessment might be an interesting and appropriate activity.

Sample Items for Tests.   Sample items for tests of word recognition, listed in Appendix A, are presented for two purposes: (1) for use as examples when constructing test items, and (2) for selective use as test items when the samples exactly match the student's curricular tasks. Most of these samples present the words and word-parts in isolation as production-level tasks, although some are selection-level. Included samples represent each task, itemized for the four subskill areas listed on the word recognition curriculum chart in Figure 5.1. The numbers of the sample items correspond with the appropriate text level cells on

the chart; each task is also presented in objective terms, coded by that same number, in Appendix A. In other words, the chart of the word recognition curriculum, the suggestions for constructing tests, the sample test items, skill objectives, and maintenance strategies are cross-referenced by task number. For example, if a student is required to master antonyms, reference Task IVE.3 in each section for both assessment and programming direction. Again, you are cautioned to examine carefully the content and the stimulus/response format of each item before electing to use one of these tasks for assessment. You should only use the sample test when the task matches the typical curricular presentation as well or better than one that you might design. The specific tasks designated by the teacher on the word recognition curriculum chart determine which tasks should be presented to the student, initially. To confirm prerequisite tasks, as well as those that may surpass expectations, examine the student's performance of tasks adjacent to the target level.

To extend assessment to include application-level tasks and strategy usage, follow testing of appropriate tasks with the questions or tasks suggested in Chapter 3. A brief example of extended assessment for two sample test items is illustrated in Figure 5.5.

Alternative Assessment Techniques.   There are two general types of alternative formats for assessing word recognition skills: word recognition in isolation and word recognition in context. Several techniques are appropriate for assessing the skills, either in or out of context.

Word Recognition in Isolation.   Word lists are the primary form of presentation for assessing recognition of words in isolation, or out of context. One procedure is to ask students to pronounce each word or word element on a list derived from curricular content. Another procedure involves asking students to select or tell the word that conforms to a specified criterion; for example, choose the word that begins with the same sound or means the same as "hop" or mark the word "jump." This is a popular task included

FIGURE 5.5   Extended Assessment of Vocabulary Relations

IVE.7	Voc. Relations: "Name five nouns each word *could* describe."	ancient	enormous	modern	miserable	patient
IVE.8	Voc. Relations: "Explain the meaning of each word."	democracy	quality	value	reputation	independence

Followup Tasks

Tell how each word applies to you personally.

With what do you associate each word?

How do you know the meaning of each word?

Use these words to summarize this paragraph . . .

in computerized assessment programs and is easily incorporated into audiotutorial assessment tasks. Assessment of phonetic analysis and some structural analysis tasks in isolation presents a special problem if words from the curriculum are used as test items because students may recognize the words as sight words and not because of their phonetic elements. Thus, nonsense words comprised of target elements are sometimes used to assess these tasks. Probes listing high-frequency words are a quick means of assessing sight vocabulary. Most techniques for assessing specific word recognition skills in isolation require considerably less time than the procedures for assessing identical elements in context.

Word Recognition in Context.   Recording and analyzing the errors a student makes when he or she reads a passage aloud is the technique used by most informal reading inventories for assessing word recognition skills in context. Another procedure involves asking students questions about the words and word elements in a passage after they read orally or silently. Questions such as these might be asked: Which two words in the story mean the same as "happy?" Can you find three words in the passage that illustrate the CVCe pattern? Which word contains the same digraph as "phone?" The passage says that birds migrate; what does migrate mean? The major difficulty in assessing word recognition in the context of com-

plete reading passages lies in the limitations of the target elements that are likely to occur in the passages. This problem is partially alleviated by presenting target elements in the context of selected sentences for the student to pronounce aloud or read, then answer questions. Cloze, or fill-in-the-blank, statements can also be used because the student must be able to pronounce or understand the meanings of the elements in order to select or produce the best elements to complete the sentences. This format is frequently used in computerized assessment programs and can be adapted for audiotutorial programs. As discussed further in Chapter 6, perhaps the cloze format offers the most practical approach to assessing application-level word recognition skills since it incorporates comprehension into the process but is not as time consuming as other in-context techniques.

When possible, word recognition skills should be assessed both in isolation and in context, and the results compared to identify instructional needs. Given ample time and opportunities to observe students reading in the classroom, diagnosticians can use checklists or rating scales of target performances to analyze and record word recognition skills both in and out of context. When the diagnostician is also the classroom reading teacher this could even save teacher and student time by making the assessment incidental to the teaching process. Sources of checklists include curriculum charts or listings of objectives, as illustrated in Figure 5.6, the skill listings that accompany informal reading inventories, or published listings such as the one by Choate (1990c).

Published Tests. Published tests may present word recognition tasks in context, or isolation, or both. By carefully comparing the student's curriculum chart to certain commercial criterion-referenced instruments, you may select specific test items that provide appropriate measures of target tasks. If you frequently use or favor a particular instrument, ensure that you carefully select test items that match the student's curriculum. The content and format of all the word recognition subtests of Brigance Diagnostic Comprehensive Inventory of Basic Skills (Brigance, 1983) readily permit identification of appropriate tasks. The student protocol itemizes the tasks, indicating with superscript numerals the grade level at which each is typically presented by major reading texts. The Blachowicz Informal Phonics Survey (Barr, Sadow, & Blachowicz, 1995) is a quick phonics test and Ekwall & Shanker (1993) present several devices for measuring word recognition performance in the appendices of *Locating and Correcting Reading Difficulties.*

The Gates-McKillop-Horowitz Diagnostic Tests (1981), and the Diagnostic Reading Scales

---

FIGURE 5.6   Checklist of Word Recognition Objectives

Directions: Highlight the objectives the student should master and then record and track the assessment and programming process.

I. SIGHT VOCABULARY	Assessment Dates/Results	Programming Dates/Results
		Developmental Corrective Maintenance

The Student:

A.   Basic Vocabulary
  .1   Points to his or her name in the list of names.
  .2   Orally reads each word from a list of primary color words.
  .3   Orally reads each word from a list of number words, 0-10.
  .4–.9 Orally reads each word from a list of basic sight words appropriate to his or her level.

B.   High Frequency Vocabulary
  .1–.2 Orally states the name of each letter when given a visual stimulus of upper and/or lower case letters.
  .3   Orally reads each word from a list of common nouns.
  .4–.6 Orally reads each word from a list of high frequency words appropriate to his or her level.

Sample objectives taken from Appendix A.

(Spache, 1981) are two, individually administered standardized tests that include measures of sight vocabulary and word analysis subskills among the subtests. Included in the Woodcock Reading Mastery Tests–Revised (Woodcock, 1987) and in the Woodcock-Johnson Psychoeducational Battery–Revised (Woodcock & Johnson, 1989) are subtests which also measure sight vocabulary, word analysis, and word meaning. The Durrell Analysis of Reading Difficulty (Durrell & Catterson, 1980) includes subtests for assessing sight vocabulary and word analysis subskills as well as a section for evaluating listening vocabulary. Although standardized instruments typically yield general information, by conducting an item analysis of test content, you can correlate the results of each test with at least a portion of the word recognition curriculum. Because many kinds of word recognition tests are available, your choices are limited only by the degree to which the test content corresponds to the student's curricular content.

Test Administration.   Regardless of the particular assessment technique selected, certain procedures facilitate the assessment process. It is important to predetermine the behaviors that will signal mastery, that is, the standards that are acceptable to the teacher. As you test, record all oral responses exactly as made for later analysis. For example, if the student says "run" instead of "ran," write it down because this may be part of a larger pattern. To avoid distracting the student and overburdening the examiner, use two copies of the test items for which oral responses are required—one copy for the student to read and one on which the diagnostician can write. Allot a reasonable amount of time for the student to respond to each task (say, a few seconds) before moving on to the next task. Prompt and probe to elicit as much information as you need and to test the student's limits by asking, for example, do you know any part of that word? If the student says the beginning sound or the prefix, use that response as a measure of phonics or structural analysis. Ask follow-up questions and assign

tasks to assess strategy usage and application-level tasks.

If, as many do, the student balks or appears uncomfortable when asked to pronounce nonsense words, offer encouragement and reassurance by stating that they are not real words and that they sound silly. If many elements are included on a single page, break the page into smaller units by using an index card to cover all but the immediate stimulus; also use the index card to help the student locate the stimulus and to pace the student from item to item. When a student begins to have difficulty, as on a list of sight words, instruct him or her to quickly look at the remaining items and just read the ones he or she knows. If the student has difficulty responding to the testing format, change the stimulus/response demands and/or the level of response and note on your copy the test item requiring change. For example, if J. E. has difficulty reading a passage aloud, ask him to pronounce three target words as you point to or write them; or if Annetta cannot tell you the meaning of a word, state or write three choices from which she may select a synonym. During assessment, carefully note and record clinical observations and student comments (e.g., appears confident explaining word meanings, anxious when asked to sound out words; makes wild guesses at unknown sight words and frequently asked how long till recess). Then consider the student's performance errors and successes along with your notes when you interpret assessment results.

Documenting Student Skill Needs.   Documenting a student's word recognition skill needs serves three main purposes: it provides a record for interested parties; it serves as a baseline for comparing subsequent assessment and programming results and as a focus for planning appropriate instructional programs; and it provides a useful summary with which to compare reading comprehension performance. Before word recognition performance is interpreted and charted, however, the accuracy of the assessment results first must be substantiated.

Substantiating Need.   In any reading task where assessment results present conflicting or incomplete data, further assessment is indicated. Most test items provide only a brief sample of performance. Confirm unusual performance on any task through comparison with the student's typical classroom performance of word recognition tasks, follow-up diagnostic observations, and additional assessment or repeated measures as needed. Remember that repeated measures are also needed to obtain reliable assessment results.

In addition to extra testing and conferences required to reconcile disparities, implementing the assessment/programming cycle provides further substantiation of the student's word recognition needs. Inaccurate or distorted perceptions of the student's skill attainment may be readily corrected throughout the programming procedures. As with assessment results in any subject area, all conclusions about the student's proficiency in word recognition should be considered tentative until confirmed through the assessment/programming cycle.

Charting and Interpreting Needs.   Record the results of assessment on the student's curriculum chart (Figure 5.1) for use in programming and in subsequent assessment. If you are using the personalized assessment plan, which was presented in Figure 3.16, or a similar plan, transfer the information to the chart. Circling in blue ink the student's tentatively identified needs and checking the tasks as the student demonstrates them serves two assessment purposes: (1) to highlight the tasks for which that student requires direct instruction, and (2) to compare the marked items with the sequence and placement of the actual tasks on the student's curriculum. You now have the information with which to evaluate the student's performance in the area of word recognition and in each subskill area and task. If the majority of a student's circled tasks are charted at two grade levels below the ones required for success in his or her present curriculum, you know that this student must have a comprehensive plan for specialized instruction in word recognition.

Circled tasks, approximating success level in all but structural analysis, indicate a more positive evaluation and suggest that the student's word recognition subskills probably do not pose a serious threat to academic progress in other subject areas. For evaluating a student's status and needs, refer to the interpretation comments presented with each suggestion for constructing test items and to the general comments about the relative importance of each subskill and task. Reserve final judgment, however, until you have compared assessment results with the student's reading comprehension skills; regardless of a student's word recognition performance, if comprehension is satisfactory, the outlook for future academic achievement is positive. The annotated word recognition curriculum chart provides valuable information for evaluating reading comprehension and also serves important initial programming and continual assessment and programming functions.

PERSONALIZED PROGRAMMING PROCEDURES

The initial step in programming is to evaluate the relative importance of the student's word recognition skill needs compared to his or her overall academic progress. First, organize the specific word recognition subskills in terms of the student's most pressing and immediate needs. The unmastered subskills and tasks that will most directly facilitate reading comprehension deserve primary program consideration. Analyze the teacher's ranking of the most deficit performances. Any skill gaps that can be rapidly filled by direct instruction provide an avenue for efficient programming. Use the annotated curriculum chart for word recognition, indicating a student's specific needs, to decide upon the initial emphasis of the word recognition program.

Selection of Content

Consider the relevance and usefulness of the word recognition subskills in deciding where to begin a program. Of the four subskill categories presented, knowledge of word meanings probably offers the student the most valuable reading strategy. Understanding the meanings of words can significantly increase reading comprehension as well as allow the student to succeed in specific vocabulary activities. The interrelationship of the student's subskills among the word recognition categories is an aid in identifying instructional priorities. The acquisition of at least a limited sight vocabulary is necessary to a student's reading progress. However, if phonic skills are intact, or if the student is making efficient use of the context clues discussed in the next chapter, an expansive sight vocabulary may be less critical. Certain phonic skills are useful tools for the student's independent decoding of new and difficult words. If the classroom curriculum treats phonetics as a separate subject or places heavy emphasis on detailed mastery, these tasks will be needed for classroom success. In general, the better his or her sight vocabulary, the less the student must rely on phonic skills; conversely, if his or her phonetic skills are intact, having a large sight vocabulary may not be as important for the beginning reader. Structural analysis skills are less vital to the beginning reader than they are to the intermediate reader. The primary student may rely on phonetic skills for affixes; in the intermediate grade program, a phonetic approach to recognition of affixes may be too slow for the student to succeed. Again, if the student has acquired many sight words, the specific structural analysis skills decrease in importance. If a student is proficient in the use of context clues (to be discussed in the next chapter), then he or she may become an efficient reader despite a lesser level of skill in each of these word recognition subskills.

Selection of Methods and Materials

To choose the reading methods with which to begin a personalized word recognition program analyze three factors: (1) the reading methods that have been used, (2) the student's word recognition subskill profile, and (3) the student's learning patterns.

The profile of a student's word recognition subskills offers important information for guiding the selection of appropriate reading methods. The student, whose sight vocabulary is significantly greater than other skills, may respond well to a look-say or whole-word instructional approach. A linguistic approach, emphasizing word families, may be indicated for the student whose phonic skills are largely confined to initial- and final-letter combinations. If a student experiences great difficulty mastering phonics, a combined whole word and linguistic program may be more appropriate. The student, whose phonetic skills are superior to all other word recognition subskills, may benefit from an auditory method that emphasizes listening, structural analysis, and phonic generalizations.

The learning patterns of the student also influence the choice of methods. The student who is primarily a visual learner will benefit from increased attention to the visual features of whole words, such as configuration and letter order. More emphasis on the phonetic features of word beginnings and endings and less emphasis on vowel sounds will be required. This same student will probably master structural components of words more quickly when the elements such as prefixes (e.g., sub- or pre-) are presented as total units by using a whole word-part approach. The strong auditory learner will probably benefit from heavy emphasis on phonics, with oral discussions of word meanings.

The selection of materials is primarily determined by skill content and availability. Using materials with which the student has previously experienced failure is not generally considered a positive practice. However, "old" materials, which are part of the curricular text, present the most valid content. These may be physically modified to mask identity or presented in new sequence. Ideally, you will locate materials that parallel the word recognition curriculum in content and sequence. The general suggestions presented in Chapters 2 and 3 are appropriate for selecting, locating, and modifying word recognition materials.

Programming for Subskills

In all areas of word recognition, new words should first be presented in context and then in isolation. This procedure ties the word meaning to the appearance of the word. Since ultimately the student is expected to use all word recognition skills in context to achieve comprehension, such presentations more closely approximate the goal of reading instruction. The new words in the reading program should be stressed and used in all other subject areas to reinforce recognition and meaning.

The instructional strategies that follow, focus on specific word recognition skills but incorporate the concept of teaching students how to learn. Most suggestions are intended as teacher-directed activities that ultimately result in student-directed learning. Thus, systematic application of the word recognition skills themselves provides valuable learning strategies for comprehending print.

Developmental Strategies

Certain instructional strategies are widely accepted as the best for introductory teaching of the specific word recognition tasks. For a contextual approach to decoding, Manzo and Manzo (1993) recommend the Dictated Story Approach. Based on discussion of an event or object, students compose a story or reaction, which the teacher records; the teacher reads the story aloud for students to edit; as students reread the story, individual words are highlighted with various markings to indicate those they do and do not know. Unknown words then become the target for specific instruction. Because the following discussion is abbreviated, you may wish to consult Rinsky (1993) about detailed suggestions for teaching the various word attack subskills. Although the four subskill areas operate concurrently during reading, they are discussed separately, here, for clarification.

Sight Vocabulary.   A whole word or look-say approach is typically used to teach sight vocabulary. That is, the teacher simply says, "Read this sentence with me. The dog is playing *with* the ball. The new word is *with*." As sight words are introduced, direct the student's attention to distinctive features of words. Stress the similarities and differences among words that the student already recognizes to reinforce "old" sight vocabulary as well as to highlight "new" word features. In this example, the student might be led to discover the differences in *with* and several known words. Later the student would be asked to name other words that look like *with*. Ask the student to outline the configuration of new words. By presenting the words in context and attending to the first letter sounds and/or distinctive endings, the student is encouraged to use context with some phonics. Discuss the meaning and guide the student to make other sentences using the new word. Focusing attention on word meanings is an important ingredient for building sight vocabularies (Harp & Brewer, 1991).

Flashcards or vocabulary cards offer the core material for presenting and teaching sight words. The content, taken from the curriculum, usually includes high-frequency word lists, such as the ones by Dolch (1942) or Fry (1980), and the specific words that occur most often in the student's core reading text. The names of text characters are included in the content, along with names of places and other words that are either irregular or for which the student does not currently have the decoding skills to unlock independently. Locate or compile a list of the most important words for the specific text and level. If the reading content includes more than a single text, as in the case of a literature- or experience-based program, list important words as they occur or guide students to keep personal sight word lists. Tachistoscopic devices, including sliding window and slotted cards, are valuable instructional aids in promoting speed of recognition. Use word cards to play the game of "Concentration" for all tasks in this area. "Go Fish" and "Bingo" may also be played using high-frequency words. Extensive experience reading and writing (Danielson & LaBonty, 1994) and repeated exposure and practice in and out of context are the most efficient strategies for helping students to remember sight words.

Phonetic Analysis.   One of the most serious errors teachers commit in phonic instruction is attaching vowel sounds when pronouncing single consonants. Too many students are taught that "b" says "buh" and "t" says "tuh." Is it any wonder, then, that some students eventually wind up in special education with a so-called sound-blending disability, dutifully trying to pronounce bat as "buh - a - tuh"?! Instead, use key words to illustrate the letter sounds that cannot be produced without adding a vowel sound. Present the sound for the letter B, for example, as the beginning sound in "boy" or another appropriate word. The analytic approach to teaching phonics provides most learners with a more usable tool for decoding new words than does the synthetic approach. Rather than learning each letter sound individually and then trying to blend the sounds into a word, the student uses the sounds in known words to decode new words. If the student recognizes the word "boy," the sound of "t" can be presented by substituting the "t" for "b"; or "Bill" can be related to the beginning sound of the known word "boy."

Focus student attention on the similarities and differences of new words and known words. Although the analytic method of phonic instruction requires the student to have an initial sight vocabulary of at least 50 words, using the analytic approach, the student can develop some semblance of independence in reading. Cunningham, Moore, Cunningham, and Moore (1995) offer three important principles for teaching phonics: Teach consonants first; begin with auditory discrimination; use an analytic approach; have students apply the sound(s) to real words and authentic reading; and remind students that the sounds are sometimes inconsistent. Searfoss and Readence (1994) add these principles: personalize lessons by using students' words and names; provide ample oral instruction and practice, and

teach only the most reliable generalizations. By using an analytic phonic approach, you may guide students to discover the more consistent rules. If the student knows many CVC words, such as *cat* and *run,* you can lead him or her to discover that the vowel sound is usually short without memorizing the rule. The student who uses context clues may not need as much specific instruction in vowel patterns as the student who is required to pronounce words in isolation. The purpose of instruction in phonics is to assist the student in the pronunciation of unknown words, based on the assumption that this procedure will also clue the student to the word meanings already in his or her oral vocabulary. If you accept this purpose, then the practice of asking students to decode nonsense words, other than for assessment, is a useless procedure. The content of the phonics program should be meaningful words.

The most useful materials for teaching phonics include word wheels, pictures, and key word lists, particularly for initial presentations. Word wheels are used to present new sound/symbol combinations and for independent practice. Pictures provide a stimulus for the student to identify letters that represent the name. With a key word list, you can readily offer alternate examples of specific sound/symbol patterns. Many reading teachers supplement the core reading program with a separate phonics program. These activities should correlate closely with the presentation sequence and content of the main reading program. They may also be used selectively with those students who require additional practice. Arthur Heilman (1993) presents numerous practical suggestions for teaching phonetic analysis.

Structural Analysis.   Instruction in structural analysis should be accompanied by direct instruction in word meaning. By examining the meaning changes created by the addition, deletion, or modification of word parts, students gain a better understanding of both word structure and meaning. Specific instruction in the meanings of prefixes and suffixes can significantly expand a student's reading vocabulary. When a new word part is introduced, present examples of its use and effect on several words. Such lessons also enhance the understanding and use of oral and written language.

The standard materials for teaching structural analysis include a list of meanings of word parts for the teacher, word wheels, and a highlighting pen or colored chalk. A list of word elements required in each grade or subject is also helpful. Use word wheels to present and reinforce the meaning changes that accompany change in word structure. With pen or chalk, highlight the specific meaningful word parts during initial presentation and review. Encourage the student to present examples of each part studied. The first grader who suggests *pl'ike* as an example of a contraction of *play* and *like* helps himself and peers to gain a better understanding of contractions as a result of the example. Similarly, the student's formation of neologisms using affixes, for example, may greatly expand class understanding of the concept as well as awaken an interest in word meanings.

Word Meaning.   Pair instruction in word meaning with lessons in all other word recognition skills. Although a young student's speaking and listening vocabulary generally exceeds his or her reading vocabulary, the student's knowledge of word meanings cannot be assumed. By exploring the meaning of each word as it is introduced, you reinforce the student who understands the meaning. This also allows you to present deeper and alternate meanings and to provide direct instruction to the student whose oral vocabulary does not include the word. Specific instruction and encouragement in the use of context clues is a standard means of expanding vocabulary knowledge. Delete target words in a sentence or paragraph, listing only the initial letter of an important word or a choice of three words. Frequently ask students to suggest other words that mean the same or opposite as the stimulus word. Semantic mapping, a more comprehensive method of expanding word concepts, and strategies for teaching the use of context are discussed in Chapter 6.

The student's experiences, both real and vicarious, the teacher's vocabulary, the dictionary, and a thesaurus are the most important materials for teaching word meanings. At the lower grade levels, picture dictionaries and text glossaries provide instructional aids. Although assigning words for which definitions are to be copied from a dictionary is not a useful practice, using the dictionary or thesaurus to find a synonym or antonym may be helpful. Use these references to contrast words for a meaningful activity. A variety of references on several ability levels allows the student to select the one most appropriate to the individual's skill level. At the intermediate grade levels, other classroom references may include books about the history of words and resources listing affix meanings, euphemisms, pejoratives, and the like.

Corrective Strategies

These corrective strategies are designed to reteach or to correct specific word recognition errors. Provisions for overlearning are incorporated into most corrective programs. The student's learning style, cited by Gibson (1991) as the overlooked variable in the phonics debate, should be considered when selecting strategies. Some students require more instruction that highlights the visual features of the words, while others require more auditory teaching. Some students may need to write the words while saying them to reinforce the appearance and sound. Visualization activities are helpful to many students. Begin instruction by verbalizing the steps of the strategies for accomplishing a few samples of each word recognition task (Searfoss & Readence, 1994). As with corrective strategies in any subject, use progress charts and contracts to provide reinforcement and motivation. Numerous additional corrective strategies for word recognition problems are presented in *Reading: Detecting and Correcting Special Needs* (Choate & Rakes, 1989).

It is essential that word recognition skills be presented as strategies for comprehending. A procedure to help students decide how and when to apply the skills strategically is WORDS Help (Choate & Rakes, 1993):

With context–Try the unknown word with context;

Only beginning sounds–Use only beginning sounds with context;

Read aloud–Read aloud the beginning and ending sound with context;

Decode by structure–Try decoding using word structure with context;

Sound it out–Sound out the word if it is still unknown;

Help!–Get help if the word remains unknown.

For must students and situations, the steps represent the sequence in which decoding skills should be applied.

A variety of intensive, specialized teaching strategies have been reported to be successful with students who experience difficulty recognizing words. Most of these techniques share the common denominator of multisensory input. Each typically lengthens the instructional period or time span. Whether you follow the exact steps proposed by Fernald (1943, 1988) or the modifications suggested by others, the basic premise is the same; involve as many of the student's senses as possible. Image writing, for example, is a corrective strategy in which the teacher pronounces the stimulus as students repeatedly say and trace with their forefingers a letter, word-part, or word written in chalk until only an image remains on the board; they then trace the image with chalk and repeat the process as needed (Rakes & Choate, 1989). The additional input provided by having the student see, say, hear, trace and/or write difficult letters and words, is believed to reinforce memory of the words. This idea supports the recommendation in the preceding section to present and use target words in spelling and other content areas. However, multisensory instruction, like other methods, must stand the test of the assessment/programming cycle before it can be proclaimed as the best method for an individual student. Some students may need only to see, say

and write a word rather than to see, say, hear, trace and write words repeatedly. The increased time required to implement a comprehensive multisensory program may limit the number of words that can be presented. Weigh this disadvantage against the degree of mastery the student demonstrates when taught with the various single and multiple-sensory methods. When it is practical to involve several senses in the presentation and illustration of new words, employ this approach as many students benefit from the extra reinforcement. For a more comprehensive discussion of these intensive methods for teaching word recognition, refer to the texts by Collins and Cheek (1993) and Manzo and Manzo (1993).

Sight Vocabulary.   In introductory corrective lessons, present only words of maximum contrast. Words that are visually similar can be phased in gradually. Lead the student to develop strategies for comparing unknown words to the sight words that are mastered. Borrowing ideas from the language experience approach, ask the student to select from a target word list a word he or she particularly wants to learn. Then have the student state a sentence using the word. The teacher or student should write the word on one side of a card and a sentence using the word on the other; the student should practice the word in isolation and in context until mastered. Since words related to a concrete image (wagon, bed) are generally easier to learn than abstract words like "the" and "but" (Hargis & Gickling, 1978; Jorm, 1977; Kolker & Terwilliger, 1981), include both types in each lesson. That is, by selecting two nouns and one or two of the more difficult abstract terms, the student is more likely to experience success. For the nouns, present pictures. Introduce abstract terms in the context of words the student knows. Present sight words as concepts, emphasizing alternate meanings.

A personal collection of words recognized on sight is reinforcing to the student. As the student learns new words, they are written on cards or are listed and added to the student's word bank. Cunningham (1988) suggests tape recording an easy book for the student to listen to and read along with until memorized; then use the words from the memorized book to begin a word bank. Use the banks to build phrases and sentences and as other instructional materials. Wilson and Cleland (1989) suggest employing the hand signs used by the hearing-impaired for teaching sight vocabulary to hearing students. They suggest that the words learned in this manner may be better remembered because of the novelty of the approach. For students whose "overanalytical habits" interfere with sight vocabulary, Bond, Tinker, Wasson, and Wasson (1994) recommend extensive experience reading relatively easy material with guidance to focus on larger word elements.

Judicious use of word banks, flashcards, word wheels, tachistoscopes, and sentences and stories containing target words is necessary for corrective teaching to be effective. For the student who requires extensive practice to master a word, vary the design of instructional materials to decrease boredom. For example, after introducing five new words in context, you might present those same five words by using a word wheel and five example sentences on Monday, a commercial tachistoscope on Tuesday, flashcards with sentences written on the back on Wednesday, sandpaper letters on Thursday, and in story context on Friday. The change in the mode of presentation should encourage the student. Direct instruction, lasting 5 to 10 minutes, in recognizing the words in isolation, followed by 10 to 15 minutes of guided practice in recognizing the words in sentence or story context presents a balanced lesson (Heilman, Blair, & Rupley, 1994). Timed practice reading letters and sight words on a regular basis is also an effective strategy for some students (Carnine, Silbert, & Kameenui, 1990).

Phonetic Analysis.   Keep phonic lessons brief but detailed, and place the sounds and words in context. Unless a student has difficulty extracting the single sounds from words, teach individual sounds from within words rather than in isolation. Tell students to use context with beginning consonants and to guess the vowel sounds within. Emphasize context and sound blending throughout the phonics program. Fuchs and Fuchs (1984b) recommend a procedure for teaching blending that helps students to hum the sounds. The personal word bank used for sight word recognition is also helpful in teaching phonics; use the words to teach specific sounds. Words that are in the student's oral vocabulary should also be used as content for phonic lessons; allow the student to use his or her typical pronunciation of each word (Richek et al., 1989). Teach phonetically regular words before the irregular ones; the irregular words that the student needs to master can be taught as sight words. Teach dissimilar phonetic elements in each lesson. The student who experiences extreme difficulty learning phonics may only need to master initial sounds, provided you build, as compensation, sufficient sight vocabulary and contextual usage habits. This student may find vowels easier to master when common syllables or phonograms are taught as total units (Spache & Spache, 1986). For difficult tasks, highlight the particular sound pattern with a felt marker and gradually fade the color cues when the student is ready. Use a visual phonics strategy to teach students what, where, and how to attend to letter clusters in words and form words by blending spelling patterns (Schworm, 1988). Capitalize on the interdependence between spelling and word recognition and on the phonetic emphasis of many spelling programs; closely parallel instruction in both areas, including similar content. Trachtenburg (1990) suggests a three-part strategy: present target sounds in the context of a literature selection; next provide explicit instruction in the phonetic element; and then read aloud or have students read a second "high quality literature selection" that emphasizes the sound(s). Although she provides a list of trade books that emphasize phonetic elements, a creative teacher can add and substitute names and words to highlight target sounds when reading aloud, illustrated by the sample story in Figure 5.7.

FIGURE 5.7   Phonics in Context: A "B" Story

Once upon a time there were three bouncing bears: big papa bear, Bobby; bossy mama bear, Bertha; and bashful baby bear; Bubba. Early one beautiful morning; bossy mama bear, Bertha, barley boiled and baked biscuits. While the boiled barley and the baked biscuits cooled, the bouncing bears bounded out the back door to gather berries in their baskets.

Structural Analysis.   Many of the corrective strategies cited for teaching phonetic analysis also apply to teaching structural analysis. Use a discovery method to teach generalizations of affixes and compound words. Present only known sight words to teach compound words. Use words from the student's word bank to make the word parts more meaningful and easier to master. Teach the student strategies to compare and contrast knowledge of specific word parts when unlocking new words. Consider having cooperative groups develop Morphemic Maps that explain the meaning of target word parts (a variation of semantic mapping discussed in Chapter 6), and then have the groups teach their maps to peers (Danielson & LaBounty, 1994). Some corrective learners may find structural analysis easier to use than phonics (Richek et al., 1989). Using a look-say approach along with a key word and the meaning of the affix, present common affixes as intact units. The value of direct teaching of syllabication is questionable. In fact, Cunningham (1979) concludes that the worth of the rules of syllabication may be primarily confined to dictionary usage. It is possible that only two rules need to be taught for decoding multisyllabic words: the rule governing the syllabic division between two consonants and the one governing division between a vowel and a consonant (Polloway & Patton, 1993).

Word Meaning.   Some features of effective word-meaning instruction for students with reading disabilities include illustrations in authentic contexts, repeated exposure to each word, instruction in contextual usage and in strategies for remembering basic word meanings, and opportunities for meaningful use (Carlisle, 1993). Instruction should be built on prior knowledge, relating new concepts to known ones. Helping students develop new concepts requires rich and varied experiences, both real and vicarious. Have students group word-bank words in categories such as naming words, action words, and things to wear (Wilson & Cleland, 1989). Provide practice in changing words with affixes in context. Emphasize the word meaning changes as well as the value of affixes in unlocking the meaning of new words. McNeil (1992) suggests presenting a new or difficult word in several defining sentences constructed with familiar words; ask the student to read the sentences, then use his or her own experience to define the word. Guide students to discuss and elaborate on new words. To make word meanings more concrete, encourage students to dramatize or act out words for each other (Richek et al., 1989), as in the sample activity in Figure 5.8. Guide small groups or pairs of students to solve analogies containing target concepts and words (Thomas & Carmack, 1990). Consider using captioned TV programs for a dynamic and effective means of expanding the word knowledge of below-average and bilingual readers (Koskinen, Wilson, Gambrell, & Neuman, 1993). The multisensory presentations facilitate

FIGURE 5.8   Word Mimes

Read each sentence aloud, but pantomime the underlined words:

Tom was angry.

This candy is bitter.

She pranced down the hall.

The principal waved to me.

learning and also build conceptual and experiential foundations for meaning. Of particular importance to the continued growth of a student's word meaning knowledge is the teacher's reinforcement of the student's spontaneous oral and written use of difficult words.

Maintenance Strategies

Maintenance strategies provide the practice and reinforcement required for generalization and application of word recognition subskills as strategies to comprehend. Computer activities offer versatile and interesting maintenance strategies for retention of task proficiency in all word recognition subskills. Numerous software programs, both commercial and in the public domain, are available for this purpose. Word processing programs can be used to provide interesting and meaningful practice. A good source for information about available instructional programs is the Technology and Media Division of the Council for Exceptional Children, 1920 Association Drive, Reston, Virginia 22091.

Samuels (1988) contends that teachers promote fluent decoding by first teaching until accuracy is achieved, next providing appropriate practice, and then motivating students to stay on task long enough to achieve both accuracy and fluency. Integrating systematic practice of target tasks with activities in all language arts facilitates automaticity. Regardless of the mode of presentation, interactive and collaborative games and activities are more appealing than undisguised rote drill. Choate and Rakes (1989) and Ekwall and Shanker (1993) present a variety of ideas for practicing word recognition skills. Additional ideas for maintenance activities follow, referenced by task number on the curriculum chart (Figure 5.1). Many of these strategies are applicable to several word recognition subskills. All strategies should be accepted, rejected, or modified according to student and teacher needs.

Sight Vocabulary.   The key to maintaining sight word skills is frequent and active practice. Activities should be varied to prevent boredom

and lessen the feeling of drill. Brief practice exercises that are timed can promote fluency and generate enthusiasm for competing with peers and self.

Basic Sight Vocabulary, (IA.1–.9 and IB.1–.6). ▪Print target words or letters on a word wheel or slot card; have student practice reading them aloud, gradually increasing speed. ▪Have each student bring a stack of cards to class; when a word or letter is unknown, the student or teacher writes it on a card. The student should be tested on individual cards by the teacher or a peer several times during the week. ▪Have student illustrate word or letter cards on the reverse side with felt-marker drawings or magazine pictures. As the student pronounces each word or letter, pictures provide a self-check. ▪Prepare duplicate cards for each target letter or word. Play matching games (e.g., "Concentration" or "Go Fish"), matching upper to upper, lower to lower, and upper to lower case letters or matching words. ▪Paste pictures illustrating a target word or letter on file folders; prepare word or letter cards to fit underneath each picture. Ask the student to match print with pictures. ▪For especially troublesome letters or words, make personal cards from sandpaper; have student trace the cards with his or her finger and then make his or her own association with something already known or mastered.

Visual Discrimination, (IC.1–.3). ▪Prepare duplicate sets of picture cards; ask students to match pairs. ▪Make or collect triplicate sets of picture or figure cards and several odd cards. Have the student find the ones that have no match. ▪From discarded samples of cloth, plastic, and wallpaper, compile sets of pairs. Have the student match pairs, or you present each pair with one odd sample and ask student to find the one that does not match. ▪Prepare sets of cards with color swatches, letters, or words, and ask the student to match or find the ones that do not match.

Phonetic Analysis.   Maintenance strategies in phonics should focus on confirming sound/symbol associations. Integrating spelling activities with meaningful practice may improve performance in both areas. Many of the suggested strategies are appropriate for building fluency in a variety of phonetic tasks.

Single Consonants, (IIA.1–.5). ▪Ask the student to cut pictures from magazines or newspapers and make his or her own chart or booklet of specific consonants. ▪List several consonants on the board; pronounce words beginning or ending with these letters and ask student to write only the target consonants. ▪Ask the student to say all the words that contain a specified sound and then indicate its position. ▪Prepare a chart of pictures only; ask the student to name the pictures and then to name or write the consonant in the target position in each name. ▪Prepare an exercise in which student must choose pictures from one column to match words in a second column; these exercises may be used to reinforce consonant sounds in any desired position: initial, medial, or final. ▪Provide cards with one consonant on each; ask student to hold up the letter heard in the specified position as you pronounce each word.

Consonant Blends, (IIB.1–.4). ▪Dictate to student words containing blends; ask student to name at least five other words that contain the same blend as the dictated word and indicate the blend's position. ▪Prepare charts of pictures of objects whose names contain blends; label pictures, omitting blends and ask student to supply blends either orally or by writing in the blanks. ▪Write several three-letter blends on the chalkboard; give student five minutes to make as many words as possible using the blends. Have student compete with peers or self on successive days.

Consonant Digraphs, (IIC.1–.2). ▪Prepare an exercise giving only the digraphs to be studied; ask student to add letters to make a word and then draw a picture to illustrate each word. ▪Provide a columned sheet headed by several digraphs; ask student to paste three pictures whose names each contain a digraph in the appropriate column. ▪Write digraphs on individual cards to give to student; ask student to display the digraph that matches each word dictated by teacher or peer.

Variant Consonants, (IID.1–.5). ▪Prepare a list of words containing variant consonants; ask student to pronounce each word and underline the variant. ▪For fun, ask student to pronounce words containing target sounds, saying each according to its most common sound. (This could also be used as a crutch for remembering the correct spelling of the words.) ▪Write the target letters on the chalkboard; give student a time limit to name or list under each heading words in which these letters are variant. Student may compete with peers or self on successive days.

Vowels, (IIE.1–.9). ▪Dictate a word from the vocabulary list and have students repeat the word; then read a list of words and have students clap when they hear a word that rhymes with or contains the vowel sound of the stimulus word. ▪Ask student to spell new words that rhyme with underlined words in sentences. ▪Prepare a page of pictures, the names of which contain the desired vowel sounds; prepare another page with headings to indicate generalizations or vowel sounds. Ask student to cut out pictures and place them under the appropriate headings. ▪Ask student to cut and paste magazine pictures so as to make booklets for vowel sounds. ▪List vowels and/or vowel combinations; ask student to use a sound to build as many words as possible. ▪Prepare an exercise in which student can place a series of dictated words under appropriate classifications; classifications may be related to the desired vowel. ▪Prepare vowel Bingo cards with sixteen squares and a vowel or vowel combination in each square; dictate words containing target sounds while the student attempts to "Bingo" by placing a marker in any square corresponding with the vowel sounds of dictated words. ▪Print words with the target vowel sounds highlighted on playing cards to use with a game board; as student draws a card he or she must pronounce the word to advance on the board.

Phonic Generalizations, (IIF.1–.3). ▪Prepare a "consonant frame" in which the student is to supply a vowel sound to form new words (c__t, n__te, g__); ask student to say the words and formulate sentences with each. ▪Give student two or three words which fit the target pattern; ask student to say or write at least five more words that fit each pattern. ▪Have student pronounce pattern words with alternate vowel sounds and compare to actual pronunciation. ▪Ask student to construct original pattern words, pronounce them, and state the possible or intended meaning.

Structural Analysis.   The goal of maintenance strategies for this subskill is to promote rapid recognition of word parts as intact units. Most activities also can be paired with spelling practice. Since associating unit meanings with appearances expands word knowledge, meanings should also be emphasized.

Root Words, Suffixes, and Prefixes (IIIA.1–.6 through IIIC.1–.5). ▪List a series of words containing various affixes; ask student to circle each root word, draw a line under each prefix or suffix, and then explain the meaning. ▪Ask student to write on the board a root word and then call on a peer to add an affix and use the new word in a sentence; if the peer correctly changes the word and uses it in a sentence, he or she may write the next root word. ▪Provide student with a list of root words on cards and an envelope of affixes that may be added to the words; ask student to list and explain as many real words as possible. ▪Prepare a list of words with affixes; ask student to write the words without prefixes and indicate how the meaning changes. (This activity may be reversed by preparing a list of unknown words and a list of known prefixes for the student to match and then give the probable meaning).

Compound Words, (IIIC.1–.2). ▪Ask student to collect pictures of objects whose names can be joined to construct compound words and mount the pictures on cards; assist the student in writing the compound words on the back of the cards. Use cards for practice. ▪Ask the student to form funny compound words and illustrate them; let peers try to guess each word from the illustration. ▪Present common compound words and ask student to read and cite all the possible meanings

that a student from another country or planet might guess for each; then have student prepare an explanation of the actual meaning of each word to present to the foreign visitor.

Contractions, (IIIE.1–.2). ▪Prepare pairs of words cards, one of which gives a contraction and the other the two words from which the contraction is formed; ask student to use the cards in various activities calling for matching and meaning. ▪Prepare a list of two words from which contractions can be formed; ask student to strike out the letters that are to be omitted in writing the contractions and write the contracted form directly under the two words. ▪Review a list of acceptable contractions; ask student to write contracted word forms that he or she uses in everyday speech that are not acceptable, hypothesizing the spelling as if they were actual contractions. (This can also be used as a lesson in spelling and written expression.)

Syllabication, (IIIF.1–7). ▪Show pictures and ask student to respond by pronouncing each name and clapping out the rhythm of the syllables; then ask student to state the number of syllables. The same strategy can be used with picture cards; ask student to pronounce the names of the pictures and to write the number of syllables under each picture. ▪Prepare a group of sentences using at least one word with two or more syllables; omit one syllable of the word and ask student to supply it (I saw a little black kit____). ▪List a group of two- and three-syllable words; ask student to divide the words into syllables and write "c's" and "v's" to indicate the sequence of consonants and vowels. Then have student circle the pattern that dictates the division into syllables and explain the rule. ▪Prepare a number of syllables on separate cards for the student to select, read, and give a word containing the syllable and its meaning; the dictionary should be consulted to verify questionable words. ▪List multisyllable words which vary in the consonant/vowel patterns of syllabication; ask student to list them in columns to indicate their classification according to pattern and then use each word in a sentence.

Syllabication, (IIIF.8–.12). ▪From a list of multisyllabic words, have students identify the accented syllable and then verify the accents by comparison with the diacritical markings in the dictionary. ▪List several multisyllabic words with the accents placed on different syllables; ask student to pronounce the words each way and then lead student to discover the generalization. ▪Select only the most important vocabulary words for the student to rewrite and mark diacritically; to make the activity more meaningful, have student verify markings and then teach the marked words to another student. Ask student to add other words having the same sound(s) as the common element(s) of the words in the list.

Word Meaning. Many of the strategies for maintaining word meaning skills can, and should be conducted orally. The objective is to incorporate the words into the students' speaking, listening, reading, and writing vocabularies. Thus, maintaining and increasing fluency in word meanings should be an integral component of all word recognition activities and instruction in other subjects as well.

Basic Vocabulary, (IVA.1–.7). ▪Prepare definitions of words that have similar meanings; ask student to write or tell two words to fit each definition. ▪Prepare pairs of words with similar meanings; ask student to use a dictionary and a thesaurus to find the similarities and differences in the meanings of each pair. ▪Present the meanings of target words in context; then have student state what the word means to him or her personally and how the student can possibly use the word in speech and/or writing.

Classification, (IVB.1–.8). ▪Ask student to name at least ten people, ten places, and ten things; read aloud the list and ask student to classify and use each in a sentence. ▪Prepare a list of four words in a series containing three words of similar classification; read aloud each series and ask student to identify the word that does not belong (for example, red, yellow, sun, and green). ▪Assist student in developing a system for classi-

fying words according to their utility or personal meaning to him or her (words I think of as happy, sad, fun, etc.); list the categories and ask the student to classify word cards or word lists and then compare lists among peers.

Pronoun Referents, (IVC.1–.2). ▪Prepare and distribute word cards with pronouns; read aloud sentences, asking student to choose the pronoun card that corresponds with the noun in the sentence. ▪Write or ask student to write a story with many proper nouns; underline proper nouns and ask student to replace nouns with pronouns. ▪Prepare a short story using incorrect pronoun referents; ask student to read carefully and change the pronouns and explain how and why they were changed.

Affixes, (IVD.1–.6). ▪Present the meanings of several on-level affixes and ask student to find words containing them; have him or her explain the literal meaning change created by the addition of the affix. ▪Have student form novel words using on-level root words and affixes; then have student explain the meanings of the new words or ask a peer to guess the meanings. ▪Prepare a brief story containing several root words to which affixes are frequently attached; ask student to add affixes to change the meaning of the story.

Vocabulary Relationships, (IVE.1–.13). ▪Write a story using only subjects and verbs; ask student to supply appropriate descriptive words to enhance the story. ▪Give student vocabulary words and ask him or her to use the dictionary or thesaurus in finding a specific number of synonyms, antonyms, or other related words, and then to choose the best and justify choice. ▪Using the classified ad section of the newspaper, clip ads that employ very descriptive words; ask student to consult the dictionary in finding synonyms, antonyms, and colloquials for the underlined descriptive words and then to write a humorous ad containing these words. ▪Discuss the most common meaning of each word on a list; have student draw pictures to illustrate humorous misconceptions that may arise if one understands only the most common meaning. ▪Help student discover the importance of setting when defining specific terms by comparing relative meanings in different countries, at different points in time. ▪Explain to student that some terms are used to make reality seem less harsh, a job more important, or the speaker sound polite; prepare a sheet with two columns entitled "blunt" and "polite." Ask the student to categorize vocabulary words under each column and then describe situations in which each would be appropriate. ▪Ask student to read the "Picturesque Speech" section from an issue of Reader's Digest; then ask him or her to coin at least three new terms to present to the class. ▪Discuss word history; help student make time lines to illustrate the influence of history on the English language. ▪Post a graffiti board and allow student to write one word that he or she thinks peers cannot define; the student who can formulate a simple definition may write the next word on the graffiti board. These words can then be classified according to meaning, emotional impact, or other categories. ▪Use a computer program to construct relationship crossword puzzles for the student to solve or have the student construct the puzzles for peers to solve.

Implementing the CBA/P Model

The curriculum-based assessment/programming cycle discussed in Chapter 3 provides the format for assessing and programming in word recognition. In addition to the major procedures recommended for all subject areas, certain elements in each step of the CBA/P process should be emphasized because of the nature of the word recognition skills and their particular role in the total curriculum.

Step 1: Analyze the Curriculum

After locating or formulating the word recognition curriculum listing, analyze the system's and the teacher's curricula, noting in particular whether the teacher typically evaluates word

recognition classroom performance orally or in writing (most teachers primarily use written tasks for their formal evaluations), and just how much emphasis the teacher places on word pronunciation versus comprehension. Mark the teacher's expectations of the specific student on the curriculum chart and proceed to assessment of skills.

Step 2: Assess Skills

Continue the teacher interview to indirectly assess student performance, asking for the teacher's view of the degree to which problems in recognizing words may be affecting reading comprehension and performance in other subjects as well. If school records indicate major fluctuations in reading performance, determine if a change in reading series or programs coincided with performance differences; if so, identify the instructional approach and emphasis of each program (e.g., code vs. meaning emphasis or highly controlled vs. slightly controlled vocabulary) for assessment and programming implications. To gain a general picture of the student's relative reading proficiency, analyze by subskill the scores on any recently administered reading tests and compare that performance with the student's reading comprehension scores on the same test; if the actual test items are available, analyze the student's response to each test item to identify decoding patterns. In addition to any work samples the teacher already has collected, ask to see the student's entire reading workbook. When analyzing work samples, look for evidence to confirm the teacher's estimates of performance and its impact on other areas, particularly in comprehension.

Based on indirect assessment data, hypothesize the nature of difficulties and also the degree of interference or facilitation that word recognition performance presents in other areas. Establish assessment priorities by placing the teacher's concerns in the context of the relative importance of the subskills; if, for example, the teacher is equally concerned about word meaning and structural analysis, begin with word meaning because of its greater utility. Directly assess the student's performance using reading workbook pages and basal text passages where feasible and select assessment tasks from other tests and/or develop test items as needed. To assess skill application and the use of strategies, follow administration of test items by having the student read words containing target elements or features in the context of reading passages, and by asking questions (e.g., How did you figure that out? What helped you?). Record the student's performance and use assessment results to begin developing a personalized word recognition program.

Step 3: Program for Assessed Needs

Use the curriculum chart (Figure 5.1) in conjunction with the personalized programming plan presented in Figure 3.17 or a similar plan to map the course for you and the specific student. Initially select those specific subskills and tasks that appear to be the most important and most likely to increase student's progress. Include one or two problem tasks and four to eight mastered tasks to increase the probability of student and teacher success.

Plan three stages of instruction, selecting teaching strategies according to student and teacher needs. As in other skill areas, consider this initial program as tentative, subject to perceived need for revision.

Developmental Instruction.   For developmental instruction to introduce new tasks, first try the strategies that are recommended in the teacher's edition of the student's basal series or the methods that the student's teacher typically uses. Following instruction, assess performance and use maintenance strategies if tasks are tentatively mastered and corrective strategies if not.

Corrective Instruction.   Begin corrective instruction with a method that is likely to match the learning needs of the student. For example, a strong emphasis on phonetic analysis may be the first approach chosen for the student who relies

heavily upon auditory stimuli for learning new words, particularly if he or she has not responded well to a whole word approach. Assess performance of programmed tasks as in Step 2; modify instructional procedures according to the assessment/programming diagram for the tasks that remain unmastered. Keep tentatively mastered tasks in the program for maintenance activities until long-term mastery is assured.

Maintenance Instruction.   Provide application and practice activities for tasks that are tentatively mastered. The student should practice the target words or elements both in isolation and in the context of meaningful passages. Continue using maintenance strategies until the student quickly and comfortably recognizes and responds to the target tasks. Then reenter the CBA/P cycle.

Step 4: Repeat the CBA/P Cycle

Reassess the student's total profile, as recorded on the curriculum charts for each academic skill area, to determine whether and which word recognitions skills should be included in an updated program. The student's rate of mastery of tasks in the cycle just completed determines the number of tasks and the estimated length of instruction to plan for the program update. The student who masters two blends in one day and retains that mastery can probably handle an additional new task during each successive and shortened cycle. Use the methods and materials that encouraged the student's mastery of tasks in the previous cycle to influence the selection of strategies for the new program. With each cycle repetition, communicate results with the student and all persons involved in his or her academic program. As the student gains proficiency in word recognition skills, gauge the effects of such gains on other skill areas. Before beginning a new cycle, carefully analyze the student's reading comprehension skills in relation to his or her word recognition skills. This will assist you to plan a balanced reading program.

SUMMARY

The major importance of word recognition sub-skills to a student's total, long-term academic progress is their contribution to the reading comprehension process. That is, the skills and strategies utilized in recognizing words and word-parts combine to form a powerful learning strategy for comprehending print. The four subskill areas—sight vocabulary, phonetic analysis, structural analysis, and word meaning—equip the student to decode the pronunciation and meaning of words. The relative importance of specific word recognition subskills and tasks to a student's most immediate academic progress is contingent upon the degree of emphasis placed on each area by the teacher and the school. However, understanding word meanings directly influences comprehension.

Procedures have been presented to assess the student's word recognition curriculum and to assess indirectly and directly the student's present level and mastery of word recognition subskills and tasks. Such assessment should be planned and interpreted in relation to similar assessment of reading comprehension skills. The personalized program that evolves from this integrated assessment is more likely to offer the student a meaningful reading program than is a generalized program. As the teacher works through the assessment/programming cycle, professional judgment and student performance will validate effective developmental, corrective, and maintenance strategies and materials so as to ensure the student's efficient mastery of word recognition tasks.

CASE STUDIES

Sample Case

Jerry is a nine-year-old student in the third grade. Indirect assessment reveals the following pertinent information:

The teacher ranks skills in word recognition and spelling as the weakest; performance is on a beginning, second-grade level. Although Jerry seems to comprehend much of what he reads, he consistently fails reading; grades are based on average scores from reading workbook, phonics workbook, and teacher worksheets. Of the word recognition subskills, sight vocabulary is ranked most proficient and phonetic analysis the least. The teacher reports that Jerry probably learns best by seeing and, perhaps, by writing. Extra help in class, a phonics tape program in the listening center, and a private tutor have been used with limited success. Work-sample analysis suggests that Jerry does not consistently apply word-attack strategies to decode unknown words.

Diagnostic Hypotheses: Jerry's major difficulty stems from the heavy auditory emphasis of the reading program; if he had mastered the rudi-ments of phonics, his sight vocabulary and word meaning proficiency would probably compensate for the weakness in phonics. Since comprehension is better than word recognition, he is probably relying heavily upon contextual clues. Therefore, assess the very basic phonic tasks.

Based on the results of indirect assessment, direct assessment proceeds in the following manner: When Jerry is observed during classroom reading instruction he does not attempt to pronounce unknown words; instead he omits them. During the student interview he is asked to discuss his analysis of word recognition performance. He states that he tries to remember how the words look, but has trouble remembering letter sounds. Direct testing is begun with selected phonics workbook pages, the source of a large portion of Jerry's failing grades.

Sample Items IIB.1, IIC.1, and IID.1–.2 are used to assess performance of tasks below the level of the workbook. The results are depicted in Figure 5.9. Testing does not extend beyond many second-grade tasks because Jerry has not mas-

FIGURE 5.9   Word Recognition Curriculum, Sample Case

WORD RECOGNITION SUBSKILLS

	K	1	2	3
II PHONETIC ANALYSIS A Single Consonants	II ✓.1 Aud. Discr. Initial ✓ Aud. Discr. Final	II ✓.3 Initial (.4) Final	II (A.5) Medical	II
B Consonant Blends		(B.1) Initial Two Letter	(B.2) Final nd,nt,st (.3) Three Letter	
C Consonant Digraphs		(C.1) Initial ch,ph, sh,th,wh	C.2 Final ck,ng	
D Variant Consonants		(D.1) k,wr,gn (.2) c,g	(D.3) s,qu,x, gh	(D.4) Silent mb,p,t,s .5 Mul.Sd.
E Vowels	E.1 Aud. Discr. Rhymes	E.2 Long (.3) Short (.4) ai,ay,ea ee,oa (.5) r-Control.	(E.6) l-Control (.7) oi,oy,ou (.8) oo .9 schwa	
F Phonic Generalizations		(F.1) CVC	(F.2) CVCe (.3) CV	

tered sufficient prerequisite tasks. Results of direct testing are compared with teacher reports, classroom observations, and work-sample analysis and found to be consistent.

A tentative word recognition program is planned. It includes the following components: The major program emphasis will be teaching initial sounds of words in context, stressing the value of combining initial sounds with context clues in decoding words. The initial priority will be three of the most elementary initial consonant blends that are not mastered. Once these are mastered, additional blends will be included. Blends will also be presented in final and medial positions. Unmastered digraphs, "ch" and "wh" will be the next priority. Initial corrective strategies will emphasize the visual features of the initial sounds. Target blends will be highlighted with felt marker, with color cues reduced when student is ready. Key picture clues will be emphasized. Jerry will be taught to visualize each blend as it is

said. Teaching materials will include the mastered sight words from Jerry's word bank, the spelling words that include the target sounds, and phonic cards containing material from a phonics workbook at a lower adjacent level. From the workbook, a key picture representing the target sound will be placed on one side of a phonic card, and three to four target words used in sentences will be placed on the reverse side. The strong visual features of computer practice will provide many maintenance strategies, since three game programs will be employed. Additional maintenance strategies will be selected as needed from those suggested for IIB.1–.4 and IIC.2. Program modifications will be determined by student performance under these conditions.

Practice Case A

Jerry's second weakest subskill area is structural analysis. He was observed to omit suffixes frequently and stumble over prefixes. The diagnostic hypotheses include: Jerry has been taught to analyze the separate letters of word parts; he probably needs to view them as whole units.

Based upon this information and the annotated curriculum chart (Figure 5.10), make the following assessment and programming decisions.

1. Where should direct testing begin and why?
2. Where do you tentatively plan to stop testing and why?
3. What materials will you use for testing and why?
4. Assume that the diagnostic hypotheses are confirmed; what will probably be the secondary (after phonetic analysis) program emphasis and why?
5. How will the secondary program priority be established?
6. What corrective strategies will you plan to use initially and why?
7. Which materials will you plan to use initially and why?

8. What maintenance strategies will you plan to use and why?
9. Which two developmental strategies will you select to introduce new tasks in subsequent program cycles and why?

Practice Case B

Suppose that Jerry's relative strengths and weaknesses among the word recognition subskills are rearranged so that sight vocabulary is ranked as fourth, or weakest, and others are ranked as follows: (1) phonetic analysis; (2) structural analysis; (3) word meaning. His reading comprehension is satisfactory when he reads first-grade level texts. Assume that indirect assessment indicates that Jerry demonstrates strong auditory performance, and that strengths and weaknesses are confirmed through observation and work-sample analysis. Based upon this information and the curriculum chart in Figure 5.11, make the appropriate assessment and programming decisions.

FIGURE 5.10   Word Recognition Curriculum, Practice Case A

WORD RECOGNITION SUBSKILLS

	K	1	2	3
III STRUCTURAL ANALYSIS	III	III	III	III
A Root Words		A.1 Basal, PP/P/1	A.2 Basal 2.1/2.2	A.3 Basal 3.1/3.2
B Suffixes		B.1 s,ed,d, t,ing .2 er,est	B.3 ly,ful	B.4 less, ness
C Prefixes			C.1 a,be,un, re	C.2 dis
D Compound Words		D.1 Basal PP/P/1	D.2 Basal 2.1/2.2	
E Contractions			E.1 Omit One Letter	E.2 Omit Two+ Letters
F Syllabication	F.1 Aud. Disc One & Two Syll			F.2 Two Consnt. .3 Affixes .4 (c)le .5 Dbl. Letter

FIGURE 5.11 Word Recognition Curriculum, Practice Case B

WORD RECOGNITION SUBSKILLS

	K	1	2	3
I SIGHT VOCABULARY	I	I	I	I
A Basic Vocabulary	A.1 Name .2 Colors Numbers	A.4 Basal, PP/P/1	A.5 Basal 2.1/2.2	A.6 Basal 3.1/3.2
B High-Frequency Vocabulary	B.1 Upper Letters .2 Lower Letters	B.3 Common Nouns .4 PP/P/1	B.5 2nd	B.6 3rd

1. What are your diagnostic hypotheses?
2. Where should direct testing begin and why?
3. Where do you tentatively plan to stop testing and why?
4. What materials will you use for testing and why?
5. Assume that your diagnostic hypotheses are confirmed; what will probably be the secondary (sight vocabulary) program emphasis and why?
6. How will the secondary program priority be established?
7. What corrective strategies will you plan to use initially and why?
8. Which materials will you plan to use initially and why?
9. What maintenance strategies will you plan to use and why?
10. Which two developmental strategies will you select to introduce new tasks in subsequent program cycles and why?
11. What specific assessment and programming plans should be made for reading comprehension and why?

ENRICHMENT ACTIVITIES

Discussion

1. Discuss the relative importance of word recognition and each word recognition subskill to the general academic success of an elementary age student; of an adolescent. Explain example tasks that are and are not important to students in each age range.
2. What are the advantages and disadvantages of including nonsense words in the content of the word recognition instructional program? In the content of the word recognition assessment plan?
3. Review the discussion of direct assessment in this chapter. Compare the suggestions for constructing tests with the suggested alternative assessment techniques. Which technique(s) would be most likely to parallel classroom tasks? Which would be fastest and least intrusive? Which would give you the most information useful for planning instruction?
4. Discuss the relative importance of direct instruction in phonetic analysis.

5. Review the assessment and programming strategies in the sample case study. Once consonant sounds are mastered, what strategies should be utilized to teach Jerry vowel sounds? What are the relative merits of teaching him vowel sounds?

Special Projects

1. Using the word recognition teacher survey (Figure 5.2), interview a third-grade teacher about the word recognition skills of his or her strongest and weakest students.

2. Practice administering to a peer the word recognition sample items for second and fourth grade in Appendix A.

3. Choose four tasks, one from each of the four word recognition subskills. For each task, construct a test item at selection, production, and application levels.

4. Practice implementing the procedures in this chapter with a student whose skills in word recognition are below grade level; if possible, use the weakest student indicated by the third-grade teacher in Activity 1.

5. Review Practice Case B. Assume that word meaning is Jerry's weakest subskill. With a peer, formulate diagnostic hypotheses; then plan direct assessment strategies using the format of the personalized assessment plan (Figure 3.16). Simulate student performance, and then plan programming in word meaning for Jerry.

CHAPTER 6

READING COMPREHENSION

JOYCE S. CHOATE
THOMAS A. RAKES

CHAPTER OBJECTIVES

This chapter is designed to enable the reader to:

1. Explain the relative importance of reading comprehension and each of its subskills to a student's academic success.
2. Describe the indirect assessment procedures and resulting data that are most relevant to a student's comprehension and general academic progress.
3. Develop appropriate plans for direct assessment of the comprehension performance of specific students.
4. Select and justify developmental, corrective, and maintenance strategies according to the assessed comprehension skills of specific students.
5. Plan a tentative reading comprehension program that is personalized for specific students.

Reading comprehension is the goal of instruction in reading and word recognition is a means to help achieve that goal. This chapter presents reading comprehension curricula organized according to measurable subskill performances that encompass the strategies for comprehension. Toward this end, comprehension is divided into four subskill categories: (1) literal, (2) interpretive, (3) critical, and (4) words in context. Being able to understand what one reads is not, in fact, a singular cognitive process, but rather an integrated thought process. This relatively unexplained cognitive area, called reading comprehension, is easier to manage for instructional purposes if approached through a more didactic treatment of invented or hypothesized subskill areas. Topics such as schema, metacognition, and specific learning strategies are appearing in instructional materials. However, it is difficult to delineate clearly the related assessment and instructional procedures with any assured degree of empirical accuracy. The rather conservative grouping of comprehension skills presented on the following pages is based upon the reading materials, literature-based programs, and curricula currently used in many schools. Incorporated within the recommended instructional practices are the implications of a substantive body of research focusing on reading comprehension (Durkin, 1993; Fielding & Pearson, 1994; Flood & Lapp, 1990; McNeil, 1992).

READING COMPREHENSION SKILLS

Much research has focused upon comprehension as a composite of skills which, as a result, requires reading comprehension to be perceived as an evolution of reader applied skills. In addition to the reader's decoding fluency, his or her affective characteristics, prior knowledge, and cultural background impinge upon comprehension. Heilman, Blair, and Rupley (1994) refer to reading comprehension as a constructive process—one in which the reader relates the text to prior knowledge and experiences to construct meaning. Metacognitive theory suggests that, in addition to skills application and mastery, a reader's strategies for assimilating and accommodating information should be considered. Such a model requires readers to ask themselves as they read: "How do I figure this out? Where is this coming from? How did the writer come up with this approach?" Active comprehension results when readers are aware of what is being learned, and how they can find out information. Because many students, special learners in particular, need structured learning experiences and direct instruction to develop active comprehension skills and strategies, both metacognitive and more traditional, skills-based comprehension strategies are recommended in this chapter.

The four major comprehension subskill categories represent the areas of cognitive performance that are suspected to be directly involved in the teaching/learning process. However, the comprehension process requires the interaction of multiple-skill mastery and, at times, a simultaneous application of skill competencies. The holis-

tic, or interactive, skills model is an important consideration in interpreting data and planning instruction. It is the current limitations of cognitive assessment that similarly limits measurement of comprehension skills. Thus, this chapter treats the measurement of comprehension skills in a more discrete fashion than is, perhaps, ideal. Within the framework of instructional strategies, you will sense both the more global treatment of reading comprehension instruction as well as attention to subskill categories.

"Reading" infers comprehension. In fact, without comprehension, reading is little more than pronouncing words. Letter and word recognition in the absence of meaning is not reading. Reading means interpreting print, either orally or silently, and interacting with text to construct meaning. Manzo and Manzo (1993) note that the processes of comprehending speech and print are similar, referring to reading and listening as a unitary process. Although the listening and reading comprehension processes may also differ somewhat, they contend that the similarities are sufficient that, in the absence of specific speech or listening difficulties, students' levels of listening comprehension may be excellent indicators of their reading comprehension or reading capacity levels.

Literal Comprehension

Generally considered the most basic or entry-level comprehension skill, literal comprehension includes reading and understanding *the lines* of text to recognize details and sequence of events. Burns, Roe, and Ross (1992) explain the literal level in terms of textually *explicit* meaning, which involves recognizing the sequence and facts that are explicitly stated in the text as well as answering factual questions. Understanding sequential order of events is a somewhat more difficult task than factual recall for some readers. It requires students to remember details but do so in an organized or sequential manner. This skill is particularly necessary when reading science, social studies, and other content subjects. Educators are occasionally criticized for focusing exclusively on the recall of facts (Guszak, 1967). Another concern is that too much time is spent testing for mastery of details and not in teaching students to read for details.

Interpretive Comprehension

Interpretive comprehension is acknowledged as reading *between the lines*. That is, interpretive reading is comprehending the information implied in the text, or understanding *implicit* meaning. Some authors refer to this second area of comprehension as inferential reading comprehension (Cunningham, Moore, Cunningham, & Moore, 1995; Lapp & Flood, 1992). Collins and Cheek (1993) state that interpretive skills require a higher level of thinking than literal skills. Interpretive comprehension includes the tasks of finding main ideas and cause and effect relationships, drawing conclusions, and summarizing from printed material. The major difference between literal and interpretive comprehension is that the second requires the reader to rely more heavily upon factors that are not always directly stated in text. The student must synthesize information from prior knowledge, context, and subtle language differences, such as syntactic and semantic variables.

Critical Comprehension

Critical comprehension results from reading *behind and beyond the lines* to evaluate the text and the reading act. In this respect, critical comprehension is reading for *transplicit* meaning. That is, critical comprehension transcends and encompasses literal and interpretive comprehension, prior experiences, and the reading process itself. Critical reading skills involve the evaluation of written material and are considered by some to represent a still higher level of thinking (Burns, Roe, & Ross, 1992). These skills are intended to develop questioning and thinking readers. They enable a student to sort relevant from irrelevant information and, on the basis of his or her knowledge, to judge the quality and accuracy of text.

Differentiating between fact and opinion, identifying author purpose and bias, and recognizing propaganda techniques (a task that interests many students) are among the critical comprehension tasks discussed in this chapter. Beyer (1987) suggests that thinking skills can be organized, introduced, and assessed. His premise is based upon viewing thinking as three major interrelated components: operations, knowledge, and dispositions. Critical comprehension, the most difficult of the three levels to teach, is often overlooked, or more likely, explained and practiced but not taught. Although infrequently directly addressed by curricular plans, the instructional implications of the results of research on thinking skills are discussed later in this chapter. In general, most low-achieving readers can be expected to experience difficulty in employing critical comprehension skills.

Over the past twenty years the meaning of critical reading or critical comprehension has expanded to include not only a set of reader-based skills but also factors involving prior knowledge and the relevance of textual material. Metacognitive analysis has added another dimension, that of the reader as a manager of knowledge. Layman and Collins (1990) provide a brief summary of the evolution of the concept of critical reading, noting the need for direct instruction that explains and demonstrates strategies, shows when and why to use them, and also provides appropriate practice.

Thus, as outlined in Figure 6.1, literal, interpretive, and critical are the three categories of reading comprehension discussed in this chapter. Again, it is important to remember that this breakdown of comprehension skills is more a classification of skills than a strict sequence. The carryover or integration of skills makes the classification logical but not necessarily cognitively accurate. It is nearly impossible to divide comprehension into discrete categories; the division merely conforms to the practices of many reading programs upon which the comprehension scope and sequence charts are often based and permits more direct measurement and improvement of the overall process.

FIGURE 6.1   Three Types of Reading Comprehension

READER'S TASK	LITERAL COMPREHENSION	INTERPRETIVE COMPREHENSION	CRITICAL COMPREHENSION
Understand and Recall	*Explicit Meanings:*	*Implicit Meanings:*	*Transplicit Meanings:*
	Facts	Conclusions	Validity
	Stated Main Idea	Unstated Main Idea	Reliability
	Sequence	Cause/Effect	Relevance
		Summary	Effect on Reading

Words-in-Context

The final category, words-in-context, is included with comprehension skills because of its direct contribution to a meaningful comprehension curriculum. The use of context is essential to all three types of comprehension—literal, interpretive, and critical. Understanding words in context represents a continuation of the word meaning and other word recognition skills discussed in Chapter 5. Contextual usage focuses on the surrounding words that define and expand the meaning of individual words. Students with reading problems may be able to decode in isolation or call words orally. It is only when they can understand words in the context of each page that the full usefulness of reading is realized. Without the ability to use context successfully, a reader has severely limited comprehension. (Additional examples of the utility and necessity for using words in context appear in Chapter 10 within the discussion of technical and nontechnical vocabulary.)

PERSONALIZED ASSESSMENT PROCEDURES

Diagnosis for program planning must include a review of the student's specific comprehension skills, subskills, and any other sources of performance-related data (e.g., work samples, teacher comments, and test records). The results from such an analysis provide the basis from which an appropriate comprehension program may be developed. In formulating this program, you should also consider reading comprehension's interrelationship with word recognition, speaking, listening, and writing skills and study strategies. The separation of reading skills is more a mechanism or convenience for instructional purposes than an indicator of how a child actually reads. Although specialized instruction in comprehension is often necessary, steps should also be taken to ensure application of specifically taught comprehension skills as strategies for reading actual story content.

Personalized assessment of reading comprehension requires that you initially establish specific content and comprehension curriculum priorities for each student. Through the use of indirect procedures you can estimate a student's current proficiency in applying specific reading comprehension subskills. To complete the personalized assessment profile, directly assess the student's competency using leveled comprehension tasks.

Curriculum Analysis

The reading comprehension curriculum chart (Figure 6.2) includes the minimal comprehension skills necessary for most readers. Beginning with the teacher survey, refer back to the curriculum chart to assess and maintain a record of a student's progress and curricular priorities.

Although most reading comprehension curricula share common elements, there may be a difference among the tasks selected and the level at which they are introduced and/or reintroduced. The comprehension subskills and tasks included in Figure 6.2 represent a typical comprehension skills grouping. In some instances, these may need to be adjusted according to your particular

FIGURE 6.2   Sample Reading Comprehension Curriculum Chart

Student's Name_____Grade_____Teacher_____School_____Date_____

Directions: Circle the specific tasks required for success at this student's current level; in the space provided list any other tasks appropriate to the existing curriculum.

Typical Text Level for Tasks

COMPREHENSION SKILLS*							
	K	1	2	3	4	5	6
I LITERAL A Details	I A.1 Listening 1st Level 4 Facts	I A.2 PP-4 Facts .3 P " .4 1st- "	I A.5 5 Facts	I A.6 6 Facts	I A.7 6 Facts	I A.8 7 Facts	I A.9 7 Facts
B Sequence	B.1 Listening 1st Level 3 Events	B.2 PP-3 Events .3 P " " .4 1st "	B.5 4 Events	B.6 5 Events	B.7 5 Events	B.8 6 Events	B.9 6 Events
	K	1	2	3	4	5	6
II INTERPRETIVE A Main Idea	II A.1 States Listening 1st Level	II A.2 PP-States .3 P-States .4 1st-States	II A.5 States	II A.6 States	II A.7 States, 3 Support Details	II A.8 States, 4 Support Details	II A.9 States, 5 Support Details
B Conclusions	B.1 Listening	B.2 PP .3 P .4 1st	B.5 2nd	B.6 3rd	B.7 4th	B.8 5th	B.9 6th
C Cause/Effect			C.1 2nd	C.2 3rd	C.3 4th	C.4 5th	C.5 6th
	K	1	2	3	4	5	6
III CRITICAL A Evaluates Material Fact/Fiction/ Opinion	III A.1 Listening 1st Level	III A.2 PP .3 P .4 1st	III A.5 2nd	III A.6 3rd	III A.7 4th	III A.8 5th .10 Propaganda	III A.9 6th .11 Propaganda
B Evaluates Author					B.1 Purpose .4 Bias	B.2 Purpose .5 Bias	B.3 Purpose .6 Bias
	K	1	2	3	4	5	6
IV WORDS IN CONTEXT A Single Words	IV A.1 Listening 1st	IV A.2 PP .3 P .4 1st	IV A.5 2nd	IV A.6 3rd	IV A.7 4th	IV A.8 5th	IV A.9 6th
B Figuratives				B.1 3rd	B.2 4th	B.3 5th	B.4 6th
	K	1	2	3	4	5	6
V ADDITIONAL SKILLS							

COMMENTS

curriculum or learner needs; an integrated listing of the language arts may be more appropriate for a whole language program. Use the teacher survey of reading comprehension skills (Figure 6.3) to document curricular expectations for each student. Part A of the comprehension survey involves teacher estimation of curricular goals, priorities, and ratings of student performance. Part B involves the indirect assessment of individual student competencies. Information is needed from both sections to complete the curriculum chart (Figure 6.2), which is the plan or data base from which to develop a reading comprehension program. The circled items on the curriculum chart represent the tasks to target for instruction. As the central record, the curriculum chart serves as a monitor for student progress and projection of future needs.

The comprehension curriculum chart and teacher survey should be used in a manner similar to that of the chart and survey provided for word recognition in Chapter 5. Begin by interviewing the teacher to gain as much information as possible about the student and curricular expectations. Using this information, mark the curriculum chart (priority items circled) to plan assessment procedures. Following the assessment, mark the curriculum chart and continue the cycle throughout the teaching-learning process.

Indirect Student Assessment

Before directly administering test items to the student, summarize, chart, and review information on the comprehension curriculum chart. By interviewing the teacher, you are sometimes able to obtain different information than is typically gained from directly testing a student. Indirect assessment gives an additional source of information with which to verify, reject, support, or extend the assessment process. The indirect survey (Figure 6.3) provides a curriculum data base (Part A) as well as an indirect preview of student behaviors (Part B).

Indirect assessment data may also include portfolios of student work. How do the samples compare to perceived achievement? Is there evidence to substantiate teacher comments, observations, or curriculum expectations? Is there an inconsistency between reported performance and its occurrence during a particular time of day or between it and the response format? These and other questions may be answered when work samples are compared with indirect and direct assessment information. The additional information improves the basis for making assessment and programming decisions. The perceptions of the teacher reflect a student's performance across time and add to the data that will be collected through direct testing.

Use the teacher interview to formulate diagnostic hypotheses for planning direct assessment procedures. The process of indirect assessment links a multiple source record of curricular priorities and perceived student performance factors with an assessment plan designed for each student.

Direct Student Assessment

Careful planning maximizes the effectiveness and efficiency of the direct assessment of a student's performance. Before interviewing and directly testing a student, consider the available data: indirect assessment information, tentative diagnostic hypotheses, and teacher priorities. An assessment planning checksheet, such as the one for Gandy in Figure 6.4, may facilitate planning and also help focus and streamline the direct assessment procedures.

Preliminary Procedures

Review the completed curriculum chart for each student. The chart will assist you in deciding which skills and levels to begin directly testing. Also note the teacher's estimate of subskills performance. If, for example, the teacher reports that Ocie can choose the correct answers, but cannot "talk about" a story, you may hypothesize that Ocie is reasonably proficient in literal comprehension. Her comprehension difficulty may stem from deficient skills in the higher levels of com-

FIGURE 6.3   Teacher Survey: Reading Comprehension Skills

Student_____Date_____
Teacher_____Interviewer_____

ADDITIONAL COMMENTS

A. ASSESSMENT OF CURRICULUM:
1. Indicate appropriate skills, subskills, and tasks on an attached reading comprehension curriculum chart.

List available text titles/levels you would consider as options:

2. List current text titles and levels in which student is expected to read with understanding:
_____
_____
_____

3. Check the primary source(s) of student's report grades in reading comprehension:
__Reading Workbook   __Oral Reading
__Teacher Tests   __Board Work
__Combination_____
__Other _____

Describe grade sources:

4. Indicate the relative importance of each subskill to student's grades in reading comprehension using 1 as the most important:
__Literal Comprehension   __Critical Comprehension
__Interpretive Comprehension   __Words in Context

Indicate time devoted to each by current curriculum and texts:

5. Describe instructional modifications in reading comprehension that you have attempted with this student:
_____
_____

Degree of success:

B. INDIRECT STUDENT ASSESSMENT:
6. Rank order this student's reading comprehension subskills using 1 as the strongest:
__Literal Comprehension   __Critical Comprehension
__Interpretive Comprehension   __Words in Context

In weakest area(s) identify the most difficult tasks for this student:

7. Check the best description of the student's emotional reaction to his or her comprehension performance:
__Over concern   __No concern
__Some concern   __Other reaction

Describe student's emotional reaction:

8. Check any other subject areas in which student's comprehension level interferes with performance:
__Word Recognition   __Spelling
__Math   __Science
__English   __Social Studies
__Other _____

Indicate why and to what extent:

9. List specifically what you want to know about this student's reading comprehension performance: _____
_____
_____

Attach representative samples of the student's work

10. Interviewer Summary: _____
_____
_____

FIGURE 6.4   Assessment Planning Checksheet for Gandy

DATES BEGUN/COMPLETED	Gandy
2/5 / 2/12	1. CURRICULUM ANALYSIS
2/5 / 2/12	2. INDIRECT ASSESSMENT
2/5 / 2/7	—General Teacher Survey; Teacher: Mrs. Mousopolores
2/5 / 2/5	•Assessment of Curriculum, Part I
2/5 / 2/6	•Estimate of Achievement, Part II
2/5 / 2/7	•Learning Patterns, Part III
2/5 / 2/7	•Academic Adjustment Survey, Part IV
2/5 / 2/7	—Specific Subject Teacher Survey; Teacher(s) & Subject(s) Mrs. M — Reading
2/5 / 2/12	—Work Samples Analysis; Subjects: Reading
2/7 / 2/9	—Other Available Data: SRA Tests 5/94; Report Cards 93 – 95, 1st grade teacher interview
2/7 / 2/12	—Curriculum Chart Marked
2/14 /	3. DIRECT ASSESSMENT

> *Target Skills for Direct Assessment:* Interpretive and critical comprehension, Gr 1 – 3; context; also word meanings
>
> *Diagnostic Hypotheses:* 1) Doesn't know or use interpretive strategies   2) Ineffective use of context; generally weak vocabulary?

2/14 / 2/14	—Observation in Classroom
2/15 / 2/15	—Student Interview
2/15 /	—Personalized Test Items
2/15 / 2/15	•To Use; Source: CBA/P Book: pp. 395 – 397; pp. 389 – 391
2/16 / 2/16	•To Adapt; Source: Reading Workbook pp. 17, 24, 43, 61
2/16 / 2/19	•To Develop; Materials Needed: Basal Reader pp. 25 – 26, 110 – 112
2/19 /	—Testing Scheduled; Data: 2/21

NOTES: Repeated 1st grade; failing social studies – check weak speaking vocabulary – check word meaning prehension. The work samples that you have analyzed provide a vital clue to sources of difficulty. You can frequently confirm or reject hypotheses on the basis of such samples. If Ocie correctly performs workbook exercises requiring her to select answers to interpretive and critical comprehension tasks, you will probably reject the hypothesis that her skills are deficient in higher levels of comprehension. To establish assessment priorities, review both the teacher's priorities and your working hypotheses.

Classroom Observations

It is important to observe students, not only during testing situations, but during the daily completion of assignments. Watching, listening, questioning, and noting comprehension-related behaviors can provided additional insight into what is seen during testing situations. Opportunities for observations are typically more numerous and nonthreatening so that the observed behaviors are reasonably accurate reflections of typical behavior.

Informal Student Interview

An informal student interview provides a direct means of gaining information from the reader about how he or she feels or reacts to comprehension related behaviors. Information from Part B of the teacher survey of reading comprehension skills (Figure 6.3) can be used to initiate student responses. The student interview also provides an excellent opportunity for obtaining information concerning students' levels of oral language usage, reading interests, attitudes about reading, and motivation for reading. Both topical and purpose-related interests affect a reader's ability to comprehend. Even a student who dislikes reading may have a favorite subject topic or hobby. It is also possible that a student does not read well because he or she dislikes the topic of required reading or frequent assignments. For example, Kyle dislikes history, but he has daily reading assignments in history. You can begin to understand why his reading interest, progress, and perhaps

his potential for improvement are decreased. This does not mean that attention to history should be limited. Instead, a special effort should be made to point out interesting aspects in history and to ensure that Kyle receives reading assignments in at least one or two other areas of higher interest. The content of the graded passages used for assessment should not be unduly weighted with historical text.

Personalized Comprehension Tests

Direct and personalized assessment of comprehension skills may be conducted by developing your own tests, using sample items from Appendix B, using commercially prepared reading tests, or by using a combination of items from all three sources. Suggestions for constructing your own comprehension tests are provided in the next few pages. Sufficient information is also provided for the judicious use of the sample test items (see Appendix B), tasks from other tests, and/or alternative assessment procedures. In all cases, the criterion for test selection is the match between the comprehension tasks and content of the curriculum.

Suggestions for Constructing Tests of Comprehension.   In contrast to the variety of materials and formats needed to assess word recognition subskills, the tools for testing comprehension are reasonably uniform. One or more passages from each level of the student's reading materials are required to construct personalized tests of comprehension. The passages from the reading materials and the comprehension questions, developed by the examiner, provide the materials for assessing all the cited comprehension subskills. To assess comprehension, ask questions much like those used in an Informal Reading Inventory (IRI). A word of caution should be noted. Although many teachers continue to use IRI type procedures, Schell (1988) cites a number of problems associated with assessing comprehension. More specifically, the accuracy of published IRIs to measure main idea and vocabulary is questioned by Duffelmeyer and Duffelmeyer (1989) and Duffelmeyer, Robinson, and Squier (1989). The following suggestions are provided for assessing comprehension in printed materials currently in use in your classroom.

Reading programs generally compile several stories from different text levels or literature books and present them either in the teacher's manual or as a separate unit. These placement inventories or informal reading tests are intended for use in determining at which level of the series a student should be placed. Although many teachers are using whole language style programs, it can still be useful to select content from the passages students are reading in their classes. You may need to alter or adapt these tests so that they will be useful for making initial text placement decisions as well as programming decisions. If you are using whole language or combination basal/literature based programs and want additional assessment suggestions, see the section on alternative assessment procedures later in this chapter and in Chapter 10.

If no published tests are available to you, the second best source is text from the reading material currently being used in class. A reader, library book, or trade book can serve as a source of test material. Select one or two short stories or portions of stories containing approximately 100 to 150 words. In most cases the passages should be taken from the student's current reading text and from texts in the same series that are two levels below and two levels above the text in use. The passages should be new (not previously read) to the student. Asking students to read outdated materials or inappropriate topics can adversely affect comprehension. Particular care should be taken to select passages that are interesting or personally relevant to students. Materials also should appeal to and reflect different cultural, ethnic, and gender groups. A copy of the passages will be needed for the teacher and the reader. Estimate the passage level appropriate for initial testing, either by using a passage one level below that of most of the student's word recognition skills, or by asking the student to read a grade-level passage at sight

(no silent prereading) and then to tell the story. One level below the one on which the student can recall most of the major story points, regardless of his or her word pronunciation, is the level at which assessment should begin. Once you determine the initial testing level, prepare passages and questions similar to the ones in Appendix B.

In addition to the suggestions in Chapter 3 for consolidating direct testing, information from two sources provides the basis for selecting the beginning level of comprehension testing: (1) the teacher's estimate of comprehension performance, and (2) the student's assessed word recognition level. Use the teacher's estimate of a student's general comprehension skills as a guide in establishing the initial level of testing. Begin testing one text level below the teacher's estimate. When most of a student's word recognition skills have been determined to be at a specific grade level, begin testing comprehension at one grade level below that of the student's word recognition skills. The level below the estimated comprehension level is suggested to prevent total frustration of the student during testing.

As a general guide to comprehension assessment, the following three-level format is useful:

- *Literal Comprehension:* Have the reader orally recall what has been read.
- *Interpretive Comprehension:* Ask the reader to explain story facts or events; use two or three questions of this type.
- *Critical Comprehension:* Ask the student to judge or evaluate events based upon information from the passage as well as his or her general knowledge; use one or two questions of this type.

The sample items for tests of comprehension in Appendix B present examples of wording and style for interpretive and critical comprehension questions.

To administer the passages, find a quiet place with few distractions. A copy of the passages for each level is needed for the reader and the examiner. The procedure should take from 15 to 20 minutes. Begin by seating the student and

FIGURE 6.5   Steps in Administering Graded Passages

1. Have student read the selection orally or silently (student choice). If the passage is read orally, carefully note the student's word recognition in context. Begin by using a passage one to two levels below the estimated level of functioning.

2. Take the selection back after reading is completed.

3. Request oral recall of the story and number the details on your copy of the passage as the student recalls what has been read.

4. If appropriate, use prompted recall questions and note responses on your copy of each graded passage.

5. Score responses based upon story content and following the criterion levels which apply to task numbers. (See Appendix B.)

6. Continue until the reader has reached a level where the overall comprehension performance falls below 70 to 75 percent accuracy. This level is referred to as an instructional level, or the level at which the student would likely benefit from instruction.

7. Consider this level as a tentative placement and the subskill levels as estimates; verify through actual student performance over several days of actual use and observed progress.

explaining the purpose of the test. Point out that no grades will be given and that after each selection is read, the student will be asked to recall the information. Ask the student whether he or she recalls more material by reading orally or silently; then request that the student read the passages in the manner that results in the better comprehension. The steps in Figure 6.5 describe the way in which the process should be conducted.

If the student's classroom teacher usually evaluates performance using oral questioning, additional tasks may be unnecessary. However, if comprehension workbook pages and written tests account for a large measure of success and if all the appropriate types of tasks were not included in the work-sample analysis, then collect representative tasks from those pages to administer to the student.

The specific suggestions that follow are numbered according to the curriculum chart (Figure 6.2), the skill objectives in Appendix B, and the programming strategies. The scoring recommendations are presented as guides and should be adjusted according to curricular demands. These are primarily production level tasks; to identify the strategies a student is using to accomplish the tasks, followup questions should be asked about the ways in which the student derived or thought

out the answers. To convert the tasks to the application level, the reading text must contain information that the student needs or wants to know.

Literal Comprehension
Recalls Details on Level, (IA.1–.9). Materials: A copy for student and one for teacher of reading text stories (one from student's text level, one from each of the two levels above and below; these materials are also the stimulus for assessment of all other comprehension tasks). *Strategy:* Ask student to read story orally or silently (student choice) and be ready to discuss and answer questions; remove story from student when finished reading and ask him or her to retell the story. (In preparation for assessing sequencing skills, Tasks IB.1–.2, number the important facts in the order they are retold.) *Interpretation:* Four important facts (IA.1–.4), five facts (IA.5), six facts, (IA.6–.7), seven facts (IA.8–.9); if student retells less than criterion number of details, follow same procedure at increasingly lower levels of texts in same series until criterion level is found. Factual recall is the building block of higher level comprehension; detail questions are the most frequently occurring comprehension task required of elementary students, particularly in the primary grades. The student who has

extreme difficulty remembering facts is not likely to succeed either in the typical comprehension curriculum or in social studies or science.

Recalls Details in Sequence, (IB.1–.9). *Materials:* The teacher's record of order in which student recalled details when retelling stories in IA.1–.9. *Strategy:* No further action is required of student; teacher compares sequence with criteria. *Interpretation:* Three facts retold in order of story (IB.1–.4), four facts in correct sequence (IB.5), five facts in correct sequence (IB.6–.7), six facts in sequence (IB.8–.9); remembering details sequentially is particularly important for certain types of material, such as directions. It also aids in understanding cause and effect. However, relative importance rests upon curricular emphasis.

Interpretive Comprehension

States Main Idea, (IIA.1–.6). *Materials:* Student copy and teacher copy of text (see IA) and teacher-formulated "explain" the main idea questions. *Strategy:* If the student did not specify the main idea while retelling the story in IA, ask student to explain a good title or state the main idea of the story. *Interpretation:* Two of three of the combination of interpretive and evaluation questions answered correctly for IIA.1–.4; for IIA.5–.6, three of four of the combination of interpretive and evaluation questions answered correctly. Because the main idea of a passage is the framework around which to build other understandings, it is one of the most important comprehension tasks. Understanding the central idea of the story enables many students to fill in the details and draw conclusions.

States Main Idea and Supporting Details, (IIA.7–.9). *Materials:* Student copy and teacher copy of text (See IA) and teacher formulated "explain" questions ("Explain the main idea and give 3–5 details to support your answer.") *Strategy:* Ask student to state the main idea of the story and cite passage details that prove or support the answer. *Interpretation:* For IIA.7, at least three support details plus five of six of the combined

interpretive and evaluation questions answered correctly; four details for IIA.8 and five details for IIA.9, plus six of seven of the combined interpretive and evaluation questions answered correctly. The addition of supportive details will often prompt students to correct their answers about the main idea. This additional task aids students by clarifying and substantiating the process of deriving the main idea. As noted above, this is a most important task to assure student success in reading class and also in the other content areas.

Draws Conclusions, (IIB.1–.9). *Materials:* Student and teacher copies of text (IA) and teacher-formulated conclusions questions. *Strategy:* Ask student to explain a logical conclusion that can be inferred or predicted from the story. *Interpretation:* Two of three of the combination of interpretive and evaluation questions answered correctly for IIB.1–4; for IIB.5–6, three of four of the combination of interpretive and evaluation questions; for IIB.7 five of six of the combination; for IIB.8–.9, six of seven of the combined questions answered correctly. The student who can perform this task is not confined by the boundaries of the story, can relate story content to personal and vicarious experiences, and gains a deeper understanding of the text.

States Cause and Effect, (IIC.1–.5). *Materials:* Student and teacher copies of text (IA) and teacher-formulated cause and/or effect questions. *Strategy:* Ask student to explain a logical conclusion that can be inferred or predicted from the story. *Interpretation:* For IIC.1–.2, three of four of the combination of interpretive and evaluation questions; for IIC.3, five of six of the combination; for IIC.4–.5, six of seven of the combined questions answered correctly. The degree of difficulty of cause and effect questions varies; the easier task requires student to determine the relationship between the cause and the effect, both of which are separately stated in the passage, although their relationship is unstated. Inferring a cause from a stated effect or an effect from a stated cause is the more difficult task. Check student's performance on both types of tasks.

Critical Comprehension

Evaluates Material: Fact, Fiction, Opinion, (IIIA.1–.11). Materials: Student and teacher copies of text (IA) and teacher-formulated evaluation questions. *Strategy:* Ask student to judge (IIIA.1–.5) or evaluate (IIIA.6–.9) the passage to decide if it is fact, or fiction (IIIA.1–.6), fact, fiction, or opinion (IIIA.7–.11), and if it contains propaganda (IIIA.10–.11), and describe how the decision was made. *Interpretation:* Two of three of the combination of interpretive and evaluation questions answered correctly for IIIA.1–.4; for IIIA.5–.6, three of four of the combination of interpretive and evaluation questions; for IIIA.7, five of six of the combination; for IIIA.8–.9, six of seven of the combined questions answered correctly. Distinguishing the veracity of text is important to adjustment and avoiding gullibility; this task provides a vital building block for making wise decisions about what is read and ultimately for becoming an informed consumer and citizen.

Evaluates Material: Author Purpose and Bias, (IIIB.1–.6). Materials: Student and teacher copies of text (IA) and teacher-formulated evaluation questions. *Strategy:* Ask student to evaluate the passage to determine the author's bias and purpose in writing it and to justify the answers. *Interpretation:* For IIIB.1 and .4, five of six of the combination of interpretive and evaluation questions answered correctly; for IIIB.2, .3, .5, and .6, six of seven of the combined questions answered correctly. Detecting the author's bias and purpose are high-level cognitive tasks that help the student evaluate the worth of reading material. When mastered, like the tasks in IIIA, these accomplishments assist the student to become an active and informed reader.

Words in Context

Single Words in Context, (IVA.1–.9). Materials: Student and teacher copies of text (IA) and teacher-formulated word meaning questions. *Strategy:* Select from the appropriate text one or more vocabulary words and the sentences in which they appear. Quote the sentence and ask student to tell the meaning of the key vocabulary word(s). *Interpretation:* 100 percent accuracy; word comprehension expands passage comprehension. The student who has limited word understanding may experience little difficulty with literal comprehension, but the depth of interpretive and critical comprehension will suffer. Use of context to attach meaning to words greatly increases reading efficiency. Contextual analysis should be strongly encouraged, with intense instruction provided the student who is not proficient in its use. (See Figure 5.1, tasks IVA–E for additional word meaning tasks.)

Figurative Words in Context, (IVB.1–.4). Materials: Student and teacher copies of text (IA) and teacher-formulated word meaning questions. *Strategy:* Select from the appropriate text one or more sentences containing figures of speech. Quote each sentence and ask student to tell the meaning of the figurative language. *Interpretation:* 80–90 percent accuracy; the meanings of figures of speech are particularly difficult for some students, especially those who favor very concrete tasks or who have limited experiences. The rate of occurrence of figurative language in the student's reading text will determine the importance of the task to student success.

Sample Items for Tests of Reading Comprehension. Sample items for testing reading comprehension are presented in Appendix B. The primary purpose for including these items is to present a model to help you construct similar items using the student's reading text. Unlike other subjects, it is improbable that these passages or items will be the same ones that appear in the student's text. The format of the questions is, however, likely to follow that of the curriculum. The subskills and tasks are similar to the traditional ones of basal reading series, and are listed in Appendix B by numbers corresponding to those on the reading comprehension curriculum chart (Figure 6.2).

Because of inaccessibility of curricular materials or time constraints, it is sometimes difficult to develop tests using the student's actual text. Under such circumstances the sample items may be useful, provided you understand that the information so derived is very tentative. The procedures for administering these items are the same as those cited for items constructed by the teacher. Ask the student to read either orally or silently, depending upon which mode usually results in his or her greater comprehension. Remove the passage from the student and follow the strategies for each task cited on the teacher's copies of the stories. Increase or decrease the difficulty level of passages, asking the student to read and recall or answer questions until each criterion-level performance has been established. Using the sample items, interpret assessment results very cautiously unless they can be verified through additional measures.

Alternative Assessment Techniques. Zabrucky and Moore (1989) caution teachers about using verbal responding alone as a means of assessing reading comprehension. Although the most common means of individual assessment, verbal response measured in isolation may be misleading. With this in mind, several alternative assessment techniques are recommended in order to help provide a more balanced or authentic analysis of reading comprehension. In each case, assessment of the strategies a student uses to facilitate comprehension can be accomplished by using followup questions, while application level performance can be assessed by using passages containing information the student wants or needs to know.

As discussed in Chapters 1 and 3, the authentic assessment and curriculum movement continues to gain the favor of a wide range of specialists—and the area of reading is no exception. Advocates encourage assessing the reading performances representative of real-world reading practices, assuming, of course, that the reading curricula focus on authentic performances. Paris and colleagues (1992) present an interesting discussion of the issues related to authentic literacy assessment. Additional descriptions and suggestions for authentic assessment practices appear in the book edited by Valencia, Hiebert, and Afflerbach (1994).

Computer-assisted assessment, such as the systems approach advocated by McEneaney (1992), may be a viable and interesting alternative to traditional assessment techniques. Another likely alternative is portfolio assessment using literacy or reading portfolios. Among the advantages cited for using portfolios are their emphasis on production, depth, and informed judgments (Calfee & Perfumo, 1993); the opportunities they provide for student self-evaluation; and their usefulness in documenting a student's literacy development across time (May, 1994).

In addition to the traditional question-answer format or retellings about what the student has read, there are several other assessment techniques that are appropriate for assessing reading comprehension. Questions can be reformatted when a student is unable to answer a particular form. Alternate questioning formats also allow for testing different types or levels of skills. Other assessment alternatives range from cloze procedures and fluency measures to more specific measures and selective use of published tests. A few uses of these alternative assessment procedures are outlined in Figure 6.6. Since the specificity of diagnostic data obtainable from each alternative varies, assessment techniques should be selected according to purpose as well as curricular match.

Selection Level Questioning. For students who have difficulty producing answers to questions, choices from which to select the correct answers present a viable alternat.ive teaching and testing format. True/false, multiple-choice, adapted cloze, and maze formats each suggest and limit the options for answers. When one of these resembles the classroom teaching and testing format, it should be considered.

Open-Ended Questioning. Questions with more than one correct answer are often used to assess reading comprehension immediately following reading of a selection. However, requiring free

FIGURE 6.6   Sample Uses of Alternative Assessment Procedures

ASSESSMENT PROCEDURE	SAMPLE USES
━ Selection-Level Questioning	Traditional IRI Assess comprehension subskills Compare oral, silent, listening comprehension Place in appropriate text level Restructure assessment tasks Assess comprehension subskills
━ Open-Ended Questioning	Assess interpretive comprehension Assess critical comprehension Assess strategy usage
━ Mediated Questioning	Restructure assessment tasks Probe limits of performance Place in appropriate text level Teach comprehension subskills
━ Thinking Aloud	Assess use of reading strategies Assess self-monitoring during reading
━ Student-Generated Questioning	Assess comprehension subskills Teach comprehension subskills
━ Sentence Verification	Obtain global estimate of reading level Assess selected comprehension subskills
━ Story Frames	Assess comprehension subskills Assess use of text structure Teach text structure and comprehension skills
━ Cloze Procedures	Obtain global estimate of reading level Place in appropriate text level Assess use of context Teach contextual use
━ Fluency Measures	Assess reading rate Obtain global estimate of reading level Place in appropriate text level Assess word pronunciation in context
━ Reading Logs	Identify interests and general performance Monitor reading progress Assess whole language development
━ Writing Samples	Assess transfer/application of comprehension Teach comprehension subskills Encourage reading/writing
━ Dynamic Assessment	Assess readiness for new reading tasks Identify facilitative cues and hints Assess strategy usage Assess while teaching
━ Strategy Usage	Assess use of reading strategies Assess self-monitoring during reading
━ Published Tests	Obtain global estimate of reading level Assess selected comprehension tasks

and written responses can cause poor readers to perform worse on measures of comprehension (Davey, 1989). One alternative to using unassisted, open-ended questioning is to allow readers to "look back" or review the text to find information when they are unable to respond from memory. This provides an additional dimension by verifying a student's ability to find an answer. At times it may be necessary to specifically point out a line, paragraph, section, or page where helpful information can be located. If students have difficulty, it may help to ask them to describe how they went about finding the information and what they did find.

Mediated Questioning.   Another adaptation that can be used to extend the typical question-answer model is the use of mediated questioning. Originating from Vygotsky's work (1978, 1981) involving cognitive learning theory and described by Wertsch (1985), this adaptation involves two levels of assessment: (1) the current level of development as indicated by unaided recall and (2) a level indicated by aided responses. For purposes of assessing comprehension, mediated questioning should be used as a follow-up when a reader is unable to successfully answer questions. This can be done by simply asking the initial question and if unanswered or answered incorrectly, follow up by providing a guiding statement. The example in Figure 6.7 typifies the use of a mediated questioning exchange following the reading of a passage.

The use of mediated questioning is suggested as a means of further clarifying what a reader can learn or figure out. The use of unaided recall limits the level and type of information received. Mediated questioning allows the examiner to move a step further and observe a student's ability to respond on a different level of cognitive functioning.

Thinking Aloud.   A logical extension of mediated questioning is a modification of what Wade (1990) refers to as "think alouds." Think alouds can be used as an interactive assessment procedure. Simplified, this procedure can be used as a

FIGURE 6.7   Mediated Questioning

Teacher: Why was the boy in the story afraid?

Student: I'm not sure.

Teacher: Think about what he said to Grandpa—does that give you a clue?

Student: Well, he said he liked his house.

Teacher: Right! And you just told me about the young boy running away—what was the last thing that happened just before he ran away?

Student: His mom told him they were moving; I guess he was scared he wouldn't like a new place and maybe wouldn't have friends and stuff like that.

---

meta-cognitive assessment tool to replace the traditional IRI assessment. Ask the student to read one to three sentences orally and then tell about what was just read. Use follow-up questions to involve the reader in generating hypotheses. At the end of a section, ask the student to retell the entire passage. The key question is: how do students use existing information? Can they relate existing information with new information? Are they able to integrate new information with existing knowledge? How do they react to new words and concepts? Do they exhibit any particular strategies for understanding what they read? Are they able to predict or anticipate upcoming events in a story? Think aloud procedures provide excellent opportunities to assess the strategy usage of the student.

Student-Generated Questioning.   Asking students to read a passage and then develop comprehension questions (and answers) about the content reverses the traditional questioning format. As a qualitative measure of student comprehension, this technique is also an important instructional strategy. Before implementation, students must be provided specific training that includes guidelines for developing different types of questions, demonstrations, coaching sessions, and then appropriate practice.

Sentence Verification.   An alternative to asking questions to assess comprehension is the sentence verification technique (SVT). As described by Royer, Greene, and Sinatra (1987), in this procedure the student is presented four types of sentences and asked to identify the ones that represent ideas from a passage just read or listened to. Sentence types include paraphrases, meaning changes, distractors, and originals. Carlisle (1989) reports preliminary findings that suggest that the SVT not only identifies students who have comprehension difficulties but also suggests reasons for their deficits based on their error patterns. This format presents selection level tasks; however, with coaching, some students can be cued to produce the four types of sentences.

Story Frames.   Story frames are discussed later on in this chapter as an instructional tool. When used for assessment purposes, story frames are simply sentences or paragraphs constructed leaving blanks where key information should be filled in. After having a student read material, the story frame is used as a stimulus for gaining feedback about what he or she understands and remembers about what was read. The purpose of using story frames is to provide a non-question format through which specific comprehension skills can be assessed. A teacher can specifically delete target portions of a story (e.g., key words, events or places) and have students fill in the appropriate information. It is possible to delete only vocabulary, facts, causes, or other specific types of information in order to assess a particular type of recall.

Cloze Procedures.   Cloze procedures can be used as both assessment and programming techniques. Cloze tasks involve deleting words (e.g., omitting every fifth or seventh word) in a passage and then asking the student to supply the missing words or semantically acceptable substitutes (Taylor, 1957) to fill the blanks. When the blanks are random, the student's performance gives an indication of his or her ability to read and understand text at a particular level of difficulty; when the deleted words are chosen according to type or conceptual load, error patterns may be discerned. Particularly appropriate for assessing and teaching contextual usage, cloze procedures as instructional strategies are discussed later in this chapter, and for assessment purposes, are described in greater detail in Chapter 10.

Fluency Measures.   According to Marston (1989), oral reading fluency, or the rate at which a student reads a passage aloud, is both a valid and reliable measure of reading comprehension, and according to Potter and Wamre (1990), is consistent with developmental reading models. Thus, one- to three-minute samplings of a student's oral reading, noting also accuracy, may be used to obtain a global picture of his or her facility for comprehending texts at a particular level of difficulty.

Reading Logs.   Reading logs can become an integral part of an ongoing assessment and instructional program as a modified portfolio. Particularly useful in classrooms where whole language programs are used, reading logs provide a means for students to monitor their own reading. Each day, have students write their descriptions, reactions, and feelings about what they are reading in a journal or notebook. The writings should be read but not graded by the teacher on a weekly basis. Positive or supportive oral comments should be shared privately with students. The use of reading logs provides a means of monitoring reading growth and encouraging reflection about reading. By not directly marking or grading logs, students are free to express themselves. These writings can, of course, be considered a mirror reflecting areas of possible instructional intervention. Using reading logs, teachers can tap into an unencumbered source of daily information about students' reactions to what they read. Peripheral benefits include an ongoing monitoring system through which to note grammatical, syntax, spelling, and language generation needs and then offer direct instruction without specific mention of the source of the evaluative information. The exact format and content of the reading logs should be structured to meet students' needs.

Writing Samples.   Writing samples are generally used as a more direct means of having students react to their reading. Samples can be taken on a weekly basis and then used to compare progress or measure growth throughout the year. Unlike reading logs, samples should be solicited and developed for specific purposes. For those who cannot generate a sample, a dictated sample or group sample can be used. To solicit a writing sample, ask students to write about: their favorite story character, a different version of a favorite story, something they read this week, one of the three topics listed on the board, or other starters that provide a basis for responding to something they have read. For a more structured approach, the teacher can choose appropriate stories and then suggest options for writing assignments to measure comprehension (Heller, 1991). It may be necessary to model such examples by actually writing a few group samples together, talking through the process, sharing ideas, and demonstrating how to accomplish the task. The standards for evaluating the concepts, style, and mechanics of the writing samples should match curricular demands and student capabilities. If appropriate, and only with the permission of the writer, samples should be posted on a board for others to enjoy. In some cases it may be more appropriate to keep a portfolio containing samples for comparison throughout the year.

Dynamic Assessment.   Although there are several models of dynamic assessment, they all revolve around a test-teach-test cycle. Like mediated questioning, the Dynamic Reading Assessment procedure (DAP) is based on Vygotsky's work (Kletzien & Bednar, 1990). This approach to assessment focuses on probing the student's readiness to master new skills based on the student's response to instruction and the particular cues and hints that facilitate learning (Lidz, 1991). Suggested as an alternative approach for assessing low achieving Hispanic students (Duran, 1989), dynamic assessment also

offers advantages for assessing reading comprehension. Implementation of dynamic assessment to measure reading comprehension performance requires first identifying appropriate cues for accomplishing component tasks (e.g., check to see if the first sentence tells the main idea), then systematically teaching and monitoring as the student reads. Although awkward as an initial testing approach, when integrated with ongoing instruction, this assessment strategy can help structure the monitoring of the teaching/learning process and yield valuable instructional information that includes the reading strategies for which a student requires explicit programming.

Strategy Usage.   In addition to asking the student how he or she derived answers or comprehended a passage or having the student think aloud while completing a reading assignment, Palincsar and Ransom (1988) suggest two other means of assessing a student's knowledge and use of strategies. The first is to observe the student tutoring a peer to read a passage. The instructions and hints that the target student provides indicate the strategies he or she is familiar with and thinks are important. A second approach is to provide scenarios of students reading (e.g., descriptions or even videotapes) and have the student evaluate the strategies used by the depicted children.

Published Tests.   Since 1970, an increasing number of informal reading inventories have been published. The most popular is the Classroom Reading Inventory (CRI) by Silvaroli (1994). It is best known because of its short administration time. Johns' Basic Reading Inventory (1988) features an easy to use format, longer passages, and more comprehension questions than the CRI. Burns/Roe Informal Reading Inventory: Preprimer to Twelfth Grade (Burns & Roe, 1992) is an easy-to-use inventory with several excellent story passages. There are perhaps a dozen or more additional published inventories that include tests for word recognition in isolation, word recognition in context, and reading comprehension for oral and/or silent reading. In addition to weaknesses cited by Duffelmeyer and Duffelmeyer (1989), several other weaknesses of published informal reading inventories have been cited. These include: (1) a lack of empirical validity based upon formal field testing, (2) the bias generated by the subjective nature of the scoring of the inventories, and (3) the lack of direct correspondence with reading materials generally used in the classroom. Clearly, the use of prepared IRIs is controversial. Johns (1993) offers an overview of the research involving IRIs in a helpful annotated reference guide.

The assessment procedures suggested in this chapter are designed to avoid the general criticisms of published IRIs, since the mismatch between student performance and instructional content can be eliminated by using curriculum-based tests (Wilson & Cleland, 1989). The primary value of these curriculum-based instruments is not placement or grade-level determination but the variety and depth of diagnostic data they provide. Profiling student performance using actual curriculum materials establishes a direct link between teaching expectations (priorities) and student performance. Even the most carefully standardized and validated test cannot claim to be directly representative of a particular student's curriculum.

Standardized tests may be useful during or after diagnostic screening or for the purpose of comparing student performances on a large scale. They should not be used to (1) determine individual student progress, (2) determine a specific instructional reading level, or (3) accurately reflect achievement in language arts, social studies, and science. Group standardized tests are helpful, however, in providing global achievement data in reading comprehension. Some of the more widely used group, standardized reading tests include: California Achievement Tests (CTB/McGraw-Hill, 1987), vocabulary and comprehension subtests; Gates-MacGinitie Reading Tests (MacGinitie & MacGinitie, 1989), vocabulary and comprehension subtests; Iowa Silent Reading Tests (Farr, 1973), vocabulary, comprehension, and speed subtests; and the Stanford Diagnostic Reading Test (Bjorn, Madden, & Gardner, 1983),

vocabulary, comprehension, word attack, and speed subtests.

An analysis of test items from certain standardized individual reading tests may reveal content similar to a student's curriculum. In this situation, occasional items may be useful for making assessment and programming decisions. These tests are examples of some of the more popular standardized individual reading instruments: Diagnostic Reading Scales (Spache, 1981), vocabulary, comprehension, word attack, and listening subtests; Durrell Analysis of Reading Difficulty-Revised (Durrell & Catterson, 1980), vocabulary, comprehension, word attack, speed, and listening subtests; and the Woodcock Reading Mastery Test, Revised (Woodcock, 1987), comprehension and word attack subtests.

Test Administration. Although assessment of comprehension is an ongoing process in the classroom, there will be times when the administration of tests should be conducted in a quiet, distraction-free location. When oral reading is sampled, two copies of the passages are needed—one for the student to read and one for the examiner to record responses. When unaided recall is the target performance, the reading passage must be removed from view during questioning. The examiner has a great deal to do with the tone and atmosphere during a testing period. A positive, supportive approach should be used. It is also very important to present tasks in a relaxed, yet professional manner. A harried or unconcerned air by the examiner is usually detected by students and their performances affected accordingly. Careful attention should be given to providing specific directions for what is expected for each test. Frequent breaks or stretch periods may be needed to limit the confining, frustration many students associate with testing. A good rule of thumb is to postpone any test if the student appears tired or unusually uncomfortable. Data gathered over a period of time using different types of reading materials and during several sessions usually yield a better sample and more representative behaviors.

Documenting Student Skill Needs. The importance of documenting observed behaviors over a sustained period of time cannot be over emphasized. Without a history of carefully recorded student performance, development of an appropriate intervention plan cannot be possible.

Substantiating Needs.   A recognizable pattern of errors and successes is often apparent in the reading performance of some students. A student may, for example, exhibit difficulty answering a particular type of question or be unable to recall a certain type of information on successive passages. For these students data interpretation is comparatively easy; simply verify results by further testing on another day, using classroom observations or perhaps a different test method. It is important to double check diagnostic findings. In fact, the curriculum-based assessment/programming cycle is based upon a continuous test/teach/retest model.

Verification is even more appropriate when a reader reveals inconsistent or random behaviors that make patterns difficult to discern. When this occurs, make temporary instructional decisions; then, through a combination of teaching and reassessment you should be able to adjust or confirm initial assessment information. Consider comprehension assessment information as tentative until the programming cycle is completed and the findings are verified. Base your progress decisions on demonstrated skill achievement, not on level or grade expectations.

Charting and Interpreting Needs.   Use blue ink to circle the student's comprehension needs on the curriculum chart. The chart can then be used as a record of ongoing needs and progress. The assessment and programming planning formats presented in Chapter 3 (Figures 3.16 and 3.17) are useful as organizational and tracking aids. In addition to these, you may want to develop your own code for entering skill needs, mastery, and other items on the comprehension curriculum chart so that the chart always reflects the student's current status. Because of the likelihood of repeated use, make additional copies of the chart.

By annotating and distributing the chart to all who are involved in a student's comprehension program, you increase the probability of coordinated and integrated personalized programming.

PERSONALIZED PROGRAMMING PROCEDURES

A student's comprehension performance should first be compared with other curriculum needs. Two separate priorities usually exist. The first is the overall level and type of skill mastery of the student. How well does the student read with understanding? In which comprehension subskills do problems exist? The second priority is the extent to which comprehension problems or strengths relate to other academic skills. A student with very weak comprehension skills will likely evidence limited progress in written expression, social studies, science, and arithmetic problem solving. Instruction in comprehension is obviously the most important need. A second student who laboriously sounds out high-frequency words has a different profile. This student's problem interferes with understanding directions in all subjects as well as with progress in general comprehension skills. Word recognition, in this case, requires more direct attention. Such a decision does not mean that comprehension is of lesser importance. It does mean that for the present time, the sight vocabulary tasks should be considered a higher priority. Thus, although a student may have a variety of strengths and weaknesses, programming decisions must be based on the overall curriculum plan, not on performance in just one or two subject areas.

Selection of Content

The order of the four major subskill areas presented on the curriculum chart (Figure 6.2) is not intended as a sequential or developmental order for instruction. The progression from literal to interpretative to critical comprehension is usually considered one of increasing difficulty. However, that does not mean that the thinking process involved in each occurs apart from any other category. It is possible for a student to miss a literal fact and still make a judgment or draw a conclusion. This interactive process is operational at all times. It is for the purposes of instructional programming and verification of mastery that reading comprehension has been artificially broken down into semiprecise categories. This allows you to concentrate on a very specific type of problem or aspect of comprehension. It also enables readers to learn to develop specific strategies for finding out information from a printed page. This type of targeted, or single skill, direct teaching is recommended for building the comprehension skills of unsuccessful readers (Carnine, Silbert, & Kameenui, 1990).

Using words in context is the most generally applied skill area within this comprehension skills curriculum. Learning to use context to understand a word or group of words is an ongoing process, requiring direct instruction and much practice. The use of context clues can be enhanced by several other subskills such as fluency, overall level of vocabulary, and interest in the material. For this reason the teaching of context must be integrated with vocabulary, comprehension, and study strategies programming. Contextual analysis is as much a strategy as it is a skill. That is, good readers develop the habit of using words to explain other words. Poor readers have to be taught to use the ideas and words to understand new or difficult words and phrases. For this purpose some direct methods of improving contextual skills are suggested. Since the report by Vineyard and Massey in 1957, educators have recognized the importance of improving comprehension through instruction in vocabulary.

In attempting to improve the teaching of comprehension, several taxonomies have been developed (e.g., Barrett & Smith, 1976; Bloom, 1956; Sanders, 1966). However, some researchers question the validity of such hierarchical categorizing of questions or thinking (Hopkins & Stanley, 1990). Schema theory, as described by Sheridan (1981), presents comprehension as a holistic process. The skills-based approach suggested

here is intended to be used in relation to the reader's prior knowledge. It is imperative that the teacher provide ample attention to cognitive preparation before assigning reading. Collins and Cheek (1993) present a detailed discussion of the dichotomy created by prescriptive teaching of comprehension and schema theory.

Selection of Methods and Materials

Deciding which materials and methods to use can be difficult. The task becomes easier if you remember that such decisions are temporary and can be altered depending upon the degree to which the student responds to the material or special method. Many of the same factors used for word recognition are also important in selecting comprehension materials or instructional strategies. Consider the types of previous instruction, individual student learning styles or learning patterns, school or district directives, gender and cultural needs of the students, and the availability of specialized materials. The student's interests, reading level, and specific comprehension needs narrow the choices of appropriate materials.

Using a text that a student has previously struggled through may be frustrating for the teacher and student. The student's memory of story lines may impede his or her reading for stated purposes. The student who already knows the outcome of each passage may show only limited interest and motivation. In addition to selecting materials of interest to diverse groups of students, consider using appropriate computer software to motivate and actively involve students in developmental, corrective, and, particularly, maintenance activities. Content textbooks can be especially appropriate materials for an integrated whole language approach that teaches interdisciplinary concepts and content along with reading, writing, listening, and speaking (Zucker, 1993). More specific suggestions for integrating comprehension and content area studies are presented in Chapter 10 of this book.

It is important to confirm that additional assistance, such as tutorial or special class instruction, is consistent and compatible with a student's regular classroom materials. Equally important is *when* specific skill instruction is presented—before the student reads a passage for a traditional approach or after he or she reads for a whole language approach. Be aware of all types of instruction that students receive in order to develop better learning activities than they have experienced previously. Because comprehension skills are directly involved in other subject areas, it is also crucial to provide targeted, pull-out types of instructional experiences, integrated (developmentally) with instruction in science, social studies, literature, and other subject areas.

Programming for Reading Comprehension Subskills

Instructional practices are intended to focus upon both directed teaching and directed or guided practice. Improving reading and listening comprehension requires similar procedures. The discussion that follows provides a basis from which you may develop your own teaching strategies. As in the previous chapter, developmental strategies are followed by corrective and then maintenance strategies.

Developmental Strategies

Several of the more popular developmental comprehension strategies are discussed in this section. For a more detailed explanation see Lapp and Flood (1992), McNeil (1992), and Tierney, Readence, and Dishner (1990).

General Comprehension. Several techniques are appropriate for teaching all levels of comprehension. These include: successful practices, thoughtful reading, memory steps, purposeful reading, QAR, schema, reading strategies, strategic listening, and the SLA. With modifications, these strategies also apply to teaching adjacent subskills. (Later in this section, strategies specific to each of the four levels of comprehension are presented.)

Successful Practices. To set the stage for student success in comprehension, Fielding and Pearson (1994) recommend four research-based instructional practices: (1) offer direct instruction in comprehension strategies, (2) encourage collaborative learning, (3) provide ample opportunity and time for students to actually read, and (4) have students discuss their reading with each other and their teacher. The first two practices, applicable to all subject areas, are an integral part of the "Principles of Programming" presented in Chapter 2. Implementing the third recommendation requires increasing both the quantity and the quality of time students spend reading. Suggestions for improvement include offering students choices of reading selections at an appropriate level of difficulty, permitting and encouraging rereading of some texts, and allocating time for students to share and discuss reading. The fourth practice calls for restructuring classroom discussion formats to give students more input and control, to encourage more personal interpretations, and to embed strategy usage instruction in the discussion process.

Thoughtful Reading. Instruction in thinking skills is especially applicable to the teaching of general comprehension skills. Beyer (1987) suggests two formats for guiding students' thought processes. The first strategy requires the teacher to introduce a specific technique (e.g., when teaching the main idea, you clue students to check the first and then the last statements of a passage). Then review the mechanics for the task. Have students read the text and attempt the task (in this case, finding the main idea). Then help them review how and why they accomplished the task as they did. The second strategy is designed to assist students to analyze their thinking. Students first state their goal and describe how they plan to use certain skills to accomplish it. They predict their success and monitor progress and procedures while performing. After task completion, they evaluate the effectiveness of the particular procedures. This strategy can also be followed with pairs of students working together. Both strategies encourage students to be active readers, that is, to be aware of and to monitor their comprehension.

Memory Steps.   Teachers are constantly trying to assist students in remembering what they read. McKowen's (1979) three steps to improve memory are useful for this purpose: (1) keep the reader's mind alert, active, and attending; (2) put what is read into the reader's own words (rehearsing/paraphrasing); and (3) organize and connect new information with existing information (assimilation and accommodation).

Purposeful Reading.   Readers should always have a specific purpose for reading. This leads to focused, thoughtful comprehension. The publishers of popular novels know what they are doing when they print excerpts of the most stimulating scenes on the book covers. The increase in sales proves that many adult readers will set as their purpose the enjoyment of those scenes and others like them! The student who is told to read a novel in preparation for a comprehensive test on it is not likely to pass the test. Similarly, the primary student who is simply told to read a story in the basal reader may set his or own purpose: "hurry up and finish so I can talk to my friend." By asking that student to read for the purpose of locating the answer to an important question, the teacher helps focus attention on comprehension. Begin, early in the school year, setting purposes for students each time they read. As soon as they appear ready, guide them to set their own appropriate purposes and then to read with those purposes in mind.

QAR. The QAR strategy combines each of the three levels of comprehension. Raphael (1982, 1986) recommends the Question Answer Relationship (QAR) technique as a means of enhancing student responses to comprehension questions. It is designed to integrate the comprehension process. Three teacher-provided cues are offered to students to assist them in comprehending and responding. These cues are: right there, search and think, and on your own. Suppose a student is unable to respond to a literal question. You

would then say, "The answer is *right there*." The directive alerts the student that the answer is on the page, directly stated. The student is given a locational aid to find the answer. You may need to point out answers to demonstrate what to do or where to look. The directive *think and search* is used to assist the student in answering interpretive questions. When a student needs information from more than one part of a selection, this directive presents a text-based, extended source of information. This interpretive process may also include the limited use of personal experiences or prior knowledge. The teacher cue provided for a critical question is *on your own*. This type of search procedure involves the use of text information, personal knowledge, and some degree of evaluative judgment. QAR provides a simplified taxonomy for guiding thinking and generating answers. The analysis of questions is an important and effective learning and comprehension strategy (Pressley & Harris, 1990).

Schema. A reader's ability to understand and interpret text is influenced by prior experience and knowledge. It is usually helpful to provide or resurrect background information for students before they begin a reading assignment. Developing a schema with a student who has limited knowledge about a topic or subject is particularly important. A student's schemata or prior knowledge may improve comprehension in two ways. As an aid to assimilation, students' schemata enable them to relate new information to a more familiar information base. When there is little prior knowledge about a topic, a process referred to as accommodation is activated. Accommodation requires the student to adjust or add new schemata in order to understand what is being read.

To activate existing knowledge, use demonstrations, illustrations, visual aids, class discussions, or relevant situations. For the student who knows little about a topic, these types of readiness experiences may be even more helpful. Some topics of study require teachers to extend the duration of lessons so as to allow more time and exposure for students to assimilate the ideas.

Reading Strategies.   Not only the skills them-selves but also their strategic use as well as other systematic strategies for accomplishing reading tasks must be explicitly taught to many students. Pearson and Dole (1987) offer useful guidelines that apply to the presentation of a variety of reading strategies. They recommend five steps: 1) Modeling and explanation; 2) guided practice; 3) further explanation; 4) independent practice; and 5) application. In order to monitor student progress and determine when and what additional instruction is needed, students should be encouraged to think aloud throughout each of the steps.

Strategic Listening.   Listening and reading com-prehension are very closely related. In many in-stances, from kindergarten through higher grades, activities suggested for reading also can be pre-sented as meaningful listening experiences. The purpose of doing so is to help students recognize and understand text-based questions, participate in discussions about text, and apply ideas. Freed from the word recognition tasks and aided by oral intonation and expression, the listener can focus on understanding. The potential transfer of listen-ing skills to reading (Searfoss & Readence, 1994) and the growing emphasis on whole language in-struction are prime reasons to increase systematic listening instruction.

Many students with and without disabilities need direct instruction in listening strategies. Brent and Anderson (1993) recommend five steps for teaching strategic listening: (1) identify the needed listening skill or strategy, (2) directly teach that skill or strategy, (3) provide supervised practice and ample discussions and debriefings, (4) review previously taught strategies, and (5) teach students how to select strategies to match the listening task. The model includes such behaviors as watching the speaker, blocking distractions, visualization, and mental association as well as traditional skills and practices such as self-assessment and collaborative learning. To guide students to reflect on the content, an addi-tional element to emphasize might be literary

conversations, or what Hennings (1992) calls the "literature talk out."

SLA.   The Structured Listening Activity (SLA) is a procedure for systematically improving lis-tening comprehension (Choate & Rakes, 1987). This strategy is a five-step process that includes (1) concept building, (2) establishing a purpose for listening, (3) reading aloud, (4) interspersed questioning, and (5) recitation. The model may be particularly helpful since it involves both the teacher and student before listening, during lis-tening, and after listening. An example of an SLA for a familiar children's story is illustrated in Figure 6.8. As can be seen, the strategy provides multiple opportunities for the teacher to model, guide, reinforce verbally, and observe students as they respond to various types of questions.

The SLA can also be adapted and extended to incorporate whole language involvement. For ex-ample, additional language activities might in-clude a variety of shared experiences such as retelling or writing the story to make it happier (or sadder, better, more exciting, and so on), writ-ing predictions and then confirming them, writing a modern-day version of the story, or reading or listening to a peer's new version of the story.

Literal Comprehension.   For some youngsters, recalling facts is a relatively simple task. Others, however, need direct instruction, practice, and en-couragement to locate and remember details. The strategies specific to this need include: literal questioning, ReQuest, detailing, story frames, and story maps.

Literal Questioning. A major means of develop-ing literal comprehension is teacher-generated questions. Admittedly, the use of too many literal or fact type questions has been criticized. Even so, such questions can assist students in learning how to answer detail or factual-based questions. Four guidelines are recommended in Figure 6.9.

Developmental instruction in reading compre-hension can be provided by modeling the type of questioning and talk-through behavior you desire in your students. Take the time to explain where

FIGURE 6.8   SLA for Three Pigs

Materials: Copy of story Band 7 visual aids—V1-3 pigs; V4 wolf; V5 straw; V6 sticks; V7 bricks; V8 pot

1. Concept building
Where do you go during a storm? Why do you feel safer inside? Why doesn't the storm bother your house? Let's talk about where pigs live; who knows? Why do you think they live there? This story is about three pigs and the new houses they build.

2. Listening purpose
Listen to decide what the pigs and the wolf do in this story that is good and what is bad.

3. Reading aloud
[Use visuals (v), prediction cues (P), and optional interspersed comprehension questions (*) at indicated points during the reading. **NOTE:** The best placement of the starred questions—during vs. after the story reading—depends upon the nature and size of the listening group.]

STORY OUTLINE		VISUALS, PREDICTIONS, AND QUESTIONS*
Three pigs^v go to seek their fortune	(V)	V1–3
The first pig^v builds her house of straw^v;	(V)	V1, V5
the wolf^v blows it down (P);	(V)	V4; (P) What do you think will happen? Why?
the pig runs to her brother's house.*	*	Why do you think she ran to her brother's house?
The second pig^v builds his house of sticks^v;	(V)	V2, V6
the wolf^v asks to come in (P);	(V)	V4; (P) What is about to happen? How do you
the wolf blows the house down;		know?
the pigs go to their big sister's house.		
The third pig^v builds her house of bricks^v;	(V)	V3, V7
the wolf^v comes to the door and (P)	(V)	V4; (P) What will he say?
asks to come in; he tries to blow the		
house down but can't*	*	Why do you think the house doesn't fall in?
The wolf begins to climb down the chimney (P);	(P)	What do you think will happen? Why?
The pigs place a pot^v in the fireplace;	(V)	V8
the wolf falls in the pot, burns his tail, and		
runs away forever*	*	Why did the wolf run away?

4. Questioning (Postponed):
A. Literal comprehension questions:
   1. What was the first house built from?
   2. Why did baby sister say she wanted a house of straw?
   3. What was the second house built from?
   4. What was the third house built of?
   5. How long did it take big sister to build her house?
   6. Which house did the wolf blow down first? Second?

B. Interpretive comprehension questions:
   1.* Why didn't the brick house fall in?
   2.* Why do you think the first pig ran to her brother's house?
   3.* Why did the wolf run away?
   4. Why do you think the third pig chose bricks for her house?
   5. Retell the story in three sentences or less.
   6. What is the main idea of this story?

C. Critical comprehension questions:
   1. Which parts of this story *could* really happen? Which parts are make believe? How do you know?
   2. Tell why you think the pigs were good or bad; tell why the wolf was bad or good.

5. Recitation
Quickly retell this story. [Lead students to verbalize the lessons learned by the three pigs and by the wolf.]

FIGURE 6.9   Guidelines for Literal Questioning

1. Ask questions for which an answer is stated and can be verified.

2. Use a prompted recall process when a student does not know an answer.

3. Focus prompted recall upon asking questions or giving cues that tap into the student's knowledge and experience rather that being based and directed toward getting a correct answer.

4. Encourage answers by: (a) using unfinished sentences and encouraging students to finish what you begin; (b) using verbal and nonverbal cues or hints as to what the answer may be; (c) providing an initial consonant orally or on the chalk board as a cue to the word or idea; and (d) collecting multiple answers, continuing even when "the correct" answer is given. Then go back and decide with the student(s) which answer is most appropriate.

---

or how you decided on a specific fact question. By modeling your thinking out loud with them, students are better able to learn how to both ask and answer literal questions.

ReQuest.   The reciprocal questioning technique (ReQuest) is intended to teach students to ask and answer questions. Manzo (1969, 1985) recommends that a student read a line or short paragraph and then ask the teacher a question or two based upon what he or she has just read. Later on one student may question another in a similar manner. By modeling appropriate literal questioning behavior and then encouraging students to generate questions, the mystery of where answers come from is somewhat less magical. Kay, Young, and Mottley (1986) report success using ReQuest with at-risk adolescent readers. For students unfamiliar with the techniques it may be helpful to begin on an individual basis to reduce stress and better learn the procedure. Tierney, Readence, and Dishner (1990) also suggest alternating the role of the questioner after each question and encouraging students to underline or check sections of text as they read so they can later return to develop questions from a preselected portion of the reading passage.

Detailing.   It helps students read purposefully if they know prior to reading a passage the elements

that are most important. These elements then identify the details that should be noted. For a narrative passage, list the main characters and tell students to read to find details about them; or for an expository passage, list the factors important to the thesis (e.g., the three main characteristics of penguins that equip them to survive their environment). This preview provides a simple framework to help students sort relevant from irrelevant facts, but is less comprehensive than story frames.

Story Frames.   Although questioning is a mainstay in encouraging and developing literal comprehension, other steps can and should be used. The use of story frames can encourage the development of literal comprehension if first modeled by the teacher as a demonstrated talk-through. After explaining and using story frames, apply the specific procedures suggested by Fowler (1982). First read the story yourself to determine the details or events. Then construct a modified cloze type of paragraph. This results in a skeleton of blank phrases for the student to fill in, as illustrated in the sample in Figure 6.10. This procedure allows teachers to develop specific lessons to elicit the exact factual information they wish to have a student locate.

Story frames can be used to replace verbal question asking, but you must demonstrate how the frames are constructed and practice complet-

FIGURE 6.10   Sample Story Frame

Directions: Based upon what your read or heard, fill in the following blanks.

In the story, _____ was not able to

_____. After

_____ tried to _____

_____, the group left. Finally,

_____.

FIGURE 6.11   Sequence Story Map

Directions: Having read or listened to the story, now fill in or tell the answers to the following questions.

1. As the morning began what happened?

_____

_____

2. After the rain what did Ocie try to do?

_____

_____

3. What two events followed the surprise?

_____

_____

4. Describe how Ocie felt just before the story ended?

_____

_____

ing several frames for different samples of text before expecting a student to fill in the information without assistance.

Story Maps.   Closely related to story frames are story maps and story grammar. To help students better understand writing structures, story maps or grammar can be used to visually display specific or overall ideas in a story or unit of study. An overall story map includes major ideas and concepts in a graphic arrangement much like a modified outline. Such an arrangement is headed by a global or umbrella concept with supporting ideas and their related facts placed below. A story map can be used to represent an entire story or to help students focus on a specific structural element such as settings or plots. When stressing the sequence of a story, for example, the teacher would first model responding to a story map, such as the one in Figure 6.11, and guide students to respond first orally and then in writing.

Imagery and Illustrations.   Combining attention to relevant text illustrations with mental imagery is an effective strategy for improving students' recall of text (Gambrell & Jawitz, 1993). Guiding students to examine illustrations carefully and also to visualize what they read periodically may enhance comprehension in the content areas. Because picture analysis and visualization are somewhat independent of the more technical and difficult aspects of reading, this strategy might be of special value to students with special needs.

Interpretive Comprehension.   The next level of comprehension involves direct teaching to improve student abilities in locating main ideas, drawing conclusions, and determining cause and effect. In addition to appropriate questioning, developmental strategies for interpretive skills include semantic webs and maps, simulation, and predictive statements. Several of these suggestions involve both reading and writing experiences. Tierney and Pearson (1983) discuss the appropriate association and natural teaching opportunities involving comprehension and composition. Some students experiencing reading comprehension problems may be unable to respond in writing. In such cases teacher-assisted oral, group, or partially guided responses may be used in place of written student responses. Not to be confused with story maps and story frames, semantic webs are usually more detailed and complex graphically than story maps.

Interpretive Questioning. Interpretive strategies can usually be found within the trade books or subject area textbooks currently being used. The use of special procedures must be coupled with careful teacher-directed interpretive questioning, prompting, and modeling of the answer process. Teacher questioning could begin with such statements as these: "If I were you I would try. . . . Have you considered looking at. . . . If you compare _____ and _____ what would be the difference? What could have happened had. . . . or How could _____ have reacted differently?" Remember that teaching interpretive skills involves both prereading and postreading questioning of a nature that requires the student to predict or see cause and effect relationships. By using fewer literal questions and, instead, developing questions that require more than one possible correct answer, the teacher encourages students to read between the lines. Reports by Hansen (1981) and Hansen and Pearson (1983) support the use of inference (interpretive) questions before and after reading to enhance reader comprehension.

Semantic Webs. One of the more promising of the procedures recommended for improving interpretive as well as literal comprehension is semantic webbing (Cleland, 1981; Freeman & Reynolds, 1980). As a technique for organizing categories of information, webbing is appropriate for use with students with and without disabilities. Lovitt (1984) suggests a four-step procedure:

1. The teacher chooses a core question that focuses the web and the inquiry.
2. Strands of the web are determined by student responses to core interpretive questions.
3. Strand supports, or wings, are the facts, inferences, and/or conclusions the students provide from the story or passage.
4. Connectors or ties between core questions and strands reflect relationships between various strands.

A sample of a simple semantic web based upon a single core conclusion about a story is presented in Figure 6.12.

To use a semantic web students must be given a purpose for reading. A core question is usually based on a single page or paragraph. Student responses are then listed on the board. Next the responses to accept, reject, or change according to the reading material are discussed. Rereading may be necessary for some students during the discussion phase. Once relationships have been clarified, the strands are added to the web around the question.

Semantic Maps. Semantic mapping is similar to webbing except that it may be more appropriate for students who require additional direction and structure. Mapping is accomplished by giving the student either a question or key phrase, several possible headings and key predictions or conclusions. Using this information, the student is guided in making decisions based upon the reading. Mapping offers the student more information from which to make decisions than webbing. Throughout the processes of both mapping and webbing the teacher models how he or she is finding, verifying, or rejecting the information for possible use in the strands.

FIGURE 6.12 Sample of a Completed Semantic Web

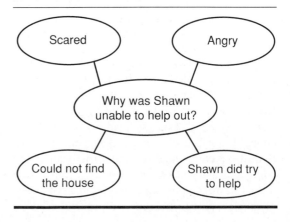

Simulation. In 1975, Herber and Nelson suggested a procedure called simulation, although it has little to do with simulations as the term is generally used. The technique comprises a series of contrived activities used to encourage the student to draw conclusions and determine cause and effect relationships. To create a simulation exercise, you must first construct words or phrases that represent possible cause and effect relationships in the assigned material. After each group of words a number is given to indicate the line from which the concept was taken. A simulation experience could look like this:

Example: storm/power loss (4)
emergency/siren (6)
help/police officers (7)

From looking at this example, you can get some idea about the story, but without reading the material you can not accurately determine if the relationships exist in the story. Perhaps the police helped, but the passage may tell about the fire department or a neighbor. As a guide for reading, students are asked to verify or reject and modify each stated cause and effect. After reading, students discuss and then decide on the basis of the passage if teacher-generated statements are reasonable. Discussion is suggested to help clarify responses for acceptance or rejection of each statement. Statements to extend the previous example might include these: Storms are unhealthy; We can expect help during an emergency; or Help is always welcome.

Critical Comprehension.   Critical reading involves evaluating what is read. Evaluation from the standpoint of the author's purpose or bias, evaluation of persuasive intent (propaganda), and evaluation as fact or opinion are all considered a part of critical comprehension. Five strategies are presented for teaching critical comprehension: critical questioning, criteria, text analysis, content turnabout, and GRP.

Critical Questioning.   Questioning can provide a useful purpose in teaching higher level comprehension skills when it is used in a manner which emphasizes process and teacher use of probed inquiry. When used with specific criteria for evaluating text, the guidelines in Figure 6.13, the first four from Rakes (1984) and the fifth from

---

FIGURE 6.13   *Guidelines for Critical Questioning*

1. **Acknowledge Responses.** Use eye contact between the respondent and the teacher to acknowledge students' answers.

2. **Allow for Answers from More Than One Student.** Collect several answers and guide students in deciding which answers are most appropriate according to what they have read and the evaluation criteria. As needed, refer back to text to verify, justify, expand, or disregard an answer. Remember, in dealing with fiction, opinions, and propaganda, there are frequently several appropriate answers.

3. **Encourage Every Pupil Response.** By allowing several students to respond together or freely in pairs or groups, you encourage participation without judgment. Responses may be given by having students raise one finger for yes and two fingers for no, color cards, or the letters "Y" and "N." Then ask for answer justification.

4. **Provide Answer Cues.** If students are reluctant or confused about how to respond, use both verbal and nonverbal hints to guide them to find or create answers. As a rule of thumb, use two to four questions (cues) or nonverbal actions (act outs).

5. **Allow for Think Time.** After asking a question, allow students from five to seven seconds to begin responding. If no response is given, begin to cue students for answers. Encourage discussion, multiple responses, and clarification.

Gambrell (1980), convey the type of involvement and student centered interaction necessary for questioning to improve critical thinking and responses.

Many teachers have a tendency to elicit answers and race on to another problem or question. By doing this, they fail to clarify why one or two answers are most appropriate and, more importantly, to leave some students wondering about the source of the answer. Teacher-directed questioning can be indispensable in teaching critical comprehension. For this to happen, however, you must focus upon helping students provide their own answers, predictions, or opinions. The teacher-directed talk through, act out, sorting of possible answers, and probing of a curious problem are necessary if critical comprehension is to be taught.

Criteria. To evaluate text, a student must have criteria against which to compare the material. These criteria may be student- or teacher-generated. Initially, the teacher may pose one rule to help students make judgments. In detecting bias, for example, tell students to watch for all positive or all negative statements. Ask them to read a selection that is obviously biased and to cite all the evidence of author bias. List the bias elements on a display chart. Help students add to the list as you guide them to discover other indices of bias. This same procedure can be followed for distinguishing fact from fiction and opinion, judging the worth of a selection, and detecting author purpose. In teaching recognition of propaganda, provide direct instruction in the different types of propaganda techniques before establishing criteria. Without criteria for evaluation, students can only express uninformed opinions.

Text Analysis. The PMI tool suggested by Edward de Bono (1985) illustrates to students the very heart of critical comprehension. Using this technique the reader can more readily weigh and evaluate text. The student first considers Positive or P points, then Minus or M points. Interesting or I features that may even be neutral are also explored. The PMI tool helps to establish criteria.

The worth of each positive, negative, and interesting feature must then be weighed. The results of such an analysis provide the content for the student to make judgments about the text.

Content Turnabout. Lessons in content areas offer excellent opportunities to teach fact, opinion, and propaganda techniques. To do this, you should: (1) provide phrase or sentence cards or chalkboard listings for a student to accept or reject, (2) ask the student to locate and describe a particular opinion or propaganda technique in a specific portion of the reading material, and (3) then use a story or passage as the stimulus for a student to rewrite information so that it reflects the opposite of the original. This strategy demonstrates how facts become fiction or opinion and how fiction can be authenticated with facts.

GRP. The final recommendation for critical comprehension is called the Guided Reading Procedure (GRP) (Manzo, 1985). The GRP is particularly well suited for social studies and science materials as well as for general fact-filled reading materials. To implement, follow steps such as these:

1. Provide a purpose for reading and advise the student to remember as much as possible; after reading have student close the book.
2. Ask the students to recall everything they can about the selection; list information on board.
3. Have the students read the information on the board and then reread the selection to add or correct the list.
4. Next, assist students in organizing the list, an outline, semantic web or map, or perhaps a diagram.
5. Using the newly organized information, ask synthesizing questions requiring use of the information to make judgments. Questions should require the evaluation of author purpose, bias, and other critical reading subskills. Student-generated questions can also be used. (This is an excellent point at which to evaluate the relevance of the information to the student, peers, and others.)

6. Administer a test to assess short-term memory. The test should be the type you typically use in class (multiple choice, essay, matching, or true-or-false questions). Discuss the answers to the questions.
7. Administer a different test on the same information two to four days later. This test could be constructed from student input.

Critical comprehension can be improved by using a process-centered questioning approach, evaluation criteria and tools, QARs, rewriting techniques, or the Guided Reading Procedure. Prediction and curiosity arousal are also important. Vacca and Vacca (1993) offer an entertaining and practical discussion of brainstorming, valuing, and problem solving techniques in the teaching of critical comprehension skills.

Words-in-Context.   The direct and daily teaching of vocabulary is a requirement of effective instruction. Learning to understand words in context, especially figurative language, can be one of the more interesting and enjoyable instructional activities. Many of the word meaning strategies in Chapter 5 are also appropriate for teaching contextual usage. In addition to these, three specific developmental strategies are particularly appropriate for improving student use of

context in understanding word meanings: cloze, possible and impossible sentences, and context specifics. All include a writing component, which can be adapted for the teacher's dictation for students who require it.

Cloze.   The cloze procedure, introduced in 1957 by Taylor, was cited as an alternative assessment strategy earlier in this chapter. As mentioned, a passage is taken from a student's textbook and words are deleted using a predetermined interval of deletion (e.g., every seventh word). The student is then asked to fill in the missing words using context clues.

Adapted cloze exercises differ from story frames mentioned earlier in this chapter. The deletions include only one or two words per blank and, in general, do not require removing as much original information as do story frames. As an instructional strategy, considerable flexibility is allowed in the choice of answers; if a word makes sense in the context of the sentence, it is "correct." Three different cloze instructional formats are presented in Figure 6.14, but regardless of the particular format, a student may complete the blanks by reading orally or silently. Oral reading is often used in checking students' responses. Reutzel (1986) suggests the use of a cloze story map technique. Other variations of

FIGURE 6.14   Three Formats for Instructional Cloze Activities

Format One: Cloze activities may be presented as a series of sentences:

1. We _____ arrived on time.
2. Most of the _____ were _____ about the score.
3. _____ we were able to _____ who won the race.

Format Two: A cloze activity can also be presented in paragraph style:

Most of the group arrived on time. Only _____ boys came _____ in late. We all _____ at them as they _____ the room. In fact, _____ were almost _____ to come in at all.

Format Three: Cloze exercises can also include cues in text.

Each time the (group, train) came near the animal, we could (see, hear) a soft whimper. Even so, it was (important, empty) that no more (time, daylight) was lost if the group was to (return, wander) to camp by nightfall.

cloze activities are explained as developmental strategies in Chapter 10.

Possible Sentences.   Possible Sentences (Moore & Moore, 1992) is a strategy that involves constructing sentences prior to reading and then modifying them according to story content. There are four basic steps that can be used for individuals or groups of students.

1. Select six to eight words from the passage. Choose problem words, key words, or words of particular interest to the student. List these words on the chalkboard.
2. Pronounce the words with the students. Then have students use one or two words in sentences. Print the sentences on the chalkboard, underlining the target words.
3. Ask students to read the story.
4. After reading is completed, use teacher-directed discussion and rereading to decide how the sentence can be modified to correlate with passage content. If the target words are used in a different context than in the story, help students to reword the sentences to match what actually happened in the story.

Impossible Sentences.   An alternative to Possible Sentences is Impossible Sentences. For this procedure, omit steps one and two in the procedures described above. After reading is completed, provide students with sentences emphasizing the target words. These should include appropriate and inappropriate use of the target words. If you wish, you can provide the impossible sentences before reading is begun. After reading, have students reword the impossible sentences. Although Impossible Sentences saves time, the longer participatory procedures for Possible Sentences are preferable.

Context Specifics.   A final concern in teaching words in context is that the written product should be left in a correct context. This means using phrases and sentences to reflect the correct or pertinent meaning for a specific lesson story. Telling or providing oral examples is not sufficient. The visual representation of the appropriate usage must be shown to maximize student learning and mastery of context. This is particularly important for emphasizing the influence of context on words with multiple meanings.

Corrective Strategies

Strategies for correcting comprehension difficulties are usually more focused than developmental methods. Many developmental and corrective strategies share common features, making a distinction difficult. Mercer and Mercer (1993) suggest an instructional continuum between the two, with the teacher modifying the strategy so as to adjust it to student needs. Unlike some content areas, comprehension is not a process that can be readily subdivided into units. Although corrective strategies necessarily involve more than one comprehension level or subskill, it is the teacher who initially directs the student to concentrate on a target task until it is accomplished, who focuses on the task through maintenance strategies, and thereafter who provides periodic review. The teacher should provide not only direct training in reading but also the specific strategies for achieving the reading tasks. For low-achieving and exceptional students, this concentrated instruction on a single comprehension item is particularly important (Burns, Roe, & Ross, 1992). Once the student achieves the objective, the focus may shift among the subskills according to needs. It is equally important to plan lessons that demonstrate the interactive nature of reading and to assist the student in integrating all mastered comprehension tasks.

Most of the highly specialized methods for teaching reading to students who require intensive instruction focus on word recognition rather than on comprehension. In so far as word recognition facilitates comprehension, the intensive approaches, such as the various multisensory methods, cited in the previous chapter are primarily indirect comprehension methods. As such, their major function in correcting comprehension performance is a supplementary one, to help students with particularly troublesome words that may be interfering with comprehension.

When planning and implementing a corrective reading program, Carnine, Silbert, and Kameenui (1990) recommend including six essential elements: extra direct instruction, early intervention, expert personnel, rapid pace, and deliberate motivation. The corrective strategies that follow are designed to provide explicit and extra instruction in both skills and strategies with the teacher incorporating the other five elements into each lesson and the overall plan.

General Comprehension Strategies.   Several corrective strategies are appropriate for teaching most of the comprehension subskills, either separately or in combinations. Although these may seem simplistic, they can be effective.

Repeated Readings.   Evidence suggests that repeated readings of a passage may improve comprehension (Amlund, Kardash, & Kulhavy, 1986; Bos, 1982). Most of the decoding of individual words takes place during the initial reading. With up to three repetitions (Beattie, 1994), comprehension tends to increase because the burden of decoding individual words is lightened, freeing the reader to attend to the meaning of the passage. However, remember to introduce this procedure with a positive explanation so as to prevent the student from becoming bored or frustrated.

Unit Boundaries.   Highlighting with a felt marker the phrase boundaries in each sentence and the thought units within each paragraph assists some students. The markings cluster the meaning units, making the passage more comprehensible. Henk, Helfeldt, and Platt (1986) suggest beginning with phrases of a few words and expanding the marked phrase length as the student becomes more proficient. Eventually encourage the students to make the markings themselves.

Focused Listening Activities.   Listening comprehension activities that focus on a specific task are a logical prelude to teaching students special techniques to accomplish the task. Before reading a short story aloud give the student a listening purpose that targets a specific task. Tell the student to listen to find out, for example, what

caused Leonard to run away (interpretive comprehension: cause and effect). If the student readily answers, ask for a description of how he or she knew the answer. If the answer is incorrect, seize the opportunity to explain or model how you know the answer. In the absence of interfering auditory disabilities, this strategy provides a foundation for developing and modeling comprehension techniques. Strategic listening and structured listening activities described earlier are easily modified to emphasize the particular tasks for which a student needs instruction and practice. Focused listening activities are appropriate as comprehension readiness strategies for students of any age and are often enjoyable for teachers and students as well.

Thought Modeling.   Modeling the thought processes that lead to a solution or answer is not a new technique. For generations teachers asked students to write a question or problem on the board and then to describe how the answer was derived. However, what is relatively new about modeling is the recognition of its contribution to improving student achievement and its integration into other than "did you do your homework" activities. Good and Brophy (1994) suggest that the teacher think aloud, verbalizing each step of the thinking process. This procedure offers students a model of the teacher's specific techniques for solving a problem or finding the answer. For corrective instruction in comprehension, the strategy is invaluable, since the steps followed in understanding text are not visible as they are in solving arithmetic computation tasks. Not only should the teacher provide a model for the various comprehension subskills and tasks, but students should also be encouraged to analyze how they formulate their answers, thereby examining the techniques that are and are not effective for them. The student who correctly answers is doubly reinforced when you care enough to ask, "How did you know that?" The student thus becomes aware of reasoning patterns that should be continued. Similarly, by examining the reasoning that led to incorrect responses (an error-analysis process) the student can discard faulty patterns and techniques. This strategy also provides peers an additional, and sometimes alternate, model for understanding what they read. It is important to guide the student's verbalizations of thought processes gently and to appreciate the diverse techniques that different learners use effectively.

Level Reduction.   As a general rule, when possible drop back one or two reading levels below the student's instructional reading level in teaching specific comprehension subskills and tasks. This lessens the concept and vocabulary load and allows the student to attend to the target task. If the student's reading level is too low to allow this tactic, conduct instruction as a listening/oral activity. The reading level of the stimulus text should be gradually increased as the student progresses.

Captioned Videos.   Captioned television programs, intended for persons with hearing impairments, offer excellent comprehension activities that also can be highly motivational. Designated as close captioned (CC) in television guides and on screen during opening credits, captioned programs can be videotaped for use in the classroom. In addition to using the tapes to teach word meanings, as discussed in Chapter 5, the tapes are appropriate for teaching and practicing a variety of reading comprehension skills and strategies. Goldman (1993) succinctly presents details and ideas for implementation in a concise booklet. He suggests leaving the sound on for the first five minutes of a program to introduce the characters and provide a mental set; then turn off the sound and guide students to read the captions. Periodically pause the program for meaningful discussions and to predict and set purposes for additional reading/viewing. Teachers should preview each program and consider constructing a study guide appropriate to student needs. Students for whom English is a second language and some students with special needs may benefit from leaving the sound on for longer periods to permit them to see and hear the script simultaneously.

Semantic Mapping.   When simplified, semantic mapping, presented as a developmental strategy, may provide the student with a useful tool. By categorizing the relationships among the various concepts, the student is organizing the information. The actual map presents the student with an extra visual cue; it may also aid the student in predicting outcomes (Sinatra, Berg & Dunn, 1985).

Story Guides.   A method for assisting the student to organize information, modified story frames are recommended for use as a corrective strategy. Fowler and Davis (1985) suggest presenting students with a simplistic frame and talking them through a familiar story. By presenting decreasingly familiar stories and increasing the difficulty of the stories, the teacher can guide the students into using the frame to organize the text at the appropriate reading level. As students progress, the story guides can be expanded to include additional elements. Variations of this approach include cutting or typing a story into sentences and helping students piece it together according to each story element, guiding students in marking each story element in the actual text as they read (Lovitt, 1984); or marking the texts for the students, coding each element by number, and gradually guiding the students in marking the elements themselves.

Self-Monitoring.   To increase student awareness of the strategies that facilitate comprehension, Lipson and Wickizer (1989) suggest five categories of behaviors to teach and reinforce: (1) pause and reflect, (2) hypothesize, (3) monitor, (4) integrate, and (5) clarify. Self-monitoring is a procedure that many students who experience reading difficulty must be directly taught. According to Brown and Palincsar (1982) self-questioning, paraphrasing, clarifying, and predicting are important strategies for students to use in monitoring their own performance while reading.

To help students self-monitor their reading, give them a self-rating checklist to follow as they read. Have them record the location of any difficult part, and ask them to indicate which of these

"READER Help" strategies they used and to rate how they worked:

Reread or read on
Examine the graphics
Ask self-questions
Do over (Start over)
Examine a mental image
Rephrase
Help: Get it!

The student ratings of strategy effectiveness provide content for lively discussions and debates and also emphasize the strategies themselves and how and when to use them.

Self-Regulation.   Students need to know what to do when they realize that they are having difficulty comprehending while reading. According to Haller, Child, and Walberg (1988), direct instruction in strategies to correct comprehension failures results in improved comprehension. Recommended strategies to teach include: relate the text to what you already know; reread confusing parts and/or preceding parts; read ahead for clarification; associate details with main ideas; consult other sources; seek help; and determine the meanings of unknown vocabulary (Gall, Gall, Jacobsen, & Bullock, 1990). Depending on the age and ability of the students, the format for sequencing and presenting these steps might look like this:

4RAG
R 1   Relate to what you know
   2   Reread
   3   Read preceding
   4   Read ahead
A Associate details with main ideas
G Get word meanings and/or help

Motivational Advancement.   A tactic suggested by Lovitt (1984), "Skip and Drill," is appropriate for use as a motivational and management strategy. Although described as a technique for improving fluency and rate, the tactic is equally applicable to comprehension subskills. Divide a text into several sections with markers or clips.

Decide on the target performance with the student, for example, to improve interpretive comprehension by 20 percent or to answer two more questions correctly. Collect baseline data by having the student read several pages and answer comprehension questions, and record this performance on a chart. Then begin the plan. If the student achieves the goal, he or she skips the rest of the passages in that section and advances to the next section. If not, the student completes the remainder of the section, reviewing the strategies for the specific task (in this case, interpretive comprehension). Not only the act of advancing through the text and "skipping some work" but also the chart and/or peer competition are reinforcing to students.

Low achieving and disinterested readers often need a variety of incentives to engage in tasks that are difficult. Ford and Ohlhausen (1988) suggest several guidelines for motivating students in group situations: (1) identify specific reinforcers for each student, (2) set a reasonable goal for each student and allow alternate means of goal attainment, (3) measure progress in relation to student ability, (4) maintain personal progress records, and (5) emphasize self-competition and group cooperation. Of these suggestions, the first is the most critical factor for deliberate planning of an incentive program.

Glossing.   Glossing refers to the notes, usually in the margins of texts, which assist the reader in understanding the important points of the passages. An adaptation of this technique offers a useful comprehension activity. For each page of a student's reading text, develop a simplified glossed sheet to illustrate specific strategies for task accomplishment. The glossing may either name the point at which specific subskill items appear or present clues coded by number or color. As students learn the code and apply the strategies, they, in turn, can prepare the glossing for a peer. For students who are comprehending text above a fourth-grade level, simplified written clues will probably be more appropriate.

Transition Text.   Transition stories, ones that contain a high percentage of words that the student recognizes, free him or her from rigorous decoding to attend to comprehension. Some supplementary and transitional texts, designed for students who are not quite ready to advance to the next level in a series of readers, are available for purchase. Teachers can compose short transitional stories for each student, based upon the words which the specific student has mastered. Another means of accomplishing the same purpose is to have a more capable reader, as a creative writing activity, compose stories using the appropriate vocabulary. This strategy benefits both the target student and the composing student who expands creative skills as well as comprehension abilities.

Peer Tutoring.   Structured programs for peer tutoring using students with special needs as tutors offer opportunities to improve both comprehension and social skills. Three tutorial formats are recommended (Maheady, Mallette, Harper, Sacca, & Pomerantz, 1994): (1) cross-age tutoring, in which older students with disabilities teach younger students with similar disabilities; (2) reverse-role tutoring, in which the older students with disabilities teach younger students without disabilities; and (3) classwide peer tutoring, a highly structured system. Common problems occurring with peer-mediated instruction include increased noise levels, student bickering, and cheating. Because each format is research-supported for improving comprehension, Maheady and colleagues suggest selecting the option that is consistent with instructional objectives, feasible for the particular situation, and enjoyable for teacher and students.

Early Intervention Programs.   Several special programs designed to intervene in reading difficulties are gaining favor. Descriptions and reports of a variety of early intervention programs are presented by Hiebert and Taylor (1994). For example, one such program, Success for All, has been especially effective in disadvantaged urban schools. This schoolwide improvement program includes preventive and interventive reading instruction. Significant gains in reading achievement are reported for kindergarten and first-grade participants, and reading gains of students in all grades increase each year their school is in the program (Slavin, Madden, Dolan, Wasik, Ross, & Smith, 1994). Reading Recovery, developed by Marie Clay and adopted as a national program in New Zealand in 1983, is a widely known early intervention program. As described by Gaffney (1994), Reading Recovery, designed to prevent school failure, is currently being implemented in several countries including the United States. In participating schools, first-grade teachers select children experiencing the most problems learning to read and write. The chosen children receive structured and intensive tutoring for 30 minutes daily from specially trained teachers. Students who continue to experience difficulty after 20 weeks of tutoring are referred to special services. Gaffney partially attributes the program's success to the strict teacher training model, wherein specifically trained university faculty train teacher leaders, who then train other teachers. Quality control is also maintained by licensure granted only to programs meeting guidelines established by Clay and the Ohio State University.

Structured early intervention programs have implications for corrective reading instruction. First, if they are successful, reading intervention could receive even more emphasis (and funding) as an early childhood concept. Second, certain features of the programs are appropriate for corrective instruction at any age level: special teacher training; curricular adaptations; the tutorial approach; highly structured small-group instruction; intervention across the grades; and schoolwide intervention facilitators.

In addition to the corrective strategies for teaching general comprehension skills, a few corrective strategies are particularly appropriate for teaching specific comprehension subskills or tasks. Presented according to subskill, some of the strategies can be modified to teach adjacent subskills.

Literal Comprehension. Corrective instruction in literal comprehension focuses on three tasks confronting students: recognizing details, locating them in text, and remembering the facts. The glossing strategy discussed earlier is particularly helpful in guiding students to find important details. Four additional strategies are described for assisting students in accomplishing the three key tasks.

WH Questions. The WH questions are the ones that occur most frequently in recalling details. Teach a student to ask these reporter questions, "who," "what," "when," "where," while reading. Give the students a list of the questions and a below-level passage to read. Use each questioning word, in the order listed, to preface a statement in the passage. Ask students to locate the answers and read them. After the students have practiced on several passages, increase passage difficulty and repeat. Then, still following the order of the list, ask questions that paraphrase story statements. When students can follow the strategy and answer correctly, guide them in using the list while reading independently, lightly checking or highlighting the answers as they are found. Gradually fade the cues as students begin to use the self-monitoring strategy.

Question Guides. Bruno and Newman (1985) describe a structured procedure for teaching literal comprehension to mainstreamed exceptional children. Using short passages on a student's reading level, the teacher writes multiple-choice detail questions, including less obvious distractor items for each successive lesson. The student is initially given a short passage to read and one simple detail question to answer. The answer to the question is highlighted in the passage. The student must demonstrate task mastery on three similar passages in a single session to progress through the plan. Over a series of lessons the highlighted cues are faded, the passages become longer, and the questions increase in difficulty. The student must defend inaccurate answers and correct them. This strategy also helps students to master content area concepts. Reciprocal questioning between a more capable reader and the target student is an effective means of correcting and practicing literal questioning and answering.

Structuring Text. To help students recognize important text parts and then organize them, specific guides are helpful. Similar to story frames, guides to text structure outline the key questions the student should answer as he or she reads. For narrative text, the outline given to students students usually contains these elements:

- When and where does the story take place?
- Who are the main characters?
- What is the story problem?
- If it is solved, how?

To teach students the structure of a particular type of text it is important to present a generic guide that applies to all passages of that type. Students trained to use such procedures often can do so independently and improve in their comprehension of text (Idol, 1987).

CAPS Plus. The effectiveness of story structure training may increase when it is paired with training in self-questioning. Griffey, Zigmond, and Leinhardt (1988) describe the use of this particular combination, noting its effectiveness. Their story structure model is CAPS: Characters, Aim, Problem, Solution. The results of their study suggest that students be taught a model and also coached to ask themselves questions about each element as they read.

Interpretive Comprehension. Guiding students through the comprehension of a story step by step may improve performance. It is important to illustrate to students the relationship of passage details to interpretive comprehension. Rupley and Blair (1989) describe a procedure that requires the student to read in order to solve teacher-posed problems. The teacher guides a discussion to relate each answer to previous answers and to provide the background for future answers. POP, Written Structure, Logic, Summarization, and Literacy Games are among the other strategies that are suggested for corrective instruction in interpretive comprehension.

POP.   To assist students in identifying the main idea of a passage, a series of "Pick or Pass" (POP) strategies is effective. These constitute a type of thought modeling using "pick" for the acceptable solutions and "pass" for questionable or unacceptable solutions. The steps to follow in implementing POP are presented in Figure 6.15.

Written Structure.   Englert and Lichter (1982) describe another procedure for teaching the main idea. They suggest providing the student with a written structure to follow for the main idea and supporting details. The model follows the "Statement-Pie" example by Hanau (1974). The statement is the main idea and the pieces of the pie are the proof, information, and examples.

Students use the pieces of the pie to formulate the main idea statement.

Logic.   To aid students in relating cause and effect, Rupley and Blair (1989) suggest logical continuation activities. Give students a sentence and request another sentence that would logically follow the first sentence. Students can also be asked to match the continuations with stimuli sentences. For drawing conclusions, omit every other sentence of a passage and ask students to supply the missing sentences that would logically fit. To help transfer the skill, ask students to read only a portion of a story and predict the remainder according to a logical fit. Reciprocal questioning, using the POP strategy for establishing logical answers, is also helpful for polishing techniques in determining cause and effect and drawing conclusions.

FIGURE 6.15   Seven Steps for Using POP

1. Present a sequence of pictures; ask student to select the one that is the most important, or "If you could only use one picture to tell this story, which one would you pick and why?" Give the picked picture a name. Model the Pick or Pass method by describing the first picture and saying something like, "This picture is not so important; I'll pass." Describe the second picture, "This picture tells some of the story. I'll pick it; it's the best one yet, but I'll check the others to be sure." Describe the third picture by saying "Picture number three is really important; now I'll pass number two and pick number three."

2. From the picture sequences, progress to a short listening story, asking the student to pick the most important sentence, verbalizing the POP strategies, and then giving the story a name. If the student has difficulty, model; if not, practice and move on to step 3.

3. Repeat step 2, but with the student orally reading similar short stories and using POP to select the most important sentences; model if needed, and then provide practice.

4. Explain that the main or topic sentence is the author's own main idea or summary statement. Repeat steps 2 and 3 using passages with topic sentences as the first sentence in the paragraph and then as the last sentence in paragraph. Ask the student to POP the main ideas using topic sentences. Gradually increase passage length and/or difficulty.

5. Explain and demonstrate that topic sentences can also occur in the middle of paragraphs and repeat steps 2 and 3, interspersing step 4 with appropriate samples. Ask student to POP topic sentences and explain main ideas.

6. Repeat the steps using four to six paragraphs. Have student find the main idea of each paragraph and then POP the main ideas of the entire passages.

7. Once the student has become proficient with preceding steps, explain that the topic sentence may not be stated; the reader may have to invent or guess what it is. Practice with passages used in previous steps, but remove topic sentences and ask student to state main ideas. Again model POP if needed.

Summarization.   To teach students to summarize, display an easy passage and a summary of it either on the chalkboard or on a transparency. First demonstrate identifying the most important information in the passage, underlining each point as you think aloud. Next, delete the unimportant information by erasing it on the board or marking through it on the transparency. Highlight the words that are left that match those contained in the sample summary. Then rephrase the important points to match the summary, thinking aloud as you do so. Finally coach students to repeat the procedures with several different passages and summaries. Guide students to derive a list of clues and procedures to follow when summarizing and post their list as a reminder for later use when they are ready for additional practice.

Literacy Games.   Games can increase interest and involvement in reading and listening activities. Richards (1993) suggests developing games that call for students to respond personally to story characters and support their opinions and thoughts with story information. She describes two appealing card games, one matching descriptive cards with story characters, and one predicting and then justifying what well-known characters would do in described situations. Peer instruction is built in, because both games are played cooperatively rather than competitively. These and other creative games can be constructed by teacher or students to reflect the literature of the particular curriculum. In addition to offering students an entertaining opportunity to improve interpretive comprehension, the cooperative games offer an excellent source for alternative assessment. Students' behavior during the game can reveal their interpretive comprehension skills, strategy usage, social skills, oral expression skills, and, across time, their rate of growth in each area.

Critical Comprehension.   Critical comprehension is particularly difficult for low-achieving students. Many of these learners tend to be uncomfortable when there is no one correct answer. They must be gently led to explore options.

Brainstorms.   Structured brainstorming sessions are the mainstay of critical comprehension. Brainstorming can be conducted with only one student and the teacher or with more students. Once all possibilities have been exhausted for a given topic, the teacher can model how to think through the selection process.

DRA and CAA.   The results of studies conducted by Sachs (1983) suggest two specific procedures for correcting and improving critical comprehension performance. The first procedure is a Directed Reading Activity (DRA) modified into a prereading activity. This model follows four steps: (1) The student selects an illustration from the text and discusses it with the teacher; (2) the student's past experiences are related to story pictures; (3) key vocabulary words are presented in context, with teacher and student reading each key sentence; the student composes a sentence with each word; this is followed by a five-minute discussion focusing on the theme of the story; and (4) the teacher reads the story title, and the student predicts the story content. The second procedure, a modified Concept Analysis Activity (CAA), is also used as a prereading activity. It also includes four steps: (1) The teacher writes the main concept of the passage on a sheet of paper; (2) teacher and student together cite examples of the concept, and the teacher lists them on the paper; (3) they cite nonexamples and list them; and (4) the student states a definition of the concept, and the teacher writes it on the paper. Sachs concludes that these two structured prereading experiences can be used to assist students in evaluating the textual information.

Rating Texts.   Asking students to rate texts on the basis of predetermined criteria is a motivational strategy. Guide students in establishing criteria for recommending or not recommending text to peers. The lower the level of student comprehension, the less complex should be the criteria. A coding system can be developed to mark the reading materials. Three stars on the spine of a text may mean that three students think the book is great. As comprehension skills increase, expand the system to include not only the appeal of the text but also an indication of whether the material is fact, fiction, bias, or propaganda.

SORT.   A strategy students can use to sort facts from fiction is SORT. Assign the task of categorizing the information in a passage according to accuracy—for naive students, identifying real versus make believe elements and for more capable students, factual elements versus opinion or propaganda. To introduce the strategy, post a list with two columns. Using the familiar children's story about the three bears, for example, head one column "real" and the other "make believe." Then guide students to systematically analyze the parts of the the story that could *really* happen and those that could not, using the SORT steps:

> **S**een or Source
> **O**r
> **R**ead in References
> **T**hink

For events to be classified as possibly real they must have been seen or verified by an authoritative source, (the S) or (the O) read about in a legitimate reference (R), or concluded by logical and defensible thinking or thought (T). Make believe elements are those so categorized using the same strategies or ones excluded because they cannot be verified. Samples of students' classification of events in the story of the three bears are depicted in Figure 6.16. As evidenced by the creative responses, students often find this an enjoyable learning activity. The strategy itself outlines the thinking process for evaluating the veracity of text.

Words-in-Context.   Many strategies for teaching and correcting word meaning skills, discussed in Chapter 5, also apply to correcting contextual usage skills. Four additional strategies are suggested for this subskill.

Structured Cloze.   Cloze activities are contextual usage activities. Modified cloze and maze activities force the student to use context clues.

FIGURE 6.16   SORTing the Three Bears: A Sampling

REAL	PROOF	MAKE BELIEVE	PROOF
A bear family with dad the biggest, mom the next, and the kid the littlest	Seen at zoo Saw videotape Read science book	Mama bear cooks porridge	Read science book Seen eating at zoo Think: If they could cook they wouldn't choose porridge! What's porridge anyway?
Bears walk in woods	Seen at zoo Read reference Think: bears walk live in woods	Bears live in house	Saw videotape Read reference Think: Where would they get money to buy it? How would they paint it?
Nosy little girl	Seen in class I'm one!	Girl going in bears' house	Think: House isn't real so she can't go in. She'd have to be stupid too and the story just said she was nosy.
Girl tastes porridge	Think: She could if she really was dumb, but I sure wouldn't	Girl sits in bears' chairs	Think: Chairs aren't real 'cause house isn't real; she can't sit in make believe chairs.

Gunn and Elkins (1979) suggest, however, that cloze tasks vary according to the level of conscious processing and reasoning ability they require. By beginning with cloze activities that use highly predictable context, you can assist students in developing reasonably reliable context techniques. As students progress, more abstract text can be used. For additional explanation and examples of cloze activities, refer to Chapters 5 and 10.

Oral Cloze.   For students who need additional instruction in contextual analysis, present cloze or modified cloze activities orally. This can be done informally by the teacher reading aloud a story. Stop reading and ask, "What word do you think will come next? Listen to see if you're correct." Or the teacher can ask the student to guess the missing word in groups of sentences. "The __?__ ran down the street. What words could fit? Listen to the next sentence and see if you guessed correctly." The teacher and student or two students may take turns quizzing each other. As each response is given, the context clues to correct answers should be discussed.

Mad Libs.   A particularly amusing strategy to both students and teachers is Mad Libs, published by Price, Stern, and Sloan Publishers. Available by mail order or from local bookstores, these consumable pads of cloze activities ask students for specific categories of words. The words are then placed in the contexts provided. For example, a student may be asked for his or her name, an action word, a number, favorite color, and favorite subject. The student who answers "Annette, eating, twenty-seven, pink, and math" would then place the answers in the context of the next page of the pad. The story would then begin with "Did you hear about Annette eating twenty-seven worms with pink eyes during math?" Since each page presents a different story, the function of context is stressed in a fanciful manner that few students find boring. Students also enjoy composing these activities for their peers. The composition of such activities can also be paired with focused instruction in written expression. The

higher-level Mad Libs refer to the word categories by parts of speech; they reinforce word function as well as context.

Travel Libs.   Travel Libs, similar to the game of gossip, is a variation of the Mad Libs activity. This game presents an enjoyable means for three or more students to practice their use of context. The teacher (or student) starts the game by writing three words on paper to begin a sentence and then whispering a request for a word of a particular category from a student. The student, in turn, whispers a response that is written on the paper and passed on. The process is repeated with each student supplying a word without knowing the context into which his or her word will be inserted until it is recorded.

Maintenance Strategies

Maintenance activities in comprehension are particularly important. The more a student reads, the better he or she is able to read. Oral and written practice is essential to improving comprehension. Subskills and tasks should be applied at reading levels that are relatively easy for the student; the difficulty-level of the text should be increased as the student masters the mechanics of the particular task. Maintenance strategies are necessary because even after mastery has been attained, students tend to lose or forget how to apply a skill. Based on a survey of several hundred readers, Rakes and Chance (1990) report that few adolescents and adult readers can name three or more specific techniques they use to remember what they read. They also note that elementary age youngsters are more likely than older readers to recognize and use comprehension strategies. Frequent use of mastered skills is necessary if students are to maintain confidence and remember what they read both in and out of the classroom.

Crawford (1993) suggests developing Structured Learning Centers (SLCs) that integrate the language skills in authentic situations. The centers should focus on real-life situations related to content topics and require the application of language skills. SLCs are particularly appropriate for students from varying cultural backgrounds and students with disabilities because they typically need ample meaningful practice applying language skills in a variety of social and environmental situations.

Microcomputers are particularly useful tools for maintaining many comprehension skills. Mercer and Mercer (1993) suggest that appropriate software programs provide effective reinforcement, practice, and drill, and recommend a few specific programs. Professional journals such as *The Reading Teacher* and *The Journal of Special Education Technology* often present reviews of the most current reading software.

Maintenance strategies for reading comprehension are presented in the pages which follow. Each strategy is referenced according to the number(s) on the curriculum chart for reading comprehension (Figure 6.2). This listing is not intended to be exhaustive but rather to provide some ideas for the teacher to manipulate according to individual teacher and student needs. Many of these activities may be conveniently designed as file folder tasks for independent practice. By using acetate overlays and transparency markers for the student's written responses, the utility of the activities is extended. Self-checking provisions also expand the practicality and effectiveness of the exercises. Choate and Rakes (1989) and Ekwall and Shanker (1993) present a variety of activities for practicing reading comprehension.

Although focused maintenance strategies are important to anchoring a student's comprehension accomplishments, a note of caution is offered: Don't so overwhelm the student with highly structured practice that you fail to provide and encourage recreational practice. The title of an article by Rakes (1973) aptly illustrates this point from a student's view: "Drill Me, Skill Me, But Please Let Me Read."

Literal Comprehension.   While it has not been proven that a student must master literal comprehension before moving to a higher level of com-

prehension, understanding and remembering factual information certainly facilitates higher order comprehension and is essential to academic success as well. Because of the frequency with which students are expected to demonstrate literal comprehension in the classroom, coaching and practice must include strategies for locating and understanding facts in text.

Recalls Details, (IA.1–.9). ▪Prepare a list of detail sentences from the student's text; underline portions of each sentence. Ask the student to either write or select from choices the "wh" question that each underlined part answers. ▪Prepare several short paragraphs or stories containing details. Ask the student to underline the words or statements that answer the "wh" questions. ▪Insert a nonsense sentence into each of several paragraphs; ask the student to read the paragraph and mark through the sentence that does not belong. ▪Have student construct descriptive riddles for classmates. Two students with similar needs can swap riddles; this affords the one who originates the riddle an exercise in attending to detail and the one who solves the riddle an opportunity to practice drawing conclusions.

Recalls Details in Sequence, (IB.1–.9). ▪Cut comic strips into individual frames and ask student to place them in one or more logical sequences. ▪Divide sentences from the student's text into two to four parts, depending upon the reading level and the sentence complexity. Ask student to number the parts in the correct sequence to form a logical sentence. ▪Write the sentences of a paragraph on sentence strips. Ask the student to place the strips in logical sequence to reconstruct the paragraph. ▪Give the student scrambled paragraphs, requesting that the paragraphs be reordered to form a logical story. Or have the student scramble a paragraph or story for a peer and make an answer key.

Interpretive Comprehension.   Developing interpretive comprehension skill, or reading between the lines, requires closely supervised practice. Whereas practice in literal comprehension easily can be monitored because of its exactness, the open-ended nature of many interpretive tasks calls for closer teacher attention to ensure that students are indeed maintaining correct performances.

States Main Idea, (IIA.1–.9). ▪Write a story title on each of several index cards; provide copies of the companion stories. Ask the student to match the titles to the stories and explain choices. ▪From each of several stories written on the student's level, write a main idea statement on one card and several supporting details on another; as an independent activity ask student to match the main ideas with the correct supporting details. ▪Have student write a fax or telegram, copying the words from a passage, to a friend explaining a story; vary the word limit using at different times 10-, 15-, 20-, and 25-word messages. Ask student to explain the choice of words. ▪Prepare a reading passage containing four to six paragraphs; construct a true/false test of main idea statements from each paragraph. Ask student to answer the test before reading and then to correct the answers after reading. This focuses the student's attention on the main points of the passage and presents a model for finding the main idea (Ekwall & Shanker, 1993). ▪Write on each of several index cards a topic sentence from the student's text. Ask the student to find the supporting sentences in the text. Reversing this activity is also appropriate. Write the supporting statements on index cards and ask the student to highlight or copy from the text the topic sentence. An explanatory discussion should follow either activity.

Draws Conclusions, (IIB.1–.9). ▪Remove the last frame of comic strips and ask the student to state or draw the probable ending and explain each. Discuss the reasons for choice. ▪Place a collection of single frame cartoons in a folder. Ask student to state or choose from three statements the events that probably occurred before the cartoon and/or those that probably followed the picture. Discuss reasons for choices. (This activity also expands sequencing abilities.) ▪Prepare sev-

eral riddles on index cards; write the solutions on index cards of a different color. Ask student to match the riddles and answers and explain each selection. ▪Tape a portion of a story. Ask student to listen to the tape and suggest three possible story endings. Then discuss the reasons for choice.

States Cause and Effect, (IIC.1–.5). ▪With peers or with teacher, have student play "Concentration." Write causes on one set of cards; on a set of cards of a different color, write the matching effects. A match is accomplished by pairing the cause with its effect, provided the student can logically explain the cause/effect relationship. ▪Have student match "if/then" statements. Prepare several short paragraphs or stories; on separate cards write the resulting effect or the precipitating cause of each passage. Ask student to match the card with the appropriate passage. An explanatory discussion should follow the activity.

Critical Comprehension.   Without regular application, the ability to read critically is not likely to fully develop and is apt to be soon forgotten. Critical comprehension involves the reader in making active decisions and responses and is a very demanding task. Students need to be encouraged to respond thoughtfully, flexibly, and creatively and then reinforced for doing so.

Evaluates Fact/Fiction/Opinion, (IIIA.1–.9). ▪List several titles, including fact and fiction. Ask student to mark the titles that could be factual with an exclamation point and those that are probably fictional with a question mark. If a title could be either, use both markings. (If the student uses an acetate overlay, the activity can be reused.) Discuss the reasons for choice. This activity can be modified as a fact versus opinion exercise by listing fact and opinion statements. ▪List several opinion statements; ask the student to restate or rewrite the opinions so that they are factual. To vary the activity, list factual statements and ask the student to revise them as opinions or as fantasy statements.

Evaluates Propaganda, (IIIA.10–.1). ▪Prepare two sets of index cards; on one write factual statements; on the other write propaganda statements. Ask student to sort or designate which are factual and which are propaganda. ▪Have the student identify the propaganda strategies used in advertising the products regularly used by the student and/or family. Discuss the influence of each strategy on the family's purchasing habits. ▪On a set of index cards mount real or contrived advertisements. Have the student circle the propaganda strategies and check the factual information. Then analyze and discuss the strategies that most appeal to the student and those that appeal least. ▪Have the student originate advertisements using specified propaganda techniques. Discuss the ads that are and are not appealing and why.

Evaluates Author Purpose/Bias, (IIIB.1–.6). ▪Using short passages from the student's text, ask the student to check the words the author uses that are positive and cross out those that are negative. Classifications such as "happy/sad" or "good/ bad" may be used. Discuss the probable reasons for the author's choice of words. ▪As an extension of the preceding activity, have the student substitute opposite words for those marked. Thus the happy words may be replaced with sad ones, and the sad ones replaced with happy ones. Then read the new story and discuss the changes. (This activity also expands the student's knowledge of word relationships.) ▪List several author purposes (make a point, entertain, give information, etc.). For students with limited abilities the purposes can be portrayed in rebus form. Have student read brief passages and decide which is the probable purpose of the author of each selection.

Single Words in Context, (IVA.1–.9). ▪Prepare a listing of sentences that contain contextual clues (synonyms, appositives, etc.) to the meaning of another word; ask student to circle the clues and check the word that is partially defined. ▪Vary the preceding activity by deleting the target word, asking the student to circle the clues and then to select from three choices the correct word for the blank. ▪List several paragraphs from the student's text. Into each paragraph, insert a word that obviously does not belong. Ask the student to read and cross out the inserted words. To vary the activity, intersperse the odd words randomly instead of putting one in every paragraph. ▪All variations of the cloze, modified cloze, and maze strategies are appropriate activities for this task. ▪For a variety of context activities for grade-levels three and up, use the computer software program, "Cloze-Plus," produced by Milliken.

Figurative Words in Context, (IVB.1–.4). ▪Develop a word bank of figures of speech as they occur in the student's text. On each word card, illustrate the literal meaning, asking the student to either draw or paste pictures to illustrate the figurative meaning. ▪Using a computer program for developing crossword puzzles, construct puzzles, with figures of speech as the stimulus and one-word synonyms as the required puzzle response. Present each figure of speech in a sentence, underlining the target word(s). ▪Tape passages from the student's text, emphasizing the figures of speech; prepare a list of the figurative language. Beside each figure of speech list a one-word synonym and two foils in random order. Ask the student to listen and circle the meaning of the target word(s). Then discuss with the student the reasons for choices, highlighting the contextual clues. As a follow-up activity have the student read the same passages in the text and explain each figure of speech.

Implementing the CBA/P Model

As in other subjects, the curriculum-based assessment/programming cycle presented in Chapter 3 is recommended as the format for assessing and programming in reading comprehension. Because reading comprehension cuts across all areas of the curriculum, particular elements in each step of the cycle should be emphasized.

Step 1: Analyze the Curriculum

In addition to identifying the general requirements of the system's and the teacher's reading comprehension curriculum, it is important to determine the extent of explicit comprehension instruction that the teacher offers. The itemization of specific comprehension skills means that they are tested but may not ensure that they are taught. Ask for specific examples of the reading strategies taught and the ways in which they are presented. Of particular interest is the teacher's philosophical approach to reading instruction: Is it primarily skill-based and a self-contained reading program? Or is a whole language approach favored? If so, how does the teacher teach and monitor skills? What is the role of basal readers in the program? What is the nature of independent comprehension activities? How much guidance does the teacher provide for workbook and seatwork activities? Compare the curricular analysis in comprehension with that in word recognition. How much emphasis does the teacher place on word pronunciation and how much on comprehension? And finally, how much direct instruction does the teacher provide for comprehending text not designated as reading materials? What are the comprehension expectations in other subjects? Answers to these questions clarify curricular demands for both the teacher and the diagnostician.

Step 2: Assess Skills

To indirectly assess student performance, continue the teacher interview. Ask for the teacher's estimate of the impact of the student's comprehension on overall academic achievement and the degree to which the student's comprehension is facilitated or impeded by his or her word recognition skills. If not previously determined, check school records to see if differences in reading performance might be related to a change in reading programs. Analyze scores on any recently administered tests to identify differences in word recognition and comprehension performances and to examine comprehension subskills. Also inspect the reading demands of tests in other areas to investigate the impact of comprehension there. Analyze work samples in reading workbooks, other written assignments in reading, and in all

subject areas to gain to confirm teacher estimates and identify performance patterns.

Using indirect assessment data, hypothesize the nature of difficulties, the impact of the student's word recognition skills on comprehension, and the degree to which his or her comprehension performances affect overall academic achievement. Establish initial assessment priorities according to the specific comprehension tasks the student must demonstrate most frequently in the classroom. In an interview with the student ask specific questions to identify his or her particular reading interests as well as understanding and use of strategies to accomplish the target tasks. Directly assess the student's performance using actual passages from classroom reading materials where possible; if time permits and preliminary data indicate, globally assess comprehension of texts for other subjects as well. Throughout testing encourage the student to think aloud the strategies he or she is using to make sense of text. Follow administration of test items with questions about strategy usage as needed. Analyze and record responses and base preliminary program planning on assessment results.

Step 3: Program for Assessed Needs

Begin programming by following the curriculum-based assessment/programming cycle (CBA/P), using the annotated curriculum chart (Figure 6.2) for content and a systematic plan (Figure 3.15). According to the student's most pressing needs, select a specific comprehension subskill and related tasks.

Select teaching strategies to accommodate student and teacher needs and plan three stages of instruction. For initial instruction, drop one or two reading levels below that at which the student reads comfortably. To improve the likelihood of student and teacher success, increase passage difficulty only when the student appears to understand and apply a systematic approach to the task using "easy" reading materials. Consider the student who understands most of the content of third-grade passages but has difficulty finding the main idea. An appropriate point at which to begin focused teaching may be main idea activities using first-grade passages.

Developmental Instruction.   When introducing new tasks and materials, first try the methods of the student's teacher or the ones suggested in the teacher's edition of the reading text. Evaluate progress by assessing performance of taught tasks in the context of whole passages, and then plan maintenance instruction for tasks that are tentatively mastered and corrective strategies for those that are unmastered.

Corrective Instruction.   Determining the specific strategy for teaching the target subskill and task depends upon the student's learning patterns. Although a strategy may be assumed to accommodate the learner's needs, its efficacy can only be substantiated by the rate and ease of the student's mastery of the task at hand. Provide explicit instruction in the strategies for accomplishing specific tasks and then coach the student in applying those strategies to comprehend whole passages. Repeat Step 2, assessment. For tasks that remain unmastered, modify instruction according to the assessment/programming cycle changing methods first, next materials, then methods and materials, and finally the task level until tentative mastery is achieved. Among the changes in reading materials to consider are substituting passages of high interest, shortening passages, and reducing the reading level of the text. To reduce the task level, shift to a selection level format, providing the student choices from which to choose responses; to increase task demands, shift to a production or application level format and to higher level text. Retain tentatively mastered tasks in the program for maintenance instruction.

Maintenance Instruction.   Maintain tentative mastery by providing application and practice activities. Begin with text that is below the student's reading level and gradually increase the level of text difficulty. Emphasize application of strategies in the context of a variety of text structures. Continue maintenance activities until the student reads and performs target tasks fluently. Then re-enter the CBA/P cycle.

Step 4: Repeat the CBA/P Cycle

As tasks are mastered, for example finding the main idea, review the curriculum chart to select additional subjects, subskills, and/or tasks that should be channeled into the updated program. It is particularly important to compare the student's reading comprehension and word recognition performances regularly. Striking a reasonable balance between the two areas, such that progress in one enhances learning in the other, is necessary for building an effective reading program. A review of the student's charted performance in science and social studies as well as in other subjects may also suggest tasks from those areas that can be readily be incorporated into a functional comprehension program. With each cycle repetition, communicate results and consult the student and all persons involved in his or her academic program. Previous CBA/P cycles provide additional information for updating the next program. The number of difficult tasks that the student can handle in one lesson, the best lesson length for him or her, the individual's learning rate, and the specific methods and materials that foster task mastery by that student offer clues to the best content and pace for subsequent programming.

SUMMARY

Reading comprehension is perhaps the most important academic skill in the elementary curriculum. The four components, literal, interpretive, and critical comprehension, and comprehension of words in context, are invaluable tools and

strategies for achievement in all other academic areas. Although understanding of all four types or levels is interactive to the extent that one seldom occurs in isolation, curricular emphasis may largely focus on recalling facts or understanding word meanings, particularly at the lower grade levels. Thus, in terms of the student's immediate academic progress, the value of each type of comprehension is relative to the focus of the reading curriculum as well as to the emphasis on each by the curricula of all other subject areas.

Specific procedures have been suggested for assessing the student's reading curriculum, his or her current level of functioning within the comprehension curriculum, and the specific tasks for which explicit instruction is needed. Not only task performances but also the comprehension strategies used to accomplish tasks are emphasized. The results of such assessment should be interpreted in relation to word recognition performance and performance in other subject areas that require extensive reading. When paired with the recommendations for programming at the three stages and selecting methods and materials to include in the assessment and programming cyclical plan, instruction in reading comprehension is more personalized. Although these procedures are not presented as a panacea for the comprehension difficulties of all students, they offer a viable system for modifying instruction according to the unique reading comprehension needs of a specific student. The likelihood of progress in many subject areas is increased.

CASE STUDIES

Sample Case: Jerry

Jerry, the focus of the sample case in Chapter 5, has made substantial progress in the personalized word recognition program described. Although detailed phonetic analysis is still somewhat difficult for him, by combining his newly acquired proficiency in using initial and final consonants with effective use of context, he is able to identify most words in the texts of third grade, his present grade placement. However, the class has begun lessons that specifically emphasize finding the main idea of short passages. Jerry is again failing reading because he seldom correctly identifies the main idea. You will recall that Jerry seems to learn best with a strong, visual approach; computer practice has been particularly effective as a maintenance strategy.

Because much is already known about Jerry's performances, indirect assessment can be reduced to obtaining the teacher's ranking of performance in comprehension subskills (Words in Context–1; Literal–2; Critical–3; Interpretive–4), brief observations, and a quick analysis of samples of Jerry's responses to comprehension exercises in the reading workbook and on teacher worksheets. These confirm that Jerry usually scores 80 to 90 percent mastery on literal comprehension but approaches main idea tasks in a haphazard fashion.

Diagnostic Hypotheses: Jerry has not mastered a systematic approach to finding the main idea; since recall of details is adequate, it is possible that he does not understand the concept of main idea. It is probable that he also has difficulty drawing conclusions and evaluating text. Therefore assess only interpretive and critical comprehension, omitting literal comprehension assessment.

Based on the results of indirect assessment, direct assessment proceeds in the following manner:

Jerry is interviewed to discuss his view of unsatisfactory comprehension grades. He states that he thinks that he is "doing it right, but the teacher doesn't." Direct testing is begun with sample passages from the first-grade reader (one grade level below the estimated level at which he can read with ease) of the series in which Jerry is currently expected to perform at third-grade level. Jerry reads the passages silently (his preference); he is asked specific "explain" and "judge" questions about the first- and then the second-grade passages. Testing does not proceed beyond second-grade level, since he evidences difficulty with the higher level questions as depicted in Figure 6.17.

A tentative comprehension program is planned, which includes these components:

FIGURE 6.17   Personalized Assessment Plan for Sample Case

Jerry
(Student's Name)

Reading Comprehension
(Academic Subjects)

Mr. Gonzales
(Teacher)

Subject Tasks# Task	Test Source	Success	Error	Assessement / Programming Implications	Dates Checked		Charted
Comp. II A.4 Main Idea	HBJ Basal p.p. 45-48		✗	No attempt – teach specific steps	$\frac{11}{11}$		
II B.4 Conclusion	''	✓		O.K.	''		
III A.4 Fact/Fiction	''	✓		"Fact because it happened to me"	''		
IV A.4 Words/Context	''	✓		Good answer	''		
II A.5 Main Idea	HBJ 91-95		✗	No attempt – teach <u>concept</u>	$\frac{11}{12}$		
" B.5 Concl.	''		✗	"Story didn't tell" (No guess)	''		
" C.1 Cause/Effect	''	$\frac{1}{2}$	$\frac{1}{2}$	One effect correct	''		
III A.5 Fact/Fic	''		✗	Can't tell why it's make believe	''		
IV A.5 Words/Con.	''	✓		Good use of context	''		

NOTES: Confirm 1st grade tasks before charting.
Teach concepts of main idea with pictures first.

The major program emphasis will be interpretive comprehension. Since finding the main idea is the task that is the source of Jerry's present distress, it will be the initial priority of the program. The concept of main idea will first be taught using primer and first-grade passages. The "Pick or Pass" (POP) procedure will be used as a corrective strategy. The POP format will be slightly changed to include more visual input; a checklist of the strategy steps will be provided for Jerry's use. Passage difficulty will be increased as he progresses. Felt markers will be used to highlight topic sentences. Practice and maintenance activities will be provided by two computer programs that stress main idea. Additional maintenance strategies will be selected from among those cited for IIA.1–.5. Program modifications will be determined by Jerry's performance under these conditions.

PRACTICE CASES

Case A

Jerry's second weakest task is drawing conclusions. Again, he approached the task in haphazard fashion. The diagnostic hypotheses include: Jerry's previous instruction has focused on literal comprehension to the detriment of interpretive comprehension; he may not understand the task, may lack a systematic approach, and/or may feel he has completed the comprehension process once details are recalled. Based upon the assessment plan in Figure 6.17, make the following assessment and programming decisions:

1. Assume that the diagnostic hypotheses are confirmed; what will probably be the secondary (after interpretive) emphasis of the comprehension program and why?
2. How will you establish the secondary priority of the program?
3. What corrective strategies will you plan to use initially and why?
4. Which materials will you plan to use initially and why?
5. Which maintenance strategies will you plan and at what levels?

Case B

Suppose that Jerry's relative strengths and weaknesses among the comprehension subskills are rearranged such that literal comprehension is the weakest subskill:

Interpretive comprehension (1)
Critical comprehension (2)
Words in context (3)
Detail comprehension (4)

Assume that the word recognition performances are ranked in the following order:

Phonetic analysis (1)
Structural analysis (2)
Word meaning (3)
Sight vocabulary (4)

Indirect assessment indicates that Jerry demonstrates strong auditory performance; relative strengths and weaknesses are confirmed through observation and work sample analysis. His teacher has circled each third-grade task on the word recognition curriculum chart in Figure 5.1, and on the comprehension chart in Figure 6.2. Based on these curricular goals and the indirect assessment data, make the appropriate assessment and programming decisions:

1. What are your diagnostic hypotheses?
2. Where should direct testing begin and why? (Hint: First decide between comprehension and word recognition.)
3. Where do you tentatively plan to stop testing and why?
4. What materials will you use for testing and why?
5. What corrective strategies will you plan to use initially and why?
6. Which materials will you plan to use initially and why?

7. If the diagnostic hypotheses are confirmed, what will probably be the secondary emphasis of the program and why?

8. How will the secondary priority of the program be established?

9. What specific assessment and programming plans for reading should be made and why?

ENRICHMENT ACTIVITIES

Discussion

1. Discuss the relative importance of reading comprehension and each type of comprehension to the general academic success of an elementary student.

2. Speculate why reading comprehension difficulties are often more difficult to correct than word recognition problems.

3. A school system sets separate and lower promotion standards for special education students who are mainstreamed than for general education students. Consider the implications of requiring a fourth-grade general education student to comprehend at a fourth-grade level, while an exceptional student mainstreamed into the same class must comprehend at a second-grade level to be promoted. Evaluate the effects of this policy on the special student, the other student, the classroom reading program, and the general classroom teacher.

4. Review the assessment and programming strategies in the sample case study. Once techniques for finding the main idea have been taught and mastered, what strategies should be utilized to teach Jerry to infer cause from effect or vice versa?

5. Pretend that you are teaching in a situation where a whole language approach is encouraged. Describe how you could go about implementing any three of the comprehension strategies discussed in this chapter using library books. What books would you choose and which portions of the material would be most appropriate for specific skills application?

Special Projects

1. Using the teacher survey on reading comprehension (Figure 6.3), interview a fifth-grade teacher about the reading comprehension skills of his or her strongest and weakest student.

2. Interview a special education resource teacher about the reading comprehension skills of his or her strongest student who is 10 to 11 years of age. Again, use the reading comprehension teacher survey. Compare the estimate of the special education student's performance with that of the strongest and the weakest readers from the fifth-grade class.

3. Obtain a scope and sequence chart for the second- or third-grade texts of two primary reading programs or reading curriculum guides. Note the similarities and differences between the two texts, and between those texts and the curriculum

chart of this book, Figure 6.2. What conclusions can be drawn from this comparison?

4. Review Practice Case B. Assume that words in context is Jerry's weakest comprehension subskill. Furthermore assume that word meaning is his weakest word recognition subskill. With a peer, formulate diagnostic hypotheses and plan direct assessment strategies. Simulate Jerry's test performance; plan an integrated reading program for him.

5. Select one or two skill areas (e.g., literal comprehension or words in context) and develop a plan for teaching the same skill area on a developmental, corrective, and maintenance level.

CHAPTER 7

WRITTEN EXPRESSION

JAMES A. POTEET

CHAPTER OBJECTIVES

This chapter is designed to enable the reader to:

1. Modify a scope and sequence chart of written expression skills to reflect the needs of a student.
2. Explain the relative importance of written expression and each subskill to a student's academic success.
3. Develop a personalized assessment plan, using both indirect and direct student assessment procedures.
4. Pinpoint student needs in written expression and determine if the needs require developmental, corrective, or maintenance strategies.
5. Develop a personalized programming plan for a student's instructional needs in written expression.

Communication is one of the most treasured human abilities because it allows us to form relationships with other people. However, communication does not come easily for many of your students. Since communication is based on the use of language, and since many low-achieving students and students with disabilities have delayed language development, or at least some difficulty in acquiring the basic skills of language, it is understandable that they have difficulty with communication.

One of the most important language and communication skills is written expression. Written expression is "a visual representation of thoughts, feelings, and ideas using symbols of the writer's language system for the purpose of communication or recording" (Poteet, 1980, p. 88). Algozzine, O'Shea, Stoddard, and Crews (1988) found that 80 percent of the employers surveyed listed the ability to write accurate messages as the number one skill an employee would need. The second most important skill, cited by 67 percent of the employers, was the ability to write requests.

The act of writing forces students to verbalize their thoughts. Weber (1990) feels that this might explain why memory experts believe that the writing process is the most effective tool for remembering information. Clearly then, it is important that all students acquire the basic skills in written expression so that their written communication will be accurate and easily understood; competency in written expression should be a goal for everyone, including people with disabilities, to the maximum extent possible.

COMPONENTS OF WRITTEN EXPRESSION

Written expression encompasses the five major components discussed briefly below. It is important to keep in mind that while some rules of written expression never seem to change, others do change to reflect current trends.

Handwriting

Handwriting, or penmanship, is a fine-motor skill used to display written expression. It is important that this skill be taught and perfected at an early age so that what is written can be easily read. If writing is illegible, then it does not communicate to another person and, in many cases, not even to ourselves. When time must be spent attending to handwriting, rather than to the *ideas* of the writing, communication is impeded. One should not have to "decode" what is written. Techniques for assessment and programming handwriting within the curriculum are presented in Chapter 8.

Spelling

Spelling is the process of transforming spoken language into written language. Spelling, like handwriting, can hinder the communication process when performed incorrectly. When reading incorrectly spelled words, our attention is diverted from the message of the communication to "decoding" what was written. Spelling, like handwriting, is taught from an early age so that it, too, can be perfected to make written language easier to read. Techniques for assessment and programming spelling within the curriculum are presented in Chapter 8.

Mechanics

Mechanics are those grammatical rules of the language that aid in clarifying the intent of the

writer. Elements of mechanics (Capitalization, Punctuation, Abbreviations, and Numbers) are taught in the traditional curriculum beginning in the first grade.

Usage

Usage deals with how the building blocks of our language are chosen and manipulated for the purpose of expressing the writer's intent. The elements of usage (see Figure 7.1) include words, phrases, clauses, sentences, and paragraphs.

FIGURE 7.1 Elements of "Usage" of Written Expression

USAGE	
Words:	When words are used correctly, the writing flows smoothly and is easy to understand.
Phrases:	Phrases are groups of words that belong together logically but cannot function as sentences because they do not contain a subject and predicate. The correct use and placement of phrases within sentences aid comprehension of the writing.
Clauses:	Clauses have a subject and a predicate; they increase the maturity level of the writing; and they help the writer focus on the precise intent of the communication.
Sentences:	A sentence is a logically related group of words containing a subject and predicate. It expresses a complete thought and can function independently of other groups of words to be understood. The sentence must be properly constructed for the writing to be clear to the reader.
Paragraphs:	A paragraph is a group of related sentences usually about one topic, often set off by an indent. Correct structure and transition between paragraphs makes the writing flow smoothly and easy to understand.

Ideation

Ideation represents the *ideas* underlying the writer's purpose and intent. The elements within this component must always be judged on the basis of the type of writing being assessed. Most writing in the schools consists of friendly and business letters, stories, reports, reviews, essays, and possibly a few poems. The first four components equally apply to all types of writing; in contrast, underlying ideas are different for each type of writing. The elements within this component include fluency, level of maturity, word choice, and style (see Figure 7.2).

TASK DEMANDS OF WRITTEN EXPRESSION

A comprehensive assessment of written expression requires the writer to perform three different types of tasks (see Types A, B, and C in Figure 7.3.) These tasks place quite different demands on the language used, the level of memory involved, and the action required to make a response.

A *receptive* task (Type A) requires *recognition* of correct answers or of errors, depending on the test directions. The student *selects* the response from several choices and marks the response on an answer sheet or perhaps underlines one of several choices. This type of task is typical of many standardized, norm-referenced tests, especially those given in group situations. Note that a student may be able to *select* the correct response or to recognize many errors in a written passage, yet make these errors when required to actually produce writing, an expressive task. Ebel and Frisbie (1991) point out that when a task requires the *selection* of an answer rather than the *production* of an answer, the thought processes may not necessarily be less complex or less difficult.

FIGURE 7.2   Elements of "Ideation" Written Expression

IDEATION

Fluency: An appropriate number of words must be written to clearly express the writer's intent. Otherwise, the reader is left with a sense of emptiness. However, superfluous words detract from the clarity of the writing. The number of words written varies with the type of writing, but generally it increases with the age of the writer (Poteet, 1979).

Four Levels of Writing Maturity:

1. Level 1, *Naming,* is characterized by the writer simply naming objects or people. A beginning narrative might be "There is a boy, a girl, a cat, a dog, and a house."

2. Level 2, *Description,* simply describes something. An example might be "The boy is running. The dog is barking. It is raining."

3. Level 3, *Plot,* is a good story with a beginning, middle and end. A more sophisticated story would present a conflict, problem, or complication that is resolved (Newcomer, Barenbaum, & Nodine, 1988).

4. Level 4, *Issue,* is the most mature level of writing because the main purpose is the discussion of some issue. The issue can be social, personal, political, or philosophical.

Word Choice: The competent writer will choose words carefully to achieve the major purpose of the writing. Trite and mundane expressions will be avoided; words that crate excitement, anticipation, and awareness of physical senses and emotions will be used.

Style: Style is probably the most personal of all elements of written expression; it is how the writer puts it all together. Although there are guidelines for improving the overall quality of the writing, it is the personal approach taken by the writer that ultimately establishes the style. The writing must be comprehensible, well organized, and well developed. Style is the personal trademark of the writer.

FIGURE 7.3   Types of Tasks for Written Expression Test Items

	TYPE A	TYPE B	TYPE C
Language Usage	RECEPTIVE (Read the item)	EXPRESSIVE (Write the item)	INTEGRATIVE (Perform the task)
Memory Demand	RECOGNITION A.1—Recognize correct answer A.2—Recognize error	RECALL B.1—Cued Recall B.2—Total Recall	COMPREHENSIVE C.1—All memory systems are used
Response Required	SELECTION A.1—Mark answer sheet • Multiple choice • True-False • Matching A.2 - Mark stimulus item • Underline • Cross out	PRODUCTION B.1—Written • Short-answer: sentence completion fill-in-the-blank B.2 - Written • Extended response, essays, narratives, term papers, reports	APPLICATION C.1—Authentic: • Use of skills in the real world. C.2 - Performance: • Generalize to new situations and purposes

An *expressive* task (Type B in Figure 7.3) requires either cued or total recall of information. The student *produces* a response, usually on a short-answer or fill-in-the-blanks test. Some expressive tasks require the student to produce an extended written response, such as a story, an essay, a personal letter, or term paper. Expressive tasks, which require that the student actually produce writing, are more valid measures of written expression than receptive tasks because skill in written expression is ultimately judged by the student's actual writing.

An *integrative* task (Type C in Figure 7.3) requires comprehensive use of memory in the *application* of knowledge and skill to real-life, real-world situations. These tasks are frequently referred to as authentic or performance tasks, as discussed in Chapter 1.

It is important to realize that students will not use in any given task all of the skills listed on a curriculum chart. For instance, skills used in writing friendly or business letters, such as writing dates and addresses, are usually not necessary in writing stories. Therefore, to assess knowledge of all curriculum skills you will have to present tasks requiring *selection, production,* and *application*

responses for each curriculum skill. It is important to have a record of your assessment of each skill in these three types of responses. The curriculum chart itself can serve as a good record of these activities. Procedures for use of the curriculum chart as a record and management tool will be discussed later in this chapter.

PERSONALIZED ASSESSMENT PROCEDURES

Personalized assessment in written expression provides the basis for deciding which skills to develop, correct, or maintain. In the section to follow, these steps will be detailed. Once these steps have been completed, then program planning for personalized instruction is readily apparent.

Step 1: Establish the Curriculum

The first step requires that you obtain a detailed scope and sequence chart or list of curriculum skills in written expression. The chart should indicate the *sequence* of skills by *grade level*. The curriculum list may reflect the skills adopted by the school system, it may be a list of skills taught in the language arts text or program, or it may be the one given in Figure 7.4. This chart gives the essential skills, listed in sequential order for each grade level (K through 6), for mechanics, usage, and ideation. These skills were collected from a variety of basal language arts texts; they are equally appropriate for older students who need remediation or review of these essential skills. Appendix C lists these skills as objectives for those readers who prefer a different format than the chart.

Handwriting and spelling, while certainly part of written expression, are not part of the written expression curriculum chart. They are addressed separately in Chapter 8 and have detailed curriculum charts of their own, because they are typically evaluated as distinct subjects on the student's report card. Direct instruction is of sufficient importance in these subjects that assessment and programming for them merits separate coverage. "Spelling in context," an item in some curricula, is discussed with integrated language arts instruction in Chapter 8. If the teacher grades spelling in context, then it must be assessed in context.

Once a curriculum chart or list is selected, additional required skills may be added as necessary. When the chart is complete to your satisfaction, make three columns beside the list of skills. Label the first column "P" for production responses, the second column "S" for selection responses, and the third column "A" for application responses. The use of these columns will be explained later. Now the curriculum chart can serve as a management tool for your assessment and instruction if you record your test findings directly on it.

Step 2: Designate Skills to Assess

Once you have your curriculum chart or list, photocopy the Teacher Survey: Written Expression in Figure 7.5, and use both to obtain information about teacher expectations and student characteristics in written expression for your target student. The teacher survey may be completed by the student's teacher or jointly with another professional, such as an educational diagnostician or a special education consultant.

It is crucial that the student's teacher note directly on the curriculum chart those skills that are appropriate for the student to learn given the learning characteristics of the student. For example, if the student is of average intelligence, the teacher may indicate that all of the skills at a certain grade are appropriate to learn. If the student is disabled, the teacher may select only those skills considered to be crucial for success at the student's grade placement. The teacher may designate the crucial skills by marking them with a highlighter or by placing a check beside them, or even by circling the items. It is important that the crucial skills be marked in some clear manner because *you initially assess only those skills marked by the teacher.* When the teacher has designated the important items on the curriculum chart, have the teacher complete section A on the Teacher Survey: Written Expression. Note that if the General Teacher Survey (see Chapter 4) has been used with this target student, it will contain valuable information about the student's learning style, school adjustment, and estimated academic performance in written expression.

Part B on the Teacher Survey: Written Expression asks for an indirect assessment of the student's skills by the teacher when the student is *not* present. To assist in completing this portion of the survey, end-of-unit exercises and other teacher assignments may provide written products for analysis. Also, do not forget to look at written products created for other teachers in different subject areas. With the interest in writing-across-the-curriculum, teachers are expecting more and more writing pieces in all subject areas. Obtaining information about the student's writing from teachers of other subject areas not only reminds those teachers of the importance of using writing in those subjects, but it also helps you to determine if errors are consistent throughout the school day and across the school curricula.

When inspecting writing completed in subject areas other than language arts, it is important to

FIGURE 7.4   Written-Expression Curriculum Chart

Student's Name_____Grade_____Teacher_____School_____Date_____

Directions: Circle the specific tasks required for success at this student's current level; in the space provided list any other tasks appropriate to the existing curriculum.

Typical Text Level for Tasks

WRITTEN EXPRESSION SUBSKILLS

	K	1	2	3	4	5	6
I MECHANICS	I	I		I	I	I	I
A Capitalization		A.1 Names, Titles .2 Days, Months .3 Begin Sentence .4 "I"	A.5 Proper Nouns .6 Letters .7 Abbreviations	A.8 Names .9 Initials .10 Time	A.11 Places .12 Peoples .13 School Subjects .14 Quotes	A.15 Outline .16 Organizations .17 Songs .18 Proper Nouns .19 Poetry	A.20 Degrees .21 Documents .22 Proper Adjectives
B Punctuation		B.1 Period .2 ? .3 Dash	B.4 Comma .5 Underline	B.6 Apostrophe .7 Underline .8 ! .9 Period .10 Colon .11 Comma .12 "—"	B.13 Comma .14 Period	B.15 Colon .16 Underline .17 Hyphen .18 Comma	B.19 Period .20 Dash .21 Comma .22 Parentheses
C Abbreviations		C.1 Personal Titles .2 Days, Months	C.3 Postal	C.4 Initials .5 Time	C.6 Names .7 Measurement .8 Address	C.9 Acronyms	C.10 Organizations .11 References
D Numbers		D.1 Phone .2 Words	D.3 Date .4 Address	D.5 Time .6 Phone	D.7 References	D.8 Roman Numerals	(Review)

	K	1	2	3	4	5	6
II USAGE	II	II	II	II	II	II	II
A Sentences	Speaking: A.1 Complete .2 Declarative .3 ?	A.4 Subj./Pred. .5 Simple .6 Declarative .7 Interrogative .8 Word Order	Review	A.9 Exclamatory .10 Compound .11 No Fragments .12 Word Order	A.13 Imperative .14 No Run-on .15 Compound Subject .16 Compound Predicate .17 Word Order	A.18 Implied Subject	A.19 Complex .20 Compound/ Complex
B Words	Speaking: B.1 Nouns .2 Verbs .3 Adjectives .4 Prep. .5 Word Order	B.6 Nouns .7 Verbs .8 Pronouns .9 Adjective	B.10 Nouns .11 Pronouns .12 Verbs .13 Adjectives .14 Figurative .15 Review	B.16 Nouns .17 Verbs .18 Verbs .19 Adjectives .20 Adverbs .21 Conjunctions .22 Review	B.23 Pronouns .24 Verbs .25 Adjectives .26 Negatives .27 Review	B.28 Pronouns .29 Adjectives .30 Prepositions .31 Adverbs .32 Nouns .33 Review	B.34 Pronouns .35 Verbs .36 Adjectives .37 Interjections .38 Nouns .39 Conjunctions .40 Review
C Phrases				C.1 Noun .2 Verb	Review	C.3 Prepositional .4 Adjective .5 Adverb	C.6 Participial
D Clauses							D.1 Main
E Paragraphs				E.1 Definition .2 Indentation .3 Sequence Within	E.4 Topic Sentence .5 Descriptive .6 Expository	E.7 Connectives Between	E.8 Expository .9 Narrative

	K	1	2	3	4	5	6
III IDEATION	III	III	III	III	III	III	III
A Fluency	Speaking: A.1 Tell Stories	Writing: A.2 15 words	A.3 30 Words	A.4 50 Words	A.5 70 Words	A.6 110 Words	A.7 115 Words
B Maturity	B.1 Names .2 Describes	B.3 Naming (Level I)	B.4 Description (Level II)	B.5 Plot (Level III)	B.6 Issues (Level IV)	Review	Review
C Word Choice		C.1 Accurate	C.2 Descriptive	C.3 Purposeful .4 Sounds	C.5 Necessary, Exact	C.6 Senses .7 Emotions	Review
D Style		D.1 Sequence Words	D.2 Organization	D.3 Event Sequence	D.4 Necessary Details .5 Cohesive	D.6 Purpose .7 Splits .8 References	D.9 Modifier Placement .10 Shifts

Note: Check subskills and tasks as mastery is demonstrated, circling additional tasks required for student's advancement.

FIGURE 7.5   Teacher Survey: Written Expression

Student_____Date_____

Teacher_____Interviewer_____

ADDITIONAL COMMENTS

A. ASSESSMENT OF CURRICULUM:

1. Indicate appropriate skills, subskills, and tasks on an attached written expression curriculum chart.

List available text titles/levels you would consider as options:

2. List current text titles and levels in which student is expected to master written expression skills: _____
    _____

3. Check the primary source(s) of student's report grades in written expression:

    __Language Arts Workbook   __Homework
    __Teacher tests   __Class writing assignments
    __Combination of sources (specify) _____
    __Other _____

Describe grade sources:

4. Indicate the relative importance of each subskill to student's grades in written expression using 1 as the most important:

    __Handwriting   __Use of words
    __Spelling   __se of phrases/clauses
    __Capitalization   __Use of sentences
    __Punctuation   __Paragraphs
    __Underlying ideas   __Fluency (number of words)
    __Level of maturity   __Abbreviations/numbers

Indicate time devoted to each in the current curriculum and texts:

5. Describe instructional modifications in written expression that you have attempted with this student: _____
    _____

Degree of success:

B. INDIRECT STUDENT ASSESSMENT:

6. Rank order this student's written expression subskills using 1 as the strongest skill:

    __Handwriting   __Use of words
    __Spelling   __Use of phrases/clauses
    __Capitalization   __Use of sentences
    __Punctuation   __Paragraphs
    __Underlying ideas   __Fluency (number of words)
    __Level of maturity   __Abbreviations/numbers

In weakest area(s) identify the most difficult tasks for this student:

7. Check the best description of the student's emotional reaction to his or her performance in written expression:

    __Over concern   __No concern
    __Some concern   __Other reaction

Describe student's emotional reaction:

8. Check any other subject areas in which student's written-expression skill interferes with performance:

    __Reading   __Science
    __Math   __Social Studies
    __Other _____

Indicate why and to what extent:

9. List specifically what you want to know about this student's written expression subskills: _____
    _____

Attach representative samples of the student's work.

10. Interviewer Summary:_____
     _____

keep in mind that particular skills are related more to some areas than to others. For instance, a general science report might require the use of more abbreviations and numbers than would be used in a report in social studies. A social studies term paper would require the use of proper sentence construction and word choice to report facts and to possibly persuade opinion. Reports and papers required in arithmetic require the proper writing and alignment of numbers as well as concise and clear sentence structure to explain findings. Discussion of the student's written product with the teacher of these subject areas can provide valuable insight into the skills the teacher requires.

Classroom observation is an important part of any assessment. Observation of a student's classroom performance during a written expression task can provide a wealth of information, such as the student's attitude and approach to the writing requirements. Some students eagerly approach the task only to get bogged down in the mechanics of writing. Others perform all sorts of avoidance behaviors, yet they easily perform the task once they begin. The student's cumulative folder showing results from certain group and individually administered tests may provide additional information about the student's writing skills.

Information about the student's skills in the language areas prerequisite to written expression should be assessed indirectly. These areas include listening comprehension, oral expression, basic reading skills, and reading comprehension. It is important to give consideration to underlying (not directly observable) causes. Process disorders such as auditory discrimination difficulty may contribute to skill deficiency and require instruction. Gregg (1991) discusses a variety of cognitive processing prerequisites to writing. Diagnostic looking and listening can provide some clues to the student's facility with listening comprehension and oral expression during classroom activities. In addition, an observation of the reading class can provide information about the student's reading skills. Coupled with the analysis of work samples, these observations are valuable in helping to determine if a deficit skill is unique to one subject area or across several subjects.

Step 3: Organize Written Expression Tests

You will have to create, develop, and organize your own set of test items to use with your students, based on their curricula. Suggestions for doing so and sample items you may use are given below.

Personalized Written Expression Tests

In effect, you will be making your own personal "Written Expression Testing Kit" to assess all the skills on your curriculum chart. You can use 4- × 6-inch spiral-bound flip cards, or you might simply use a three-hole notebook. Design your pages so that the test item is on one side and the teacher directions and correct answers are on the adjacent page, allowing the kit to be propped up so that the student and the teacher can read at the same time without either seeing the other page. Many individual achievement tests (KeyMath, Kaufmann Test of Educational Achievement, etc.) are designed in this manner. Review the format of one of these tests before you organize your own kit.

Response Levels

Remember, for a *comprehensive* set of test items you will need three items for selection responses, three items for production responses, and three items for application responses for each skill on the curriculum chart or list. Note that one test item (a sentence) may be created to cover several skills at the same time. These test items may be developed over a period of time; you can begin your CBA with only a few production items to assess the critical skills for your target student. Before we look at developing test items requiring production responses, let's look briefly at the other two types of test items.

Application Responses.   Application responses are given to test items or situations found in real-life, real-world environments. For some students, usually those who are younger, teachers make *simulations* of the real world within the classroom. *Application responses always require the student to DO something that is common in life outside of school.* Some examples are writing checks, letters to friends, business letters, and memos; personal messages to friends, such as in greeting cards; messages and instructions to others (friends, parents, children); addresses for letters and cards; and job applications.

Each profession or job position usually requires some type of writing. Nurses require daily charting of patients; physicians write orders and prescriptions; managers must place requisitions for materials; people in the business world write contracts, bids, and specifications for particular jobs; and electronic mail on personal computers is becoming common in both personal and business activities. It is apparent that tests requiring application of knowledge and skills can cover several skills in only a few items. For instance, a test item asking the student to address an envelope to a friend requires the use of several skills (capitalization, punctuation, and numbers).

Selection Responses.   Items requiring students to *select* an answer, such as filling in a bubble on an answer sheet or underlining an incorrectly punctuated sentence (rather than actually producing writing), are used to help you determine if the student *knows* the skill. If a skill is used incorrectly when the student writes something, selection items can be given to help you determine if the student can *recognize* correct use of the skill even though it was not used correctly when writing was produced.

Any task requiring the student to write (a production response) can be changed to a task requiring a selection response. For example, to assess the student's knowledge of capital letters in names of organizations, songs, and proper nouns, instead of dictating the sentences as you would in a production task, present the sentence in writing on the chalkboard or on a prepared handout with no capital letters in the sentence. Then simply ask the student to circle the letters that should be capitalized.

Production Responses.   The production tests require the student to produce writing. The writing is then analyzed to determine use of skills noted on the Written Expression Curriculum Chart (Figure 7.4) and by using the Ideation Evaluation Questions (see Figure 7.6).

At the primary level, the student can be asked to write either a thank-you letter or a story. The younger and less experienced writer should probably be asked to write a letter, since that form is typically introduced before story writing in the language arts curriculum. Some general directions to the student for writing a thank-you letter are given; feel free to change the exact wording so the student can understand the task:

> *Pretend someone gave you a gift for your birthday. Write a friendly thank-you letter, and be sure to tell the person why you like your present. Use correct capitalization and punctuation. If you use any abbreviations or numbers, write them correctly also.*

The student at the primary level, with some experience in writing stories, should be given that opportunity, using a picture as a stimulus. Choose two or three pictures in color showing some action by children of the same gender and age as the writer. If the student is still writing at the end of 20 minutes, ask him or her to end the story in the next two or three minutes. If the student is hesitant about writing or finishes after only a few words, encourage a longer story but do not give any suggestions for content. For students who have difficulty creating a story, ask them to write about a recent experience such as a field trip, a special event at school, a family event, or the like.

Some students are hesitant to write because of poor spelling. Make it clear that no spelling help will be given and that the story will not be graded on spelling. After the student has finished writing the story, ask for it to be read aloud. Note any deviations from what was written and words that are grossly misspelled. The notes are best written on

FIGURE 7.6   Ideation Evaluation Questions

Student's Name _____

Check the type of writing that is being evaluated:

__Friendly letter   __Narrative   __Expository   __Descriptive   __Story

__Report   __Review   __Essay   __Business letter   __Poem   __Other

A. **FLUENCY**—Are enough words and sentences written to:
1. *adequately* convey the writer's ideas and purpose?   __YES__SOMEWHAT__NO
2. *appropriately* represent fluency for:
    (a) an average, nondisabled student of the writer's same age in the regular curriculum?
          __YES__SOMEWHAT__NO
    (b) the writer?   __YES__SOMEWHAT__NO
         (Number of words written _____)
         (Number of sentences written _____)

B. **LEVEL OF MATURITY**—(Check only if writing is a narrative)
__Level 1—Naming   __Level II—Description
__Level III—Plot   __Level IV—Issue
Is the level appropriate for age/grade placement?   __YES__SOMEWHAT__NO

C. **WORD CHOICE**—Are specific words expressly chosen to achieve the writer's *purpose* for a specific audience, on a specific *occasion*?   __YES__SOMEWHAT__NO

D. **STYLE**—
1. *Organization:* Is the writing well organized with a clear beginning, middle, and end?
          __YES__SOMEWHAT__NO
2. *Development:* Are the *main idea* and *purpose* clear, accurate, and complete?
          __YES__SOMEWHAT__NO
    Is the *sequence* logical and orderly?   __YES__SOMEWHAT__NO
    Is the composition *cohesive* (no superfluous ideas and no errors in logic)?
          __YES__SOMEWHAT__NO
    Are sufficient *details* (examples, proofs, reasons) and *supplementary ideas* used to support or de-
    velop the main idea or purpose?   __YES__SOMEWHAT__NO
3. *Comprehensibility:*
    Is the composition easily understood (no shift in tense, person, number, or point of view; no split in-
    finitives; clear pronoun reference; proper location of modifiers, prepositional phrases, adjective
    clauses)?   __YES__SOMEWHAT__NO

E. OVERALL IMPRESSION
Is the overall impression favorable (effective, interesting, creative)?
          __YES__SOMEWHAT__NO

Check any area below that requires remedial attention:

__Spelling   __Handwriting   __Capitalization   __Punctuation

__Abbreviations   __Numbers   __Other (specify)

NOTES:

a separate sheet. Instructions such as these should be given to the student in a manner that will be understood; exact wording is not important.

> *Choose one of these pictures and write a story about it. I want you to write the story all on your own, so do not use a dictionary. Spell the words the best you can. You will not be graded on your spelling. If you make a mistake, put a line through it; do not erase. You have about 20 minutes to write the story. Take a few minutes to plan your story before you begin. Write the best story you can.*

For older students, the task and the directions are the same. The difference is that the content of the pictures selected by the teacher must match the interest and maturity level of the student.

Suggestions for Constructing Test Items

Suggestions follow for constructing your own items. They are coded with the skill numbers on the Curriculum Chart. These suggested items are valid only to the extent that they match the skills offered in the student's actual curriculum.

Mechanics

Capitalization: First Names, Titles, Days, Months, Beginning of Sentence, "I," (IA.1–.4). *Materials:* Paper, pencil. *Strategy:* Dictate sentences using words students can spell. Cover each skill. *Interpretation:* 100 percent accuracy. These beginning skills are necessary for all future writing, especially personal and business letters.

Capitalization: Proper Nouns—streets, cities, states, places, book titles, holidays; Letters—salutation, closing; Postal Abbreviations, (IA.5–.7). *Materials:* Paper, pencil. *Strategy:* Dictate sentences using words students can spell, covering all proper nouns listed above. Ask student to write a short friendly letter using salutation and closing. Have student address an envelope using the correct postal abbreviation. *Interpretation:* 100 percent accuracy. These second-grade skills are important for future writing, especially personal and business letters.

Capitalization: Family Names, Initials in People's Names; Time of Day; Famous Places;

Organizations and Businesses; Song Titles; Proper Nouns—geographic, trade names, ethnic groups, degrees, documents, proper adjectives, (IA.8–.13, IA.16–.18, IA.20–.22). *Materials:* Paper, pencil. *Strategy:* Create and dictate sentences that cover each skill and employ words the student can spell. *Interpretation:* 100 percent accuracy. These skills are necessary in future formal and informal writing of a general nature and in personal notes.

Capitalization: First Word in Direct Quote, (IA.14). *Materials:* Paper, pencil. *Strategy:* Have student read from basal reader a selection using direct quotes. Then have student create and write a short dialogue between two or more people. *Interpretation:* 100 percent accuracy. It is necessary to write direct quotes correctly so the reader will know who is talking and what is being said.

Capitalization: Outlines, (IA.15). *Materials:* Paper, pencil. *Strategy:* Have student outline a speech with three major sections, each with two subdivisions. *Interpretation:* 100 percent accuracy. Correctly written outlines help organize thoughts for later speaking and writing.

Capitalization: Organizations, Songs, Proper Nouns, (IA.16–.18). *Materials:* Paper, pencil. *Strategy:* Dictate sentences containing the skills, such as "I belong to the American Heart Club"; "The band played 'America the Beautiful'"; "We went to Italy"; "I like Campbell's soup." *Interpretation:* 100 percent accuracy. The good writer will use capitals correctly in a variety of types of writing, both informal and formal.

Capitalization: Poetry—first word in each line of verse, (IA.19). *Materials:* Paper, pencil. *Strategy:* Dictate a poem or have student write one already known, such as "Twinkle, Twinkle Little Star." The poem should have a least two lines. *Interpretation:* 100 percent accuracy. Capitalization in poems follow conventional rules. These rules must be used in future writing.

Capitalization: Degrees, Documents, Proper Adjectives, (IA.20–.22). *Materials:* Paper, pencil. *Strategy:* Dictate sentences for student to write using target skills, such as "My brother is Tom Johnson, Ph.D." "Have you seen the U.S.S. Constitution?" "We bought some Amish cheese." *Interpretation:* Capital letters are used in a variety of places. The good writer must know when to use them properly. Readers are distracted from the intent of the writing when words and letters are not properly capitalized.

Punctuation: Periods—after personal titles, initials, abbreviations, professional degrees, (IB.1, IB.9, IB.14, IB.19). Materials: Paper, pencil. *Strategy:* Dictate sentences or have student create sentences using each skill. *Interpretation:* 100 percent accuracy. These skills cover basic punctuation skills necessary to future writing. The use of the period to end the sentence is necessary to avoid writing run-on sentences. The other uses of the period reflect conventional mechanics.

Punctuation: Question Mark; Dash in telephone number; Exclamation Mark; Colon in time of day, salutation, to designate speaker, to indicate "the following," reference works; Hyphen to divide words at end of sentence; Dash to replace "to," as in 1952–1992, (IB.2, IB.3, IB.8, IB.10, IB.15, IB.17, IB.20). Materials: Paper, pencil. *Strategy:* Dictate or ask student to write sentences that use each of these skills. The task must not be one of copying. *Interpretation:* 100 percent accuracy. Each of these skills are vital for proper written expression throughout the elementary grades.

Punctuation: Comma—city/state, day/year, salutation, complementary close; items in series; to set off direct quote, introductory words, noun of address; following transition words; before coordinating conjunctions; to set off dependent clauses, confusing items, appositives; in reference of published works; set off incidental words, phrases, or clauses; set off modifiers as necessary to clarify the message, (IB.4, IB.11, IB.13, IB.21). Materials: Paper, pencil. *Strategy:* Dictate or ask student to create and write sentences or other appropriate tasks that make use of each of the above skills. *Interpretation:* 100 per-

cent accuracy. The correct use of the comma is necessary so that the intent of the writer is correctly perceived by the reader.

Punctuation: Underline—names of ships in water, sea, and air; book titles; art, music, and drama titles (IB.5, IB.7, IB.16). Materials: Paper, pencil. *Strategy:* Dictate sentences that require the student to use underlining in each of the above instances. Use titles familiar to the student, if possible. *Interpretation:* 100 percent accuracy. Underlining is a new skill for many students. It makes the words stand out and appear more important, and is the proofreading mark editors use to put words into italics in books. Show the students an example of italics. When the writing is not to be printed, underlining is used conventionally.

Punctuation: Quotation Marks—direct quotes, emphasis; Parentheses, (IB.12, IB.22). Materials: Paper, pencil. *Strategy:* Dictate sentences or ask student to write an appropriate task that requires correct use of these skills. *Interpretation:* 100 percent accuracy. Correct and conventional use of quotations and parentheses permit the reader to know the exact intent of the writer.

Abbreviations: Personal Titles; Days & Months; Postal; Initials in names; Time of day; Names—people (Jr.), natural things (Mt. Ranier); Measurement; Addresses; Acronyms and common terms; Organizations; in Reference Works, (IC.1–.11). Materials: Paper, pencil. *Strategy:* Dictate sentences or ask the student to write an appropriate task that requires each skill. *Interpretation:* 100 percent accuracy. The correct and conventional use of abbreviations is necessary so the reader can understand what was written. The legality of a document depends upon the correct use of abbreviations as well as proper content.

Numbers: Telephone; Words for numbers less than 10; Date/Year; Addresses; Time; Telephone Area Code; Reference Works; Roman Numerals, (ID.1–.18). Materials: Paper, pencil. *Strategy:* Dictate sentences or ask student to write an appropriate task that requires the use of each of these skills. *Interpretation:* 100 percent accuracy. Writing numbers correctly is one of the most important written expression skills because of the way the information is used. Personal notes, telephone messages, and other informal notes can be a matter of life or death, thus accuracy is vital. In research, it is necessary to be able to find the correct reference to obtain the desired information quickly. It is necessary to address packages correctly so they reach their proper destination. Correct use of numbers is essential in personal, informal, and formal writing.

Usage

Sentences: Speaking—using Complete, Declarative, and Interrogative Sentences, (IIA.1–.3). *Materials:* None. *Strategy:* Tell student to use complete sentences to describe something in the classroom. Have student ask another student about what was described. *Interpretation:* 100 percent accuracy. Oral expressive language is a prerequisite skill to good written expression.

Sentences: Subject and Predicate; Simple; Declarative; Interrogative; Word Order; Exclamatory; Compound; No Fragments; Imperative; No Run-on; Compound Subject; Compound Predicate; Implied Subject; Complex; Compound/Complex, (IIA.4–.20). *Materials:* Pencil, paper. *Strategy:* Dictate sentences and ask student to create and write sentences that assess the above skills. The current language arts books may be consulted for examples. *Interpretation:* 100 percent accuracy. Different types of sentences make the writing more interesting to read. The structure of the sentences, however, must be accurate. These skills are basic to good writing and will be used in future writing. They should be mastered completely.

Words: Nouns; Verbs; Adjectives; Prepositions; Word Order, (IIB.1–.5). *Materials:* None. *Strategy:* Engage the student in conversation, asking for descriptions about the room, locations of objects, and general information. Note the use of the different types of words in the response given.

Interpretation: 100 percent accuracy; all types must be used. The correct use of words when speaking is prerequisite to correct use when writing. Each type of word has a purpose different from the others.

Words: All Parts of Speech—Nouns, Verbs, etc., (IIB.6–.40). *Materials:* Paper, pencil. *Strategy:* Inspect the current language arts text for examples of sentences and activities using the parts of speech appropriate for the student's grade level. Dictate sentences or ask the student to write tasks that require the appropriate use of the parts of speech. *Interpretation:* Words must be correctly used in good writing. Knowing the parts of speech helps the writer determine how to use the word correctly. Correct word usage makes the writing easier to understand.

Phrases: Noun; Verb; Prepositional; Adjective; Adverb; Participle; Main Clause, (IIC.1–.6, IID.1). *Materials:* Paper, pencil. *Strategy:* Ask the student to write one or more sentences using the targeted skills. *Interpretation:* 100 percent accuracy. It is important to know that a phrase (a group of words) can act as different parts of speech within a sentence. By using phrases as parts of speech, one makes the writing more interesting to read. The proper use of clauses is required for more complex sentence structure in future writing.

Paragraphs: Definition; Indentation; Sequence Within; Topic Sentence; Descriptive; Expository; Connectives; Narrative, (IIE.1–.9). *Materials:* Paper, pencil. *Strategy:* Assign a writing task using story starters, purposes, and topics appropriate for the student. The current language arts text may be consulted for examples. The assigned task should illustrate knowledge of the above skills used in good paragraphs. *Interpretation:* 100 percent accuracy. The use of topic sentences, sequence within and between paragraphs, and different types of paragraphs, depending on the purpose of the writing, are all necessary skills for good written expression. Skill in using good paragraphs makes the task of writing longer pieces easier. Also, when the piece flows easily from beginning to end because of well-constructed paragraphs, the entire writing is more easily understood and enjoyed by the reader.

Ideation: Speaking; Telling Stories; Naming and Describing objects and actions, (IIIA.1; IIIB.1–.2). Materials: None. Strategy: (1) Ask the student to tell others a story about something of interest. The student should use enough words so that the story is understood by the listener. (2) Ask the student to name and describe objects and actions of other students in the classroom. *Interpretation:* 100 percent accuracy. Words used in speaking should be the correct ones to portray the discussed object and to describe the actions of others. The correct use of words in oral expression is a prerequisite for correct writing.

Level of Maturity: Labeling objects; Descriptive sentences; Plot; Issue, (IIIB.3–.6). Materials: Paper, pencil. Strategy: Have the student do the following: Write a list of objects and people in a picture of interest, use the word list in sentences and arrange the sentences in a chronological or meaningful sequence, add sentences to the ones written to make a plot with a beginning, middle and end. *Interpretation:* 100 percent accuracy. The level of maturity must develop from simply writing the correct name of objects; to writing correct descriptive sentences; to formulating a well-established plot with a beginning, middle, and end; to developing a piece that discusses some issue of importance (political, social, moral, educational, etc.). The level of maturity of the writing is influenced by acquisition of all the other skills in written expression. As new skills are learned, the maturity level should increase.

Word Choice: Accurate Words; Descriptive Words; Purposeful Words; Words of Sounds; Use of Necessary and Exact Words; Words of the Senses and Emotions, (IIIC.1–.7). Materials: Paper, pencil. Strategy: Assign an appropriate writing task to assess knowledge of the different uses of proper word choice. Consult the current language arts texts for examples of tasks. *Interpretation:* 100 percent accuracy of correct word choice and usage for the assigned task. Use of the correct word, in addition to the correct parts of speech as in IIIB, can make the difference between an outstanding piece of writing and a mediocre one.

Style: Sequence; Organization; Detail; Cohesiveness; Clarity of Purpose; Pronoun Preference; Placement of Modifiers; No Split Infinitive; No Shifts in Point of View, (IIID.1–.10). Materials: Paper, pencil, a variety of colored pictures. Strategy: Choose three pictures, in color, you think would be interesting to the student. Ask the student to choose one of the pictures and write a story about it. Give no help with spelling. Have the student write for 15 to 20 minutes. *Interpretation:* Adequate display of each skill appropriate to the student's grade placement. Style reflects the individualism of the writer. Yet, there are certain conventions of style, reflected in the target skills, that the writer must master so the writing can be easily understood and enjoyed by the reader.

Sample Items for Tests of Written Expression. Specific sample items are presented in Appendix C that you can use if time is not available to create items or to find test items published elsewhere. These items are coded to match the sequence of skills on the Written Expression Curriculum Chart (Figure 7.4). They require the student to recognize and select correct and incorrect usage rather than to produce a sentence using the skill.

These items take the form of friendly letters and assess skills at approximately grades one and two. The student is to circle each error on the page. Depending on the age and achievement level of the student, consideration should be given to having the student correctly rewrite the letter, although this procedures is not necessary for the task at hand. In the appendix, a teacher's copy of these letters shows the correct responses and the curriculum skill matched to the written expression curriculum chart (following the errors).

Test items requiring selection responses for grades three through six are presented in multiple-choice format, requiring the student to underline the correct answer. The teacher may read the instructions for each item to those students who cannot read on their own.

You are reminded to use authentic performance assessment tasks so that the student can have the chance to *apply* the specific curriculum skills learned in situations where real-life applications are studied.

Step 4: Obtain a Sample of the Student's Writing

If you have not used the Student Interview (Figure 4.9) questions as part of the General Teacher Survey (see Chapter 4), when you first meet the student for the assessment it is a good idea to spend a few minutes getting acquainted and learning what the student thinks about written expression. During this interview, you might have some questions prepared to ascertain the student's attitude toward writing, specific skills that are troublesome, the value placed on writing, and instructional strategies the student finds meaningful. Other questions you might use are suggested in Figure 7.7. A direct, face-to-face interview provides information you cannot obtain from any other source. Also, it suggests to the student that you care enough to spend individual time with him or her.

It is necessary to obtain a representative sample of the student's writing. The sample is then analyzed to determine what curriculum skills are known and used by the student. Additional assessment must be conducted to assess knowledge and application of skills not used in the sample. If students are reluctant to write, you might change the task slightly (for instance, let the student choose a picture or a story starter) or assign the task at a different time when the student is more willing. Regardless, it is imperative to obtain a sample so that you have a base from which to begin instruction and additional assessment.

This first writing sample should require the student to integrate as many curriculum skills as possible. Examples of good tasks are writing a story, letter, essay, or term paper, depending on the grade level of the student. The writing task used for the initial production assessment must be highly motivating for the student in order to elicit the best writing possible. Therefore, it is necessary that you know your student's interests before selecting the story starter for narratives and the purpose and audience if other formats are used. Conduct the assessment in an informal, yet businesslike manner so that the process is fun for both you and the student. Instructions for obtaining a written sample of a story were given in Step 3.

Step 5: Analyze the Written Sample

Analyses of short writing samples can be used for multiple assessment and programming purposes, including screening and even eligibility decisions (Parker, Tindal, & Hasbrouck, 1991). The written sample is first evaluated by answering the Ideation Evaluation Questions (see Figure 7.6). Be sure to answer each question. The evaluation of ideation is the most subjective of all the components; it is essentially a holistic approach. Evaluating ideation must always be conducted with the writer's age and grade placement in mind. For comparison purposes, it is helpful to be familiar with the writing of other students of the same age and grade as the target student. Also, it is important to know what specific skills have been taught as part of the student's language arts curriculum. Keeping these factors in mind will

FIGURE 7.7   Some Questions about Written Expression to Use for the Student Interview

1. What kinds of writing do you do in class?
2. Which of these do you enjoy?
3. Which do you not like?
4. What type of writing do you do best?
5. What type of writing assignment do you not like?
6. What about writing is hard for you?
7. What could the teacher do to make writing more fun for you?

make the subjective judgments more reliable and valid. Inexperienced teachers are advised to consult with teachers who have taught language arts to similar students.

After answering items of the ideation section, use your curriculum chart or list to analyze Mechanics and Usage. Circle all *mechanics* errors of capitalization, punctuation, abbreviation, and number directly on the written sample. Underline all errors of *usage*. Use a wavy line to underline misspelled words, including those repeatedly misspelled. It is not a good idea to return the student's writing to the student if it has been marked with many errors.

Step 6: Document Test Results

For curriculum-based assessment and programming to be effective, it is necessary that you document results of your assessment to show skills the student knows and those to be learned. A good record-keeping system is vital to this procedure. Choose one of your own, or use the one suggested in this chapter. In either case, make sure that it is easy to use and easily understood by you, the student, the parent, and other professionals. Consider using colored markers or highlighters directly on the curriculum chart, with each color representing a separate type of response, instructional strategy, or some other meaning. Your documentation can be a valuable tool to explain your student's progress to others and also helps you to make decisions about when to reprocess the student through the CBA/P cycle. One approach to documenting your test results is given here:

1. Place your curriculum chart or skills list beside the student's written sample. Make sure the chart or list shows those skills designated by the teacher as appropriate for the target student. Place a check mark on the chart or list beside the skills selected by the teacher.
2. Examine the errors you marked on the written sample. Find the skills on the curriculum chart that represent the errors and mark them by *underlining the skills on the curriculum chart.*

These skills require your attention for direct teaching.
3. Note the skills on the chart or list that are checked but *not* used in the writing sample. Circle these. They are the skills to assess next.

Step 7: Continue Assessment

Dictate sentences for the student to write that contain the skills checked by the teacher on the curriculum chart or list but that were not used by the student in the first writing sample. Some sample items you may use are given in Appendix C. Remember, always begin your assessment with tasks that require the student to produce writing (that is, initial test items should require production responses).

Begin testing of these checked skills at the student's grade placement. For older students, begin testing at the grade level where most errors were made. If you are conducting the assessment while teaching, you will be able to assess only a few skills at a time. You will have to schedule a few minutes each day to test the remaining skills. Otherwise, once all skills at the student's grade placement have been assessed, continue assessing the remaining skills with a check, moving one-by-one toward the lower grade levels. Continue in this manner until *all* skills have been assessed.

After dictating test items for the student to write, analyze the responses. For correct responses, mark the curriculum chart with a "+" in the column marked "P" for production responses. For incorrect responses, put a "−" in the same column. For the known skills (the ones with a "+"), plan maintenance instructional strategies for review. For the unknown skills (the ones with a "−"), further assessment must be conducted using test items that require a selection response. This procedure is the next step.

Step 8: Continue Assessment for Selection Responses

Examine the curriculum chart or list and note those items that were missed during the dictation tests. Gather test items to assess these skills. Remember, these items must require selection responses wherein, for example, the student underlines or circles the errors or the correct answers to questions. You may use items found in workbooks or even in other tests. You may create your own items, write them on the chalkboard, and ask the student to circle the errors in the sentence. The objective is to determine if the student can recognize errors (or correct use) of the curriculum skills missed in the dictation items. Be sure to assess each target skill on the curriculum chart or list. Sometimes, several skills can be assessed in one sentence to save time. For those items responded to correctly, mark the curriculum chart with "+" in the "S" column (for *selection* responses). For incorrect items, put "–" in the same column.

Plan to teach the student to actually use (write in a sentence) the skills correctly recognized. First, have the student *copy* sentences in which the skills are correctly used. Then, have the student use the skill in a fill-in-the-blank exercise. When the student can do these exercises correctly, reassess the skill using dictated sentences. Correct responses for these dictated sentences will be marked with "+" in the "P" column to indicate successful production responses. These skills will be reviewed via your maintenance instructional strategies. If the student cannot successfully complete the dictation exercises, return to the copy exercises and then the fill-in-the-blank exercises until success is met. Those items marked as incorrect with "–" in the "S" column require your instruction. You will plan developmental strategies to teach these as new skills.

Alternative Assessment Approaches. Although this text advocates direct assessment of specific curriculum skills actually taught, there are other approaches taken to the assessment of written expression. Luftig (1989) discusses a variety of analytical techniques; McLoughlin and Lewis (1994) give a variety of instruments used in assessment, and Taylor (1993) reviews tests used to assess written expression.

Fluency Measures. Most assessment approaches look at fluency in one way or another. Fluency can mean the number of items written in a piece (i.e., the number of letters, words, correctly spelled words, letter sequences, sentences, etc.) as well as the number of items written within a certain time span resulting in a measure of rate of writing. Obviously the more words written the higher the rate of writing. Rate is a useful measure in written expression. For instance, a student may write three words correctly in a very legible handwriting, but if it took five minutes to write the three words there would be an obvious problem requiring remediation. Figure 7.8 presents some approaches to assessment concerned with fluency.

Checklists. Informal checklists are available to assist in the assessment of basic skills in written expression. Checklists can be used to structure diagnostic observations, facilitate success and error analysis of work samples and test performance, and document student performance (Choate, 1990a). Checklists for assessing written expression usually are based on an analysis of a written sample (Poteet, 1980; Weiner, 1980).

Published Tests. Published formal and informal tests of written expression should be used only to the extent that the skills assessed match the skills taught in the classroom. If a comparison is needed between a given student and the "national average" for a given grade or age level, then a norm-referenced test must be used. Most group tests mentioned earlier meet this requirement. The best score for comparing a given student with the national norm is the percentile rank. For example, a student who earns a percentile of 36 has performed as well or better than 36 percent of the students, similar to his or her age or grade, on whom the test was normed.

In general, the teacher is well advised to assess curriculum skills by developing his or her own tests that precisely match what has been taught. For those students who are performing above their current grade level, skills may be assessed

FIGURE 7.8   Fluency Measures of Written Expression

Type-Token Ratio—The number of different words (tokens) is divided by the number of words actually written. The resulting ratio, if high, suggests that many different words were used in the passage. High ratios suggest a more mature writing than compositions with low type-token ratios.

T-Units—Assesses the number of *sentences* written. The T-unit is one main (independent) clause with all subordinate (dependent) clauses attached to or embedded within it (Hunt, 1965). If the word *and,* or presumably any other coordinating conjunction, is used between two main clauses, it is included in the second main clause. T-units are marked directly on the writing with vertical lines. Sentence fragments can be set off with brackets. Clauses can be designated by parenthesis with the type of clause written above it. This type of marking allows the teacher to establish the number of ideas used in the writing; merely counting the number of terminal markers (periods, question marks) as sentences will not give this information. The T-unit has been used as a measure of "syntactic maturity" by some researchers. It is especially useful in evaluating Ideation. The T-unit allows the teacher to determine the "sentence sense" of a student who begins a passage with a capitalized word and writes one long run-on sentence covering the entire page, ending it with a period at the bottom of the page.

   Houck and Billingsley (1989) asked normally achieving and learning disabled (LD) students in grades 4, 8, and 11 to take 20 minutes to write about a trip that would be fun to take. The LD students in grades 4 and 11 wrote less complex and fewer T-units than the achieving students. The reader is referred to this excellent article for a more complete analysis of other variables of written expression.

Curriculum-Based Measurement—Tindal and Parker (1989) looked at eight different variables relating to written expression on a 6-minute writing sample of special education students. Holistic judgment on a scale of 1 to 7 was also used to rate the writing. The percentage of words correctly spelled and correctly sequenced were the two most influential variables when the teachers used holistic evaluation.

by simply selecting test items for the higher grade levels and then administering them in the sequence shown on the written expression curriculum chart being used. The skills that are unknown would then become the new skills to be taught. This procedure is to be followed regardless of the student's current grade placement because it allows both assessment and programming to be truly personalized and ensures that the curriculum chart remains the assessment and programming management tool.

   Once a specific skill in the curriculum has been mastered, the teacher should conduct authentic performance assessment. This form of assessment requires the student to apply the learned skill in "real-life" situations.

PERSONALIZED PROGRAMMING PROCEDURES

Once assessment data have been collected, the teacher then personalizes the programming by ranking those skills the student must learn into priorities for instruction. Content, methods, materials, and specific strategies must be chosen carefully to match each student's identified skills to learn.

Step 9: Program and Recycle

After all the skills designated as appropriate for the student by the teacher (and noted by your check) on the curriculum chart or list have been assessed, select the *critical* skills for immediate instruction. Critical skills are those required for success in the student's classroom. Start with grade level skills and gradually add those at lower grade levels.

Your instructional goal is for the students to correctly *use* (produce) all required skills in writing tasks. Use the information in the "P" column to help you select the skills to teach. If the skill is marked with "–," schedule it for instruction. Monitor progress, and mark the skill with "+" when it is mastered; then, select the next skill marked with "–," teach it, mark it with "+" when mastered, and continue in this fashion. Be sure to follow this procedure also with those skills used incorrectly in the initial writing sample.

As the student masters the curriculum skills and you record the "+" in the "P" column, have the student demonstrate the skill in a task requiring an application response. Remember, these tasks are real-life, real-world situations. With evidence of successful performance, record a "+" in the application column labeled "A."

Selection of Content

To establish the sequence, or priorities, of instruction, one consideration may be to teach the most deficient skills first. Another consideration may be to teach the deficient skills in the order in which they occur on the Curriculum Chart.

The components of written expression discussed within this chapter may be used as a guide for determining which skills receive priority instruction. *Mechanics* contains the basic skills and is therefore closely related to most classroom tasks. The elements of mechanics that are the most basic include capitalization and punctuation. It would seem logical, from this perspective, that skills in capitalization and in punctuation would at least comprise a major part of priority instruction. With these skills the student can write basic sentences. The actual expression of ideas in writing, regardless of misspellings or lack of skills, must always be a daily activity especially in the earlier grades.

The next priority skills would be those listed under Sentences (sentence sense, different types of sentences, and syntax) within the component of "Usage." As sentences are developed and expanded, along with correct capitalization and punctuation, the maturity level of the writing is improved.

Selection of Methods and Materials

Once the skills have been ranked into a sequence for instruction, the teacher must decide what method of instruction with what materials is best for the student.

The assessment data can be useful in making decisions about specifics of instruction. For instance, knowing the student's interests can help guide the teacher's selection of the story starters and pictures for narrative writing. Observations of selection and production responses may suggest that the student favors one over the other. Also, observation of the student's peer interaction can assist in determining if independent or small-group assignments are preferred. Observation of fine-motor skills can help determine the appropriate size pencil and lined paper to be used. By giving careful attention to a variety of assessment data, one can match the methods and materials used to the student's learning style and interests in such a way that the student is eager to perform the writing tasks.

The use of computers in teaching written expression is an interest of many professionals. Male (1994) gives many strategies that teachers have used. It is an appropriate reference for using the computer with students who have a disability. In a study comparing handwritten stories with word-processed stories on a computer, MacArthur and Graham (1987) found that fifth- and sixth-grade students with learning disabilities performed equally well on both. However, the word-processing stories were written much slower, at less than half as fast as handwritten stories. Yet many of the students preferred composing on a word processor. The authors recommend that systematic typing instruction be provided as a part of any major use of word processing when used in the instruction of writing.

Computers can be used effectively to teach not only the basic skills in writing but also editing and proofreading skills. There are several word-processing programs available that are suitable for different ages. Editing and proofreading skills can be explored by using spelling and grammar checking programs. The teacher must review these programs carefully before using to be sure they are age- and skill-level appropriate. Some programs create more confusion than clarity for the very skills they are trying to teach. Therefore, evaluation of the programs is important.

Montague and Fonseca (1993) offer several suggestions for helping students improve writing by using computers in a computer-assisted composition (CAC) environment. They note that the use of CAC is naturally reinforcing and that it facilitates revisions, helps poor readers write, facilitates discussion about writing, offers a good alternative for students with handwriting problems, and helps students become independent writers.

Programming for Written Expression Subskills

Creative writing should be introduced as early as possible in the student's school career, preferably in kindergarten. The emphasis in the early grades, grades one and two especially, must be on the expression of personal ideas, *not* on mechanics or usage! Written skills, as noted on the curriculum chart, should be learned as techniques or tools to be used by the writer to express his or her ideas clearly to the reader. Note that it is the *ideas* that are of paramount importance, not the skills. Therefore, incorrect spelling, poor handwriting, and incorrect mechanics and usage all take second place to a writing sample that reveals a student's personal composition. As students mature, they will find it important to use the skills as tools, so that their most important ideas can be communicated effectively to others to achieve their purpose.

Most development strategies found in many classroom proceed in the opposite manner, putting the attainment of the skill before the freedom to express ideas in writing. Many young writers find this type of instruction drudgery and simply tune out because it is too much of a chore. Writing should be taught as fun and enjoyable. It must *not* be highly censured or corrected in the early years. Similarly, we should expect more writing from students than is currently obtained. Students should write daily for a minimum of 30 minutes each day (Graves, 1985). When the task is enjoyable and nonpunitive, students usually will be eager to express their ideas.

Every written product needs a reader. The writer must share his or her product with someone. Reading the product aloud to others is the best way to share in the early grades because many students cannot read the writing of fellow students because of handwriting, misspellings, and a host of other reasons. Written letters, memos, invitations, and the like should be sent to someone. Stories should be posted on bulletin boards or "published" in collections covered with a durable material such as wallpaper; instructions for making fudge should be followed by some aspiring cook. Writing, then, has a purpose—communication.

Communication is best achieved when the writer knows who the reader (the audience) will be. Everyone writes differently for different readers. Therefore, the first pre-writing activity should be to establish the audience. Usually it is the writer's classmates for descriptive, narrative, or expository writing. Consequently, classmates can often best serve as critiques of the first draft and make valuable suggestions for improvement.

Developmental   Strategies. Developmental strategies are those instructional activities to teach the basic foundations of good writing in some developmental sequence. These strategies are used to introduce new skills. Regardless of the types of students being taught, the instruction can be provided within a basic framework of effective instruction. The procedures which follow incorporate much of that framework.

Group Lessons.   In the early grades, the best developmental strategy is to have a set time each day for writing class. It should be a group activity at first; individualized personalized writing will grow from this activity. Each class should begin by oral discussion of a topic about which to write. The best topic is a common experience such as a field trip. This oral discussion sets the stage for thinking about what to write. It can lead to the development of an outline to organize the writing.

Once the discussion is completed, students should dictate the story, and the teacher should write it on the chalkboard. Most students should make some contribution to the story. The teacher should read the finished story to the class. Then, the class should discuss how to improve the story. In the early grades, the change of a word here and there will be sufficient. In the later grades, the technique of slotting can be used for sentence expansion and adding parts of speech such as adjectives, adverbs, phrases, and even clauses, thus making the writing more mature. An example of slotting is: The _____ dog ran down the street. The students can be asked to list words to describe the dog. These words are placed below the slot. Not only single adjectives, but also phrases and even clauses can be listed to describe the dog more accurately. The class can select the best choice(s) to write in the slot.

The teacher uses this oral discussion time to introduce new writing skills after every student's attention is focused on the task and a brief interactive review of learned skills is conducted. Each new skill, then, is introduced within the context of a piece of writing, just as a new word is introduced within the context of a sentence. The teacher must point out why the new skill is important and how it will make the students' writing better. In other words, the goal and the purpose of the lesson is explicitly stated for the students.

The new skill within the dictated story should be written on the chalkboard or on an overhead projector. In this manner the teacher models by writing the skill as the students watch. The use of colored chalk to highlight the major aspect of the skill (such as a capital letter or a comma) is sound instruction. Young students should copy the illustrated example and read it aloud as a group or individually to a friend. The example should be kept in the student's notebook or writing folder as a model for future reference.

The teacher must be sure that the student can produce the new skill correctly in an expressive writing task before assigning independent work as practice for the new skill. Students should not be allowed to practice errors! The teacher should ask the students to use the new skill on tasks while he or she actively monitors (checks) the students' work. This procedure allows for corrective feedback to students while giving information to the teacher to help determine if the instruction should be repeated for some or all of the students.

Depending on the grade level, the teacher should then assign independent work to write a piece using the new skill and integrating it with the previously learned skills. Here the individual personalized instruction can be implemented by having each student choose his or her own topic or mode of writing.

As a new skill is introduced, the teacher should make a chart entitled "My Writing Skills" and put the skill on the chart. The skill may be posted as a question such as "Did I begin each sentence with a capital letter?" The chart should always remain in full view of the class for reference.

The use of oral discussion to determine how the initially dictated story can be improved paves the way for editing and proofreading, processes that should result in rewriting as a normal part of the writing process. In the early grades, a one-time revision will probably suffice; in higher grades several revisions may be necessary before the student feels that his or her product is just right.

Free Writing.   In addition to the group writing lesson, there should be time during the school day for "free writing" when the students can write for the fun of it, without preplanning and without any specific learning objective. It is a time when mistakes can be made and risks can be taken without censure. Many students use this free writing time to keep a school journal (diary) or to write a story. Interactive journals between student and teacher or among peers can be used to increase enthusiasm and expand communication skills (Gaustad & Messenheimer, 1991); interactive journals also offer opportunities for detecting individual instructional needs. Some students may want to write as a team to produce a mystery story or play. A standard part of the writing produced during the free writing time should be self-evaluation, which requires proofreading and rewriting, or *proofwriting*. The students should keep their writing in a special writing folder that is available to them during any free time.

It usually takes the students several days to finish the first draft, which should then be proofread and rewritten. The teacher should be available as a consultant to assist in any problem and to offer solicited advice. Time should be set aside by the teacher for students to share what has been written.

Specific Teaching Procedures.   With this particular philosophy of writing, specific steps are presented as developmental strategies appropriate for use with all students. These steps are based on ideas influenced by procedures used in the Academy for Effective Instruction sponsored by the Council for Exceptional Children (Archer, et al., 1989) and by "Individualized Language Arts: Diagnosis, Prescription, and Evaluation" developed in the Weehawken, New Jersey public schools (Ezor, 1974). This publication was developed by teachers and is an excellent source of many kinds of instructional strategies. The steps presented in Figure 7.9 represent a general approach toward teaching new writing skills in the curriculum sequence. These developmental strategies, then, can be generalized by the teacher whenever any specific skill needs to be introduced to the student.

The sequence outlined in Figure 7.9 works well and should become an expected activity for writing class. Figure 7.10 summarizes procedures for the teacher and the student to ensure effective teaching and effective learning based on the principles and approaches discussed. See Archer and Gleason (1990) for an excellent and more detailed account of using these effective teaching procedures.

The teacher may want to use practical writing at various times, depending on the age of the students, to maintain interest and variety. Some topical ideas include check writing, friendly letters, party invitations, thank-you notes, job applications, personal diary, mail-order letters to purchase something, note taking, letters of complaint, a manual of directions, recipes, and articles for a classroom newspaper. Such tasks can serve as "authentic performance assessment" to determine if the learned skills can be generalized to real-life situations. Students often enjoy illustrating their final story. If illustrations are to be part of the story, space for the drawings must be planned in the final copy.

Learning Strategies.   The teaching of strategies has become a popular instructional approach to many learning problems. A strategy is a "series of ordered steps to solve a particular problem or complete a task" (Archer, et al., 1989). Archer and Gleason (1990) note that a variety of strategies to help students learn (learning strategies) have been created; they list common characteristics of learning strategies and give a discussion of many strategies to help students achieve school success, organization, and learning. Included in their discussion are strategies for learning skills in written expression.

Self-instruction strategies in written expression have been developed by Graham and Harris (Graham & Harris, 1987, 1989; Graham, Harris, & Sawyer, 1987; Harris & Graham, 1985, 1988, 1992). Many of these strategies were developed for use with students who have learning disabilities, but they would apply to any type of learner.

FIGURE 7.9   Teaching Written Expression

1. ***Experiences.*** The writing should be based on some first-hand personal experience of the student or group of students. The experience may be a field trip, a school convocation, community event, etc. The experience should be interesting enough to motivate an exciting discussion.

2. ***Discussion.*** The teacher leads the group in a general discussion of the experience asking "wh" questions (who, what, when, where, why). The purpose of the discussion is to develop ideas to use in the writing. Some questions may include: Who will be in the story? When did it happen (what year)?, What happened in the story?, When did it happen (sequence)?, Where did the action take place?, Why did the main event happen?, How did it happen (give details, feelings, etc)?

3. ***The Writing Task.*** The teacher specifies the writing task, making clear to all students the *type* of writing (story) the *purpose* (to inform and entertain), the *audience* (age of peers). The teacher may write the specific requirements on the chalkboard for all to see. A task may be: An informative and entertaining story about a fire drill written for other third graders.

   The oral discussion is the stimulus for the story. With older and more mature writers, story starters may include a few sentences that lead to an uncompleted story. Other story starters are pictures or a short paragraph specifying the task. Newcomer, Barenbaum, and Nodine (1988) point out that the use of a sequence of three pictures to elicit written stories resulted in more successful writing possibly because of the visual reminder of a beginning, middle, and an ending, especially for students with memory limitations.

4. ***Plan.*** The content of the story should be planned before writing is started. Attention should be given to the sequence of events in the story. Note-taking skills and outlining can be taught as tools to help the writer at this stage. These skills help students to organize and develop the story. The importance of this step cannot be overemphasized. Many learning disabled students begin to write without any time given to planning or even thinking about what they want to write (MacArthur & Graham, 1987; Wong, Wong, & Blenkinsop, 1989).

5. ***Write.*** The students should use their plans which may include outlines, sentences, or notes in writing the first draft. The teacher should accept what the student writes for the first draft in a positive manner. If the story is dictated orally by young students for the teacher to write on the chalkboard, it should be read aloud and copied by all students.

6. ***Proofread.*** Proofreading is often best done one or two days after the first draft has been written. A story can be written on the chalkboard, and the group can discuss how it may be improved. There should be only one new skill taught at this time (for instance, sentence expanding by using phrases or clauses). Have the students say the changes to be made, then write them on the chalkboard. Have the students read the story aloud, then copy the story.

7. ***Rewrite for Improvement.*** For disabled and low-achieving students, a second draft will probably be sufficient to show improvement. In any case, the students should feel that the story is "just right" before they consider it finished. The teacher should select one or two for posting on the bulletin board. All students should save their writing in their writing folder.

A variety of strategies are presented by Ellis and Lenz (1987). They present the WRITER strategy to monitor written errors. Each letter is to remind the learner of a step to do. It incorporates the COPS strategy by Schumaker, Nolan, and Deshler (1985). The strategy asks the student to **W**rite on every line, **R**ead for meaning, **I**nterrogate yourself using COPS (check for **C**apitalization, the **O**verall appearance, **P**unctuation, and **s**pelling), **T**ake the paper to someone to proofread, **E**xecute the last draft, and **R**eread for the last time. The *keyword* approach is used to serve as a mnemonic for recalling the steps in the strategy. It would seem that the letters

FIGURE 7.10   Effective Teaching and Effective Learning of Written Expression Skills

TEACHER	STUDENT
Choose a new skill to teach (Developmental Strategy) or an old skill to reteach (Corrective Strategy), then:	
1. Gain the attention of the student.	1. Am I paying attention?
2. Review related skills previously learned.	2. Do I know all preskills?
3. State goal of lesson and WHY it is important.	3. Why is this new skill important to me? • Can I give an example?
4. Show the student how to use new skill. • Model, using chalkboard. • Tell what you're doing as you do it. • Go slowly. • Make sure the student is attending.	4. Am I watching? • Do I understand what to do? • Do I need to ask anything?
5. Have the student do an example with you. • Give lots of verbal prompts so few mistakes are made.	5. Am I on task (doing what the teacher says)?
6. Have student do examples without your help. • Monitor the work. • If error, go back to #4. • If correct, praise the student.	6. Am I doing my best work?
7. Assign independent work requiring use of preskills and the new skill.	7. Am I paying attention? • Am I on task? • Am I doing my best work?

in the keyword would permit the recall of steps more efficiently if the letters stood for an important word in the step of the strategy. Creating a good keyword with this requirement is no easy task. In any case, teachers and students are encouraged to develop their own keywords for strategies important for learning a skill. For example, if students are told to "fire up!" and get involved in writing a story as an assignment, the TORCH strategy might be used as shown in Figure 7.11.

Corrective Strategies.   Corrective strategies are those instructional activities used to reteach a skill that has been forgotten, that is used incorrectly, or that is sometimes used correctly and sometimes not used correctly. Campbell, Brady, and Linehan (1991) provide an excellent description of some of the writing errors made by stu-

dents with mild disabilities. Corrective strategies are used to correct such errors in writing. These strategies can be presented to the entire class or to a group of students if a particular skill appears difficult to remember. Most often, the strategies are used with an individual student in a personalized way. Corrective strategies should follow the procedures given in Figure 7.12.

Some students have "written" many things before they entered school. Graves (1983) notes that children actually want to write; they have made numerous marks on numerous things such as walls, pavement, and newspapers with crayons, pencils, and chalk. Their marks are their unique personal statements, just as writing is. However, this natural desire to write is dampened by insistence on correct spelling, handwriting, grammar, and punctuation early in the school experience, thus requiring the teacher to use a variety of

FIGURE 7.11   Fire-Up for Stories: The TORCH Strategy for Narrative Writing

T = THINK about a plot for the story. Be sure it has a beginning, a middle, and an end. It has to have some conflict that is resolved. Write notes as you think so you don't forget.

O = ORDER the events in the story so that they make sense and follow each other logically. You can number the notes in sequence that you jotted down when you were THINKing. Add or delete events as you see fit. Then write the story.

R = REVISE after you read it to yourself silently AND aloud. Have a friend read it and offer suggestions for improvement. You decide if the suggestions add or detract from what you wanted the story to do. This step is proofreading. Then rewrite your story with the changes YOU want to make.

C = CHECK for the COPS strategy and any other changes you think are necessary. This step is the last check before turning it in to the teacher.

H = HAND your story in when it is due!

corrective strategies to rekindle the students' natural desire to write.

Providing cues and prompts for students who have difficulty getting started and organizing their writing can be a great help. Graves and Hauge (1993) suggest that the teacher first determine if students can identify the major story grammar elements (main character, setting, problem, plan, and ending) when listening to a story. Then, coach those who have difficulty with this task, using a cuing system checklist to help them when they write their stories. Stevens and Englert (1993) give an excellent summary of questions students can ask themselves when developing the subprocesses of writing. Some of their questions include:

Planning: Who am I writing for?
Organizing: How can I group my ideas?
Drafting: Did I include all my categories?
Editing/Revising: Does everything make sense?

Most corrective strategies suggest that writing experiences should begin as soon as the student enters school. The themes of the writing should come from the student's own experiences or thoughts. The clustering technique, spontaneous writing, and short conferences can help students organize their own ideas for writing. Writing should be done each day, beginning with a short period of time that gradually increases. Initially, attention should not be paid to spelling, mechanics, and punctuation; the emphasis should be placed on the intent of the communication. Some students view a speller or dictionary as a valuable aid even when correct spelling is not emphasized. Uncorrected errors gradually assume correctness in the same developmental sequence as does the writing; for students with problems in written expression, the rate of improvement is slow. Reinforcement of writing is best achieved from peers when students share their writing with them either orally or as "published" products. After interests and motivation for writing are well established, then skills for the development of good writing techniques and the mechanics of writing can be gradually taught.

Written expression instruction for students who are bilingual poses a set of unusual circumstances. In their review of literature about language-minority students and special education, Gersten and Woodward (1994) emphasize three points to keep in mind when specifically teaching written expression to students with a language difference. First, the tasks must be highly interesting and make sense to the student so he or she can link prior knowledge to the writing tasks assigned. Second, the student must understand the

FIGURE 7.12   Using Corrective Strategies in Written Expression

1. Choose *one* error made by the student and point it out in the student's writing. Explain that the skill is an important one and tell why it is best to use the skill correctly. Make it very clear to the student that the goal of the lesson is to use the skill correctly. Note the skill on the skills chart displayed somewhere in the room. A skill on the chart for a young writer may be: Always end a sentence with a period.

2. Model correct usage of the skill. Write it *in context* in a sentence (or paragraph) on the chalkboard, on large tagboard if it is to be used with a small group, or on the student's paper for him or her to keep in the writing folder. Highlight the skill in color.

3. Have the student read aloud the example that was written by the teacher to illustrate the reviewed skill.

4. Have the student illustrate his or her knowledge of the reviewed skill by writing it in an isolated task (for example, in only one sentence). Monitor the writing very carefully providing corrective feedback and reinforcement. Provide prompts so that the skill will more than likely be used correctly. Ask the student to use the skill in a different task as you provide additional prompts if necessary.

5. Ask the student to illustrate his or her knowledge and use of the skill in another task. Do not provide any prompts since this task will serve as a check on the student's achievement of the skill without your help. Make sure the student can do the skill correctly before assigning independent work using the skill.

6. Have the student use the skill within the context of a larger piece of writing as an assignment of independent work.

7. Have the student proofread the writing to determine if the skill was used correctly. Ask the student to choose a friend to proofread the writing for the specific skill under review. The student can write across the top of the paper "Proofread for comma usage in a series of three or more," for example.

---

concepts underlying the writing instruction. Teaching the concepts is no easy task; it requires redundancy, use of simple and declarative sentences, checks of comprehension, physical gestures, and visual cues. The teacher wants to ensure that the concepts are mastered. Third, the complexity of writing instruction and required tasks should be increased. The use of slotting techniques can increase sentence length for both words and phrases, while sentence-combining techniques can aid in developing complex sentences and thoughts.

Most students will require corrective strategies when they are learning the basic skills of writing. These corrective strategies may be used with all skills listed on the curriculum chart. All learned skills must be maintained at a level that makes them available for use as needed. In the next section, strategies are presented to help maintain those skills.

Maintenance Strategies. Maintenance strategies are those instructional practices used to en-

sure that learned skills are practiced and available for immediate use. The best maintenance strategy is to require that the student write something each day. The assignments should vary to maintain interest and to practice different skills that have been learned.

The following maintenance strategies are coded to match the skills on the curriculum chart (Figure 7.4). These strategies are suggestions and should be accepted, rejected, or modified according to student or teacher needs.

Mechanics
Capitalization, Punctuation, Abbreviations Numbers, (IA.1–.7, IB.1–.5, IC.1–,3, ID,1–,4). List skills taught on chalkboard. Have student copy skills and write an example beneath each. Keep papers in notebook for reference. Have student write one or more friendly letters containing all skill learned.

Capitalization, Punctuation, Abbreviation (Names and People's Initials), (IA.8–.9, IB.9,

IC.4–.6). ▪Have student draw a square to represent the house where he or she lives and write in the full names (including initials) of families who live on both sides of the street or who live above and/or below the student in an apartment. Have student write sentences using the full names of the neighbors such as "The Johnsons invited the Marvin F. Smiths to a party."

Capitalization, Punctuation, Abbreviations and Numbers, (IA.10, IB.10, IC.5, ID.5). ▪Ask students to write the time of day on the chalkboard using correct capitalization and punctuation. ▪Have student keep a schedule for three days showing the time of day in morning and afternoon when each class begins.

Capitalization of Proper Nouns, (IA.11 .13). Write sentences using capital letters (beginning of sentences, school subject, peoples, important places and things). Have student circle each and explain reason for capital letters to another student. ▪Have student find ten examples of capitalized proper nouns from a social studies text and make a list. Have student write a sentence using each example found in the social studies text.

Capitalization, Punctuation Using Quotation Marks, (IA.14, IB.12). ▪Have student copy one page of dialogue from appropriate text. ▪Have student create one page of dialogue about some topic of interest.

Capitalization, Numbers (Roman Numerals), (IA.15, ID.8). ▪Have student read a short story and outline it properly. ▪Have student create a short story, outline it, then write it in a narrative form.

Capitalization, (IA.16–.18, IA.20–.22, IB.19). ▪Write an example of each of these skills on the chalkboard: organizations, song title, geographic location, trade names, ethnic groups, professional degree, documents, and proper adjectives. Have student copy the example and state what it is. ▪Have student write sentences using as many examples as possible in one sentence. The crazier the sentence, the better. ▪Have student write a silly

short story using all the examples in as few sentences as possible.

Capitalization (Poetry), (IA.19). ▪Have student copy a short poem from a book of poems appropriate for the student's grade placement. ▪Ask student to compose a short poem about a topic of interest. Each line is to begin with a capital letter.

Punctuation (Apostrophe in contractions, possessives, and plurals, Underlining Titles, Exclamation Mark, Hyphen at end of sentence, Abbreviations in Addresses), (IB.6–.8, IB.16–.17, IC.8). ▪Write examples of each on chalkboard and have student copy. Student must write a sentence, using only one example in each sentence. ▪Have student write a thank-you letter to an uncle who sent a present of fifty dollars for the student's birthday. Use all examples in the letter.

Punctuation (Comma—separate items in a series of three; in a direct quote; introductory words; noun of address; following translational words; before coordinating conjunction; to set off main clauses; to separate confusing items; to set off incidental words, phrases, or clause; to set off modifiers), (IB.11, IB.13, IB.18, IB.21). ▪Inspect student's current language arts text to determine which comma usages are appropriate. Write an example of each on chalkboard. Have student copy the example and label each. ▪Have student write three sentences using each example from above.

Punctuation (Period—Abbreviations of Measurements), (IB.14, IC.7). ▪Have student measure perimeter of classroom and write the dimensions on the chalkboard using correct abbreviations and punctuation. ▪Have student draw floor plan of his or her house and label it with proper dimensions.

Punctuation, Abbreviations, Numbers in Reference. (IB.15, IB.20, IB.22, IC.11, ID.7). ▪Select bibliographical information appropriate to student's grade level from the current language arts text. List all on the chalkboard and have student copy. Have student read library materials that use these reference skills. ▪Assign a two-page research project that requires the use of as many reference skills as possible.

Abbreviations of Acronyms and Organizations, Area Code in Phone Number, (IC.9–.10, ID.6). ▪Have student list three or more acronyms and abbreviations or organizations. ▪Have student play secretary and write telephone messages to presidents or organizations in five different states. ▪Have student find the area codes for five relatives who live in five different states.

Usage

Speaking Sentences, (IIA.1–.3). ▪Encourage student to use complete sentences when talking with other students and when telling stories in front of class. Have student use sentences that describe and ask questions. ▪Have student relate a story to a small group of students. Student should use complete sentences and describe actions of a major character. ▪Have student listen to a story told by a classmate. Student is then to ask the storyteller three questions about the story.

Sentence Structure, (IIA.4–.20). ▪Determine which sentence type is appropriate for student's grade level from the current language arts text. Write an example of each on the chalkboard. Have the student copy each example and label it. ▪Have student write three sentences of each example on the chalkboard. Have the student write a one-page short story. With a red pencil, label each sentence on the paper.

Speaking Words, (IIB.1–.5). ▪Ask student to tell class some exciting event in the student's life. Encourage student to use a variety of words (nouns, verbs, adjectives, prepositions) in the correct order when speaking. ▪Ask classmates to tell stories in front of the class; have students listen and remember the different types of words that were used.

Words (Different Parts of Speech), (IIB.6–.40). ▪Inspect the written expression curriculum chart or the language arts text and determine the different parts of speech appropriate for the student to be using at the current grade level. List

these on the chalkboard. Have student copy these and write examples of each. ▪Have student write three sentences for each part of speech listed on the chalkboard. ▪Have two students write a short essay or story on some topic of interest. Have students exchange papers and label each part of speech with red pencil.

Words (Adjectives), (IIB.26, IIB.29, IIB.36). ▪Have student take a short story written by another student and add adjectives to modify every noun and pronoun in the story. Have the student read the story aloud to a classmate who must critique it to see if it sounds stilted or free-flowing. Point out that overuse of adjectives can detract from the story content, while proper use of adjectives can add to the mental imagery of a story.

Phrases (Noun, Verb, Preposition, Adjective, Adverb, Participle), (IIC.1–.6). ▪Inspect the written expression curriculum chart or the language arts text and determine which type of phrase the student should know at the current grade level. Write these phrases on the chalkboard. Have student copy the phrases and label each. ▪Have student write three sentences using each phrase. ▪Have student write a one-page short story, using each phrase. Underline all phrases and label them when the story is complete.

Main Clause, (IID.1). ▪Write a sentence on the chalkboard and underline the main clause. Have student write three sentences and underline the main clauses in the sentences. ▪Have student read a story written by a classmate and underline all main clauses with red pencil. ▪Have student read an article in a favorite magazine and underline all main clauses in that article.

Style (Point of View), (IID.10). ▪Have students think of some important and meaningful experience they had as a child and write a one-page descriptive narration of that experience. ▪Have students exchange papers and write the experience submitted by a classmate from the point of view of the child in the narration. Encourage the use of sensory words and adjectives and adverbs that relate to the feelings of the child in the narrative. Let another classmate read the short story and guess the age of the main character.

Paragraphs (Definition, Indention, Sequence within Topic Sentence, Connectives between Paragraphs), (IIE.1–.4, IIE.7). ▪Have student circle examples of each skill in a favorite magazine. ▪Have student write a short story with at least three paragraphs. Have student underline examples of each skill on the paper. ▪Have student underline examples of each skill on another student's short story. Have students discuss those skills underlined and determine how those skills not used could be placed in the story.

Paragraphs (Main Idea in an Expository Paragraph), (IIE.8). ▪Have student conduct research using books, encyclopedias, other students, etc., about a topic of interest in science and keep notes regarding the source of the information. Have student select the one topic gleaned from the research that is the most interesting and list details he or she learned from the research to support and expand upon the chosen one topic. Have student write the the chosen topic in a topic sentence expressing the main idea in a paragraph. The list of supporting details must be incorporated into sentences to finish the paragraph. ▪Have student rewrite the paragraph, first putting the topic last and then in the middle of the paragraph. Discuss with student the effect that this relocation has on other sentences and determine if any of the supporting detail sentences need rewriting or relocating. Have other students read the different paragraphs and determine which structure is the easiest to comprehend.

Ideation

Speaking (Telling Stories, Naming and Describing objects), (IIIA.1, IIIB.1–.2). ▪Have students tell a story, trying to increase the number of words used and correctly giving the name and description of objects. ▪Have students count or tally the number of different objects named or described by other students. ▪Have students tell another story, using more words than used in the previous story by naming and describing more objects.

Fluency (Number of Words Written), (IIIA.2–.6). ▪Inspect the written expression curriculum chart for the average number of words written for the student's grade placement. Have student write a short story, using at least the number of words appropriate for the grade level. ▪Have students write a one-paragraph short story. Have students rewrite the story of a classmate and increase the number of words by adding nouns, verbs, and adjectives to the story. Have older students increase the number of words in the paragraph by using additional phrases and clauses in appropriate places.

Level of Maturity (Labeling objects, Description, Plot, Issue), (IIIB.3–.6). ▪Determine which level of maturity is appropriate for the student's current grade level. Have student write a short story. Have a classmate rewrite the story, constructing it at the next higher level of maturity. For instance, if student A wrote a story at Level I, Naming, student B would rewrite the story at Level II, Description.

Word Choice (Accurate, Descriptive, Purposeful, Sounds, Necessary, Senses, and Emotions), (IIIC.1–.7). ▪Have all students write a short story about some topic and then exchange papers. Have students underline words that are descriptive, unique to the story, and represent sounds, senses, and feelings. Have student cross out all unnecessary and trite words and expressions.

Word Choice (Descriptive), (IIIC.2). ▪Have student sit by a window and watch what is going on outside. Have student make a list of words that describe what is seen in terms of feelings, temperature, time, etc. A review of adjectives and adverbs can precede this assignment. Have the student write a vignette to describe what was seen, using the descriptive words listed.

Word Choice (Necessary, Exact), (IIIC.5). ▪Have student write a five-line advertisement. Remind the student that the trick is to pack as much information in five lines as possible because it costs money to buy advertising space in a newspaper. After the ad has been written, have student telephone a local paper to determine what the ad would cost. Then, have the student rewrite the ad so that it costs half of what the original ad would cost.

Style (Sequence Words, Organization, Sequence of Events, Details, Cohesiveness, Clarity of Purpose, Reference, Modification, No Split Infinitives or Shifts in Tense, Person, or Point of View), (IIID.1–.10). ▪Inspect the written expression curriculum chart or the language arts text used by the student. Determine those components of style that are currently covered in the text. List these on the chalkboard. ▪Have the student copy these in a notebook for easy reference. ▪Have student read a story from a favorite magazine and underline examples from the list on the chalkboard. ▪Have student write a story about a favorite picture. Have another student underline the skills used by the student in the story.

Style (Organization, Event Sequence, Necessary Detail), (IIID.2–.4). ▪Have three students work together to plan a class party. Have them list in sequence the things that have to be done to prepare for a party. A review of simple flow-charting techniques may help certain students in planning. After the list is completed, review it with students and suggest any necessary changes. ▪Have students write a brief paper on how to give a party. Let class members read the paper and decide if they would like to do what the paper suggests.

Style (Purpose), (IIID.6). ▪Have student read a brief column in a newspaper, noting that the first paragraph is a summary with each additional paragraph being less important to the main purpose of the column. Have the student report on some school or community event, such as a fire in a neighborhood house. Ask the student to submit his or her piece to the school newspaper for publication. ▪Have student ask five other students what makes them laugh, cry, get angry, or express some other deep emotion. Have student use one or more of the findings to write a one-page story for the purpose of eliciting that emotion from a reader. Have other students read the story and determine if it accomplished the intended purpose.

Implementing the CBA/P Model

Begin the program by following the CBA/P cycle as explained in Chapter 3. After assessment has been completed, needs prioritized, and appropriate methods and materials selected, instruction is the next order of business.

Instruction generally begins with a discussion of some meaningful experience to write about with examples given by the teacher of the specific skills to be taught. Then the student plans and writes the assignment. One or two drafts are proofread and rewritten and the final draft is read by the intended audience. A new task with new skills is then assigned.

SUMMARY

Skills in written expression allow us to communicate our ideas for others to read. The components of handwriting, spelling, mechanics, usage, and ideation equip the student with skills to facilitate this communication.

Procedures have been provided to establish a curriculum scope and sequence in written expres-

sion and to assess the curriculum. Indirect and direct student assessment procedures were then specified. Developmental, corrective, and maintenance instructional strategies based on the assessment information were offered. These procedures complete the assessment/programming cycle in written expression.

CASE STUDIES

This section presents three examples of writing by students in the elementary grades. In the Sample Case a complete analysis and suggestions for programming are offered. (The writer thanks Ms. Deanna Cothren for her evaluation of this student.) In the two Practice Cases the reader is instructed to do the analysis and programming.

Sample Case: Jerry

Jerry is an eight-year-old male in the second grade. He has been identified as learning disabled and attends the learning disabilities Resource Room for two hours of instruction each week. He is a pleasant boy and puts forth much effort. He is right-handed and has good fine and gross visual-motor skills.

Jerry's IQ on the Slosson Intelligence Test, Revised is 91, suggesting ability in the lower limits of the average range. Expected skills could logically be those appropriate for the middle of the second grade.

Results of the Slingerland Screening Test for Identifying Children with Specific Language Disability (Form B), suggest that he has good skills in handwriting, visual perception, and visual memory when no spelling or writing is required. However, Jerry shows marked deficits in his ability to integrate writing with auditory and visual memory. He also lacks the attention skills necessary for processing information effectively.

School medical screening tests indicate that Jerry's auditory and visual acuity are normal. Also, his skills in listening comprehension and oral expression are age appropriate.

Results of reading evaluations show that his total reading score on the Woodcock Reading Mastery Test-Revised lies at the 29 percentile and is described as a mild deficit. Results of the Individual Evaluation Procedures in Reading (IEP–r) suggest a preprimer level for independent and instructional levels in both oral and silent reading. Frustration levels were noted at the

Primer level. Specific difficulties were noted in vocabulary development and word-attack skills. The apparent use of context cues aided his oral and silent comprehension to the middle second-grade level.

Jerry's written sample was analyzed by inspecting the first- and second-grade skills on the curriculum chart to determine those skills that were used correctly and incorrectly and those used inconsistently. The appropriate column was marked directly on the chart. The ideation evaluation questions were completed, and the obvious needs were written on the bottom of the page. Figure 7.13 shows Jerry's written sample.

Jerry was asked to write a story about a picture. His oral reading of what he wrote is as follows: "The boys and girls (title). One day the boys and the girls was going to the play place and play with the toys. They saw a dog and a bird. They went home. The end (tag)."

FIGURE 7.13   Jerry's Written Sample

Jerry wrote very quickly and the quality is below standards for a second-grade student. Most letters were correctly formed but of inconsistent height with some capital letters being the same height as small letters. The spacing between letters in a word was adequate, but the spacing between words was inconsistent. He did not center the title at the top of the page or indent. He showed only one reversal. However, possibly to avoid reversing "b" and "d," he used the capital form each time he wrote those letters. His overall quality of handwriting is similar to a student at the first-grade level. (See Chapter 8 in this book for additional assessment and programming ideas for handwriting.)

Jerry misspelled 12 of the 28 words in the body of his story for a 43 percent error rate. Most errors were attributed to his poor visual memory and his lack of ability to apply phoneme-grapheme relationships to the spelling of words. The misspelled words are not generally spelled phonetically but were correctly pronounced when read aloud. His spelling errors were consistent with his observed difficulties on the Slingerland test. Most of his misspelled words are those that are learned at the first-grade level. See Chapter 8 in this book for additional assessment and programming ideas for spelling.

Jerry's writing shows no use of capitalization to begin sentences (IA.3). He did not use the period to end his sentences (IB.1). He wrote the digit "1" for the number word "one." Jerry was successful in his use of nouns, pronouns, and verbs with the one exception of subject-verb agreement ("boys and girls was going"). Words were used in their correct place in the sentence, suggesting an adequate knowledge of syntax and oral language usage. The story consists of three sentences, two simple and one complex.

Jerry's written story of 28 words suggests only slightly lowered fluency for a second-grader. His story is rated at Level III level of maturity but is merely suggestive of a simple plot. His choice of words is similar to first-grade writing, possibly because of his difficulty with spelling. He chose the awkward expression "play place" because he could not spell "playground."

His story indicates some organization skill with sentences since they do express a central idea and are in correct sequence. Additional detail could have been added, and the sentences could have been expanded by using additional descriptive words and phrases to make the story more mature. It is easily understood. The overall impression is that the story is quite immature for a second-grader and below his expected level of middle second grade. Figure 7.14 shows the ideation Evaluation Questions form completed for Jerry.

Assessment results were noted on the Curriculum Chart. Inspection of the written sample also suggests that vocabulary development with correct spelling and handwriting are two related language arts skills that need corrective instruction.

In mechanics, the priority skills to teach are I.A.3, the use of capital letters at the beginning of sentences, I.B.1, the use of the period at the end of sentences, and I.D.2, the use of number words in sentences instead of the digits. A review of developmental and corrective strategies presented earlier in this chapter can give ideas for appropriate instructional activities. A review of maintenance strategies would also be valuable once the skills have been reviewed and practiced. Ratings on Jerry's Ideation evaluation questions suggest that he has some ability in this area that may need further development in the future. Skills in this area do not require the immediate attention so necessary for the other deficit skills.

Because of the number of first- and second-grade skills not used in his story, it would be important to assess these unused skills with tests requiring selection responses such as the sample items given in Appendix C. It is necessary to follow these with tests requiring production responses to determine if Jerry can use the skills in actual writing.

FIGURE 7.14   IDEATION Evaluation Questions for Jerry

Student's Name ___Jerry_____

Check the type of writing that is being evaluated:

__ Friendly letter   ✓ Narrative   __ Expository   __ Descriptive   ✓ Story   __ Report   __ Review
__ Essay   __ Business letter __ Poem   __ Other

A. FLUENCY Are enough words and sentences written to
    1. *adequately* convey the writer's ideas and purposes?   __Yes ✓ Somewhat __No

    2. *appropriately* represent fluency for
      a. an average, nondisabled student of the writer's age in the regular curriculum? __Yes __Somewhat ✓ No
      b. the writer?   __Yes __Somewhat ✓ No
        (Number of words written _28_)
        (Number of sentence written _3_)

B. LEVEL OF MATURITY (Check only if writing is a narrative)
    __ Level I Naming   __ Level II Description
    ✓ Level III Plot   __ Level IV Issue

    Is the level appropriate for age/grade placement?   __Yes ✓ Somewhat __No

C. WORD CHOICE Are specific words expressly chosen to achieve the writer's
purpose for a specific audience?   __Yes ✓ Somewhat __No

D. STYLE
    1. *Organization:*
      Is the writing well-organized with a clear beginning, middle, and end? ✓Yes __Somewhat __No

    2. *Development:*
      Are the *main idea* and *purpose* clear, accurate, and complete? __Yes ✓ Somewhat __No
      Is the *sequence* logical and orderly? ✓Yes __Somewhat __No
      Is the composition *cohesive* (no superfluous ideas and no errors in logic)? ✓Yes __Somewhat __No
      Are sufficient *details* (examples, proofs, reasons) and *supplementary ideas* used
      to support or develop the main idea or purpose? __Yes ✓ Somewhat __No

    3. *Comprehensibility:*
      Is the composition easily understood (no shift in tense,
      person, number, or point of view; no split infinitives; clear pronoun reference;
      proper location of modifiers, prepositional phrases, adjective clauses)? __Yes ✓ Somewhat __No

E. OVERALL IMPRESSION
Is the overall impression favorable (effective, interesting, creative)? __Yes ✓ Somewhat __No

    Check any area below that requires remedial attention:
    ✓ Spelling   ✓ Handwriting   ✓ Capitalization
    ✓ Punctuation   __ Abbreviations   __ Numbers
    __ Other _____

Comments:

Practice Case: Tiffany

Tiffany is an 11-year-old female who is repeating the fifth grade. She is an underachiever in most school subjects, but the teacher does not feel that she is disabled. The teacher asked her to write a story about a picture by Norman Rockwell, showing a family going and returning from the beach in a car. Additional achievement information is not available. Use the assessment and programming procedures mentioned throughout this chapter to analyze Tiffany's story shown in Figure 7.15. Make your notations directly on that page. Complete the ideation evaluation questions and mark the Curriculum Chart appropriately. Add any necessary summary remarks on the bottom of the page.

Since Tiffany is repeating the fifth grade, skills at the sixth-grade level would not be expected. Begin your analysis with the fifth-grade level skills. Be sure to check skills below the fifth-grade level that are in obvious need of remediation.

Practice Case: Carol

Carol is mildly retarded and a student in a full-time special education program. She is eight years old and is quite verbal. Use the procedures discussed throughout this chapter to assess her written expression sample shown in Figure 7.16 and to plan for programming. Try to decipher the words she wrote before checking what she read aloud in Figure 7.17.

FIGURE 7.15 Tiffany's Written Sample

Tiffany 11

The story looks like their going on a long family trip for they can have some fun they went to a circus that was two miles away from their home they saw lots of things after the circus was close they went 1 miles to their grand parents house they spend a hole day away from home when they left their grandparents house their mother went two sleep she was very tired and the children was Bord when they left the were very eixited about it because they want to tell their friends.

FIGURE 7.16   Carol's Written Sample

She got in a fot
She got a bok oe
hre ne is us srr
S hre s or on tod
hre har is mis up
hre sos or mis up
She had to go to the
prss of is
hre rib b is or mes up

FIGURE 7.17   Carol's Reading of Her Written Sample

She got in a fight.

She got a black eye.

Her knee is sure scraped.

Her shoes are untied.

Her hair is messed up.

Her socks are messed up.

She had to go to the principal's office.

Her ribbons are messed up.

ENRICHMENT ACTIVITIES

The following activities are designed to allow you to develop and enrich the skills you learned in this chapter. The discussion issues require your thinking about the content of the chapter and its general implications. The reinforcement activities are practical, action-oriented tasks that may concern current practices in your local schools and state.

Discussion

1. Explain why written expression is considered to be the last phase of language development. What are the necessary prerequisite skills for adequate development of written expression? What is the relationship of instructional strategies to the development of written expression? Can a given instructional strategy be considered "correct" or "incorrect" within the developmental sequence of language and written expression?

2. Discuss the effect of spelling and handwriting on written expression. What are the effects from the writer's perspective and from the reader's perspective? How important are these related skills? How much instructional time should be devoted to these skills in relation to the instructional time allocated for teaching written expression?

3. Discuss the reasons for poor performance in written expression by disabled students. Do students with different disabilities perform differently? Why? What are the characteristics of written expression that are unique to specific disabilities? What characteristics are seen among several disabling conditions?

4. Discuss several things the teacher can do to help the student remember to use a particular skill such as placing a comma after items in a series. Which skill is forgotten the most frequently by students just learning to write, by junior high students, and by senior high school students? Why? How can it be taught so that the student does NOT forget to use it?

5. Explain how written expression fits into the "whole language" approach to teaching the language arts. Do you agree with this approach or do you think it should be taught as a separate subject area? Why? What are the advantages and disadvantages of both approaches?

Special Projects

1. Contact the department of special education in your state and determine if a curriculum in written expression is suggested for the different disabling conditions. Do the same at the local school level. Obtain a copy of the curriculum guidelines and note if it specifies the number of minutes per day or week for teaching written expression. If not, where in the curriculum should this academic area be taught?

2. Organize a team composed of yourself and two others. Each team member will interview teachers asking them to describe the most common characteristics of their students' writing. One team member should interview a learning disabilities teacher and a teacher of the mentally retarded at the elementary, middle school, and senior high school level (six interviews). Another team member should interview a teacher of the physically disabled and a teacher of the emotionally disturbed (six interviews). The third team member should interview a teacher of the deaf and a teacher of the blind at the three levels (six interviews). Set a time for the team to meet and discuss the findings. Determine the common characteristics across all disabilities and those that are unique to only certain disabilities. Make a final report to your class and include implications for instruction.

3. Interview the managers of several local fast food restaurants or other favorite places of employment of young people in the community. Think of five questions to ask regarding employment of the disabled. At least two of the questions should relate to the student's skills in written expression. For instance, you may ask the manager his or her impression of the applicant's skills, based only on the handwriting used in completing the application form for employment What impression does spelling have when reading the application form? Are written expression skills required on the job? Are any disabled students currently employed at that location? Write a summary of your interview and report your findings to your peers.

4. Visit a special education classroom and obtain permission from the teacher to ask one of the students to write a story for you. Ask the teacher if there are three pictures that may be used as a story starter for the student. Have the student select one of the pictures and write a story about it. Inspect the product using the frame

of reference discussed in this chapter. Write what you would perceive as the appropriate instructional strategies for the student. Share your ideas with the student's teacher and solicit feedback. Discuss your findings with your peers.

5. Collect several language arts textbooks, all from one grade level, that include instruction in teaching written expression. Examine each text to determine if it includes any activities that can be used as an authentic performance assessment. Put these activities in an "Authentic Performance Assessment" file to use with your students in the future. If the text does NOT have any such activities, take the activities in the book and extend them to be authentic performance assessments. Put the activities you created in your file also to use at a later time.

CHAPTER 8

SPELLING AND HANDWRITING

LAMOINE J. MILLER

CHAPTER OBJECTIVES

This chapter is designed to enable the reader to:

1. Explain and give at least three examples of each of the spelling and handwriting subskills common to most spelling and handwriting curricula.
2. Describe several procedures for indirect assessment of a student's spelling and handwriting performance.
3. Develop appropriate plans for the direct assessment of the spelling and handwriting performance of specific students.
4. Select and justify developmental, corrective, and maintenance strategies according to the assessed spelling and handwriting skills of specific students.
5. Plan a tentative personalized spelling and handwriting program for specific students.

Spelling is a skill area that can impact on both writing and reading performances. Mercer and Mercer (1993) point out that spelling a word is much more difficult than reading it. Reading is a decoding process in which the reader gains clues from the visual stimulus. Spelling, however, is an encoding process and provides the student with no visual clues. Lerner (1993) states, "the student who is poor in decoding words in reading is almost always poor in spelling" (p. 447). Handwriting also has a direct impact on written expression. Students with illegible handwriting have difficulty communicating their thoughts and ideas in writing. The importance of spelling and handwriting cannot be ignored since they are support skills and fundamental to successful performance in the other subject areas of the core and collateral curricula. Barbe, Lucas, and Wasylyk (1984) and Phelps and Stempel (1987) suggest that about 20 percent of spelling errors are due to handwriting illegibilities. Although there is a strong relationship between spelling ability and good handwriting, it is inappropriate to suggest that good handwriting causes good spelling, or that improved legibility in handwriting will bring about a corresponding change in spelling ability.

SPELLING

Spelling words correctly is important for several reasons. It permits the writer to communicate effectively in written form and allows him or her to function competently in other areas of the curriculum as well as throughout life. It enables the speller to pursue a broad range of educational and employment options and increases self-esteem as well. Poor spelling, however, may interfere with an individual's employment opportunities, educational achievement, and interpersonal relations. In addition, poor spelling results in an unfavorable impression on the public, which considers poor spellers to be uneducated or careless.

Correct spelling is a mechanical skill, and, like any other mechanical skills, will decline if not continually used. To maintain and continue to improve their spelling skills, students must write frequently. After all, the only reason students learn to spell is to communicate clearly their ideas in writing. As Hillerich (1977) so aptly stated, "If they aren't going to write there is no point in wasting precious instructional time in learning to spell" (p. 302).

The current trend toward full inclusion will necessitate individualized instruction in both spelling and handwriting. Numerous professionals (e.g., Masters, Mori, & Mori, 1993; Meese, Overton, & Whitfield, 1994; Mercer & Mercer, 1993; Polloway & Smith, 1992) recommend a limited word list (five-to-ten words) weekly for students with special needs. In addition, rather than using *fixed lists* (a new set of words each week), a *flow list* is recommended. The number of words is limited on a flow list; as the student masters each word, it is dropped from the list, and a new word is added.

Spelling Subskills

The subskills in spelling may be grouped into five major components with numerous tasks comprising each component. These five major compo-

nents are reflected in the spelling curriculum chart (Figure 8.1) as readiness, basic words, auditory recognition of phonemes, graphemes, and structural analysis. An important, but often overlooked, component of spelling is the development of adequate readiness skills for formalized spelling instruction. The development of readiness skills in spelling is as crucial as developing readiness skills in other subject areas. Tiedt and Tiedt (1987) recommend developing spelling readiness through discrimination training, memory training, sound blending and auditory closure. Norton (1993) recommends considering the student's developmental spelling level. According to Henderson and Templeton (1986), children's invented spellings are of assistance in identifying which of five developmental stages children proceed through as they acquire spelling ability. Henderson (1990) identifies these stages as: Stage 1—Preliterate word knowledge in which the student uses symbols to represent words—students scribble, draw, imitate writing and learn letters; Stage 2—Letter-name spelling, the student begins to spell alphabetically; Stage 3—Within-word pattern, the student begins to assimilate word knowledge and conventional alternatives for representing sounds; Stage 4—Syllable juncture, the student increases understanding and usage of word patterns and the doubling principle—student is beginning to write fluently, use multisyllabic words, and spell a large collection of words correctly; and Stage 5—Derivational principles, the student's knowledge of the English orthographic system and spelling rules is extensively developed. This student has become a more abstract thinker, uses multiple-meaning words and homophones, and shows a greater awareness of roots, prefixes, and suffixes.

Students with special needs who have difficulty learning to spell pass through the same developmental stages at a slower rate than their normal achieving peers (Polloway & Smith, 1992). It is important that all teachers understand these stages are natural, and that students must be allowed to experiment and take risks with language to improve their spelling (Texas Education Agency, 1991). For students with special needs,

FIGURE 8.1   Sample Spelling Curriculum Chart

Student's Name _____ Grade _____ Teacher _____ School _____ Date _____

Directions: Circle the specific tasks required for success at this student's current level; in the spaces provided list any other tasks appropriate to the existing curricula.

Typical Text Level for Tasks

*SPELLING SUBSKILLS	K	1	2	3	4	5	6
I READINESS	I	I	I	I	I	I	I
A Motor Coordination	A.1 See Hdwr. 1B.1-.3						
B Visual Discrimination	B.1-3 See Hdwr. IC.1-.3						
C Auditory Discrimination	C.1-.2 See W.R. IIA.1-.2						
D Manuscript/ Letters	D.1 See Hdwr., IIA.1-C.4						

	K	1	2	3	4	5	6
II BASIC WORDS	II	II	II	II	II	II	II
A High Frequency		A.1 1st	A.2 2nd	A.3 3rd	A.4 4th	A.5 5th	A.6 6th
B Grade Level		B.1 1st	B.2 2nd	B.3 3rd	B.4 4th	B.5 5th	B.6 6th
C Numbers			C.1 1-6,8,10	C.2 7,9,60	C.3 11-15,20,50	C.4 16-19,21+	
D Colors			D.1 6 Primary		D.2 2 Primary pink, purple		
E Days					E.1 All		
F Months					F.1 All		

	K	1	2	3	4	5	6
III PHONEMES, AUDITORY REC.	III	III	III	III	III	III	III
A Consonants		A.1 Initial .2 Final					
B Digraphs		B.1 All					
C Vowels		C.1 All					

	K	1	2	3	4	5	6
IV GRAPHEMES	IV	IV	IV	IV	IV	IV	IV
A Single Consonants		A.1 Initial .2 Final					
B Blends		B.1 2 Letter .2 3 Letter		B.3 spr		B.4 spl	
C Digraphs			C.1 th,ch,sh,wh				
D Variants			D.1 n/kn;k/c; h/wh;z/s;ng; nk;f/ff;l/ll s/ss&ce;ch/ tch;Silent w, l,k,h,g,t,b	D.2 kw/qu;r/wr; j/ge;x/cks/ks; s/c;se;z/se	D.3 g/j;g/gh; k/ch;tw;g/gu; squ;n/gn;f/ph &gh;z/ze & ex	D.4 sh/ci,si,& ti;j-dge si/sh	D.5 sk/sch; skr/scr/sh/ch
E Short Vowels		E.1 Init,Med.					
F Long Vowels		F.1 Open Syll .2 CVCe					
G Special Vowels			G.1 2 together .2 r-Control .3 schwa er;or;ar .8 variant:ay; y;ie,igh;ow; oy;au,aw;ou; ou,ow,oo,u,ou oo,ew,ou,ue	G.4 schwa:le .9 avariant:ui	G.5 schwa:e,a, ai,u,o,ou;il, al,el .10 variant: oar	G.6 schwa:on, en,an,ain tion,sion; 11 variant eigh	G.7 schwa:io

(continued)

FIGURE 8.1 *(continued)*

					Typical Text Level for Tasks		
*SPELLING SUBSKILLS							
	K	1	2	3	4	5	6
V STRUCTURAL ANALYSIS	V	V	V	V	V	V	V
A Inflectional Suffix			A.1 No Change s,es .2 Dbl. Finl Cns ed;er;ing	A.3 Dbl. Finl. Cns. est .4 Drop Finl. E + ing .5 y to i + es			
B Derivational Suffix				B.1 ly,ful	B.2 ness	B.3 ment,ous,y ish,ive,ist ant,able,less ent,ible,ence age,ance,ture	B.4 ward,ary ion,ity
C Prefix					C.1 re,un	C.2 dis,pre,ex in,de,en,pro con,com	C.3 mis,im,ad ab,sub,sus
D Word Forms			D.1 Compounds .2 Homophone	D.3 Compounds .4 Contrac'ns .5 Homophone	D.6 Compounds .7 Contrac'ns .8 Homophone	D.9 Compounds .10 Contrac'ns .11 Homophone	D.12 Compounds .13 Contracn's

VI ADDITIONAL
    ANALYSIS

COMMENTS

NOTE: Check tasks as they are mastered, circling additional tasks required for student's advancement.

the spelling curriculum will depend on the individual student's needs as perceived by the IEP committee. Browder and Snell (1993) suggest that teachers generate vocabulary lists with direct relevance to daily living (e.g., Dolch word lists, phonetically regular words, survival words).

Skill Interdependence

The dependence of spelling readiness on the development of reading and writing readiness skills cannot be underestimated. The development of visual and auditory discrimination skills required in reading are also necessary for developing good spellers. The writing skills important to spelling are fine-motor coordination and writing manuscript or cursive letters legibly. Because of the similarity between spelling readiness skills and those for reading and handwriting, the sample items for tests of spelling in Appendix D do not include readiness tasks, but rather refer the reader to the readiness items in Chapter 5 and to the handwriting section of this chapter. Because of the importance of readiness to spelling, it is identified on the curriculum chart as the first subskill area with references to word recognition and handwriting. The second subskill is basic words and consists of high frequency and grade level words. The third subskill of spelling, auditory recognition of phonemes, is closely related to reading, but moves one step beyond to actual formulation of the letters represented by the phonemes. The specific tasks require auditory recognition of consonants, both in initial and final position, digraphs, and vowels. Graphemic representation of phonemes comprises the fourth subskill component on the curriculum chart (Figure 8.1). This includes single consonants, two and three letter blends, digraphs, variant consonants, vowels (long and short), r-controlled vowels, schwa, and variant vowels. The final component presented on the chart is structural analysis. This subskill includes inflectional suffixes, derivational suffixes, prefixes, and word forms. Tests representing each task within a subskill area are presented for the reader's convenience in the sample items for tests of spelling in Appendix D.

HANDWRITING

The quality of a person's handwriting is a visible, concrete sign of literacy. The person who cannot write, or writes poorly, is held in low regard by society and is likely to have a poor self-image. Wasylyk (1984) states, "Today's 'hurry up' society is a major cause of illegible handwriting" (p. 128). Illegible handwriting is costing U.S. businesses millions of dollars annually because of the ambiguities and misrepresentations that occur in bookkeeping, billings, order forms, messages and numerous other areas. The U.S. Post Office reports that millions of pieces of mail wind up in the "dead letter office" due to illegibilities in handwriting. Many school children today do not know how to write legibly because they have not been taught the mechanics of handwriting. Howell, Fox and Morehead (1993) contend that handwriting instruction consists largely of students copying exercises without and explanation or demonstration by the teacher. Handwriting is one of the most neglected areas of the elementary school curriculum and may result from the fact that few teacher training programs train teachers to teach handwriting (Graham, 1986). It should be recognized that the majority of children who require special education can learn good handwriting. As Milone and Wasylyk (1981) state, "Barring a severe intellectual or visual disability, or an orthopedic condition that involves the hands and arms, there is no reason why exceptional children cannot succeed at penmanship" (p. 59).

Handwriting Subskills

Handwriting skills may be divided into the following three areas: (1) readiness, (2) manuscript, and (3) cursive (see Figure 8.2). Various prerequisite skills are necessary if students are to learn to write successfully. The prerequisite skills include: eye-hand coordination, small muscle development, grasping the writing instrument, basic strokes, letter perception, and orientation to printed language (Mercer & Mercer, 1993; Polloway & Smith, 1992). Before formal instruction in letter formation is introduced, it is essen-

FIGURE 8.2   Sample Handwriting Curriculum Chart (Traditional)

Student's Name_____Grade_____Teacher_____School_____Date_____

Directions: Circle the specific tasks required for success at this student's current level; in the spaces provided list any other tasks appropriate to the existing curricula.

Typical Text Level for Tasks

*HANDWRITING SUBSKILLS							
	K	1	2	3	4	5	6
I READINESS I		I	I	I	I	I	I
A Concepts	A.1 top,middle bottom,left right,shapes						
B Strokes	.1 -;l;back o, front o;/ \						
C Motor	C.1 Fine .2 Eye-hand .3 Grasp						
	K	1	2	3	4	5	6
II MANUSCRIPT II		II	II	II	II	II	II
A Survey		A.1 Pretest					
B Lower-Case Letters		B.1 l,i,t .2 o,c,a,e .3 r,m,n,u,s .4 v,x,w,k,z .5 d,h,f,b .6 g,y,p,q,j		REVIEW			
C Upper-Case Letters		C.1 L,I,T,H E,F .2 O,C,G,Q .3 A,M,N,K, V,W,X, Y,Z .4 B,R,D P,S,J,U		REVIEW			
D Numerals		D.1 0-9					
	K	1	2	3	4	5	6
III CURSIVE III		III	III	III	III	III	III
A Survey				A.1 Pretest			
B Precursive				B.1 under, over, down curves slant, check strokes			
C Lower-Case Letters				C.1 i,u,t,e,s, w,r,p .2 l,b,f,h,k .3 a,c,d,o,g,q .4 g,j,q,f,y,z .5 n,m,v,x,y,z .6 r,v,b,w		REVIEW	
D Upper-Case Letters				D.1 O,C,D,E,A .2 H,K,M,N, W,X,U,V, Y,Z,Q .3 I,J .4 T,F,S,G,B .5 P,R,L		REVIEW	

IV ADDITIONAL
   SKILLS

COMMENTS

NOTE: Check tasks as they are mastered, circling additional tasks required for student's advancement.

tial that students learn the basic strokes of letter forms. Students who have mastered the basic strokes of manuscript, will learn the letter forms much faster; since the basic strokes are the major criteria for evaluation of letter forms, they are a great aid to self-evaluation. These six basic strokes include horizontal line, vertical line, backward circle, forward circle, slant right line, and slant left line. Figure 8.3 represents upper- and lower-case letters from a typical handwriting program (Zaner-Bloser, 1993).

The handwriting curriculum for students with severe disabilities should include alphabet recog-

nition, which may be introduced along with typing or computer skills. During handwriting instruction, letter strokes should be task-analyzed and taught along with verbal prompts. Students who demonstrate little or no communicative abilities or reading or writing skill may require facilitated communication. According to Browder and Snell (1993), facilitated communication involves teachers' use of hand-over-hand or hand-on-forearm support of students as they communicate through one of several ways: (a) pointing at pictures, (b) pointing at letters or objects, or (c) typing.

FIGURE 8.3   Zaner-Bloser Manuscript Style

Used with permission from the publisher, Zaner-Bloser Inc., Columbus, OH, copyright 1993.

Manuscript

There are a number of reasons why manuscript writing is the preferred style of writing to be taught to primary grade children. Those who favor manuscript writing claim it is more legible than cursive, is similar to book print, requires fewer movements, and is easier to learn. Although instruction in manuscript begins in first grade, the emphasis continues through second grade and is periodically reviewed through the upper grades.

Cursive

Cursive letter forms are introduced after the students have demonstrated mastery of manuscript letters and fluency in the use of these letters. As is true with manuscript, the basic strokes in cursive writing should precede instruction in how to make the letter forms. The five basic strokes of cursive letter forms include slant line, undercurve, downcurve, overcurve, and checkstroke. Once the student has mastered the basic strokes, he or she is ready for the presentation of the letters in sequential order, based on the strokes required in each letter. As soon as the student has learned the basic strokes and mastered the letter form taught, opportunities should be provided for practice in using the letter in meaningful situations (Ariel, 1992; Polloway & Smith, 1992). The suggestions presented in this chapter for improv-

ing handwriting are condensed. A more in depth treatment for improving handwriting may be found in Hammill and Bartel (1990), Mercer and Mercer (1993), Norton (1993), and Saland (1994).

Alternate Styles

An alternate instructional handwriting program that is rapidly gaining popularity is the D'Nealian Handwriting program that was introduced in 1978 by Thurber and Jordan (1991). This program consists of an upper- and lower-case manuscript alphabet that is designed for ease of writing that leads directly into cursive writing with little difficulty. The manuscript letters are the basic forms of corresponding cursive letters, and the majority of the letters are formed with one continuous stroke. The manuscript letters are slanted as are the cursive letters, thereby requiring little additional instruction when learning cursive. The downward stroke is perhaps the most important in forming the manuscript letters, as can be seen in the sample written by Bobby, a first grader who has almost mastered D'Nealian manuscript (Figure 8.4). Three important strokes for students to learn in the cursive program are the uphill stroke, overhill stroke and the sidestroke, which are similar to the undercurve, overcurve, and the check stroke in traditional cursive writing. A

FIGURE 8.4   Sample of Bobby's D'Nealian Manuscript

Work Sample Analysis: Bobby has good letter formation and letter spacing; needs additional instruction in letter slant, especially "i, ., and w."

FIGURE 8.5   McDougal, Littell Manuscript Style

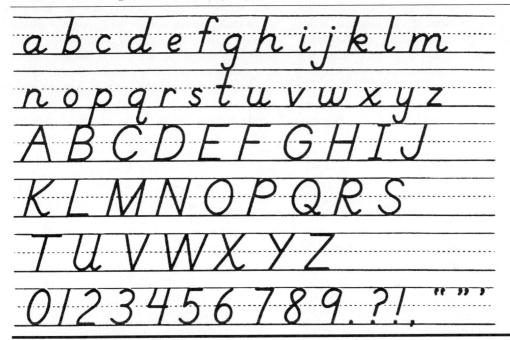

Used with permission from the publisher, McDougal Littell Handwriting Connections, McDougal, Littell, 1993.

new program, *McDougal, Littell Handwriting Connections* (1993) features similar shapes and slant for both manuscript and cursive letters, uses a continuous stroke, and has simplified cursive capital letters (McBride, 1992). Figure 8.5 illustrates the upper- and lower-case letters from this program. Although this chapter focuses primarily on traditional manuscript and cursive writing, practitioners using the D'Nealian or McDougal, Littell programs are referred to the teacher's manual (Thurber and Jordan, 1991; McDougal, Littell, 1993) for correcting handwriting difficulties encountered.

Although there are variations in each program, the purpose of both programs is to make the transition between manuscript and cursive writing easier, more efficient, and more legible (McBride, 1992; Thurber, 1993). However, Graham (1992) reviewed the research and the claims espoused by both programs and concluded . . . "there is no creditable evidence that the new, slanted manuscript alphabets make a difference for students in general or for special needs students in particular. The transition to cursive writing does not appear to be enhanced by using a special alphabet like D'Nealian." (p. 8).

PERSONALIZED ASSESSMENT PROCEDURES

Determining the student's spelling and handwriting curriculum and specific spelling and handwriting skills is necessary for accurate assessment and programming. The information provided from these sources will establish a base for preparing a spelling and handwriting program which is likely to improve the student's performance in these skills. As described in Chapter 3, the assessment/programming cycle specifies the necessary steps for implementing an effective instructional program.

Curriculum Analysis

The spelling and handwriting curriculum that determines the student's success in the classroom must be clearly stated in terms of subskills and tasks listed. This skill listing becomes the basis for determining the student's spelling and handwriting needs. An accurate listing is essential if the student's spelling and handwriting needs are to be met. The spelling and handwriting curriculum charts (Figures 8.1 and 8.2) list the skills typically taught in kindergarten through sixth grade. Although the spelling and handwriting series may differ in the order of presentation of the skills, the charts list the skills at the level most frequently-introduced among the elementary curricula. Those using the D'Nealian or McDougal, Littell handwriting programs should refer to the recommended instructional procedures in the teacher's manual.

It is necessary to identify what is required and what is available to the specific student in spelling and handwriting. This process may be facilitated by completing the teacher survey for spelling and handwriting (Figure 8.6). With survey in hand, ask the teacher to designate, on a curriculum chart, those spelling and handwriting skills that the target student must master at the level of concern. A variety of sources such as the scope and sequence chart of the classroom spelling and handwriting series, the charts presented in Figures 8.1 and 8.2, and curriculum charts by state and local school departments may be used in developing a specific student's chart. Teacher designation of the necessary spelling and handwriting skills on the chosen curriculum chart will provide the skill content for assessment. The important skills should be clearly marked on the chart to provide you with a listing of the specific areas in which assessment techniques must be developed. Charting the spelling and handwriting curriculum does not end with the survey, but continues throughout the assessment/programming cycle.

Several items on the teacher survey (Figure 8.6) are particularly important for assessing the curriculum at this time. The first question that requires specification of the spelling and handwriting skills expected of the student should be completed by the interviewer. Those specific subskills and tasks identified are recorded on the cur-

riculum chart with colored pen. The fourth question identifies those spelling and handwriting skills the teacher considers most important for determining the student's grades. During this interview it is important to identify how the teacher determines the student's grades in both spelling and handwriting. Are the grades based solely on the student's performance in the spelling and handwriting period, or are the grades based on the student's performance across content areas? If spelling is graded across content areas, is the student permitted to use the dictionary? If the word processor is used, is it permissible to use the spell checker? If the teacher does not have a formal instructional period in handwriting, how does the teacher determine the student's grade? Is the student permitted to use manuscript above third grade? The tenth question, the interviewer summary, ensures that the information collected from the teacher is accurate and has been clarified. Once the spelling and handwriting curriculum charts and the teacher survey are completed, the teacher is provided copies of the curriculum charts for continuous monitoring of the student's progress.

Indirect Student Assessment

Prior to conducting direct assessment, you can obtain valuable information about the target student's spelling and handwriting skills through indirect assessment. Analyzing relevant data from sources that are not directly observable, or may not be identified through direct assessment, can provide important information for formulating the diagnostic hypotheses. The result of the teacher interview will indicate those subskill areas which the teacher perceives to be most difficult for the student. Examining samples of the student's daily written work in spelling and handwriting and in other subject areas will provide clues for identifying the student's difficulty. The student who exhibits poor spelling and handwriting skills across content areas presents a different problem than the student who meets the teacher's criteria on spelling and handwriting papers but not in other

FIGURE 8.6   Teacher Survey: Spelling and Handwriting

Student _____ Date _____
Teacher _____ Interviewer _____

| A. | ASSESSMENT OF CURRICULUM: | ADDITIONAL COMMENTS |

A. ASSESSMENT OF CURRICULUM:

   1. Indicate appropriate skills, subskills, and tasks on an attached spelling and handwriitng curriculum chart.

   2. List current text titles and levels in which student is expected to master spelling and handwriting. _____
_____

   3. Check the primary source(s) of student's report grades:

ADDITIONAL COMMENTS

List available text titles/levels you would consider as options:

Describe grade sources:

Spelling:	*Handwriting:*	*Spelling:*	*Handwriting:*
___ Workbook _____		___ Teacher Tests _____	
___ Board Work _____		___ Homework _____	
___ Daily Work _____		___ Written Reports _____	
___ Combination _____		___ Other _____	

   4. Indicate the amount of time devoted to each subject by the current curriculum and texts per week.

Indicate time devoted to each by current curriculum and texts:

Spelling:	*Handwriting:*	
___Basic Words	___Letter Formation	___Slant
___Phonemes, Auditory	___Line Quality	___Spacing
___Graphemes	___Vertical Quality	
___Structural Analysis	___Alignment/Proportion	

   5. Describe instructional modifications that you have attempted with this student: _____
_____

Degree of success:

B. INDIRECT STUDENT ASSESSMENT:

   6. Rank order this student's spelling and handwriting subskills using <u>1</u> as the strongest in each area.

In weakest area(s) identify the most difficult tasks for this student:

Spelling:	*Handwriting:*	
___Basic Words	___Letter Formation	___Slant
___Phonemes, Auditory	___Line Quality	___Spacing
___Graphemes	___Vertical Quality	
___Structural Analysis	___Alignment/Proportion	

   7. Check the best description of the student's emotional reaction to his or her performance in each area.

Describe student's emotional reaction:

Spelling:	*Handwriting:*	*Spelling:*	*Handwriting:*
_____Over concern _____		_____No concern _____	
_____Some concern _____		_____Other reaction _____	

   8. Check any other subject areas in which student's spelling or handwriting interferes with performance.

Indicate why and to what extent:

Spelling:	*Handwriting:*	*Spelling:*	*Handwriting:*
___ Reading _____		___ Social Studies _____	
___ Math _____		___ Science _____	
___ English _____		___ Other _____	

   9. List specifically what you want to know about this student's spelling or handwriting performance. _____
_____

Attach representative samples of the student's work.

   10. Interviewer Summary: _____
_____

written work. The teacher's comments on the general teacher survey (see Chapter 4) and on the seventh question of the spelling and handwriting survey (Figure 8.6) will provide information concerning the student's learning characteristics and school adjustment. An accurate assessment of the student's spelling and handwriting difficulties through indirect assessment will narrow the focus and provide direction for developing appropriate assessment strategies.

Teacher Perceptions

Questions six through ten of the teacher survey (Figure 8.6) request the teacher to indicate those subskill areas in spelling and handwriting that appear to be most difficult for the student and interfere with the student's performance in other content areas. The teacher's response to these questions should shape and narrow the focus for direct assessment and save valuable time as well.

Available Data

All sources of available data are valuable—school records, recently administered tests, teacher's responses to the general teacher survey (Figure 4.4 and 8.6), and daily work samples. A detailed analysis of the student's daily work in both spelling and handwriting as well as other subject areas provides clues for identifying the student's major difficulties. Weekly spelling samples (test papers) are readily available and provide the basis for identifying consistent spelling errors. Other sources of written work should also be analyzed to verify noted spelling errors. Figure 8.7 is a story written by Chad, a ten-year-old fourth-grader. Notice the types of errors and the consistency of the errors. Those errors that appear to be consistent should be further analyzed, looking for clues that might account for the misspellings, such as incorrect application of a spelling generalization, illegible letters, etc. The teacher's comments on the general teacher survey (Figures 4.3 and 4.4) and on the seventh question of the spelling and handwriting survey (Figure 8.6) will provide specific information concerning the student's learning characteristics and school adjustment as it relates to these areas.

Organizing and classifying the information obtained through indirect assessment facilitates the formulation of diagnostic hypotheses to be validated through direct assessment. Diagnosticians, who are pressed for time, may streamline direct assessment if an accurate analysis of the student's spelling and handwriting difficulties are used to develop the diagnostic hypotheses. You may have noticed through error analysis that Joey does not close the following letters: a, o, g, q, b, d, and p. Rather than assess Joey on all of his manuscript letters, assess only those that are poorly formed. Assess both in isolation and in context. This may also apply to spelling. If, for example, in error analysis you notice that Mary consistently leaves off the silent "e," then develop a list of silent "e" words and assess that skill.

FIGURE 8.7 Story Written by Chad, a Ten-Year-Old Fourth-Grader

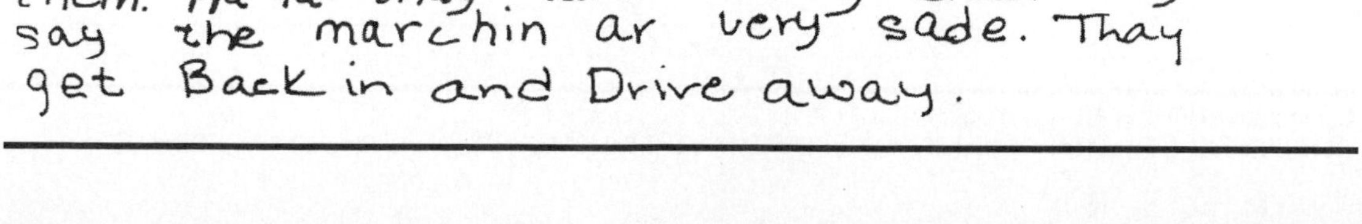
The Mar sons ar coming from another
plant. They ar craring andles to Eirth
whin thay get to Eirth Thay get out
to stish ther legs. Then thay have a
pinknk. dot ut every doby lags at
them. Ha ha thay have funny eirs. Thay
say the marchin ar very sade. Thay
get Back in and Drive away.

Direct Student Assessment

Direct assessment consists of three major tasks: (1) observing the student in the classroom setting, (2) conducting the student interview, and (3) administering and interpreting the personalized tests. Prior to initiating direct assessment, diagnosticians can save valuable time by collecting and interpreting indirect assessment data, formulating diagnostic hypotheses, determining assessment priorities, and developing an assessment plan.

Preliminary Procedures

The information collected through informal means, work samples, teacher interview, and error analysis will serve as the base for formulating the diagnostic hypotheses to be confirmed through the assessment process. Conducting error analyses on daily work samples of the student's spelling and handwriting papers provides direction and focus for direct assessment.

Work Sample Analysis. Research by Fuchs, Fuchs, Hamlett, and Allinder (1991) emphasizes the importance of analyzing students' spelling responses to develop better instructional programs. To conduct error analyses in spelling, it is helpful to know the most common types of errors students make. According to Ariel (1992), Miller (1990), Miller, Choate, and Rakes (1993), Norton (1993), Polloway and Patton (1993), Spache (1941), and Tindal and Marston (1990), there are certain spelling errors that are commonly found in students' spellings. These common spelling errors arc indicated in Figure 8.8.

Once the student's spelling errors have been analyzed by type, Gable and Hendrickson (1990c) recommend one of the following approaches for categorizing the spelling errors: (1) syllable, (2) sound cluster, (3) letters-in-place, or (4) letters in sequence. Tindal and Marston (1990) recommend analyzing a student's spelling errors using the "letter in sequence" method since it may be more sensitive to student growth. Detailed descriptions on how to use these approaches are pro-

FIGURE 8.8   Most Common Spelling Errors

SPELLING ERROR	EXAMPLE
1. A silent letter is omitted	(change-chang)
2. A sounded letter is omitted	(band-ban)
3. A double letter is omitted	(better-beter)
4. A single letter is added	(alright-allright)
5. Letters are transposed or reversed	(handle-handel)
6. Subsitution for a phonetic vowel	(whey-whay)
7. Substitution for a phonetic consonant	(city-sity)
8. A complete phonetic syllable substitution	(enough-enuff)
9. A complete phonetic word substitution	(here-hear)
10. A nonphonetic vowel substitution	(went-want)
11. A nonphonetic consonant substitution	(storm-storn)

vided in Gable and Hendrickson (1990c) and Tindal and Marston (1990).

Stowitschek and Stowitschek (1990) have developed a handwriting error analysis matrix to assist teachers in identifying letter formation attributes and communicating letter analysis to their students. They include 11 handwriting problems on their matrix (e.g., letters too large, letters too small, letters too close together). In addition to looking for error clusters, these authors suggest a correction procedure that permits students to self analyze and correct their own handwriting errors. Miller, Choate, and Rakes (1993) have developed a handwriting checklist to use while observing a student as he or she writes. This checklist will assist in pinpointing specific handwriting difficulties. The point at which to begin direct assessment is located by synthesizing all information to identify problematic elements. Data, relevant to the student's spelling and handwriting performance, will be used in developing the diagnostic hypotheses.

Diagnostic Hypotheses. Suppose that the teacher's major concern, expressed on the teacher survey, indicates Jerry's performance is consistently poor on the weekly spelling test. She also notes that his writing is nearly illegible. From your analysis of his work samples in spelling, you note that many of his errors appear to be caused by poorly formed letters. Although spelling is a major concern, from your work sample analysis, you might hypothesize that the first priority assessment task is handwriting, and spelling is the second priority. Indirect assessment of the handwriting product permits classifying errors in terms of alignment, slant, and line quality. Figure 8.9 is a sample of handwriting from Christie, a seventh-grader. Notice the non-fluency in her writing, the lack of slant and the incorrect letter formations. Analyzing the student's written product serves the primary purpose of formulating

diagnostic hypotheses to be tested through direct assessment. Ranking these hypotheses in order of importance to the student's progress in spelling or handwriting is necessary to facilitate planning for direct assessment. Error analysis and systematic observation will provide clues that will help in determining at which point direct assessment is necessary. In some instances, it may be necessary to conduct additional assessment to substantiate the diagnostic findings in both spelling and handwriting.

Assessment Plan. Efficient use of teacher and student time needs to be considered when planning for direct assessment. Classroom observations for spelling will likely occur during the student's spelling test. For handwriting, however, it will be beneficial to observe during formal handwriting instruction and another period of

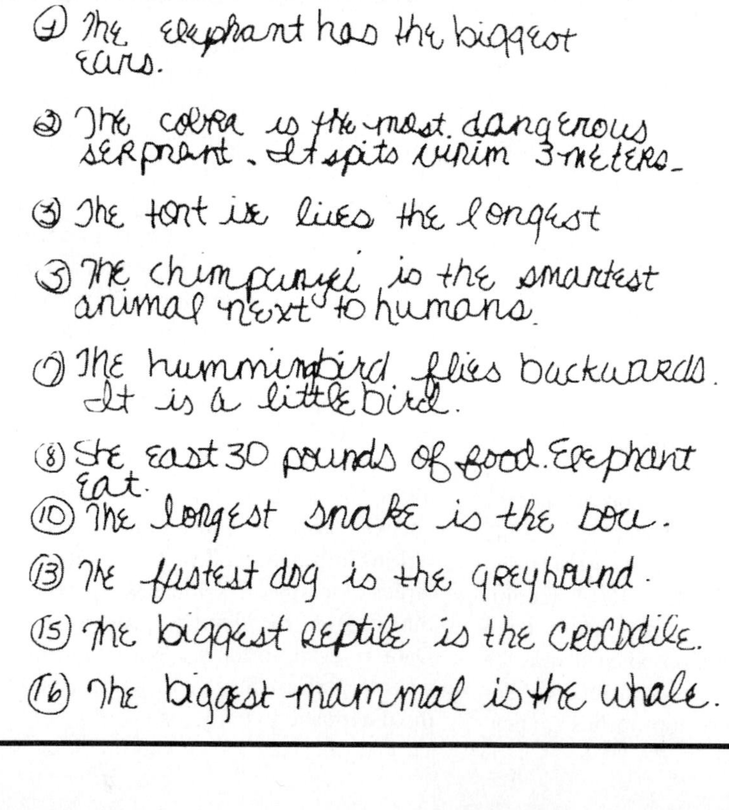

FIGURE 8.9   Sample Handwriting of Christie, Seventh-Grader

less structured writing. Plan the student interview so that it does not remove the student from those subject areas in which extreme difficulty is occurring.

To begin direct assessment in spelling, plan to use high frequency and grade-level words. If the student spells 50 percent or less correct at the current grade level, decrease grade levels until the student achieves 75 percent correct. At this level, note by using error analysis, the types of spelling patterns which appear to be problematic for the student. Randomly select writing samples from other curriculum areas and note spelling errors through error analysis. Are they consistent with the high-frequency and grade-level words just administered? Validate hypotheses by administering sample item tests for those spelling patterns that appear to be problematic in grade-level words.

Direct assessment in handwriting may begin with a pretest. Pretests, similar to those suggested in Personalized Spelling and Handwriting Tests listed in this chapter, are recommended (IIA.1 and IIIA.1). These Personalized Spelling and Handwriting Tests are provided as examples and should be utilized only if they match curricular tasks or when the teacher lacks the time or skill required to develop personalized tests from the student's actual curricula. Select either the manuscript or cursive pretest based on your knowledge of the student's current grade placement. For those students who are making the transition from manuscript to cursive, both pretests may be administered. In all cases where handwriting is a concern, direct observation of the student's performance is necessary (Mercer, 1992; Mercer & Mercer, 1993; Miller, Choate, & Rakes, 1993; Polloway & Patton, 1993). During this observation, particular attention must be given to letter formation, grasp of writing instrument, position of paper, and posture. Once pretests have been administered, randomly select writing samples from other written assignments. Compare the student's pretest performance with these samples. Are there consistencies in letter formation, alignment, size, and slant that need correction? If so,

develop your direct assessment tasks to substantiate these findings.

Classroom Observations

Observation of the student should occur in those classes the teacher indicated to be problematic for the target student. This will necessitate observing the student in spelling during the dictated spelling test. Particular attention should be given to those conditions under which the student is expected to perform. Does the student respond within the allotted time? Is the student's response immediate? Is the student attentive and prepared?

Classroom observation is critical for an accurate assessment of handwriting difficulties. Although students are adept at making letters "look correct," actual observation will detect those letters formed incorrectly. Additional factors which may contribute to illegible handwriting and may not be identified through analysis of the written product include the student's grasp of the writing instrument, posture, writing fluency and position of the writing paper.

Observing the student during teacher directed spelling and handwriting instruction will indicate whether the student follows teacher directions, rushes through the activity, wastes valuable response time, or lacks interest in the instructional task.

Informal Student Interview

Additional information regarding those variables which interfere with the student's spelling and handwriting performance may be obtained through an informal student interview. The preferred instructional methods as well as spelling and handwriting activities may also be determined through the interviewing process. "What do you like best in your spelling and writing lessons?" "What is the most difficult activity to complete in spelling and handwriting?" "Do you like to practice your spelling/handwriting?" "How do you study your spelling words?" Here, you are attempting to find out if the student has a systematic strategy for learning and remembering unknown words. The information obtained through the student interview may provide additional clues which will require verification through additional direct assessment.

Personalized Tests

To complete direct assessment, several procedures will be required. The spelling and handwriting materials used in the classroom are the most logical sources for developing relevant test items. Items from the sample spelling and handwriting tests, listed in Appendix D, which correlate with the classroom curriculum, may also be used. In some instances, selected items from other criterion-referenced instruments may be more appropriate and, therefore, selected for the assessment task. The critical factor in selecting the assessment task is similarity to the curriculum activities required of the student in the classroom.

Suggestions for Constructing Tests. To develop original tests, it is necessary to have a copy of the student's spelling and handwriting text. These texts, the teacher's guides, accompanying workbooks and skill activities, plus any supplementary aids provide the materials for personalized assessment of spelling and handwriting skills. For each task specified on the student's spelling and handwriting curriculum charts, a strategy must be designed to assess proficiency. The following suggestions for constructing spelling and handwriting test items are cross-referenced with the spelling and handwriting curriculum charts (Figure 8.1 and 8.2). If a different curriculum list is used, the tasks should be renumbered to correspond to that list. These suggestions are for constructing production level tasks. To assess application level tasks, have the student use the spelling words to write an integrated story or select five words and have the student construct a sentence using these words. To assess strategy usage, have the student verbally describe the process used to remember words. However, only the suggestions that parallel curricular format should be used to construct assessment tasks.

Spelling: Readiness

Readiness, (IA.1–ID.1). Use suggestions from word recognition, items IC.1–IC.3 and IIA.1 and .2 and the suggestions from handwriting, Items IB.1 and IIA.1–IIC.4.

Spelling: Basic Words

High-Frequency Words, (IIA.1–.6). Materials: Appropriate grade-level spelling text, word list in back of book. Select 15 high-frequency words from this list (and, in, like, she, etc.). *Strategy:* Ask student to write each word as you pronounce it, use in a sentence and pronounce it again. *Interpretation:* 75 percent accuracy. If the student consistently spells less than 50 percent correct, the list is entirely too difficult, and the teacher must move to a lower level text until the criterion level is established.

Grade-Level Words, (IIB.1–.6). Materials: Student spelling text at appropriate grade level, word list in back of book. Select 20 words, each representing a different spelling pattern from the word list. *Strategy:* Have the student write each word as you dictate the list. *Interpretation:* 75 percent accuracy. Use the same interpretation used previously. However, since you have selected pattern words, you should be able to determine which spelling patterns are a possible source of difficulty through error analysis.

Number Words, (IIC.1–4). Materials: Student spelling text. Select all number words contained in appropriate grade-level speller. *Strategy:* Student writes words as you dictate them. *Interpretation:* 90 percent accuracy. Number words are frequently used words that may require additional practice for mastery.

Color Words, (IID.1–.2). Materials: Student spelling text. Select all color words appropriate to student's grade level. *Strategy:* Dictate words and have student write them. *Interpretation:* 90 percent accuracy. Color words are important enough to require mastery. Select appropriate word-learning strategy and teach it to student.

Days of the Week, (IIE.1). Materials: Student spelling text. Select the names of the seven days of the week. *Strategy:* Dictate the names of the seven days of the week and have the student write them. *Interpretation:* 100 percent accuracy. If student experiences difficulty with this task, select the corrective strategy for teaching multisyllabic words.

Months of the Year, (IIF.1). *Materials:* Appropriate grade level spelling text. Prepare a list of the 12 months of the year. *Strategy:* Dictate the names of the months and have the student write them. *Interpretation:* 100 percent accuracy. Use same corrective strategy as for days of the week.

Spelling: Auditory Recognition of Phonemes

Initial Consonants, (IIIA.1.). *Materials:* Student spelling text. Prepare a list of words, each beginning with a different consonant. Include all consonants. *Strategy:* Pronounce each word and have the student write the letter that begins each word. *Interpretation:* 100 percent accuracy. Phoneme/grapheme association is essential prior to formal instruction in spelling and, therefore, must be firmly established. If student experiences difficulty, investigate task in Word Recognition.

Final Consonants, (IIIA.2). *Materials:* Student spelling text. Prepare a list of words, each ending with a different consonant. Include all ending consonants. *Strategy:* Have the student write the letter for the ending sound heard in each word as you pronounce them. *Interpretation:* 100 percent accuracy. Student should not experience difficulty if preceding task is mastered.

Digraphs, (IIIB.1). *Materials:* Student spelling text. Select eight to twelve words containing digraphs. *Strategy:* Have the student write the digraph contained in each word you pronounce. *Interpretation:* 100 percent accuracy. This may be a difficult task for some students. If the skill is firmly established in reading, it should not present a problem in spelling.

Vowels, (IIIC.1). *Materials:* Student spelling text. Develop a list of words which contain both short and long vowel sounds. *Strategy:* Have the student write the letter for the vowel sound heard in each word you pronounce. *Interpretation:* 100 percent accuracy. Mastery of this skill is most important for correct spelling. If the student performs below criterion, additional teaching and reinforcement activities must be initiated to achieve mastery.

Spelling: Graphemes

Initial Consonants, (IVA.1). *Materials:* Student spelling text. Develop a list of words, each beginning with a different consonant. *Strategy:* Have the student write the words as you dictate them. *Interpretation:* 90 percent accuracy. Check for correct spelling of all words with particular emphasis given to the correct initial letter.

Final Consonants, (IVA.2). *Materials:* Student spelling text. Develop a list of words each with a different ending consonant. *Strategy:* Dictate the words and have the student write them. *Interpretation:* 90 percent accuracy. Same as the preceding task but with emphasis now on the ending consonant.

Two Letter Blends, (IVB.1). *Materials:* Student spelling text. Develop a list of words containing all of the two letter blends. *Strategy:* Have the student write the words as they are dictated. *Interpretation:* 90 percent accuracy. If this skill has been mastered in reading, the student should experience little difficulty. Concern should be in noting whether the two letter blends are spelled correctly.

Three Letter Blends, (IVB.2–.4). *Materials:* Appropriate grade-level spelling text. Develop a list of words containing three letter blends. *Strategy:* Dictate the list of words and have the student write them. *Interpretation:* 90 percent accuracy. Same as preceding task, only concern should be directed at correct spelling of three-letter blends.

Digraphs, (IVC.1). *Materials:* Student spelling text. Develop a list of words containing digraphs in both initial and final position. *Strategy:* Student writes words as they are dictated. *Interpretation:* 90 percent accuracy.

Correct spelling of the words is important, but particular emphasis should be directed at correct spelling of the digraphs.

Variant Consonant Spellings, (IVD.1–.5). *Materials:* Appropriate grade-level spelling text. Develop a list of words which contain variant consonant spellings. The curricular demands chart, currently in use in your system or school, will be invaluable in assisting with this task. *Strategy:* Dictate the words and have the student write them. *Interpretation:* 90 percent accuracy. This may be a difficult task for some students. Through error analysis, note which variant spellings give the student difficulty and reteach those spelling generalizations.

Spelling: Vowels

Short Vowels, Initial and Medial Position, (IVE.1). *Materials:* Student spelling text. Develop a list of words containing the short vowel sound in both the initial and medial position. *Strategy:* Have the student write the words as you dictate them. *Interpretation:* 100 percent accuracy. According to Spache (1941), phonetic substitution for a vowel is a common spelling error that students exhibit. Any noted vowel substitutions may require reteaching vowel sounds.

Long Vowels, Single Open Syllable, (IVF.1). *Materials:* Student spelling text. Develop a list of words containing the long vowel sound in a single open syllable. *Strategy:* Dictate words and have student write them. *Interpretation:* 100 percent accuracy. Correct spelling will indicate student's understanding of the long vowel sound in an open syllable. If the student experiences difficulty, reteach the long vowel sounds.

CVCe Words, (IVF.2). *Materials:* Student spelling text. Develop a list of words containing the CVCe pattern. *Strategy:* Have the student write the CVCe pattern words as they are dictated. *Interpretation:* 100 percent accuracy. Students experiencing difficulty with this task should be retaught the following phonics generalization: the silent "e" at the end of a word makes a short vowel long.

Special, Two Vowels Together, (IVG.1). *Materials:* Student spelling text. Develop a list of words containing two adjoining vowels. *Strategy:* Dictate the words and have the student write them. *Interpretation:* 90 percent accuracy This may be a difficult task for some students. Many students omit the silent vowel. Highlighting, color coding, or any method for directing the student's attention to the two vowels may be helpful.

R–Controlled Vowels, (IVG.2). *Materials:* Appropriate grade-level spelling text. Develop a list of words in which the vowel sound is controlled by "r." *Strategy:* Dictate the words and have the student write them. *Interpretation:* 90 percent accuracy. Mastery of this task is particularly difficult because of the different spellings of the same sound. Any noted difficulties should be corrected immediately by presenting visual comparisons of the difficult words.

Schwa, (IVG.3–.7). *Materials:* Appropriate grade-level spelling text. Develop a list of words from the appropriate level spelling text that contain the schwa sound. *Strategy:* Pronounce the words and have the student write them, marking the schwa sound. *Interpretation:* 80 percent accuracy. Note any students experiencing difficulty with this task and reteach the meaning of the schwa.

Variant Vowels, (IVG.8–.11). *Materials:* Student spelling text. Develop a list of words containing variant vowel sounds from the appropriate grade-level text. *Strategy:* Dictate the words and have the student write them. *Interpretation:* 90 percent accuracy. This is a difficult task for poor spellers. Note students experiencing difficulty and reteach the appropriate rule with examples.

Spelling: Structural Analysis

Inflectional Suffixes, No Base Word Change, (VA.1). *Materials:* Student spelling text. Develop a list of words in which the root word does not change when adding "s" or "es." *Strategy:* Dictate the words and have the student write them. *Interpretation:* 90 percent accuracy. If the student has difficulty with this task, teach the following phonics generalization: the plural of most nouns is formed by adding "s" to the noun; however, nouns ending in "s, x, sh" and "ch" are made plural by adding "es."

Inflectional Suffixes, Double Final Consonants (VA.2–.3). Materials: Student spelling text. Prepare a list of words in which the final consonant is doubled before adding "er, ed, ing," or "est." *Strategy:* Have the student write the words as they are dictated. *Interpretation:* 90 percent accuracy. Reteach the following generalization for students who demonstrate difficulty with this task: double the final consonant before adding the suffix if you have one syllable ending with a consonant preceded by a short vowel.

Inflectional Suffixes, Drop Final "e," (VA.4). *Materials:* Student spelling text. Develop a list of words in which the final "e" is dropped before adding a suffix. *Strategy:* Dictate the words and have the student write them. *Interpretation:* 90 percent accuracy. Teach the following phonics generalization to students experiencing difficulty with this task: in a word ending with a silent "e," drop the "e" before adding a suffix beginning with a vowel. If the suffix begins with a consonant, do not drop the "e."

Change "y" to "i," (VA.5). Materials: Student spelling text. Prepare a list of words in which "y" is changed to "i" before adding "e." *Strategy:* Have the student write the words as they are dictated. *Interpretation:* 90 percent accuracy. There are two phonics generalizations to be re-emphasized if the student has difficulty with this task: (1) in words ending in "y" preceded by a consonant the "y" changes to "i" before adding any ending except "ing" or "ist"; and (2) words ending in "y" preceded by a vowel, keep the "y" and add the suffix.

Derivational Suffixes, (VB.1–.4). Materials: Appropriate grade-level spelling text. Develop a list of words with derivational suffixes. *Strategy:* Dictate the words and have the student write them. *Interpretation:* 90 percent accuracy. If the four preceding tasks are mastered, the student will experience little difficulty with this task.

Prefixes, (VC.1–.3). *Materials:* Appropriate grade-level spelling text. Prepare a list of words containing prefixes at the appropriate grade-level. *Strategy:* Ask the student to write the words as they are dictated. *Interpretation:* 90 percent accuracy. Any student experiencing difficulty should be retaught the prefixes and their meanings.

Word Forms, Compound, (VD.1, VD.3, VD.6, VD.9, VD.12). Materials: Appropriate grade-level spelling text. Develop a list of compound words. *Strategy:* Dictate the words and have the student write them. *Interpretation:* 90 percent accuracy. Students who experience difficulty with this task should be taught the meaning of compound. Start with simple root words which may be combined. Additional strategies may be found in the section titled, "Programming for Spelling and Handwriting Skills."

Word Forms, Contractions, (VD.4, VD.7, VD.10). Materials: Appropriate grade-level spelling text. Develop a list of contractions from student's spelling text. *Strategy:* Dictate the contraction words and have the student write them. *Interpretation:* 90 percent accuracy. Students experiencing difficulty with this task should be retaught the meaning of contraction and provided additional practice in forming contractions in writing.

Word Forms, Homophones, (VD.2, VD.5, VD.8, VD.11, VD.13). Materials: Appropriate grade-level spelling text. Develop a list of homophones with accompanying sentences. *Strategy:* Dictate the word; use it in a sentence; and dictate again. *Interpretation:* 90 percent accuracy. To be successful with this task, the student must use the context of the sentence in which the homophone is embedded. Students experiencing difficulty with this task will require reteaching of the meaning and spelling of the homophones.

Handwriting: Readiness
Concepts/Directions, (IA.1). Materials: Pencil, paper and models of basic shapes (✚ ● ■ ▬ ▲). *Strategy:* Ask student to identify by pointing, drawing lines etc., the top, middle, bot-

tom, left edge, and right edge of the paper. Present shapes, ask student to name or examiner name and have student point to named shapes. *Interpretation:* 100 percent accuracy. Since these are prerequisite writing skills, mastery must be demonstrated before formal writing instruction begins.

Basic Manuscript Strokes, (IB.1). *Materials:* Model of basic strokes from student's writing series (⊒ |ᐟ ◯ ↘◯ ⟋). *Strategy:* Present model of basic strokes. Ask student to name, trace, and copy these strokes. *Interpretation:* Teacher's professional judgment as to whether student's performance meets the criteria for current grade level. Research indicates that basic strokes should be taught prior to letter forms in order to master manuscript writing. Students who have mastered the basic strokes will quickly master the letter forms.

Motor Coordination, Fine Motor, (IC.1). *Materials:* No special materials are necessary. Teacher observation of student's performance in any, or all, of the following activities: zipping, buttoning, screwing caps on small jars, tying bows, etc. *Strategy:* Observe student's performance in fine-motor activities. *Interpretation:* Teacher's professional judgment. Those students who have difficulty holding a pencil properly often lack a high degree of small muscle control. Further development of fine-motor control may be necessary.

Eye-Hand Coordination, (IC.2). *Materials:* Pencil and mazes. *Strategy:* Ask the student to follow the maze without touching the exterior lines. *Interpretation:* Teacher's professional judgment of adequate performance. Students who can perform successfully on this task have the prerequisite eye-hand coordination skills to begin handwriting instruction.

Grasp of Writing Instrument, (IC.3). *Materials:* Pencil and paper. *Strategy:* Give student pencil and paper and ask him or her to draw a picture, write his or her name, or perform any other age-appropriate task. *Interpretation:* Teacher's judgment of correct grasp of writing in-strument. The pencil should be loosely gripped with the fingers above the shaved tip about an inch from the point. Only the index finger should rest on top of the pencil.

Handwriting: Manuscript

Manuscript Pretest, (IIA.1). *Materials:* Pencil, lined paper (appropriate size), and a model of the following sentence for the student to copy: "The quick brown fox jumps over the lazy dog." *Strategy:* Ask student to copy the model sentence. *Interpretation:* Teacher's professional judgment about whether student's performance is acceptable for current grade placement. This sentence contains all of the letters of the alphabet. Evaluate student's performance in the following five areas: (1) letter formation: observe student forming the letters to make sure he or she is using the correct strokes and starting points; (2) alignment and proportion: this refers to the evenness of the letters along the baseline and along the tops of the letters. All letters of the same size should be of the same height; (3) vertical quality: the manuscript letters should be vertical; there should be no slant; (4) spacing: there should be enough space between words to insert one lower case *o.* There should be enough space between sentences to insert two lower case *o*'s. Spacing between letters should be less than spacing between words; (5) line quality: in evaluating line quality, concentrate on the smoothness, evenness, and thickness of the pencil or pen line.

Manuscript, Lower Case l, i, t, (IIB.1). *Materials:* Pencil and line paper. *Strategy:* Ask student to print the lower case *l, i,* and *t.* as you name them. *Interpretation:* Evaluation criteria established by teacher's current handwriting series. Note how vertical stroke is made. It should always be made from top to bottom. Also note size of the letters: *l,* full space, *i,* half space, and *t,* three-fourths space.

Manuscript, Lower Case o, c, a, e, (IIB.2). *Materials:* Pencil and line paper. *Strategy:* Ask student to print the following lower case letters as you name them: *o, c, a, e. Interpretation:*

Evaluation scale for current handwriting series. Note size, which should be one-half space, and whether student used the backward circle (counterclockwise) to form the letters.

Manuscript, Lower Case r, m, n, u, s, (IIB.3). *Materials:* Pencil and lined paper. *Strategy:* Ask student to print the following lower-case letters as you name them: *r, m, n, u, s. Interpretation:* Evaluation scale from current handwriting series. Observe size one-half space; vertical stroke with forward curve for *r, m,* and *n;* vertical stroke with undercurve for *u;* and backward to forward curve for *s.*

Manuscript, Lower Case v, w, x, z, k, (IIB.4). *Materials:* Pencil and lined paper. *Strategy:* Ask student to print the following lower case letters as you name them: *v, w, x, z, k. Interpretation:* Evaluation scale from current handwriting series. Size of all letters should be one-half space except k, which is a full-space vertical stroke with one-half slant lines. Note whether all slant lines are formed from top to bottom.

Manuscript, Lower Case d, f, h, b, (IIB.5). *Materials:* Pencil and lined paper. *Strategy:* Ask student to print the following lower case letters as you name them: *d, f, h, b. Interpretation:* Evaluation scale from current handwriting series. Observe letter formation and size. All letters should be full space with the backward and forward circle (*d* and *b*), hump (*h*), and cross (*f*) one-half space.

Manuscript, Lower Case g, y, p, q, j, (IIB.6). *Materials:* Pencil and lined paper. *Strategy:* Ask student to print the following lower case letters as you name them: *g, y, p, q, j. Interpretation:* Evaluation scale from current handwriting series. Note size, the tails of these descender letters should be one-half space below the baseline. The upper portion should be one-half space above the baseline.

Manuscript, Upper Case L, I, T, H, E, F, (IIC.1). *Materials:* Pencil and lined paper. *Strategy:* Ask student to print the following upper case letters as you name them: *L, I, T, H, E, F.*

Interpretation: Evaluation scale from current handwriting series. Note size and letter formation. Letters should occupy the full space from headline to baseline. The vertical strokes should be made from top to bottom and the horizontal strokes from left to right.

Manuscript, Upper Case O, C, G, Q, (IIC.2). *Materials:* Pencil and lined paper. *Strategy:* Ask student to print the following upper case letters as you name them: *O, C, G, Q. Interpretation:* Evaluation scale from current handwriting series. All letters should be one space in height. They should be made with the backward circle stroke that begins at the two o'clock position.

Manuscript, Upper Case A, M, N, K, V, W, X, Y, Z, (IIC.3). *Materials:* Pencil and lined paper. *Strategy:* Ask student to print each of the following upper case letters as you name them: *A, M, N, K, V, W, X, Y, Z. Interpretation:* Evaluation scale from current handwriting series. All letters should be one space in height. All vertical and slant lines in these letters should be made from top to bottom. Horizontal lines should flow from left to right.

Manuscript, Upper Case B, R, D, P, S, J, U, (IIC.4). *Materials:* Pencil and lined paper. *Strategy:* Ask student to print the following upper case letters as you name them: *B, R, D, P, S, J, U. Interpretation:* Evaluation scale from current handwriting series. All letters should be one space in height. The loops on B, P, and R should be one-half space. All vertical strokes should start from top to bottom except in U, which contains a push-up stroke.

Numerals 0–9, (IID.1). *Materials:* Pencil and lined paper. *Strategy:* Ask student to print the numerals *0–9* as you name them. *Interpretation:* Evaluation scale from current handwriting series. All numerals should be one-half space in height. Backward curves and circles are used in *0, 6, 8,* and *9.* All vertical and slant lines start from top to bottom. All horizontal lines start from left to right. The curves in *2, 3,* and *5* are made clockwise.

Handwriting: Cursive

Cursive Pretest, (IIIA.1). *Materials:* Pencil or pen, lined paper, and a model of the following sentence for the student to copy: "Most boys and girls can fix zippers quickly whenever they jam." *Strategy:* Ask student to copy the sentence in cursive writing. *Interpretation:* Evaluation scale from current handwriting series. This sentence contains all of the lower case cursive letters. Evaluate student's performance in the following four areas: (1) letter formation: observe student forming the letters and note whether correct strokes are used; (2) alignment and proportion: the tops of all minimum letters should be even and one-half space high; (3) slant: all upper and lower case cursive letters should have about a 20–30 degree slant. The slant should be uniform; (4) spacing: to judge spacing use the following guidelines: (a) between letters: just enough space for the oval part of the numeral 9; (b) between words: the beginning stroke of a word should start directly beneath the ending stroke of the preceding word; (c) between sentences: enough space for an upper case oval *O.*

Basic Cursive Strokes, (IIIB.1). *Materials:* Model of basic cursive strokes from student's current writing series. *Strategy:* Present model of strokes, ask student to name, trace, and copy these strokes. *Interpretation:* Teacher's professional judgment about whether student's performance meets the norm for current grade level. Under-curve ⌣, overcurve ⌢, downcurve ⌐, checkstroke ✓, and slant stroke ⫽ are the building blocks for cursive letter forms and should be taught as a prerequisite to cursive writing.

Cursive, Lower Case i, u, t, e, s, w, r, p, (IIIC.1). *Materials:* Pencil or pen and lined paper. *Strategy:* Ask the student to write in cursive the following lower case letters as you name them: *i, u, t, e, s, w, r, p. Interpretation:* Evaluation scale from current handwriting series. The undercurve is used more than any other basic stroke, and, therefore, letters beginning with this stroke are taught first. It is used in every lower

case cursive letter except *z.* Observe slant of letters; there should be a slant of 20–30 degrees. All letters should be one-half space in height except t, which should be three-fourths space high.

Cursive, Lower Case l, b, f, h, k, (IIIC.2). *Materials:* Pencil or pen and lined paper. *Strategy:* Ask student to write in cursive the following letters in lower case as you name them: *l, b, f, h, k. Interpretation:* Evaluation scale from current handwriting series. All of these upper loop letters should be one full space in height; the upper loop should cross at mid-space. Note uniformity of slant.

Cursive, Lower Case a, c, o, d, g, q, (IIIC.3). *Materials:* Pencil or pen and lined paper. *Strategy:* Ask student to write in cursive the following letters in lower case as you name them: *a, c, o, d, g, q. Interpretation:* Evaluation scale from current handwriting series. The down curve is used to begin these six letters. It is part of the backward oval and must begin with a slide left motion before it curves down; if this is not done, the oval will become too straight, and the oval in the letters will be left open. All letters should be one-half space high except d in which the slant stroke is three-fourths space high. Note uniformity of slant

Cursive, Lower Case g, j, q, f, y, z, p, (IIIC.4). Materials: Pencil or pen and lined paper. *Strategy:* Ask student to write in cursive the following lower case letters as you name them: *g, j, q, f, y, z, p. Interpretation:* Evaluation scale from current handwriting series. These seven letters are the descender letters. The descenders should reach one-half space below the baseline. Note uniformity of slant.

Cursive, Lower Case n, m, v, x, y, z, (IIIC.5). *Materials:* Pencil or pen and lined paper. *Strategy:* Ask student to write in cursive the following lower case letters as you name them: *n, m, x, v, y, z. Interpretation:* Evaluation scale from current handwriting series. The overcurve is used in forming these six letters. Too straight an overcurve will make and *m* look like *w* and *n* like *u*. Note size and slant of these letters.

Cursive, Lower Case r, b, v, w, (IIIC.6). *Materials:* Pencil or pen and lined paper. *Strategy:* Ask student to write in cursive the following lower case letters as you name them: *r, b, v, w. Interpretation:* Evaluation scale from current handwriting series. These letters all include the checkstroke which involves a slight retracing. Note size and uniformity of slant.

Cursive, Upper Case O, C, D, E, A, (IIID.1). *Materials:* Pencil or pen and lined paper. *Strategy:* Ask student to write in cursive the following upper case letters as you name them: *O, C, D, E, A. Interpretation:* Evaluation scale from current handwriting series. The down curve oval is used in forming these letters. Letters should be one full space in height. Observe for correct letter formation and slant.

Cursive, Upper Case H, K, M, N, W, X, U, Y, Z, V, Q, (IIID.2). *Materials:* Pencil or pen and lined paper. *Strategy:* Ask student to write in cursive the following upper case letters as you name them: *H, K, M, N, W, X, U, Y, Z, V, Q. Interpretation:* Evaluation scale form current handwriting series. These 11 letters all begin with the cane stroke. Note whether student uses correct starting point and has uniform slant in these letters. All letters should be one space high.

Cursive, Upper Case I, J, (IIID.3). *Materials:* Pencil or pen and lined paper. *Strategy:* Ask student to write in cursive the following upper case letters as you name them: *I, J. Interpretation:* Evaluation scale from current handwriting series. These two letters contain the upper loop, clockwise oval. Observe correct starting position and slant.

Cursive, Upper Case T, F, S, G, B, (IIID.4). *Materials:* Pencil or pen and lined paper. *Strategy:* Ask student to write in cursive the following upper case letters as you name them: *T, F, S, G, B. Interpretation:* Evaluation scale from current handwriting series. These letters may be referred to as boat letters due to their ending

stroke. All letters should be made one space high with the boat ending one-half space high. The boat ending in *B* should be one-fourth space high.

Cursive, Upper Case P, R, L, (IIID.5). *Materials:* Pencil or pen and lined paper. *Strategy:* Ask student to write in cursive the following upper case letters as you name them: *P, R, L. Interpretation:* Evaluation scale from current handwriting series. These three letters begin with the undercurve stroke and contain the slant stroke. Note student's formation of these letters.

Handwriting: D'Nealian and McDougal, Littell

Manuscript/Cursive Lower and Upper Case. *Materials:* Pencil or pen and lined paper. *Strategy:* Strategies similar to those suggested for traditional manuscript and cursive writing may be used. However, the letter groupings, presented in the D'Nealian and McDougal, Littell teacher's manuals, should be followed. *Interpretation:* Evaluate according to the procedures specified for each letter grouping in the teacher's manual (McDougal, Littell 1993; Thurber & Jordan, 1991).

Sample Items for Tests.   The sample items for tests, included in Appendix D, offer suggestions to the reader for developing similar original tests. The test items are numbered according to the subskills and tasks listed on the spelling and handwriting curriculum charts (Figures 8.1 and 8.2). The test items presented in this chapter are production-level tasks. To assess application-level performance, have the student write a story using all of the spelling words. To assess strategy usage, ask the student to verbally describe how the word was remembered. You may choose selected items from the sample tests as assessment tasks if they correspond closely with specific tasks the target student is required to perform in the classroom. It is most important that you observe the student's performance when administering the handwriting test items. The student's finished product (letter) may look correct, but without direct observation you will not know whether the letter was formed correctly. Incorrectly formed letters will slow the student's writing fluency and may affect the student's performance in other content areas. Those letters incorrectly formed will be recorded on the curriculum chart and identified as target tasks for program intervention.

Directions for administering the sample items for tests of spelling and handwriting are presented at the beginning of each subskill for spelling and each task for handwriting. Provide the student with appropriate materials before administering the test items.

Alternative Assessment Techniques.   The typical format for assessing a student's spelling skills is the dictated spelling test. Alternative assessment techniques may include oral spelling, spelling in context, and selection responding. Handwriting skills may be assessed using a published handwriting scale. However, most teacher's evaluate a student's handwriting skills on the basis of what they consider to be "average" or "typical" for a particular grade level. Similar to spelling, alternative assessment techniques may include writing in context and selection responding.

Spelling Alternatives.   Oral spelling is an appropriate alternative if you suspect that a student's fine-motor coordination or visual-motor abilities are interfering with the student's spelling performance. Asking a student to verbally describe why a misspelled word was written the way it was may help detect a faulty spelling strategy, while asking him or her to describe how correctly spelled words were remembered may help detect successful strategies. Asking the student to write three sentences containing the target word or spelling in context, is one technique for assessing spelling at the application level. Another technique is to assess spelling in lengthier writing assignments in which the student must use the target words in context (e.g., use your spelling words to write a story). For students experiencing extreme difficulty at the production level, consider reducing the task level and assessing spelling at the selection level. Several assessment formats are applicable here. Present the target word along with three misspellings of the word and have the student identify the correctly spelled word. A second option is similar to the cloze procedure used in reading. The target word is omitted from a sentence and a standard sized blank is inserted. Three to four spellings of the target word are listed below the blank. The student selects the correct spelling of the word. Many norm-referenced tests use one of these strategies because they are easy to administer and score, and offer the potential for sampling many words at the same time. The use of word processors is a third option that can help students improve their spelling skills. There are a variety of software packages designed specifically to facilitate spelling. Mercer and Mercer, (1993) have described some of the more popular programs.

Handwriting Alternatives.   An assessment technique that yields particularly useful information is the three-sample technique (Ariel, 1992; Mercer & Mercer, 1993; Polloway & Smith, 1992). Obtain three samples of the student's handwriting under varying conditions: "typical," "best," and "fastest." Compare these three writing samples and note significant differences. The "typical" sample indicates the student's current writing used in daily writing tasks. The "best" sample indicates the student's knowledge of how to write correctly given sufficient time and incentive; and the third sample, "fastest," indicates how the student performs under pressure, since this is a timed sample. A dictation or application format may also prove beneficial for locating letters that appear problematic in context. "Write this sentence as I dictate it," or "Write three words that contain the letter h," are examples of application-level tasks. As in spelling, selection-level tasks are appropriate for assessing handwriting at a reduced task level. Present one correctly formed letter along with three incorrect representations of the same letter. Ask the student to select the correctly formed letter. However, selection formats provide less useful information than product formats for correcting illegible handwriting.

Published Tests. In some instances, you may elect to use published criterion-referenced measures that correlate with the spelling tasks listed on the curriculum chart. The spelling section of the Brigance Diagnostic Comprehensive Inventory of Basic Skills (Brigance, 1983), the spelling section of the Hudson Education Skills Inventory (Hudson, Colson, Welch, Banikowski & Mehring, 1989), and the Spellmaster Assessment and Teaching System (Greenbaum, 1987) may present possible test items. Although handwriting tests are limited, there are several available from which to choose. Examples of such published assessment devices include the Basic School Skills Inventory-Diagnostic (Hammill & Leigh, 1983), the Zaner-Bloser Evaluation Scales (1984), and the Test of Written Language-2 (Hammill & Larsen, 1988). Again, in selecting items for assessing spelling or handwriting skills, choose only those that are similar in task demands to those required of the student in the classroom.

Test Administration. Based on your indirect assessment data, you should have a good estimate of where the student is performing in spelling. Prior to direct assessment, prepare your lists of grade-level and high-frequency words at grade level, two grade levels below and one level above. Use the criteria set forth in the Preliminary Procedures section of this chapter as a guide in completing direct assessment. Allot sufficient time for the student to respond to each dictated word. Once the dictated part of the test is completed, ask follow-up questions; select misspelled words and ask the student to verbally describe how the word was learned. This will assist you in identifying any faulty spelling strategies the student may be using. To administer the pretest in handwriting, you need a copy of the sentence that contains all the manuscript or cursive letters (see Handwriting IIA.1 and IIIA.1). Attention should be focused on letter formation, position of the paper, grasp of the writing instrument and posture. Make sure desk and chair are the appropriate size and are comfortable for the student. Record

all clinical observations for use in interpreting your assessment results.

Documenting Student Skill Needs. Information obtained from indirect assessment must be verified through direct assessment. In some cases, there may be a significant discrepancy between the two sets of data. When such situations arise, conduct further diagnostic assessment to verify the significance of these discrepancies.

Substantiating Needs. As mentioned in the preceding section, whenever discrepancies occur in the assessment data, additional assessment should be completed in an attempt to clarify these discrepancies. This may necessitate repeated assessments in a specific skill area to verify previously obtained data. However, these repeated measures will assist you in substantiating specific skills needs and, at the same time, obtain reliable assessment results. Further verification may be obtained by following the recommended steps in the assessment/programming cycle, direct observations, and during informal chats with the classroom teacher.

Charting and Interpreting Needs. After spelling and handwriting skills have been assessed and needed skills identified, record these skills on the curriculum charts (e.g., those in Figures 8.1 and 8.2). The assessment results should be recorded on the same curriculum charts the teacher and interviewer completed from the teacher survey (Figure 8.6). Following this procedure will allow you to make a comparison between the student's actual skill performance and the teacher's expected mastery level for these skills. Significant differences will indicate those skills in need of immediate instructional intervention. Figure 8.10 provides the steps to follow in beginning direct assessment in spelling.

PERSONALIZED PROGRAMMING PROCEDURES

The spelling and handwriting assessment results will provide direction for instructional program

FIGURE 8.10   How to Begin the Assessment Process in Spelling

1. Select 15 high frequency and 20 grade level words at each of the following levels:
   a) grade level
   b) one grade level above
   c) two grade levels below
2. Begin at grade level and administer words by dictation
3. Determine criterion: more than 75% correct, move to next higher level, less than 75% correct, move to next lower level.
4. Obtain criterion then analyze error patterns
5. Begin additional direct assessment on identified error patterns
6. Record consistent error patterns on curriculum chart
7. Develop instructional plan

planning. To maximize the student's progress through the spelling and handwriting curriculum, focus attention on those skills which are in need of direct instruction. The learning characteristics and special needs of the student will determine which methods and materials will be selected to promote student success.

There will likely be some adolescents with mild disabilities on an Individual Transition Plan who have not mastered basic skills in spelling and handwriting. Gajar, Goodman, and McAfee (1993) contend that basic skills instruction loses none of its importance as these students progress from the elementary to the secondary school. To assist these students, Lerner (1993) suggests using shorthand dictionaries, electronic spellers, computer spell checkers, and the *Bad Speller's Dictionary* (Krevisky & Linfield, 1963) in which words are arranged alphabetically according to their common misspellings.

Selection of Content

The initial step to program for spelling is to evaluate the relative importance of the student's spelling skill needs to his or her overall academic progress. An analysis of the student's error patterns should provide clues for program intervention and indicate spelling patterns that are not mastered. Knowledge of spelling patterns, introduced in the curriculum at various levels, may assist in ranking unmastered skills in need of direct instruction (Greenbaum, 1987; Mercer & Mercer, 1993).

Spelling

After diagnosing the student's error patterns, the major task is to implement an effective intervention program. Experts agree that there is no single, correct way to teach spelling for all children (Polloway & Smith, 1992; Smith, Finn, & Dowdy, 1993). What may work to one child's advantage may work to another child's disadvantage. Consideration must be given to the student's perceptual or modality strengths and other aspects of learning style. Students who can readily visualize words in their correct form may profit from repeated exposure to whole words rather than practice in phonetic analysis. Students who have not learned to use visual imagery to improve their spelling performance may benefit from imagery instruction. Pressley and his associates (1990) provide a number of imagery strategies for assisting these students. Similarly, students who are non-visual should be taught through a method that utilizes their strong auditory or kinesthetic modalities. According to Dunn & Dunn, 1993, teachers favor teaching methods they find most helpful to themselves. Realizing this may be the case, teachers should make provisions for students who have different modality strengths to allow for maximum spelling progress.

Handwriting

Those handwriting skills in need of direct instruction must also be ranked in order of their importance to the student's progress. Instruction in basic strokes, manuscript, or cursive (whichever is appropriate), will likely be one of the more valuable means for improving handwriting. Manuscript and cursive letters are complex visual symbols that may tax the cognitive, perceptual, and motor skills of many children. However, the basic strokes that make up these letters are much less complex. Students can learn to write these strokes comparatively easily; once the basic strokes have been mastered, they serve as building blocks for forming letters (Milone & Wasylyk, 1981). Research in handwriting has shown repeatedly that the majority of illegibilities are due to errors in letter formation. These errors are the result of incorrectly formed basic strokes. Illegible handwriting can be improved by analyzing the basic strokes incorrectly made within each letter and reteaching the correct form of these strokes. A second factor to consider in improving illegible handwriting is direct teaching.

Handwriting simply must be taught. The teacher must develop a sequentially planned presentation before practicing letter forms if the program is to be effective. Too often teachers have assigned pages in practice books without any direct instruction (Howell, Fox, & Morehead, 1993). As Barbe, Lucas and Wasylyk (1984) state, "The adage that practice makes perfect is not true; practice only makes permanent" (p. 5). Handwriting practice is necessary, but, to be effective, it must be preceded by direct instruction. A student's handwriting cannot improve unless he or she practices the correct letter forms. A third factor to consider in improving handwriting is to teach students to diagnose their own handwriting difficulties. They should be taught to evaluate their handwriting in relation to letter formation, alignment/proportion, spacing, uniform slant, and line quality (Ariel, 1992; Mercer & Mercer, 1993; Polloway & Patton, 1993; Smith, Finn, & Dowdy, 1993). Teachers have several options available in teaching students how to evaluate their handwriting: the evaluation procedures recommended by the writing series currently in use, commercially prepared handwriting scales and plastic overlays that contain printed tolerance levels of each letter, or their personal evaluation procedures.

Selection of Methods and Materials

The methods and materials selected must match the student's learning characteristics and special needs. In selecting methods and materials, ask and answer the following questions: Do they follow the scope and sequence of skills presented in the classroom curriculum? Does their instructional pace match the student's learning rate? Do the materials provide for reinforcement and feedback? Will the student be able to work independently with the materials? A spelling series is readily available in most schools. These texts should be considered tools or classroom aids to assist the teacher in teaching spelling. A major disadvantage of spelling series is that teachers rely too heavily on them (Barbe, Francis & Braun, 1982). The spelling series do not teach spelling—teachers do. Although there are disadvantages to using a spelling series, there are also several advantages: they provide a basic word list, activities that correlate with the words, suggested games, and an overall structure for the spelling program.

When materials are scarce and budgets limited, you may be required to develop your own instructional resources. Locating used and outdated materials in teacher workrooms, closets, and media centers, then revising and adapting them for program use can be quite effective. The major concern is that the materials correlate with the curriculum.

Programming for Subskills

Although spelling is one of the most thoroughly researched areas in the language arts, Loomer & Fitzsimmons (1989), and Vallecorsa, Zigmond and Henderson (1985) report that teachers seldom use research-supported practices in their classrooms. There is a serious gap between the existing research in spelling and its application in the classroom. According to Graham and Miller (1979), spelling instruction should be teacher-directed, contain a variety of instructional options, and should be based on a foundation of research evidence. Before selecting an instructional strategy, you are encouraged to review those confirmed procedures of spelling instruction, cited in Figure 8.11, for inclusion in your plans. Few spelling series include all of these research supported procedures. However, the *Useful Spelling Program* (Loomer, 1990) does incorporate only those learning techniques that have research support.

Teachers should make a concerted effort to include spelling as part of an integrated language arts program. For students to retain and master their spelling words, the words should be reinforced throughout the total curriculum (Ariel, 1992; Mercer, 1992; Polloway & Patton, 1993). However, Graham (1985) indicates that poor spellers do not acquire many words outside of the period set aside for spelling. Miller, Choate, and Rakes (1993) and Wood (1993) provide numerous strategies for assisting students to integrate their spelling words in daily written work.

As mentioned previously, handwriting is one of the most neglected areas of the elementary school curriculum. Many students with illegible writing simply have not learned the mechanics of handwriting. The close relationship of handwriting to other subject areas mandates formal instruction in developing handwriting skills. Direct teaching, corrective feedback, and supervised practice are essential ingredients in any handwrit-

FIGURE 8.11   Research on Spelling Procedures

CONFIRMED BY RESEARCH	UNCONFIRMED BY RESEARCH
Using a test-study-test method	Using a study-test method
Learning spelling words by a synthetic approach	Writing spelling words in the air
Presenting words in list or column form	Learning words by syllables
Requiring students to correct their own spelling or test under teacher direction	Presenting words in sentence paragraph form
Teaching students a systematic word-learning strategy for learning new words	Allowing students to devise their own methods for studying spelling words
Using motivational spelling games	Writing words numerous times to aid retention
Presenting and testing a few words daily	Studying the "hard spots" within words
Providing practice to develop proofreading skills	Using oral spelling to learn words
Allotting 60 to 75 minutes per week for spelling instruction	
Teaching only those spelling rules that apply to a large number of words	
Increasing a student's dictionary skills	
Improving a student's auditory and visual imagery	
Providing frequent opportunities to apply across the curriculum	

Source: Adapted from "Spelling Research and Practice: A Unified Approach" by S. Graham and L. Miller, October 1979. *Focus on Exceptional Children.* Copyright 1979 by Love Publishing Company. Reprinted by permission.

ing program and must be included for improving the student's handwriting skills.

Students with handwriting difficulties should be encouraged to write legibly, not only during handwriting instruction, but on daily writing tasks as well. Supporters of the whole-language movement would recommend teaching a handwriting skill when the child needs it for some other task rather than during a separate instructional period in handwriting. Graham (1992) contends that an important part of handwriting instruction is capitalizing on "teachable moments." For example, as students are working on a creative story, the teacher circulates and observes students' writing. The teacher may notice several students forming letters incorrectly and can immediately provide instruction to correct these deficiencies. However, Graham would submit that, for students with special needs, these "teachable moments" will not be enough. Teachers need to provide direct instruction in handwriting during the handwriting period and capitalize on "teachable moments" during other written tasks.

Developmental Strategies

The instructional strategies presented in the following section are those considered to be the best of professional and research supported techniques. These developmental strategies are presented for teacher use and may be adapted and modified as needed. They are general strategies that are to be included in every spelling and handwriting program when first introducing a student to a task or concept.

Spelling Strategies: *Test-Study-Test Procedure.* Numerous Studies (Loomer, 1990) support the test-study-test approach to spelling instruction. This procedure recommends beginning a unit of instruction with a test that identifies those words each student does not know how to spell. Barbe and others (1982) recommend letting students take the test "cold." This will give you a better estimate of the student's preinstruction level of ability. This procedure allows you to individualize spelling according to student needs, since the student will concentrate on the spelling words missed on the pretest.

Self-Correcting Test Procedure. This technique reportedly is responsible for 90–95 percent of children's spelling achievement. The field research (Loomer & Fitzsimmons, 1989) indicates this procedure is the single most worthwhile learning activity devised to date and is appropriate for all ages and abilities. Students take a spelling test with no previous exposure to the word list. The student then corrects his or her own test as the teacher spells each word orally or writes it on the board. Horn (1976) recommends that teachers retest and have students make corrections immediately following the initial test in order to show students what they have learned from their first correction. This procedure has several advantages: it individualizes spelling for the student as he or she studies only those words misspelled; it provides immediate feedback to students; and it promotes motivation.

Word Learning Strategies. An organized method for studying each misspelled word is paramount to good learning. The field research summarized by Loomer (1990) confirms there should be a systematic approach whereby students learn to study each word. Too often students are asked to study misspelled words without being given a systematic, word-learning strategy, or they are required to write their spelling words some magical number of times. A systematic approach involves pronunciation, visual imagery, oral and written reinforcement, and systematic recall of words. Students should be given the opportunity to use their spelling words in all written work to enhance and maintain spelling ability. Graham and Miller (1979) cite the following as effective procedures for improving spelling performance. You may select the one that matches the student's learning characteristics. First, you should familiarize the student with the steps involved in the word-learning strategy. Repeat the steps until the student performs them automatically. That is, when Tim is studying a word he has misspelled, he automatically implements the steps provided by the word-learning strategy to learn the word. Figure 8.12 outlines a sampling of word-learning strategies that may be used to enhance a student's spelling performance.

Presenting Words in Column or List Form. Spelling should be taught as spelling, and words to be learned should be presented in list or column form. Loomer (1990) contends that teachers appear to be confusing some goals of spelling with reading goals because they insist on teaching the meaning of each spelling word. Teachers are urged to recognize that the meanings of most spelling words in the typical spelling program have already been learned through the student's

reading and composition program. Directing attention to meaning distracts the student from concentrating on the spelling word. Research (Allred, 1984) demonstrates that it is most efficient to present words for study in list or column form, since such a method requires students to focus their attention upon each word as a separate problem. E. Horn (1960) states, "Research has consistently shown that it is more efficient to study words in list than in context. Words studied in lists are learned more quickly, remembered longer, and transferred more readily to new context" (p. 1338).

Spelling the Whole Word. When the student misspells a word, his or her attention should be

---

FIGURE 8.12   Word-Learning Strategies

A. Fitzgerald Method (Fitzgerald, 1951)

1. Look at the word carefully.
2. Say the word.
3. With eyes closed, visualize the word.
4. Cover the word and then write it.
5. Check the spelling.
6. If the word is misspelled, repeat steps 1 through 5.

B. Horn Method 1 (E. Horn, 1919)

1. Look at the word and say it to yourself.
2. Close your eyes and visualize the word.
3. Check to see if you were right. If not, begin at step 1.
4. Cover the word and write it.
5. Check to see if you were right. If not, begin at step 1.
6. Repeat steps 4 and 5 two more times.

C. Horn Method 2 (E. Horn, 1954)

1. Pronounce each word carefully.
2. Look carefully at each part of the word as you pronounce it.

3. Say the letters in sequence.
4. Attempt to recall how the word looks, then spell the word.
5. Check this attempt to recall.
6. Write the word.
7. Check this spelling attempt.
8. Repeat the above steps if necessary.

D. Visual-Vocal Method (Westerman, 1971)

1. Say the word.
2. Spell the word orally.
3. Say word again.
4. Spell word from memory four times correctly.

E. Gilstrap Method (Gilstrap, 1962)

1. Look at the word and say it softly. If it has more than one part say it again part by part, looking at each part as you say it.
2. Look at the letters and say each one. If the word has more than one part, say the letters part by part.
3. Write the word without looking at the book.

Source: Adapted from "Spelling Research and Practice: A Unified Approach" by S. Graham and L. Miller, Oct. 1979. *Focus on Exceptional Children.* Copyright 1979 by Love Publishing Company. Reprinted by permission.

directed at forming a correct visual image of the whole word. Dividing words into parts or syllables has not proven to be a superior technique for assisting students in learning to spell. The student should concentrate on each whole word as a specific learning problem. Some spelling series attempt to improve spelling ability by calling attention to "hard spots" within a word. Research has shown this practice to be of little value (Loomer & Fitsimmons, 1989). It is important for teachers to realize that students learn words as whole units and not as individual parts.

Individualize the Spelling Program.   You can effectively individualize the spelling program by utilizing a pretest without making major modifications in the program format currently used in the classroom. Moreover, by presenting the pretest (trial test) on Monday, rather than Wednesday, as recommended by numerous spelling programs, you focus the student's attention on those words he or she misspelled. This minor change will provide the student additional days to master unknown words. Students should also keep a log of words they had difficulty mastering. This procedure will further focus their attention on individual spelling words.

Spelling Conscience.   Although many spelling programs omit this component, research indicates the desire and concern to spell correctly are crucial to spelling improvement (Barbe et al., 1982; Graham & Miller, 1979; Hillerich, 1977). Techniques and procedures that enhance student interest and motivation should be incorporated into the spelling program. These may include: (1) informing students that spelling is a courtesy to the reader and that correct spelling should exist in any important writing, (2) confining the spelling vocabulary to the student's immediate and future writing needs, (3) focusing student attention only on those words he or she is unable to spell, and (4) encouraging self-satisfaction with correctly spelled papers. More important than any of these techniques or procedures is the classroom teacher. If the teacher considers correct spelling important, then it is likely that the students in his or her class will become good spellers.

Handwriting Strategies: *Readiness.*   The readiness skills of importance to handwriting include concepts of top, center, bottom, left, and right; recognition of basic shapes; fine-motor and eye-hand coordination; proper grasp of the writing instrument; and ability to produce the basic manuscript strokes. Numerous, informal activities that regularly occur in the classroom may be used for teaching the basic concepts and shapes. Modeling and demonstration are two of the more effective techniques for teaching these concepts (Ariel, 1992; Mercer, 1992; & Wood, 1993). Fine-motor and eye-hand coordination may be developed through numerous chalkboard and art activities. Additional ideas for developing these skills may be found in the teacher's guide of the handwriting series used in the classroom. The most effective procedures for assisting the student in grasping the pencil properly are modeling and demonstration. Proper formulation of the basic manuscript strokes will be achieved through chalkboard demonstration, modeling, and supervised practice.

Manuscript.   Instruction in manuscript writing requires the teacher to ensure that students are prepared for the writing task. The following variables contribute to legible manuscript handwriting.

- *Posture:* The student should sit upright in the desk with the lower back against the back of the seat and both feet flat on the floor. The upper back and shoulders should lean forward, with the forearms extending on the table surface and with the nonwriting hand holding the paper at the top. The eyes should be approximately 12–15 inches from the paper.
- *Paper:* For manuscript writing, the position of the paper for a right-hander should be parallel with the bottom edge of the desk. The student should be taught to slide his or her paper up as he or she moves down the paper.

The strokes should be directed toward the center of the body. For the left-handed student, the paper should be slanted to the right with the lower right corner pointed toward the center of the body. The stroke movement should be toward the left elbow.

Alignment/proportion: The evenness of the letters along the baseline and tops of the letters is referred to as alignment. In primary-level manuscript, the maximum letters touch the headline, and minimum letters are one-half space. The relationship in height of the letters to each other and to the writing space is referred to as proportion.

Vertical quality: In manuscript writing there should be no slant. If the paper is positioned as mentioned previously with proper strokes, there should be no slant in the writing unless they are using the D'Nealian or McDougal, Littel manuscript. If using the D'Nealian or McDougal, Littell Handwriting programs, both upper and lower case manuscript letters have a 15- to 20-degree slant to the right.

Spacing: A rule of thumb to follow for proper spacing is: in words the widest space is between two straight line letters; a slightly smaller space should exist between a circle letter and a straight line letter; and the smallest space should occur between two circle letters. There should be enough space between words to insert one lower case *o*. Proper spacing between sentences should allow for two lower case *o*'s.

Line quality: Manuscript writing should have a good line quality. This refers to the evenness, smoothness, and thickness of the pen or pencil line. A heavy line may indicate the student is applying too much pressure or grasping the writing instrument too tightly. If the line quality varies or shows inconsistencies, it may indicate the student is writing too rapidly or is tired. If the line quality is too light, it may indicate the writing instrument is too hard or too fine.

Letter formation: Poor letter formation is one of the major causes for illegible handwriting. Therefore, correct letter formation must be of primary importance in the instructional program. The letters should be overlearned in isolation through repeated practice and then written in context. Presented in Figure 8.13 are some strategies that may be used to teach letter formation (Graham & Miller, 1980).

Cursive. According to Polloway and Smith (1992), the emphasis on handwriting has been limited for several decades. This lack of emphasis may be the result of the general perception that handwriting instruction is unimportant or due to teachers' limited knowledge of how to teach handwriting skills. Milone and Wasylyk (1984) suggest that the critical ingredient in handwriting success is instruction. Therefore, teachers who wish to improve the handwriting of their students must provide direct supervised instruction. The most appropriate time to introduce cursive writing into the curriculum is still a debatable issue. Graham and Miller (1980) recommend introducing cursive writing after manuscript writing has been mastered. This mastery can occur when cur-

---

FIGURE 8.13   Letter Formation Strategies

1. ***Modeling:*** The teacher demonstrates the formation of the letter on the chalkboard, while the student observes and pays attention to beginning and ending strokes.

2. ***Tracing:*** Student traces over models of the letter, progresses to dashed letters that are gradually faded, and finally writes the letter without a model.

3. ***Copying:*** Student copies letter from model.

4. ***Self-correction:*** Student learns to self evaluate using the text model, wall chart, or plastic overlay.

5. ***Reinforcement:*** Teacher provides verbal and written reinforcement for correctly formed letters.

sive writing is not introduced until the beginning of third grade. Instruction in cursive writing requires the teacher to ensure that students are prepared for the writing task. The following variables contribute to legible cursive writing:

Paper: The paper should be slanted approximately 60 degrees for both right- and left-handed students. The right-handed student tilts the paper to the left with the lower left corner pointing toward the center of the body. For the left-handed student, the paper is tilted 60 degrees to the right with the lower right corner pointing to the center of the body and the writing stroke pulled toward the left elbow.

Slant: There should be a slant of about 20–30 degrees in cursive writing. Irregular slant is usually caused by not positioning the paper correctly on the desk.

Spacing: There should be consistent spacing between letters, words, and sentences in cursive writing. Spacing between letters should allow for the oval part of the numeral 9.

Line quality: Factors contributing to poor line quality were discussed in the preceding section on manuscript writing.

Alignment: Irregular alignment may be caused by slanting the paper too much or positioning the paper so that the lines on the paper are horizontal to the bottom of the desk.

Size: Irregular size may be due to several reasons such as holding the pencil with the thumb straight, using only arm movement, and holding the pencil too close to the point.

Corrective Strategies

Corrective strategies will be required for those students whose spelling and handwriting performance are consistently below expectations. These strategies are more highly structured and systematic than the developmental strategies and require more direct and one-to-one instruction. Additional corrective strategies for spelling and handwriting are presented in *Teaching Students*

with Learning and Behavior Problems (Hammill & Bartel, 1995) and *Teaching Students with Learning Problems* (Mercer & Mercer, 1993).

Spelling Strategies.   *Word-Learning Strategies.* As previously mentioned, students who experience difficulty in learning to spell usually have not developed a systematic procedure for learning new words. The word-learning strategies, presented in Figure 8.14 are more structured and intensive and may be used as corrective strategies.

Spelling: Readiness.   As mentioned earlier in this chapter, the readiness skills in spelling are highly related to readiness skills in reading and handwriting. In fact, readiness skills in reading and handwriting are prerequisites to spelling readiness. Therefore, the reader is referred to reading subskill items IC.1–IC.3 (Figure 5.1), and to handwriting subskill items IC.1–IC.3 and IIA.1–IIC.4, (Figure 8.2), for suggestions in developing the readiness skills for spelling.

Spelling: Basic Words.   To teach multisyllabic words, Sofge (1975) recommends these four procedures:

1. Tape record the words. Pronounce the word, pronounce it syllable by syllable.
2. At the same time, have the words written on individual color-coded cards.
3. As the taped words are pronounced syllable by syllable, student writes each syllable in a different color.
4. Practice daily until student is ready to be tested.

This process may be adapted to teach many specialized words. For students who profit from multisensory stimulation, use of the **Language Master** may be helpful. Purchase blank cards and laminate them. This permits a wide variety of uses for minimal cost. If the student has not demonstrated a systematic means of learning words, then select a word-learning strategy and teach it. The steps in the technique must be overlearned so the student applies them automatically

FIGURE 8.14 Corrective Word-Learning Strategies

A. **Method for Visual Learners (Radabaugh & Yukish, 1982)[1]**

1. Student is shown the word on a card or list and given the name.

2. Student looks at the word, says it, spells it, and says it again.

3. The word is removed, and the student spells it from memory.

4. After spelling it two or three times more, student writes it from memory and checks the word against the stimulus card.

B. **Method for Audiotry Learners (Radabaugh & Yukish, 1982)[2]**

1. Teacher says the word, spells it, then says it again.

2. Child says the word, spells it.

3. Teacher repeats.

4. Child repeats several times if necessary before writing.

5. Child then writes the word from memory.

C. **Fernald Method Modified[2]**

1. Make a model of the word with a crayon, grease pencil, or magic marker, saying the word as you write it.

2. Check the accuracy of the model.

3. Trace over the model with your index finger, saying the word at the same time.

4. Repeat step 3 five times.

5. Copy the word three times correctly.

6. Write the word three times from memory correctly.

D. **Cover and Write Method[1]**

1. Look at the word, say it.

2. Write word two times.

3. Cover and write one time.

4. Check work.

5. Write word two times.

6. Cover and write one time.

7. Check work.

8. Write word three times.

9. Check work.

10. Check work.

E. **Fitzsimmons and Loomer Method (Fitzsimmons & Loomer, 1978)[3]**

1. Present visual stimulus of word with correct pronunciation to establish correct visual-aural impression.

2. Student closes eyes attempting to visualize the word while pronouncing it and again attempting to recall how it looked.

3. Student opens eyes and looks at word to see if spelled correctly.

4. Focus attention to word and correctly pronounce it again.

5. Student closes eyes, visualizes word, and spells it orally.

6. Look at the model and check for correct spelling.

7. Write the word several times, each time covering the previous spelling. If incorrect, repeat steps 1–7.

F. **Copy-Cover-Compare (Hansen, 1977; McCoy & Prehm, 1987)**

1. Student copies the word, saying each letter silently, noting distinctive features.

2. Student covers the word and writes it from memory.

3. Student compares the word with original spelling for correctness. If incorrect, errors are corrected.

4. Student repeats steps 1 through 3 five times more for each word.

---

[1]Data from Radabaugh, M. T., & Yukish, J. F. *Curriculum and Methods for the Mildly Handicapped* (Boston: Allyn and Bacon, Inc., 1982), p. 117. Reprinted by permission.

[2]Data from Graham, S., & Miller, L. "Spelling research and practice: A unified approach," *Focus on Exceptional Children* (October, 1979), p. 11. Reprinted by permission.

[3]Fitzsimmons, R. J., & Loomer, B. M. (1978). *Excerpts from spelling: Learning and instruction-research and practice.* (Wellesley, MA: Curriculum Associates, Inc., 1978). Reprinted by permission.

in learning words. Select a word-learning strategy which matches the student's learning characteristics.

Auditory Recognition of Phonemes.   The following strategy has been adapted from Gillingham and Stillman (1977) and may be used with severely disabled spellers who have not established the grapheme/phoneme correspondence.

Teacher	*Pupil*
1. Presents card with grapheme and names letter.	1. Repeats letter.
2. Shows card, gives sound.	2. Repeats sound.
3. Shows card.	3. Gives sound.
4. Makes sound.	4. Gives letter name.
5. Writes letter, explains formation.	5. Traces and copies letter, writes from memory and writes with eyes closed.
6. Makes sound.	6. Writes letter.

These steps are followed until the phoneme/grapheme association is firmly established.

Selected worksheets from reading workbooks may be used for reteaching these skills. Select worksheets which present one task or concept. For initial consonants, select worksheets containing pictures with the name of the pictured object written beneath each illustration. The word beneath the picture has the initial consonant missing. The student writes in the correct initial consonant. This exercise may be adapted to include all subskills in this section. Adding taped lessons to correspond with the written lessons is helpful to some students since this procedure allows for both auditory and visual input. Students who have difficulty with phoneme/grapheme associations need to hear the phonemes frequently.

Graphemes.   Prepare a list of word families using the pattern to be retaught. Highlighting the pattern in each word. Example: Silent "t" in watch, witch, hitch, and match. Teach the whole word, drawing attention to the pattern. If the student's spelling errors indicate poor phonics ability, select a multisensory word-study technique such as the Fernald Method (1943, 1988) and teach it. This student must see the word, hear the word, say the word, spell the word orally, and write the word. The following strategy may be used with students who spell nonphonetic words phonetically (e.g., "enuff" for "enough").

1. Develop a list of words which are not entirely phonetic.
2. Expose for a few seconds, one at a time.
3. Student writes the word in large script from memory.
4. Check for correct spelling.
5. Finger trace the word.
6. Write from memory.

Structural Analysis.   Provide for overlearning and shorten assignments. As words are mastered, select new words and review previously learned words. For students who have not learned the rules for formulation of derivatives ("comeing" for "coming"), stress imagery. Teach generalizations for forming tenses and adding suffixes. For example, words ending in a silent "e" drop the "e" before endings beginning with vowels (hope and hoping), but do not change before endings beginning with consonants (close and closely).

Develop a list of words in which the final consonant is to be doubled before adding a suffix. Using a felt marker, write each word on a 3" x 5" card. Leave space between the double letters and cut each card in half with a different angle so that only those two parts will match (cut /ting).

For students who have difficulty mastering spelling, it is particularly helpful to provide distributed practice (Graham & Voth, 1990; Masters Mori, & Mori, 1993; Reith, Axelrod, Anderson, Hathaway, & Fitzgerald, 1974). That is, by moving the pretest to Monday, as recommended in the previous section, you give two additional days of study time. For example, suppose a student misspells 16 words on the pretest. To incorporate distributed practice, divide those 16 words into four groups of four (the student has four days to learn these words before the final test). Dividing the misspelled words into small groups and providing the appropriate word-learning strategy will increase the probability of student success in learning these words as opposed to studying all 16 words (massed practice) each day.

Handwriting Strategies. *Readiness.* Those students who experience difficulty learning the basic concepts will require direct instruction with concrete objects prior to moving to pencil/paper tasks. For example, using objects in the classroom, the teacher might say, "place your box of crayons on the left side of your desk," or "place your pencil at the top of your desk." Numerous structured activities may be utilized in teaching recognition of basic shapes. Concrete objects offer an initial starting point. After introducing one shape, ask the student to identify classroom objects having a similar shape. Gradually introduce the second shape, the third, etc. Matching activities, frequent verbalizing, use of templates, and chalkboard activities will help in establishing this skill. Fine-motor and eye-hand coordination skills can be improved through a variety of art activities such as cutting, coloring, finger painting, writing in sand or salt, tracing, sketching, etc. A wide selection of commercial programs are also available to enhance the development of fine-motor and eye-hand coordination. The proper grasp of the writing instrument may be obtained through modeling, teaching the student to self-verbalize the correct grasp, or color coding as recommended by Radabaugh and Yukish (1982). The key factor for success in correct formation of basic strokes is supervised practice. Providing directional clues and color coding the beginning and ending points of the basic strokes may prove most beneficial.

Manuscript. An effective method for improving a student's handwriting is to teach the student how to evaluate his or her own handwriting. Stowitschek and Stowitschek (1990) have developed a correction procedure that permits students to self-analyze and correct their own handwriting errors with relative ease. It is important to impress upon the student the elements that constitute good handwriting. These elements include letter forma-tion, slant, alignment and proportion, size, spacing, and line quality. The student should be taught how to evaluate each of these elements as they relate to their own handwriting. For those students who have particular difficulty in letter formation, it may be helpful to teach one of the strategies in Figure 8.15 suggested by Graham and Miller (1980). Teachers using the D'Nealian program (Thurber & Jordan, 1991) should apply suggestions in the "Special Needs" section, while teachers using the McDougal, Littell program (1993) should capitalize on the "Corrective Strategies" provided in the teacher's manuals to assist students experiencing handwriting difficulties.

Cursive. Newland (1959) analyzed handwriting illegibilities and found that 11 letters (*a, b, d, e, h, i, m, n, o, r,* and *t*) are responsible for about 50 percent of all the handwriting illegibilities. These illegibilities concern four types of difficulties: (1) failure to close letters, (2) closing looped strokes, (3) looping nonlooped strokes, and (4) using straight up strokes rather than rounded strokes. Teacher awareness of these difficulties may provide major directions for corrective instruction. The correction of one variable will automatically correct another. Those variables, discussed in relation to developmental strategies, are presented in relation to corrective procedures:

> *Paper:* Place two strips of masking tape on the student's desk, slanted in the appropriate direction for students who have difficulty keeping the correct tilt to their paper. There should be just enough space between the strips of tape for the paper to slide up easily as the student moves down the paper. If you do not wish to use the masking tape try the following procedure. The nonwriting hand should be extended diagonally across the writing surface. The lines on the paper should slant in the same direction (parallel) as the fingers of the nonwriting hand.
>
> *Slant:* If there is too much slant in the writing, it usually is caused by slanting the paper too much. Writing that has little or no slant is usually the result of holding the paper so

FIGURE 8.15   Corrective Letter Formation Strategies

A. Fauke Approach (Fauke, Burnett, Powers, & Sulzer-Azaroff, 1973)

1. Teacher writes the letter, and student and teacher discuss its formation.
2. Student names the letter.
3. Student traces the letter with a finger, pencil, or magic marker.
4. Student finger traces a letter made from yarn.
5. Student copies the letter.
6. Student writes the letter from memory.
7. Teacher rewards the student for correctly writing the letter.

B. Progressive Approximation Approach (Hofmeister, 1973)

1. Student copies the letter using a pencil.
2. Teacher examines the letter and, if necessary, corrects by overmarking with a highlighter.
3. Student erases incorrect portions of the letter and traces over the teacher's highlighter marking.
4. Student repeats steps 1-3 until the letter is written correctly.

C. Furner Approach (Furner, 1970)

1. Student and teacher establish a purpose for the lesson.

2. Teacher provides the student with many guided exposures to the letter.
3. Student describes the process while writing the letter and attempts to visualize the letter as another child describes it.
4. Teacher uses multisensory stimulation to teach the letter form.
5. Student compares his or her written response to a model.

D. VAKT Approach

1. Teacher writes the letter with crayon, while the student observes the process.
2. Teacher and student both say the name of the letter.
3. Student traces the letter with the index finger, simultaneously saying the name of the letter; completes successfully five times.
4. Student copies and names the letter successfully three times.
5. Student writes and names the letter correctly three times from memory.

E. Neidermeyer Approach (Niedermeyer, 1973)

1. Student traces a dotted representation of the letter twelve times.
2. Student copies the letter twelve times.
3. Student writes the letter as the teacher pronounces it.

Source: Adapted from "Handwriting Research and Practice: A Unified Approach" by S. Graham and L. Miller, Oct. 1980. *Focus on Exceptional Children.* Copyright 1980 by Love Publishing Company. Reprinted by permission.

that the lines are horizontal. Correctly positioning the paper will assist students who are experiencing difficulty with correct slant.

Spacing: To obtain uniformity of space between words, the beginning stroke should begin directly beneath the ending stroke of the preceding word. Space between sentences should allow for an oval.

Line quality: Line quality, which may be either too dark or too light, can be corrected by

teaching the student this procedure. Ask the student to bend his or her thumb so sharply that the tip of it lifts the pen in the hand and to grasp the pen far enough back from the point to allow the two little fingers to curl under and carry the hand across the paper.

Alignment: As mentioned previously, correcting one variable may automatically correct another. In this case, positioning the paper correctly on the writing surface will assist in correcting alignment difficulties.

Size: Correct size can be obtained by "digging" the thumb nail into the pencil. This action lifts the pencil in the hand and allows the right degree of finger movement. Holding the pencil far enough back from the point allows the nails of the two little fingers to carry the hand comfortably across the paper.

Maintenance Strategies

Maintenance strategies are used when a student has partially mastered a skill and requires additional practice, drill, and reinforcement for mastery to occur. A wide range of supplementary materials may be used for this purpose. Careful selection is required, however, so that the needed task or concept is being reinforced. The creative teacher will modify and vary these strategies to maintain student interest and motivation.

Maintenance strategies should lead to application of the learned skill or concept in natural settings across the curriculum. Teachers may use one or all of the following strategies to enhance application of skills and concepts taught: (1) scripted lessons, (2) simulations, or (3) guided practice. Wood (1993) suggests that, in teaching application, initial examples should be representations of the skill or concept, and a variety of examples should be presented to represent the full range of divergence; also, additional presentations should include both examples and nonexamples and should clarify for the student what is distinctive about the skill or concept. An example of application across people and settings is as follows: the student has been practicing spelling words in the resource room through guided practice and simulations. The general education teacher administers the weekly spelling test and makes sure these words are used and reinforced in various classroom writing assignments in science, social studies, and reading. Similarly, in handwriting, correct formation of a letter is taught by demonstration, tracing, and guided practice in the resource room. The general education teacher and parents require the correct formation in all written work in both classroom and homework assign-ments. Miller, Choate, and Rakes (1993) have identified numerous spelling and handwriting activities to assist students who experience difficulty in applying learned skills and concepts in these two areas.

Spelling: Readiness

Readiness, (IA.1–ID.1). The reader is referred to word recognition subskill items IC.1–IC.3 and IIA.1 and .2 (Figure 5.1) and handwriting subskill items IC.1–IC.3 and IIA.1–IIC.4 (Figure 8.2) for maintenance strategies at the readiness level.

Spelling: Basic Words

Basic Words, (IIA.1–IIF.1). ▪*Find a Word:* These puzzles vary in difficulty and may be located at the local news or teacher's supply store. The student scans the page, looking for key letters and learns to recognize the word in a variety of positions. These puzzles usually focus on a special topic such as days of the week, months of the year, etc. ▪*Spelling Tic-Tac-Toe:* A game board with twenty-five squares is required. Two or four players each with a partner may participate. The weekly list of spelling words is on individual cards that contain both the words and sentences incorporating the words. A player draws a card and reads the word and the sentence. The opponent writes the word. If the spelling is correct, he or she marks any square chosen on the board. The first player to obtain five squares in a row either horizontally, vertically, or diagonally is the winner. ▪*Who Can Spell It?* Label objects in the room with color words or any category of words needing reinforcement. Intermittently throughout the day have short spelling sessions. As the students become proficient in one category add a new category. Using the basic words for the week, play word games such as Hangman, Password and Scrabble. Modify directions and rules to meet your students' needs.

Spelling: Auditory Recognition of Phonemes

Auditory Recognition of Phonemes, (IIIA.1–IIIC.1). ▪*Card Match:* Prepare index cards each with one consonant and a wild card. Prepare a second set that has pictures beginning with each consonant. Shuffle the cards and deal to three or more players. The players check for pairs that match and lay them on the table. The first player picks a card from the player on his or her left. The game continues until all cards have been matched and one student is left holding the wild card. Before a student can lay a pair on the table, he or she must pronounce the word and give the initial sound. This game may be adapted for a variety of sounds. ▪*Partners:* Divide the students into pairs, one acting as the teacher and the other the student. Provide each teacher with a list of words containing troublesome phonemes. The teacher pronounces the word, and the student orally states and writes the letter name of the troublesome sound. ▪*Extra Practice:* Numerous activities from reading workbooks and beginning spelling series may be selected to develop this skill. Additional sources may include old workbooks, selected activities in commercial kits, and duplicating and taped programs.

Spelling: Graphemes
Graphemes, (IVA.1–IVG.11). ▪*Word Wheels:* Construct word wheels similar to those used in reading activities. Write words containing the spelling pattern to be learned (e.g., blends, variant consonants, vowels, etc.). The student spins the wheel to form a word, pronounces it, closes eyes and visualizes word, writes word, and checks with model for accuracy. This may be played with two students, each monitoring the others responses. ▪*Computer Assisted Instruction (CAI).* CAI should not be overlooked as a viable means for assisting students in maintaining newly acquired spelling skills. According to Mercer & Mercer (1993), Reid (1988), and Walberg (1990) many software packages are available to review and reinforce existing academic skills. ▪*"IE" or "EI":* This strategy may be used to reinforce and strengthen the recognition and the spelling of *ie* and *ei* words. Prepare a list of words containing ie and ei. Type the list omitting the *ie* or *ei* from each word. The student completes the words.

Example: __ther (either), qu__t (quiet), rel__f (relief).

Spelling: Structural Analysis
Structural Analysis, (VA.1–VD.13). ▪*Crosswords:* These may be located at your local newsstand, drugstore, or grocery store. Purchase several levels of difficulty. There are crosswords for synonyms, antonyms, homonyms, and a variety of other word forms. To solve the puzzle the student must spell the answers correctly. ▪*Compound Words:* Make up two columns of simple words that can be made into compound words. The student matches the word from Column 1 to the appropriate word in Column 2 and writes the word. Example:

Column 1	Column 2	Writes Word
fish	time	_ _ _ _ _
night	hook	_ _ _ _ _

This strategy may also be adapted for prefixes and suffixes. ▪*Suffixes:* Prepare a list of sentences using the suffixes from the weekly spelling list. Type the sentence but omit the suffix. Students must complete the sentence. Example: John was very help_ _ _ in finding my coat (ful). Tim's care_ _ _ _ errors lowered his grade (less). A variation of this strategy is to prepare the sentences omitting the spelling word and inserting a standard size blank. Type beneath each blank four words with only one spelled correctly. The student circles the correctly spelled word.

Handwriting: Readiness
Readiness (IA.1–IC.3). ▪*Concepts:* Mini informal teaching sessions throughout the school day may be used to reinforce the concepts of left-right, top, center, and bottom. Example: "Mary, draw three circles down the right edge of your paper." "Tom, write your name across the top of your paper." ▪*Shapes:* Matching concrete objects and pencil or paper tasks may be used to reinforce shape recognition. Numerous commercially prepared readiness books have appropriate activities for reinforcing this skill. ▪*Fine-Motor and Eye-Hand Coordination:* May be reinforced through

chalkboard writing, sketching, coloring, tracing, and numerous common classroom art activities. Modeling and frequent reminders will be helpful in establishing the correct grasp of the writing instrument. Modeling, tracing, slashed, dot-to-dot, and copying exercises along with supervised practice will enhance learning the proper formation of the basic strokes.

Handwriting: Manuscript

Manuscript, (IIA.1–IIB.6). ▪Select practice activities from those recommended by commercial handwriting programs. ▪Supervised practice is essential for developing legible and fluent handwriting. ▪Frequent reminders concerning writing posture, paper position, and grasp of the writing instrument are required. ▪Teach students how to evaluate their own handwriting in terms of alignment, line and vertical quality, spacing, and size. ▪Provide written feedback to the student concerning specific areas needing improvement. ▪Encourage legible handwriting in all written tasks to facilitate transfer of what has been stressed in handwriting to other required written assignments.

Handwriting: Cursive

Cursive, (IIIA.1–IIID.1). ▪Many maintenance strategies recommended for manuscript apply to cursive writing as well. These strategies include supervised practice, self-evaluation, and requiring legible handwriting across subject areas. ▪Supervised practice is particularly important when the student is making the transition from manuscript to cursive. As was previously stated in this chapter, practice does not make perfect, it only makes permanent. Therefore, it is most important for the teacher to supervise all aspects of the student's written work to ensure the formulation of the letters is learned correctly. ▪Teach the student to self-evaluate his or her written work and provide corrective feedback. ▪Those strategies unique to cursive writing include positioning the paper with the correct slant, correct slant of the letters, and letter size. Use frequent reminders throughout the school day to encourage students to practice correct paper position, letter slant, and

letter size. The reader interested in obtaining additional strategies for use in spelling instruction is referred to Mercer and Mercer (1993), Barbe, Francis, and Braun (1982), and Miller, Choate, and Rakes (1993); and in handwriting to Barbe, Lucas, and Wasylyk (1984), Mercer and Mercer (1993), Morsink (1989), McBride (1992), and Thurber (1993).

Implementing the CBA/P Model

In Chapter 3, the curriculum-based assessment/ programming cycle was described in detail. This section describes the CBA/P process as it relates to spelling and handwriting.

Step 1: Analyze the Curriculum

Determining just what the spelling and handwriting curricula are is an essential first step. Investigate whether the teacher adheres closely to the adopted spelling text, or whether the teacher adds what he or she considers important to the spelling curriculum. If so, then these additional skills must be included on the student's curriculum chart. In handwriting, however, research suggests that little formal instruction occurs above fourth-grade level. Therefore, it is critical to identify the exact curriculum the teacher uses in handwriting if you wish to improve the student's handwriting skills. In both areas, you need to know the teacher's criteria for evaluating performance. Because spelling and handwriting are support skills, they must be used in all written work. Determine whether the teacher only grades performance on specific spelling tests and handwriting lessons or if the spelling and handwriting are evaluated in all written work. Then plan assessment procedures accordingly.

Step 2: Assess Skills

Use information obtained from the teacher survey to determine to what extent spelling and handwriting are interfering with the student's other academic areas. Analyze recently administered tests and compare results with present day work samples. Note discrepancies, if any, and use this information to plan direct assessment strategies. After reviewing all indirect assessment data, formulate diagnostic hypotheses. In prioritizing the diagnostic hypotheses, take into consideration the teacher's concerns, expressed on the teacher survey, and all supporting indirect assessment data. Begin direct assessment with the student's current spelling text and handwriting curriculum, using an assessment format that parallels the teacher's expectations. Use as a guide those procedures set forth in Preliminary Procedures found in this chapter. Particularly with spelling, use followup questions (e.g., Why did you spell _____ like that? How did you learn that word?). Chart the student's performance on the spelling or handwriting chart and develop the personalized program for spelling and/or handwriting.

Step 3: Program for Assessed Needs

Select for programming those spelling or handwriting subskills that appear to have the greatest impact on the student's academic progress. Select one or two tasks needing instruction along with six to eight tasks that are mastered to increase the student and teacher's chances for success. Plan instruction for three stages: developmental, corrective, and maintenance.

Developmental Instruction. For introducing new tasks, follow the regular spelling curriculum and whatever handwriting curriculum the teacher has indicated is being used in the classroom. The typical spelling activities found in basal series, or other series that are similar, are appropriate for developmental instruction. Assess student performance after instruction. Maintenance strategies should be provided for tasks that appear to have been mastered, while unmastered tasks should be targeted for corrective strategies.

Corrective Strategies. To implement corrective instruction, begin with a method that matches the student's learning characteristics. If the student appears to be visual, select a method for teaching that emphasizes visual clues for both spelling and handwriting. Give the teaching method sufficient time to produce effects and then assess student's performance. Modify instructional procedures described in the CBA/P model set forth in Chapter 3. First, modify your method. For example, if the word-learning strategy you selected does not improve Billy's spelling scores, then select one that involves a different sensory channel. If this does not prove to be effective, modify the materials. This may mean copying the spelling activities from the basal text and cutting into small units or using the word processor and CAI software programs. Teach and assess. If, at this point, the student is not successful, modify both methods and materials. In this case, select methods that emphasize a different sensory channel and materials that are multisensory (e.g., Language Master or Computer). Teach and assess again. Should the task remain unmastered, reduce your task level and provide selection level tasks.

Maintenance Strategies. Tasks that appear to be tentatively mastered should remain in the program with maintenance strategies until long-term mastery can be demonstrated. This will require numerous drill and practice activities that need modification and variation in order to maintain student interest and motivation.

Step 4: Repeat the CBA/P Cycle

Once the student demonstrates tentative mastery of the skills in the initial program, update the entire program, using the student's curriculum chart determine which skills next need instruction. Continue to use those methods and materials in which the student was successful in the initial program. Communicate the student's performance to all persons involved in the student's academic program as well as the student.

The spelling and handwriting program is implemented when the curriculum has been determined, skill assessment has been completed, and a tentative instructional program has been developed. The program will focus on those subskills and tasks, identified by the teacher survey and through assessment, as most deficient and in need of direct intervention. Teaching strategies, based on the student's learning characteristics and special needs, will be selected for use in program intervention. Newly acquired skills that require drill and practice will become the target of maintenance strategies and remain in the program until mastery has occurred. Those subskills and tasks requiring corrective strategies remain in the program and will be recycled through Step 3 of the assessment/programming cycle as described in Chapter 3. As the student masters specific subskills and tasks, they will be recorded on his or her curriculum chart and new subskills and tasks will be added to the program.

SUMMARY

Although considered support skills, the importance of spelling and handwriting to the student's academic progress is their impact on written expression. Students who are poor spellers and have illegible handwriting cannot communicate their ideas and thoughts in writing. Factors which contribute to poor spelling and illegible handwriting were emphasized in this chapter. Procedures for assessing the student's spelling and handwriting curricula and the student's present level of mastery within each of these areas were presented.

Following the steps outlined in the assessment/programming cycle will enhance the student's chances for achieving mastery of spelling and handwriting skills. Recommendations were also offered for selecting instructional methods for teaching the needed subskills and tasks at three stages of instruction: developmental, corrective, and maintenance.

CASE STUDIES

Sample Spelling Case

Shawn's fourth-grade teacher, Mrs. Hall, is concerned because Shawn has been performing below grade level in spelling since she entered the fourth grade. Shawn has consistently scored between 60 and 65 percent correct on her final tests, even though Shawn insists she studies her spelling words each evening. Mrs. Hall ranked auditory recognition of phonemes as the strongest subskill and basic words as the weakest. Shawn was observed on two different occasions during spelling instruction and the following was noted: Shawn completes her text activities with acceptable marks but experiences difficulty when words are dictated, as on her final test. Work-sample analysis and observations verified these findings.

Diagnostic Hypotheses: Shawn's spelling difficulties may be the result of attempting to spell words she cannot read, or she has not mastered the prerequisite skills for the fourth-grade level words.

Based on Mrs. Hall's rating on the teacher survey, observation, and work sample analysis, basic words will be used for the initial assessment. In interviewing Shawn, the examiner learned that Mrs. Hall administers the pretest on Wednesday and that each student is required to write his or her spelling words five times each. Direct assessment began with sample item IIA.4, Basic Words: High Frequency, Grade 4 (Appendix D). However, before Shawn was asked to spell the words, she was requested to read all the words. She completed this task with no difficulty. The results of Shawn's performance are shown in Figure 8.16.

Shawn's performance on the direct assessment items was consistent with her classroom performance. From an analysis of Shawn's performance, several error patterns emerge; Shawn has not mastered vowel digraphs as applied to spelling or the more advanced skill of spelling words correctly that contain suffixes.

FIGURE 8.16   Shawn's Spelling Test

Name __Shawn_____ Grade __4__ Age __9__

Date ___1/4_____ Examiner ___Mrs. Hall_____

Observations _____

Item IA.4

1.	kne	knee
2.	mounton	mountain
3.	beautifull	beautiful
4.	sudden	
5.	famous	
6.	pound	
7.	brekfast	breakfast
8.	kitchen	
9.	carefull	careful
10.	young	
11.	ocen	ocean
12.	reson	reason
13.	cousin	
14.	families	
15.	awfull	awful
16.	sale	
17.	hang	
18.	esy	easy
19.	case	cause
20.	whole	

In developing a spelling program for Shawn, the major emphasis will be reteaching vowel digraphs as applied in spelling. Instruction in suffixes will begin after Shawn has demonstrated partial mastery of the vowel digraphs. In addition Shawn will be taught a word-learning strategy to use in learning new words rather than have her write them each five times. Mrs. Hall has agreed to move the pretest to Monday so that Shawn will have more time to learn the words misspelled. Mrs. Hall will determine how many misspelled words Shawn will work on each evening (distributed practice) rather than have her study all of her misspelled words each evening.

Sample Handwriting Case

Adam's third-grade teacher, Miss Holt, has been attempting all year to get Adam to improve his cursive writing. Miss Holt indicated on the teacher survey that Adam's letters are poorly formed and have inconsistent slant. She indicated that constant reminders to Adam to improve his handwriting have not helped. A review of Adam's daily written work confirms that he does have an inconsistent slant and some of his letters are not correctly formed. From observing Adam in the classroom, the examiner also learned that he positions his paper on the desk incorrectly. During the interview with Adam, he indicated to the examiner he could not remember how to write some of his letters so he would have to look up at the model Miss Holt had placed above the chalkboard.

Diagnostic   Hypotheses: Adam's   poorly formed letters suggest he has not mastered the basic cursive strokes. His inconsistent slant appears to be the result of not positioning his paper correctly on his desk.

Direct assessment will begin by sampling Adam's writing of the letters. The examiner asked Adam to copy the sentence from the sample item IIIA.1 (Appendix D). The results of Adam's performance are shown in Figure 8.17.

Miss Holt's description of Adam's performance is verified in direct assessment. He does have letter formation difficulties and the slant of his letters is inconsistent. Although assessment of upper case letters is necessary, enough information has been collected to begin a tentative corrective program. The upper case letters will be assessed as time permits.

The initial program will focus on correct letter formation, making sure he has mastered the basic cursive strokes before introducing specific letters. In analyzing Adam's performance, the examiner

FIGURE 8.17 Adam's Cursive Pretest

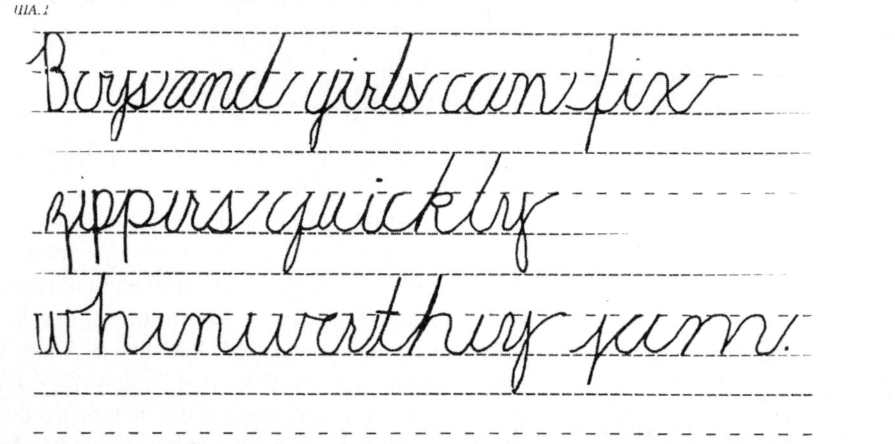

noted that all his backward oval letters (*a, o, d, g, q*) lack closure. A letter formation strategy is selected from the corrective strategies to help Adam learn the correct letter formation. A corrective procedure is also taught to Adam for correctly positioning his paper on his desk. Miss Holt has agreed to provide corrective feedback to Adam and to teach him how to evaluate his own handwriting skills.

Practice Cases

Case A: Spelling

Shawn's second error pattern was noted in suffixes. She added an extra letter to each word with a suffix. Look at her misspellings again (Figure 8.16) and answer the following questions:

1. What additional assessment would you recommend and why?
2. Which sample item from Appendix D would you select for additional assessment?
3. Realizing that the sample items in Appendix D are limited, what additional sources would you refer to for verifying this error pattern?

4. What correction strategy would you recommend and why?
5. Once Shawn has partially mastered this skill, what maintenance strategies would you select and why?

Case B: Handwriting

Adam's writing indicates he has more than just backward oval difficulties in forming letters. Based on his performance (Figure 8.17), what additional assessment and programming are necessary to improve Adam's handwriting?

1. Which additional set of letters needs reteaching?
2. Which sample items for tests of handwriting would you select to verify his performance and why?
3. What additional resources might be used to complete the assessment?
4. What additional strategies would you recommend to Miss Holt? Why?
5. How can you help Adam with spacing?

ENRICHMENT ACTIVITIES _____

Discussion

1. Discuss the importance of incorporating distributed practice into a program for underachieving spellers.

2. Discuss how you would select a specific word-learning strategy for a particular student. What learner characteristics need to be considered?

3. It is customary for teachers to require students to write their spelling words some "magical" number of times. Discuss the value of this practice. Justify your response with supported research.

4. Many left-handed students are "hook" writers. Why does this occur? Suggest how you would teach a left-handed student to write in order to prevent his from occurring.

5. Discuss different procedures you might use to assist a student in grasping the writing instrument correctly.

Special Projects

1. Observe a spelling lesson in a general classroom and note whether the self-correction procedure is being implemented. Select a day to observe when the "trial" or "final" test is being administered.

2. Interview a fourth-grade teacher and identify his or her procedures for teaching spelling. Are they research supported? Use Figure 8.11 to assist you in determining your answers.

3. Select a student, fourth grade or above and administer the pretest in cursive writing found in Appendix D. Evaluate in terms of letter formation, alignment, spacing, line quality, and slant.

4. Return to Chad's written story (Figure 8.7) and classify his spelling errors according to type as discussed in the Preliminary Procedures of this chapter. Note the consistency of the error types.

5. Locate Christie's handwriting sample (Figure 8.9) and evaluate in terms of slant, line quality fluency, and letter formation. Where would you begin to improve her handwriting? Justify your response.

CHAPTER 9

BASIC MATHEMATICS

BRIAN E. ENRIGHT

CHAPTER OBJECTIVES

This chapter is designed to enable the reader to:

1. Assess the basic mathematics curriculum in the areas of readiness, number facts, whole number computation, fractions, decimals, and problem solving.
2. Indirectly assess a student's basic mathematics skills through analysis of the teacher survey on basic mathematics, current test information, work samples, observations, and student interview.
3. Directly assess a student's mastery of those basic mathematics skills required by the curriculum through administration and interpretation of original mathematics tests, selected sample test items, and other tests.
4. Chart a student's basic mathematics skills, subskills, and task needs on the curriculum chart.
5. Program for a student's basic mathematics needs, adhering to charted needs and following best practice procedures.
6. Revise and modify the basic mathematics program based upon student performance.

Basic arithmetic is one of the fundamental building blocks of all of elementary education. Learning to think mathematically is essential in the world in which we live and will be even more important in the world where our students will work. The power of the tools that are becoming available, today, will either increase our productivity or will cause us to make catastrophic errors. The determining factor will be the ability to ask the right questions and recognize obvious mis-takes. As Arcavi and Schoenfield (1992) point out, there is a need to create learning environments in which mathematical sense is natural.

BASIC MATHEMATICS SKILLS

Basic mathematics is made up of a set of parts that go together to form the foundation of higher mathematics. Basic arithmetic can be subdivided into two component parts: first, the computational component that includes both number facts and number computation; second, basic problem solving, the true purpose of mathematics. Each of these will be treated separately.

Computation

Computation is the manipulation of given numbers according to a preset rule to determine a predictable outcome. That is to say that only one outcome (answer) is acceptable. Computation can be subdivided into three broad areas: readiness skills, number facts, and algorithms. Readiness skills are essential here, as in other areas, because these skills lead to or block future number manipulation. The recognition and comprehension of numbers, one-to-one correlation, and the joining of sets of objects must be internal to a child's system before number facts or number computation can be accomplished. Similarly, number facts must be built upon the readiness skills. The most fundamental set of data in computation is referred to as number facts. Number facts are isolated bits of information that can be used in the computation process much the same as sight vocabulary is used in the reading process. Also, as with sight words, number facts must be immediately recalled during the computation process if they are to be useful. There are 390 of these isolated bits of information with which a student must learn to work. These number facts are often not learned, or are learned in a faulty way that leads to incorrect answers difficult to analyze.

Number computation constitutes various manipulations of these number facts according to a set of rules whose application will result in some predictable result. Number computation can be divided two ways. First, it can be divided into the areas of whole numbers, fractions, and decimals. Secondly, each of these three areas can be subdivided into addition, subtraction, multiplication and division. A difficulty in computation can begin in any of these 12 areas. When a difficulty occurs, it most frequently will carry over into the following levels. For example, if a student has difficulty with multiplication of whole numbers,

that student will have problems with complicated division of whole numbers, because multiplication is required as a skill in long division. Similarly, that student will have difficulties in the manipulation of fractions and decimals whenever multiplication is required. It is essential in this example to address the difficulty in multiplication of whole numbers first. This example demonstrates the sequential nature of computation skills. Computation skills are tools for solving problems. There are very few individuals (past the age of nine or ten) who walk around practicing multiplication. However, if you are in a store buying ten items at $4.20 each and the clerk asks you for $52.00, multiplication becomes useful. What is being said is that number computation is not very useful on its own but draws its utility when applied to solving mathematical problems. This is not to say, however, that computation is unimportant. In fact, computation is very important. It should be considered a tool necessary for the proper development of the final product. Many experts are downplaying the significance of computation in favor of problem solving. Clearly, problem solving should be the cornerstone of any mathematical curriculum; however, cornerstones are set in place by the correct use of tools. Computation is that set of tools for arithmetic.

Computation may be divided into four major subskill areas, as listed on the basic mathematics curriculum chart in Figure 9.1. Each of these subskill areas consists of sets of specific skills placed in sequential order. These sets of specific skills are listed later in this chapter when specific strategies for assessment and programming are presented. These strategies are very important because they enable you to discern the point in these sets of skills where the student begins to fail and toward which you must focus the intensity of the corrective instructional program.

Problem Solving

Problem solving is the application of a process or organized framework of thinking in order to understand some previously unknown situation.

FIGURE 9.1   Sample Basic Mathematics Curriculum Chart

Student's Name_____Grade_____Teacher_____School_____Date_____

Directions: Circle the specific tasks required for success at this student's current level; in the space provided list any other tasks appropriate to the existing curriculum.

Code:	reg = Regrouping	~~reg~~ = No Regrouping	Fr = Fraction	Den = Denominator
	R = Remainder	~~R~~ = No Remainder	dec = Decimal	hrz = Horizontal Form
			d = Number of digits in number	

Typical Text Level for Tasks

MATHEMATICS SUBSKILLS	K	1	2	3	4	5	6
I READINESS	I R.1 Same Sets .2 More, Less .3 Counts obj to 10 .4 Joins sets to 10 .5 Counts-100 .6 Concept-10 .7 Recognizes to 100 .8 Writes-100 .9 Summatizes	I	I	I	I	I	

	K	1	2	3	4	5	6
II NUMBER FACTS	II	II	II				
A Addition		A.1 0-5+0-5	A.2 6-9+6-9				
B Subtraction		B.1 0-5–0-5	B.2 0-9–0-9				
C Multiplication				C.1 1,2,3,5x0-10	C.2 0-10x0-10		
D Division					D.1 1-90÷1-9		

	K	1	2	3	4	5	6
III WHOLE NUMBER COMPUTATION	III	III	III	III	III	III	III
A Addition		A.1 1d+1d=<10 .2 1d+1d=>10 .3 1d+1d+1d=<10 .4 2d+1d;~~reg~~	A.5 2d+1d;reg 1s .6 2d+2d;~~reg~~ .7 2d+2d; reg 1s .8 2d+2d;reg 1s, 10s .11 3d+3d;reg 1s .12 3d+3d;reg 1s, 10s	A.9 2d+2d+2d;reg 1s .10 2d+2d+2d; reg 1s, 10s			
B Subtraction		B.1 1d-1d .2 1d-Self .3 1d-0 .4 2d<20-1d; ~~reg~~ .5 2d-1d;~~reg~~ .6 2d-2d;~~reg~~	B.7 2d-1d;reg 10s .8 2d-2d;reg 10s .9 3d-3d;~~reg~~	B.10 3d-3d;reg 10s .11 3d-3d;reg 100s .12 3d-3d;reg 10s, 100s .13 3d(0in1s)-3d .14 3d(0in10s) -3d .15 3d(0in1, 10s) -3d			
C Multiplication			C.1 1dx1d	C.2 2dx1d;~~reg~~ .3 3dx1d;~~reg~~ .4 2dx1d;reg 1s .5 2dx1d;reg 1s, 10s .6 3dx1d;reg 1s .7 3dx1d;reg 10s .8 3dx1d;reg 1s, 10s .9 3dx1d;reg all	C.10 2dx2d;~~reg~~ .11 2dx2d;reg1s .12 2dx2d;reg .13 3dx2d;~~reg~~ .14 3dx2d;reg	C.15 3dx3d;~~reg~~ .16 3dx3d;reg 1s, 10s .17 3dx3d;reg all .18 3d (0in10s) x2d;reg	
D Division				D.1 1d÷1d~~R~~ .2 2d(0in1s) ÷1d~~R~~ .3 3d(0in1s, 10s)÷1d~~R~~ .4 2d÷1d;~~reg~~~~R~~ .5 1d÷1d;R .6 2d÷1d~~R~~ .7 3d÷1d;~~reg~~~~R~~ in 1st 2d	D.9 3d÷1d;reg~~R~~ .12 3d ÷1d;R .14 2d÷2d~~R~~ .15 2d÷2d;R .16 3d÷2d;R .17 3d÷2d~~R~~ .18 3d÷2d;R .19 4d÷2d;R .20 4d÷2d, 0in quotient~~R~~	D.21 4d÷3d;R	D.22 5d÷3d;R

FIGURE 9.1   *(continued)*

MATHEMATICS SUBSKILLS							
	K	1	2	3	4	5	6
III WHOLE NUMBER COMPUTATION (Con't.) D Division	III	III	III	III .8 2d÷1d;reg R̸ .10 2d÷1d;R .11 3d÷1d R̸ .13 3d (0in10s) ÷1d R̸	III	III	
	K	1	2	3	4	5	6
IV FRACTIONS A Conversion	IV	IV	IV	IV	IV A.1 Improper to whole # .2 Improper to mixed # .3 To simplest form	IV A.4 2 Fr to LCD, LCD in 1 Fr .5 2 Fr to LCD, LCD in 0 Fr .6 2Fr to LCD,x Factors for LCD .7 3 Fr to LCD,2 like Den. .8 3 Fr to LCD, LCD in 0 FR	IV
B Addition					B.1 2 Like Fr;hrz .2 2 Like Fr;hrz =whole/ mixed #	B.3 3 Like Fr;hrz .4 2 Unlike Fr; LCD in 1 Fr .5 2 Unlike Fr; no LCD .6 2 Unlike Fr; LCD≠x Den .7 3 Fr; 2 like Den .8 3 Unlike Fr .9 Mixed # + Fr; hrz .10 2 mixed #'s	
C Subtraction					C.1 1 Fr-Like Fr	C.2 Fr-Unlike Fr; LCD in 1 .3 Fr-Unlike Fr; no LCD .4 Fr-Unlike Fr; LCD≠ x Den .5 Mixed #-Fr; reg .6 Mixed #-Fr; reg .7 Mixed #-Mixed #;reg .8 Mixed #-Mixed #;reg .9 Mixed #-Mixed #;reg;hrz	
D Multiplication						D.1 FrxLike Fr .2 FrxUnlike Fr .3 FrxImproper Fr .4 FrxWhole# .5 FrxMixed#	D.6 Mixed # x Mixed x
E Division						.1 Fr÷Fr .2 Fr÷Unlike Fr .3 Fr÷Whole # .4 Whole #÷Fr	E.5 Mixed #÷Fr .6 Mixed #÷ Mixed#
	K	1	2	3	4	5	6
V DECIMALS A Addition	V	V	V	V	V	V A.1 .0+.0;reg .2 .0+.0;reg .0 .3 .00+.00;reg .4 .00+.00;reg .00 .5 .00+.00;reg .0,.00 .6 .00+.00;reg .7 .00+.0;reg .0 .8 .00+.0;reg .0;hrz .9 Mixed + .00 .10 Mixed + Mixed; reg .11 Mixed + Mixed reg;hrz	V

(continued)

FIGURE 9.1   *(continued)*

MATHEMATICS SUBSKILLS							
	K	1	2	3	4	5	6
V DECIMALS (Cont.)	V	V	V	V	V	V	V
B Subtraction						B.1 .0-.0;reg .2 .00-.00;reg .3 .00-.00;reg .4 .00-.0 .5 Mixed-.0;reg .6 Mixed-.0;reg .7 Mixed-.00;reg .8 .0-.00;reg .9 Mixed-.00;reg .10 Mixed-.00;reg hrz .11 Mixed-Mixed;reg	
C Multiplication						C.1 .Whole # x .0 .2 .0 x .0	C.3 .00x.0;reg .4 Mixed x.0;reg .5 Mixed x.00;reg .6 Mixed x Mixed;reg
D Division							D.1 .0÷1d Whole #;reg .2 .00÷1d Whole #;reg .3 .00÷1d Whole #;reg .4 Mixed (with .0) ÷ Whole # .5 Mixed (with .00) ÷ Whole # .6 Whole # ÷ .0 .7 Whole # ÷ .00 .8 Mixed ÷ .0 .9 Mixed ÷ .00 .10 Mixed÷Mixed
E Conversion of Percent to Decimals							E.1 % to Whole # .2 % to .00 .3 % to .0 .4 % to Mixed Dec.
	K	1	2	3	4	5	6
VI PROBLEM SOLVING	VI	VI	VI	VI	VI	VI	VI
A Reads and Understands		A.1 1st grade	A.2 2nd grade	A.3 3rd grade	A.4 4th grade	A.5 5th grade	A.6 6th grade
B Organizes		B.1 1st grade	B.2 2nd grade	B.3 3rd grade	B.4 4th grade	B.5 5th grade	B.6 6th grade
C Correct Operation		C.1 1st grade	C.2 2nd grade	C.3 3rd grade	C.4 4th grade	C.5 5th grade	C.6 6th grade
D Computes Answer		D.1 1st grade	D.2 2nd grade	D.3 3rd grade	D.4 4th grade	D.5 5th grade	D.6 6th grade
E Checks Answer		E.1 1st grade	E.2 2nd grade	E.3 3rd grade	E.4 4th grade	E.5 5th grade	E.6 6th grade
VIII ADDITIONAL SKILLS							

COMMENTS

NOTE: Check subskills and tasks as they are mastered, circling additional tasks required for student's advancement.

How problem solving is approached probably varies more than any other area of the curriculum. In some cases, the curriculum is centered around the computation skills. In other cases, the program is based on whether the problem is a one-step or two-step problem. The approach taken here is a more generic one that should be applicable to the other approaches and also provide useful diagnostic information. This approach is built around a set of procedures for problem solving. The approach includes five steps or parts:

1. To study the problem and find what is sought
2. To organize the information within the problem
3. To develop an action strategy for solving the problem
4. To select and apply the correct computational or other skill
5. To evaluate the answer for correctness and reasonableness

The utility of this approach in a diagnostic process originates with the increased ability to determine the cause of incorrect final answers. That is, when the final answer is incorrect, the examiner must be able to determine at which point the error began. If a student's error occurs only in step 4, then the correction should be directed at computational skills. If, however, the student's error originates during step 1 and the student does not truly understand what is being asked for, then the remediation efforts will focus more on reading and comprehension skills. Studying the step or steps with which a student is having difficulty will lead to the final design of the course of study for a student in problem solving as is the process in all other curriculum areas.

PERSONALIZED ASSESSMENT PROCEDURES

Assessment for program planning should include the critical examination of the student's mathematics skills. The results of such assessment provide the basis for planning a mathematics program that will foster gains in student achievement.

In mathematics, as in other skill areas, to personalize the assessment procedure one should first establish the content and sequence of the basic mathematics curriculum within which the student must function. Establishing the student's relative proficiency in performing specific arithmetic tasks provides additional individualized information. Directly assessing the student's performance of curricular tasks further ensures that the assessment procedures are indeed personalized (Howell, 1986; Gable, Enright, & Hendrickson, 1991).

Central to any assessment used to develop a program for a student is the process of error analysis (Ashlock, 1990; Clarkson, 1992; Enright, 1983, 1985, 1986, 1989; Enright, Gable, & Hendrickson, 1990). Error analysis is the study of the student's mistakes. The premise of error analysis is that students develop incorrect or faulty ways of doing mathematics much the same way that other students develop correct ways of performing the same skills. Based on this thesis, the error pattern a student demonstrates provides the evaluator with information regarding how the incorrect answer was derived. Once this is known, the teacher is able to alter instruction to correct the problem. Error analysis and its ramifications are so essential to corrective instruction that all suggestions for corrective instruction in this chapter are based on the results of this process. Enright (1985) suggests seven error clusters (Figure 9.2) that organize student errors in a logical manner.

Curriculum Analysis

Most basic mathematics curricula include similar elements. The degree of emphasis may differ, and there may be a slight variance in the levels at which specific tasks are introduced. The first five items of the teacher survey on basic mathematics (Figure 9.3) assess the curriculum in terms of what is expected of a student in the area of basic mathematics skills. The teacher is asked to designate on a curriculum chart those mathematics subskills and tasks that the student must master at

FIGURE 9.2   Error Clusters in Arithmetic Computation

Regrouping 1: Writes entire sum of each column without regrouping.

$$\begin{array}{c|c} 2 & 8 \\ + & 8 \\ \hline 2 & 16 \end{array}$$

REGROUPING

This cluster of errors shows that the student has little understanding of *place value* or the arithmetic steps to show it.

Process Substitution 18: Adds using multiplication process.

$$\begin{array}{r} 42 \\ + \quad 3 \\ \hline 75 \end{array}$$

PROCESS SUBSTITUTION

In this error cluster, the student changes the *process* of one or more of the computation steps and creates a different algorithm that results in an incorrect answer.

Omission 123: Computes decimal fractions as if they were whole numbers and omits decimal point.

$$\begin{array}{r} .3 \\ + \quad .4 \\ \hline \odot \ 7 \end{array}$$

OMISSION

This cluster of errors is indicated when a student *leaves out* a step in the process or *leaves out* a part of the answer. An omission error differs from a process substitution error by representing an *incomplete* rather than a *different* algorithm.

Directional 154: Writes sum of all digits.

$$\begin{array}{r} 4\ ^+ 2 \\ + \quad 3^+ \\ \hline 9 \end{array}$$

DIRECTIONAL

In this error cluster, the computation is correct, but the steps are performed in the wrong *direction and/or order.*

Placement 167: Reverses digits in sum.

$$\begin{array}{r} 9 \\ + \quad 6 \\ \hline 15 \end{array}$$

PLACEMENT

These errors are often computed accurately, but because the numbers are written in the wrong *place,* the answers will be incorrect

Attention to Sign 188: Subtracts.

$$\begin{array}{r} 4.75 \\ - \oplus \quad .62 \\ \hline 4.13 \end{array}$$

ATTENTION TO SIGN

By ignoring the *sign,* the student performs the wrong operation. This generally occurs when the student uses the "shape" of the item as his or her sole clue to which operation to perform.

Guessing 204: Copies addends from top to bottom as sum.

$$\begin{array}{r} 1 \\ + \quad 2 \\ \hline 21 \end{array}$$

GUESSING

In this cluster, the errors often lack logical quality, indicating a *lack of basic understanding* of the processes or skills being assessed.

Source: From ENRIGHT® *Diagnostic Inventory of Basic Arithmetic Skills,* © 1983 Curriculum Associates, Inc. ENRIGHT® is a registered trademark of Curriculum Associates Inc. Adapted and reprinted by permission.

different levels. The curriculum chart on which the responses are recorded may be the school's published mathematics curriculum, the scope and sequences chart of the basal mathematics text used for computational instruction, or the basic mathematics curriculum chart (Figure 9.1).

The first item, in Figure 9.3, calling for teacher judgement of mathematics skills necessary for the target level, is the most important information requested. The teacher should be encouraged to add specific skill demands from his or her mathematics curriculum to the chart, noting minimum competencies where applicable. Items two through five, describing instructional options and teacher priorities, require discussion for complete answers.

The teacher's designation of the skills, subskills, and tasks that are necessary for the student to progress in mathematics provides the skill content for assessment. The circled items on the chart, representing the content of the curriculum, provide the diagnostician with a listing of the specific mathematics tasks for which assessment techniques must be developed.

Indirect Student Assessment

Assessment of the student's mathematics skills can be initiated through indirect assessment procedures. These indirect methods include the continuation of the teacher survey on basic mathematics (Figure 9.3) to determine the teacher's estimate of specific mathematics skill needs and the analysis and interpretation of available data from other sources.

Teacher Perceptions

The second portion of the teacher survey on basic mathematics requests the teacher to indicate his or her perception of the student's skills. Of particular importance to the assessment of the student's overall program is any suggestion of mathematics difficulties interfering with performance in other subject areas such as science. If indicated, direct assessment of the student's mastery of these related skills is needed. Representative samples of the student's class work should

be collected for the skills cited in item 6 as strongest and for those cited as weakest.

Available Data

All available data should be carefully reviewed before any direct assessment is conducted. As noted in Chapter 4, the general teacher survey, the school adjustment survey, and the student interview can provide valuable information.

One of the most valuable sources of indirect assessment is actual samples of the student's written class assignments. The most readily analyzed samples are the basic mathematics activities that the student has completed in the arithmetic workbook. Samples of the student's recent chapter tests from the math program also present a good source of student performance. In addition, attention should be paid to the nature of the student's answers. In math, wrong answers may be the result of basic number fact error, an error in the computation algorithm, or an error in not understanding the question being asked. Such differences will greatly alter the direction taken during direct assessment as well as during program planning.

Direct Student Assessment

Before direct assessment begins, the teacher should: (1) interpret the data collected using indirect assessment means, (2) formulate diagnostic hypotheses, (3) establish assessment priorities, and (4) develop streamlined plans for direct assessment.

Preliminary Procedures

Analysis of the information relevant to the student's mathematics performance should generate tentative diagnostic hypotheses. The teacher may have noted multiplication of whole numbers as Marisa's greatest problem and division of whole numbers as her next weakest area. Through analysis of work samples, it had been determined that Marisa regularly regroups incorrectly and frequently writes the wrong answer to a particular fact (e.g., $6 \times 7 = 47$). Also, through observation, the teacher discovers that Marisa counts on her

FIGURE 9.3   Teacher Survey: Basic Mathematics

Student_____Date_____
Teacher_____Interviewer_____

A.   ASSESSMENT OF CURRICULUM:

    ADDITIONAL COMMENTS

1. Indicate appropriate skills, subskills, and tasks on an attached basic mathematics curriculum chart.

    List available text titles/levels you would consider as options:

2. List current text titles and levels in which student is expected to master basic mathematics:

_____
_____
_____

3. Check the primary source(s) of student's report grades in mathematics:
   __Mathematics Workbook   __Homework
   __Teacher tests   __Board Work
   __Combination _____
   __Other _____

    Describe grade sources:

4. Indicate the relative importance of each subskill to student's grades in basic mathematics using 1 as the most important:
   __Number Facts   __Fractions
   __Whole Number Computation   __Decimals
   __Problem Solving   __Other _____

    Indicate time devoted to each by current curriculum and texts:

5. Describe instructional modifications in mathematics that you have attempted with this student:

_____
_____

    Degree of success:

B.   INDIRECT STUDENT ASSESSMENT:

6. Rate this student's mathematics subskills using 1 as mastered, 2 as currently developing, and 3 as unknown:
   __Number Facts   __Fractions
   __Whole Number Computation   __Decimals
   __Problem Solving   __Other _____

    In weakest area(s) identify the most difficult tasks for this student:

7. Check the best description of the student's emotional reaction to his or her mathematics performance:
   __Over concern   __No concern
   __Some concern   __Other reaction

    Describe student's emotional reaction:

8. List any other subject areas in which student's mathematics skill interferes with performance:

_____ _____ _____ _____

    Indicate why and to what extent:

9. List specifically what you want to know about this student's mathematics skills: _____
_____
_____

    Attach representative samples of the student's work.

10. Interviewer Summary:_____
_____
_____

fingers. In establishing assessment priorities, the first step may be a test of multiplication number facts, timed to eliminate any form of finger counting. The next step may be to directly assess multiplication of whole numbers to determine at which exact step in multiplication the problem begins. This could lead to focusing the assessment priorities on a fairly specific area. A fourth preliminary procedure entails formulating direct assessment plans. Suggestions for planning streamlined assessment in mathematics include: (1) use sample items in Appendix E that match the student's curriculum to confirm the student's ability quickly; (2) having focused on a subskill, select items from the student's curricular materials, or create additional items to measure that skill and use them to confirm the exact point of difficulty; (3) study the student's incorrect responses to determine if there is a precise reason for the incorrect response.

Classroom Observations

The student should be observed during one or more mathematics classes and also during any other subject in which mathematics might be used. Science is a natural second subject. Care should be taken to observe if the student is participating in the lesson. Ideally, an observation should be made during a lesson in which a skill is being reviewed and also during a lesson when a new skill is being introduced. Note whether the student participates, asks questions, and the nature and quality of any questions asked. Frequently, students who have serious problems in mathematics will try "to disappear" during a mathematics lesson. Determine if the student is copying the examples down correctly or working with the manipulatives correctly. If instruction is significantly above the present skill level of the student, you may observe that student to be doing a lot to appear busy while not really keying into the lesson. Collect any work the student attempted or completed during the observations. Analyze how much work was completed compared with other students in the same group. Also,

check for correctness and general types of errors that might have been made. The information obtained through observation will assist in planning the informal interview with the student as well as narrow the focus of direct testing.

Informal Student Interview

An informal interview with a student can provide valuable insight into factors that may interfere with performance in mathematics. Some students may be burned-out on workbooks. Others may indicate that they can do the skills but not at the pace required. There are students who have a great fear of math (called math phobia); this should become obvious during an interview. Through the interviewing process, one can also determine the student's response to instructional methods and preference for activities. The questions on Part B of the teacher survey on basic mathematics (Figure 9.3) may be used as content for this interview. Restate these questions on a level students will understand and to which they will respond.

Personalized Mathematics Tests

Creating tests using the classroom math materials is the most likely means of collecting relevant assessment data. Certain sample items for tests of basic mathematics in Appendix E may be selected if they correlate with the classroom curriculum. Subtests from other published assessment instruments may be similarly chosen. Select tests or parts of tests that measure those skills students must master within the curriculum. In other words, tests and their parts can be directed by you rather than you being directed by them.

Suggestions for Constructing Tests of Mathematics. The math text, the teacher's guide, accompanying workbook and skills activities, plus any supplementary math aids can provide the materials for personalized assessment of mathematics skills. Use of grade-level texts below the student's actual grade level is often needed. Actual workbook pages can be used to assess mathematics skills. Pages should be selected that represent the workbook's most frequently used format for the skill being measured. If the student is usually required to show all the steps of a multiplication problem rather than the answer, then such an exercise is appropriate for assessment purposes. One word of caution is needed. Sometimes workbook pages cover a variety of skills. If this is the case, these pages should be omitted because they will confuse the assessment process. Therefore, check each workbook page very carefully.

The following suggestions for the design of original assessment tasks are numbered according to the basic mathematics curriculum chart (Figure 9.1). If an alternate curriculum listing is followed, the tasks may be renumbered accordingly. Note that the readiness and computation test items are production-level tasks, while the problem solving items are application-level tasks. The scoring criteria are presented as guides and should fluctuate with each student's curriculum.

Readiness

Readiness, (IR.1–.9). Materials: Student arithmetic text or arithmetic workbook and a set of manipulatives. Select two items per skill and write or type them in a worksheet form, leaving adequate room to solve each problem. *Strategy:* Ask student to complete each problem. The student should use the manipulatives to demonstrate the skill where applicable. No problem is to be skipped. *Interpretation:* Both items in each pair must be correct. Score each pair separately. Stop after two skills have been missed. The first skill at which a student is unsuccessful is the skill at which instruction would begin. Carefully note the student's error pattern because it will, to a great extent, determine the instructional strategy. It is very important to note that students who have serious problems at this level should not progress to any higher level of instruction in mathematics. Students who do not demonstrate solid readiness skills will only be able to develop splintered skills and/or defective skills.

Number Facts

Addition, Subtraction, Multiplication, Division, (IIA–IID). Materials: There are 390 basic facts. Randomly select 50 for each of the four operations. List these for written group assessment or on flash cards for individual assessment. *Strategy:* Ask student(s) to answer each item as quickly as possible. *Interpretation:* 100 percent accuracy; if the assessment is done individually, allow three seconds per response. If the assessment is a group one, allow two minutes for activity. The operations for which the student scores 100 percent accuracy within the time limit should be credited. Any level that falls below 100 percent accuracy needs to be assessed further. This is done by compiling a second set of fifty facts in the same manner as the first fifty and assessing each fact. Create a list of known/unknown facts. This can later be used to determine each student's math fact practice program.

Whole Number Computation

Addition, Subtraction, Multiplication, Division, (IIIA–IIID). Materials: Student arithmetic text or arithmetic workbook. Select two items per skill and write or type them in a worksheet form, leaving adequate room to solve each problem. *Strategy:* Ask student to solve each problem. No problem is to be skipped. *Interpretation:* Both items in each pair must be correct. Score each pair separately. Stop after two skills have been missed. The first skill at which a student is unsuccessful is the skill at which instruction should begin. Carefully note the student's error pattern. Math-fact errors can be controlled by utilizing the fact chart during computation. This should be done only if the student did not know the math facts for that operation. The student's error pattern will, to a great extent, determine the instructional strategy.

Fractions

Conversion, Addition, Subtraction, Multiplication, Division, (IVA–IVE). Materials: Student arithmetic text or arithmetic workbook. Select two items per skill and write or type them in a worksheet form, leaving adequate room to solve each problem. *Strategy:* Ask student to compute each problem. No problem is to be skipped. *Interpretation:* Both items in each pair must be correct. Score each pair separately. Stop after two skills have been missed. The first skill at which a student is unsuccessful is the skill at which instruction should begin. Carefully note the student's error pattern. The student's error pattern will, to a great extent, determine the instructional strategy.

Decimals

Addition, Subtraction, Multiplication, Division, Conversion of Percents to Decimals, (VA–VE). *Materials:* Student arithmetic text or arithmetic workbook. Select two items per skill and write or type them in a worksheet form, leaving adequate room to solve each problem. *Strategy:* Ask student to compute each problem. No problem is to be skipped. *Interpretation:* Both items in each pair must be correct. Score each pair separately. Stop after two skills have been missed. The first skill at which a student is unsuccessful is the skill at which instruction should begin. Carefully note the student's error pattern. Math-fact errors can be controlled by utilizing a fact chart during computation. This should be done only if the student did not know the math facts for that operation. The student's error pattern will, to a great extent, determine the instructional strategy. If the student is not successful with multiplication of decimals, do not go on to conversion of percents to decimals.

Problem Solving

Reads and Understands, Organizes Facts, Correct Operation, Computes Answer, Checks Answer, (VIA–VIE). *Materials.* Student arithmetic text or arithmetic workbook. Select two items per skill and write or type them in a worksheet form, leaving adequate room to solve each problem. *Strategy.* Ask student to solve each problem. No problem is to be skipped. *Interpretation:* Both items in each pair must be correct. Score each pair separately. Stop after two

skills have been missed. The first skill at which a student is unsuccessful is the skill at which instruction should begin. A student may progress to a higher level in one of the procedural steps than he or she does in the other steps. This is perfectly acceptable and should be carefully monitored for instructional implications. The examiner either can test all five steps in a given grade level and then progress to the next grade level, or can choose to test a particular step (e.g., understanding the problem) through various grade levels. In either case, stop within a procedural step after the first error for that particular step. Carefully note the student's error pattern. Math-fact errors can be controlled by utilizing a fact error chart during computation. This should be done only if the student did not know the math facts for that operation. The student's error pattern will, to a great extent, determine the instructional strategy. (For step D use subtests from sections I–V as appropriate by grade level.)

Sample Items for Tests of Basic Mathematics. The sample tests for basic mathematics, listed in Appendix E, are primarily taken from the ENRIGHT® Diagnostic Inventory of Basic Arithmetic Skills (1983) with the permission of Curriculum Associates, Inc. These sample tests represent the skill placement tests from that inventory. They may be used to survey the student's ability or as a guide in developing more in depth tests. They may also be used to determine where, in that inventory, the teacher should look for further assessment. The sample tests for readiness, conversion of percents to decimals, and problem solving are not taken from ENRIGHT (1983) and should only be used when they reflect the curriculum of the classroom. Like the suggestions for constructing test items, these readiness and computation tests contain production-level tasks; however, the problem-solving tests are application-level tasks that utilize a selection format. In all cases, the teacher should select and/or develop tests that best reflect what is being taught.

Each sample test item is cross-referenced with the basic mathematics curriculum chart

(Figure 9.1) and also shown as an objective in Appendix E. This organization should help you in developing both the assessment plan and the programming plan. Make a copy of those tests appropriate for each student. (The answers for these tests follow the sample tests themselves.)

As was discussed earlier in this chapter, you are encouraged to use the teacher survey as well as any samples of the student's work to make an initial determination of what to test. It should be noted that each subtest only briefly samples designated subskills. Because the sample items are limited, unusual performance on any subtest should be confirmed through comparison with the student's typical classroom performance, follow-up diagnostic observations, and additional assessment.

The student summary sheet presented in Figure 9.4 is very useful in synthesizing much data. It should be attached as a cover page to any sample tests and/or work samples. This form should expedite finding the sources of the problems and correcting them. Also useful is a more

FIGURE 9.4   Student Summary Sheet for Basic Mathematics

Name_____Date_____

A.   Area of Concern (circle one or two)

    I.   Readiness

    II.   Number Facts

    III. Whole Number Operations

    IV. Fractions

    V.   Decimals

    VI. Problem Solving

B.   Specific Skills to Remediate

    1.

    2.

    3.

    4.

    5.

C.   Types of Errors

COMPUTATION:	PROBLEM SOLVING:
1. Careless	1. Ignores question
2. Number facts	2. Uses extraneous data
3. Regrouping	3. Leaves out facts
4. Process substitution	4. Acts without a plan
5. Directional	5. Selects wrong operation
6. Omission	6. Doesn't check work
7. Placement	
8. Attention to sign	
9. Guessing	

detailed checklist of common arithmetic errors (Enright, 1990).

Alternative Assessment Techniques.   There are several viable alternatives to assessing basic mathematics. The suggestions given earlier will help standardize the process of curriculum-based assessment. However, sometimes it is necessary to evaluate students in a non-standard way. This section considers alternative ways to assess basic computation and problem solving. The purpose in using these alternative assessment strategies is to more accurately evaluate the thinking process behind the paper and pencil procedures.

Unfortunately, mathematics problems are made up of many steps and an error can occur at any one of these steps. The error can be sporadic (i.e., it occurs rarely) or the error can be systematic (i.e., the error occurs all the time). Systematic errors can be founded in the lack of understanding the basic concepts of mathematics or in the procedure of the algorithm. In other words, some students do not understand what they are doing; others, who understand, can still consistently fail because they have not learned the steps. Because there are many possible causes of error, it is frequently useful to implement alternative methods to unlock the error or at least verify what previous assessment has suggested.

Computation in Isolation.   Frequently computation errors can be evasive. This can occur when the student either makes several different errors in a single problem or when the student makes several different errors in several examples of the same skill. When this occurs, it is useful to have the student "talk through" the problem. As the student talks through a problem, several things quickly become clear. Students who have not mastered the basic number facts frequently miss one or two facts in a problem, causing an incorrect answer. This error can be quickly observed and measures taken. Other times, the student will leave out a step, or place the step out of order. This too can be noted and appropriate review using flowcharts might be implemented. Other students may not understand the concept of the

operation at all. When this occurs, the diagnostician can bring the use of manipulatives into the assessment process. This use of manipulatives is, itself, an alternative to traditional assessment procedures.

Assessing the most successful method for a particular student to learn new computation skills is also important. Once an error pattern or simply the lack of a skill is determined, several different techniques can be tried out, observing how the student benefits from each one. The rate at which new skills can be introduced can be determined, as well as whether new skills are better introduced for that learner using manipulatives or other learning strategies.

Problem Solving.   Assessing the five steps of problem solving should assist in identifying at which step in the procedure the student breaks down. However, it is also useful to know how the student puts the whole process together. This can be accomplished in several ways. First, the student may talk through the process. Arcavi and Schoenfeld (1992) suggest having the students identify what they are doing, why they are doing it, and how it is helping them. This procedure will reveal the strategies and the thought processes the student is using. Secondly, have the student draw a picture of what the problem is all about. Many students think better visually, and this will again demonstrate their thinking process. Third, having the student generate problems which require preset action can show if the student understands the concept. For example, have the students generate problems which require the action of "comparing to find a difference" (e.g., given two people of different heights, find how much taller one person is than the other). Lastly, to check on understanding and strategy usage, observe and analyze the explanations the target student uses to teach a peer to solve sample problems.

Published Tests.   The ENRIGHT Diagnostic Inventory of Basic Arithmetic Skills (Enright, 1983), the Brigance Diagnostic Comprehensive Inventory of Basic Skills (Brigance, 1983), the Multi-Level Academic Skills Inventory and the

Multi-Level Academic Survey Tests (Howell, Zucker, & Morehead, 1982, 1985), present well-documented test items. By carefully comparing the student's curriculum chart to certain commercial criterion-referenced instruments, the diagnostician may select specific test items that provide appropriate measures of target skills required by the curriculum.

Test Administration.   Certain procedures are common to all testing—mathematics assessment is no exception to that rule. It is critical to identify exactly which skills are to be assessed. *Exactly* is the operative word. If addition with regrouping is to be assessed, then the items being used must focus on that skill and that skill only. Other skills will be assessed later. Once the skills have been selected, mastery must be defined. What will the level of accuracy and rate of performance be? For the strands within mathematics which appear to be sequential, it makes no sense to have the student work skills above his/her level of ability. Therefore, after consistent errors are located, stop testing in that strand. If any part of the assessment is done orally, make sure to record everything that is said. It is a good idea to use a tape recorder if the oral part of the test is substantial. Error patterns should be examined carefully (Ashlock, 1990; Enright, 1989; Gable & Hendrickson, 1990a). As will be discussed later, error analysis is the key to unlocking the reason behind much of student failure in mathematics.

It is perfectly acceptable to break up a page of work into smaller sections. This can keep the task from overwhelming the student who is not very successful. Be sure to make careful note that the task was broken down and the reason that this action was taken. If the student is more successful with shorter tasks, this will have a direct effect on the design of future lessons. If the student performs no differently with shorter tasks, this, too, is important information.

One must consider all aspects of the assessment situation in order to make useful suggestions for future instruction. Consider which skills were missed, but also under what circumstances,

at what rate, with what effect. All aspects will play an important role in curriculum planning.

Documenting Skill Needs.   Documentation of mathematics assessment results is essential for several reasons: It provides a record of how the student was performing at a given point in time for all appropriate parties to review; it establishes a baseline of performance against which to compare all future assessment, both summative and formative; it serves as justification for the development of a particular instructional program; and it allows the integration of information from the various aspects of mathematics, as well as from other areas of the curriculum such as reading and language arts. In addition, documentation provides a base for substantiation of the accuracy of the information before it is charted.

Substantiating Needs.   Mathematics skill needs are substantiated through the additional testing that may be required, conferring with the teacher, and throughout programming. All skills should be considered tentative until substantiated through the assessment/programming cycle.

Observation of the student's computation performance in the classroom is vital to accurate assessment. Both success and error patterns must be recorded and analyzed. Through error analysis the mastered portions of a task may be identified. In addition, by identifying a student's error pattern, the teacher is able to tailor corrective instruction for a more rapid acquisition of skills.

Charting and Interpreting Needs.   Once the student's mathematics skill needs are tentatively identified, they should be charted on the mathematics curriculum chart. Circle the specific subskills, so as to highlight needs and compare them with those required by the curriculum. It is important to use the same curriculum chart to record both curricular demands and diagnosed subskill needs to allow for this comparison. If the majority of a student's circled subskills are charted at two grade levels below the ones checked as necessary for success in the curriculum, one can assume that the student will have continual difficulty in basic mathematics without a comprehensive plan for specialized instruction.

PERSONALIZED PROGRAMMING PROCEDURES

The first step in programming is determining the relative importance of the student's basic mathematics skill needs to his or her overall academic progress. The specific basic mathematics subskills must be ranked in terms of the student's most pressing and immediate needs. The unmastered subskills and tasks that will most directly facilitate mathematics problem solving deserve primary program consideration.

Selection of Content

The importance of the various basic mathematics subskills must be considered in deciding where to begin a program. Of the six subskill categories presented, it is very difficult to rank one above the others. If number facts are partially learned, a brief intense program to master them should be considered. Such a program need not take up more than two or three minutes a day. By utilizing some of the corrective strategies proposed later in this chapter, the teacher can facilitate rapid student gain in computation skills. The acquisition of number facts and computation skills can be accomplished at the same time as the acquisition of problem-solving skills. One may use a typical 35-minute period to address the relative importance of each by allocating: (1) 3 minutes for number facts drill, (2) 15 minutes for computation skills, and (3) 17 minutes for problem solving.

Selection of Methods and Materials

The choice of methods with which to begin a personalized instructional program in basic mathematics is a difficult one. Many good suggestions for the development of such a program can be found in the writings of Burton (1992), Capps and Cox (1991), Fennell (1992), Graeber and Baker (1992), Howell (1986), Jensen (1993), Owens (1993), Pressley and associates (1990), Rivers and Bryant (1992), Silbert, Carnine, and Stein (1990), and Spikell (1993). If emphasis is to be put on readiness skills, almost certainly the program should be geared to the use of manipulatives as a method. However, if the emphasis is on number facts, drill should be the dominant instructional mode (whether oral and/or written). If the emphasis is on computation, some combination of manipulative activities and error pattern analysis should be employed. The focus should not be the number of computations performed, but rather the manner in which the computations are completed. Skilled problem solving combines all the skills mentioned plus group interaction and the mastery of an investigative procedure. The reader is referred to an article by Lambie and Hutchens (1986) for additional ideas on adapting math instruction.

If the student has failed using the basal series and is very anxious about its use, it should be avoided. A temporary transfer into a supplementary series that is skill-specific for quick acquisition of skills and then a gradual reentry into the basal series may provide a comfortable environment in which to learn and maintain progress. If the need is to provide corrective instruction, be very careful that the material covers only the skill desired. Also build materials into the program that regularly review all skills learned. A series that accomplishes these things is the ENRIGHT Computation Series (1985, 1986). Three problem-solving programs that provide for assessment and remediation are *SOLVE: Action Problem Solving* (Enright, 1987), *Developing Key Concepts for Solving Word Problems* (Panchyshyn, 1986), and *Problem Solving Experiences in Mathematics* (Charles, 1985).

Programming for Subskills

Programming for basic mathematics skills must be considered an integrated process in that number facts, computation skills, and problem solving all work together. The first two serve as tools during problem solving. Because the teaching of most computation skills is similar, computation will be addressed in this section as one entity. Programming will be divided into: (1) developmental strategies, (2) corrective strategies, and (3) maintenance strategies. Wherever it is appropriate to use a specific strategy across skill areas, it is noted.

Developmental Strategies

Certain instructional strategies are widely accepted as appropriate for introductory teaching of specific mathematics computation skills. They are presented in the following sections under the headings of readiness, number facts, computation, and problem solving. Some of these strategies are repeated under corrective strategies (especially with number facts), since they can also be useful in this area. For one of the most detailed and excellent presentations of the teaching of mathematics, consult *Today's Mathematics* by Heddens and Speer (1992) for specific suggestions.

Readiness.   Readiness is the act of beginning to think mathematically. The foundation for learning eadiness skills is the certain understanding of one-to-one correlation. At first, it is useful to line objects up to be counted. This helps the student touch each in sequence. Make sure the student does not count too fast; children who can rote count (say one to ten) may count faster than they touch the objects, thus, counting to eight when there may be only five blocks. The teacher may need to hold the student's hand and help him or her touch each object while counting. Once this has been accomplished, moving objects out of line to present them in a more natural way will also serve to confirm mastery of this skill.

To develop the skill of joining sets together, the teacher can simply divide the group of objects the student has been counting into two sets. The student should count one set and then the other set, and lastly, put the sets together and count that new set.

Rote counting is an oral skill and can be practiced in small groups. The teacher must listen very carefully to each child's contribution. Children will often speak just after their peers. This is frequently a means for them to learn from the group. It is not necessarily a bad practice and probably should not be discouraged. However, if this does persist, the teacher might pull that student aside to listen to him or her individually. One technique that helps children is actually seeing their progress. The teacher might write the numbers from 1 to 100, and using a blue highlighting pen, trace through the sequence as far as the student can rote count without error. After some practice (possibly two or three weeks), check again and move the highlighting through as many more numbers as the student can then rote count without error. This provides the student with information about what he or she knows as well as a continuous progress report.

Number Facts.   Number facts are bits of information much like sight words. They need to be recalled instantly to be of much use later in computation. However, in their initial learning, number facts should have meaning. This meaning can be acquired by relating number facts to the joining of sets. For example, create two sets of three objects each. Have the student count the objects in the first set and write the number (3). Write a "+" for the student to show the adding together of groups (3 +). Have the student count the number of objects in the second set and write the number (3) after the "+" (3 + 3). Write the equal sign after the problem (3 + 3 =) and have the student count all the objects together. Have the student write the answer (6) after the problem. Next is a very important step frequently ignored. Have the student read the problem with the answer (3 + 3 = 6). The student has only been counting up to this point. Now, he or she is reading a number fact. Reading a number fact will help store it for future retrieval. The teacher may want to create a worksheet with 20 sets of blank problems (__+__=__) and let the student fill in the blanks while using objects. This is a particularly good activity for paired learning with two students. Later, the process can move to worksheets with a number of facts on them. The teacher should always emphasize speed during these activities so as to encourage the student to move away from counting (either block or figures). As with rote counting, the use of choral reaction and some means of continuous record keeping can be very helpful.

Computation.   One basis for a strong understanding of computation is to have successfully mastered readiness and number facts. This provides the student with the one-to-one correlation relationship as well as a good sense of place value. The use of commonly available concrete objects is still necessary for the introduction of addition and its inverse, subtraction. Cutting pies into halves, fourths, or eighths and adding those components or subtracting them will enhance working with fractions. The use of manipulatives over time is essential so that students will become both comfortable with their use and will be able to truly develop the understanding of the process necessary later for application. It is, however, necessary to bridge the gap between the use of manipulatives and the abstract concepts of mathematics (Heddens, 1986). It should be noted that the manipulatives are not just for young learners; the methods are useful for middle school students and beyond. Once a fundamental understanding has been developed, the next step is to master the algorithm. An algorithm is a set of steps or procedures for successfully completing a task. Although there are probably several possible algorithms for any skill (and it is probably useful to introduce all forms to above average children), it is helpful to keep the possible algorithms simple and limited. Taking a wordy algorithm and changing it to a brief visual road map is also useful. This is discussed again under corrective strategies and a sample will be provided there.

One of the fundamental understandings that a student must develop is the concept of the equation. It is very important that a student realize that each side of an equation is equal. This may seem obvious to teachers, but it is not obvious to the student as a beginning learner. Many times teachers will create two groups of objects and then, to demonstrate addition, will put the groups together and have the student count how many there are. This practice is useful in beginning the concept, but to move further the teacher should arrange the two groups, create an = sign, and have the student take from a separate pile of objects the number equal to the objects in the two groups. Next the student should write the equation. As a developmental activity, the student should learn to write and use an equation after he or she has learned what an equation is through the use of manipulatives. This fundamental understanding could then lead to the use of reverse operations. The student could learn to build on the understanding that 5 + 3 = 8 so that he or she also knows that 8 − 3 = 5.

Problem Solving.   The developmental teaching of problem solving is a complicated process. Problem solving should focus on the use of realistic problems. Encourage students to share real mathematical problems they encounter. Also have students help generate problems they find interesting. This helps build interest in the initial stages of problem solving.

Problem solving was introduced earlier in this chapter as a five-step procedure. For the purpose of addressing the developmental teaching of problem solving, each step will be explained separately. Three additional steps are necessary. First, the teacher must lead the students through these steps one at a time. The need to reach a final answer must be replaced by the desire to learn how to attain many answers after the student has developed the essential set of skills in problem solving. Reward the attempt at the step being learned. If the student is learning to "organize information," try to avoid using that information until the learning process enters that stage. Simply put, make the student realize the importance of the step in which he or she is working.

Second, problem solving must focus on real-life situations. Students must see the true implications of problem solving to their lives. Students will attend to problems that stress issues they can relate to in their daily lives. Life skills of shopping, entertainment, or hobbies are good choices. Also, this is an opportunity to bring in content from other areas of the curriculum, especially science and social studies.

Third, the teacher must allocate enough time in the daily plan for problem solving. If problem solving does not receive a high priority and if it is not allocated a specific time slot each day, then it will probably not always be taught. If the attitude is taken that problem solving will be taught after (if) we finish computation, then problem solving won't get taught. It must be a priority item in the curriculum. It is quite possible that students will work harder on computation skills when they realize how these skills can help them in problem solving.

The first step in problem solving is to understand the problem. Certainly the skills discussed in Chapters 5 and 6 can be very helpful here. Have the student practice underlining the question within the problem. By separating what must be found from what is given, the student can begin the search. Have the student rewrite or tell what is asked in his or her own words. This practice also enables the teacher to discern that the student does understand what is being sought (Choate, 1990b).

Since visualization frequently aids in understanding a situation, have the student draw a picture of the problem. (Drawing a picture is also useful for generating interest in the process.) Check to see that the student included all parts of the problem in the picture. If the problem mentions eight birds, for example, make sure that there are eight birds in the picture rather than just some birds. This will help the student to attend to detail, a task so critical in problem solving. The student can also act out the problem. By having small groups of students actually perform the problem, better understanding can occur. It is not necessary to do all these steps for every problem, but it is useful for a student to be able to choose among these aids in understanding the problem.

Therefore, each should at least be practiced by all students.

The second step in problem solving is to organize the information given into some workable format (Szubinski & Enright, 1992). As in reading comprehension, this may be as simple as listing the facts, or as complex as putting those facts into tables, charts, or graphs. When the student first lists the facts, ensure he or she lists them all. Do not let the student leave any out because "they don't seem important," since this habit can lead to leaving out very important facts later on. Once the student has listed all the facts, he or she can go back and cross out any facts that are clearly not needed. At this point in the instructional process, it is useful to select problems that contain extraneous information. Practice sorting useful and useless information will speed up the process. The student should justify dropping any information. Students can be taught to put this information into tabular form. Teach the student that creating tables, charts, and graphs is no more than listing the facts in categories so that they may be studied better and understood more easily. Also make a conscious, systematic effort to provide problems for which there are insufficient data—facts that have to be located outside of the problem in order to solve the problem. These facts could be found in a newspaper, an encyclopedia, or simply by gathering information in the classroom. Remember, real-life problems seldom come with all the data needed for solution.

The third step in problem solving is to develop a plan (Miller & Beattie, 1992). A plan is a student's systematic means of solving a problem. Even though there may be several ways to solve a problem, an acceptable plan is systematic, not based on guesswork. The student should write the plan in simple outline form. A useful question is to ask the student how he or she would solve this kind of problem outside of school. Of course, we must provide real-life problems that students would want to solve outside of school. For example, "You go to a movie with $6.50; after you pay $3.50 to get in, do you have enough money for a drink and popcorn? How do you know?" Think about it; this is relevant to students, and most could tell you what the drink and popcorn cost from their experience.

The fourth step, to compute the problem, is discussed under the heading Computation throughout this chapter. There are additional considerations. Problems must be selected that require computation skills that a student has mastered (Enright & Beattie, 1993). Although this will require a significant degree of individualization, it can be achieved by using problems from existing programs where computation is controlled. Also, calculators can be employed while the student is developing the computation skills, provided the student at least understands how to select the correct computation skill. To determine this, have the student practice selecting the correct equation from several possible operations.

The final step in problem solving is to determine if the answer is correct (Gable, Evans, & Evans, 1993). A calculator can easily be used to determine the accuracy of the computation. However, to determine whether the answer fits the problem, the student will need to go back to the first step and compare the answer (which should be written in the form of a complete statement) to the question being asked. This match up is frequently assumed but much less often done and can lead to "computationally correct" answers that have nothing to do with the problem. Before the students write the answer in a complete thought, have them write the question.

Having students write their own problems will make the student more familiar with each part of the problem. The process of writing, editing, and rewriting clearly helps students understand the component parts of problems and their interrelationships, become better problem solvers (Wang & Willoughby, 1991), and it offers an integrated program as well.

Corrective Strategies

Corrective strategies are those used to reteach a concept skill after it has been incorrectly learned. Although this sounds rather obvious, nowhere is

it better demonstrated than in arithmetic. Students can memorize facts incorrectly, from $4 + 2 = 5$ to $6 \times 7 = 46$. In a far more complex manner, students develop incorrect algorithms for solving computation items. These incorrect algorithms are called error patterns. Ashlock (1990) describes various error patterns and demonstrates the analysis of them. Enright (1983, 1988) expands upon that work and identifies 233 error patterns responsible for many of the difficulties students are having in computation. He later subdivides the 233 errors into 7 categories based on instructional similarities. These seven categories will be the focus for corrective strategies in computation. The reader may wish to consult Enright (1985, 1986) for more detailed information regarding strategies for remediating error patterns. In addition, strategies will be presented to deal with unsuccessful problem solving skills.

Number Facts.   Any of the strategies discussed under developmental strategies, when targeted for individual need, are appropriate here. In addition, two simple strategies seem helpful. One, using two grids (Figures 9.5 and 9.6) to represent addition and subtraction or multiplication and division respectively, has the student highlight each answer he or she knows. Base this strategy on at least two tests of number facts. As the student progresses, have him or her continue to highlight the grid. This practice initially shows students that indeed they know some facts and also helps them to trace later success. Another method that helps individualize number facts quickly is the use of number fact rings. Use any ring (metal shower-curtain rings or key rings that open easily are good) to hold fact cards. In their spare time, students can pair up to practice these facts. Students should always state their math fact as a complete idea. Thus, when asked "$3 + 2 = ?$," they should respond "$3 + 2 = 5$." This recitation can help code that piece of data for later retrieval.

Computation.   As was stated earlier seven clusters of error patterns have been identified. This section of the chapter presents each error cluster and suggests strategies for correcting each.

FIGURE 9.5 Table of Basic Facts for Addition and Subtraction

±	0	1	2	3	4	5	6	7	8	9
0	0	1	2	3	4	5	6	7	8	9
1	1	2	3	4	5	6	7	8	9	10
2	2	3	4	5	6	7	8	9	10	11
3	3	4	5	6	7	8	9	10	11	12
4	4	5	6	7	8	9	10	11	12	13
5	5	6	7	8	9	10	11	12	13	14
6	6	7	8	9	10	11	12	13	14	15
7	7	8	9	10	11	12	13	14	15	16
8	8	9	10	11	12	13	14	15	16	17
9	9	10	11	12	13	14	15	16	17	18

FIGURE 9.6 Table of Basic Facts for Multiplication and Division

÷ ⁄ ×	0	1	2	3	4	5	6	7	8	9
0	0	0	0	0	0	0	0	0	0	0
1	0	1	2	3	4	5	6	7	8	9
2	0	2	4	6	8	10	12	14	16	18
3	0	3	6	9	12	15	18	21	24	27
4	0	4	8	12	16	20	24	28	32	36
5	0	5	10	15	20	25	30	35	40	45
6	0	6	12	18	24	30	36	42	48	54
7	0	7	14	21	28	35	42	49	56	63
8	0	8	16	24	32	40	48	56	64	72
9	0	9	18	27	36	45	54	63	72	81

Source: From ENRIGHT® *Diagnostic Inventory of Basic Arithmetic Skills,* © 1983 Curriculum Associates, Inc. Adapted and reprinted by permission.

Cluster 1: Regrouping. Regrouping errors are errors in which a student's mistake takes place on one or more of the steps required to regroup successfully in a math problem. It may be that the student fails to regroup and records the total answer below the problem, regroups the wrong value, or perhaps does record the ones value but fails to regroup the tens value. The following are three examples of regrouping errors (there are at least seven such errors):

27	27	27
+ 35	+ 35	+ 35
512	71	52

Each wrong answer means something. The fact that each has to do with regrouping helps in two ways. First, it may be possible to group a few students together with similar problems. Second, the focus of the corrective lesson will be similar.

Strategy 1: Grid Paper. Provide the student with graph paper or write the problem in grids. You may wish to label the columns. Emphasize that only one numeral can go in a box.

Strategy 2: Color Boxes. Draw boxes for the parts of the answers to be inserted. Place a green box over the tens column and a red box under the ones column. Also draw these boxes to the right side of the problem so that the student must first record the partial sum next to the problem and then record it in the problem. After drawing the initial boxes, have the student draw the boxes for the rest of the problems. This causes the student to begin to internalize the process. The student should have to ask the question, "Is the answer greater than 9?" each time he or she adds.

Strategy 3: Chip Trading. Provide the student with manipulatives such as interlocking blocks and a space that will only hold 9 blocks. When the student has more than nine of these he or she must trade a set of ten for a ten block which then moves to the ten's column. Chip trading can be done with various colored poker chips, provided the student can visualize the relationship of color to value. Also money can be used. However, money sometimes presents the problem that ten pennies equals something smaller. Students must know the value of the coins for this to be effective.

Cluster 2: Process Substitution. Errors produced under this cluster are a result of the student changing one or more steps in the computation process, thus, creating a new and defective algorithm. A student may add using the multiplication process or add the divisor to the dividend to form the quotient. (There are at least 105 of these types of errors.)

   Strategy 1: Structure the Problem. Draw a line to separate the various columns of an addition problem. This brings the student's attention back to the ones, tens, etc.
   Strategy 2: Alphabet Use. Use the alphabet to order steps in a problem. Students follow the ABC order to things. Combining this idea with Strategy 1 increases how each will work.
   Strategy 3: Flowcharts. This idea works well with many kinds of errors but it best suits process substitutions. Create a flowchart similar to the one in Figure 9.7, which shows the steps a student should follow. Make enough copies so that a student can write on the chart and from time to time replace it. Since one of the characteristics of students who make this kind of error is their inability to move in a step-by-step fashion, have them use a place holder to mark where in the flowchart they are at any time. Almost anything can be used as a placeholder (a coin is often preferred).

Cluster 3: Directional. In the steps the computation is correct, but the steps are performed in the wrong direction.

$$
\begin{array}{r}
50 \\
+\ 37 \\
\hline
510
\end{array}
\quad = \quad
\begin{array}{l}
5 + 0 = 5 \\
3 + 7 = 10
\end{array}
\qquad
\begin{array}{r}
12 \\
\times 23 \\
\hline
24 \\
36 \\
\hline
384
\end{array}
$$

   Strategy 1: Lines. Draw solid line between the columns in addition and subtraction to emphasize the place value and the columns made for these operations.
   Strategy 2: Letter Use. As a supplement to Strategy 1, letter the columns A and B to show the student in which order they should be added.
   Strategy 3: Color Code. Use a color-coded grid to reverse the pattern shown in multiplication, with green for the boxes and first multiplier, and red for the boxes and second multiplier.

Cluster 4: Omission. This is a set of error patterns in which the student leaves out one or more steps in the algorithms.

$$
\begin{array}{r}
45 \\
-2 \\
\hline
3
\end{array}
\qquad
\begin{array}{r}
50r2 \\
3\overline{)172} \\
\underline{15} \\
2
\end{array}
$$

   Strategy 1: Highlighting. Use colored highlighting pens to stress both columns. Use green for the one's column and red for the ten's column.
   Strategy 2: Reminder Boxes. For either of the previous problems, reminder boxes are useful. Set up the problem with the boxes in place for the student to see.

FIGURE 9.7   Multiplication Flowchart

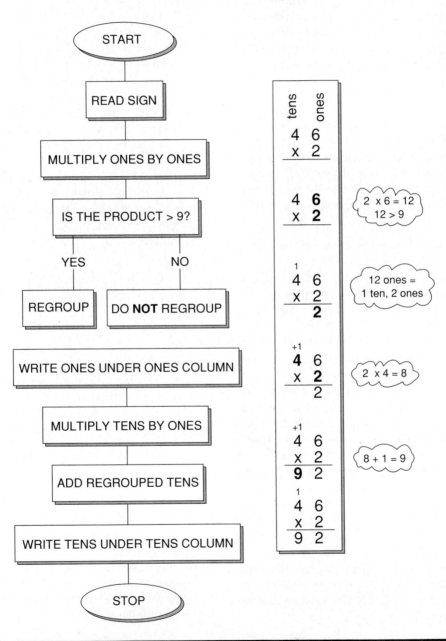

Is the Product > 9? Regroup

Source: From ENRIGHT®, *Diagnostic Inventory of Basic Arithmetic Skills,* © 1983 Curriculum Associates, Inc. Adapted and reprinted with permission.

Strategy 3: Partial Answer. Show a partial answer through the point of the error. In the division example, show the subtraction and bringing down of the next digit. It is useful to do this in a different color for emphasis.

Cluster 5: Placement. In this set of error patterns the student computes correctly but places the answer in the wrong place.

$$
\begin{array}{r}
12 \\
\times\, 23 \\
\hline
36 \\
24 \\
\hline
70
\end{array}
\qquad
\begin{array}{r}
820\text{r}2 \\
3\overline{)246} \\
\underline{24} \\
06 \\
\underline{6} \\
0 \\
0
\end{array}
$$

Strategy 1: Graph Paper. Graph paper or grids are useful here. Fill the space where the problem is occurring with a zero to hold that space open.

Strategy 2: Key Thought. Use a key thought. After demonstrating the process correctly, have the students come up with a short phrase to help them remember the correction.

Strategy 3: Place Holder. Find something to use as a place holder. When students have to determine where to place the answer in the division process have them use a "pincher" clothespin to hold the place until they are ready to write the answer.

Cluster 6: Attention to Sign. In this set of error patterns the student does not attend to which sign is used. This is not a mathematical error but does result in incorrect answers. (Some students who do this also ignore punctuation in reading.)

Strategy 1: Sign Find. Prepare a practice page with all four signs listed to the left of each problem. Before the student computes, he or she must match the sign to the problem.

Strategy 2: Color Code. Write the sign in a different color to emphasize it. Gradually do fewer and fewer signs in different colors.

Strategy 3: Tracing. Have the student trace the sign three times with his or her pencil before doing the computation.

Cluster 7: Guessing. In this set of error patterns the student demonstrates no fundamental understanding of the problem at all.

Strategies: For this type of error pattern it is necessary to go back to the developmental process in readiness and use basic concrete objects. Many of these students have not yet mastered the one-to-one correlation or the concept of joining sets.

Problem Solving. Problem solving has been addressed in this chapter as a five-step process with each step leading to the successful completion of the problem. Therefore, if the student is unsuccessful in his or her attempt to solve the problem, the cause for the error should be located in one or more of the steps. For example, Burrows (1987) points out that unrecognized reading errors often interfere with the process needed in problem solving. That is the reason that the sample tests on problem solving provided in this text assess each individual step in the procedure rather than just check for a correct answer to the total problem. The latter will tell you that your students have difficulty in problem solving, whereas the former will tell you at which step your efforts must be applied for corrective instruction. If several students in your class have problems with a particular step they can be grouped for instruction in this area.

Step 1: Understanding the Problem. As was stated in the discussion of developmental strategies, many of the suggestions made in Chapters 5 and 6 apply here. In addition the further testing of math vocabulary is very useful at this point. For example, assess to see if a student having difficulty with subtraction problems understands the math meaning of *difference*.

Create multiple-choice practice items that list two or more choices for the question being asked. This will help the student who has underlined the question but does not truly understand what it means.

Step 2: Organizing the Facts. Start by underlining the facts for the student and then have the student write them in a list. Have the student number the list and go back and count the underlined facts in the problem. This practice will help develop attention to details. To start this stage, provide a numbered list in which the numbers correspond to the exact number of facts in each problem. Pairing two students at this step will help provide a cross-check and free you for other instruction. When paired students work together, they should first attempt the task separately and then compare notes. This procedure should also be followed in teaching students to recognize extraneous data.

Step 3: Making a Plan. This is probably the most difficult step to correct because it entails higher level thinking skills. Separate the strategies listed earlier in the discussion of developmental teaching and analyze each task. Each will require significant practice. Using a process of fading, provide the student (or team of students) with a sample problem whose plan of action is completed. Next provide a similar problem that requires the student to work out the last step. Continue this process, deleting one additional step at appropriate times. After this has been accomplished, omit each step of the problem one at a time. Each time one plan of action has been learned, introduce another plan. Always continue the previous plan as a reinforcement procedure.

Step 4: Computing the Answer. The extensive strategies already listed in this chapter for correcting computation-error patterns are also useful here. In addition, two other strategies are appropriate. First, provide the student with multiple-choice problems with answers varying widely. This will provide a point of comparison for the student. As stated earlier, students with error patterns in computation can still learn problem solving skills at the same time the computation error patterns are being remediated. To reduce stress for the student, use calculators. This assistance should be monitored closely so that the use of the calculator can gradually be diminished and replaced with the new computation skills as they are learned. Calculators, as well as computation skills, are tools students should be able to use interchangeably.

Step 5: Checking the Answer. Checking one's answer in problem solving is a complicated process because the student must ensure not only that the answer is accurate but also that it makes sense. (Is the answer reasonable?) This implies, as it should, a higher level thinking skill.

Provide the student with a problem followed by a restatement of the question and a pair of answers. Each possible answer should have the correct numerical answer, but only one should match the question. If the question asks how many miles did a plane travel, one answer should be in miles and one answer could be in hours. Such a strategy should help the student in determining the rightness or reasonableness of answers.

Maintenance Strategies

Often, students do not retain the skills they have learned. This frequently occurs because after the initial learning there is not adequate review in most basal programs. Certain strategies can be very useful in maintaining a skill and building fluency.

Periodic Review.   Probably the most fundamental strategy is review . . . systematic, periodic review. Many people refer to this as spiraling, that is spiraling back to a lower skill and bringing it back up. Some programs have maintenance books developed for practicing all previously learned computations skills every few lessons. If these are not available, create worksheets that demonstrate spiraling by choosing problems from previous lessons.

Math Bees. Math bees are a quick way to practice skills orally. Remember that each student should only be asked problems from his or her repertoire of skills.

Pop Quizzes. Give unannounced pop quizzes on previously learned skills. This is really just a variation of spiraling, but it takes on importance because it's a "quiz."

Scrapbooks. Have students build individual scrapbooks of skills they have learned. As each new task is mastered, have each student list the name of the skill at the top of each page, writing several examples of the skill on the page. This exercise could be used to help the teacher during math bees.

Calculators. Calculators are very powerful tools that can enhance the learning process or impair it. There are three benefits of using calculators to check work: (1) It provides the student with immediate feedback; (2) it is a reinforcing activity for many students; and (3) it frees the teacher from having to correct papers constantly. When checking the answers with a calculator, the student should circle any incorrect answers, not correct them, so that the teacher can analyze the error patterns.

Computers. There are many programs available for computation on computers. Teachers should be very careful in the selection of programs. Study the content and the curriculum implications more than the attractive graphics. Many programs, for example, automatically put the student's answer where it is supposed to go, even if this place is not where the student would have put it. This has the effect of masking students' errors, with the probability that they will surface later. Study the management component of the software. If the software does not provide the teacher with continuous information about student progress, he or she has no way of judging its use-

fulness. The computer is the ideal tool to enact the practices, mentioned earlier, concerning testing, teaching, and monitoring number facts. Unfortunately, few programs do this.

Problem Solving. The way that problem solving has been addressed in this chapter lends itself to a maintenance program. By building one step upon another the student must perform each previous step in order to go on to the next. Obviously, when a new step is introduced the former steps will be worked out for the student so that he or she can concentrate on the new step. But as soon as the new step is learned, all work up to and including that step should be done by the student. Therefore, if a strategy in step 3 were being introduced to the student, then steps 1 and 2 should be done for the student. Once the student understands the strategy, steps 1 and 2 should be done by the student before another strategy for step 3 is introduced. This constant controlling and then releasing of control allows a student to commit his or her full attention to the step being learned, and then to integrate that step into the steps already learned. It also provides continuous practice of already learned steps. In addition, as was mentioned earlier, writing problems of their own helps students extend and maintain their understanding of the important component parts of word problems (Fennell, 1992).

Implementing CBA/P Model

The curriculum-based assessment/programming cycle discussed in Chapter 3 provides the format for assessing and programming in basic mathematics as it does in all content areas. It is essential to follow the steps in the model as they were outlined in Chapter 3. Certain elements in this model are specific to mathematics instruction and are discussed here.

Step 1: Analyze the Curriculum

After locating or formulating a basic mathematics curriculum listing, analyze the teacher's and the system's curricula, paying particular attention to how assessment is typically done. Frequently, mathematics assessment is conducted in group settings, using a written format. Especially important is the determination of whether the teacher gives partial credit and thus if any form of error analysis is used. In addition, it is important to determine how much emphasis the teacher places on computation versus problem solving. Mark the teacher's expectations of the specific student on the curriculum chart and proceed to assessment of skills.

Step 2: Assess Skills

Use the teacher interview to indirectly assess student performance in mathematics. Ask the teacher to what degree computation problems are interfering with problem solving and to what degree math facts are causing difficulty. Check available school records to determine if there have been any major shifts in mathematics performance over time and, if so, if these shifts correlate to changes in text books. Frequently different text books take wholly different approaches to the instruction of mathematics. For example, one series might emphasize the use of manipulatives during skill acquisition while another stresses drill. The student under study might do better in one and that could account for differences in performance. Also, note if differences in performance correlate to specific years in school (e.g., the student who did not appear to have any real problems in mathematics until fourth grade). Remember that in fourth grade all math programs introduce many more abstract skills and also greatly increase the reading load for students. It is critical to evaluate work samples at this stage. Evaluate the student's mathematics workbook. This sets the stage for what is expected. You will quickly note if the student consistently misses problems; if there is an excessive number of erasures in each lesson; or if the student's error pattern can be isolated. This will save a significant amount of time later.

Using all the results from indirect assessment, hypothesize the nature of the student's mathematics problem. Determine what the emphasis of the next stage of assessment should be based on the apparent relationship of the different parts of

mathematics for this specific student. If the student does not have difficulty with certain elements of the mathematics curriculum, skip over those areas, only going back later if necessary. If, on the other hand, the student appears to have trouble with all areas of the curriculum, start with the lowest area and eliminate. If facts appear to be a difficulty, they can confound any results found in higher skills. Test facts, and if there are difficulties, provide a fact table during the testing of computational skills. Also, a calculator can be used while testing problem solving if computation skills are weak. Record the student's performance and use the assessment results to begin planning a personalized basic mathematics program.

Step 3: Program for Assessed Needs

To plan and implement a personalized mathematics program, follow the steps of the personalized programming plan described in Chapter 3 in conjunction with the curriculum chart. In selecting program content, make a concerted effort to strike a reasonable balance between instruction in computation and problem solving. Remember that skills in number facts, computation, and problem solving can be taught and learned concurrently. Utilize manipulatives at each step of developmental instruction. Manipulatives can make a major difference for students who have conceptual difficulties. Emphasize the role of number computation skills as tools to solve problems. Incorporate direct instruction in the vocabulary of mathematics into each and every lesson. As you work through the personalized plan, watch closely for specific error and success patterns and program for these accordingly.

Developmental Instruction.   Developmental instruction is used for the purpose of introducing new skills. Attempt to remain as close to traditional instruction for that student to determine how successful it is for the student. Then compare the effect of using the ideas from the basal series the student is currently in with the use of more hands-on materials. This will provide an assessment base for future developmental planning.

Corrective Instruction. The student's error pattern(s) will determine the initial approach to corrective instruction. For example, some students' errors are based in procedural/organizational areas. For these students, flowcharts to assist them in structuring their work may be most appropriate. Other students' error patterns might indicate conceptual difficulties (i.e., regrouping or place value confusion). For these students the use of manipulatives might be most appropriate. What must be understood is that no one way will be most appropriate with all students.

If the student continues to have significant difficulty, change the method and/or the materials being used. Do not, however, change materials or methods too quickly. Students, who have established error patterns, will often take somewhat longer to master the correct method than if they were learning a new skill. That is, confusion and misunderstanding take some time to replace. If mastery still does not occur, go back and reevaluate the task being attempted; it may be necessary to further break down the task, or reinforce earlier tasks, before attempting the target task.

Maintenance Instruction. For skills to be maintained in basic mathematics it is necessary to integrate the new skill with other previously acquired mathematics skills and to use these newly acquired skills frequently. Other new skills can and should be introduced while newly learned skills are in the maintenance stage. Especially important during the maintenance phase of a mathematics skill is its use in other settings and the extension of the skill through various means. For example, if the student has just learned to compute double digit addition with regrouping, the student could practice writing word problems that would require that task for their solution. This has

the effect of both extending the skill to a new level and practicing the skill through different means (writing). This also helps the student truly understand how important the new skill is and why it was learned.

Step 4: Repeat the CBA/P Cycle

To determine which mathematics skills should be included in any updated program, reassess not only the mathematics needs but also the student's total profile (Gable, Enright, & Hendrickson, 1991). Mathematics is integrated with many other skill areas, and these areas will influence the mathematics skills selected. The student who masters the majority of number facts and many computation skills may require a shift in his or her program to more strongly emphasize problem solving. The rate at which new skills had been developed or error patterns eliminated will suggest the best pace of instruction. By evaluating the different methods and/or materials used in each cycle, selection of future methods and materials will be more and more effective. Lastly, evaluate the interrelationship of the various components of the mathematics curriculum. All of the subareas must develop together.

Communication is an essential component of assessment. At the end of each cycle and the beginning of the next, communicate to the student exactly what has happened. Explain why there has or has not been a change in methods. Have the student help record information and especially progress. At the same time communicate with other appropriate persons, in particular, other teachers who are involved with the student and the student's parents. A continuous flow of information about attempts and progress will build rapport and positive relationships.

SUMMARY

The major importance of the arithmetic computation subskills to a student's total long-term academic progress is their contribution to the problem-solving process. The subskill areas, readiness, number facts, and arithmetic computa-

tion, equip the student to utilize his or her problem-solving strategies successfully and help him or her to develop a foundation for problem solving. Much like reading, mathematics has many interdependent skills. These skills must work in harmony and develop in harmony. Programs which only stress one aspect of mathematics (even an area as important as problem solving) will not assist a student in total mathematics development.

Procedures for assessing the student's basic mathematics curriculum and the student's present level and mastery of basic mathematics subskills and tasks have been presented. Recommendations were offered for alternative assessment strategies. One area that was emphasized included not only the assessment of content, but, concurrently, the assessment of how the student best learns and which strategies they bring to different mathematics problem situations. Recommendations were offered for the selection of instructional methods for teaching the needed mathematics subskills and the strategies for accomplishing them. The following case studies should help guide the reader through typical assessment and programming sessions.

CASE STUDIES

Sample Case: Morgan

Morgan is a nine-year-old student in the third grade. The results of indirect assessment indicate the following pertinent information:

The teacher ranks basic mathematics skills as follows: number facts (2), whole number skills (2), fraction skills (3), decimal skills (3), and problem solving skills (2). Skills in whole-number computation and number facts are the weakest areas at approximately beginning second grade. The teacher notes that Morgan has mastered readiness skills and addition skills. He seems to learn best with a visual, structural format. A meaning-based approach with heavy emphasis on manipulation has been used with only limited success. Observation and work samples reveal that Morgan mixes his steps. Morgan is now only ready to begin to develop the first steps in problem solving.

Diagnostic Hypotheses: *Morgan's major difficulty stems from his lack of transfer from manipulative to structural usage. Although he understands the relationship in number facts, he has not yet committed them to memory.*

Based on the results of indirect assessment, direct assessment proceeds in the following manner:

Morgan is interviewed to discuss computation. He states that he has no problem when working with manipulatives (even large sets) but gets "mixed up" when he works "harder" subtraction problems. Direct testing is begun with selected subtraction workbook pages. Sample items IIB and IIIB in Appendix E are used. The results are compared with teacher reports and are found to be consistent. Morgan is making a number of regrouping and process substitution errors in upper level subtraction as depicted in Figure 9.8. He also has mastered less than half of the subtraction facts.

A mathematics program that includes these components is planned:

1. A subtraction drill in which number facts will be introduced ten at a time on a ring. Morgan will write these himself from his number-fact record sheet. He will be tested daily without the use of manipulatives.
2. A subtraction computation program in which the use of flowcharts will be emphasized. Also one problem on each page will be color-coded to remind Morgan of how the steps work.
3. A basic problem solving program that introduces the first step in problem solving. This program will stress problems that Morgan can illustrate to help him understand what is being asked.

FIGURE 9.8   Morgan's Summary Sheet for Basic Mathematics

Name _____ Morgan _____ Date _____ 11/11 _____

A.   Area of Concern (circle one or two)

   I.   Readiness

   (II.)   Number Facts

   (III.)   Whole Number Operations

   IV.   Fractions

   V.   Decimals

   VI.   Problem Solving

B.   Specific Skills to Remediate

   1. Subtraction number facts

   2. Subtraction computation

   3.

   4.

   5.

C.   Types of Errors

COMPUTATION:		PROBLEM SOLVING:
1. Careless		1. Ignores question
2. Number facts		2. Uses extraneous data
3. Regrouping ✓✓✓✓		3. Leaves out facts
4. Process substitution ✓✓✓		4. Acts without a plan
5. Directional		5. Selects wrong operation
6. Omission		6. Doesn't check work
7. Placement		
8. Attention to sign		
9. Guessing		

Practice Case: Paco

The teacher's analysis of Paco's strengths and weaknesses among mathematics subskills indicates that number facts and readiness skills are his weakest points. Indirect assessment indicates that he demonstrates strong auditory preference and that the strengths and weaknesses are confirmed through observation and work sample analysis.

Based upon the summary sheet in Figure 9.9, make the appropriate assessment and programming decisions.

1. What are your diagnostic hypotheses?
2. Where should direct testing begin and why?
3. At what point do you tentatively plan to stop testing and why?

FIGURE 9.9   Paco's Summary Sheet for Basic Mathematics

Name _____Paco_____ Date _____12/4_____

A.   Area of Concern (circle one or two)

(I.)   Readiness

(II.)   Number Facts

III.   Whole Number Operations

IV.   Fractions

V.   Decimals

VI.   Problem Solving

B.   Specific Skills to Remediate

1.   + 1 – Number facts

2.   Joining sets

3.   Counting to 100

4.

5.

C.   Types of Errors

COMPUTATION:

1.   Careless ✓✓✓✓

2.   Number facts

3.   Regrouping ✓✓✓✓✓✓✓✓✓✓

4.   Process substitution

5.   Directional

6.   Omission

7.   Placement

8.   Attention to sign

9.   Guessing ✓✓✓

PROBLEM SOLVING:

1.   Ignores question

2.   Uses extraneous data

3.   Leaves out facts

4.   Acts without a plan

5.   Selects wrong operation

6.   Doesn't check work

4. What materials will you use for testing and why?

5. If the diagnostic hypotheses are confirmed what will probably be the secondary (number facts) program emphasis and why?

6. How will the secondary program priority be established?

7. What corrective strategies will you plan to use initially and why?

8. Which materials will you plan to use initially and why?

9. What specific assessment and programming plans should be made and why?

Practice Case: Katie

Consider the data in Figures 9.10 and 9.11. Answer the following questions as completely as possible. What additional information would be helpful?

1. What are your diagnostic hypotheses?

FIGURE 9.10   Teacher Survey for Katie

Student ___Katie___ Date ___2/21___
Teacher ___Mrs. Laird___ Interviewer ___P.J. Thomas___

A. ASSESSMENT OF CURRICULUM:

1. Indicate appropriate skills, subskills, and tasks on an attached basic mathematics curriculum chart.

2. List current text titles and levels in which student is expected to master basic mathematics:
   ___XYZ Basal___
   _____
   _____

3. Check the primary source(s) of student's report grades in mathematics:
   ✓ Mathematics Workbook   ___ Homework
   ✓ Teacher Tests   ___ Board Work
   ___ Combination _____
   ___ Other _____

4. Indicate the relative importance of each subskill to student's grades in basic mathematics using _1_ as the most important:
   _2_ Number Facts   _3_ Fractions
   _1_ Whole Number Computation   _4_ Decimals
   _1_ Problem Solving   ___ Other _____

5. Describe instructional modifications in mathematics that you have attempted with this student:
   ___Third tutoring — meeting 1 to 1___
   _____

B. INDIRECT STUDENT ASSESSMENT:

6. Rate this student's mathematics subskills using _1_ as mastered, _2_ as currently developing, and _3_ as unknown:
   _1_ Number Facts   _3_ Fractions
   _2_ Whole Number Computation   _3_ Decimals
   _2_ Problem Solving   ___ Other _____

7. Check the best description of the student's emotional reaction to his or her mathematics performance:
   ___ Over concern   ___ No concern
   ✓ Some concern   ___ Other reaction

8. List any other subject areas in which student's mathematics skill interferes with performance:
   ___Science___   _____   _____   _____

9. List specifically what you want to know about this student's mathematics skills: _____
   ___What can she do and where should___
   ___I start teaching___

10. Interviewer Summary: _____
    _____
    _____

ADDITIONAL COMMENTS

List available text titles/levels you would consider as options:

Describe grade sources:

Indicate time devoted to each by current curriculum and texts:

Degree of success:
   Poor

In weakest area(s) identify the most difficult tasks for this student:

Describe student's emotional reaction:

Indicate why and to what extent:

Attach representative samples of the student's work.

FIGURE 9.11 Katie's Summary Sheet for Basic Mathematics

Name _____ Katie _____ Date _____ 2/28 _____

A. Area of Concern (circle one or two)

    I.   Readiness

    II.   Number Facts

   (III.) Whole Number Operations

    IV. Fractions

    V.   Decimals

   (VI.) Problem Solving

B. Specific Skills to Remediate

1. Multiplication / Regrouping
2. Division / Remainders
3. Understanding the question
4. Selecting operations
5.

C. Types of Errors

COMPUTATION:		PROBLEM SOLVING:
1. Careless		1. Ignores question ✓✓✓✓✓
2. Number facts ✓✓		2. Uses extraneous data
3. Regrouping Mult. ✓✓✓✓✓✓		3. Leaves out facts
4. Process substitution		4. Acts without a plan
5. Directional		5. Selects wrong operation ✓✓✓
6. Omission		6. Doesn't check work
7. Placement Div. ✓✓✓✓✓		
8. Attention to sign		
9. Guessing		

2. Where should direct testing begin and why?
3. At what point do you tentatively plan to stop testing and why?
4. What materials will you use for testing and why?
5. If the diagnostic hypotheses are confirmed, what will probably be the secondary (number facts) program emphasis and why?
6. How will the secondary-program priority be established?
7. What corrective strategies will you plan to use initially and why?
8. Which materials will you plan to use initially and why?
9. What specific assessment and programming plans should be made and why?

ENRICHMENT ACTIVITIES

Discussion

1. Discuss the importance of basic mathematics and each subskill to the general academic success of elementary students.
2. Speculate why students who have received special services may evidence more growth in computation skills than in problem-solving skills.
3. Discuss the relative importance of providing direct instruction in number facts.
4. Discuss the circumstances under which the use of manipulatives would be the preferred method of instruction.
5. Discuss and give examples of the difference between students who experience conceptual difficulties in mathematics with students who have organizational difficulties in mathematics.

Special Projects

1. Using the teacher survey for basic mathematics (Figure 9.3), interview a third-grade teacher about the basic mathematics skills of his or her strongest and weakest students.
2. Practice administering to a peer the second, third and fourth grade sample items for tests of basic mathematics in Appendix E.
3. Obtain a copy of a formal basic mathematics curriculum chart from a local school system and compare it with Figure 9.1; note similarities and differences in the subskill, task, and grade levels. What conclusions can be drawn from this comparison?
4. Practice implementing the procedures in this chapter with a student who has evidenced need in arithmetic computation skills; if possible, use the weakest student indicated by the third-grade teacher in the first activity.
5. Select a student who has no apparent difficulty with computation but is experiencing difficulties with problem solving. Assess the various subskills from problem solving and design a first cycle program for that student.

CHAPTER 10

CONTENT AND STUDY STRATEGIES

THOMAS A. RAKES

CHAPTER OBJECTIVES

This chapter is designed to enable the reader to:

1. Explain the importance of content and study strategies.
2. Describe the indirect and direct assessment strategies that are most appropriate for subskill areas in content and study strategies.
3. Develop appropriately integrated intervention strategies for developmental, corrective, and maintenance level use.
4. Plan a personalized content and study strategies program for specific students.

This chapter includes selected content and study strategies appropriate for use with at-risk elementary and adolescent-age learners. For the purpose of providing classroom examples, science and social studies are highlighted. Keep in mind that many of the suggestions for assessment and intervention are applicable to other content areas as well as science and social studies.

The necessity of directly teaching study strategies has been touted by experts in many disciplines. Some effective strategies for improving students' learning have been validated (Meltzer 1993; Pressley & Harris, 1990). As a result of research efforts underway, others soon will be identified. The present literature abounds with suggestions for tactics, strategies, and techniques for improving learning or study strategies. Although

some authors explain differences between study skills, study strategies, and study tactics, the term *study strategies* is used in this book to describe what Wade, Trathen and Schraw (1990) refer to as "a configuration of study tactics used together in a purposeful way to accomplish a particular learning task" (p. 147). Good study strategies are so important that, without them, students will not be able to continue to learn varied subject matter through successive levels of difficulty. While reading specialists, special educators, and cognitive psychologists haggle over clear differences among similar, but different, terminology, this chapter addresses the use of study strategies in general, without accentuating subtle differences between study techniques and study skills or among study, cognitive, and learning strategies.

Of more importance is the concept of infusing the curriculum with study strategies.

Teaching study strategies is most effective when planned techniques are applied while students are actually learning content area information. Learning skills in isolation and later intervening to integrate or transfer a particular study strategy for use in a subject area may be an unnecessary duplication of time, training, and effort for teachers and students. The appropriate use of study strategies in different subject areas can be most effective when applied or infused while studying in the content areas. The interventions that are recommended in Chapter 10 are intended to be taught as a part of content area studies and not as separate units or pull-out lessons. When students learn content information, study strategies should be demonstrated, applied, and if necessary, adapted and retaught. Thus, instruction in the use of study strategies is recommended as a part of instructional lessons in each subject area. Discussion of curricula begins by reviewing representative content area skills.

SCIENCE AND SOCIAL STUDIES SKILLS

Content subjects such as science and social studies are generally recognized as the collateral curriculum. Mastery of these subjects is dependent upon mastery of both basic skills and the specified study and content skills presented in the curriculum chart, Figure 10.1. This chart is not intended to be comprehensive. The categories included are representative of the types of specialized skills most important in the two subjects. They provide an excellent beginning point from which you may adapt or expand your own curriculum according to the needs of your students and local curriculum guidelines. For more comprehensive checklists of science and social studies skills, see Rakes and Choate (1990) and Smith and Smith (1990).

Content area curricula typically reflect a mixture of textbooks, local school-curriculum guides, and national standards or guidelines. Some recent science curricula, for example, stress hands-on activities, with specific direction provided from projects such as the Elementary Science Study (ESS), the Science Curriculum Improvement Study (SCIS), or standards published through the National Science Teachers Association (Cain & Sund, 1989). In social studies, the National Council for the Social Studies sets national standards. In each curricular specialty area, a professional organization supports national guidelines or standards. These standards should be considered as part of curriculum analyses but should be tempered by the degree to which the local school and classrooms adhere to the standards.

Vocabulary

Both science and social studies curricula include technical and nontechnical vocabulary which are necessary as pronunciation and meaning-based functions. No other specific area is more vital to content area success than vocabulary. Some textbooks point out key terminology before each chapter. Beyond this, very little specific vocabulary training is usually provided in most classes. The development of multiple meanings, varied contextual usage, and the sheer volume of vocabulary make mastery essential. The major source of specific vocabulary instruction is not often the particular materials but depends upon the teacher instead. Unless specialized words are pronounced, explained, and taught prior to reading, success will be limited for many students. Nontechnical vocabulary can sometimes cause greater problems than the technical words within subject-area reading materials. This is true because of the many unusual ways in which familiar words can be used. For example, in science, words such as *float, rare, composition,* or *change* have a very different meaning in the laboratory or during an experiment. In the middle grades, there are numerous common words appearing in the textbooks, but these words are often used in unfamiliar ways. The process of assimilating new information is one type of task; a more difficult learning task is that of accommodating information when new information is inconsistent or very

FIGURE 10.1 Sample Content and Study Strategies Curriculum Chart

Student's Name_____Grade_____Teacher_____School_____Date_____

Directions: Circle the specific tasks required for success at this student's current level; in the space provided list any other tasks appropriate to the existing curriculum.

Typical Text Level for Tasks

SCIENCE SKILLS

	K	1	2	3	4	5	6
I VOCABULARY	I	I	I	I	I	I	I
A Technical		A.1 Pronounce .2 Define	A.3 Pronounce .4 Define	A.5 Pronounce .6 Define	A.7 Pronounce .8 Define	A.9 Pronounce .10 Define	A.11 Pronounce .12 Define
B Nontechnical		B.1 Pronounce .2 Define	B.3 Pronounce .4 Define	B.5 Pronounce .6 Define	B.7 Pronounce .8 Define	B.9 Pronounce .10 Define	B.11 Pronounce .12 Define
II PROBLEM SOLVING	II	II	II	II	II	II	II
A Problem Identification			A.1 Listen/ explain, oral	Review	A.2 Read/explain, oral	Review	A.3 Read/explain, write
B Problem Solution			B.1 Listen/ explain, oral	Review	B.2 Read/explain, oral	Review	B.3 Read/explain, write
III ADDITIONAL SKILLS							

SOCIAL STUDIES SKILLS

	K	1	2	3	4	5	6
I VOCABULARY	I	I	I	I	I	I	I
A Technical		A.1 Pronounce .2 Define	A.3 Pronounce .4 Define	A.5 Pronounce .6 Define	A.7 Pronounce .8 Define	A.9 Pronounce .10 Define	A.11 Pronounce .12 Define
B Nontechnical		B.1 Pronounce .2 Define	B.3 Pronounce .4 Define	B.5 Pronounce .6 Define	B.7 Pronounce .8 Define	B.9 Pronounce .10 Define	B.11 Pronounce .12 Define
II GRAPHIC AIDS	II	II	II	II	II	II	II
A Maps			A.1 Neighborhood	Review	A.2 State, Nation	Review A.3 W.Hemis,World	
B Graphs			B.1 Bar	Review	B.2 Circle	Review	B.3 Line
III ADDITIONAL SKILLS							

(continued)

FIGURE 10.1   Sample Content and Study Strategies Curriculum Chart *(continued)*

STUDY STRATEGIES

I ORGANIZATION	K	1	2	3	4	5	6
	I	I	I	I	I	I	I
A Categorizing	A.1 Size, Shape, Color .2 Pictures	A.3 by words	A.4 Words and Concepts				
B Alphabetizing		B.1 by 1st letter		B.2 by 1st & 2nd letters	B.3 by 3 letters		B.4 by 4+ letters
C Directions		C.1 Oral		C.2 Written			

II BOOK USE	K	1	2	3	4	5	6
	II	II	II	II	II	II	II
A Book Handling		A.1 Posture	A.2 Proper Handling .3 Keeps Place				
B Book Parts		B.1 Title page .2 Title .3 Page Numbers	B.4 Table of Contents		B.5 Index		

III REFERENCES	K	1	2	3	4	5	6
	III	I!I	III	III	III	III	III
A Dictionary				A.1 Guide Words .2 Locates Words	A.3 Pronounce Words .4 Meanings		
B Encyclopedia					B.1 Locates information		
C Card Catalog							C. Locates: .1 by Author .2 by Title .3 by Subject

IV STUDY HABITS	K	1	2	3	4	5	6
	IV	IV	IV	IV	IV	IV	IV
A Outlines from Reading					A.1 Main Idea .2 Details	A.3 Semantic Mapping	A.4 Summary Paragraph
B Study Strategies						B.1 Notes from Reading	B.2 Notes from Listening .3 Strategy
C Reading Rate Adjustment						C.1 Different Purposes	C.2 Skims .3 Scans
D Specific Strategies	D.1 Grade Level Tasks	D.2 Grade Level Tasks	D.3 Grade Level Tasks	D.4 Grade Level Tasks	D.5 Grade Level Tasks	D.6 Grade Level Tasks	D.7 Grade Level Tasks

COMMENTS

NOTE: Check tasks as mastery is demonstrated, circling additional tasks required for student's advancement.

different from existing information or meaning. It is the accommodation process that is frequently a problem for special learners.

Problem Solving

One specific science skill that is an integral part of most science curricula is problem solving. The abilities to identify, explain, and ultimately provide solutions all contribute to the scientific method. They also provide a minimal base from which a student may go about the study and application of scientific concepts. Although many science textbooks provide opportunities to apply problem solving, too few are designed to actually teach a student the thinking skills involved in problem solving. More likely, the experiences are of a practice nature.

Graphic Aids

A crucial subskill in social studies involves satisfactory interpretation and use of graphic aids. Numerous maps and graphs are traditionally provided in social studies material. The concern is: Do the graphics enhance reader understanding? The volume and depth of economics, government, civics, and history data make the efficient use of graphic material a very important skill to master. Efficient use of graphic aids must be taught directly. It is not unusual to hear someone say, "This chart or figure only complicates the ideas." However, most readers are interested in color and simplified representations of difficult numerical and abstract material. Appropriate use of graphics to expand understanding of text is exemplified in the graphics presented in one of the of the comprehensive newspapers, distributed on a national basis.

STUDY STRATEGIES

Using reading, locational, and study-type skills for the purpose of obtaining information are important functional reading or study strategies. Admittedly, several competencies discussed as

study skills could reflect an even broader scope. Although exact skill categories may vary, there is widespread agreement that study strategies are an integral part of the learning process (Alvermann & Phelps, 1994; Collins & Cheek, 1993; Ryder & Graves, 1994). Mastery of basic study strategies is usually necessary for the successful progression through most sequentially organized subject area programs and text-based study areas. The components generally considered a part of study strategies instruction include locational, informational, and applied skills that enable students to gain information from the numerous resources available in school. The grouping or leveling of study strategy competencies in this chapter is intended to provide a practical means for assessing specific levels of study strategies and subsequently program-appropriate interventions for individual learners.

Study strategies are generally considered enabling skills and, as discussed in Chapters 1 and 2, are categorized in this book as part of the support curriculum. They are taught through the use of procedures directed toward skills mastery and/or the development of subject area knowledge. Heilman, Blair, and Rupley (1994) suggest that study strategies should be learned as needed by using classroom materials and assignments. Pairing study strategy instruction with subject area content enables the learner to experience the utility of study skills in a practical, applied manner.

Although study strategy worktexts, kits, and a few books are available, most youngsters receive the majority, if any, of their study strategy instruction as a part of the reading program. Thus, application of practical, content-based study strategies is sometimes introduced, but seldom systematically taught and applied as part of many reading/language arts programs. It is important to focus on teaching students when, why, and how to apply skills of the subject areas—reading, written expression, spelling, handwriting, mathematics, science, and social studies (Chapters 5–10)—as *strategies* to accomplish authentic tasks. Skill practice should then be embedded in authentic contexts to offer a holistic skills approach (Brophy, 1992). An important goal of this chapter is to provide information that will help students become good strategy users. The intent is not only to highlight many useful learning strategies, but to also describe the processes through which teachers may assist students to understand and use learning strategies on a regular basis when studying in the content areas.

Over the years, different scope and sequence lists have been recommended by educators and publishers (Barbe, 1961; Karlin & Karlin, 1987; May, 1994; Rogers, 1984). There are similarities but no consistent agreement on which study skills to include in each category, nor is there a specific sequence to be maintained on a grade by grade basis. In this text study strategies are divided into four major subskills: (1) organization, (2) book use, (3) references, and (4) study habits, as can be seen in Figure 10.1.

Although there is overlap between grade levels, the first two subskills, organization and book use, are generally considered primary-level skills (grades kindergarten through 3). References and study habits, for the most part, are representative of competencies emphasized at elementary levels 4 through 6, but also include some overlap between primary and intermediate levels. This leveling of skills should in no way limit their use for junior and senior high school special learners who are functioning below grade placement. Several of the subskills are necessary for successful reading in subject area material.

Organization

Organization and locational skills are important primary-level abilities that enable young students to complete assignments and generally function in a self-reliant manner. The ability to categorize information and ideas has been divided into four basic areas moving from: (1) size, shape, and color, to (2) pictures, to (3) words, and finally to (4) words and concepts.

Using varied shapes and colors for classification tasks is relatively commonplace. The use of

pictures for the purpose of grouping by type, use, function, or other categories is also a favorite activity used in primary-grade classrooms. The classification of words and words/concepts requires some degree of explanation, since the two involve similar but different skills.

The ability to categorize words by their shape, initial or final letter, or perhaps by their function (e.g., color words, food words, or names) represents an entry-level ability not exclusively found under the study strategies category. Categorizing by words and concepts requires the student to use both word recognition knowledge and the appropriate concepts associated with each word. There may be more than one possible category or group within which a word will fit. As a meaning-based experience, such activities represent a basic study skill that may precede a student's progression into other study skills.

Learning to alphabetize is an initial study skill necessary for developing numerous word usage, word meaning, and locational tasks. The ability to locate information in an index, dictionary, encyclopedia, or other reference material is dependent upon the use of alphabetical order. Alphabetizing is usually learned by beginning with the first letter, and then later by progressing to the first and second letters and so on.

Oral directions call for almost daily attention if students are to learn to listen carefully to them and remember what they hear. Following directions may be particularly difficult for low-achieving and disabled learners. These students may require visual aids to supplement oral directions and oral explanations to accompany written directions. By beginning with simple verbal directions for one or two tasks and reinforcing correct responses, the teacher can gradually increase the length and complexity of the directions. Physical difficulties can cause a student to struggle in following directions. In some instances, the young child is not aware of the difficulty or its origin.

Written directions are often taught through a combined listening and silent reading procedure. Once students have learned to follow along silently as directions are read to them, they can begin to develop some degree of independence in following written directions. Some youngsters require repeated reassurance to continue or even initiate a task. Often additional assistance, illustration of task, or follow-up is required.

Book Use

Book handling and book parts represent a group of subskills requiring attention to keeping one's place, caring for books, and other tasks ranging from locating a page number or title to using an index, glossary, or illustrative parts in a book. Learning to use book parts is often neglected because of teacher priorities in developing ideas, information, or subject-related competency.

References

Systematic instruction in the use of references (and study habits) is necessary to increase reader comprehension of text (Adams, Carnine, & Gersten, 1982). The use of reference sources includes a variety of school and nonschool related tasks. Learning to use dictionaries, encyclopedias, and card catalogues are activities that primarily occur in school. As mentioned in the beginning of this chapter, functional reading for the purpose of finding specific information is necessary for success in school. Mastery of a variety of reference skills is required for the pursuit of information of many different types.

Study Habits

The final study strategies category includes planned study techniques. This grouping of skills involves both specific study techniques, systems, and strategies recommended for use while learning and studying for tests and the ideas, habits, and other suggestions that may improve one's ability to remember information.

Learning to outline requires the reader to first determine the main idea(s) for the material. From this point, the student needs to connect details to each major topic or idea. The process is often initiated by providing students with a partially completed outline or map and guiding them through the process of matching topics with details. Semantic maps and summarizing are also techniques for developing written outline skills.

Many special systems are recommended to help students study. One of the most often mentioned is called SQ3R—Survey, Question, Read, Recite, and Review (Robinson, 1961). Learning to take notes, developing work habits, and organizing for efficient study are all part of what can be called the art of studying and preparing for tests.

The ability to adjust one's reading rate for different purposes is important, particularly for those who wish to save time and still obtain the necessary information. Techniques involving skimming for the overall message or scanning for one or two specific pieces of information must be taught directly and practiced regularly. The student who attempts to read mathematics problems at the same pace as the school paper may become frustrated. These skills—skimming, scanning, and reading for varied purposes—are among those frequently neglected in school.

Study strategies are considered an integral part of content area skills, including science, social studies, and other subject areas. Each subject area also contains skills and specific strategies peculiar to that area of study. Science and social studies are highlighted in this book as representative of the content areas. In addition to study skills, subject-specific skills and strategies are necessary for success in each content area.

Specific Strategies

This category refers to particular combinations or individual tactics or techniques students use for a given purpose. Any of the strategies described in developmental, corrective or maintenance categories can be used in a specific situation. For example, effective use of technology is a learning strategy that cuts across all subjects yet may differ by subject. The category of specific strategies is included to encourage metacognitive functioning by requiring students to develop an awareness of what strategy they are using, and, to an equal degree, involve teachers in being sure they can identify the strategy or skill they are teaching or expecting students to use for an assignment or to learn in a particular content area.

PERSONALIZED ASSESSMENT PROCEDURES

Assessment of study and content area skills includes the observation and documentation of the student's perceived and demonstrated ability to perform on curriculum-based measures. Data resulting from the assessment are then used to plan a content and study program appropriate in terms of the student's needs, one that, in turn, will provide a realistic basis for achievement gains. By using the suggested assessment procedures, you should be able to develop new curricular experiences or modify existing materials and programs for most students. Assessment of content and study strategies should be conducted after the assessment of reading comprehension and word recognition skills. This will allow for a better understanding of a student's overall reading abilities and also provide an excellent opportunity for a comparison of related skills.

Curriculum Analysis

The content and study strategies curriculum chart should be used by an interviewer to begin the process of documenting the study and content area expectations for each student. Depending upon the situation, the curriculum sequence you select may consist of the school's curriculum guide, the program scope and sequence chart, or the sample curriculum chart in Figure 10.1. The teacher survey of content and study strategies in Figure 10.2 should be used for every student. Keep in mind the exit behaviors that are required for promotion, minimum competence standards, or other school guidelines. If needed, add skills to the list, depending upon requirements in each school or program of study. Throughout the assessment and programming cycle, the skills chart will be helpful for recording what is needed for a

student to continue to improve content and study strategies.

Indirect Student Assessment

Initial procedures for personalizing the assessment of content and study strategies include obtaining and analyzing student work samples. In the content areas there may be little direct written evidence beyond observations, with the exception of isolated assignments that require a student to display competence using content skills. If there is a lack of actual classroom work samples, follow the data base provided in the teacher survey and curriculum chart (Figures 10.1 and 10.2). Several of the academic adjustment items on which the teacher rates the student involve the foundations of study strategies and study habits (see Figure 4.4). Through classroom observation, you can confirm any difficulties noted in the categories of organization and independence. It can also be helpful to ask yourself the following three questions: (1) Which strategies have been taught? (2) Can you describe the strategies that you have observed students actually using? (3) Can you describe the task-specific strategies that you expect your students to use? Answering these three questions about students will help you prepare for direct assessment. Begin the direct testing of a student's content and study strategy competency according to the ranked grouping of skills.

A conscious effort should be made to focus on the global functioning of each student before beginning specific skills analysis and during the assessment process as well. Such a mindset further reinforces the need to conduct assessment within the context of integrated procedures involving students in assessments that, as nearly as possible, replicate actual learning or classroom learning situations. Although it is possible to measure some discrete skills, it is the composite use of several skills that enables a student to learn. Patterns that may point to hypotheses about what a student can or cannot accomplish are particularly noteworthy throughout indirect and direct assessment.

FIGURE 10.2   Teacher Survey: Content and Study Strategies

Student_____Date_____

Teacher_____Interviewer_____

ADDITIONAL COMMENTS

A. ASSESSMENT OF CURRICULUM:

1. Indicate appropriate skills, subskills, and tasks on an attached study and content area skills curriculum chart.

List available text titles/levels you would consider as options:

2. List current text titles and levels in which student is expected to master skills.
    Science: _____

_____

    Social Studies: _____

_____

3. Check the primary source(s) of student's report grades in each subject:

Science:	*Social Studies:*	*Science:*	*Social Studies:*
__ Projects	_____	__ Workbook	_____
__ Reports	_____	__ Board Work	_____
__ Teacher tests	_____	__ Homework	_____
__ Combination	_____	__ Other	_____

Describe grade sources:

4. Indicate the amount of time devoted to each subject by the current curriculum and texts per week.
    Science: __In Class   __Homework __Total
    Social Studies: __In Class   __Homework __Total

Indicate time devoted to each by current curriculum and texts:

5. Describe modifications in that you have attempted with this student:

_____

_____

Degree of success:

B. INDIRECT STUDENT ASSESSMENT:

6. Rank order this student's study and content subskills using *1* as the strongest subskill in each area:

Science:	*Social Studies:*	*Study Strategies:*
__Vocabulary	__Vocabulary	__Organization
__Problem Solving	__Graphics	__Book Use
		__References
		__Study Habits

In weakest area(s) identify the most difficult tasks for this student:

7. Check the best description of the student's interest in his or her performance in each area:

Science:	__High	__Moderate	__Low	__Variable
Social Studies:	__High	__Moderate	__Low	__Variable
Study Strategies:	__High	__Moderate	__Low	__Variable

Describe student's emotional reaction:

8. Check any other subject areas in which student's study skills interfere with performance.
    __Math   __English   __Social Studies
    __Reading Comprehension   __Spelling   __Science
    __Other _____

Indicate why and to what extent:

9. List specifically what you want to know about this student's performance in each area:
    Science: _____
    Social Studies: _____
    Study Strategies: _____

Attach representative samples of the student's work.

10. Interviewer Summary:_____

_____

Direct Student Assessment

After interpreting the data from indirect means, developing diagnostic hypotheses, and determining the assessment priorities, you are ready to plan for efficient assessment. Because of the importance of both technical and nontechnical vocabulary to a student's understanding of social studies and science, begin your plan with vocabulary. Give the student five words at each level, increasing the difficulty until the student misses one or two. The level at which one of the five words is missed will probably be the source of the most useful assessment information; present an additional 15 words and the specific skills for the subject.

Unlike other areas within the curriculum, content area skills have not generally been assessed with the directness applied to the testing of mathematics or word recognition skills. There are few resources for checking a student's competency in specific study skills or mastery of vocabulary in science or social studies. Of those available resources, most are directed toward an eighth grade or higher level pupil. Even at this higher level, the resources primarily consist of "here's how" information; they lack ample sample tests and explanations for curriculum-based use (McWilliams & Rakes, 1979; Roe, Stoodt, & Burns, 1991; Ryder & Graves, 1994). The suggestions that follow and the sample test items in Appendix F are intentionally directed toward primary- and intermediate-grade audiences. The target group may, of course, include older learners functioning at lower achievement levels. It is helpful for teachers to construct subject area tests, using teaching materials available in the school. The best assessment is one based upon actual materials intended for instructional purposes in the school. In some cases, if the existing sample items in Appendix F are appropriate, use them. However, optimum use of assessment rests in instruments and procedures that are keyed to instructional materials currently in use in the classroom. With this in mind, the sample items serve as models that, when used with suggestions

for constructing tests, will assist in the development of personalized curriculum-based tests for specific classroom use.

Preliminary Procedures

Preparing for direct assessment involves the gathering and interpretation of information from numerous sources including other teachers, school records, samples of student work, observational notes, and parental comments. It is also important to consider curriculum requirements as well as other special academic or social needs that may be involved. The purpose of examining an assortment of existing information sources is to better understand how to appropriately conduct a more meaningful direct assessment. Rather than attempting to test so many possible areas associated with content and study strategies, indirect assessment enables us to narrow the field of inquiry to a reasonable number of skills.

Classroom Observations

In addition to periods during which specific assessment procedures are administered, it is important to observe students during instructional lessons involving the use of content and study strategies. On-the-spot observations provide the truest opportunity to verify the use or non-use of specific strategies. Are students able to determine or select for themselves, which strategy should be used in a particular lesson? Do students use different strategies for different subject areas? Does there appear to be a planned or organized manner in how students go about studying or completing an assignment in mathematics, science, or social studies? Because content and study strategies can be so much a part of daily instructional exchanges, teachers have an ongoing opportunity to verify or analyze student proficiency in content and/or study strategies. No personalized assessment is complete without verification through classroom observations. Before beginning a review of informal testing procedures, take a few minutes to look over the information provided in the sample teacher survey for Wade that appears in Figure 10.3.

FIGURE 10.3   Sample Teacher Survey: Wade

Student __Wade James__ Date __4/16__
Teacher __Klein__ Interviewer __T. Rakes__

A. ASSESSMENT OF CURRICULUM:

ADDITIONAL COMMENTS

1. Indicate appropriate skills, subskills, and tasks on an attached study and content area skills curriculum chart.

List available text titles/levels you would consider as options:

2. List current text titles and levels in which student is expected to master skills:

Science: _____THE EARTH AND PLANETS_____

Social Studies: _____OUR NEW LANDS_____

PEOPLE OF THE
WORLD

3. Check the primary source(s) of student's report grades in each subject:

Science: *Social Studies:*   *Science:*   *Social Studies:*
✓ Projects _____   __ Homework _____
__ Reports _____   __ Board Work _____
✓ Teacher Tests ✓_____   ✓ Homework _____
__ Combination _____   __ Other _____

Describe grade sources:

Mainly Tests

4. Indicate the amount of time devoted to each subject by the current curriculum and texts per week:

Science: __1.5__ In Class   __1__ Homework   __2.5__ Total
Social Studies: __2.5 hr__ In Class __2.5__ Homework   __5__ Total

Indicate time devoted to each by current curriculum and texts:

5. Describe modifications in that you have attempted with this student:
__Study Guides (science); more use of maps, projects in__
__social studies; small group work in both areas__

Degree of success:

Limited

B. INDIRECT STUDENT ASSESSMENT:

6. Rank order this student's study and content subskills using __1__ as the strongest subskill in each area:

Science: *Social Studies:*   *Study Strategies:*
__1__ Vocabulary   __2__ Vocabulary   __3__ Organization
__2__ Problem Solving __1__ Graphics   __1__ Book Use
                          __4__ References
                          __2__ Study Habits

In weakest area(s) identify the most difficult tasks for this student:

Inquiry; indepen-
dent studies

7. Check the best description of the student's interest in his or her performance in each area.

Science: __ High ✓ Moderate __ Low __ Variable
Social Studies: __ High __ Moderate __ Low ✓ Variable
Study Strategies: __ High __ Moderate ✓ Low __ Variable

Describe student's emotional reaction: Related to
topic and peer
reactions.

8. Check any other subject areas in which student's study skills interfere with performance:

__ Math   ✓ English   ✓ Social Studies
✓ Reading Comprehension __ Spelling   ✓ Science
__ Other _____

Indicate why and to what extent:

On homework,
tests

9. List specifically what you want to know about this student's performance in each area: _____
Science: __Level of problem solving__
Social Studies: _____
Study Strategies: __Number of and type of strategies used.__

Attach representative samples of the student's work.

10. Interviewer Summary: _____

Informal Student Interview

As in other areas, some information from the teacher survey (Figure 10.2) should be helpful as a guide for the student interview. Because of the similarity between some academic adjustment behaviors and study skills and habits, certain items in the general teacher survey on which the student was rated (Figure 4.4) may provide appropriate content for the interview discussion. Often a student will voice a definite preference for either social studies or science. When this occurs, the reasons for the preference should be analyzed. When conducted in a friendly, informal manner, the interview can set the stage for the student's cooperation and best performance during testing.

Personalized Tests

Personalized tests using actual classroom materials are an excellent source of practical diagnostic information. The sample test items in Appendix F, as well as other published tests, may be used in conjunction with your own personally developed tests. Because of the variety and range of related skills that could be involved, no single listing, checklist, or predetermined skills sequence is appropriate for a particular student. The use of personalized tests is necessary if you are to develop intervention plans that are effective and indeed developed around the specific strengths and weaknesses of your students. Once the test development strategies are mastered, you will have gained a variety of assessment tools for studying each student. From this personalized analysis, appropriate intervention strategies can be developed and implemented.

Suggestions for Constructing Tests.   The next several pages feature specific suggestions for making your own assessment instruments. Each section corresponds to a section on the curriculum chart (Figure 10.1). At the end of this section suggestions are made for using alternate, ongoing types of assessment procedures.

Keep in mind that the decision concerning which test items to administer should be based upon consideration of information from the teacher survey and other data sources. It is highly unlikely that any student will be required to complete test items for every area within the study and content area skills curriculum. It is also advisable to view the diagnostic process as a continuous process that includes samples of behaviors over a period of time and includes a number of measurement opportunities for the same skills in different subjects using different materials and taken at different times of day.

Begin direct assessment of skills that are indicated according to findings on your indirect assessment. Target skill areas are those that appear to be symptomatic as students go about using their content and study strategies. It may be useful to review the section on preliminary procedures in Chapter 3 as well as the five suggestions for administering tests. This section begins with a few suggestions for assessing representative content area skills in science and social studies, followed by suggestions for assessing study strategies.

Science and Social Studies: Vocabulary

Technical: Pronounces Vocabulary, (IA.1, IA.3, IA.5, IA.7, IA.9, IA.11). Materials: Current science and social studies textbooks equal to, above, and below expected level of student performance; select twenty words from the glossary or index; list these technical words vertically on a page. *Strategy:* Ask student to pronounce each word. *Interpretation:* 75–80 percent accuracy; proper pronunciation is necessary and slang, partial pronunciation, or synonyms can not be accepted.

Technical: Defines Vocabulary, (IA.2, IA.4, IA.6, IA.8, IA.10, IA.12). Materials: Same books for pronunciation. *Strategy:* Point to each word and ask student to give the meaning for the word. If this fails, ask the student to use the word in a sentence that clearly demonstrates an understanding of the word. *Interpretation:* 70 percent accuracy; each word must be defined in relation to text meaning. Use of a nonscientific context or ambiguous explanation should not be counted as correct.

Nontechnical: Pronounces Vocabulary, (IB.1, IB.3, IB.5, IB.7, IB.9, IB.11). Materials: Select three to four currently used science or social studies textbooks and pick four to five words of a nontechnical but science or social studies related nature and list on a page. *Strategy:* Ask student to pronounce each word. *Interpretation:* 80 percent accuracy; correct pronunciation is required.

Nontechnical: Defines Vocabulary, (IB.2, IB.4, IB.6, IB.8, IB.10, IB.12). *Materials:* Same books as for pronunciation. *Strategy:* Ask student to explain each word or use it in a meaningful sentence. *Interpretation:* 80 percent accuracy; student use of each word should reflect understanding. It is appropriate to probe for more information.

Science: Problem Solving

Identifying a Problem: Listening/Oral Explanation, (IIA.1). *Materials:* Adopted science textbook for class. *Strategy:* Ask student to listen as a passage is read and then be prepared to describe orally the problem discussed in the passage. *Interpretation:* 100 percent accuracy; a limited attention span and poor listening or speaking skills may hamper student response. Difficulty or unfamiliarity with locating a problem can also cause a student to exhibit unsatisfactory performance.

Reading/Oral Explanation, (IIA.2). *Materials:* The adopted science text. *Strategy:* Ask student to read a passage or selection and be prepared to describe the problem in the story. *Interpretation:* 100 percent accuracy; students who have difficulty reading with understanding or providing oral responses may experience difficulty.

Reading and Written Explanation, (IIA.3). *Materials:* Adopted science book for grade five; select a one or two page selection that contains a problem. *Strategy:* Ask student to read the material and be prepared to write a short description of the problem. *Interpretation:* 100 percent accuracy; the task involves reading comprehension, writing, and identifying problems. Any of the three areas can cause poor student performance.

Science: Providing Solutions

Listening/Oral Explanation, (IIB.2). *Materials:* Use a different passage from the same text as above. *Strategy:* After reading passage to the student and having the student explain the problem orally, ask for possible solutions. *Interpretation:* 100 percent accuracy; any reasonable solution is acceptable.

Reading/Oral Explanation, (IIB.1). *Materials:* Use a different passage from the same text as above. *Strategy:* Ask student to read the selection and explain the problem orally; next ask for possible solutions. *Interpretation:* 100 percent accuracy; one or more solutions should be accepted. Proposed solutions should be based upon information given in the story and not be guesses.

Reading/Written Expression, (IIB.3). *Materials:* Same passage as above. *Strategy:* Having already read the passage, ask the student to provide a written example; next, ask the student to recommend two possible solutions. *Interpretation:* 100 percent accuracy; accept one acceptable solution or creative alternative. Acceptability should be based primarily upon the answers, not on grammar or mechanics.

Social Studies: Graphic Aids

Reading Maps: Neighborhood, (IIA.1). *Materials:* Sketch of an area around school; label the major items. *Strategy:* Ask student to point out places on the map; using the map, have the student show how to get to _____. *Interpretation:* 90 percent accuracy; student should locate places, routes, and directions. Evidence of guessing or hesitancy should be noted.

Reading State or National Maps, (IIA.2). *Materials:* Select a state or U.S. map from a fourth- grade social studies textbook. *Strategy:* Ask student to point out specific cities, rivers, and other landmarks; ask student to use the map key. *Interpretation:* 80 percent accuracy; mastery of map usage should be evident; student responses should appear confident and unconfused.

Reading Western Hemisphere or World Maps, (IIA.3). *Materials:* Use a sixth-grade text and select a map of the Western Hemisphere or the world. *Strategy:* Ask student to use the map and answer questions about places, landmarks, and other features specific to the map. *Interpretation:* 80 percent accuracy; oral responses should reveal a clear understanding of the map content. Long delays or confusion in answering should not be experienced if mastery is indicated.

Interpreting Bar Graphs, (IIB.1). *Materials:* Use a bar graph from a fourth-grade social studies textbook or daily paper. *Strategy:* Ask student to answer three or four questions requiring use of information from the graph. *Interpretation:* 75–80 percent accuracy; student responses should be based upon graphic information without using discussion or narrative text.

Interpreting Circle Graphs, (IIB.2). *Materials:* Use a circle graph from a fifth-grade textbook or newspaper. *Strategy:* Ask student to look at the graph and answer three to four questions based on the graph. *Interpretation:* 75–80 percent accuracy; circle graphs can be confusing unless the student is able to interpret the map key, judge proportional size, and relate to percentages. A slower rate of response may be expected while maintaining a minimum level of accuracy.

Interpreting Line Graphs, (IIB.3). *Materials:* Use a line graph from a sixth-grade textbook. *Strategy:* Ask student to look at the graph and answer three-to-four questions about the information. *Interpretation:* 75–80 percent accuracy; line graphs are difficult to read. More time may be necessary to note small changes in data between intervals.

Study Strategies: Organization

Categorizing: By Size, Shape, Color, (IA.1–.3). *Materials:* Use four-to-eight common objects. *Strategy:* Ask student to group items by categories. *Interpretation:* 100 percent accuracy; student should group objects quickly and explain why the grouping is correct.

Categorizing by Pictures, (IA.2). *Materials:* Use magazines, catalogs, or other picture sources; cut out six-to-ten pictures of objects that can be logically grouped into two or three categories; paste each picture on a 3" × 5" index card. *Strategy:* Ask student to place pictures in piles by categories. *Interpretation:* 100 percent accuracy; student should group pictures quickly, accurately, and explain why they grouping is correct.

Categorizing by Words and Concepts, (IA.3–.4.). *Materials:* Books or word lists used in class; six-to-ten words that begin or end with the same letter or that are related in concept (e.g., animals, tools, plants); print each word on a 3" × 5" index card. *Strategy:* Ask student to stack word cards that begin or end with the same letter or are similar or related by concept. *Interpretation:* 90 percent accuracy; student should exhibit little confusion and his or her groupings should reflect a conceptual level of understanding or meaningful relationships.

Alphabetizing: By First, Second or More Letters, (IB.1–.4.). *Materials:* Words from books or materials used in class; print each word on a 3" × 5" index card and place in piles of four to eight words. *Strategy:* Shuffle the cards and ask students to arrange the cards by one, two, or three letters. *Interpretation:* 80 percent accuracy; without assistance student should arrange the words. This skill is a prerequisite for dictionary use. This task can be transferred to a pencil and paper task by asking students to look at a mixed list of words and reorder the words by rewriting the list.

Following Oral Directions, (IC.1). *Materials:* Use four-to-six small items (e.g., chalk, pencil or book). *Strategy:* Ask student to complete a series of two or three item directions involving moving, turning, or picking up the objects. *Interpretation:* 100 percent accuracy; student should complete tasks without repeated help or requests for assistance. Attending to oral tasks is essential for completing assignments and independent work.

Following Written Directions, (IC.2). *Materials:* Directions printed on a chalkboard or paper; the readability and complexity of the directions should be appropriate for the student. *Strategy:* Have student read and follow the directions. *Interpretation:* 100 percent accuracy; after reading student should pick up a pencil, draw a circle, turn around twice, or perform similar direction sequences.

Study Strategies: Book Use

Book Handling: Good Posture, (IIA.1). *Materials:* Observation of students reading. *Strategy:* On three or four different occasions observe students reading; see if they sit up straight, keep feet on floor, hold book properly, and sit relatively still. *Interpretation:* Varies; unless students are able to sit still and appear comfortable while reading, completion of assignments will be difficult.

Handles Books Carefully and Keeps Place While Reading, (IIA.2–.3). *Materials:* Book. *Strategy:* During several days observe students reading; notice if students are careful with books (bending, twisting, or abusing pages, and covers); see if students keep place while they read. *Interpretation:* Varies but should reveal good judgment and careful treatment of books. Students should keep place with or without a marker. The manner in which students store, carry, or turn pages reflects their book handling skills.

Locates Title Page, Title, and Page Numbers, (IIB.1–.3). *Materials:* Book. *Strategy:* Using their books, ask students to point out title page and title; have students turn to page_____ and page _____. *Interpretation:* 100 percent accuracy; as a prerequisite for book handling students must respond quickly and without repeated assistance.

Uses Table of Contents and Index, (IIB.4–.5). *Materials:* Book. *Strategy:* Ask student to turn to the index or table of contents; ask for the page number on which two or three topics can be found. *Interpretation:* 90 percent accuracy; student should locate topical information using the index or table of contents without hunting through actual chapters. Typically students will be able to use a table of contents, then an index.

Study Strategies: References

Uses Guide Words and Word Entries, (IIIA.1–.2). *Materials:* Dictionary. *Strategy:* Ask student to point out an entry or guide word on a page. *Interpretation:* 100 percent accuracy; student should turn through several pages quickly rather then searching down columns on several pages before finding the correct page and entry.

Pronounces Words, (IIIA.3). *Materials:* Dictionary. *Strategy:* After locating a word, have student give an alternate pronunciation for three-to-four words. *Interpretation:* 80 percent accuracy, using unfamiliar words. Students will need help in using the pronunciation key if this task is troublesome.

Determines Meanings, (IIIA.4). *Materials:* Dictionary. *Strategy:* After locating a word, ask student to state the first and second meanings; it is best to try using three or four different words that may be unfamiliar. *Interpretation:* 80 percent accuracy; locating meanings for words is an important skill for developing writing and vocabulary skills. It is helpful to ask students to use the words in a sentence to ensure understanding.

Encyclopedia: Locates Information, (IIIB.1). *Materials:* Encyclopedia. *Strategy:* First, ask student to select the correct volume for a specified topic; next ask students to point out the page or section in the book that contains the requested information. *Interpretation:* 100 percent accuracy; if student is unable to complete either of these tasks, verify competency of the two other skills. Locating information in an encyclopedia is dependent, in part, upon mastery of alphabetizing and dictionary use.

Uses Card Catalog: Locates Information by Subject, (IIIC.1–.3). *Materials:* Library card catalog and/or computerized data base. *Strategy:* Ask student to locate a book about _____. *Interpretation:* 100 percent accuracy; use of the card catalog is required to conduct research or locate books in the library.

Study Strategies: Study Habits

Outlining from Reading: Main Ideas and Details, (IVA.1–.2). Materials: Textbook. *Strategy:* Ask student to read a paragraph or two and state the main idea(s) and two-to-three important supporting details. *Interpretation:* 80 percent accuracy; there should be a clear indication that the responses are consistent with the material.

Semantic Mapping, (IVA.3). Materials: Textbook. *Strategy:* Ask student to read a page or two and write down key words that represent the most important ideas. Ask student to place the words with the broader concepts (overall ideas) above those words representing smaller ideas or facts. *Interpretation:* 80 percent accuracy; test is used to see if students can classify ideas in a reading selection using single words instead of phrases or sentences. The ability to do so reflects a high degree of vocabulary and concept development.

Summarizing, (IVA.4). Materials: Textbook. *Strategy:* After reading a one-to-two page selection, students should write a 50–100 word summary. *Interpretation:* 90 percent accuracy; summary writing is required to maintain notes and study ideas. If the student experiences difficulty, ask for the summary to be dictated.

Study Techniques: Takes Notes from Reading, (IVB.1). Materials: Textbooks. *Strategy:* Ask students to take notes on a unit or chapter as they read. *Interpretation:* 80 percent accuracy, but may vary; inability to take notes may represent a problem involving comprehension and or writing.

Takes Notes from Listening, (IVB.2). Materials: An information source (e.g., textbook, notes). *Strategy:* Ask students to listen for five-to-seven minutes and take notes on the important ideas. *Interpretation:* 80 percent accuracy; students should write down most major points. Note whether students tried to write down everything, nothing, or only selected ideas.

Adjusting Reading Rate: Reads for Different Purposes, (IVB.3). Materials: Two or three different types of reading material that are about the same length. *Strategy:* Ask student to read silently for three-to-five minutes in each of two-to-three different materials (history, science, literature). Then ask student to tell about what was read. Notice if one is read more quickly than the others. *Interpretation:* 80 percent accuracy, but varies; expect to see some materials read at a much slower, careful rate. Other materials may be read more quickly (e.g., magazines, short stories, or library books).

Skimming, (IVC.2). Materials: Article or one to two pages from a textbook. *Strategy:* Ask student to quickly read the material to attain an overall idea about what is important. *Interpretation:* 90 percent accuracy; performance should indicate an ability to read quickly for overall understanding.

Scanning, (IVC.3). Materials: Article or one to two pages from a textbook. *Strategy:* Ask student to quickly read the material to find out two to three specific pieces of information or facts. The student should be told which facts to find. *Interpretation:* 90 percent accuracy; notice if student is trying to read the entire selection or is searching for the important information.

Specific Strategies, (IVD.1–.7). Materials: Appropriate content material; access to appropriate technology. *Strategy:* Ask the student to perform a particular task using a specific strategy that he or she has been taught. Either have the student verbalize the steps as they are used or ask that the steps be explained prior to task performance and note the correct use of the strategy. *Interpretation:* The key to interpreting performance is whether the student has been taught specific strategies for accomplishing the tasks and whether task performance is accurate. If specific strategies have been taught but are not used effectively, identify the source of error for corrective instruction; if the student performs target tasks correctly at a reasonable rate, with or without verbalized strategies, he or she is making effective use of strategies. If strategies have not been taught, do not fault the student, but do plan instruction in the specific strategies needed for target tasks. Repeat assessment to identify strategy usage for a variety of tasks.

Sample Items for Tests.   The sample test items in Appendix F represent the subskills and tasks on the curriculum chart and are numbered accordingly. These items may be used as they are presented if they match the student's curriculum. They can be altered to meet specific learner needs or used as a model for the development of completely new test items that more nearly reflect the content of a particular area. If you decide to use any of the items, be sure that the level of difficulty for each task most nearly matches that of the identified task in the curriculum. Because the sample items are comparatively short, remember to use additional sources and/or observations to confirm unusual performance. Heilman, Blair and Rupley (1994) and Lapp and Flood (1992) provide additional elementary-level suggestions for developing assessment and teaching strategies in the study and content area curriculum. For use with students in the middle and upper grades, suggestions can be adapted from other sources for specific tasks (e.g., Alvermann & Phelps, 1994; Karlin & Karlin, 1987; Langer, 1986; Rakes & Smith, 1992; Roe, Stoodt & Burns, 1991).

Alternative Assessment Procedures.   While it is important to use specific assessments as a part of an evaluation program, it is can also be helpful to include procedures that are, in some ways, less specific and more global or authentic in nature. The accumulation of information in a systematic manner can be of value in conducting a through assessment. Alternative assessments should be included as a means of gaining "everyday" information over a period of time instead of using only information gathered during specific testing or isolated observation situations. One important strategy currently associated with alternative assessment is the use of portfolios.

Content Portfolio Assessment.   Portfolios are intended to be used in addition to specifically constructed tests, checklists, and planned interviews and observations. The use of portfolios is a valuable means of gathering and maintenance of subject area information. In the subject areas, a portfolio can take the form of a folder or notebook containing samples of student work as well as daily logs of student reactions to what is being studied. Have students enter their responses to assignments, homework, tests, or other assignments. In science, students can summarize each experiment or lab experience and enter any lingering questions or "grand" observations they believe are important. A history teacher can ask students to keep a running dialogue or critical reaction about one or two historical characters or events each week. When used weekly, these writings can provide a basis for discussion and serve as clues to which areas need to be reviewed or retaught. Students can be encouraged to keep group digests of particular topical studies that can be discussed or shared throughout a particular area of study.

Portfolios provide a flexible format for students to offer an ongoing contribution to their own learning. By providing personalized reactions, students can actually provide a self-monitoring or mirror of their progress. It may be appropriate to maintain a dual portfolio system: one containing work samples related directly to curricular objectives and progress through completed assignments; and another containing student-generated reactions, ideas, summaries, and written recitations of information. Student-generated portfolios should not typically be graded as a paper or project. Their contents should be read on a regular basis but not marked by the teacher. Positive, private oral comments are appropriate. The contents of student developed portfolios should be used as another source of data from which you can see what types of knowledge are being gained. Are misconceptions or incomplete knowledge resulting from a particular unit of study? Are student's reacting with favor, disinterest or boredom when certain topics are covered?

Once students realize their thoughts will not be used against them, most will actually enjoy entering their reactions on paper. For those students who have difficulty writing, it may be necessary to talk in small groups and even have them develop a group journal. In some instances, a few sessions, where different students share their ideas, will be enough to help students gain an idea about what to write for themselves.

Anecdotal Journals. It is also appropriate for teachers to maintain a portfolio of daily ideas, reactions, and observations. These can be more of an anecdotal record or combination including student behaviors and teacher reactions to what worked or instructional procedures. Some teachers use their notebooks to summarize student reactions after they review what their students have written. Teacher portfolios are not usually intended to serve as discipline records or demerit ledgers. For more information about using portfolios see Abruscato (1993), Flood and Lapp (1989), Herman, Aschbacher, and Winters (1992), Jongsma (1989), and Pierce and O'Malley (1992). Examples of formats that can be used as portfolio observation or response forms are displayed in Figure 10.4.

Strategic Interviews. As a spin-off from Reading Comprehension Interviews (RCI), strategic interviews can be conducted to gain helpful information from students (Wixson, Bosky, Yochum & Alverman, 1984). Strategic interviews should be conducted with students immediately before or immediately following the completion of a learning task. The purpose of using

Figure 10.4   Sample Portfolio Observation/Reaction Format

STRATEGY OR SKILL OBSERVATION OBSERVATION FORM

(Completed by teacher)

Student: ____Toby Cross____   Class: ____Science____

Date	Question/Problem	Result	Strategies Used	Suggestions
10/12	Why did the air rise?	Possible cause plus logical support for response	Notes; Graphic in book	None
10/21	What could have prevented oxidation?	Confusion; one unrelated cause	Rereading; Scanned for key word in text	Use of index; Was there a recent experiment involving oxidation?

CRITICAL EVENTS LOG

(Completed by students)

Student: ____Yolanda Mendez____   Class: ____American History____

Date	Unit/Topic	Source of Information	Reaction	Reason/Justification
12/4	Revolutionary War	Text	Positive	Necessary; poorly planned: dedicated Continental Army
12/6	Boston Harbor	Text; Report Incident	Very positive	Four specific reasons: no response from England; frustration by the colonists . . .

three-item interviews is to obtain direct, content specific information about how a student intends to use one or more study strategies to complete a task or after completion, what strategy a student used to complete a task. To construct question items for your interview it is necessary to decide which types of strategies you wish to survey. Categories could include strategies such as text noting, memory aids, organizational procedures, and summarizing. A few sample items that would be appropriate for use in pre-learning and post-learning strategic interviews are sketched in Figure 10.5.

Abbreviated Performance. In addition to using portfolios and strategic interviews one instruction-based suggestion is worth considering as an alternative to traditional testing procedures: abbreviated performance. The concept of abbreviated performance involves limiting the unit of measured performance. This requires a student to demonstrate use of a skill or strategy using less than a paragraph, chapter, or unit of textual infor-

---

FIGURE 10.5   Strategic Interview Questions

The assignments involve studying about different types of machines. The students were told that they would be given examples and then expected to name the type of machine that is represented by the example (e.g., seesaw lever).

Prelearning Items:

1. What do you know about simple machines?

2. Can you name any? If so, can you think of an example of one common use?

3. What can you do to help you remember information about the different types of machines? (If the student has no ideas suggest 1–2 strategies.)

Postlearning Items:

1. Describe what you did to help remember the different types of machines.

2. Did you try more than one way to remember the information? Explain.

3. Can you think of any other strategies that would be helpful in learning this information?

---

mation. Instead of having a student outline or gloss a section in a textbook, provide one paragraph or a few sentences. For those who do not particularly favor outlining, marginal glossing is a technique that has been used by publishers in social studies and science texts for several years. Singer and Dolan (1980) provide a description of teacher-constructed glosses with examples. Students can be taught to gloss by using side margins in text or handout materials. The technique calls for noting key words and then writing brief explanations in the margin, as illustrated in the sample in Figure 10.6. Then, if appropriate, increase the volume of text and require replication of the outline or glossing. By slowly increasing the unit of knowledge (amount of information to be learned), students are more likely to master a strategy.

Published Tests. Although there are a number of commercially available informal and standardized tests that include sections or subtests on science, social studies and other subject areas, such tests are typically not curriculum-based. Many published tests are intended to test global skills in group settings on a one-, two-, or three-time basis. If published tests are used, great care should be taken to follow instructions in test manuals and be sure that results are used for the purposes stated by the authors (i.e., not for student comparisons, measuring individual progress or for making instructional decisions about students for whom the test(s) were not intended and validated). There is perhaps, some value in selecting items that are directly related to your curriculum. However, in picking and choosing items you will then be violating any validation or reliability a test offers. In the content areas, the breadth of content and factors such as item density, readability, effects of timed administrations, and a lack of match with the curriculum often render published tests inappropriate for making programming decisions for individual students.

Test Administration.   Gathering information about student performance involves constructing

FIGURE 10.6   Sample of Glossed Passage

"Supply lines were cut off."	At one time the entire force was unable to reach their main supply line. This caused the troops to *ration* what food and other supplies	
ration: use very little; save up for later	they had until the weather broke. Then a small group moved secretly by night until they were finally able to locate their main force. By that time their *nemesis* had nearly surrounded their tiny outpost.	"The weather changes and was better."
		nemesis: enemy

and using tests to measure specific skills as well as the development of checklists and portfolios for use as part of an ongoing, curriculum specific means of documenting and monitoring student progress. Tests should be administered during a period of time that is relatively short and in an environment that is nonthreatening to students. Sometimes a degree of privacy is necessary. In some classrooms data can be gathered as a part of the day-to-day instructional process without calling unusual attention by announcing "this is a test" or "come on over here Yu, I need to check to see if . . . " Keep in mind that information collected through testing should be based upon curricular needs and gained in a manner that is consistent with realistic, classroom response modes. Insofar as possible, testing should occur as an integral part of the instructional process and not as a period of interrogation or threat to students. Mediated instruction, discussed in Chapter 6, can also be helpful since it involves testing, instructing, or providing information related to the area currently being assessed, and then retesting.

Documenting Student Needs.   In earlier sections of this chapter you have been reminded about the importance of recording observational information and using portfolios to document student performance. To carry record keeping a step further, you may find it helpful to develop checklists or document inventories for your own tests and student requirements. Unless protocols and other documentary information is recorded and maintained, the development and revision of intervention plans cannot be appropriately moni-

tored. Programming must be based upon a record of measured performance and this performance can only be useful if care is taken to record assessment information.

Substantiating Needs.   The concept of on-going assessment is acutely important because content is quickly forgotten and study strategies not used regularly tend to vanish. Demonstrated mastery of a particular study strategy represents a point in time when success was recorded. Applied in another subject area or after a period of time, it will be necessary to verify mastery. Even when mastery has been demonstrated, maintenance level programming is appropriate.

Specific assessment sessions are not always needed. It is helpful to use instructional periods during which information is being taught to informally diagnose needs. Whether or not content and study strategies need to be retaught, maintained, or introduced for the first time, demonstrated applications and progress are expected as a part of the programming cycle.

Charting and Interpreting Needs.   The proper interpretation of assessment information is just as important as constructing or administering tests correctly. There may be occasions when other teachers or other specially trained individuals should be contacted in order to provide another point of view. Evaluative judgements are relative and, to some degree, subjective. Therefore, interpretation of student performance must be done carefully and include accurate scoring and charting of patterns and, when necessary, following up with additional testing or referral. Be particularly sensitive to assessment results when they are inconsistent or skewed to any extreme. It is usually advisable to continue assessing until some degree of explainable behaviors can be described and verified.

It is helpful to circle a student's skill needs on the curriculum chart. Used as an ongoing record, the curriculum chart is a handy means of monitoring progress. The assessment and programming formats presented in Chapter 3 (Figures 3.16 and 3.17) also facilitate tracking student progress.

PERSONALIZED PROGRAMMING PROCEDURES

Content area skills have been traditionally limited to supplementary instruction intended to teach content (e.g., science concepts or social studies ideas). By specific and direct instruction, content area skills can be strengthened. Instruction in study strategies is best conducted through the use of books and materials available in the classroom. In fact, the overall utility and mastery of study skills may be enhanced by including such instruction within daily lessons to support most areas and topics. In addition to integrating reading and study strategy instruction within subject area lessons, instruction should focus on real-life, authentic issues and environments. For example, social studies lessons that focus on current local or national events help students see the practicality of what they are learning. Lessons should emphasize relevance and immediate applications of concepts to students' current situations.

Selection of Content

Even though content and study strategies vary according to difficulty levels and types of skills, direct instruction is usually necessary for student mastery. Typically, content and study strategies are included within reading and language arts instruction. Indeed, the wide application of such skills to subject areas is logical. However, in many instances, teachers are forced to begin with the most important subskills and hope there is

time for the rest. Outlining is particularly valuable because of the wide utility of the skill. The classification or ordering of ideas and events is required in many subjects. The single content subskill area of greatest importance is mastery of technical and nontechnical vocabulary. Reading is based on meaning, and a strong vocabulary serves to make learning easier. Those students, who are unable to master basic content and study strategies (vocabulary in particular), are likely to find other language and reading-related tasks and procedures difficult. Although it is not possible to delineate the most important subskill for all students, mastery of outlining, summarizing, vocabulary, and efficient use of specific strategies are among the most important.

Selection of Methods and Materials

Determining specific methods and selecting materials for personalizing a content and study strategies program should be based upon (1) observed needs of the student, (2) level of application considering age and ability of the student, (3) types of materials available in a particular school or intervention program, and (4) visible consideration for the needs of diverse learners (Grossman, 1995). Rudell (1993) and Herber and Herber (1993) provide excellent suggestions for using diversity as an instructional resource in the content areas.

When considering a specific approach or learning experience, you must remain sensitive to the types of previous instruction a student has received. Plan to use available materials for developmental and maintenance strategies also. For corrective efforts it is appropriate to use classroom materials and specialized materials constructed and organized by achievement level for subskill instruction.

A discussion of teaching materials and methods would be incomplete without attention to the role of learning styles. A host of prominent researchers have reported successful learning based on attention to learning styles. Among these, Brunner and Majewski (1990) describe a New

York study involving mildly disabled high school subjects. Others including Carbo (1990) in reading and writing and Perrin (1990) in dropout prevention have added to the increasing research and rationale for using learning styles as a basis for developing instructional interventions. Viewed from such positive perspectives, the concept of learning styles has great appeal. Perhaps equally as convincing, however, are the questions raised about learning styles in reports such as Snider's "What We Know About Learning Styles From Research in Special Education" (1990). Snider, referring to learning styles as aptitude treatment interactions, pointedly calls for careful consideration and voices a skeptical view of assessment instruments or instructional programs that rely on learning styles as a basis for making decisions but do not provide clear and applicable valid and reliable research for support. Thus, as discussed in Chapters 3 and 4, certain elements of learning style strengthen the integrity of the assessment and programming process. However, even the elements considered in Figure 4.3, Learning Patterns, should be approached cautiously until validated through successive CBA/P cycles.

The need for accommodating individual differences and determining instructional interventions based upon an ongoing, curriculum-based process is clear. The intent of the sample tests and suggestions for test construction that follow is to offer a variety of informal, curriculum-based techniques that may help in the selection of instructional strategies. Rather than propose one or two programs for everyone, the model proposed in this book requires the use of a variety of assessment options through which better instructional decisions can be made. The degree and intensity of attention given to learning styles is left to the judgment of each teacher.

Programming for Content and Study Strategies

The range of topical, readability, and format differences in subject area textbooks is great. When the diversity and range of student abilities is also

considered, teachers are faced with a manageable but difficult instructional dilemma. One structure for prioritizing content and selecting methods to meet diverse student needs is the Planning Pyramid (Schumm, Vaughn, & Leavell, 1994). With the most essential content as its base, the pyramid features optional and graduated points of entry according to degrees of learning. Regardless of the exact planning mechanics, instructional decisions should be made by using curriculum-based information on a student-by-student basis. Some students cannot read their textbooks. When dealing with low-achieving students, it is necessary to use study guides, advance organizers, audio and visual displays, and reteaching-review procedures. Pearson (1982) cites the need for "independent strategies" and recommends explicit instruction. As a framework, several models have been recommended as reflective of an appropriate learning cycle (Archer et al., 1989; Deshler & Schumaker, 1986; Mosenthal, 1988; Roe, 1992). In this book, a four-step CBA/P cycle is used as the framework through which a diagnostic-prescriptive process occurs. Review Chapter 3 for an extended explanation of this cycle.

Skilled study in any subject requires skilled thinking. Brandt (1984) suggests eight guidelines for focusing student thinking skills. These include:

1. Plan specific experiences to accomplish goals.
2. Provide structured experiences for students to process information.
3. Ask broad, open-ended questions.
4. Provide think-time before requiring answers.
5. Analyze student responses for justification, elaboration, classification, and thought processes.
6. Encourage students to formulate their own questions.
7. Model thinking processes.
8. Encourage students to model, compare, and contrast thought processes.

Whimbey (1984) offers a specific format for improving thinking skills. Although originally designed for college students, the basic procedure can be adapted for elementary and middle-school students. The strategy is called Thinking Aloud Paired Problem Solving (TAPS). TAPS involves pairs of students reading aloud, explaining the thought process used for finding solutions, then alternating roles or tasks.

As previously noted, the teaching of content and study strategies should be integrated within the context of subject area instruction whenever possible. The practice of including content area subskills is efficient and offers a more authentic application of skills to content. Direct application is particularly important for special learners (Archer & Gleason, 1990; Schumaker & Deshler, 1988). The continuation of skills development can also be enhanced by informing the student about the advantages of using certain study and content skills. Tadlock (1978) relates the need-to-know concept to improving student information processing systems. The following discussion begins with developmental techniques, then progresses to corrective methods, and concludes with maintenance strategies for study and content are skills.

Developmental Strategies

Just as study strategies are initiated within the materials and regularly planned content area lessons, so are other content area skills. Vocabulary (technical and nontechnical), problem solving, and graphic aids are highlighted for the content areas. Although science and social studies strategies are emphasized, they can be adapted to other subject areas.

As an introductory learning experience, developmental procedures should be initiated on a regular basis beginning in the primary grades. For special learners developmental instruction refers to first-time instructional experiences using a specific skill. As such, much time is needed to explain, demonstrate, and then guide the student through mastery and then application of a skill.

Content Vocabulary. Of primary concern in science and social studies, as well as in other content areas, is the need to preteach both technical and nontechnical words that may have an unusual meaning or use in a selection. Teachers often spend too much time presenting technical terms and exclude difficult nontechnical words. List-group-label (Taba, 1967), also called semantic mapping (Johnson & Pearson, 1984), modified cloze experiences, and the mnemonic keyword method (Mastropieri & Scruggs, 1988) are examples of prereading techniques that help establish a vocabulary network for assisting students. Each strategy involves both the student and the teacher in prereading experiences or applied reading of a specific nature. Each strategy can be used as both an introduction to the material and as a vocabulary-building experience.

List-Group-Label. This procedure was created specifically to help students handle technical vocabulary in science and social studies (Readence & Searfoss, 1992). This five-step plan has been modified for use with low achievers:

1. *Stimulus.* Discuss the area of study (unit, chapter, or partial chapter). Use key vocabulary from the material as you discuss the content. Cite the interesting information and highlight main ideas. Then, print a one-word topic on the chalkboard.
2. *Student Response.* Have a student think of words or expressions related to the topic. In some instances you may provide some related words and phrases as examples. The responses should be listed on paper or on the board.
3. *Review.* Reread each word or phrase on the list.
4. *Categorizing.* Have the student use groups of two or three words that can be regrouped according to something they have in common. List the words under this common label or phrase.
5. *Application.* Use the words and labels to again discuss the material to be read.

List-group-label encourages student involvement prior to reading. It helps build concepts and vocabulary knowledge in a participatory manner. The outlined plan can be shortened to include three simple steps to use as a part of a content lesson: (1) listing, (2) grouping, and (3) follow-up or categories.

Note that vocabulary journals or other "look-it-up," "write a sentence" assignments have not been discussed. Such teacher commands are generally not appropriate and may represent busy work, not teaching behaviors. In fact, the use of such do-it-yourself procedures may be of less value than doing nothing at all. In Figure 10.7 is an example of information as it could appear using the simplified list-group-label procedure.

Modified Cloze Experiences. As an instructional strategy, a modified cloze technique can be used to improve vocabulary and comprehension (Jongsma, 1971). As an aid to vocabulary development, several alternatives are possible through the cloze process of having a student use contextual analysis skills to insert meaningful words into blanks. A modified cloze or maze exercise is

not like the cloze procedure typically used as a placement or readability measure. Unlike a cloze test taken directly from a textbook, a modified cloze practice can be developed from the book or from other sources. Exercises can be expressly written to use designated words or ideas. Gunn and Elkins (1979) suggest the use of a modified cloze technique to help students functioning on a third grade or higher level. They discuss three influencing factors or guidelines for using cloze exercises as instructional tools: (1) the type of cloze exercise to be used, (2) the nature of the language interaction, and (3) the transfer of strategies to other reading. Each of these guidelines is helpful when constructing a modified cloze exercise.

In using this procedure, the first consideration is to begin with a cloze exercise that allows the reader to fill in at least 40–50 percent of the missing words. For the student to be successful the use of one or more of five different formats may be

FIGURE 10.7   Simple List-Group-Label For Animals

Listing:	grizzly	alligator	horse
	panther	rattler	cobra
	pelican	deer	turtle
	dove	dog	woodpecker
	parrot	lizard	eagle
Grouping:	grizzly	dove	cobra
	panther	pelican	rattler
	deer	woodpecker	alligator
	dog	parrot	turtle
	horse	eagle	lizard
Categorizing:	*Mammals*	*Birds*	*Reptiles*
	deer	dove	alligator
	dog	eagle	cobra
	grizzly	parrot	lizard
	horse	pelican	rattler
	panther	woodpecker	turtle

necessary. The five suggested instructional cloze formats are shown in Figure 10.8; they are sequenced from the easiest (Format 1) to the most difficult (Format 5, which offers learners no choices or hints except the context of the material itself). The selection of an appropriate format should be based upon the perceived level of success for each student. The overall goal is to improve vocabulary and comprehension. For this to happen a format that allows for successful student completion is necessary.

In addition to format, the interval of deletion can affect student success. In the samples in Figure 10.8, an interval of 3–5 words is used. If this is too difficult for a student, the interval can be extended to a range of 7, 10, or even 12 words.

FIGURE 10.8   Five Modified Cloze Formats

Format One (The correct word choice is provided near each blank):

> Bryan was (very, happy) careful not to (see, disturb) the cubs while they were (quietly, quickly) sleeping.

Format Two (An initial consonant is provided along with a short blank for each letter of an appropriate word):

> Bryan was v_____ careful not to d_____
> the cubs while they were q_____ sleeping.

Format Three (Word clues are represented by a short blank for each letter of an appropriate word):

> Bryan was _ _ _ _ careful not to _ _ _ _ _ _ _
> the cubs while they were _ _ _ _ _ _ _
> sleeping.

Format Four (Word clues provided in an answer box):

> Bryan was v_____ careful not to d_____
> the cubs while they were q_____ sleeping.

Answer Box			
very	hurriedly	quietly	disturb

Format Five (No word clues provided):

> Bryan was _____ careful not to _____the
> cubs while they were _____ sleeping.

When used as a teaching technique, the cloze exercise can reflect a deletion format that allows for both student success and practice using a particular word or grouping of words.

A second consideration, the nature of the language interaction, involves deciding which words to omit. When used as an instructional technique, and not for testing, the cloze technique involves the deletion of certain words, regardless of the interval of deletion. Gardner (1975) for example, found that some upper grade students have difficulty using logical connectives in expository science material. In this instance, it may be helpful to use exercises that delete only connectives in a short selection. The option regarding what to omit is determined by which concept words, terms, descriptives, or other vocabulary you wish to teach.

The final guideline for the transfer to other reading situations is vital. Upon completion of a modified cloze exercise, have the student read a similar passage or selection that incorporates the content and vocabulary used in the cloze technique. This allows for an immediate application of reading using a natural and uninterrupted prose format.

Mnemonic Keyword Method.   Used as a type of elaborative learning strategy, the mnemonic keyword method has been used successfully with learning disabled students (Scruggs, Mastropieri, McLoone & Levin, 1987). The use of mnemonic instruction involves having students relate familiar words and ideas with target words. In social studies, for example, students might find the three branches of government easy to remember by using the keyword activitiy in Figure 10.9. Used effectively, students will need assistance in learning to adapt important information into a mnemonic device. This strategy could also be used as a maintenance strategy. Specific strategies for learning mnemonically are described in the book by Mastropieri and Scruggs (1991).

Writing for Concepts.   A number of writing activities are appropriate for expanding students' vocabulary knowledge. Palmer, Hafner, and Sharp (1994) emphasize the role of writing in

FIGURE 10.9   Example of a Mnemonic Keyword: Remembering the Three Branches of the Federal Government

---

J E L (pronounced jell)

Judicial—as a judge in a court

Executive—as large executive desk for the President

Legislative—as in law making, legislative body

---

their book, *Developing Cultural Literacy through the Writing Process.* They present a variety of activities amenable to adaptations for low-achieving students.

Problem Solving.   This area is one of the most difficult subskill areas to deal with directly since effective instruction in problem solving must utilize the context of the subject areas (e.g., mathematics, science). Areas of comprehension involving inference and critical reading are frequently involved in problem solving. Thinking skills, as discussed in Chapter 6, are considered to be a part of the problem-solving process. As an overall developmental strategy teachers should maximize the use of oral or written experiences. In accord with Whimbey's (1984) suggestions concerning the need for thinking aloud and discussion, encourage the following student actions: (1) elaborating or going beyond a particular answer by adding explanation, (2) predicting or hypothesizing about outcomes before or after reading, (3) combining sources to yield a single result or conclusion, and (4) encouraging multiple responses to classroom questions instead of always seeking a single or preferred "right" answer to all problems

Although thinking experiences can be included in lessons, a more planned, integrated approach is generally preferred. The actual learning or development of problem solving comes from brain storming, discussion, and guided reasoning between teacher and students. Bereiter's call for teaching thinking as opposed to teaching about thinking applies equally well to problem solving

(1984). Asking a student to consider consequences or to look beyond the words of a text requires much teacher guidance and daily attention within the subject area lesson itself. This can be accomplished by going beyond the literal, factual review of information and extending the questioning and examples into a prediction and reasoning phase. In an explanation of thinking strategies, Beyer (1987) discusses three levels of cognitive operation and classifies thinking strategies under these headings: Problem solving, decision making, and conceptualizing. His skill categories include more than 20 different skill areas. Clark (1990) provides a discussion of six aspects of thinking he believes are necessary to help students focus on the thinking process. These six strategies are: scanning and focusing; creating categories and classes; inducing propositions from facts; activating conceptual knowledge; predicting and planning; and developing procedures.

A final recommendation for problem solving is to include an action or application problem as frequently as possible. In many content area lessons a situation can be turned into a problem. Develop a problem as it existed in the past and assist a student in finding out how "they" could have solved the problem. Dated information can be applied to today's conditions and yield guided discussions and practice in finding alternatives to problem situations. Whenever possible, use familiar or current happenings in the school or local environment to illustrate the usefulness of problem-solving skills. Suggestions in Figure 10.10 may be helpful in assisting students to develop and improve problem-solving skills.

Graphic Aids.   Students often become frustrated because the aids seem to complicate the expression of information rather than clarify meaning. Take time to explain graphic aids as they appear in the textbook. Bean and Pardi (1979) suggest, as a prereading step, conducting a five-minute survey of headings, pictures, tables, and graphs. When a graph is used in social studies, take the additional time to explain the

FIGURE 10.10   Suggestions for Improving Problem-Solving Skills

1. **Ask questions;** students need practice asking questions.
2. **Develop models;** use diagrams or drawings to illustrate possible solutions.
3. **Concentrate on the big picture;** worry about the overall problem and do not let details delay ideas.
4. **Be patient;** do not fret if answers take time.
5. **Be creative;** consider how something has never been done before.
6. **List possible solutions;** by listing possible actions and then reviewing them, valid options are identified.

information and then, most importantly, require the student to demonstrate understanding by interpreting some part of the graph. Use classroom maps and graphs on the chalkboard or overhead transparencies to demonstrate how to locate information. It is almost always necessary to extend textbook use of graphic aids for them to be learned. Few textbooks provide sufficient detail to explain how to interpret graphics.

One of the major reasons students have not developed their content area skills is the limited attention given to the study skills area. Ideas for developing study habits, technical vocabulary, graphic aids, problem solving, and other associated skills may be found in several resources. Extended discussions of developmental strategies for the content areas are presented by Alvermann and Phelps (1994), Herber and Herber (1993); Tierney, Readence and Dishner (1990); and Vacca and Vacca (1993).

Study Strategies: *Organization and Book Use.* Categorizing, alphabetizing, following directions, book handling, and book parts represent prerequisite subskills for using reference sources and completing assignments. Instruction generally moves from the concrete or simple application level to the more abstract or complicated tasks.

The completion of assigned work depends upon a specific student following both oral and written directions. Remedial or low-achieving learners characteristically require constant reminders and repeated directions. To assist students to perform, the teacher should display patient modeling and use sequentially developed learning experiences. Developmental lessons are generally approached by first providing a skills base from which more difficult study skills may be developed.

Introduce instructional procedures within daily lessons as part of the classroom program. Be sure to use readily available organizational materials within instruction manuals and teacher's editions. The two major sources of developmental activities include: (1) the manuals accompanying content and reading texts and (2) teacher-generated opportunities that exist within many lessons on a daily basis. Organizational skills will usually be noted in the books and should be taught. This condition will exist for all developmental skills discussed in this chapter. Be sure to use the instructional experiences already provided in the materials. Check the skills sequence carefully before beginning a lesson to see if and where such skills are included. Since many content area textbooks do not include enough instructional attention for students to master organization and other study skills, you must provide such instruction.

There are many opportunities for teaching categorizing, alphabetizing, and book handling. First present the content information and ask students to make judgments about how it might be classified. Initially, it may be necessary for you to model how to categorize the information yourself so that students can actually see the categorization process. Throughout the day, take the time to seek oral and then written responses. In kindergarten and first grade, combining categorizing and alphabetizing in one lesson is not recommended. After mastery of each, items or words can be categorized and then alphabetized.

The completion of assigned work in the classroom depends on the student's being able to first listen and then follow oral directions and second, to read and follow written directions. Obviously the student's listening and reading competency must be equivalent to the readability level of the directions. This is often not the case. Directions accompanying materials can be written on a level higher than that of the student's instructional reading level. When this occurs, following directions is largely a reading comprehension problem. If comprehension is the problem, it may be necessary to review information in Chapter 6.

To teach students to follow directions, the teacher should begin by reading the directions and adding explanations and examples. This should be followed by having the student perform the task (to verify his or her understanding) or by having him or her repeat the directions. The cycle appears simple. However, problems occur if time is not taken to give clear directions and then to follow up by requiring student response. (As in the case of other organizational skills, directions can be taught within regular lessons by taking the time to specifically use examples, modeling, and learner response.) It may be necessary to spend time each day "practicing" following directions. These "short interval" lessons can precede almost any planned lesson. Remember, when students understand what is expected, they should be able to tell you or show you what they are going to do or what they were asked to do. Part of the problem students have following directions is related to understanding. It is often useful to have a student first read the directions silently. Then, go over the directions with the student. An additional factor to consider involves the important habit of paying attention. For this, frequent teacher-directed experiences are necessary to develop the discipline required to follow directions.

Using parts of a book requires the teacher to spend time teaching (showing, asking, verifying) students to find page numbers, topics, and titles. This is perhaps one of the easier study skills to teach. Nearly every lesson provides an opportunity to model and assist students in using book parts. It is also relatively easy to observe student progress in doing so. The presentation or teaching strategy required here is to ensure that students have opportunities to use book parts in all their subjects. Do not reserve usage of book parts for just one subject. The application of this skill can be mastered more easily when it is taught by using a variety of subject area textbooks.

There are two obvious requirements in order for a student to use a textbook successfully. First, the student needs to know how to read the particular text. Secondly, the student needs to know how to find information quickly through the use of the table of contents and index. Nearly every book students use for reference or for subject area study includes at least a few standard sections. This means that the instructional material necessary for teaching the proper use of book parts is already available. What is not generally available is direct guidance from the teacher. Do not be so concerned about teaching the facts that you fail to encourage and provide direct instruction in using book parts.

References.   Reference skills are generally not taught directly until organizational and book-handling skills have been mastered. Because reference skills are extension skills, they require the use of materials (card or computer catalog), books (dictionary or encyclopedia), or media in addition to textbooks. Developmental procedures involve: (1) giving a student a purpose for needing additional information, (2) demonstrating the utility of a resource (e.g., dictionary or encyclopedia), and (3) monitoring student use of such resources. Most critical to the teaching of reference skills is the necessity for students to realize the value in being able to find information easily.

It is sometimes helpful to initially require students to work with each other in locating a specific kind of information. For example, ask students to find out how many rivers are in a particular state. Let them answer and also have them suggest how they could find out this information. Then you use an encyclopedia or atlas to illustrate the usefulness. Repeat this format for other situations requiring the use of reference tools. Stimuli for what to look for can be taken from topics being studied in science, social studies, reading, or other areas.

Study Habits. The teaching of study habits is based upon the assumption that a student has attained some level of mastery for each of the other study skills areas. Students approach studying in a variety of ways. Too often however, their approach includes several inefficient behaviors or routines.

No matter how skillful one becomes in locating information, recording, organizing notes, summarizing, and planning are the tools that permit the use of the information. Too often the meaningful teaching of study habits is postponed until the students have mastered other skills. Because study habits are necessary for successful progress in the content areas, they must be taught throughout the academic program. Typically study habits are not a priority until grade four or five. Guided instruction in study habits should be provided in all subject areas.

As a developmental experience, learning to outline provides a conceptual plan of information. It may help in the comprehension process and also expedite the process of taking satisfactory notes. Partial or incomplete outlines should be used to guide students through initial stages of outlining. Providing major headings and selected supporting facts makes the student's task of completing an outline not only easier but also more understandable. Use the chalkboard to demonstrate and decide together (teacher and student) what goes where. Such a procedure gives the student a visual, participatory model through which to learn to construct an outline.

Essential to the successful performance of older students (those performing beyond the primary grades) is mastery of note taking and the ability to use time wisely. Much time can be wasted getting ready to study and in cramming or attempting to remember a mass of information. Good notes and a workable study technique can actually make studying easier and improve achievement. Students can benefit from learning a study technique and applying that technique directly in content material. Brazee (1979) reports support for integrating mastery of a study technique with the teaching of specific subject areas. The following study techniques are recommended: (1) REAP—Read, Encode, Annotate, Ponder (Eanet & Manzo, 1976); (2) PANORAMA—Purpose, Adapting rate to material, Need to pose questions, Overview, Read and relate, Annotate, Memorize, and Assess (Edwards, 1973); (3) SQRQCQ—Survey, Question, Read, Question, Compute, Question (Fay, 1965); and (4) EVOKER—Explore, Vocabulary, Oral reading, Key ideas, Evaluation, and Recapitulation (Robinson, 1961).

The abbreviated study technique in Figure 10.11 is intended for use with low achievers and students with disabilities. The procedure is called Preview, Read, and Express (PRE). Each of the three steps can be applied as generally described.

Students need the opportunity to rehearse, restate, verify, and/or question ideas. Use class time to acquaint students with one or more of the study

FIGURE 10.11   Preview, Read, and Express (PRE)

1. *Preview.* To begin, turn through the material with the student. Attention should be given to major headings, difficult terminology, graphics, and summary ideas. At this time a purpose or expectations should be shared and the chalkboard or overhead projector used to provide a visual model or representation of ideas and key words.

2. *Read.* Reading guidance may be necessary as a student reads. Offer assistance by answering questions, pronouncing words, and providing general encouragement. It may be necessary to break a reading assignment into short sections and move on to step three. You can also have the students read along silently as you read to them. After covering the material, move to the last step.

3. *Express.* An expressive discussion reinforces or clarifies what has been read. The major purpose is to help a student develop the process of remembering ideas and understanding concepts. Evaluation of what was read is not the aim. During this stage lead the discussion so that the student is responsible for at least half of the conversation.

techniques. Low-achieving students, in particular, need all the organization and time-saving aids they can develop. Simply spending more time in an unorganized fashion will not necessarily improve academic performance. Begin by selecting one chapter or short section from a textbook and, after presenting a study technique, guide a student through using the technique in a specific material. The process should be repeated until a student is able to apply the technique with minimal assistance.

Everyone does not need to become a rapid reader. It is helpful, however, to be able to read quickly for specific purposes. Unless students can skim and scan, they may be forced to read everything at a slow, plodding pace and perhaps, become bored. This can lead to running out of time and eventually giving up. The use of short-interval learning experiences can be very effective in improving skimming and scanning. For this purpose the student should be given a short paragraph or two and asked to read quickly to gain an overall idea about the passage. To provide guided practice in scanning, ask the student to read quickly to find out two or three pieces of information in a passage. You need to underline or highlight areas in the reading to provide cues during early presentations or practice sessions. Short interval guided practice involves using short reading passages to apply certain techniques, instead of using several pages or an entire chapter. Special students learn best by using an abbreviated sampling of content. After the skill (skimming, scanning, or outlining) has been mastered to some degree, longer sections can be introduced gradually. This procedure can be presented as a game with two or more students competing to tell the main idea or locate other requested details in a selection.

Some students perform poorly on tests because they lack knowledge, study strategies for test preparation, or specific test-tasking skills; this tends to cause anxiety or frustration during test situations. Some useful test-taking guidelines are presented in Figure 10.12. For more specific suggestions, refer to *Teaching Test Taking*

FIGURE 10.12   Strategies for Improving Test-Taking Skills

1. Match test formats with teaching/learning formats. If open-ended discussions are the primary lesson format, then tests should follow a similar format.

2. Provide students with study guides and discussion sessions reflecting the information to be learned and the format in which learning will be tested.

3. Provide students with modeling through the use of talk-through sessions in which the teacher and then students read and think aloud while solving or determining answers to sample test items.

4. Use daily cooperative study times for students to work in pairs or small groups to ask and answer questions about a particular topic of study. Monitor these 5–10 minute sessions and then adjust future instruction accordingly.

5. Guide students to make up their own test items for a practice test; routinely use one or more student test items to develop the actual test.

Skills: Helping Students Show What They Know (Scruggs & Mastropieri, 1992).

Specific Strategies.   When teaching content or a specific learning task, be sure to also teach an appropriate learning strategy to facilitate completion of the learning. For very simple tasks, have students describe how they would go about learning the information. For more difficult tasks, have students demonstrate to you or another student how to go about learning specific information. Ask students to verbalize and/or write down how to complete an assigned task. Suggestions for developing student checklists for specific strategies are presented in Figure 10.13. When appropriate, stress strategic use of technology. A variety of study strategies are described by Gall, Gall, Jacobsen, and Bullock (1990) and by Gaskins and Elliot (1991). Pressley and his colleagues (1990) present validated cognitive strategies for teaching

FIGURE 10.13   Suggestions for Developing
Student Checklists of Specific Strategies

1. Model the use of a mastered or currently studied strategy at least 5–6 times.

2. Use oral comment and board notes to reflect how you go about using the strategy.

3. After 3–4 modeling sessions, elicit student input to help clarify or verify what they would do next. If they are unable to make suggestions, offer two or three choices and ask them to guess which one would work best.

4. Monitor students as they work in pairs, listening and watching each other list how they go about applying a specific strategy.

5. Guide students to record individual checklists.

6. Provide additional teacher or student modeling of strategy use as needed.

7. Coach students as they apply and check off strategies in different contexts.

students how to learn and study in each of the major curricular areas.

Corrective Strategies

The purpose of providing corrective instruction is to reteach or teach in alternate format skills that have been introduced but not applied in a consistent manner. Corrective instruction is usually provided on a selective basis. Student performance can be satisfactory in book handling but not in book parts or satisfactory in dictionary use but unsatisfactory in using an encyclopedia.

Many students will need corrective intervention to improve performance in science, social studies, and other content areas. Because of the difficulty and the lack of attention given to content area strategies, these skills usually constitute a portion of the program for many low achievers. Corrective strategies may necessitate a slower pace, more redundancy, lower reading levels, and more active involvement and reinforcement than developmental strategies for instruction in the content areas. Focused and highly structured field trips and simulations are valuable experience

builders for students (Morsink, 1989; Polloway & Patton, 1989). It is particularly important to highlight the relevance and usefulness of content area skills to the individual student in his or her study of subject areas. As in the case of study strategies, corrective procedures dictate teaching beyond what is usually found in textbook materials. To do this requires the use of additional resources.

Content Area Strategies: *Vocabulary.* Specific vocabulary study and record keeping are necessary for some students. Present vocabulary and concepts on several different levels if students are grouped by ability (Morsink, 1989). Begin with actual hands-on experiences when possible, use concrete examples, and add any abstract terms gradually (Cooter & Reutzel, 1994). Directed experience in keeping vocabulary journals and in playing games that match vocabulary to concepts can be interesting for students. Remember to (1) convey the importance of key vocabulary, (2) provide daily exposure to content-related vocabulary, (3) use the vocabulary in an applied situation, and (4) offer a variety of different ways to learn content area vocabulary. To teach concepts, Schulz and Carpenter (1995) recommend using a language experience approach. Following informational presentations, they suggest having students summarize the key points or write stories about the major concepts. Mangieri and Corboy (1992) offer nearly a dozen suggestions for vocabulary improvement in the content areas. They recommend learning experiences on the levels of recognition, meaning, and relationship. Although you are probably familiar with such games as word search, word scramble, and crossword puzzles, are you familiar with checklist or classification?

Checklist is a strategy that involves the use of two or three categories listed on the right of a page. On the left are several key concepts. The student should be assisted in checking under one or more columns depending on the concept, application, or meaning of the key word on the left. A possible vocabulary checklist for social studies is presented in Figure 10.14.

FIGURE 10.14   Sample Vocabulary Checklist

Directions: Review the categories listed below. If a term or item fits a particular category on the left, check under the appropriate column. In some instances more than one check may be needed for one category.

CATEGORIES

Terms	Transportation	Food	Protection
1. airplane	✔		
2. convoy	✔		✔
3. trucking	✔		
4. bandage			
5. shipment	✔		
6. canning		✔	✔
7. farming		✔	
8. freight	✔		
9. police			✔

Some of the words may fit into more than one category. It may be necessary to use words with only one clear placement. By adding a fourth column such as "Examples," "My Use," "What It Means to Me," or another title that suggests the personal relevance to the individual student, the concepts will be more readily understood. Helping the students to organize the information is also a memory aid. A classification type example has been use. However, a checklist can be constructed, using types, tactics, reasons, regions, or numerous other headings.

A contextual type of corrective experience results from developing sentences with one or two technical or nontechnical words omitted. Leave a blank for each word and provide possible answer words in parentheses or at the bottom of the page. If a student is unable to select the appropriate word, include an initial consonant for each blank to make responses easier. After completing the sentences, have the student read the sentences orally.

Problem Solving.   There are those who refer to thinking skills as problem solving skills. Problem solving means thinking that is directed toward the solving of a problem. As a corrective strategy, problem solving requires a more targeted approach than when used as a developmental strategy. Polya (1957) identifies four heuristics as important or worthy of teaching. These include: (1) use a graph or diagram to represent the problem, (2) restate the problem, (3) break the problem into parts, and (4) relate a known problem of a simpler nature to the one you are trying to solve. Additional direct teaching can be focused upon areas of problem solving reported by Nickerson (1984) and taken from Project Intelligence. This outline of skills includes five specific areas under the category of problem solving: (1) linear representations, (2) tabular representations, (3) representation by simulation and enactment, (4) systematic trial and error, and (5) thinking out and its implications.

One popular corrective strategy is to use a single paragraph or description of an event or situation as a stimulus. Begin by initially reading the material to the student. Before reading, ask the student to listen carefully for: (1) what is happening, (2) what is the problem, and (3) what can be done to improve the situation. The preceding three steps all assume that the student can determine central ideas, knows what a problem is, and is able to generate solutions. In some instances a student may have difficulties with any one or all three areas. (Refer to Chapter 6 for additional comments concerning improving comprehension.) For problem determination you may need to provide several discussion sessions dealing with problems the student encounters daily. After establishing a background for recognizing a problem, generate ideas for finding solutions through discussion. Start with simple problems and move on to more complex problems. In science, examples such as the following may be used: "It's raining outside, and we have to go home. Can you tell me about a possible problem we may have? If so, how can we solve the problem?" You may need to discuss several reality-based problem situations before using printed materials that portray immediate or reality-based problems. Next move into more content-specific reading selections but continue to read to the student at first. Then gradually move to a point where you read a portion of the material and then the student reads the rest. A final step involves the student reading and solving problems independently. As proficiency increases, provide a list of the steps the student should follow to solve problems. The complexity of the steps may be gradually increased as the students progress.

Grouping so as to work in pairs or teams can be helpful after a student has demonstrated understanding of the problem-solving process. Until that point, guided instruction and talk-through of ideas and predictions are necessary on a regular basis. Cooperative learning experiences can be successful when used for short time periods and when students are given a structure or very clear directions and examples as to what is expected.

Graphic Aids.   For a student who is experiencing difficulty understanding maps and graphs, several strategies may be helpful. Maps, globes, and charts that are highly textured provide an extra aid to students. Encourage students to feel the different features, and to visualize the features as they touch them. Begin targeted lessons using a map or graph of something familiar to the student. Graphs showing the number of boys and girls in each class, the number of teachers in each grade, or even the color of shoes in the room offer a concrete starting point.

Have students create a graph with you. As the graph is completed, you can pause and request help placing information and matching it for size or importance. Giving students a graph and asking them to change information based upon different numbers can be an excellent directed experience. Maps can be similarly created.

Some attention to vocabulary is also necessary to use graphic aids successfully. Learning to use keys, map legends, directions, intervals, bottom and side headings, all require some specialized knowledge of vocabulary applied to maps and graphs. Use a game format by forming teams, pointing to a portion of a map and requesting in-

formation about what this is, what this is called or in which part (N, S, E, W) the largest lake is located. To teach these content skills present, gain a recognition response, gain a "show me" response, and review the point again. This, or a similar cycle, is necessary to pattern a response and to establish a positive memory base for continued efforts.

When using corrective procedures present a map or graph containing fewer items of information than when using development procedures. If these are understood, more information can be added. In recent years, the integration of subject area content and the use of graphic aids has become preferred practice. Segmented instruction in pull-out or nonrelated reading materials is typically not as effective as when lessons include graphic aids and proper graphic aids instruction as a part of the content study. To be effective, corrective efforts require teacher directed guidance and feedback through modeling, talk throughs, written and oral recitation, as well as explicit instructional experiences, before expecting independent or more collaborative type student responses.

A major problem with using corrective strategies is that many of the ideas suggested in content area literature are presented for middle- and upper-grade use. You may need to review these strategies and adapt, revise, or simplify them in order to use them with younger students. Do not automatically reject a potentially helpful topic or title because it carries a secondary or middle-grade designation. To adapt, use reading materials, make the response format easier, and/or spend more time modeling and guiding the learner through application of the skill.

The need for targeted instruction in the content areas represents the key difference between corrective strategies and developmental and maintenance strategies. Corrective strategies are used as special teaching efforts focused toward the mastery of a content area skill and informing the student of the need and rewards of improving the skill. In addition to considerable time and effort on your part, special printed resources (e.g., dictionaries, maps, graphs), and student involvement opportunities must be provided.

Study Strategies.   *Organization and Book Use.* For the student experiencing difficulty categorizing it is necessary to develop a hands-on selection of picture and word cards. The file can be developed with the students by having them select and cut pictures from a catalog. The pictures should be pasted on 3" × 5" cards and then used in a variety of matching or identifying experiences. Letter and shape cards can also be used. Use 10–15 minute daily sessions requiring students to respond orally and match similar figures. Unlike developmental experiences, corrective intervention requires the teacher to state, show, and guide student responses during a lesson. Corrective lessons also differ from developmental ones in that more repetition and repeated instruction of similar tasks may be required.

Students who display difficulty categorizing words according to their meaning may be able to categorize words by beginning or ending letters. If not, categorizing by pictures or by concrete objects will be necessary. The factor to recognize is that at some level most students are able to categorize. Begin instruction at a point where responses are essentially correct and then proceed to higher or harder tasks, based upon a demonstrated point of successful responses. The same sequential basis is generally applied to learning to alphabetize.

Begin corrective instruction on a manageable, "can do" level and slowly move through tasks requiring the student to complete longer and longer directed tasks. A cardinal mistake involves requiring a student to do what a teacher wants without sufficient regard for the learner's established level of performance. For example, a teacher may say, "Now I told you to print your name in the left corner, skip two lines, and be sure to indent before each heading." A student may not know how to indent, which side is left, where the corner is, or what a heading looks like. Begin by using simple directions and then, after gaining success, move on to longer directives. Demonstrate each

task and explain carefully before having a student attempt a new task. By including both oral and visual clues, you enable students to understand directions better. Provide frequent reminders such as, "Remember, this morning we completed the _____." Students can benefit from hearing or seeing a previous lesson that required a similar level of mastery. It provides a mind set and a familiar basis through which transfer of learning can occur.

References.   Many students have not received sufficient direct instruction in using references. Offer concentrated skill-specific assistance. Develop lessons focusing in the area of concern or use a published kit or worktext directed toward dictionary and other reference use. A talk-through procedure usually helps illustrate how to use a source. For example, a teacher may say, "Allan, I need to check on the spelling (or meaning) of this word. Where can I find help?" If there is no response, display the dictionary (book or screen) and state: "This reference can help us be sure we have this word spelled correctly. Please help me find it." The talk through procedure is a teacher/student interaction procedure requiring immediate implementation of a modeled skill.

Study Habits.   Instruction for improving study habits requires the teacher to provide specific in-school guided study instruction and practice. A specific outlining procedure or study technique must be selected, taught, and applied under supervision. Unless repeated guided practice is provided, study habits or test-taking skills will not improve significantly. Teachers sometimes make assignments and then do not observe, direct, and encourage students to follow through as they work. For corrective action to be successful, you must monitor the creation of outlines and then offer immediate assistance and encouragement. Giving a student partially completed outlines to be finished step-by-step with your direct assistance is a useful strategy. The clues and assistance should be gradually reduced as the student progresses. To model note-taking techniques, listen to an audio tape with the student. Both teacher and student should take notes and then compare. Explain the techniques and then ask the student to listen and take notes again, correcting them according to a personal model. With continued practice and corrective feedback, a student can eventually take notes in class, comparing and correcting them according to a teacher or peer model. Teaching a student abbreviations for high-frequency words may also lighten the note-taking load. Demonstrating a column format may simplify note taking for some youngsters. Supply the students with formatted sheets, with a small column for the main ideas and a large column for the supporting details. Give the students practice sessions, asking them to list the notes in the appropriate columns (Bos & Vaughn, 1994). This strategy may also be used to improve outlining techniques. The study habits area requires in-class time and direct teacher guidance as students attempt to apply suggested techniques or varied reading rates.

To focus corrective instruction on specific study strategies, it may be necessary to conduct a task analysis when a student is unable to perform a task or demonstrate acceptable performance. Success and error analysis should be conducted using a specific strategy until the students reaches a point where a breakdown in performance occurs. In the application of a study strategy, a student could be asked: "What will your next step be?" "Show me how you plan to outline or summarize this section." "Tell me the difference between remembering today's information and the introductory information from last week." Perhaps a student is experiencing difficulty on a more concrete level. If, for example, a student experiences difficulty alphabetizing a list of cities, it would be possible to begin by having the student alphabetize using one letter, then the first two letters, then using the first three letters, and so on until a level of proficiency is reached.

Students with special needs especially have to use strategies effectively in two areas: taking tests and using technology. In addition to activities presented earlier for helping students prepare for tests (see Figure 10.13), a mock testing situation two days before an actual test may be helpful. Have students take the mock test, and then form student teams to assume the role of teachers as they score, correct, and reteach as needed.

In their description of technology trends and the implications for students with disabilities, Sawyer and Zantal-Wiener (1993) note the potential for increased independence and greatly enhanced communication, learning, demonstration of knowledge and skills, and overall functioning. Lewis (1993) discusses different types of technology, analyzes benefits, and recommends usage for students with special needs. In order to facilitate access to and instruction for effective use of technology, the classroom teacher must be technology-literate and regularly collaborate with technology experts to harness the power of technology to compensate, communicate, motivate, and advocate for students with disabilities.

Personalized student-constructed lists can be used as a means of both helping a student to better understand and develop strategies for learning as well as providing teachers with a glimpse of how students go about completing or learning a certain task. As a metacognitive type of blueprint have students, either orally or in writing, list what they are doing as they study a portion of text, review a map or look over a section (chapter) for a specific purpose. In order for students to learn to chart their thoughts it is usually necessary for teachers to provide five to six (or more) talk-through sessions during which they model for the student, what they are thinking and how they are going about a specific learning task. It is also helpful for teachers to model the use of a strategy that is currently being taught as a concrete means of reinforcing the usefulness of glossing, key words or some other study technique. Basic guidelines should be recommended to students to help them prepare strategy monitoring lists. Such lists help students remember what they did, serve as a reminder of the kinds of things they can do to learn, and incorporate the goal of strategy attribution training (Graham, 1991; Stevens & Englert, 1993)—acknowledgment that success (or failure) is attributable to use (or nonuse) of key strategies.

In addition to metacognition as it applies to reading and writing, metacognitive strategies can be used in a more global sense. Smey-Richman (1988) uses a literature-based discussion to suggest several strategies for low achievers. Among the suggested strategies are think alouds, student generated questions, paraphrasing, retelling or rewriting, and most importantly, the necessity for teacher modeling. Teacher modeling can include sharing ideas for planning how to begin an assignment, explaining the labeling or categorizing scheme they use or talking about how they decide what approach to take for an assignment or learning task. Visual imagery and verbal mediation strategies, such as self-instruction, mnemonics, and self-questioning are recommended by C. Smith (1994). Deshler and Schumaker (1986) recommend numerous structured learning strategies validated for specific tasks and content as do Harris and Graham (1992) and Roditi (1994). For students performing at the elementary levels, Archer and Gleason (1990) describe a variety of study strategies designed for low achievers.

Maintenance Strategies

Maintenance strategies are necessary to ensure long-term mastery of tasks. Once learned, a skill is not likely to be retained unless programmatic efforts are made to review, reinforce, and expand competencies. Study and content area skills can be maintained through the use of regular application level experiences requiring the student to demonstrate mastery. Maintenance experiences may include less teacher involvement, more student interaction with peers, or more independent practice than corrective experiences. Through the use of textual aids, library aids, and direct teacher intervention, maintenance is possible. In some instances textbook publishers provide resource guides and computer software that specifically integrate maps, graphs, reference, vocabulary and problem solving skills in an interactive format. Local toy retailers also offer a variety of reference and trivia-style games that use a game board and question cards to cue student responses.

The following suggested maintenance strategies offer a sample of the type and range of experiences that may be used to improve performance in content and study strategies. Before deciding to use them, be sure to modify or adapt them according to individual student needs. Many of these same activities can be applied to other content areas such as language arts or mathematics.

Science and Social Studies
Vocabulary Pronunciation, (IA.1–.11, odd numbers and IB.1–.11, odd numbers). ■Have students select words they think are unusual, new to them, or important for understanding the topic. Print words on cards, study lists, or keep in a notebook. Allow pairs of students to play games pronouncing the words. ■Have students pick three- to-five words from a list and then, over a period of one or two days, keep track of how many times and where they see the word used. It is also helpful for the teacher to check a student's words for mastery at least every five to ten days. ■Use selected activities from Word Recognition IA.4–IB.6 for maintenance strategies (Figure 6.1).

Vocabulary Definition, (IA.2–.12, even numbers and IB.2–.12, even numbers). ■Use the same word cards or lists as for pronunciation. Have students form teams or work in pairs, taking turns selecting words for peers to explain or use appropriately in sentences. Add an element of suspense by allowing students to "bluff" for one to two turns (by saying "I Pass"). If a student misses the next turn, then two points instead of one are deducted from the overall score. ■Ask students to use a designated number of their special words during a conversation. Vary this activity by having students tape mock conversations, using key words. Then give peers a list of possible words and have then underline the ones used as they listen to the tape. ■Select strategies from Word Recognition, IVA.1–IVE.7.

Science

Problem Solving, (IIA.1–IIB). ▪Give students simple problems and five to seven possible solutions. Have then follow the POP strategy (see Chapter 6, corrective strategies) to choose the best solutions. ▪Read an interesting selection to the students. Designate at least one student as a judge and the remainder as the audience. Give the audience a set time to develop possible solution(s) to passage problems. Let the judge determine the best solutions. ▪Give pairs of students reality problems but omit some necessary facts. Have them quiz each other and verify to identify missing data. ▪List problems and one solution to each. Have teams of students formulate at least one alternate solution. Reverse the strategy by supplying a solution and having students describe three possible problems that created the need for the solution. ▪Give student pairs or teams a list of possible problems and solutions. Ask them to explain the problem they think is most nearly the same as the one in a reading passage and to justify their selections. ▪Have student groups read labels from any product that has directions. Ask them to explain the problem the products are intended to rectify or improve. ▪Ask more proficient students to draw or diagram solutions to problems. ▪For enjoyment give student pairs or teams problems and ask them to describe possible solutions 20 years ago, now, and 20 years from now. Guide students to use the library to research possibilities.

Social Studies

Maps, (IIA.1–.3). ▪Select a map that relates to something or some area which the student is or will be studying. Use a map that can be pinned or marked. Use a reciprocal question format between peers or between student and teacher to ask questions about the map. These can include directions, distances, names, or almost any element on a map. ▪Use newspapers as an inexpensive source of maps to be "used up" in a hands-on fashion. Ask students to mark maps according to directions or to plan the quickest route from one point to another. ▪Simulate a trip, tracking progress on a map, and planning the itinerary.

Graphs, (IIB.1–.3). ▪Ask students to compare and contrast the same information on a bar, circle, or line graph. ▪Newspapers and magazines are excellent sources of graphic material. Use such disposable sources to ask students to annotate the graphs ("Use the red marker and check the year in which . . . ; Underline the category that represents . . ."). The active response mode is reinforcing. ▪Have students convert information displayed in one form, such as a bar graph, to a different form such as a line or circle graph. ▪Have students look at two different graph formats of the same information and explain why one format may be easier to understand than another format. ▪Have students collect data and then enter them into a computer software program that constructs graphs. Then have them exchange graphs for reciprocal questioning and discussion.

Study Strategies: Organization

Categorizing, (IA.1–.4). ▪Write words on the chalkboard and show an object or name a category. Have students go to the board and circle the word that goes with each object or name as presented. Have another student explain why the choice is or is not accurate. ▪List categories and items; ask students to group items under the appropriate heading. As students progress, use categories that are increasingly similar. ▪Select additional maintenance strategies from those listed for Word Recognition, IV.B.

Alphabetizing, (IB.1–.4). ▪Begin by using the first letter, then first and second letter and so on. Ask students to compare the words on word cards with a stimulus word and decide which comes first. ▪Have teams of students compete in alphabetizing groups of words. The names of classmates, school subjects, spelling words, or other school-related terms with personal meaning are appropriate. ▪Give students lists of words that are partially alphabetized and ask them to edit and correct the lists. Present increasingly difficult lists. ▪Have students keep their word recognition "word banks" in alphabetical order.

Following Directions, (IC.1–.2). ▪Hold a "direction bee"; begin by orally giving one direction to the first participant. Proceed as in a spelling bee, increasing the complexity of the directions and tasks until a winner is declared. ▪Give simple directions on audio tape, gradually adding more and more tasks to remember. At a listening center have students listen and perform each task. Include "fun" directives such as, "Get a drink of water; put a sticker on your friend's paper." Have students repeat each item orally when following oral or taped directions. ▪Have students explain written directions to a classmate or when necessary to you to verify understanding.

Study Strategies: Book Use
Book Handling, (IIA.1–.3). ▪Model and demonstrate proper posture and care of books, and then ask a student to do the same for less proficient students. ▪To practice keeping place while reading or following along as others read orally, guide students who need it to use a paper card as a marker or a finger to mark or underline the line currently being read. Demonstrate proper use (i.e., moving the marker vertically down the page, but not horizontally). ▪Frequently reinforce proper book handling to promote the habit.

Book Parts, (IIB.1–.5). ▪Routinely direct practice by asking: "On what page does today's lesson begin? What page comes before today's lesson? What is the page number of the last page in this lesson? Count three pages into today's lesson and tell me what the first sentence says; what page are you on?" ▪Give students lists of ten page numbers and time how long it takes each student to find all the pages; chart performance. ▪Periodically ask students to use the table of contents or index in their classroom texts to locate pages, page numbers, chapters, or topics you request. ▪Use pairs of students to ask each other to locate information. ▪Using books of particular interest to students, develop lists of topics and ask students to locate the page numbers.

Study Strategies: References
Dictionary, (IIIA.1–.4). ▪Give students lists of words and ask them to underline the two guide words for each list. ▪Have students use the dictionary to contrast the meanings of similar word pairs or trios. Students sometimes enjoy using a thesaurus to follow the same procedures. ▪Give students specific words to locate in the dictionary and then pronounce them according to markings. ▪Have students add to their word banks the new words that they can pronounce. Then have them locate the meaning of each word and dictate a personal sentence to write on the back of the word card. ▪Use the word cards for reciprocal questioning between classmates. ▪Underline target words in sentences; have students decide which definition in the classroom dictionary explains each word as it is used in the sentence context. The student can write the page number and the number of that definition beside each sentence.

Encyclopedia, (IIIB). ▪Give students specific topics and ask them to locate the correct volume to use. Give students topics that do not have entries of their own. ▪Have students list several entries and volumes in which to look. Groups of students may be asked to rank the possible entries in terms of which are the most likely candidates. Have students list topics of special interest, and then cite the volumes to check. ▪Give students a topic and have them compare two encyclopedias for quantity and quality of topic treatment.

Card Catalog, (IIIC.1–.3.). ▪Using only one type of card at a time, have students locate a book by subject, author, or title; have students repeat the process using a computerized data base. ▪Have students locate a book related to a specified book. ▪Give students an interesting list and send them on a scavenger hunt in the library. For example, have them find and bring to class a book about dogs, one by Jim Ham's brother, etc., or as many books and articles as they can locate about a specified topic.

Study Strategies: Habits
Outline from Reading, (IVA.1–.2). ▪Provide a skeletal outline of brief sections of their texts for

students to complete. ▪Give students an annotated outline to complete about a passage. List as follows with blanks following each entry: I. Main Idea; A. Detail; B. Detail; II. Main Idea, etc. ▪Pair practice with strategies suggested for Comprehension II. A. (Figure 6.1). Gradually phase out skeletal outline clues.

Semantic Mapping, (IVA.3). ▪Begin with easy material; have students substitute map parts for phrases in simple outlines. ▪Have students construct a semantic map for a portion of text and give to a peer to study before reading. Ask the peer to modify the map based on the text, and then ask the first student to reread both passage and map to verify information. ▪Supply partially completed maps and fade cues as students progress.

Summary Paragraph, (IVA.4). ▪Give students a simple outline of textbook material. Have students write or dictate a summary paragraph using the topic sentence and supporting details. ▪Prepare summary paragraphs that contain surplus information. Have students read the selection and then cross out the excess wording and/or rewrite the paragraph. ▪Have pairs of students work together to summarize material. Let one student form the outline, the other the paragraph, and then both edit the paragraph together.

Study Techniques, Note Taking, (IVB.1–.3). ▪Give students brief passages and ask them to highlight with two felt markers the key concepts in one color and supporting details in another color. Then ask students to copy their highlights as notes. ▪Use out-lining strategies cited for IVA.1–.2. ▪Select practice strategies from Readence, Bean, and Baldwin (1981).

Reading Rate Adjustment, (IVC.1–.3). ▪Ask students to read quickly the headings of a passage and select the main ideas from six choices. Let

students chart their time. ▪Use the highlighting strategy in IVB.1–.3 for main idea (skimming) or specific information (scanning). Give students three minutes to find the answers to main idea or specific information questions. ▪Set a 15-minute time limit to read a passage and prepare for a quiz.

Specific Strategies, (IVD.1–.7). ▪Have students quietly verbalize each step of specific strategies as they accomplish appropriate tasks; provide personal listings of the steps as reminders. ▪When students demonstrate adequate mastery of content or study strategies, increase the level of difficulty of the material being studied. ▪Have students, either individually or in teams, teach a younger student strategic use of some form of technology. ▪Coach students to apply a more sophisticated level of a previously mastered strategy (e.g., requiring a student to deal with a more complex problem-solving task).

Implementing the CBA/P Model

The assessment and programming cycle offers the structure within which the necessary minimum study and content area skills can be taught. The time needed for mastering some of these skills may be less than that required to acquire proficiency in other curriculum areas. The importance of using and updating the study and content area skills curriculum chart (Figure 10.1) is evident. By using the chart you can accurately monitor both the quantity and quality of student progress. As in other areas, consider mastery temporary until proven otherwise. Remember that the use of study strategies is generic and applies to a variety of subject areas. A CBA/P plan specifically for content and study strategies is outlined in Figure 10.15. Note the integration of content and study strategy assessment and programming.

FIGURE 10.15   Sample Curriculum-Based Assessment/Programming Plan for Content and Study Strategies

1. **Analyze Curriculum**
   - Decide which skills on the curriculum chart (Figure 10.1) are to be used.
   - Review text or topic units of study and decide which study strategies are most important for each subject area.
   - Decide what minimum levels of performance are necessary.
2. **Assess Content and Study Strategies**
   - Gather indirect assessment information.
   - Develop skill-specific tests using subject area vocabulary and content.
   - Develop a plan of on-going assessment; include which skills, strategies, and test formats (e.g., checklists, portfolios, skill tests) to use.
   - Conduct direct assessment by administering skill-specific tests, checklists, and other appropriate items using subject area texts and other curricular resources.
   - Observe strategy usage in content context and analyze using checklist.
   - Interpret findings showing mastered and unmastered skills performance.
   - Document findings.
3. **Program for the Content/Study Strategies Needed**
   - Prioritize unmastered skills and strategies.
   - List mastered skills and strategies.
   - Based on assessment data, develop a plan for three stages of integrated content/study strategy instruction: developmental, corrective, and maintenance.
   - Begin teaching according to the plan, modifying instruction according to student performance.
   - Document progress as the plan is used.
4. **Repeat CBA/P Content/Study Strategies Cycle**

SUMMARY

The priority given to content and study strategies is admittedly less than that of some other subject areas, such as reading, writing, mathematics, and spelling. Without direct teaching of content and study strategies, however, the chances for continued academic growth beyond a basic skills level are seriously jeopardized.

The procedures in this chapter reflect ideas for assessment and programming that can be used, adapted, or expanded for use in several subject areas. A small number of published resources are available from school districts and a few publishers. Most content and study strategies are taught by classroom personnel, using many teacher-constructed materials. This chapter contains sufficient assessment and intervention strategies to assist teachers in developing their own personalized materials.

CASE STUDIES

Sample Case: Thelma

Thelma is a thirteen-year-old fifth-grader. She is cooperative and interested in school. Results from the indirect assessment reveal the following information:

Thelma's teacher considers her to be a mixture of highs and lows. She ranks her use of meaning vocabulary as unsatisfactory. Thelma's weak dictionary skills and poor study habits also contribute to her increasing problems. Thelma works hard in school but is very disorganized. She frequently leaves her work unfinished. Her overall word-recognition level is approximately grade 4.0. Her comprehension level is estimated at 5.8.

Diagnostic Hypotheses: *An inadequate vocabulary and poor study habits appear to be the major areas of difficulty. Because her comprehension is stronger than her vocabulary, Thelma has apparently not learned to use the dictionary. Perhaps her word-mastery skills are not high enough to sustain her as she begins to move farther into content area reading assignments. Poor organization skills may also interfere with other study skills.*

During the student interview, Thelma stated that she usually felt hurried in completing school assignments but really wanted to do better. Since her overall level of word recognition was suspected to be low, direct assessment began with technical and non-technical vocabulary in social studies (IA.3–.8 and IB.3–.8). Thelma's performance revealed a fourth-grade level in technical vocabulary and a third-grade level in nontechnical vocabulary. Additional assessment was conducted in using book parts (IIB.3–.5), references (IIIA.1–.4), and study habits (IVA.1–.2).

Based upon the information provided, a preliminary program can be developed. Since Thelma's nontechnical vocabulary is two years below grade placement (3.0) it will be necessary to begin a study daily file or log of new words learned in social studies. The social studies area was selected, since her teacher puts strong emphasis in this area. Thelma will be guided in the development of a "key word" collection of the special meanings of terms in social studies. A portion of the words will be given to her by the teacher. In addition to these textbook generated words, we will ask Thelma to contribute other words related to social studies. These will be found in magazines, newspapers, or library books. At least two times per week Thelma will confer with her teacher to discuss her words and demonstrate her ability to use them. During these conferences her teacher will help Thelma discuss problem words and also, guide her in developing a phrase or main-idea list to accompany each word. These techniques should help Thelma remember and use the words.

Thelma will also be guided in planning her time more wisely. Her willingness to cooperate and her comparatively high level of reading comprehension indicate some degree of ability to complete tasks. A somewhat stronger and better organized peer will be paired with Thelma. Thelma can also benefit from direct practice using the dictionary. This can be done by using a variety of games in which words are called out (with page numbers) and having her participate in quickly finding stimulus words. She will also spend ten minutes each day practicing how to locate words in the dictionary and in selecting words for another student to locate. This type of shared give and take will provide an interactive atmosphere for Thelma to apply dictionary locational skills. Since Thelma can alphabetize by first and second letters, she is capable but unaccustomed to using an index, glossary, or dictionary format to find words. The opportunity for guided practice should help her improve in a relatively short period of time.

Practice Case A: Danny

Danny is a seven-year-old boy enrolled in grade one for the second time. His teacher reports that he is still having difficulty with initial organization, following directions, and book-handling skills. Based upon the curriculum chart (Figure 10.3), answer the following questions.

1. If more testing is required, what areas will you include?
2. If the preliminary problems are confirmed, what type of curriculum will you recommend?
3. What specific corrective strategies or materials will you plan?
4. If Danny demonstrates satisfactory performance on the organization and book-handling tests, what other causes or areas will you need to investigate?
5. What other sources of information will you need to add to the sample test item results?

Practice Case B: Lori

Lori, a ten-year-old fifth grader has been referred to you. Her teacher describes her as a strong literal thinker unable to solve problems. Of additional concern is Lori's limited ability to understand illustrations in her science, mathematics, and social studies textbooks.

1. Which test items would you suggest be administered to Lori from the sample items in Appendix F?
2. If, for example, a major problem is noted in map reading above grade three, what would you recommend for beginning corrective instruction?
3. Describe the possible difficulty involved if Lori can identify problems but not offer solutions beyond a grade four level; if she can identify and solve problems on a second-grade level.
4. How will you proceed if Lori is able to solve problems at a sixth-grade level?
5. You have confirmed that the original indirect assessment data is accurate. Describe what strategies and materials you would suggest to help Lori.

ENRICHMENT ACTIVITIES

DISCUSSION

1. How can mastery of study and content area skills help all students and special learners, in particular?
2. Which study and content area tasks are the most important in the curriculum or instructional programs with which you are familiar?
3. Describe when and how you were taught study skills. Evaluate this instruction.
4. Why do you think so little attention is generally given to the teaching of study and content area skills?
5. Why is it necessary to teach study strategies in actual content materials?

Special Projects

1. Interview a teacher of a regular elementary class and a special education teacher about study and content area skills; determine if they spend time teaching and realize the need for these skills.
2. Observe a student and interview the teacher to complete the teacher survey on study and content area skills (Figure 10.2).
3. Analyze the study and content area instructional components of two or three science or social studies textbooks currently in use in a local school. Compare content and sequence with the curriculum chart in Figure 10.1.
4. Based on the information in this chapter on portfolios, select 1–2 study related skill areas and develop portfolio forms for use in a class.
5. Select an appropriate textbook, and develop cloze exercises using at least two different formats. If possible, find a student and work with the student to complete the 6–8 item exercises. Then describe, in writing, what you find out.

CHAPTER 11

SYNTHESIZING ASSESSMENT *AND* PROGRAMMING

JOYCE S. CHOATE

You may feel that you have been given more than you ever wanted to know about assessment and programming. You may be thinking, "Is all of this really necessary? How practical is it?" It is also possible that you still have questions about organization, content selection, the time and effort requirements, keeping track of more than one student's needs and progress, the physical arrangements, juggling the students to accomplish the task, and maintaining the students and your own enthusiasm. These are all legitimate concerns that will be addressed. However, before approaching these very practical issues, let us put the need for personalized assessment and programming in perspective.

ASSESSMENT AND PROGRAMMING IN PERSPECTIVE

> *Is all this really necessary?*
>
> The authors of this text believe that most of it is.

The reciprocal relationship of assessment and programming establishes the need to intertwine the two. Perhaps you will not follow the exact steps suggested. In fact, you probably should not. Your assessment and programming strategies should be selected according to the unique needs of each student. What will work for you will also be governed by the specific profile of your school system and your particular setting. You should find, however, that the assessment principles (Chapter 1) and the programming principles (Chapter 2) are helpful in choosing your strategies. As you implement your strategies, consult the assessment/programming cycle (Chapter 3) to decide upon the special combination that best suits your students and situation. Because the content of your assessment and programming will be the curriculum, much of it will have been preselected by your system and by the professional biases of you and your fellow educators. It is up to you to identify that content.

The Principles and the CBA/P Cycle

> *How do the principles of assessment and programming relate to the CBA/P Cycle?*
>
> They are the foundation of the cycle.

Another look at the assessment and programming principles and the curriculum-based assessment/programming (CBA/P) cycle may clarify the interrelationships. The assessment and programming principles are abbreviated in Figure 11.1 for your review and then placed in the context of the CBA/P cycle in Figure 11.2.

FIGURE 11.1 Assessment and Programming Principles

PRINCIPLES OF ASSESSMENT	PRINCIPLES OF PROGRAMMING
▬ Be purposeful	▬ Utilize resources
▬ Relate to curriculum	▬ Follow general curriculum
▬ Assess skills and strategies	▬ Teach skills and strategies
▬ Set priorities	▬ Set priorities by student needs
▬ Use appropriate techniques	▬ Base on assessment and update
▬ Go from general to specific	▬ Pace per learning rate
▬ Analyze errors	▬ Adjust to student needs
▬ Substantiate findings	▬ Follow learning style
▬ Record and report	▬ Coordinate program
▬ Improve continuously	▬ Actively teach for mastery

▬ Efficiently manage assessment and programming process

FIGURE 11.2 Principles in the CBA/P Cycle

Step 1: Analyze Curriculum
▬ Relate assessment to curriculum
▬ Assess what and how
▬ Follow general curriculum
▬ Set priorities by student needs
▬ Go from general to specific

Step 2: Assess Skills
▬ Follow ALL Assessment Principles and these Programming Principles:
▬ Utilize resources
▬ Follow general curriculum
▬ Adjust to student needs
▬ Coordinate program
▬ Manage efficiently

Step 3: Program for Assessed Needs
▬ Follow ALL Programming Principles and these Assessment Principles:
▬ Be purposeful
▬ Use appropriate techniques
▬ Determine effective strategies
▬ Analyze errors
▬ Substantiate findings
▬ Record and report
▬ Improve continuously
▬ Manage efficiently

As can be seen in the two figures, many of the assessment principles are directly related to the programming principles and some apply to more than one step of the cycle. Of course, these principles apply to assessment and programming outside the model as well, but they are the framework of the present model. When implementing the CBA/P model, the principles also provide the substance for making a number of key decisions.

Cycle of Decisions

Decisions, decisions . . . Who makes them and when and how?

You do after carefully considering all data.

Within the CBA/P cycle there are several key points at which decisions must be made. These decisions involve where to start and stop, what content and which procedures to use, when to use them, and how to go about it. The decision points are outlined for each step of the cycle.

Step 1: Analyze the Curriculum
  Your task is to identify the student's true curriculum. Once a curriculum is identified your decision is: Is this the true curriculum? The teacher interview and direct observations across time in the classroom (during

direct assessment) are the sources for verifying the curriculum. Thus, your initial decision must be based on eliciting from the teacher a plausible estimate of the student's curriculum; you will have to make the final decision after observing, interviewing, and working with the student. Meanwhile, with a rough estimate in hand, move on to assessment.

Step 2: Assess Skills

Your task is to identify the specific skills to assess and then implement the best assessment approach for identifying the student's performance of key tasks. Your decisions are: which tasks to assess first, which assessment procedures to use, and when to discontinue assessment and move on to programming. Data upon which to base your selection of the tasks to assess first are the student's overall performance profile, the teacher's stated priorities, the student's implied or expressed priorities, work sample analyses, and observed performances. Data for deciding which direct assessment procedures to use come from student records, the teacher's report of curricular expectations, and the teacher's and student's reports of the ways in which performance is typically evaluated in the classroom, as well as availability of assessment items and materials, time constraints, and your professional inclinations. The decision to proceed to programming must be based on your determination that you have obtained sufficient data with which to initiate or continue a personalized program.

Step 3: Program for Assessed Needs

Your task is to select and implement the best methods for producing student progress. Your decisions for programming parallel the ones you made for assessment: which tasks to teach first, which methods to use, and when to discontinue teaching particular tasks and begin a new cycle. The assessment data provide the substance for deciding which tasks to teach. The placement of the tasks on the curricular continuum identifies which ones to teach first. Deciding upon the best method is not quite so simple. First select the instructional stage according to the student's prior experience with each task (new task or a previously taught one) and the student's performance of each task (mastered or tentatively mastered). Remember, for new tasks, first try developmental instruction; for previously taught tasks that are unmastered, offer corrective instruction; and for tentatively mastered tasks provide maintenance instruction. Initially select methods similar to ones that have been successful with that student or with similar students in the past. Also consider the nature of the tasks, the student's learning style, time, space, and resource constraints, and teaching style. Regularly assess progress, graph it, and compare the student's progress with your pre-established goals. Base your decision to change methodology and/or materials or task level on comparisons between charted progress and goals; when the rate of progress is too slow to reach scheduled goals, the need for change is evident. Base the decision to shift a task from developmental or corrective instruction to maintenance instruction on the student's consistent performance of the task with the degree of accuracy specified by the curriculum.

Step 4: Repeat the CBA/P Cycle

Your task is to repeat the cycle at the appropriate time. The decision is identifying the best time. Data for making this decision come from the results of previous assessment and programming activities (e.g., the student's learning rate, the number of new tasks he or she can handle at one time, and the number of tasks at the developmental and corrective stages), suggestions from the student and other persons involved in the process, and curricular demands.

Decisions about what content to include in each repetition of the CBA/P cycle must also be based upon the relative value to the student of each task and also each subject.

Content in Perspective

> *How do you select the most important content?*
>
> According to its relative value to the student.

When the content for both assessment and programming is drawn from the curriculum, all the content is relevant to academic needs. However, curricula contain vast amounts of content. How do you weigh the comparative value of the various subject areas? You must consider not only the student's relative position on the curricular continuum in each subject but also the role of each subject within the total curriculum. In Chapter 1, four classifications of the subjects areas were presented: core curriculum, collateral curriculum, support curriculum, and enrichment curriculum.

The first three classifications comprise the academic curriculum, the focus of this book. As depicted in Figure 11.3, the core subjects, particularly reading and written expression, are the learning tools for all other academic areas. As a core subject, mathematics is unique in that it represents a separate discipline that may or may not be required for other subjects. However, all core subjects are the major contributors to general literacy. The subjects of the collateral curriculum contain the content to be learned using the skills of the core and support curricula; in addition, collateral subjects may require subject-specific skills. The support curriculum contains the skills and strategies with which to learn and evidence learning in the other curricular areas. The interrelationships among curricular areas present strong support for deliberately integrating curricula.

Core Curriculum

The core curricular subjects carry the most weight in decisions about academic progress of students. You will recall that the core curriculum includes the foundation subjects of reading, writ-

FIGURE 11.3   Academic Curricular Interrelationships

	CORE CURRICULUM			COLLATERAL CURRICULUM		SUPPORT CURRICULUM			
	READ	WREX	MATH	SOC STU	SCIENCE	SOCIAL	SPELL	HDWR	STUDY
Core Curriculum									
Reading	—	R/L	L	L	L	L/P	R/L	L	R/L
Written Expression	R/P	—	P	P	P	L/P	P	P	L/P
Basic Mathematics	R	P	—	R	L/P	L/P		P	L
Collateral Curriculum									
Science	R	R	R/L	R		L/P			
Social Studies	R	R	R	—	R	R/L/P			
Support Curriculum									
Social Skills	L/P	L/P	L/P	R/L/P	L/P	—	L/P	L/P	L/P
Spelling	R/L	R/L/P		P	P	L/P	—	P	P
Handwriting	P	R/P	P	P	P	L/P	P	—	P
Study Strategies	R/L	L	L	L	L	L	L	L	—

L = Learning Tool
P = Performance Tool
R = Related Area

ten expression, and mathematics. These areas are not only vital to the academic progress of students at the elementary levels but also entail critical survival and consumer skills throughout the life of the students. The first of these, reading, assumes major importance from the very beginning of formal instruction.

Children expect to learn to read when they enter school because they have been told that they will. At the primary-grade levels, reading, encompassing both word recognition (Chapter 5) and comprehension (Chapter 6), plays a central role in a student's academic life. Teachers, parents, and peers tend to judge students' general academic success by their reading accomplishments. As students reach third- and fourth-grade level materials, they are expected to read well enough to learn some content independently. This means reading without assistance to improve their reading skills, to discover concepts, and to understand directions for performing tasks in all subject areas. The demands for independent reading and learning increase with each grade level. Thus, a reading problem significantly compounds students' difficulties at each successive level, both in reading and in other subject areas. Both learning and performance of all the language arts, particularly written expression, are interrelated with reading achievement. Whenever a student experiences difficulty in any subject, other than handwriting or arithmetic computation, the student's reading skills should be verified to determine if the problem is subject-specific or a reading problem. Sometimes correction in reading must occur concurrently with, or even before, correction in other basic subjects.

Written expression (Chapter 7) or "language" as it is known in many elementary curricula, is the second of the core subjects. Closely interrelated with all the language arts, instruction and evaluation of written expression performance occur in every subject area. Thus, it is an integral part of the academic curriculum from the first day of school. At the primary-grade levels, the development of ideas and their expansion and discussion lay the foundation for future writing. In the early

grades, students must not be constrained by the "rules" of good writing. Creative and spontaneous oral and written expression should be encouraged and positively reinforced. Direct instruction in the subskills of written expression must be introduced gradually. For students with learning problems, progress will be slow; but with good instruction it will be developmentally in step with the typical sequence of skill acquisition. Word processing computer and typewriter programs especially designed for the young writer should be introduced to students as soon as possible in their school career as alternative vehicles for written expression. These programs free students to express their ideas, since they enable the important "proofwriting" task to be accomplished later with ease. As the upper grade levels are approached, increased demands are made on students for communication of ideas and knowledge through writing. Often the evaluation of students' learning is based on their written products; students who have not learned to communicate their knowledge in writing may be penalized. Many people judge the intelligence of others by what and how they write. Educators, then, must ensure that the early school curriculum is both flexible and integrated in order that positive and exciting groundwork can be laid for the skill building necessary for effective written communication, a skill vital for success both in school and in everyday living.

Like reading and written expression, basic computational skills (Chapter 9) are viewed as early indices of academic success. Computation is not only an important discipline but more importantly a tool needed for problem solving. In recent years, problem solving has come to the forefront of elementary curricula, with emphasis on the application and thinking skills appearing at earlier levels. These problem solving skills are necessary not only for academic achievement but also for successful functioning in later life. Because of the typical school presentation of problems as "math reading problems," reading proficiency is prerequisite for progress in this area. If a student exhibits difficulty, reading skills should be verified. If reading skills are intact, then the student may not have mastered a systematic strategy for solving problems. At the upper elementary levels, difficulties in problem solving may interfere with progress in science and, to a lesser degree, in social studies.

Collateral Curriculum

The collateral curriculum is designed to expand students' knowledge and understanding from the basic or core subjects into the content fields. When compared to the core subjects, science and social studies (Chapter 10) are not prerequisite; instead these content areas rest upon the skills gained in the core curriculum. Beginning in the middle grades, however, priorities start to shift, elevating the importance of the collateral subjects. When considered in terms of significance to student progress from grade to grade, these subjects assume an added dimension, and documented mastery is usually required. Reading and study strategies are particularly important to progress in content subjects. The student who is proficient in all the core subjects can master the content areas if concepts and specific skills are clearly presented. The inclusion of science and social studies in the curriculum is important yet clearly not as vital as that of reading, written expression, and mathematics.

Support Curriculum

The support curriculum, social skills, spelling, handwriting, and study strategies, enables students to perform the tasks required by the core and collateral curricula. Failure in these areas does not usually mean automatic grade retention. However, difficulties here often manifest themselves as problems in other subjects.

Although not a traditional academic area, social skills (Chapter 4) are vital to successful academic functioning and also assist students in learning to get along with themselves and others. Appropriate social skills support and facilitate performance in all academic areas. Conversely, inadequate social functioning is apt to impede academic progress as well as alienate peers and

teachers alike. And, as so clearly explicated by Robert Fulghum's "Credo" in *All I Ever Need to Know I Learned in Kindergarten* (1988, pp. 5–8), the value of the social skills learned at school extends far beyond the walls of the classroom.

Mastery of spelling and handwriting (Chapter 8) enables students to improve performance in other curricular areas. Poor spellers usually demonstrate misspellings in all written work and generally receive lower grades than good spellers. Students with spelling difficulties may lose considerable time attempting to locate unknown words in the dictionary. These students may also limit their expression of ideas in writing to only those words they know how to spell. In addition, society tends to view poor spellers as uneducated, lower class citizens. Therefore, teaching students to be proficient spellers provides them with important school and life skills.

The impact of handwriting on students' written assignments cannot be overlooked. Considerable time is lost by teachers in attempting to grade papers of students whose writing is illegible. Teachers tend to award higher grades to assignments that are clearly and legibly written, even though the content may be lacking. In some instances, a student's rate, or fluency, of writing may be so slow and laborious that he or she seldom completes daily written assignments. Unfinished papers in any subject usually mean lowered or even failing grades, depending on the extent of incompleteness. In extreme cases, students should be taught to use the typewriter or computer as a substitute for handwriting. This becomes a consideration when direct instruction and corrective strategies have not been successful. Mastery of both spelling and handwriting skills support students' performance in all subject areas.

Study strategies apply to nearly all the core and collateral curricular components. However, because study strategies are not designated as true curricular subjects with a direct grade assigned, these vital learning skills occupy a peculiar and tenuous position: Mastery is widely acknowledged as important to academic success, yet neither skill nor content teachers claim ownership for instruction. To be effective, instruction in study strategies must be systematically integrated with instruction in each subject area on a daily basis. Proficiency in using technology is a particularly critical study skill area. By necessity teachers should attend to assessment and programming in this area, even in the early grades. A record of poor achievement in any subject may be caused by inadequate application of the strategies for accomplishing component tasks; poor performance in two or more subjects may result from an overall lack of basic study strategies. Like social skills, spelling, and handwriting, study strategies enable students to improve skills and performances in all curricular areas.

Enrichment Curriculum

When compared to the core curriculum, the enrichment curriculum is substantially less vital to general academic performance. However, for many students with special needs, the enrichment subjects serve as the bright spot of the school day, when they can perform at or above the level of their age peers. Perhaps the most important function of the creative arts and physical education is the expansion and enhancement of students' present and future lives.

If you find the more practical side of your nature asking probing questions about where and how to begin, read on.

ORGANIZING FOR ASSESSMENT AND PROGRAMMING

> *Where do you begin?*
>
> With organization.

In assessment and programming, as in any worthwhile endeavor, organization can not only increase your effectiveness, but also help to maintain your sanity! Assuming you have the resolve to implement the CBA/P process, acquiring and organizing needed tools and organizing the

setting and yourself are the next steps. Selected materials, supplies, and equipment will simplify your professional life.

Materials

> *What materials are needed to implement CBA/P?*
>
> Curricula and textbooks for sure.

Certain materials are vital to the success of the CBA/P process. These include the curriculum chart, the textbooks for appropriate levels, the teacher's edition of the texts, and the workbooks. Among the materials that will enhance your assessment and programming capabilities are discarded books and computer programs.

1. The Curriculum Chart. The most important material in the assessment/programming process is the written curriculum. Locate a curriculum chart, guide, or skills listing for your school system. Get your very own copy of this document. (If you are unable to identify such a document, refer to Chapter 2 for suggestions. Consider chairing a school or system committee to develop a chart or listing.)

2. Textbooks. Because textbooks play such a central role in the delivery of most curricula, you need copies of the texts at the target level and copies of those one to two levels above and below. If you cannot secure copies of your own, locate the textbooks (try the storerooms, other teachers, central depository), and arrange to borrow or at least gain access to them.

3. Teacher's Edition of Textbooks. The edition of the texts designed for teachers contains vital information, such as instructional objectives, teaching suggestions, answer keys, and sometimes actual tests. You may have to borrow some of these on an overnight basis, because spare copies are seldom kept in schools.

4. Workbooks. Many written assignments required of students come from workbooks,

particularly in reading and math. Inquire about their use in each subject, and then locate copies. Schools often keep a few extra copies of workbooks for transfer students. Beg or borrow a copy of each workbook as needed. Workbooks are excellent sources of both assessment stimuli and programming content.

5. Discarded Texts. Although not essential, discarded textbooks, teacher's editions, workbooks, learning labs, and the like are often invaluable. You can modify these to fit your purpose. For assessment, representative tasks can be located and then marked, cut and pasted, reorganized, or consumed by students. For use in programming, similar modifications are possible. For the target level and for two levels above and below, locate discarded materials. These materials may also be used to form the nucleus of parallel programming.

6. Computer Software. Three types of software facilitate the assessment/programming process: diagnostic programs, instructional programs, and management systems. Management systems simplify recording and monitoring results and progress and may also include templates for communicating progress. Publishers of some basal series offer software packages correlated with their textbooks. Some instructional programs also include assessment components that either branch to different tasks and levels according to student performance or present summative evaluation tasks or both; many programs tabulate correct responses. Authoring programs offer opportunities to customize tests and educational activities. Check with supervisors to identify the programs available in your system. Inquire about licensing agreements for particular programs and also about the accessibility of educational software that is in the public domain. Consult computer networks or your local computer dealer for information about opportunities to share programs. Particularly for maintenance purposes, com-

puter activities offer a nice change of format or pace.

Supplies

What kind of supplies are needed?

School and office supplies.

Standard school and office supplies are useful for modifying instructional materials to fit assessment and programming purposes. The brief listings that follow include a few of the more obvious supplies. You will probably modify the lists themselves as you implement the CBA/P process.

For Consumable Materials

Consumable materials can easily be adapted to conform to various assessment or programming purposes and individual student needs. Many materials can be modified using a few standard supplies such as these.

— Blue pen: For recording on the curriculum chart a student's skills as they are mastered.
— Felt tip markers: To section off parts of activity sheets, cross out unnecessary items, and design original activities.
— Highlighter pens: To emphasize target tasks.
— Scissors: To remove parts of activity sheets or cut out portions of exercises or activities for mounting elsewhere.
— Glue, tape: For mounting or compiling activity parts to develop new tasks and activities.
— Stapler: To combine pieces into a whole activity and pages into booklets.
— Index cards: To use as place keepers, list special instructions, and to develop as flashcards, word-bank cards, and the like.
— File folders: To organize tasks, completed work, and record sheets for each student's portfolio.

To maximize utility, collect and organize the supplies in a compartmentalized box, drawer organizer, or similar caddy so that they are easily transported from site to site.

For Nonconsumable Materials

Unlike consumable worksheets and discarded texts, certain materials such as current textbooks, borrowed materials, non-replaceable materials, and the like, must not be defaced because of financial, ethical, and practical considerations. However, the manner in which the materials are presented can be adapted to modify them for assessment and programming purposes and meet individual student needs. Among the basic supplies for adapting nonconsumable materials are these.

— Acetate overlays: To place over pages for student to mark responses.
— Transparency or grease pens: To mark on overlays so that materials are reusable.
— Answer sheets: To use as an alternative to acetate overlays for student responses.
— Removable sticky notes: To temporarily mark or annotate materials.
— Pencils with erasers: To make necessary marks on activities, and then erase them later, and for students to use with answer sheets.
— Index cards: To use as place keepers, shield off unnecessary tasks, list special instructions, and to develop as flashcards, word-bank cards, and the like.
— File folders: To organize completed acetate overlays, special instructions, and record sheets for each student's portfolio.

Modifying instructional materials requires careful editing of existing materials. By redesigning and restructuring the materials on hand, you can develop ones that fit the personal assessment and programming needs of specific students.

Equipment

What about equipment?

It depends upon the setting.

Like materials, equipment can also simplify your task. If you are a traveling diagnostician, then you will probably want only minimal equipment. However, diagnostic-prescriptive teachers, whether they are itinerant or stationary, need some basic equipment. One special piece of equipment that most educators already have is a stop watch or watch with a second hand for assessing and building fluency in the most basic skills. The need for other equipment depends on the particular setting. Rather than attempting, here, to furnish a model classroom, we suggest a few traits that expedite the acquisition of equipment.

— Resourcefulness: Be resourceful and constantly alert to possible acquisitions.
— Practicality: Retrieve the unused audiovisual devices from the storeroom or library.
— Assertiveness: Speak out for the new equipment as it arrives at your school; dare to ask for the new computer or software.
— Imagination: Recognize potential file boxes at the grocery store (file containers are essential to organizing your CBA/P materials and the cartons and display boxes that the grocer will discard are free and readily available).
— Heroism: Rescue the neighbor's TV or refrigerator carton before the garbage collectors arrive.
— Frugality: Canvas garage and yard sales for equipment bargains.
— Creativity: Construct extra bookcases from crates or bricks and boards.
— Philanthropy: Ask students to donate old headphones from discarded stereos and radios.

As illustrated by these few examples, acquiring equipment is a matter of outlook: identify what you must have and what you would like to have, and then remain alert to the potential options for acquiring it.

The Setting

What kind of setting is best?

A carefully structured one.

The organization of the instructional setting is a major determinant of the quality of assessment and programming activities that can occur. A setting that is carefully structured to facilitate interaction and minimize distractions encourages on-task and productive behaviors. Students need an orderly environment in which everything and everybody has a designated place and defined roles. Among the factors that enhance the overall organization of the setting are advantageous placement of materials, supplies, and equipment, as noted in previous sections, and the arrangement of areas for specific purposes, establishment of routines, and the grouping practices itemized in later sections.

Self

What else needs to be organized?

YOU do!

The organization of any process is directly related to the organization of the person in charge. Certainly, a major contributor to the organization of the director (the diagnostician and/or teacher) is the availability of necessary materials and equipment. However, among the other factors that contribute to overall organization are routines, time management, and the feelings of self-organization. To increase the feelings and the reality of self-organization, try these suggestions:

- Make lists. Before implementing the CBA/P cycle with an individual student, make a list of what you need to do and the sequence in which you plan to do it. Then, as each task is completed, check it off to signal completion and also to reward yourself. Although the forms presented in the preceding chapters (e.g., Figures 3.16, 3.17, 4.10) can be used for this purpose, your list may be as informal as numbered tasks on a scratch sheet of paper. Lists make tasks seem more manageable and impart a sense of being in control of the tasks not controlled by them. The key is the security in the routine of planning, knowing that you have done so, and having a script to follow and the sense of accomplishment afforded by checking off the tasks as completed.

- Catalog materials. Develop a listing of available materials that may be appropriate for students with special needs and note their locations. If the holdings of the media or resource center, book depository, or school library are on computer, highlight a hard copy and ask for a printout of only the ones you marked.

- Develop forms. Fill-in-the-blank forms not only save time and effort but they also help organize thoughts to ensure that the vital elements are included. Develop such forms for requesting information for the teacher survey, analyzing and recording student performance, communicating progress, and the like; then make several copies of each form.

- Build a comfortable nest. If you are operating in a single location, arrange a particular spot for the convenience of you and your student(s). Organize materials, supplies, and equipment to facilitate assessment and programming. Make provisions for privacy and limit distractions. If you must travel to several locations, organize a central "nest" or office in which to do your paperwork and also make specific arrangements for organized work space in those locations.

- Organize paperwork in a loose-leaf notebook. Place all forms, checklists, record forms, curricular listings, and the like in a loose-leaf notebook. Use subject dividers to label the papers and also develop an index of the contents.

— Organize key materials in a file. Use a file cabinet if you work out of a single site and a portable file box if you travel among sites. Storage cabinets at a central location are also useful for organizing and storing bulky and extra materials or ones that are used only occasionally.

— Organize key supplies in a caddy. Supplies that you use regularly to modify tasks and record results should be organized together and should be easily transportable. Place a few of each item in the caddy and store the remainder at a central location.

— Establish routines. In addition to regularly making and using lists, establishing and then following other routines structures the CBA/P process and also facilitates student performance. Routinize each step of the cycle according to your unique situation. Habitually organize all materials and supplies and use a planning checklist before each session and summarize and record results immediately following each session.

— Develop and maintain a current wish list. List everything you ever wanted along with descriptions, uses, all purchasing information, and prices. If you use a word processor, categorize items according to price ranges. Update your list regularly and keep it handy at all times. Then, when administrators suddenly find themselves with money that must be spent by a certain date or the parent organization indicates the desire to fund worthy projects, you are ready. It is the person whose wish list is complete who often gets the goodies.

— Know your individual organization style—its strengths and weaknesses—and then adapt management strategies accordingly. For help analyzing your style, consider consulting resources such as *How to Be Organized in Spite of Yourself* (Schlenger & Roesch, 1990).

One of the most valuable tips for acquiring resources, enhancing your feelings of organization, and expanding your expertise is to network with colleagues.

COLLABORATION FOR ASSESSMENT *AND* PROGRAMMING

> *Who has the expertise to stay on top of all this?*
>
> You do. . . . if you network.

Networking with interested colleagues is efficient as well as essential for sharing resources and expanding expertise. With the constant expansion of telecommunication capabilities, networking on a local or even global basis is relatively quick and easy. Whether you collaborate with one colleague in your school, three in your district, or 11 nationwide, the collective problem-solving process and resultant exchange of information and resources can greatly enhance knowledge and skills and expand the resources for all participants. Regardless of scope or the particular collaborative approach selected, the steps for implementing the collaborative process are essentially the same:

— Identify colleagues involved in the assessment/programming process who are also interested in improving the process.
— Identify and share success and problem areas as well as resources.
— Establish a collaborative plan that capitalizes on each participant's expertise.
— Analyze the most significant mutual problems, and prioritize them.
— Discuss and analyze potential interventions, and then select appropriate ones.
— Develop and implement an action plan.

Evaluation criteria should be jointly established and then applied in judging the success of each procedure. The final step in the collaborative process is planning and then implementing any needed modifications.

SPECIAL PROBLEMS—PARTIAL SOLUTIONS

> *What about those perpetual problems that educators encounter daily?*
>
> Intervene before they occur.

Inherent in almost any worthwhile interactive endeavor are a number of recurring problems, particularly troublesome for the person in charge. There never seems to be enough time or energy to accomplish the goals; keeping up and monitoring the activities and progress are problematic; constant attention to necessary elements can be difficult; gaining the cooperation of all involved persons is not an easy task; and maintaining enthusiasm throughout the bad and good times is a constant battle. Because of the extraneous demands that are placed on educators and the nature and needs of students involved, the CBA/P process is subject to all these problems and more. However, certain procedures can be used with those presented in earlier sections to minimize some of these problems before they abort the process. As the title of this section implies, the suggestions are not intended as a panacea for solving all the problems that emerge, but rather as a precaution for lessening the load.

Time and Energy

> *Who has the time and energy to do all this?*
>
> You do . . . with a little help.

Collaboration conserves some time and energy, but by also *stretching* your time you expand opportunities for assessment and programming activities and possibly create spare time as well. There are three basic methods of stretching your time, and each conserves your energy as well: you can save time, control time, or make time. Although the three methods sometimes overlap, here they are considered separately.

Method 1: Save Time

- Identify major time consumers (e.g., paperwork, creating or modifying assessment tasks and instructional activities, giving instructions, and the like), target the essential tasks for streamlining, and get rid of the ones that you can.
- Conduct a time and motion study to identify the most efficient placement of materials, supplies, and equipment, and then place them accordingly.
- Develop templates for recurring paperwork, leaving blanks to personalize each form; use carbon paper or the computer for written activities.
- Color code materials and supplies for quick identification and sorting; use colored dots to code programs in progress to quickly identify the current status of a particular student and to cue you for the next action needed.
- Collaborate to identify and implement additional time-saving procedures.

Method 2: Control Time

- Organize yourself.
- Set goals for yourself and your students; record the goals and display them.
- Make "to do" lists for you and your students and prioritize the tasks by numbering them; then use the lists as checklists of accomplishments and to set schedules.
- Schedule each week in advance using the "to do" lists; identify tasks as easy, average, or difficult and plan to attempt the difficult tasks during prime time, the easy ones during "down" time, and the average tasks in between.
- Compete with yourself to beat self-imposed deadlines.
- Collaborate to identify and implement additional strategies to control time.

Method 3: Make Time

- Collaborate to develop and institute procedures for making time.
- Make full use of resource and support personnel. Use paraprofessionals, student teachers, and volunteers to free you from

secretarial tasks (e.g., duplicating materials, recording progress, or modifying materials according to your instructions) and numerous chores that divert your attention from the assessment/programming process.

— Train student helpers. When appropriate, coach students to organize their materials and work, check and evaluate their performance, and chart their progress.

— Establish routines. Develop efficient routines to accomplish recurring assessment and programming tasks; to eliminate the need for repeated instructions to students, label the areas where materials and supplies should be stored, post rules, and display instructions for regular routines.

— Double up. Small group assessment and/ or programming, when appropriate, makes time. Some tasks, particularly those requiring written responses, can be presented to several students at once. Subskills in the mechanics of written expression, for example, may be assessed in this way. During the same ten minutes, each of five students can write the answers to different levels of computation exercises. Personalized maintenance activities can be differentiated according to student need but accomplished by each of several students at the same time.

Keep a weekly list of brief assessment and programming tasks you wish to accomplish with specific students. Then steal or make time for them. Every classroom has momentary lulls while awaiting the bell. With list in hand, use those three to five minutes to check a student's task mastery or provide a brief maintenance activity.

A variety of helpful suggestions for efficiently managing time are presented in *Time Management for Teachers* (Collins, 1987).

When you stretch your time, acquire essential materials, organize the setting and yourself, and network with colleagues, you save considerable energy and expand your capabilities as well. In addition to the assistance gained through collaboration, you conserve even more time and energy by soliciting help from others and accumulating and organizing your materials. First, recruit friends, family, older students, or parents to assist you.

Next, if you have not already done so, organize the materials on hand into file folders and onto bookshelves. Then coerce your recruits into helping you accomplish the following:

— Begin to develop a test file; add to it as each school year progresses. Swap files with your colleagues.

— Develop meaningful instructional activities that can be accomplished by students independently; make them self-checking where possible. Exchange these with colleagues.

— Set aside an afternoon for a sharing party for colleagues to swap and copy materials. Organize materials immediately.

— As you develop activities, code them according to objectives or skill numbers on the curriculum.

— Cross-reference textbooks with the curriculum and your other materials.

— Compile a "Master List of Materials" coded by curricular skills.

— Make your materials reusable when possible. Unless it is necessary to preserve the instructional value of an activity, do not consume or allow students to consume the materials.

— Make maximum use of technology. Create a bank of alternative assessment and programming strategies. Insofar as possible and practical, utilize the computer for tasks that can be readily modified to meet emerging needs of students. Saved documents may be modified to meet the needs of future students, yet another instance of time and energy conservation.

Tracking System

Who keeps up with all this?

Until you train your help, you do.

You obviously need written checklists of where each student has been, where each is now, and where he or she needs to go. You will have to decide on the record-keeping system that best suits your needs. You may prefer to develop group charts for specific subjects, listing the specific skills in columns beside the students' names. Whether you decide on individual curriculum charts, skills listings, or a different format, once initiated, again collaborate and recruit volunteers to record progress. If you train and then supervise the students themselves, they will often be reinforced by recording their progress. At the beginning or end of each week, review the records to confirm that they are current and to rearrange priorities if necessary.

If a system for tracking the specific skill mastery of students is already in force in your school, you are among the fortunate few. Some schools use computers to maintain comprehensive and detailed records of students' achievements. If your school does not presently have a formal tracking system, you may wish to suggest instituting one in which detailed records follow the students throughout their academic years.

The Student Juggle

How do you juggle the other students while attending to the needs of only one?

You carefully orchestrate the
environmental elements.

By carefully arranging the physical setting, the types of instructional activities, and the students themselves, it is possible to attend to the special needs of several students at the same time.

Instructional Environment

The environment in which CBA/P occurs sets the tone for all the activities. Since the importance of and suggestions for structuring the instructional environment have been incorporated into discussions throughout this book, only a few brief descriptors of desirable environments are offered here as reminders.

- Safe: The environment is structurally and psychologically safe and feels safe to students.
- Free: The climate is one of acceptance in which students feel free to risk difficult tasks and free to fail occasionally.
- Enticing: The setting is interesting and appealing and attracts students to it and to the learning process as well.
- Goal-directed: Goals are formulated, displayed, and clearly evident in the organization and in all activities.
- Rewarding: Students succeed at some tasks everyday and are reinforced for doing so.
- Orderly: School and classroom rules are established and enforced; all activities are conducted in an orderly manner.
- Routinized: All activities are conducted in an orderly manner; classroom rules and specific routines are established and followed for housekeeping chores (e.g., storing materials), traffic patterns (e.g., how to get to the pencil sharpener), noninstructional tasks (e.g., getting a drink of water), beginning each task, ending each task, and the like.
- Nondistracting: Distractions are controlled either by elimination (e.g., enforcement of classroom rules and routines) or by compensation (e.g., carrels to screen off visual distractions, white noise to screen out extraneous noises, or seating arrangements to avoid distractions).
- Organized: The physical setting, including materials, supplies, and equipment, is conveniently arranged to facilitate performance; the person in charge appears (and is in fact) organized and confident; students are guided to organize their materials and routines.

Admittedly, the perfect environment seldom exists in the real world of schools. In fact, few settings approach perfection. If you must assess and program in a crowded or noisy room, on the stage in the auditorium, or in the lunchroom during cleanup, you will have to exercise considerable ingenuity to overcome these barriers. However, almost any instructional environment can be at least improved particularly by grouping practices and the arrangement of the setting.

Room Arrangement

Room dividers are essential to arranging the physical setting so as to maximize the classroom teacher's opportunities for personalizing assessment and programming. Low bookshelves, file cabinets, teaching boards, and study carrels partition off areas of the classroom. A rug may be used to define an area. A similar effect is achieved by facing the students' chairs in different directions. Why do you want room dividers? These help to minimize distractions and facilitate grouping and learning at special centers, the vital components of personalized classrooms.

Learning Centers

In addition to the area for large group instruction, classrooms need areas for small group instruction. These smaller teaching stations are the site of personalized assessment and programming. Learning centers are important structures for individual and small-group learning. The parameters of the centers are defined by the room dividers. If space and/or equipment are scarce, a shelf, student desk, or window ledge may be designated as a learning center. Learning centers designed for three purposes are suggested: (1) listening activities, (2) specific skills instruction, and (3) reward activities.

1. *Listening Centers.* Although little assessment will occur here, except for audiotutorial assessment, listening comprehension, or auditory readiness tasks, if you provide self-directed skill activities that meet the assessed needs of a few students, you will also be freed to attend to the needs of other students. The instruc-

tional activities of a listening center can be varied according to individual needs by having each student use a headset to listen to a different tape or by having several students listen to the same tape.

2. *Skill Centers.* These are subject centers that emphasize the content of a specific subject. Skill centers are appropriate sites for individual or small-group assessment and programming, using the materials placed at the center for the specific subject. Like the instructional strategies presented in Chapters 5 through 10, three stages of instruction are possible in each center.

   — Developmental instruction, or direct instruction, where the teacher, assistant, and/ or achieving peer provide individual or small-group instruction.
   — Corrective instruction that, like developmental teaching, offers direct instruction but perhaps at a slower pace and using parallel or modified materials.
   — Maintenance instruction presenting supervised and meaningful independent practice that is self-directed and self-checking.

   Two levels of assessment are also possible at these centers: initial and ongoing assessment.

3. *Reward Centers.* As the name implies, these are intended for rewarding students for skill attainment and appropriate behavior. For students who are particularly reinforced and interested in the content of the listening or skill centers, activities at those centers may be used as a reward. For other students, however, a separate center that presents different activities of interest may be required. A computer center can be established as a skill center or a reward center or both. The specific interests of the students will establish the nature of the activities that are appropriate for reward centers.

Certain management procedures can enhance the utility of learning centers. Suggestions include: place centers conveniently to facilitate traffic flow and minimize distractions; construct centers so they appeal to and attract students; establish a system for determining who goes to which center and when; establish rules for center use and maintenance; provide differentiated tasks and activities at each center to accommodate various levels of performance and interests; frequently change at least a few components at each center to ensure continued appeal; develop a system to monitor student progress; and place materials at each center that can be used for assessment as well as programming.

Grouping Students

Careful arrangement and organization of the instructional materials at the learning centers facilitate the grouping of students for assessment and programming. The juggling of students is accomplished by organizing them into groups according to their specific or common academic needs. This maximizes teacher contact and effectiveness. Instructional groups may be formed according to skill needs, activity levels, or common interests. Membership in such groups should be considered temporary; students should transfer to other groups as they progress or their needs change. There are two basic types of instructional groups: homogeneous and heterogeneous.

Homogeneous Groups. Most small-group instruction focuses on homogeneous groupings. Several students with similar skill needs are taught at the same time. Assume three students are having difficulty finding the main idea of reading passages; the teacher may present focused and corrective instruction to this group in the reading center while other students are involved in maintenance activities at the various learning centers. At the same time that such programming is occurring, assessment of task mastery of these three students is conducted to determine whether each one requires additional corrective instruction or maintenance activities. Specific students sometimes require individual instruction that focuses on a particular task. However, so as to conserve teacher-contact time, that student should be channeled into a small group as soon as he or she is able to benefit from such instruction. With homogeneous grouping,

the teacher is able to teach precisely what specific students need in order to progress. This means that students are less likely to be held back or passed over by lock-step instruction.

Heterogeneous Groups. Heterogeneous grouping of students with different achievement levels is appropriate for several purposes. Five students who share a special interest in rocks, for example, may be grouped together for a learning project at the science center. For interactive learning, reciprocal teaching groups of three to seven students may be formed. From materials of different levels of difficulty, but parallel concepts, instruction can be provided a group of several students. Using the format of a spiral curriculum, it is possible to instruct a group of students in the common concepts of materials of different categories.

For instructional groupings and learning centers to function efficiently, specific guidelines for deciding who does what, when, and where must be established. Often, as the teacher works with one group of students, members of other groups have questions or need assistance. A system for attracting teacher attention without disruption is helpful. For example, needy students may display a number or sign. By keeping the students in view and moving around among them, the teacher can orchestrate the learning activities. Classroom rules must be developed, preferably with student participation, and consistently enforced if distracting behaviors are to be avoided. As mentioned throughout this text, contingency contracts are particularly effective for managing behavior, directing goals, and generating student cooperation.

Student Cooperation

How do you convince students to cooperate?

Collaborate with them to make decisions

Anyone who has ever dealt with a resistant student understands the importance of student attitude in the educational process. Students who are cooperative and enthusiastic are likely to perform better on any task than those who are reluctant to participate. A few suggestions for encouraging students to cooperate are these:

- Collaborate with students to make decisions about both assessment and programming.
- Establish with each student appropriate weekly and daily goals.
- Develop contingency contracts with the student.
- Evaluate with the student all permanent products.
- Have the student check off tasks as they are accomplished.
- Discuss the student's progress with him or her on a regular basis.
- Make tasks short, varied, and manageable.
- Be sure that students succeed on at least some portion of each task.
- Reward appropriate behaviors.
- Guide the student to chart progress and, depending upon the circumstances, either display the chart on a bulletin board or inside the front cover of the student's work folder; regularly discuss progress with the student.
- Maximize active student engagement and overall involvement.
- Ask for student suggestions for improving assessment and programming procedures, use the ideas that are practical, and explain your reasons for not using any suggestions.

Remember, students who learn and then utilize study strategies are equipped to perform more tasks independently, which in turn is likely to increase cooperation and enthusiasm as well.

Teacher Enthusiasm

How do you maintain your enthusiasm and productivity?

You pamper yourself.

Your own enthusiasm is *crucial* to the success of the assessment and programming process. The suggestions in earlier sections, particularly those for organization, also contribute to drive and zeal. A few specific recommendations for generating and maintaining your enthusiasm are these:

- Organize your materials, supplies, equipment, setting, and most importantly, yourself.
- Conserve your time and energy and save yourself for those tasks that only you can do.
- Utilize resources to the fullest extent, using technology and delegating tasks whenever practical and appropriate.
- Arrange the instructional environment such that success is inevitable.
- Encourage student cooperation by actively involving students in the process and rewarding their efforts.
- Set weekly goals and daily objectives for yourself and check them off as they are accomplished.
- Order your tasks so that each day you attempt a few easy ones first, then the difficult ones, and finally the others.
- Each day adhere to your schedule but include at least three special times to relax (i.e., three "sanity seizers").
- Count your accomplishments each day and bask in the glow of your achievement.
- Inventory your accomplishments at the end of each month and savor your victories.
- Attend and participate in a state or national professional conference at least once a year.
- At least once a month, consult a resource that will broaden your knowledge base and enhance your personal and professional growth. For example, consider reading publications outside or peripheral to your specialty field, such as *Compact Classics* (Anderson, 1993), *Reaching Out* (Johnson, 1993), or *Lions Don't Need to Roar* (Benton, 1992).
- Identify at least one colleague who is a kindred spirit with whom to communicate on a regular basis and share materials, ideas for improvement, and individual successes and failures.
- Join a discussion group to exchange ideas regularly via a local, national, or global telecommunications network (e.g., Internet).

▬ Compile a list of potential self-rewards and regularly select one with which to reward yourself.

As director of the assessment and programming process, remember that your enthusiasm is contagious—expose the students to it and let them catch it.

POSSIBILITIES OF PERSONALIZED ASSESSMENT *AND* PROGRAMMING

> *What are the potential benefits to you and the students?*
>
> Many and varied.

A large percentage of the student population experiences academic difficulty. Curriculum-referenced assessment for instructional planning is a major approach suggested for improving the student success rate (Will, 1986). Although curriculum-based assessment and programming practices have primarily focused on low achievers and students with disabilities, these strategies are also appropriate for use with all students.

A number of possible benefits of curriculum-based assessment and programming have been presented here and elsewhere. Some of these are listed for your review:

1. *Relevance.* Because the curriculum is the hub of the process, students are judged by and taught exactly what they need to learn to succeed in school.
2. *Student Opportunity.* Conditions of assessment and programming are manipulated such that the opportunities for student success are increased.
3. *Efficiency.* This approach makes efficient use of the time of both teachers and students; teachers assess and provide instruction in precisely what each student needs to know.
4. *Continuity.* Day-to-day and year-to-year continuity are incorporated into sequenced curricular assessment and programming.

5. *Destigmatization.* When students are compared with the curriculum on a "skills mastered/skills needed" basis, some stigmatizing labels are avoided.
6. *Nonbiased Assessment and Teaching.* Because students are measured by the curriculum, bias is reduced in both testing and teaching.
7. *Continual Adjustment.* Student performance is regularly monitored and instruction then adjusted according to student needs.
8. *Accountability.* When student progress is continuously tracked, teachers, students, and parents know what each student did not, did, and probably will accomplish at any given time.
9. *Teacher Satisfaction.* Teacher satisfaction tends to increase with the knowledge that student needs are being met and as student performances improve.
10. *Test Utility.* Increasing the instructional relevance of assessment enhances its utility as a testing tool. In addition to measuring student progress, curricular assessment has been suggested for use in screening, referral, IEP planning, and program evaluation decisions. Curriculum-based measures have also been standardized and used as an integral component of the evaluation procedures for identifying students who are eligible for special education services (Germann & Tindal, 1985; Shinn, 1989b).

As noted in Chapter 1, curriculum-based assessment/programming can be both valid and reliable, and of paramount importance, it complies with IDEA. In addition, as indicated in previous discussions of trends toward authentic curricula and performance assessment, the model offers the flexibility to readily accommodate change.

Further discussions of the benefits, theory, and practice of curriculum-based assessment are presented in a special issue of *Exceptional Children* (Tucker, 1985) and in publications by King-Sears (1994), Salvia and Hughes (1990), Shinn (1989c), Shapiro and Derr (1990), and Tindal and Marston

(1990). Howell, Fox, and Morehead (1993) also include instructional interventions in their book.

Lest the list of possible benefits sound like an advertisement for yet another diet plan or wonder drug, reconsider the limitations addressed as specific concerns earlier in this chapter. This is a comprehensive approach that requires informed decisions as well as organizational and collabora- tive skills, time and effort, record keeping, and careful arrangement of the instructional setting. The end product is fitting the curriculum to the students, not the students to the curriculum. Personalizing assessment *and* programming offers not only exciting possibilities for improving student success but also opportunities for successful teaching.

Word Recognition

Word Recognition Skill Objective

I. Sight Vocabulary

  A. Basic Vocabulary - The student:

    .1   Points to his or her name in a list of names.

    .2   Orally reads each word from a list of primary color words.

    .3   Orally reads each word from a list of number words, 0–10.

    .4–.9   Orally reads each word from a list of basic sight words appropriate to his or her level.

  B. High Frequency Vocabulary - The student:

    .1–.2   Orally states the name of each letter when given a visual stimulus of upper and/or lower case letters.

    .3   Orally reads each word from a list of common nouns.

    .4–.6   Orally reads each word from a list of high frequency words appropriate to his or her level.

  C. Visual Discrimination - The student:

    .1   Matches like shapes when given pictures of basic shapes.

    .2   Matches like letters from a visual stimulus of random letters.

    .3   Matches like words from a visual stimulus of random words.

II. Phonetic Analysis

  A. Single Consonants - The student:

    .1   States whether initial consonants are the same or different in each pair of teacher-dictated words.

    .2   States whether final consonants are the same or different in each pair of teacher-dictated words.

    .3   Pronounces the single sound, or names another word beginning with the same sound when given a list of words beginning with single consonants.

    .4   Pronounces the single sound or names another word ending with the same sound when given a list of words ending with single consonants.

    .5   Pronounces the single sound or names another word with the same sound in medial position when given a list of words containing single consonants in medial position.

  B. Consonant Blends - The student:

    .1   Pronounces each word and the target blend from a list of words beginning with two-letter blends.

    .2   Pronounces each word and the target blend from a list of words ending in nd, nt, and st.

    .3   Pronounces each word and the target blend from a list of words containing three-letter blends.

    .4   Pronounces each word and the target blend from a list of words containing medial blends.

  C. Consonant Digraphs - The student:

    .1   Pronounces each word and the target digraph from a list of words containing ch, ph, sh, th, wh.

    .2   Pronounces each word and the target digraph from a list of words ending in ck and ng.

  D. Variant Consonants - The student:

    .1   Pronounces each word and digraph and names the silent letter from a list of words containing kn, wr, gn.

    .2   Pronounces each word and states whether the sound is hard or soft when given a list of words containing the hard and soft sounds of "c" and "g."

    .3   Pronounces each word and names the variant consonant when given a list of words containing the variants s, qu, x, gh.

    .4   Pronounces each word and states the silent letter(s) when given a list of words containing the silent mb, p, s, t.

    .5   Pronounces each word and names the target consonant(s) when given a list of words containing consonants with multiple sounds.

E. **Vowels** - The student:

.1   States whether each pair of teacher dictated words rhymes.

.2   Orally produces the long sound for each vowel presented visually.

.3   Orally produces the short sound for each vowel presented visually.

.4   Pronounces each word when given a list of words containing vowel digraphs at appropriate level.

.5   Pronounces each word when given a list of words in which the vowel sound is controlled by "r."

.6   Pronounces each word when given a list of words in which the vowel sound is controlled by "l."

.7   Pronounces each word when given a list of words containing diphthongs.

.8   Pronounces each word when given a list of words containing variant vowel sounds of "oo."

.9   Pronounces each word when given a list of words containing the "schwa" sound.

F. **Phonic Generalizations** - The student:

.1   Pronounces each word when given a list of words containing the CVC pattern.

.2   Pronounces each word when given a list of words containing the CVCe pattern.

.3   Pronounces each word when given a list of words containing the CV pattern.

III. *Structural Analysis*

A. **Root Words** - The student:

.1–.6 Identifies and pronounces the root of each word when given a list of words at appropriate level.

B. **Suffixes** - The student:

.1   Orally reads each word and states each suffix when given a list of words containing suffixes s, ed, d, t, ing.

.2   Orally reads each word and states each suffix when given a list of words containing suffixes er, est.

.3   Orally reads each word and states each suffix when given a list of words containing suffixes ly, ful.

.4   Orally reads each word and states each suffix when given a list of words in which the final "y" is changed to "i" before adding a suffix.

.5   Orally reads each word and states each suffix when given a list of words containing suffixes less, ness.

.6   Orally reads each word and states each suffix when given a list of words containing suffixes able, ment, ty, th, al, ist, ive, ize, or, ion, tion, age, y.

.7   Orally reads each word and states each suffix when given a list of words containing suffixes ish, ant, ent, ance, ence, ten, eous, our, ious, ation, ible, re.

C. **Prefixes** - The student:

.1   Orally reads each word and states each prefix when given a list of words containing prefixes a, be, un, re.

.2   Orally reads each word and states each prefix when given a list of words containing prefix dis.

.3   Orally reads each word and states each prefix when given a list of words containing prefixes pre, ex, in, mis, sub.

.4   Orally reads each word and states each prefix when given a list of words containing prefixes non, com, con, post, tri, de, trans, bi, inter, per, super, pro.

.5   Orally reads each word and states each prefix when given a list of words containing prefixes on, im, ad, ab, an, tele, contra.

D. **Compound Words** - The student:

.1–.6 Orally reads and states component words from a list of compound words at appropriate level.

E. **Contractions** - The student:

.1   Orally reads each word and states the two words for which each contraction stands when given a list of contractions with one letter omitted.

.2   Orally reads each word and states the two words for which each contraction stands when given a list of contractions with two or more letters omitted.

F. **Syllabication** - The student:

.1   States the number of syllables in each word when given teacher-dictated one- and two-syllable words.

.2   Orally reads and states where each word should be divided into syllables when given a list of words containing two single consonants.

.3   Orally reads and where each word should be divided into syllables when given a list of words containing affixes.

.4   Orally reads and states where each word should be divided into syllables when given a list of words ending in a consonant plus "le."

.5   Orally reads and states where each word should be divided into syllables when given a list of words containing double consonants.

.6   Orally reads and states where each word should be divided into syllables when given a list of words containing blends and digraphs.

.7   Orally reads and states where each word should be divided into syllables when given a list of words that follow the CV pattern.

.8   States which syllable is accented when given a list of teacher-dictated words.

.9   Orally reads and states which syllable(s) should be accented when given a list containing two-syllable words.

.10   Orally reads and states which syllable(s) should be accented when given a list of words containing affixes.

.11   Orally reads and states which syllable(s) should be accented when given a list of words containing syllables that follow the CV pattern.

.12   Orally reads and states which syllable(s) receive primary accent and which receive secondary accent when given a list of words containing two or more accented syllables.

IV. Word Meaning

A. Basic Vocabulary - The student:

.1–.6   Demonstrates understanding or states a word of similar meaning for each basic vocabulary word dictated by the teacher.

B. Classification - The student:

.1   States the category to which each belongs when given a set of pictures.

.2   States the category to which each belongs when given a list of nouns.

.3   States the category to which each belongs when given a list of direction words.

.4–.9   States the category to which each belongs when given list of words at the appropriate level.

C. Pronoun Referents - The student:

.1   Points to or orally reads the pronoun that stands for each noun dictated by the teacher when given a list of the pronouns they, it, she, he.

.2   Points to or orally reads the pronoun that stands for each noun dictated by the teacher when given a list of the pronouns them, we, him, her.

D. Affixes - The student:

.1–.6   Orally reads and tells the meaning of the affix when given a list of words containing affixes at appropriate level.

E. Vocabulary Relationships - The student:

.1   Orally describes each picture using at least five appropriate descriptors when given a series of pictures of home and school.

.2   Orally reads from a word list a synonym for each word dictated by the teacher.

.3   Orally reads from a word list an antonym for each word dictated by the teacher.

.4   Orally reads the sentences and points to the appropriate homonym when given a list of sentences with a word missing and a pair of homonyms.

.5   Reads orally, correctly pronouncing the underlined homographs when given a list of sentences.

.6   Uses each word in oral sentences to demonstrate at least three different meanings when given words with multiple meanings.

.7   Orally reads all possible descriptive combinations from a list of nouns, verbs, adjectives, and adverbs.

.8   Explains the meaning of each abstract term when given a list of sentences containing abstract terms.

.9   States the meaning of each term when given a list of sentences containing colloquial terms.

.10   Explains the meanings of each word when given a list of sentences containing real and contrived neologisms.

.11   States the noneuphemistic equivalents for a list of euphemisms.

.12   States and explains the pejoratives from a list of words.

.13   States the origin or history of each word on a word list.

SAMPLE ITEMS FOR TESTS OF WORD RECOGNITION

Directions: Read to student the instructions for each item. Circle the number of each item administered; mark the unknown items with an X.

SIGHT VOCABULARY

IA.1,	Basic: "Point to your name."	(On a separate page, print five first/last name combinations, including the student's name.)				
IA.2,	Basic: "Point to the word I say."	red yellow	orange brown	green black	blue purple	
IA.3,	Basic: "Point to the word I say."	six four	nine seven	one five	ten eight	three two
IA.4,	Basic: "Read these words aloud."	daddy puppy	cap hide	ball on	mother run	home fish
	(P): "Read these words aloud."	near dish	surprise boy	his at	let man	girl him
	(1): "Read these words aloud."	story fall	truck can't	guess drop	hand gone	fight bus
IA.5,	Basic (2.1): "Read these words aloud."	handle mouth	park sure	sweet wife	minute bottle	bottom live
	(2.2): "Read these words aloud."	bridge foot	easy visit	love yard	someone inside	idea large
IA.6,	Basic (3.1): "Read these words aloud."	church swirl	immediate patient	shadow castle	attention harm	impatient neighbor
	(3.2): "Read these words aloud."	bean dare	football fortune	cousin ought	certain cause	television check
IA.7,	Basic: "Read these words aloud."	scramble merchant hinge wealth	route typewriter grumble seventy	symbol youth grove character	creak regular balance flood	announce president everyone describe
IA.8,	Basic "Read these words aloud."	wharf distinguish prairie resolution	ignore advertise rhythm plastic	fascinating boundary forge navigator	shrewd amazement image mineral	voyage budge frantic bureau
IA.9,	Basic: "Read these words aloud."	devour suspicion crisis offense	specialist tournament exploration investigation	sacrifice representative journal conserve	college quarry amateur riot	discussion microphone reflection appearance
IB.1,	High Frequency: "Say each letter	X H U C N T Y F K A Z M G D I O R V B L P W E J Q S				
IB.2,	High Frequency: "Say each letter name."	h z t q r b l f i o k e g m v c p w x s y a j n d				
IB.3,	High Frequency: "Say each word."	boy name car	children men dog	mother brother boy	girl sister father	

SIGHT VOCABULARY (*continued*)

IB.4	High Frequency: (PP) "Say each word."	and down big can	come have you fast	get look we want	see not I the	here up of for	go on is red
	(P) "Say each word	will me yes said	but went are came	when us away with	my walk they did	she some in like	it ran he saw
	(1) "Say each word."	into going call was	by three so had	there find could new	am read him about	again never all must	around from be may
IB.5,	High Frequency: "Say each word."	much use any them	if don't would once	grow five first start	buy been sleep because	or these always their	under when done very
IB.6,	High Frequency: "Say each word."	carry which	today write	eight try	large hurt	only myself	both goes
IC.1,	Visual Discrim: "Match the shapes."						
IC.2,	Visual Discrim: "Match the letters.	h b y a	m d m d	b f	p p	u h	c u	n o b q
IC.3,	Visual Discrim: "Match the words.	cot sun	house cat	make milk	horse drink	sun bring	bring horse	cat cot

IC.2 remaining: q w a f / q n w o c
IC.3 remaining: cat milk drink / cot make house

PHONETIC ANALYSIS

IIA.1,	Consonants: "Say *yes* if the 2 words begin the same, and *no* if they don't."	(Practice items: "Tom/Tom"; "Tom/Mom") READ ALOUD TO STUDENT bat/jat can/can hat/sat fun/fun did/lid man/ran pat/pot go/so tot/not yell/well
IIA.2,	Single Consonants: "Say *yes* if the 2 words end the same, and *no* if they don't."	(Practice items: "dot/dot"; "dot/Don") READ ALOUD TO STUDENT bum/bun and/and bag/back car/car miss/mess hit/hit cup/cub egg/egg has/have bell/belt
*IIA.3,	Single Consonants: "Say these nonsense words; they end in the sound of *ū*."	bu cu du fu gu hu ju ku lu mu nu pu qu ru su tu vu wu yu zu
*IIA.4	Single Consonants: "These begin with the sound of *ŭ;* say them."	ub ud uf ug uk ul um un up ur us ut uv uz
*IIA.5,	Single Consonants: "These begin with *mū* and end with *ĕt;* say them."	muvet mudet muget mubet mufet muzet muket mumet mupet muset mutet muret munet mulet
*IIB.1,	Consonant Blends: "These end with *ū;* say them."	blu snu plu dru clu smu flu gru sku cru glu tru stu bru slu pru spu fru

*Student may try to form actual words; give credit if the sound is correct in the position tested, regardless of how the "word" is pronounced.

PHONETIC ANALYSIS (*continued*)

*IIB.2,	Consonant Blends: "These begin with *u;* say them."	und	ust	unt			
*IIB.3,	Consonant Blends: "These end with *u;* say them."	splu	stru	scru	thru	shru	spru
*IIC.1,	Cons. Digraphs: "These end in *u;* say them."	chu	shu	phu	thu	shu	
*IIC.2,	Cons. Digraphs: "These begin with *u;* say them."	ung	uck				
*IID.1,	Cons. Variants: "These end in *u;* say them."	wru	gnu	knu			
IID.2,	Cons. Variants: Say the 2 sounds for each letter."	c	g				
*IID.3,	Cons. Variants "Say each nonsense word."	pigh	zas	xarm	forquer		
*IID.4,	Cons. Variants: "Say each nonsense word."		famb	psat	hestle	misle	
*IID.5,	Cons Variants: "Say each nonsense word."	lupped	botture	olcint	ramtion		

IIE.1,	Vowels: "Say *yes* if the 2 words rhyme, and *no* if they don't."	(Practice items: "fat/cat"; "fat/kit") READ ALOUD TO STUDENT:				
		fun/but	tot/hot	bun/ben	rate/ate	hope/mope
		hit/nut	tub/cut	map/mop	bean/mean	pipe/ripe
IIE.2,	Vowels: "Say the long sound of each."	a	e	i	o	u
IIE.3,	Vowels: "Say the short sound of each."	a	e	i	o	u
*IIE.4,	Vowels: "These nonsense words begin with *n;* say them."	nai	nea	nay	nee	noa
*IIE.5,	Vowels: "These nonsense words begin with *n;* say them."	nur	nir	nor	nar	ner
*IIE.6,	Vowels: "These nonsense words begin with *n;* say them."	nol	nel	nal	nil	nul
*IIE.7,	Vowels: "These nonsense words begin with *n;* say them."	noi	now	noy	nou	

*Student may try to form actual words; give credit if the sound is correct in the position tested, regardless of how the "word" is pronounced.

PHONETIC ANALYSIS (*continued*)

*IIE.8,	Vowels: "Say this nonsense word 2 ways.	noo			
IIE.9,	Vowels: "Say the words 2 ways."	a	the	an	
*IIF.1,	CVC: "Say these nonsense words."	res	kot	bap	
*IIF.2,	CVCe: "Say these nonsense words."	ame	ime	ume	eme	ome
*IIF.3,	CV: "Say these nonsense words."	ko	je	fy	di

STRUCTURAL ANALYSIS

IIIA.1,	Root Words: "Say each root word."	along	stopped	away	trying	about
IIIA.2,	Root Words: "Say each root word."	remember	inside	wonderful	softly	ahead
IIIA.3,	Root Words: "Say each root word."	unusual	costless	impossible	television	
IIIA.4,	Root Words: "Say each root word."	argument	prevent	seventy	describe	submarine
IIIA.5,	Root Words: "Say each root word."	navigator	collection	amazement	boundary	celebration
IIIA.6,	Root Words: "Say each root word."	courageous	reflection	customary	appearance	desperation
*IIIB.1,	Suffixes: "Say these; the root is reb."	reb-s	reb-ed	reb-d	reb-t	reb-ing
*IIIB.2,	Suffixes: "Say these; the root is reb."	reb-er	reb-est			
*IIIB.3,	Suffixes: "Say these; the root is reb."	reb-ly	reb-ful			
*IIIB.4,	Suffixes: "Say these; the root is reb."	reb-less	reb-ness			
*IIIB.5,	Suffixes: "Say these; the root is reb."	reb-able reb-ist	reb-ment reb-ize reb-age	reb-ty reb-or	reb-th reb-ion reb-y	reb-al reb-tion
*IIIB.6,	Suffixes: "Say these; the root is reb."	reb-ish reb-ten reb-ible	reb-ant reb-eous reb-re	reb-ent reb-our reb-ive	reb-ance reb-ation	reb-ence reb-ious
*IIIC.1,	Prefixes: "Say these; the root is reb."	a-reb	be-reb	un-reb	re-reb	
*IIIC.2,	Prefixes: "Say these; the root is reb."	dis-reb				
*IIIC.3,	Prefixes: "Say these; the root is reb."	pre-reb	ex-reb	mis-reb	in-reb	sub-reb
*IIIC.4,	Prefixes: "Say these; the root is reb."	non-reb de-reb super-reb	com-reb trans-reb pro-reb	con-reb bi-reb	post-reb inter-reb	tri-reb per-reb

*Student may try to form actual words; give credit if the sound is correct in the position tested, regardless of how the "word" is pronounced.

STRUCTURAL ANALYSIS (*continued*)

IIIC.5,	Prefixes: "Say these; the root is reb."	on-reb	im-reb tele-reb	ad-reb	ab-reb contra-reb	an-reb
IIID.1,	Compounds: "Say the 2 words in each."	something	birthday	cowboy	maybe	onto
IIID.2,	Compounds: "Say the 2 words in each."	himself	anything	upon	anyone	lighthouse
IIIE.1,	Contraction: "Say the 2 words for which each stands."	it's	you're	I'm	he's	isn't
IIIE.2,	Contraction: "Say the 2 words for which each stands."	you'll	I'd	we've	can't	won't
IIIF.1,	Syllabication "How many syllables does each word have?"	READ ALOUD TO STUDENT pet	funny	red	see	running
IIIF.2,	Syllabication: "Say each word and tell where to divide the syllables."	blanket	signal	distance	pasture	history
IIIF.3,	Syllabication: "Say each word and tell where to divide the syllables."	excite	careful	obey	across	forward
IIIF.4,	Syllabication: "Say each word and tell where to divide the syllables."	able	circle	gentle	uncle	singled
IIIF.5,	Syllabication: "Say each word and tell where to divide the syllables."	letter	yellow	surround	borrow	arrive
IIIF.6,	Syllabication: "Say each word and tell where to divide the syllables."	gather	complete	weather	machine	hundred
IIIF.7,	Syllabication: "Say each word and tell where to divide the syllables."	secret	polite	ocean	pilot	gopher
IIIF.8,	Syllabication: "Listen then say the accented syllable."	wic'/ture	hes'/sy	mer/pens'	na/pun'	blad'/bus
IIIF.9,	Syllabication: "Say the words."	cur/tain	mar/ry	fig/ure	bal/co/ny	
IIIF.10,	Syllabication: "Tell which syllable is accented."	subnatch	routely	exdoubt	youthage	blamement
IIIF.11,	Syllabication: "Say the words."	va/mert	si/lawn	fe/reth	bo/led	di/brote
IIIF.12,	Syllabication: "Say the words as marked."	pay'/ler/hud"	fe/ril'/u/nat"	sko'/maf"/er		

WORD MEANING

IVA.1,	Basic Vocab.: "Show me. . .	. . . the TOP of the page; the BOTTOM of the page; the LEFT side of the page; the RIGHT side."
	"Put the pencil . . .	. . . ON the page; UNDER the page; OVER the page."

WORD MEANING (*continued*)

IVA.2,	Basic Vocab.:" "Point to the word that means . . . hat/mama baby dog/house/father."	puppy car	cap home	table mother	daddy boat
	. . . plate/food/Mr./ close/everything	near all	fun way	man dish	dinner am
	. . . fuss/van/fairy tale/ first/run."	story hand	race truck	fight next	fall pig
IVA.3,	Basic Vocab.: "Read the word that means . . . jug/knob/zoo/over/smart."	park handle	wife minute	bottle above	wise river
IVA.4	Basic Vocab.: "Read the word that means . . . like/simple/thought/ letter/mad."	easy magic	love angry	point smell	idea mail
IVA.5,	Basic Vocab.: "Read the word that means . . . hurt/sadden/instant/ under/find."	borrow patient	harm beneath	discover disappoint	immediate shadow
IVA.6,	Basic Vocab.: "Read the word that means . . . reason/say/should/ wealth/push."	shove record	ought speak	piano chew	cause fortune
IVA.7,	Basic Vocab.: "Read the word that means . . . path/remainder/joint/ complain/emblem."	hinge announce	route grumble	merchant describe	symbol balance
IVB.1,	Classification: "Point to the pictures that show . . . toys/farm animals/outside things."				
IVB.2,	Classification: "Tell if each word is a person, place, or thing."	READ ALOUD TO STUDENT school brother	garden chair	bed farmer	baby table
IVB.3,	Classification: "Point to the words that tell about . . . things to wear/pets/how someone feels."	happy cat	hat sad	puppy cap	shoe fish
	"Point to the words that tell about . . . things in a house/on a farm/ seasons of the year."	winter field	roof dish	fence tractor	kitchen summer
	"Read the words that tell . . . what to take on a picnic/body parts/ how someone feels."	nose basket	lemonade frightened	face arm	excited lunch
IVB.4,	Classification: "Read the words that tell about . . . buildings/ transportation/how someone feels."	castle bicycle	calm automobile	helicopter museum	church wise

WORD MEANING (*continued*)

IVB.5,	Classification: "Read the words that tell about . . . family/ body parts/food."	stomach cousin	bean mouth	daughter sandwich	chin vegetable	
IVB.6,	Classification: "Read the words that tell about . . . references/ communication/careers."	magazine dictionary	merchant musician	author messenger	telephone champion	
IVB.7,	Classification: "Read the words that tell about . . . earth/ government/careers."	geology constitution	citizen horizon	astronomer universe	military atmosphere	
IVB.8,	Classification: "Read the words that tell about . . . careers/ architecture/sports."	trophy tavern	cathedral spectator	sculptor shrine	auditorium tournament	
IVC.1,	Pronoun Referent: "Read the word that could mean . . . father those women/that house/ my aunt."	they	he	she	it	
IVC.2,	Pronoun Referent: "Read the word that could mean . . . you and me/a lady/ Ann & Sue/a fisherman."	them	him	her	we	
IVD.1,	Affixes: "Tell how each affix changes the word meaning."	dog<u>s</u>	say<u>ing</u>	writ<u>er</u>		
IVD.2,	Affixes: "Tell how each affix changes the word meaning."	care<u>ful</u>	soft<u>ly</u>	<u>be</u>side		
IVD.3,	Affixes: "Tell how each affix changes the word meaning."	warm<u>ness</u>	<u>dis</u>appear	care<u>less</u>		
IVD.4,	Affixes: "Tell how each affix changes the word meaning."	poll<u>ution</u>	<u>sub</u>marine	special<u>ize</u>		
IVD.5,	Affixes: "Tell how each affix changes the word meaning."	<u>non</u>sense	<u>inter</u>state	<u>tri</u>angle		
IVD.6,	Affixes: "Tell how each affix changes the word meaning."	right<u>eous</u>	respons<u>ible</u>	<u>contra</u>dict		
IVE.1,	Voc. Relations: READ ALOUD	"Tell at least 5 things about . . . your house; . . . your classroom."				
IVE.2,	Voc Relations: "Read the word that means almost the same as . . . shut/basement/yell/ know/tossed."	threw	cellar	shout	close	learn

WORD MEANING (*continued*)

IVE.3,	Voc. Relations: "Read the word that means NOT the same as. . .below/ crooked/light/brave/wet."	heavy	above	afraid	dry	straight
IVE.4,	Voc. Relations: "Point to the word that belongs in each blank."	She has a new_____of shoes. (pair, pear) He_____the horse. (rode, road) The wind_____over the trees. (blue, blew) A_____is a beautiful animal. (dear, deer) He_____how to read. (knew, new)				
IVE.5,	Voc. Relations: "Say the underlined word in each sentence."	He <u>wound</u> up the clock. I <u>live</u> uptown. The <u>wound</u> will heal.	We used <u>live</u> bait. Please don't <u>tear</u> the page. A <u>tear</u> was in her eye.			
IVE.6,	Voc. Relations: "Explain another way in which the underlined words may be used."	He will <u>direct</u> the play. The diver will <u>surface</u>. Did you <u>notice</u> her book?	The <u>patient</u> was ill. Don't <u>crowd</u> into the room. Please <u>welcome</u> the visitor.			
IVE.7,	Voc. Relations: "Name five nouns each word *could* describe."	ancient	enormous	modern	miserable	patient
IVE.8,	Voc. Relations: "Explain the meaning of each word."	democracy	quality	value	reputation	independence
IVE.9,	Voc. Relations: "Tell the meaning of the underlined word in each sentence."	We are having a <u>social</u>. Don't <u>doublecross</u> me!	I <u>frequent</u> the movies. The class <u>climate</u> was tense.			
IVE.10,	Voc. Relations: "Explain the *probable* meaning of each word."	zipful	edzoocate	instructural	excramination	
IVE.11,	Voc. Relations: "Explain a more polite way to say each word."	gamble	miser	sweat	riot	crude
IVE.12,	Voc. Relations: "Explain why each word might be considered negative."	tavern	amateur	confidence	nuclear	
IVE.13,	Voc. Relations: "Give the origin or history of *five* of these words."	WATS motel	sandwich astronaut	submarine telephone	automobile scuba	

Reading Comprehension

Reading Comprehension Skill Objectives

I. ***Literal Comprehension***

    A. **Details -** After reading a passage at the appropriate level, the student:

        .1–.4 States four important facts.

        .5   States five important facts.

        .6–.7 States six important facts.

        .8–.9 States seven important facts.

    B. **Sequence -** After reading a passage at the appropriate level, the student:

        .1–.4 Arranges in correct sequence three events,

        .5   Arranges in correct sequence four events.

        .6–.7 Arranges in correct sequence five events.

        .8–.9 Arranges in correct sequence six events.

II. ***Interpretive Comprehension***

    A. **Main Idea -** After reading a passage at the appropriate level, the student:

        .1–.6 Orally explains the main idea.

        .7   Orally explains the main idea, stating three support details.

        .8   Orally explains the main idea, stating four support details.

        .9   Orally explains the main idea, stating five support details.

    B. **Conclusions -** After reading a passage at the appropriate level, the student:

        .1–.9 Orally explains at least one logical conclusion that can be drawn from the text.

    C. **Cause/Effect -** After reading a passage at the appropriate level, the student:

        .1–.4 Orally explains one cause and/or effect that can be logically inferred from the text.

III. ***Critical Comprehension***

    A. **Evaluates Material -** After reading a passage at the appropriate level, the student:

        .1–.9 Evaluates the content, stating whether the passage is fact, fiction, or opinion and orally justifying the choice.

        .10–.11 Orally explains the propaganda techniques used by the author, orally justifying the answer(s).

    B. **Evaluates Author -** After reading a passage at the appropriate level, the student:

        .1–.6 States the author's possible purpose and/or bias, logically defending oral answers.

IV. ***Words in Context***

    A. **Single Words -** After reading a passage at the appropriate level, the student:

        .1–.9 States the meaning of a target word as it is used in the context of the sentence and passage.

    B. **Figurative Terms -** After reading a passage at the appropriate level, the student:

        .1–.4 Explains the meaning of a target figure of speech as it is used in the context of the sentence and passage.

SAMPLE ITEMS FOR TESTS OF READING COMPREHENSION

(Student Copy)

PrePrimer

"We have a surprise," said Tom.
"It is big."

"I do not see it.
Where is it?" said Jim.

"Outside," said Tom.

"What is it?" said Jim.

"You will see," said Tom.

"Is it red? Is it blue?
What is it?" said Jim.

"It is not red. It is blue.
You will see," said Tom.

"Is it funny?" said Jim.

"No, but it is fun.
It is in the box.
The box is big.
Come see," said Tom.

Source: From *Pathfinder: Allyn and Bacon Reading Program,* Level 8, "Surprises and Prizes," by Robert B. Ruddell et al., Copyright © 1978 by Allyn and Bacon. Used by permission.

(Student Copy)

"What big trucks!" said Dave.
   "They are so high!"

"You can look inside," said a man.

Mike and Dave went inside
   a big truck.

"What a big truck this is,"
   said Mike.

"We are up so high!" said Dave.

"Look over here," said a man.

Dave and Mike looked at the man.

"Wave at me," said the man.
   "You are on TV."

Dave said, "Dad!
   Mike and I are on TV."

The man had Ann wave, too.

Now they were all on TV.

Source: From *Pathfinder: Allyn and Bacon Program,* Level 8, "Surprises and Prizes," by Robert B. Ruddell et al., Copyright © 1978 by Allyn and Bacon. Used by permission.

(Student Copy)

First

One day there was a pet show.

Rosa came with her very big dog.

Pat came with her very
    little dog.

Ann came with her dog.

But her dog was not big,
    and not little.

Rosa said, "My dog is best.
    He is very big."

"My dog is best," said Pat.
    "She is very little.
    She is pretty."

"This is my dog,"
    said Ann.
    "Her name is Happy."

Pat's dog and Rosa's dog
    ran after each other.

But Ann's dog did tricks.

Ann said, "Happy, sit up."

And Happy sat up.

Ann said, "Happy, jump."

And Happy jumped.

"Happy is the best dog here,"
    said Rosa.

Source: From *Pathfinder: Allyn and Bacon Reading Program,* Level 9, "Upside and Down," by Robert B. Ruddell et al., Copyright © 1978 by Allyn and Bacon. Used by permission.

(Student Copy)

Second

Once there was a little town.

It was on the side of a mountain.

Near the little town was a mine.

The men of the town worked in the mine.

They worked very hard.

They worked deep down in the mine.

The little town looked sad.

There were hardly any trees.

There were no flowers.

And all the buildings were old.

The library was very old.

It was gray and dark.

Nobody ever went there.

A boy named Rob had a surprise.

He was on the way to school.

He saw a fine new sign that said:

FREE LIBRARY.

COME ONE! COME ALL!

A lady was standing at the door.

She had a big smile.

"Hello," said the lady.

"I'm Ms. Plunkett, and I love books.

Do you like to read?"

"Not much," said Rob.

"I don't think books are much good."

"Maybe you will," said Ms. Plunkett.

"I'm going to make this a library you will love."

Source: From *Pathfinder: Allyn and Bacon Reading Program,* Level 1O, "Inside and Out," by Robert B. Ruddell et al., Copyright © 1978 by Allyn and Bacon. Used by permission.

(Student Copy)

Third

One day Elephant fell into a pit. "Help!" cried Elephant.

The animals ran and looked into the pit. "We can't help you, Elephant," they said. "You are too big. And the pit is too deep."

The animals could not help Elephant. One by one they went away.

"Elephant!" called Monkey from the top of the pit. "I'll get you out."

"But how?" asked Elephant. "You are so little."

"Not too little," said Monkey, and away she ran.

Soon Monkey came back. She had a ladder with her. Elephant tried to climb up the ladder. But when he got on it, the ladder broke.

"It's no use," said Elephant. "How will I get out of this pit?"

"You will see," said Monkey, and away she ran.

Night fell before Monkey came back. She had a rope with her. Elephant took hold of the rope. Then Monkey pulled on it. But Monkey could not pull Elephant out of the pit.

"It's no use," said Elephant. "How will I get out of this pit?"

"You will see," said Monkey, and away she ran.

Fourth

"Nothing has happened today," said Susan.

"But today isn't over," said Mr. Miles. "Maybe something will happen yet."

Susan and her dad were in the Miles' garage. Susan looked at the big tow truck. On it was painted:

THE FRIENDLY MILES.

Sometimes Susan helped her dad as he drove around. It was fun to ride in the truck. Sometimes she and her dad helped people when their cars were stuck. Sometimes they had to fix flat tires or fan belts. Susan was always a big help to her father.

Mr. Miles received a frantic call. "Hello," said Mr. Miles. "A plane is on the freeway? We'll come right away." Mr. Miles smiled at Susan and said, "Let's go; we have an airplane to save."

There was a plane right in the middle of the freeway! Cars could not get around it. The police were there to handle the traffic.

First, Susan helped her dad get a police car back on the road. Then she helped position the airplane on the highway.

When the plane took off, all the people cheered. They all said, "Thanks to the friendly Miles, everything is running smoothly."

Fifth

"Coming," Amanda called. She took a last look at the stage. Everything had to be where it belonged. In the past, stage hands had misplaced vital props. There could be none of that now. Tomorrow was opening night.

The stage was set for the first scene. Everything seemed to be in order. Amanda walked over to the switchboard. She turned off the lights and headed for the stage door. She paused and glanced across the darkened auditorium, then left. It was late, nearly 11:45. Fortunately it was school vacation and she could sleep as late as she wanted.

Amanda had loved the theater for a long time. When she was five, her father took her to see *The Nutcracker.* The lighted production of the classic fairy tale had enchanted her. Over the years Amanda enjoyed many plays. Now, as a young woman, she was an actress.

As she neared her car, she could still remember the applause from her last effort nearly a year ago. Her thoughts were in another world. Her mind twirled as she thought of opening night, her lines and then, without warning . . .

Source: From *Pathfinder: Allyn and Bacon Reading Program,* Level 22, "Over the Horizon," by Robert B. Ruddell et al., Copyright © 1978 by Allyn and Bacon. Used by permission.

Sixth

One dark night Troy Weaver was in a haze. He was flying alone in an old single engine airplane. It was cold, damp, and the darkness made it almost impossible to see. The weather had been poor all afternoon, with the strong headwinds causing Troy to take much longer for this trip than he had expected. In fact, he was nearly sixty minutes late; and by his calculations, he had at least another fifteen or twenty minutes before reaching Orlando.

As if the cold, dark night wasn't enough to worry about, what about fuel? How much extra had been used fighting the strong winds? And of course, the extra hour of flying time for such a small plane gave Troy plenty of reason to tighten up and become uneasy. Perhaps dropping to a lower altitude would improve visibility and maybe even get him out of the heavy winds.

Down he came, lower and lower. Still no lights or dark images of movement or buildings. In fact the ground below was glazed almost like a mirror. At about 1,000 feet he leveled off, searched and strained to grab the brief moonlight shadows he could. Then it happened without warning. Quietly, breathtakingly, the lone engine sputtered, hissed and then became silent. No more fuel and no way to see a spot to land.

A cold sweat turned instantly into panic as the plane began to fall from the heavy clouds. Oh no, no ground at all; it's water, nothing but water! Troy knew he must be way off course, and even worse, there was nowhere to land. Troy took what he felt was his last deep breath as the plane began to plunge into the water and then, he woke up. Man, what a dream!

SAMPLE ITEMS FOR TESTS OF READING COMPREHENSION

(Teacher Copy)

PrePrimer

INTRODUCTION: *Read this story to find out about the boy's surprise.*

I. Literal Comprehension
__ *A.2 Details* (4): Retell this story.

_____ "We have a surprise," said Tom. "It is big."

"I do not see it. Where is it?" said Jim.
_____ "Outside," said Tom.

"What is it?" said Jim. "You will see," said Tom.
_____ "Is it red? Is it blue? What is it?" said Jim.

_____ "It is not red. It is blue. You will see," said Tom.

_____ "Is it funny?" said Jim. "No, but it is fun."

_____ It is in the box. The box is big. Come see," said Tom.

B.2 Correct Sequence:
__ 3 answers in correct sequence.

II. Interpretive Comprehension
__ *A.2 Main Idea:* Explain what this story is about.
__ *B.2 Conclusions:* Explain three things that the surprise might be.

III. Critical Comprehension
__ *A.2 Fact/Fiction:* Judge this story to decide if it could really happen? Why or why not?

IV. Word Meaning in Context
__ *A.2 Single Words:* What did Tom mean when he said OUTSIDE ?
__ What is a SURPRISE?

Source: From *Pathfinder: Allyn and Bacon Reading Program,* Level 8, "Surprises and Prizes," by Robert B. Ruddell et al., Copyright © 1978 by Allyn and Bacon. Used by permission.

Primer

INTRODUCTION: *Read this story to find out about an exciting day.*

I. Literal Comprehension

__ *A.3 Details* (4): Retell this story.

_____ "What big trucks!" said Dave. "They are so high!"

_____ "You can look inside," said a man. Mike and Dave went inside a big truck.

_____ "What a big truck this is," said Mike. "We are up so high!" said Dave.

_____ "Look over here," said a man. Dave and Mike looked at the man.

_____ "Wave at me," said the man. "You are on TV."

_____ Dave said, "Dad! Mike and I are on TV."

_____ The man had Ann wave, too. Now they were all on TV.

B.3 Correct Sequence:
__ 3 answers in correct sequence.

II. Interpretive Comprehension

__ *A.3 Main Idea:* Explain what this story is about.
__ *B.3 Conclusions:* Explain three reasons why the TV man probably chose these children to be on TV.

III. Critical Comprehension

__ *A.3 Fact/Fiction:* Judge this story; could it really happen? Why or why not?

IV. Word Meaning in Context

__ *A.3 Single Words:* The story tells about trucks that are so HIGH; what does HIGH mean?
__ The children in the story are ON TV; what does ON mean?

Source: From *Pathfinder: Allyn and Bacon Reading Program,* Level 8, "Surprises and Prizes," by Robert B. Ruddell et al., Copyright © 1978 by Allyn and Bacon. Used by permission.

(Teacher Copy)

First

INTRODUCTION: *Read this story to find out about a special kind of show.*

I. Literal Comprehension
__ *A.4 Details* (4): Retell this story.

> One day there was a pet show.
> Rosa came with her very big dog.
> Pat came with her very little dog.
> Ann came with her dog. But her dog
> ____ was not big, and not little
>
> Rosa said, "My dog is best. He is very big."
> "My dog is best," said Pay. "She is very little.
> ____ She is pretty."
>
> ____ "This is my dog," said Ann. "Her name is Happy."
>
> ____ Pat's dog and Rosa's dog ran after each other.
>
> But Ann's dog did tricks. Ann said, "Happy,
> sit up." And Happy sat up. Ann said, "Happy, jump."
> ____ And Happy jumped.
>
> ____ "Happy is the best dog here," said Rosa.

B.4 Correct Sequence:
__ 3 answers in correct sequence.

II. Interpretive Comprehension
__ *A.4 Main Idea:* Explain what this story is about.
__ *B.4 Conclusions:* Explain why each of the three dogs MIGHT win first prize in the pet show.

III. Critical Comprehension
__ *A.4 Fact/Fiction:* Judge this story; to decide if it could really happen; why or why not?

IV. Word Meaning in Context
__ *A.4 Single Words:* Two children in the story say their dog is BEST; what does BEST mean?
__ What did Pat probably mean when she said her dog is PRETTY?

(Teacher Copy)

Second

INTRODUCTION: *Read this story to find out about a surprise for a little town.*

I. Literal Comprehension
__ *A.5 Details* (5): Retell this story.

____ Once there was a little town. It was
on the side of a mountain.
Near the little town was a mine. The men of
the town worked in the mine. They worked very
____ hard. They worked deep down in the mine.
The little town looked sad. There were hardly
____ any trees. There were no flowers.
And all the buildings were old. The library was
____ very old. It was gray and dark. Nobody ever went there.
A boy named Rob had a surprise. He was on the way to
school. He saw a fine new sign that said:
____ FREE LIBRARY. COME ONE! COME ALL!
A lady was standing at the door. She had a big smile.
"Hello," said the lady. "I'm Ms. Plunkett, and I love
____ books. Do you like to read?"
____ "Not much," said Rob. "I don't think books are much good."
"Maybe you will," said Ms. Plunkett. "I'm going to make
____ this a library you will love."

B.5 Correct Sequence:
__ 4 answers in correct sequence.

II. Interpretive Comprehension
__ *A.5 Main Idea:* Explain a good title for this story.
__ *B.5 Conclusions:* Explain three ways Ms. Plunkett may make the library one Rob will love.
__ *C.1 Cause/Effect:* Explain two reasons why Rob may think books aren't "much good."

III. Critical Comprehension
__ *A.5 Fact/Fiction:* Judge this story to decide if it could really happen; why/why not?

IV. Words in Context
__ *A.5* What did Ms. Plunkett mean when she said she LOVED books?
__ The men in the story worked in the MINE; what is a MINE?

Source: From *Pathfinder: Allyn and Bacon Reading Program,* Level 10, "Inside and Out," by Robert B. Ruddell et al., Copyright © 1978 by Allyn and Bacon. Used by permission.

(Teacher Copy)

Third

INTRODUCTION: *Read this story to find out what happens to the elephant.*

I. Literal Comprehension
__ *A.6 Details* (6): Retell this story.

____ One day Elephant fell into a pit. "Help!" cried Elephant.
The animals ran and looked into the pit. "We can't help you,
Elephant," they said. "You are too big. And the pit is too deep."
____ The animals could not help Elephant. One by one they went away.
"Elephant!" called Monkey from the top of the pit. "I'll get you
____ out." "But how?" asked Elephant. "You are so little."
"Not too little," said Monkey, and away she ran. Soon Monkey came
____ back. She had a ladder with her.
Elephant tried to climb up the ladder. But when he got on it, the
ladder broke. "It's no use," said Elephant. "How will I get out
____ of this pit?"
"You will see," said Monkey, and away she ran. Night fell before
____ Monkey came back. She had a rope with her.
Elephant took hold of the rope. Then Monkey pulled on it. But
____ Monkey could not pull Elephant out of the pit.
"It's no use," said Elephant. "How will I get out of this pit?"
____ "You will see," said Monkey, and away she ran.

B.6 Correct Sequence:
__ 5 answers in correct sequence.

II. Interpretive Comprehension
__ *A.6 Main Idea:* Explain a title for the story.
__ *B.6 Conclusions:* Explain why you think the monkey did or did not come back.
__ *C.2 Cause/Effect:* Explain what caused the ladder to break.

III. Critical Comprehension
__ *A.6 Fact/Fiction:* Evaluate the story; name 3 events which could be real and 3 which are make-believe.

IV. Words in Context
__ *A.6 Single Words:* What was the PIT in the story?
__ *B.1 Figurative:* In the story, what does NIGHT FELL mean?

Source: From *Pathfinder: Allyn and Bacon Reading Program,* Level 10, "Inside and Out," by Robert B. Ruddell et al., Copyright
© 1978 by Allyn and Bacon. Used by permission.

(Teacher Copy)

Fourth

INTRODUCTION: *Read about Susan's and her father's unusual job.*

I. Literal Comprehension
___ *A.7 Details* (6): Retell this story.

> "Nothing has happened today," said Susan. "But today isn't over,"
> ____ said Mr. Miles. "Maybe something will happen yet."
> Susan and her dad were in the Miles garage. Susan looked at the
> ____ big tow truck. On it was painted: THE FRIENDLY MILES.
> Sometimes Susan helped her dad as he drove around. It was fun to
> ride in the truck. Sometimes she and her dad helped people when
> ____ their cars were stuck.
> Sometimes they had to fix flat tires or fan belts. Susan was always a
> ____ big help to her father.
> Mr. Miles received a frantic call. "Hello," said Mr. Miles. "A plane
> ____ is on the freeway?
> We'll come right away." Mr. Miles smiled at Susan and said, "Let's
> ____ go; we have an airplane to save."
> There was a plane right in the middle of the freeway! Cars could not
> ____ get around it. The police were there to handle the traffic.
> ____ First, Susan helped her dad get a police car back on the road.
> ____ Then she helped position the airplane on the highway.
> ____ When the plane took off, all the people cheered. They all said,
> "Thanks to the friendly Miles, everything is running smoothly."

B.7 Correct Sequence:
___ 5 answers in correct sequence.

II. Interpretive Comprehension
___ *A.7 Main Idea:* Explain the main idea of the story; give 3 support details.
___ *B.7 Conclusions:* Explain 3 reasons people liked Mr. Miles.
___ *C.3 Cause/Effect:* Explain why the plane was on the freeway.

III. Critical Comprehension
___ *A.7 Fact/Fiction:* Evaluate the story to decide if it is fact, fiction, or opinion; tell why.
___ *B.1 Author Purpose:* Evaluate the author's portrayal of Mr. Miles; is he successful; why/why not?
___ *B.4 Author Bias:* Evaluate and justify author feelings about daughters.

IV. Words in Context
___ *A.7* What is a FRANTIC call?
___ *B.2* Define RUNNING SMOOTHLY.

Source: From *Pathfinder: Allyn and Bacon Reading Program,* Level 10, "Inside and Out," by Robert B. Ruddell et al., Copyright © 1978 by Allyn and Bacon. Used by permission.

(Teacher Copy)

Fifth

INTRODUCTION: *Read this story to learn about a young woman and a play.*

I. Literal Comprehension
__ *A.8 Details* (7): Retell this story.

    ____ "Coming," Amanda called. She took a last look at the stage. Everything had to be where it belonged. In the past, stage hands had misplaced vital props.

    ____ There could be none of that now. Tomorrow was opening night.

    ____ The stage was set for the first scene. Everything seemed to be in order.

    ____ Amanda walked over to the switchboard. She turned off the lights and headed for the stage door. She paused and glanced across the darkened auditorium, then left.

    ____ It was late, nearly 11:45. Fortunately it was school vacation, and she could sleep as late as she wanted.

    ____ Amanda had loved the theater for a long time. When she was five, her father took her to see *The Nutcracker.* The lighted production of the classic fairy tale had enchanted her.

    ____ Over the years Amanda enjoyed many plays. Now, as a young woman, she was an actress.

    ____ As she neared her car she could still remember the applause from her last effort nearly a year ago.

    ____ Her thoughts were in another world. Her mind twirled as she thought of opening night, her lines and then, without warning . . .

B.8 Correct Sequence:
__ 6 answers in correct sequence.

II. Interpretive Comprehension
__ *A.8 Main Idea:* Explain the main idea of the story; support your answer with at least 4 details.
__ *B.8 Conclusions:* Explain 3 events which might happen next in the story.
__ *C.4 Cause/Effect:* Explain the effect on Amanda's behavior of the stage hands misplacing the props.

III. Critical Comprehension
__ *A.8 Fact/Opinion:* Evaluate the story; describe how you know if it's fact, fiction, or opinion.
__ *A.10 Propaganda:* Evaluate how the story makes you feel about stage hands; why?
__ *B.2 Author Purpose:* Evaluate the story to describe 3 possible purposes the author might have had for writing it; justify your answers.
__ *B.5 Author Bias:* Evaluate how the author may feel about plays; qualify your answer.

IV. Words in Context
__ *A.8 Single Words:* What does it mean when someone is ENCHANTED?
__ *B.3 Figuratives:* What is meant by her mind TWIRLED?

Source: From *Pathfinder: Allyn and Bacon Reading Program,* Level 22, "Over the Horizon," by Robert B. Ruddell et al., Copyright © 1978 by Allyn and Bacon. Used by permission.

(Teacher Copy)

Sixth

INTRODUCTION: *Read to find out about Troy Weaver's adventure.*

I. Literal Comprehension

__ *A.9 Details* (7): Retell this story.

_____One dark night Troy Weaver was in a haze. He was flying alone in an old single engine airplane.

_____It was cold, damp, and the darkness made it almost impossible to see.

_____The weather had been poor all afternoon, with the strong headwinds causing Troy to take much longer for this trip than he had expected.

_____In fact, he was nearly sixty minutes late; and by his calculations, he had at least another fifteen or twenty minutes before reaching Orlando.

_____As if the cold, dark night wasn't enough to worry about, what about fuel? How much extra had been used fighting the strong winds?

_____And of course, the extra hour of flying time for such a small plane gave Troy plenty of reason to tighten up and become uneasy.

_____Perhaps dropping to a lower altitude would improve visibility and maybe even get him out of the heavy winds.

_____Down he came, lower and lower. Still no lights or dark images of movement or buildings. In fact the ground below was glazed almost like a mirror.

_____At about 1,000 feet he leveled off, searched and strained to grab the brief moonlight shadows he could.

_____Then it happened without warning. Quietly, breathtakingly, the lone engine sputtered, hissed, and then became silent. No more fuel and no way to see a spot to land.

_____A cold sweat turned instantly into panic as the plane began to fall from the heavy clouds. Oh no, no ground at all; it's water, nothing but water! Troy knew he must be way off course, and even worse, there was nowhere to land.

_____Troy took what he felt was his last breath as the plane began to plunge into the water and then, he woke up. Man, what a dream!

B.9 Correct Sequence:
__ 6 answers in correct sequence.

II. Interpretive Comprehension

__ *A.9 Main Idea:* Explain what happened to Troy in this story; give 5 details to support your answer.
__ *B.9 Conclusions:* Explain why Troy dropped to 1,000 feet.
__ *C.5 Cause/Effect:* Explain what happened to Troy because of flying too long.

III. Critical Comprehension

__ *A.9 Fact/Opinion:* Evaluate the story; describe how you know if this could really happen to Troy.
__ *A.11 Propaganda:* Evaluate the story's propaganda for an airline company's advertisement; justify your answer.
__ *B.3 Author Purpose:* Evaluate the story ending; why do you think the author ended the story this way; justify your answer.
__ *B.6 Author Bias:* Evaluate the story to decide the author's probable feelings about single engine planes; justify your answer.

IV. Words in Context

__ *A.9 Single Words:* What is meant by HEADWIND?
__ *B.4 Figuratives:* What was meant by FIGHTING the wind?

Written Expression

Written Expression Skill Objectives

I. Mechanics

A. Capitalization

.1–.4 In a friendly letter, the student correctly capitalizes names of people and their personal titles, days and months, the beginning word in a sentence, and "I."

.5 The student correctly capitalizes proper nouns of places, book titles, streets, cities, states, and holidays in dictated sentences.

.6–.7, B.4, C.3, D.3–.4 In a friendly letter, the student writes capital letters in the salutation, closing, and postal abbreviations; uses correct punctuation (comma) in the date; and writes numbers correctly in the address.

.8–.9, B.9, C.4 The student correctly capitalizes family names and middle initials of people when writing dictated sentences.

.10, B.10, C.5, D.5 On request, the student correctly writes the time of day using digits, the colon, and capital letters for A.M. and P.M.

.11–.13,.16–.18,.22 Given dictated sentences, the student writes capital letters for proper nouns for places, peoples, school subjects, organizations, song titles, geographical locations, trade names, ethnic groups, and proper adjectives.

.14 (See I.B.12)

.15, B.14, D.8 Given a chapter to read in a text, the student outlines the chapter using correct capitalization, punctuation, and roman numerals.

.19 The student capitalizes the first word in each line of verse when writing an original poem.

.20–.21 Given dictated sentences, the student uses correct capitalization for professional degrees and documents.

B. Punctuation

.1–.2, C.1–.3, D.3–.4 When writing a friendly letter, the student uses correct punctuation for periods after personal titles, end of sentences, abbreviated days and months, and the question mark; correct abbreviations for personal titles, days, and months; and correct numbers in writing the date and address in the letter.

.3, D.1,.6 Upon request, the student correctly writes his or her area code and telephone number.

.5,.7,.16 Given dictated sentences, the student correctly underlines names of ships, books, and titles of art, music, and drama.

.6 The student correctly writes the apostrophe in contractions, possessives, and plurals of words in dictated sentences,

.8 Given dictated sentences, the student correctly uses the exclamation mark.

.9 (See IA.9)

.10 (See IA.10)

.11,.13,.18,.21 Given dictated sentences, the, student correctly uses the comma to separate three or more items in a series; in a direct quote; to separate introductory words, noun of address, independent clauses, confusing items, appositives; and to set off incidental words, phrases, or clauses and modifiers.

.12 In a written short story, the student correctly uses quotation marks to indicate direct quotes of a speaker and to give emphasis to a word.

.14, C.7 After measuring the perimeter of a room, the student writes the dimensions using the correct abbreviations punctuated properly.

.15 The student correctly uses the colon in writing assigned business letters, plays, and references.

.17 The student correctly uses the hyphen to divide words at the right margin of an assigned essay.

.19 (See IA.20)

.20,.22, C.11, D.7 In writing bibliographic references, the student correctly uses the dash, parentheses, abbreviations, and numbers.

.22 The student correctly uses parentheses to illustrate supplemental information in dictated sentences.

C. **Abbreviations**

.1–.3   (See IB.1)

.4   (See IA.9)

.5   (See IA.10)

.6   Given a list of dictated names of people with abbreviations (Mr. John Doe, Jr., Harry Smith, Sr.), the student correctly writes the names.

.7   (See IB.14)

.8   In a friendly letter, the student correctly uses abbreviations in the address.

.9–.10 Given a dictated list of full names, the student correctly writes the appropriate acronym or abbreviation.

.11   (See IB.20)

D. **Numbers**

.1,.6   Upon request, the student correctly writes his or her telephone number, including area code.

.2   Given dictation, the student correctly writes the words for numbers less than ten and other numerical words ("second," "half") that are appropriate for the student's reading level.

.3–.4   (See IA.6, IB.1)

.5   (See IA.10)

.7   Given an article in a published journal, the student writes the proper references for the article.

.8   (See IA.15).

II. *Usage*

A. **Sentences**

.1–.3   The student uses complete, declarative, and interrogative sentences when speaking in front of class and with others.

.4–.20 In an expository or narrative writing assignment and in friendly and business letters, the student correctly uses the types of sentences appropriate for his or her grade placement.

B. **Words**

.1–.5   The student correctly uses a variety of types of words when speaking in front of the class and with others.

.6–.40 In a writing assignment, the student correctly uses a variety of words appropriate for the student's grade placement.

C. **Phrases**

.1–.6   In a writing assignment, the student correctly uses a variety of phrases appropriate to his or her grade placement.

D. **Clauses**

.1   The student underlines all main clauses in a magazine article selected by the teacher.

E. **Paragraphs**

.1   The student circles each paragraph in a magazine article selected by the teacher.

.2–.4,.7 In a short story assignment of at least three paragraphs, the student correctly indents each paragraph, uses proper and logical sequence within each, writes a clear topic sentence for each, and uses proper connectives for transition between paragraphs.

.5   The student writes a descriptive essay at a technical and quality level appropriate for his or her grade placement

.6,.8   The student writes an expository essay at a technical and quality level appropriate for his or her grade placement.

.9   The student writes a narrative essay at a technical and quality level appropriate for the student's grade placement.

III. *Ideation*

A. **Fluency**

.1   The student tells a story using enough words so that it is easily understood by the listener.

.2–.7   In a written essay, the student uses the minimum number of words appropriate for his or her grade level.

B. **Maturity**

.1–.2   The student names and describes objects accurately when telling stories and in general conversation.

.3   Given an appropriate story starter such as a picture of interest, the student writes a list of nouns appropriate for the story.

.4   Given an appropriate story starter, the student writes simple sentences describing the story.

.5   Given an appropriate story starter, the student writes a complete plot with a clear beginning, middle, and end.

.6   Given an appropriate story starter, the student writes a complete story or essay that relates some issue or major point to the reader.

C. **Word Choice**

.1–.3   Given an appropriate writing assignment, the student uses accurate, descriptive, and purposeful words for the particular assignment.

.4   Given an appropriate writing assignment, the student writes words that convey the sounds of our language such as "hiss," "crunchy," etc.

.5   Given an appropriate writing assignment, the student writes words that are necessary for the purpose of the writing, not using trite or unnecessary words, terms, or phrases.

.6–.7   Given an appropriate writing assignment, the student writes words that describe and elicit sensory and emotional reactions.

D. Style

.1   Given an appropriate writing assignment, the student uses words (such as "first," "next," "following," etc.) that give logical and correct sequence to the written product.

.2–.3   Given an appropriate writing assignment the student uses good organization and logical sequence of events in the writing.

.4–.5   Given an appropriate writing assignment, the student incorporates a necessary amount of detail to support the main idea or purpose, using ample connectives and juncture words to give cohesion to the writing.

.6   Given an appropriate writing assignment, the student clearly expresses the purpose or main idea of the writing.

.7–.9   Given an appropriate writing assignment, the student makes correct use of infinitives, clear pronoun reference, and proper location of modifiers including words, phrases, and clauses.

.10   Given an appropriate writing assignment, the student maintains consistent tense, person, number, and point of view.

SAMPLE ITEMS FOR TESTS OF WRITTEN EXPRESSION

Student's Name_____Grade_____Teacher_____

I. MECHANICS
    A.1-.4   (Capitalization)
    B.1-.3   (Punctuation)
    C.1-.2   (Abbreviations)
    D.1-.2   (Numbers)

Directions: Circle all mistakes in capitalization, punctuation, abbreviations, and numbers in the letter below. Sometimes the correct marks or letters have been omitted. Put a circle where they should be. Then, copy the letter so it is correct.

apr 1, 19____

Dear jim,

    Our class went to the airport last wednesday   mr wilson drove the school bus
Have you been to the airport   we saw 5 big airplanes. The teacher and i flew 1
They let rover help us. april fool!
    Our new phone number is 765 4321. Call me next tue if you can.

Your pal,

Les

I. MECHANICS
    A.5-.7   (Capitalization)
    B.4-.5   (Punctuation)
    C.3   (Abbreviations)
    D.3-.4   (Numbers)

Directions: Follow directions for above letter.

97 pipin lane
New Albany in 47119
December 3 19____

dear aunt betty

    Thanks for the birthday check! I am going to buy the book when we were very young with the money. We went to louisville to see grandmother on thanksgiving day and rode the belle of louisville. It was cold. Last week we drove over to ohio. Tomorrow our class is going to the circle theater for a concert. It seems like I'm always going somewhere. I think it's fun.
    Thanks again for remembering my birthday.

your niece

Sally

IA. CAPITALIZATION

Directions: Copy each sentence on your own paper using correct capitalization or point to each error and explain correction to teacher.

    ___.8   The smiths moved in next door to us.

    ___.9   My favorite writer is robert l. stevenson.

    ___.10   My class goes to lunch at 10:45 am.

    ___.11   (a) He lives near mt. raier.

               (b) We visited boulder dam this summer.

    ___.12   Many hispanic people live in america.

    ___.13   My brother is studying geometry and spanish.

    ___.14   John asked, "what can I do now?"

    ___.15   (Outline) I. transportation

                        A. cars

                        B. planes

    ___.16   (a) She made a donation to the boy scouts of america.

               (b) His brother owns jim's speedy car wash.

    ___.17   The band played auld lang syne at midnight

    ___.18   (a) They plan to vacation in ireland.

               (b) Do you have any kleenex?

               (c) The story of the jews at Masada is a heroic one.

    ___.19   (Poem: The Swallow by Christina B. Rossetti)

                  fly away, fly away over the sea,

                        sun-loving swallow. for summer is done;

                  come again, come again, come back to me,

                        Bringing the summer and bringing the sun.

    ___.20   Her brother is Thomas B. Bosman ph.d.

    ___.21   Have you seen a copy of the bill of rights?

    .22   Do you like spanish music?

IB. PUNCTUATION

Directions: Copy each sentence on your own paper using correct punctuation or point to each error and explain correction to teacher.

    ___.6   (a) He didnt want to go to school.

               (b) The girls dog ran away.

               (c) All the students papers were good.

    ___.7   Have you read Treasure Island?

    ___.8   Ouch. You pinched me.

    ___.9   Richard M Nixon resigned from office.

    ___.10   I must meet my mother at 1015 this morning.

    ___.11   (a) He plays football baseball and soccer.

               (b) "I read my homework" Susie bragged.

    ___.12   (a) I need to study more, he said.

               (b) His sorrow lasted about one minute.

    ___.13   (a) Yes I can go to the movies with you.

               (b) She can go with you tomorrow Maria.

               (c) However I cannot stay for the entire game.

               (d) I ride the bus to school and I ride it home.

    ___.14   (a) His room is 10 ft long by 12 ft wide.

               (b) I Foods

                    A Fruits

                    B Vegetables

    ___.15   (a) (Business letter) Dear Mr, Edwardo

IB. PUNCTUATION *(continued)*

        (b) (Plays) Mary Hello, Bill. How are you?

                    Bill Fine, Mary. And you?

        (c) (References) Boston Allyn & Bacon.

____.16   Have you seen the Mona Lisa?

____.17   Sometimes when we write, we have to sep

____   arate words at the end of the line.

____.18   After he woke up he grabbed a bite to eat.

____.19   Her sister, a dentist, is Mary Lou Harrison D D S

____.20   The store is open from 9:30 6:00.

____.21   (a) After he called James Allen ate supper.

        (b) Betty his aunt is living with them.

        (c) (Reference)

           Smith D. & Jones J. (1986). *Welcome home.*

             Ashland: Nebus Publishing Co.

        (d) You may at your discretion eat lunch first.

        (e) Happy with her progress thus far she took a rest.

____.22   Her hair even though it was grey was admired by all.

IC. ABBREVIATIONS

Directions: On your own paper write the correct abbreviations for the following or tell your teacher the correct abbreviations.

____.1   Mister, Misses (wife of . . .).

____.2   Monday, Wednesday, Friday; January, March, August

____.3   Postal abbreviations for: Tennessee, Oklahoma, California.

____.4   Initials for middle name: Charles "Edward" Smith.

____.5   10:30 "in the morning"; 10:30 "in the evening."

____.6   Bill Smith, "Junior."

____.7   27 "feet"; 14 "inches."

____.8   Post Office Box 27; Rural Route 3.

____.9   Television, Unidentified Flying Object, Citizen's Band.

____.10   Federal Bureau of Investigation, Internal Revenue Service.

____.11   Volume, page, and others, for example.

ID. NUMBERS

Directions: On your own paper write the correct numerals for the following or tell your teacher the correct numerals.

____.1   Your telephone number.

____.2   Three, Fifteen, Twenty-seven, Sixty-four, Eight hundred nine.

____.3   Today's date.

____.4   Your address.

____.5   The time of day now.

____.6   Your area code.

____.7   Volume and page number of encyclopedia beginning with letter of your last name.

____.8   Roman numerals for: 7, 15, 42, 50, 100.

II: USAGE - Recognition Sample Items

IIA. SENTENCES

____.1-.3 (Point to something in the classroom and tell student to describe it in complete sentences. Then have student ask another student questions about what was described.)

IIA. SENTENCES *(continued)*

___.4 Underline the complete sentence;
  (a) The little grey cat.
  (b) I can ride a bike.
  (c) A big horse.

___.5 Underline the simple sentence:
  (a) Running down the road.
  (b) The dog barked, and then he ran away.
  (c) She has a new doll.

___.6 Underline the telling (declarative) sentence:
  (a) Washing his face.
  (b) The sky is blue.
  (c) Turn left here.

___.7 Underline the asking (interrogative) sentence:
  (a) My sister is sick.
  (b) The little old man.
  (c) Are you going to the party?

___.8 Underline the best sentence:
  (a) He went to the store.
  (b) Store to he went the.
  (c) To the went he store.

___.9 Underline the exclamatory sentence:
  (a) She is pretty.
  (b) It was hot!
  (c) Turn into this driveway.

___.10 Underline the compound sentence:
  (a) He is in the next room.
  (b) Going to town.
  (c) She asked the class, but no one answered.

___.11 Underline the complete sentence (not a fragment):
  (a) She lives next door to me.
  (b) The big horse.
  (c) Running into the room.

___.12 Underline the sentence with the best word order:
  (a) The boy ate the ice cream cone wearing the blue shirt.
  (b) Wearing the blue shirt the boy ate the ice cream cone.
  (c) The boy wearing the blue shirt ate the ice cream cone.

___.13 Underline the imperative (command sentence):
  (a) Here he comes.
  (b) Charles is the treasurer.
  (c) Close the door.

___.14 Underline the sentence that is *not* a run-on sentence:
  (a) He closed the door and stayed in his room.
  (b) He went to town, and he bought some candy and so he got very tired and he started walking home and he sat down and cried.

15 Underline the compound subject: The boy and girl sat together.

___.16 Underline the compound predicate: The dog barked and ran.

___.17 Underline the sentence with the correct word order.
  (a) I and Bill rode the horses.
  (b) Sue, Jack, and I walked to town.

___.18 Where is the subject in this sentence? Fix the tire.

___.19 Underline the complex sentence:
  (a) The old woman lived in a shoe.
  (b) The teacher reviewed the lesson plans before she began the class.
  (c) He rode the horse, and he went fishing.

IIA. SENTENCES *(continued)*

____.20   Underline the compound/complex sentence:

   (a) Because the dog was barking, the old woman went to the cupboard to get the poor dog a bone, but the cupboard was bare.

   (b) Marilou won first prize.

   (c) After the race was over, we drove home.

IIB. WORDS

____.1   Nouns.

   (a) Point to various people and things in the classroom and tell the student to say their names.

   (b) Point to a group of people and things in the classroom and ask the student what they are (the student must use plurals in the response).

   (c) Tell the student to say as many days of the week and months that he or she knows.

____.2   Verbs. Tell the student to say a sentence using an action word.

____.3   Adjectives.

   (a) Point to various objects in the room and ask the student to tell the color of the objects.

   (b) Show the student pictures of students with different expressions and ask him or her to describe the way the people in the pictures feel. If no pictures are available, the teacher may use a variety of facial expressions (happy, sad, angry).

   (c) Hand the student various objects that have different textures and tell him or her to say how they feel (rough, smooth, cold, soft, hard, fuzzy, etc.)

   (d) Place two objects of different sizes in front of the student. Choose one and say: "This one is *small,* the other one is _____." Have the student say the word that you omit. Use objects that can be big, small, tall, short, etc. Also point to one and say: "This one is tall, but this one is _____" (taller). Put three objects in front of the student and say: "This is tall, this is taller, but this one is the _____" (tallest).

   (e) Show the student two sets of two pictures or objects and say: "These two are the same." Point to the second set and say: "These two are *not* the same; they are *different.*" Show the student another set of two pictures or objects. Point to each and ask: "Are these two the same or are they different?"

____.4   Preposition.

   (a) Place a pencil on a book and say: "The pencil is *on* the book." Place it under the book and say: "The pencil is *under* the book." Place the pencil on the book and ask: "Where is the pencil?" Place the pencil under the book and ask: "Where is the pencil now?"

   (b) Give the student a crayon or pencil and a piece of paper with various objects drawn on it. Have the student put a mark *on* the _____, *under* the _____, *over* the _____, *between* the two _____, *on top of* the _____, *in front of* the _____, *behind* the _____, *to the left of* the _____, *to the right of* the_____, and to put a circle *around* the _____.

   (c) Using the student's responses to item .4, point to each response, and have the student tell you where the mark is (i.e., "on the box").

____.5   Word Order. Place four pictures or objects in front of the student. Point to each in order and say: "This is first; this is second; this is next; and this is last." Point to each in a different order and ask the student to tell which position it has.

IIB. WORDS (*continued*)

___.6   (a) Underline all nouns:
    Bill hit the ball over the fence.
    (b) Underline all nouns:
    Mr. Jones drove the school bus Tuesday.
    (c) Underline all nouns:
    Two boys had birthdays in March.
    (d) Underline the noun:
    He hit one to me.

___.7   (a) Underline the verb:
    She walks two miles every day.
    (b) Underline the correct verb:
    The cat (drink/drinks) his milk every day.
    (c) Underline the correct verb:
    I (work/worked) for three hours yesterday.
    (d) Underline the correct verb:
    The girls (is/are) here every day.
    (e) Underline the correct verb:
    I (give/gave) the paper to her last week.
    (f) Underline the correct verb:
    They (hit/hits) the ball harder than we do.

___.8   Circle the words that stand for real people:
    I one you it she

___.9   (a) Underline the adjective:
    Garfield is a happy cat.
    (b) Underline the correct adjective:
    Bill is (taller/tallest) than you.
    (c) Underline the correct adjective:
    Charles is the (taller/tallest) boy here.

___.10 Underline the nouns:
    The children are playing football.

___.11 Underline the pronouns:
    Did it scare you?

___.12 Underline the verbs:
    He has one, but we have two.

___.13 Underline the adjective:
    The shirt looks strange on her.

.14 Underline the words that make a figure of speech:
    She was mad as a wet hen.

___.15 Underline the correct words in the following sentences:
    (a) The boys have (went/gone) to town.
    (b) They do not have (no/any) money.
    (c) The books (is/are) where they (was/were) yesterday.

___.16 Underline the nouns:
    The girl's poem was about liberty.

___.17 Underline the pronouns.
    Who has their music with them?

___.18 Underline all verbs:
    They will drive tomorrow if it isn't snowing.

___.19 Underline the adjective:
    Bill has a good book.

___.20 Underline the adverbs:
    Why are you walking slowly?

___.21 Underline the coordinating conjunction:
    She went to town, and she bought some shoes.

IIB. WORDS *(continued)*

____.22 Underline the correct words:
  (a) She will (learn/teach) us how to swim.
  (b) He sings very (good/well).
  (c) Mother had (went/gone) to town before Dad (come/came) home.

____.23 (a) Underline the interrogative pronoun:
  Which do you want?
  (b) Underline the neuter pronoun.
  The rock was so heavy he could hardly lift it.

____.24 (a) Underline the linking verb:
  She is happy.
  (b) Underline the infinitive:
  I plan to visit Italy this summer.
  (c) Underline the helping (auxiliary) verb:
  I am going to visit my grandmother.
  (d) Underline the past participle:
  He has eaten the apple.
  (e) Underline the verbs that show present perfect tense:
  I have run so fast that I am exhausted.
  (f) Underline the present participle:
  They are swimming in the pond.
  (g) Underline the verbs that show the progressive tense:
  She is playing the flute in the symphony.

____.25 Underline the predicate adjective:
  She is happy.

____.26 Underline the correct word to avoid double negatives:
  He does not have (no/any) pencils.

____.27 Underline the correct words:
  (a) We went to (their/there) house.
  (b) She (don't/doesn't) need (for/four) different pencils to (write/right) her report.
  (c) Betsy wants one of (them/those) apples (two/to/too).

____.28 (a) Underline the subjective-case pronouns:
  I, him, your, they, she, ours, them
  (b) Underline the objective-case pronouns.
  he, her, we, them, theirs,
  (c) Underline the possessive-case pronouns:
  ours, I, his, me, she, hers.
  (d) Underline the demonstrative pronouns:
  this, he, that, hers, its, those
  (e) Underline first person pronouns:
  he, them, I, them, we
  (f) Underline the unnecessary word:
  Jack he lives in Hawaii.

____.29 (a) Underline the comparative adjective:
  Mine is better than yours.
  (b) Underline the unnecessary word:
  His is most best of all.
  (c) Underline the definite adjectives:
  mine, this, its, those, she
  (d) Underline the indefinite adjectives:
  she, some, mine, few, pretty

____.30 Underline the preposition:
  The dog is on the floor.

IIB. WORDS *(continued)*

____.31 (a) Underline the adverb:

His mother will be very happy.

(b) Underline the comparative adverb:

He walked more quickly than Jim.

(c) Underline the superlative adverb:

He walked most quickly of all the boys.

(d) Underline the prepositional phrase:

The girl ran into the house.

____.32 Underline the direct object (noun complement):

He drove the car.

____.33 Underline the correct words:

After he (drank/drunk) the water, he (sit/sat/set) the glass on the table.

____.34 (a) Underline the relative pronoun:

The man who you saw was my father.

(b) Underline the indefinite pronoun:

Each may go to the store.

(c) Underline the reflexive pronoun:

Did you hurt yourself?

(d) Underline the intensive pronoun:

Are you yourself going?

(e) Underline the pronoun complement:

I would like to be him.

(f) Underline the pronoun that shows correct agreement:

There is a car in the parking lot with (its/their) lights on.

____.35 (a) Underline the words to show past-perfect tense:

He had finished washing the car when it started raining.

(b) Underline the words to show future perfect tense.

He will have finished washing the car by the time they arrive.

(c) Underline the transitive verb:

Sam hit the ball.

(d) Underline the intransitive verb:

The dog died.

____.36 (a) Underline the phrase that acts as an adjective:

He was a poor boy from the country.

(b) Underline the adjective that modifies the pronoun:

The flowers made her happy.

(c) Underline the participle that acts as an adjective:

He passed the reading test.

(d) Underline the complement of the subject, the predicate adjective:

She is excellent

____.37 Underline the interjection:

Hey! Stop that.

____.38 (a) Underline the complement of the subject, or the predicate noun:

Maria is a teacher of children with disabilities.

(b) Underline the complement of the verb, or the indirect object:

He gave Mary the ball.

____.39 Underline the subordinating conjunction:

He went to the game, although he wanted to stay home.

____.40 Underline the correct words:

It (don't/doesn't) make any difference.

I have (swam/swum) that river many times.

He (sure/surely) is a good speaker.

IIC. PHRASES

___.1   Underline the noun phrase:
          The big brown dog barked at the mailman.

___.2   Underline the verb phrase:
          The last biscuit has been eaten.

___.3   Underline the prepositional phrase:
          He went to the store.

___.4   Underline the adjective phrase:
          She is the girl with the blond hair.

___.5   Underline the adverb phrase:
          They just arrived from town.

___.6   Underline the participial phrase:
          She went walking down the street.

IID. CLAUSES

___.1   Underline the main (independent) clauses.
          I have a cat, and I have a dog.
          He went to town, but he did not buy anything.
          After she came home, she went to sleep.

IIE. PARAGRAPHS

___.1   Which of the two sentences is true?
          (a) A paragraph is a group of sentences about one main topic or idea.
          (b) A paragraph is a group of words about many different things.

___.2   Which paragraph below is indented?
          (a) The little boy wanted to bring the little puppy home. He knew that his
              Dad would not let him keep it. After thinking about it he decided to
              forget the idea.
          (b)   The little boy wanted to bring the puppy home. He knew that his
              Dad would not let him keep it. After thinking about it. he decided to
              forget the idea.

___.3   Write the letters of the sentences in the best order to make a good
          paragraph.
          (a) The dog yelped and ran toward home.
          (b) The kite was flying high in the sky.
          (c) The kite took a nosedive and landed on Spotty.
          (d) Suddenly the string broke.

___.4   Underline the topic sentence in the following paragraph:
              Jeff had fun at the amusement park. First he rode the log slide, and then
          he rode the rocket. After that he saw one of the musical shows. Just
          before he left, he got a hot dog and some cotton candy. When he got
          home he went right to sleep,

___.5   Which of the following two paragraphs is descriptive writing?
          (a) The afternoon was gorgeous! The sun warmed the new daffodils
              and the blue sky made a brilliant contrast with the cotton puffs that seemed
              to hang motionless. The damp grass smelled of the early morning rain.
              Blue violets polka-dotted the entire back yard. What a day for a picnic!
          (b) Everybody needs a pocket calculator! Why should we bother with long
              division that takes so long when the answer can be had in seconds? Of
              course you have to punch the right buttons. But that is certainly a lot
              easier than doing long division.

___.6   Which of the above paragraphs in item .5 is an example of expository
          writing?

II3. PARAGRAPHS (*continued*)

___.7   Underline the connective words in the following paragraph:

One day Dave decided to go to town. First he got dressed and rode his bike to Main Street. Next, he parked his bike and started walking down the sidewalk. He saw many things he wanted. He decided to buy a new model airplane. When he started to pay for it, he realized that he did not bring any money. He got on his bike and rode around for a while. Finally, he decided to go home.

___.8   Which of the two paragraphs below is an example of expository writing?

(a) The first thing to do to make ice cream sauce is to heat the milk until it is warm and then add the butter. Pour in the chocolate chips and sugar and stir until melted. Let it boil. Add one teaspoon of vanilla. Pour over ice cream.

(b) The little kitten seemed lost in the big house. It was all alone. He just sat and looked around. Soon he scrambled to the back room. There he found an empty spool. It was fun to play with it. It would roll away and then roll back. The kitty seemed much happier after he found his new friend.

___.9   Which of the two paragraphs in item .8 is an example of narrative writing?

III: IDEATION - Sample Items

IIIA.2-.7 (Fluency), B.3-.6 (Maturity), C.1-.7 (Word Choice), D.1-.10 (Style).

Directions: Write a short story about a picture your teacher will give to you. Spell the words on your own. If you make a mistake put a line through it. Do not erase. You have about twenty minutes to write your story. Take a few minutes to plan your story before you begin. Write the best story you can.

A. Fluency
___.1   Ask the child to tell you a story. Enough words should be used to make the story understandable and to cover important points in the story.
___.2   15 words written
___.3   30 words written
___.4   50 words written
___.5   70 words written
___.6   110 words written
___.7   115 words written

B. Maturity
___.1   Ask child to name objects in the classroom. Check for accuracy.
___.2   Ask child to describe objects in the classroom. Check for accuracy.
___.3   Lists of objects, sometimes within a sentence (Level I-Naming).
___.4   Unrelated descriptions, simple sentences (Level II-Description).
___.5   Beginning, middle, and end; a good plot (Level III-Plot).
___.6   Good story dealing with an issue; makes a point (Level IV-Issue).

C. Word Choice
___.1   Words are accurate for the situation and story line.
___.2   A variety of descriptive words are used.
___.3   Wide vocabulary, some unusual words specific for writer's purpose.

C. Word Choice *(continued)*

___.4   Words to elicit sounds, onomatopoeia.

___.5   No superfluous words or trite expressions.

___.6   Words reflecting use of the senses (smells. sounds. texture, etc.).

___.7   Words reflecting states of emotion (anger, love, confusion, etc.).

D. Style

___.1   Sequence words used (first. next, following, then, later, etc.).

___.2   Well-organized (clear beginning, middle, end sections).

___.3   Sequence is logical and orderly.

___.4   Sufficient details (examples, proofs, reasons) and supplementary ideas to support or develop the main idea or purpose.

___.5   Plot is cohesive; no superfluous ideas; no errors in logic.

___.6   The purpose or main idea is clear, accurate, and complete.

___.7   No split infinitives.

___.8   References are clear; no ambiguous pronoun references.

___.9   Modifiers (words, phrases, clauses) placed logically for clarity.

___.10   No shifts in point of view, tense, person, or number.

TEACHER'S KEY TO SELECTED ITEMS

SAMPLE ITEMS FOR TESTS OF WRITTEN EXPRESSION

I. MECHANICS
  A.1-.4 (Capitalization)
  B.1-.3 (Punctuation)
  C.1-.2 (Abbreviations)
  D.1-.2 (Numbers)

Teacher: The correction is underlined in the letter below. Following each correction is the number of the skill.

<u>Apr.</u>**(A.2)(B.1)(C.2)** 1, 19____

Dear <u>Jim</u>, **(A.1)**

Our class went to the airport last <u>Wednesday,</u> **(A.2)(B.1)** <u>Mr.</u> **(A.1)(B.1)(C.1)** <u>Wilson</u> **(A.1)** drove the school <u>bus.</u> **(B.1)** Have you been to the <u>airport?</u> **(B.2)** <u>We</u> **(A.3)** saw <u>five</u> **(D.2)** big airplanes. The teacher and <u>I</u> **(A.4)** flew <u>one.</u> **(B.2)(D.2)** They let <u>Rover</u> **(A.1)** help us. <u>April</u> **(A.2)** fool!

Our new phone number is 765<u>-</u>4321. **(B.3)(D.1)** Call me next <u>Tue.</u> **(B.1)(C.2)** if you can.

Your pal,

Les

I. MECHANICS
  A.5-.7 (Capitalization)
  B.4-.5 (Punctuation)
  C.3 (Abbreviations)
  D.3-.4 (Numbers)

Teacher: See scoring comments regarding the above letter.

97 <u>pipin lane</u> **(A.5)(D.4)**
New <u>Albany, IN</u> **(B.4)(A.7)(C.3)** 47119 **(D.4)**
December 3<u>,</u> **(B.4)** 19____ **(D.3)**

Dear <u>Aunt Betty,</u> **(A.6)(B.4)**

Thanks for the birthday check! I am going to buy the book <u>When We Were Very Young</u> **(A.5)(B.5)** with the money. We went to <u>louisville</u> **(A.5)** to see grandmother on <u>Thanksgiving</u> **(A.5)** day and rode the <u>Belle of Louisville.</u> **(B.5)** It was cold. Last week we drove over to <u>Ohio.</u> **(A.5)** Tomorrow our class is going to the <u>Circle Theater</u> **(A.5)** for a concert. It seems like I'm always going somewhere. I think it's fun.

Thanks again for remembering my birthday.

<u>Your</u> **(A.6)** <u>niece,</u> **(B.4)**

Sally

I. MECHANICS

Teacher: Place a check beside the skill number for each incorrectly copied item. In the Capitalization section, the underlined letters indicate the correct response. In the Punctuation section, the sentences have been written correctly.

IA. Capitalization

____.1-.4 (see informal letter: Dear Jim)

____.5-.7 (see informal letter: Dear Aunt Betty)

____.8   The <u>S</u>miths moved in next door to us.

____.9   My favorite writer is <u>R</u>obert <u>L</u>. <u>S</u>tevenson.

____.10   My class goes to lunch at 10:45 <u>A</u>.<u>M</u>.

____.11   (a) He lives near <u>M</u>t. Ranier.

            (b) We visited <u>B</u>oulder <u>D</u>am this summer.

____.12   Many <u>H</u>ispanic people live in <u>A</u>merica.

____.13   My brother is studying <u>G</u>eometry 101 and <u>S</u>panish 247.

____.14   John asked, "<u>W</u>hat can I do now?"

____.15   (Outline) I. <u>T</u>ransportation

                  A. <u>C</u>ars

                  B. <u>P</u>lane

____.16   (a) She made a donation to the <u>B</u>oy <u>S</u>couts of <u>A</u>merica.

            (b) His brother owns <u>J</u>im's <u>S</u>peedy <u>C</u>ar <u>W</u>ash.

____.17   The band played <u>A</u>uld <u>L</u>ang <u>S</u>yne at midnight.

____.18   (a) They plan to vacation in <u>I</u>reland.

            (b) Do you have any <u>K</u>leenex?

            (c) The story of the <u>J</u>ews at Masada is a heroic one.

____.19   (Poem: The Swallow by Christina B. Rossetti)

                <u>F</u>ly away, fly away over the sea,

                    <u>S</u>un-loving swallow, for summer is done;

                <u>C</u>ome again, come again, come back to me,

                    Bringing the summer and bringing the sun.

____.20   Her brother is Thomas B. Bosman <u>Ph</u>.<u>D</u>.

____.21   Have you seen a copy of the <u>B</u>ill of <u>R</u>ights?

____.22   Do you like <u>S</u>panish music?

IB. Punctuation

____.1-.3 (see informal letter: Dear Jim)

____.4-.5 (see informal letter: Dear Aunt Betty)

____.6   (a) He didn<u>'</u>t want to go to school.

           (b) The girl<u>'</u>s dog ran away.

           (c) All the students<u>'</u> papers were good.

____.7   Have you read <u>"</u>Treasure Island<u>"</u>?

____.8   Ouch<u>!</u> You pinched me.

____.9   Richard M<u>.</u> Nixon resigned from office.

____.10   I must meet my mother at 10<u>:</u>15 this morning.

____.11   (a) He plays football<u>,</u> baseball<u>,</u> and soccer.

           (b) "I read my homework," Susie bragged.

____.12   (a) <u>"</u>I need to study more.<u>"</u> he said.

           (b) His <u>"</u>sorrow<u>"</u> lasted about one minute.

____.13   (a) Yes<u>,</u> I can go now.

           (b) She can go with you tomorrow<u>,</u> Maria.

           (c) However<u>,</u> I cannot stay for the entire game.

IB. Punctuation *(continued)*

       (d) I ride the bus to school, and I ride it home.

___.14 (a) His room is 10 ft, long by 12 ft, wide.

       (b) (Outline) I, Foods

                   A, Fruits

                   B, Vegetables

___.15 (a) (Business letter) Dear Mr. Edwardo: (colon–salutation)

___.15 (b) (Plays) Mary: Hello, Bill. How are you?

                  Bill: Fine, Mary. And you? (colon–plays)

___.15 (c) (References) Boston: Allyn & Bacon. (colon–references)

___.16 Have you seen the <u>Mona Lisa</u>? (underline–works of art)

___.17 Sometimes when we write, we have to sep-arate words at the end
of the line. (hyphen–end of line syllabication)

___.18 After he woke up, he grabbed a bite to eat.
(comma–to separate the main clause)

___.19 Her sister, a dentist, is Mary Lou Harrison D,D,D,
(period–professional degrees)

___.20 The store is open from 9:30–6:00. (dash)

___.21 (a) After he called James, Allen ate supper.
(comma–separate confusing words)

___.21 (b) Betty, his aunt, is living with them.
(comma–set off appositives)

___.21 (c) (Reference) Smith, D., & Jones, J. (1986). <u>Welcome home</u>.
Ashland: Nebus Publishing Co. (comma–in references)

___.21 (d) You may, at your discretion, eat lunch first.
(comma–set off incidental words)

___.21 (e) Happy with her progress thus far, she took a rest.
(comma–set off modifiers)

___.22 Her hair (even though it was grey) was admired by all.
(parentheses)

IC. Abbreviations

___.1 Mr., Mrs.

___.2 Mon., Wed., Fri.; Jan., NW., Aug.

___.3 TN, OK, CA

___.4 Charles E. Smith

___.5 10:30 AM; 10:30 PM

___.6 Bill Smith, Jr.

___.7 27 ft.; 14 in.

___.8 P.O. Box 27; R.R. 3

___.9 TV, UFO, CB

___.10 FBI, IRS

___.11 Vol., p., et al., e.g.

ID. Numbers

___.1 check student's response

___.2 3, 15, 27, 64, 809

   .3 check student's response

___.4 check student's response

___.5 check student's response

___.6 check student's response

___.7 check student's response

ID. Numbers *(continued)*
____.8 VII. XV, XLII, L, C

II. USAGE

IIA. Sentences
____.1-.3 check student responses
____.4   complete sentence ....b
____.5   simple sentence c
____.6   telling (declarative) sentence ....b
____.7   asking (interrogative) sentence c
____.8   the best sentence ....a
____9   exclamatory sentence ....b
____.10   compound sentence c
____.11   complete sentence (not a fragment) ....a
____.12   sentence with the best word order c
____.13   Imperative sentence c
____.14   Not a run-on sentence ....a
____.15   Compound subject ....boy and girl
____.16   Compound predicate ....barked and ran
____.17   Word order ....b
____.18   There is no subject, it is implied.
____.19   Complex sentence ....b
____.20   Compound/complex sentence ....a

IIB. Words
____.1   (a) noun ....check student's response
           (b) noun ....check student's response
           (c) noun ....check student's response
____.2   verbs ....check student's response
____.3   (a) adjective ....check student's response
           (b) adjective ....check student's response
           (c) adjective ....check student's response
           (d) adjective ....check student's response
           (e) adjective ....check student's response
____.4   (a) preposition ....check student's response
           (b) preposition ....check student's response
           (c) preposition ....check student's response
____.5   word order ....check student's response
____.6   (a) all nouns ....ball, fence
           (b) all nouns ....Mr. Jones, bus, Tuesday
           (c) all nouns ....boys, birthdays, March
           (d) the noun ....one
____.7   (a) verb ....walks
           (b) correct verb ....drinks
           (c) correct verb ....worked
           (d) correct verb ....are
           (e) correct verb ....gave
           (f) correct verb ....hit
____.8   pronouns ....I, one, you, she
____.9   (a) adjective ....happy
           (b) correct adjective ....taller
           (c) correct adjective ....tallest
____.10   nouns ....children, football

IIB. Words (*continued*)

___.11	pronouns	. . . .	it, you
___.12	verbs	. . . .	has, have
___.13	adjective	. . . .	strange
___.14	figure-of-speech	. . . .	mad as a wet hen
___.15	(a) correct word	. . . .	gone
	(b) correct word	. . . .	any
	(c) correct words	. . . .	are, were
___.16	nouns	. . . .	poem, liberty
___.17	pronouns	. . . .	who, their, them
___.18	verbs	. . . .	will drive, isn't (snowing)
___.19	adjective	. . . .	good
___.20	adverbs	. . . .	why, slowly
___.21	coordinating conjunction	. . . .	and
___.22	(a) correct word	. . . .	teach
	(b) correct word	. . . .	well
	(c) correct word	. . . .	gone, came
___.23	(a) Pronoun (interrogative)	. . . .	which
	(b) Pronoun (neuter)	. . . .	it
___.24	(a) Verb Forms (linking verb)	. . . .	is
	(b) Verb Forms (infinitive)	. . . .	to visit
	(c) Verb Forms (auxiliary)	. . . .	am
	(d) Verb Forms (past participle)	. . . .	eaten
	(e) Verb Forms (present perfect tense)	. . . .	have run
	(f) Verb Forms (present participle)	. . . .	swimming
	(g) Verb Forms (progressive tense)	. . . .	is playing
___.25	Predicate adjective	. . . .	happy
___.26	Avoid double negatives	. . . .	any
___.27	Review (irregular words)	. . . .	their, doesn't, four, write, those, too
___.28	(a) Pronouns (subjective case)	. . . .	I, they, she
	(b) Pronouns (objective case)	. . . .	her, them
	(c) Pronouns (possessive case)	. . . .	ours, his, hers
	(d) Pronouns (demonstrative case)	. . . .	this, that, those
	(e) Pronouns (first person)	. . . .	I, we
	(f) Pronouns (superfluous)	. . . .	he
___.29	(a) Adjectives (comparative)	. . . .	better
	(b) Adjectives (superfluous)	. . . .	most
	(c) Adjectives (definite)	. . . .	this, those
	(d) Adjectives (indefinite)	. . . .	some, few
___.30	Preposition	. . . .	on
___.31	(a) Adverbs (definition)	. . . .	very
	(b) Adverbs (comparative)	. . . .	more
	(c) Adverbs (superlative)	. . . .	most
	(d) Adverb Form (prepositional phrase)	. . . .	into the house
___.32	Noun (noun complement/direct object)	. . . .	car
,33	Review (irregular words)	. . . .	drank, set
___.34	(a) Pronouns (relative)	. . . .	who
	(b) Pronouns (indefinite)	. . . .	each
	(c) Pronouns (reflexive)	. . . .	yourself
	(d) Pronouns (intensive)	. . . .	yourself
	(e) Pronouns (complement)	. . . .	him
	(f) Pronouns (agreement)	. . . .	its
___.35	(a) Verbs (past-perfect tense)	. . . .	had finished
	(b) Verbs (future perfect)	. . . .	will have finished

IIB. Words *(continued)*

(c) Verbs (transitive) . . . . .hit
(d) Verbs (intransitive) . . . . .died

___.36 (a) Adjectives (phrase) . . . . .from the country
(b) Adjectives (modify pronoun) . . . . .happy
(c) Adjectives (participle) .reading
(d) Adjectives (predicate adjective) . . . . .excellent

___.37 Interjection . . . . .Hey!

___.38 (a) Nouns (complement of subject/predicate noun) . . .teacher
(b) Nouns (complement of verb/indirect object) . . . . .Mary

___.39 Subordinating conjunction .although

___.40 Review (irregular words) . . . . .doesn't, swum, surely

IIC. PHRASES

___.1 Noun phrase . . . . .The big brown dog
___.2 Verb phrase . . . . .has been eaten
___.3 Prepositional phrase . . . . .to the store
___.4 Adjective phrase . . . . .with the blond hair
___.5 Adverb phrase . . . . .from town
___.6 Participial phrase . . . . .walking down the meet

IID. CLAUSES

___.1 Main clauses (independent) . . . . .I have a cat, I have a dog,
he went to town, he did not buy anything, she went to sleep.

IIE. PARAGRAPHS

___.1 Definition . . . . .a
___.2 Indentation . . . . .b
___.3 Sequence within . . . . .b, d, c, a
___.4 Topic sentence . . . . .Jeff had fun at the amusement park.
___.5 Descriptive writing . . . . .a
___.6 Expository writing . . . . .b
___.7 Connective words within . . . . .first, next, when, finally
___.8 Expository writing . . . . .a
___.9 Narrative writing . . . . .b

III. EVALUATION

(Key is given with the sample items)

Spelling and Handwriting

Spelling Skill Objectives

I. *Readiness*

A. Motor Coordination

.1 (Refer to Handwriting Objectives IC.1-IC.3.)

B. Visual Discrimination

.1–.3 (Refer to Word Recognition Objectives IC.1-IC.3.)

C. Auditory Discrimination

.1–.2 (Refer to Word Recognition Objectives IIA.1 and .2.)

D. Manuscript Letters

.1 (Refer to Handwriting Objectives IIA.1-.4.)

II. *Basic Words*

A. High Frequency - The student:

.1–.6 Writes each word as pronounced by the examiner from a list of high-frequency words appropriate to his or her level.

B. Grade Level - The student:

.1–.6 Writes each word as pronounced by the examiner from a list of grade-level words appropriate to his or her level.

C. Number - The student:

.1–.4 Writes each word as pronounced by the examiner from a list of number words appropriate to his or her level.

D. Color - The student:

.1–.2 Writes each word pronounced by the examiner from a list of color words appropriate to his or her level.

E. Days of Week - The student:

.1 Writes each word as pronounced by the examiner from a list of the days of the week appropriate to his or her level.

F. Months of the Year - The student:

.1 Writes each word as pronounced by the examiner from a list of the months of the year appropriate to his or her level.

III. *Auditory Recognition of Phonemes*

A. Consonants - The student:

.1 Writes the initial letter of each word pronounced by the examiner from a list of words beginning with single consonants.

.2 Writes the letter for the ending sound heard in each word pronounced by the examiner.

B. Digraphs - The student:

.1 Writes the first two letters of each word pronounced by the examiner.

C. Vowels - The student:

.1 Writes the letter representing the vowel sound heard in each word pronounced by the examiner.

IV. *Graphemes*

A. Consonants - The student:

.1 Writes the word pronounced by the examiner from a list of words containing all initial consonants.

.2 Writes the word pronounced by the examiner from a list of words containing all final consonants.

B. Consonant Blends - The student:

.1 Writes each word pronounced by the examiner from a list containing all two-letter blends.

.2–.4 Writes each word pronounced by the examiner from a list containing three-letter blends appropriate to his or her level.

C. Digraphs - The student:

.1 Writes each word pronounced by the examiner from a list of words containing digraphs.

D. Variant Consonants - The student:

.1–.5 Writes each word pronounced by the examiner containing the variant consonants appropriate to his or her level.

E. Vowels: Short - The student:

.1   Writes each word pronounced by the examiner from a list of words containing short vowels.

F. Vowels: Long - The student:

.1   Writes each word pronounced by the examiner containing long vowels.

.2   Writes each word pronounced by the examiner from a list of CVCe words.

G. Vowels: Special - The student:

.1   Writes each word pronounced by the examiner from a list of words containing double vowels.

.2   Writes each word pronounced by the examiner from a list of words containing r-controlled vowels.

G. Vowels: Special - The student:

.3–.7 Writes each word pronounced by the examiner in which the schwa affects the vowel sound from a list of words appropriate to his or her level.

.8–.11 Writes each word pronounced by the examiner from a list of words containing variant vowel sounds appropriate to his or her level.

V. *Structural Analysis*

A. Suffixes - The student:

.1   Writes each word pronounced by the examiner in which "s" or "es" is added without changing the base word.

.2–.3 Writes each word pronounced by the examiner in which the final consonant is doubled before adding the suffix.

.4   Writes each word pronounced by the examiner in which the final "e" is dropped before adding the suffix.

.5   Writes each word pronounced by the examiner in which "y" is changed to "i" before adding the suffix.

B. Derivational Suffixes - The student:

.1–.4 Writes each word pronounced by the examiner from a list of words containing derivational suffixes appropriate to his or her level.

C. Prefixes - The student:

.1–.3 Writes each word pronounced by the examiner from a list of words containing prefixes appropriate to his or her level.

D. Word Forms - The student:

.1,.3,.6,.9,.12 Writes each word pronounced by the examiner from a list of compound words appropriate to his or her level.

.4,.7,.10 Writes each word pronounced by the examiner from a list of contractions appropriate to his or her level.

.2,.5,.8,.11,.13 Writes each word pronounced by the examiner from a list of homophones appropriate to his or her level.

Handwriting Skill Objectives

I. *Readiness*

    A. **Concepts and Directions** - The student:

        .1   Draws and writes the appropriate response to the examiner's oral directions.

    B. **Basic Manuscript Strokes** - The student:

        .1   Copies the basic manuscript strokes from a model.

    C. **Fine Motor Coordination** - The student:

        .1   Writes the basic strokes with correct starting position.

        .2   Draws a straight line and a curved line between two parallel lines to teacher-expected criteria.

        .3   Grasps the writing instrument correctly.

II. *Manuscript Writing*

    A. **Manuscript Pretest** - The student:

        .1   Prints the model sentence which contains all of the letters of the alphabet, as presented by the examiner.

    B. **Manuscript: Lower Case** - The student:

        .1   Prints the vertical-stroke letters as dictated by the examiner.

        .2   Prints the backward circle-stroke letters as dictated by the examiner.

        .3   Prints the vertical-stroke with forward curve, undercurve, and backward-to-forward curve letters as dictated by the examiner.

        .4   Prints the slant-line letters as dictated by the examiner.

        .5   Prints the full space backward-and-forward circle, hump-and-cross letters as dictated by the examiner.

        .6   Prints the descender letters as dictated by the examiner.

    C. **Manuscript: Upper Case** - The student:

        .1   Prints the vertical-and-horizontal stroke letters as dictated by the examiner.

        .2   Prints the backward circle-stroke letters as dictated by the examiner.

        .3   Prints the slant-line letters as dictated by the examiner.

        .4   Prints the loop letters and push up stroke letter as dictated by the examiner.

    D. **Numerals** - The student:

        .1   Prints the numerals from 0–9 with correct beginning strokes as they are dictated by the examiner.

III. *Cursive Writing*

    A. **Cursive Pretest** - The student:

        .1   Writes the model sentence which contains all of the letters of the alphabet, as presented by the examiner

    B. **Basic Cursive Strokes** - The student:

        .1   Copies the basic cursive strokes from a model.

    C. **Cursive: Lower Case** - The student:

        .1   Writes the undercurve letters as dictated by the examiner.

        .2   Writes the upper-loop letters as dictated by the examiner.

        .3   Writes the down-curve letters as dictated by the examiner.

        .4   Writes the descender letters as dictated by the examiner.

        .5   Writes the overcurve letters as dictated by the examiner.

        .6   Writes the checkstroke letters as dictated by the examiner.

    D. **Cursive: Upper Case** - The student:

        .1   Writes the down/curve oval letters when orally dictated by the examiner.

        .2   Writes the cane-stroke letters as they are dictated by the examiner.

        .3   Writes the upper loop, clockwise oval letters as dictated by the examiner.

        .4   Writes the boat letters as they are orally dictated.

        .5   Writes the undercurve stroke letters as dictated by the examiner.

SAMPLE ITEMS FOR TESTS OF SPELLING AND HANDWRITING

SPELLING: I. READINESS

IA.1, Motor Coordination, Gr. K.	(Refer to Handwriting Items IB.1-IC.3.)
IB.1-.3, Visual Discrim., Gr. K.	(Refer to Word Recognition Items IC.1-IC.3.)
IC.1-.2, Auditory Discrim., Gr. K.	(Refer to Word Recognition Items IIA.1-.2.)
ID.1, Manuscript Letters, Gr. K/1.	(Refer to Handwriting Items IIA.1-IIC.4.)

SPELLING: II. BASIC WORDS

Directions: Provide student with blank sheet of lined paper numbered appropriately.
Directions to student: "I'm going to pronounce some words I want you to write. I will pronounce the word, use it in a sentence, and pronounce it again."

IIA.1, High Frequency, Gr. 1.

1. the	4. he	7. are	10. it	13. we	16. like
2. in	5. you	8. them	11. not	14. them	17. she
3. on	6. me	9. and	12. they	15. is	18. went

IIA.2, High Frequency, Gr. 2.

1. away	4. my	7. look	10. like	13. sing	16. going	19. run
2. work	5. was	8. come	11. keep	14. has	17. had	20. his
3. not	6. that	9. tell	12. dog	15. from	18. may	

IIA.3, High Frequency, Gr. 3.

1. yours	4. better	7. their	10. fine	13. should	16. also	19. learn
2. write	5. must	8. little	11. close	14. done	17. knew	20. can't
3. high	6. cannot	9. city	12. I'm	15. it's	18. those	

IIA.4, High Frequency, Gr. 4.

1. knee	4. sudden	7. breakfast	10. young	13. cousin	17. sale
2. mountain	5. famous	8. kitchen	11. ocean	14. families	18. hang
3. beautiful	6. pound	9. careful	12. reason	15. climb	19. easy
				16. cause	20. whole

IIA.5, High Frequency, Gr. 5.

1. freeze	4. cellar	7. dozen	10. journey	13. model	17. several
2. ache	5. village	8. measure	11. science	14. direction	18. sentence
3. bloom	6. rough	9. avoid	12. doubt	15. officer	19. destroy
				16. dawn	20. regular

IIA.6, High Frequency, Gr. 6.

1. palace	4. safety	7. split	10. breathe	13. material	17. temperature
2. success	5. foreign	8. project	11. quarrel	14. style	18. dangerous
3. orchestra	6. pigeon	9. machine	12. silence	15. principal	19. excitement
				16. dictionary	20. accept

IIB.1, Grade Level, Gr. 1.

1. can	4. him	7. apple	10. jam	13. met	16. up	19. pan
2. did	5. bake	8. fan	11. kitten	14. no	17. rope	20. sun
3. but	6. go	9. home	12. let	15. end	18. in	

II.B.2, Grade Level, Gr. 2.

1. show	4. thick	7. stretch	10. loose	13. taught	16. scare	19. turn
2. block	5. spray	8. slight	11. friend	14. sound	17. tore	20. collar
3. bread	6. cheese	9. grew	12. whose	15. noise	18. march	

IIB.3, Grade Level, Gr. 3.

1. spring	4. cage	7. rocks	10. biggest	13. babies	16. nose	19. runner
2. quit	5. suit	8. cattle	11. friendly	14. helpful	17. raise	20. news-
3. wren	6. ease	9. skating	12. popcorn	15. weren't	18. taking	paper

IIB.4, Grade Level, Gr. 4.

1. squirrel	4. age	7. pencil	10. alone	13. aren't	16. quickness	19. metal
2. ghost	5. tough	8. size	11. employ	14. board	17. uncertain	20. wrong
3. geography	6. guard	9. repair	12. fare	15. unless	18. everybody	

IIB.5, Grade Level, Gr. 5.

1. foolish	4. roommate	7. speechless	10. loan	13. certain	16. excellent	19. delicious
2. define	5. amusement	8. disapprove	11. predict	14. native	17. neighbors	20. luggage
3. frozen	6. enforce	9. television	12. splash	15. prolong	18. complain	

IIB.6, Grade Level, Gr. 6.

1. comical	3. million	5. boundary	7. screen	11. quality	14. impossible
2. onion	4. backward	6. schedule	8. parcel	12. capitol	15. suspended
			9. subway	13. misrepresent	16. absent
			10. fixture		

IIC.1, Numbers, Gr. 2.

1. five	3. four	5. six	7. ten
2. eight	4. one	6. two	8. three

IIC.2, Numbers, Gr. 3.

1. nine	2. seven	3. sixty

IIC.3, Numbers, Gr. 4.

1. fifteen	2. eleven	3. twelve	4. fourteen	5. fifty	6. thirteen	7. twenty

IIC.4, Numbers, Gr. 5.

1. eighteen	3. forty	5. eighty	7. seventy
2. sixteen	4. seventeen	6. nineteen	8. ninety

IID.1, Colors, Gr. 2.

1. white	2. brown	3. yellow	4. blue	5. black	6. red

IID.2, Colors, Gr. 4.

1. orange	2. gray	3. purple	4. pink

IIE.1, Days of Week, Gr. 4.

1. Tuesday	2. Friday	3. Wednesday	4. Monday	5. Sunday	6. Thursday	7. Saturday

---

IIF.1, Months of the Year, Gr. 4.

1. March	3. February	5. May	7. October	9. September	11. August
2. June	4. November	6. July	8. January	10. December	12. April

---

SPELLING: III. AUDITORY RECOGNITION OF PHONEMES

Directions: "As I pronounce these words, you are to listen for the *first* sound that you hear in each word. Then write on your paper the letter that makes that sound."

IIIA.1, Initial Cons., Gr. 1.

1. <u>f</u> an	4. <u>b</u> ear	7. <u>j</u> ello	10. <u>n</u> urse	13. <u>y</u> ellow	16. <u>m</u> ilk	19. <u>v</u> ine
2. <u>k</u> ite	5. <u>h</u> ome	8. <u>c</u> orn	11. <u>g</u> irl	14. <u>s</u> un	17. <u>p</u> ig
3. <u>z</u> oo	6. <u>w</u> ork	9. <u>d</u> oll	12. <u>l</u> eg	15. <u>t</u> oy	18. <u>r</u> abbit

IIA.2, Final Cons., Gr. 1:

"As I pronounce these words, listen for the *last* sound you hear in each word. Then write the letter that makes that sound on your paper."

1. bi <u>g</u>	4. ra <u>t</u>	7. bi <u>b</u>	9. bel <u>l</u>	11. clas <u>s</u>	13. ca <u>p</u>
2. pe <u>n</u>	5. sa <u>d</u>	8. of <u>f</u>	10. o <u>x</u>	12. sta <u>r</u>	14. ra <u>m</u>
3. ha <u>v</u> e	6. kic <u>k</u>				

IIIB.1, Digraphs, Gr. 1:

"Write the *first two* letters of each word I pronounce."

1. <u>ch</u> air	2. <u>sh</u> oes	3. <u>wh</u> istle	4. <u>th</u> orn

IIIC.1, Vowels, Gr. 1:

"Listen for the *vowel* sound you hear in each word I pronounce. Then write on your paper the letter that makes that sound."

1. b <u>a</u> ke	3. r <u>i</u> de	5. g <u>o</u>	7. <u>a</u> pple	9. t <u>o</u> p
2. <u>u</u> p	4. b <u>e</u> d	6. <u>u</u> se	8. P <u>e</u> te	10. b <u>i</u> t

SPELLING: IV. GRAPHEMES

IVA.1, Initial Cons., Gr. 1:

"I'm going to pronounce some words I want you to write.
I will pronounce the word, use it in a sentence, and pronounce it again."

1. cat	4. went	7. see	10. log	13. did	16. just	18. zoom
2. you	5. kit	8. has	11. pan	14. view	17. got	19. man
3. not	6. bed	9. red	12. take	15. fat		

IVA.2, Final Cons., Gr. 1:

1. pig	3. ball	5. car	7. bed	9. pot
2. top	4. kick	6. pen	8. ham	10. bib

IVB.1, Cons. Blends, Gr. 2.

1. stop	4. skip	7. fly	10. green	13. draw	16. play
2. black	5. swim	8. glass	11. close	14. brown	17. pretty
3. tree	6. spin	9. free	12. sleep	15. snap	18. crow

IVB.2, Cons. Blends: 3 Letter, Gr. 2.

1. stream	2. street

IVB.3, Cons. Blends: 3 Letter, Gr. 3.

1. spring	2. strip

IVB.4, Cons. Blends: 3 Letter, Gr. 5.

1. splash	2. splice

IVC.1, Digraphs, Gr. 2.

1. chair	2. fish	3. with	4. which	5. she	6. them

IVD.1, Var. Cons., Gr. 2.

1. know (kn)	6. piece (s-ce)	11. bell (sil-l)	16. who (wh-h)
2. watch (ch-tch)	7. know (sil-k)	12. kept (k-c)	17. think (nk)
3. light (sil-gh)	8. sing (ng)	13. was (z-s)	18. catch (sil-t)
4. off (f-ff)	9. tell (l-ll)	14. limb (sil-b)	19. glass (s-ss)
5. wrote (sil-w)	10. neck (k-ck)	15. whose (sil-h)	

IVD.2, Variant Cons., Gr. 3.

1. queen (kw-qu)	3. box (ks-x)	5. please (z-se)	7. wrap (r-wr)
2. socks (ks-cks)	4. horse (s-se)	6. large (j-ge)	8. city (s-c)

IVD.3, Variant Cons., Gr. 4.

1. edge (g-j)	4. right (gh)	7. enough (gh-f)	10. school (k-ch)
2. twice (tw)	5. prize (ze-z)	8. square (squ)	11. gnaw (gn)
3. knives (es-z)	6. guess (g-gu)	9. phone (ph-f)	

IVD.4, Variant Cons., Gr. 5.

1. ancient (ci-sh)	2. patient (ti-sh)	3. mansion (si-sh)	4. bridge (dge-j)

IVD.5, Variant Cons., Gr. 6.

1. schooner (sch-sh)	2. parachute (ch-sh)	3. scream (scr-skr)

IVE.1, Short Vowels, Gr. 1.

1. and	3. pup	5. got	7. up	9. jam
2. in	4. on	6. pig	8. den	

IVF.1, Long Vowels, Gr. 1.

1. me	2. go

IVF.2, Vowels: CVCe, Gr. 1.

1. like	2. cake	3. home	4. mule

IVG.1, Vowels: Special Gr. 2.

1. eat (ea)	2. boat (oa)	3. soil (oi)	4. sleep (ee)	4. rain (ai)

IVG.2, Vowels: R-Controlled, Gr. 2.

1. hear (ir)	3. her (ér)	5. door (ôr)	7. pair (ãr)	9. deer (ir)	11. share (ãr)
2. short (ôr)	4. more (ôr)	6. hurt (ér)	8. yard (är)	10. girl (ér)	12. your (ôr)

IVG.3, Vowels: Schwa, Gr. 2.

1. over (er-ər)	2. color (or-ər)	3. dollar (ar-ər)

IVG.4, Vowels: Schwa, Gr. 3.

1. needle (le-əl)	2. bundle (le-əl)

IVG.5, Vowels: Schwa, Gr. 4.

1. parents (e-ə)	3. camel (el-əl)	5. animal (al-əl)	7. along (a-ə)	9. famous (ou-ə)
2. common (o-ə)	4. circus (u-ə)	6. pupil (il-əl)	8. afraid (ai-ə)	

IVG.6, Vowels: Schwa, Gr. 5.

1. button (on-ən)
2. mission (sh-ən)
3. fiction (sh-ən)
4. organ (an-ən)
5. decision (zh-ən)
6. curtain (ain-ən)
7. dozen (en-ən)

IVG.7, Vowels: Schwa, Gr. 6.

1. fashion (io-)

IVG.8, Variant Vowels, Gr. 2.

1. day (ā-ay)
2. boy (oi-oy)
3. due (ōō-ue)
4. low (ō-ow)
5. tie (ī-ie)
6. room (ōō-oo)
7. fly (ī-y)
8. down (ou-ow)
9. crawl (ô-aw)
10. few (ōō-ew)
11. thought (ô-ou)
12. you (ōō-ou)
13. light (i-igh)
14. should (ŏŏ-ou)
15. pull (ŏŏ-u)
16. puppy (ē-y)
17. found (ou-ou)
18. book (ŏŏ-oo)
19. caught (ô-au)

IVG.9, Variant Vowels, Gr. 3.

1. fruit (ōō-ui)
2. suit (ōō-ui)

IVG.10, Variant Vowels, Gr. 4.

1. board (ôr-oar)

IVG.11, Variant Vowels, Gr. 5.

1. neighbor (ā-eigh)

SPELLING: V. STRUCTURAL ANALYSIS

Directions: "I'm going to pronounce some words I want you to write. I will pronounce the word, use it in a sentence, and pronounce it again."

VA.1, Suffixes: No Base Word Change, Gr. 2.

1. walks
2. matches

VA.2, Suffixes: Double Final Cons., Gr. 2.

1. canned
2. runner
3. getting

VA.3, Suffixes: Double Final Cons., Gr. 3.

1. biggest

VA.4, Suffixes: Drop Final E, Gr. 3.

1. writing
2. making

VA.5, Suffixes: Change Y to I, Gr. 3.

1. stories
2. carries

VB.1, Derivational Suffixes, Gr. 3.

1. nearly
2. helpful

VB.2, Derivational Suffixes, Gr. 4.

1. darkness

VB.3, Derivational Suffixes, Gr. 5.

1. dangerous
2. foolish
3. constant
4. active
5. excellent
6. eighty
7. dizzy
8. artist
9. allowance
10. enjoyable
11. agreement
12. shortage
13. feature
14. careless
15. invisible

VB.4, Derivational Suffixes, Gr. 6.

1. onions	2. activity	3. summary	4. forward

VC.1, Prefixes, Gr. 4.

1. repeat   2. until

VC.2, Prefixes, Gr. 5.

1. discovered	3. excuse	5. depart	7. protect	9. enjoyed
2. include	4. confess	6. compare	8. pretend	

VC.3, Prefixes, Gr. 6.

1. improve	2. admitted	3. misread	4. abstract	5. subtract	6. suspect

---

VD.1, Compound Words, Gr. 2.

1. outside   2. football

VD.3, Compound Words, Gr. 3.

1. firemen   2. pancakes

VD.6, Compound Words, Gr. 4.

1. everyone   2. schoolhouse

VD.9, Compound Words, Gr. 5.

1. salesman   2. streetcar

VD.12, Compound Words, Gr. 6.

1. lemonade   2. understood

VD.4, Contractions, Gr. 3.

1. wasn't	3. I've	5. can't	7. doesn't	9. they'll	11. it's
2. haven't	4. don't	6. weren't	8. he'll	10. couldn't	12. I'm

VD.7, Contractions, Gr. 4.

1. we'll	3. aren't	5. won't	7. didn't	9. let's
2. hadn't	4. you're	6. wouldn't	8. we're	10. hasn't

VD.10, Contractions, Gr. 5.

1. what's	3. he'd	5. she'll	7. you've	9. she's
2. they're	4. here's	6. we've	8. who's	10. you'd

VD.2, Homophones, Gr. 2.

1. bare	3. buy	5. know	7. two	9. too	11. to	13. bear
2. write	4. weak	6. right	8. week	10. by	12. no	

VD.5, Homophones, Gr. 3.

1. ate	3. meet	5. meat	7. hole	9. wood	11. eight	13. road
2. knows	4. whole	6. rode	8. blue	10. nose	12. blew	14. would

VD.8, Homophones, Gr. 4.

1. peace	3. bored	5. threw	7. board	9. piece	11. sail
2. sale	4. stares	6. tail	8. stairs	10. tale	12. through

VD.11, Homophones, Gr. 5.

1. past	3. heal	5. night	7. brakes	9. steel	11. knight	13. waste
2. loan	4. steal	6. waist	8. passed	10. lone	12. heel	14. breaks

VD.13, Homophones, Gr. 6.

1. cents	3. steak	5. sense	7. thrown	9. pain	11. throne
2. pane	4. pale	6. principal	8. pail	10. principle	12. stake

HANDWRITING: I. READINESS

IA.1, Concepts/Directions, Gr. K.

Directions: Provide student with pencil and unlined paper and say: "(1) Draw a line across the *top* of your paper. (2) Draw a circle in the *middle* of the paper. (3) Write your name at the *bottom* of the paper. (4) Write the number one on the *left* side of your paper. (5) Write the number 2 on the *right* side of your paper."

Examiner: Give student a second sheet of paper and say: "(1) Draw me a *square* right here (examiner points to position). (2) Draw me a *circle* right here (examiner points to position). (3) Draw me a *triangle* right here (examiner points to position). (4) Draw me a *cross* right here (examiner points to position)."

IB.1, Basic Manuscript Strokes, Gr. K.

Directions: Provide models of the basic manuscript strokes and ask student to *trace* and then *copy* these strokes.

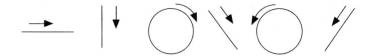

IC.1, Fine Motor Coordination, Gr. K.

Directions: Observe student's performance on preceding tasks. Note that the vertical and slant lines should be made from top to bottom; the horizontal line should be made from left to right.

IC.2, Eye-Hand Coordination, Gr. K.

Directions: Ask student to draw a straight line between two designated points and then draw a line between two parallel, curved lines.

IC.3, Grasp of Writing Instrument, Gr. K.

Directions: Hand student pencil and paper and ask him or her to write his or her name on the paper. Observe student's grasp of the writing instrument.

HANDWRITING: II. MANUSCRIPT

IIA.1, Pretest, Gr. 1.
Directions: Provide student with pencil, appropriate size lined paper and a model of the following sentence: **"The quick brown fox jumps over the lazy dog."** Observe student's letter formation, alignment, spacing, vertical quality, and line quality. Have the student copy the sentence.

IIB.1, Lower Case (l,i,t), Gr. 1.
Directions: "Print these letters in lower case as I name them: l, i, t."

IIB.2, Lower Case (o,c,a,e), Gr. 1.
Directions: "Print these letters in lower case as I name them: o, c, a, and e."

IIB.3, Lower Case (r,m,n,u,s), Gr. 1.
Directions: "Print these letters in lower case as I name them: r, m, n, u, and s."

IIB.4, Lower Case (v,w,x,z,k), Gr. 1.
Directions: "Print these letters in lower case as I name them: v, w, x, z, and k."

IIB.5, Lower Case (d,f,h,b), Gr. 1.
Directions: "Print these letters in lower case as I name them: d, f, h, b."

IIB.6, Lower Case (g,y,q,p,j), Gr. 1.
Directions: "Print these letters in lower case as I name them: g, y, q, p, and j."

IIC.1, Upper Case (L,I,T,H,E,F), Gr. 1.
Directions: "Print these letters in upper case as I name them: L, I, T, H, E, and F."

IIC.2, Upper Case (O,C,G,Q), Gr. 1.
Directions: "Print these letters in upper case as I name them: O, C, G, and Q."

IIC.3, Upper Case (A,M,N,K,V,W,X,Y,Z), Gr. 1.
Directions: "Print these letters in upper case as I name them: A, M, N, K, V, W, X, Y, and Z."

IIC.4, Upper Case (B,R,D,P,S,J,U), Gr. 1.
Directions: "Print these letters in upper case as I name them: B, R, D, P, S, J, and U."

IID.1, Numerals (0-9), Gr. 1.
Directions: "Write these numerals as I name them: 0, 1, 2, 3, 4, 5, 6, 7, 8, 9, and 10."

HANDWRITING: III. CURSIVE

IIIA.1, Pretest, Gr. 3.
Directions: Provide student with pencil, appropriate size lined paper and a model of the following sentence: **"Boys and girls can fix zippers quickly whenever they jam."** Observe student's letter formation, alignment, slant, spacing, and line quality. Have student copy the sentence.

IIIB.1, Precursive Strokes, Gr. 3.
Directions: Provide student with a model of the cursive basic strokes and have him or her copy them. Note whether student begins each stroke at the appropriate position.

IIIC.1, Lower Case (i,u,t,e,s,w,r,p), Gr. 3.
Directions: "Write these letters in lower case cursive as I name them: i, u, t, e, s, w, r, and p."

IIIC.2, Lower Case (l,b,f,h,k), Gr. 3.
Directions: "Write these letters in lower case cursive as I name them: l, b, f, h, and k."

IIIC.3, Lower Case (a,c,d,o,g,q), Gr. 3.
Directions: "Write these letters in lower case cursive as I name them: a, c, d, o, g, and q."

IIIC.4, Lower Case (g,j,q,f,y,z), Gr. 3.
Directions: "Write these letters in lower case cursive as I name them: g, j, q, f, y, and z."

IIIC.5, Lower Case (n,m,v,x,y,z), Gr. 3.
Directions: "Write these letters in lower case cursive as I name them: n, m, v, x, y, and z."

IIIC.6, Lower Case (r,v,b,w), Gr. 3.
Directions: "Write these letters in lower case cursive as I name them: r, v, b, and w."

IIID.1, Upper Case (O,C,D,E,A), Gr. 3.
Directions: "Write these letters in upper case cursive as I name them: O, C, D, E, and A."

IIID.2, Upper Case (H,K,M,N,W,X,U,V,Y,Z,Q), Gr. 3.
Directions: "Write these letters in upper case cursive as I name them: H, K, M, N, W, X, U, V, Y, Z, and Q."

IIID.3, Upper Case (I,J), Gr. 3.
Directions: "Write these letters in upper case cursive as I name them: I and J."

IIID.4, Upper Case (T,F,S,G,B), Gr. 3.
Directions: "Write these letters in upper case cursive as I name them: T, F, S, G, and B."

IIID.5, Upper Case (P,R,L), Gr. 3.
Directions: "Write these letters in upper case cursive as I name them: P, R, and L."

Basic Mathematics

Basic Mathematics Skill Objectives

I. **Readiness** - The student:

R.1 Points to equal sets.

R.2 Writes > or < to indicate the greater of 2 numbers, 1–10.

R.3 Counts objects to 10.

R.4 Joins sets to 10.

R.5 Counts to 100.

R.6 Demonstrates sets to 10.

R.7 Reads numbers to 100.

R.8 Writes numbers to 100.

R.9 Summarizes sets to 10.

II. **Number Facts**

A. **Addition** - The student quickly, and without counting:

.1 Adds numbers 0–5 to 0–5.

.2 Adds numbers 0–9 to 0–9.

B. **Subtraction** - The student quickly, and without counting:

.1 Subtracts numbers 0–5 from 0–5.

.2 Subtracts numbers 0–9 from 0–9,

C. **Multiplication** - The student quickly, and without counting:

.1 Multiplies numbers 1–3 and 5 by 0–10.

.2 Multiplies numbers 0–10 × 0–10.

D. **Division** - The student quickly, and without counting:

.1 Divides numbers 1–90 by 1–9.

III. **Computation of Whole Numbers**

A. **Addition** - The student adds:

.1 Two numbers with sum less than 10

.2 Two 1-digit numbers, with sum greater than 10

.3 Three numbers with sum less than 10

.4 2-digit number to a 1-digit number, with no regrouping

.5 2-digit number to a 1-digit number, regrouping ones

.6 Two 2-digit numbers, with no regrouping

.7 Two 2-digit numbers, regrouping ones

.8 Two 2-digit numbers, regrouping ones and tens

.9 Three 2-digit numbers, regrouping ones

.10 Three 2-digit numbers. regrouping ones and tens

.11 Two 3-digit numbers, regrouping ones

.12 Two 3-digit numbers, regrouping ones and tens

B. **Subtraction** - The student subtracts:

.1 1-digit number from a 1-digit number

.2 1-digit number from itself

.3 Zero from a 1-digit number

.4 1-digit number from a 2-digit number less than 20

.5 1-digit number from a 2-digit number, with no regrouping

.6 2-digit number from a 2-digit number, with no regrouping

.7 1-digit number from a 2-digit number, regrouping tens

.8 2-digit number from a 2-digit number, regrouping tens

.9 3-digit number from a 3-digit number, with no regrouping

.10 3-digit number from a 3-digit number, regrouping tens

.11 3-digit number from a 3-digit number, regrouping hundreds

.12 3-digit number from a 3-digit number, regrouping tens and hundreds

.13 3-digit number from a 3-digit number with zero in the ones place

Source: From ENRIGHT® *Diagnostic Inventory of Basic Arithmetic Skills,* © 1983 Curriculum Associates, Inc. Adapted and reprinted by permission.

.14   3-digit number from a 3-digit number with zero in the tens place

.15   3-digit number from a 3-digit number with zeros in the ones and tens place

C.   **Multiplication -** The student multiplies:

.1   Two 1-digit numbers

.2   2-digit number by a 1-digit number, with no regrouping

.3   3-digit number by a 1-digit number, with no regrouping

.4   2-digit number by a 1-digit number, regrouping ones

.5   2-digit number by a 1-digit number, regrouping ones and tens

.6   3-digit number by a 1-digit number, regrouping ones

.7   3-digit number by a 1-digit number, regrouping tens

.8   3-digit number by a 1-digit number, regrouping ones and tens

.9   3-digit number by a 1-digit number, regrouping ones, tens, and hundreds

.10   2-digit number by a 2-digit number, with no regrouping

.11   2-digit number by a 2-digit number, with regrouping caused by the ones place digit of the multiplier

.12   2-digit number by a 2-digit number, with regrouping

.13   3-digit number by a 2-digit number, with no regrouping

.14   3-digit number by a 2-digit number, with regrouping

.15   3-digit number by a 3-digit number, with no regrouping

.16   3-digit number by a 3-digit number, with regrouping caused by the ones place digit and the tens place digit of the multiplier

.17   3-digit number by a 3-digit number, with regrouping caused by all digits of the multiplier

.18   3-digit number with zero in the tens place by a 2-digit number

D.   **Division -** The student divides:

.1   1-digit number by a 1-digit number, with no remainder

.2   2-digit number with zero in the ones place by a 1-digit number, with no remainder

.3   3-digit number with zeros in the ones and tens places by a 1-digit number, with no remainder

.4   2-digit number by a 1-digit number, with no regrouping or remainder

.5   1-digit number by a 1-digit number, with remainder

.6   2-digit number by a 1-digit number, with no remainder

.7   3-digit number by a 1-digit number in which the first two digits of the dividend are divisible by the divisor, with no regrouping or remainder

.8   2-digit number by a 1-digit number, with regrouping but no remainder

.9   3-digit number by a 1-digit number, with regrouping but no remainder

.10   2-digit number by a 1-digit number, with remainder

.11   3-digit number by a 1-digit number, with no remainder

.12   3-digit number by a 1-digit number, with remainder

.13   3-digit number with zero in the tens place by a 1-digit number, with no remainder

.14   2-digit number by a 2-digit number, with no remainder

.15   2-digit number by a 2-digit number, with remainder

.16   3-digit number by a 2-digit number, in which the first two digits of the dividend are divisible by the divisor, with remainder

.17   3-digit number by a 2-digit number, with no remainder

.18   3-digit number by a 2-digit number, with remainder

.19   4-digit number by a 2-digit number, with remainder

.20   4-digit number by a 2-digit number, with zero in the tens place of the quotient and no remainder

.21   4-digit number by a 3-digit number, with remainder

.22   5-digit number by a 3-digit number, with remainder

IV.   *Fractions*

A.   **Conversion of Fractions -** The student converts:

.1   Improper fraction to a whole number

.2   Improper fraction to a mixed number

.3   Fraction to its simplest form

.4   Two fractions to the LCD, with the LCD included within one fraction

.5   Two fractions to the LCD, with the LCD not included

.6   Two fractions to the LCD, when the LCD is not determined by multiplying the denominators

.7   Three fractions to the LCD, with two like denominators and one different

.8   Three fractions to the LCD, with the LCD not included

B.   Addition of Fractions - The student adds:

.1   Two like fractions (in horizontal form)

.2   Two like fractions (in horizontal form), converting the answer to a whole or mixed number

.3   Three like fractions (in horizontal form)

.4   Two unlike fractions, with the LCD included within one fraction

.5   Two unlike fractions, with the LCD not included

.6   Two unlike fractions, when the LCD is not determined by multiplying the denominators

.7   Three fractions, with two like denominators and one different

.8   Three unlike fractions

.9   Mixed number and a fraction (in horizontal form)

.10   Two mixed numbers

C.   Subtraction of Fractions - The student subtracts:

.1   Fraction from a like fraction

.2   Fraction from an unlike fraction, with the LCD included within one fraction

.3   Fraction from an unlike fraction, with the LCD not included

.4   Fraction from an unlike fraction when the LCD is not determined by multiplying the denominators

.5   Fraction from a mixed number, with no regrouping

.6   Fraction from a mixed number, with regrouping

.7   Mixed number from a mixed number with no regrouping.

.8   Mixed number from a mixed number, with regrouping

.9   Mixed number from a mixed number, with regrouping (in horizontal form)

D.   Multiplication of Fractions - The student multiplies:

.1   Fraction by a like fraction

.2   Fraction by an unlike fraction

.3   Fraction by an improper fraction

.4   Fraction by a whole number

.5   Fraction by a mixed number

.6   Mixed number by a mixed number

E.   Division of Fractions - The student divides:

.1   Fraction by a like fraction

.2   Fraction by an unlike fraction

.3   Fraction by a whole number

.4   Whole number by a fraction

.5   Mixed number by a fraction

.6   Mixed number by a mixed number

V.   *Decimals*

A.   Addition of Decimals - The student adds:

.1   Two tenths decimals, with no regrouping

.2   Two tenths decimals, regrouping tenths

.3   Two hundredths decimals, with no regrouping

.4   Two hundredths decimals, regrouping hundredths

.5   Two hundredths decimals, regrouping hundredths and tenths

.6   Hundredths decimal and a tenths decimal, with no regrouping

.7   Tenths decimal and a hundredths decimal, regrouping tenths

.8   Tenths decimal and a hundredths decimal, regrouping tenths (in horizontal form)

.9   Mixed decimal and a hundredths decimal

.10   Two mixed decimals, with regrouping

.11   Two mixed decimals, with regrouping (in horizontal form)

B.   Subtraction of Decimals - The student subtracts:

.1   Tenths decimal from a tenths decimal, with no regrouping

.2   Hundredths decimal from a hundredths decimal, with no regrouping

.3   Hundredths decimal from a hundredths decimal, with regrouping

.4   Tenths decimal from a hundredths decimal

.5   Tenths decimal from a mixed decimal, with no regrouping

.6   Tenths decimal from a mixed decimal, with regrouping

.7   Hundredths decimal from a mixed decimal with no regrouping

.8   Hundredths decimal from a tenths decimal, with regrouping

.9   Hundredths decimal from a mixed decimal, with regrouping

.10   Hundredths decimal from a mixed decimal, with no regrouping (in horizontal form)

.11   Mixed decimal from a mixed decimal, with regrouping

C.   **Multiplication of Decimals -** The student multiplies:

.1   Whole number by a tenths decimal

.2   Tenths decimal by a tenths decimal

.3   Hundredths decimal by a tenths decimal, with regrouping

.4   Mixed decimal by a tenths decimal, with regrouping

.5   Mixed decimal by a hundredths decimal, with regrouping

.6   Mixed decimal by a mixed decimal with regrouping

D.   **Division of Decimals -** The student divides:

.1   Tenths decimal by a 1-digit whole number, with no regrouping

.2   Hundredths decimal by a 1-digit whole number, with no regrouping

.3   Hundredths decimal by a 1-digit whole number

.4   Mixed decimal with tenths by a whole number

.5   Mixed decimal with hundredths by a whole number

.6   Whole number by a tenths decimal

.7   Whole number by a hundredths decimal

.8   Mixed decimal by a tenths decimal

.9   Mixed decimal by a hundredths decimal

.10   Mixed decimal by a mixed decimal

VI. ***Problem Solving* -** Given grade-level problems, the student:

A.1–.6 Reads with understanding

B.1–.6 Organizes the facts

C.1–.6 Selects the correct operation

D.1–.6 Computes the answer

E.1–.6 Checks the answer for accuracy

SAMPLE ITEMS FOR TESTS OF BASIC MATHEMATICS

I. Readiness

Note: You may have to read these to the students.

I.R.1

Are these the same?

I.R.2

Use >or< to show which is more.

a. 5 ☐ 2   b. 7 ☐ 9

I.R.3

Count how many objects are in each box.

I.R.4

How many are in both boxes?

I.R.5

Count as far as you can.

I.R.6

Show me (objects or fingers):
a. 5   b. 8

I.R.7

Read these numbers.
a. 36   b. 84

I.R.8

Write your numbers to 100 (provide separate
paper or use back of this page).

I.R.9

Using your own fingers, show student the number of fingers indicated below
for 2 seconds and have him or her tell how many. There should be
no counting.

a. 3   b. 1   c. 7   d. 2   e. 8

II. NUMBER FACTS

II A.1-.2

1+0=____	1+2=____	3+4=____	0+9=____	4+7=____
5+8=____	6+8=____	1+7=____	8+6=____	9+8=____
3+7=____	5+4=____	6+6=____	4+6=____	1+8=____
9+1=____	0+4=____	0+2=____	6+4=____	8+9=____
7+3=____	3+1=____	1+5=____	3+6=____	4+5=____
3+2=____	8+7=____	3+3=____	8+8=____	5+9=____
2+0=____	2+5=____	5+3=____	8+3=____	0+7=____
9+9=____	7+7=____	9+2=____	5+0=____	0+5=____
7+8=____	1+3=____	2+6=____	5+2=____	6+1=____
4+4=____	3+5=____	0+1=____	4+3=____	8+5=____

II B.1-.2

1-0=____	3-2=____	7-4=____	9-9=____	11-7=____
13-8=____	14-8=____	8-7=____	14-6=____	17-8=____
10-7=____	9-4=____	12-6=____	10-6=____	9-8=____
10-1=____	4-4=____	2-2=____	9-6=____	17-9=____
10-3=____	4-1=____	6-5=____	16-8=____	9-5=____
5-2=____	15-7=____	6-3=____	11-3=____	14-9=____
2-0=____	7-5=____	8-3=____	5-0=____	7-7=____
18-9=____	14-7=____	11-2=____	7-2=____	5-5=____
15-8=____	4-3=____	8-6=____	7-3=____	7-1=____
8-4=____	8-5=____	1-1=____	10-4=____	13-5=____

Source: From ENRIGHT® *Diagnostic Inventory of Basic Arithmetic Skills,* © 1983 Curriculum Associates, Inc. Adapted and reprinted by permission.

II. NUMBER FACTS (*continued*)

II C.1-.2

7×6=____	5×1=____	6×2=____	5×6=____	7×5=____
9×4=____	5×5=____	9×7=____	4×1=____	7×0=____
7×4=____	3×9=____	5×7=____	7×2=____	0×8=____
2×8=____	0×0=____	2×9=____	8×4=____	3×0=____
6×0=____	8×1=____	6×9=____	0×8=____	8×2=____
4×2=____	2×2=____	2×1=____	9×6=____	1×6=____
6×7=____	7×1=____	4×8=____	6×5=____	6×3=____
2×4=____	2×7=____	0×3=____	1×4=____	9×0=____
0×6=____	9×3=____	7×9=____	4×0=____	9×5=____
3×8=____	9×1=____	2×3=____	1×1=____	4×9=____

II D.1-.2

27÷9=____	42÷7=____	32÷4=____	0÷5=____	21÷7=____
6÷2=____	18÷6=____	9÷9=____	14÷7=____	2÷2=____
21÷3=____	7÷7=____	35÷5=____	8÷2=____	12÷3=____
6÷6=____	20÷4=____	3÷1=____	0÷1=____	5÷5=____
72÷8=____	36÷6=____	50÷5=____	90÷9=____	40÷8=____
18÷3=____	18÷9=____	16÷2=____	16÷8=____	1÷1=____
0÷7=____	0÷6=____	2÷1=____	56÷7=____	14÷2=____
28÷7=____	42÷6=____	0÷2=____	54÷6=____	24÷3=____
8÷8=____	15÷5=____	72÷9=____	24÷8=____	40÷4=____
70÷7=____	24÷4=____	8÷4=____	12÷4=____	28÷4=____

Source: From ENRIGHT® *Diagnostic Inventory of Basic Arithmetic Skills,* © 1983 Curriculum Associates, Inc. Adapted and reprinted by permission.

III. WHOLE NUMBER COMPUTATION

IIIA.1-.12, Addition

.1	4 +5	*.2*	6 +7	*.3*	1 6 +1	*.4*	74 +5	*.5*	57 +5	*.6*	65 +22
.7	37 +59	*.8*	68 +74	*.9*	28 45 +14	*.10*	35 56 +64	*.11*	637 +256	*.12*	589 +345

IIIB.1-.15, Subtraction

.1	8 -5	*.2*	6 -6	*.3*	5 -0	*.4*	15 -9	*.5*	77 -5	*.6*	86 -34
.7	76 -8	*.8*	52 -35	*.9*	675 -443	*.10*	753 -236	*.11*	539 -172	*.12*	846 -379
.13	590 -246	*.14*	806 -472	*.15*	600 -357						

IIIC.1-.12, Multiplication

.1	8 ×7	*.2*	23 ×3	*.3*	637 × 1	*.4*	19 ×4	*.5*	58 ×9	*.6*	229 × 4
.7	241 × 4	*.8*	259 × 3	*.9*	394 × 9	*.10*	31 ×13	*.11*	23 ×39	*.12*	65 ×37

IIIC.13-.18, Multiplication

.13	312 ×23	*.14*	357 ×48	*.15*	113 ×323	*.16*	343 ×274	*.17*	548 ×634	*.18*	403 ×49

Source: From ENRIGHT® *Diagnostic Inventory of Basic Arithmetic Skills,* © 1983 Curriculum Associates, Inc. Adapted and reprinted by permission.

III. WHOLE NUMBER COMPUTATION *(continued)*

IIID.1-.12, Division

.1 $3\overline{)9}$ *.2* $6\overline{)90}$ *.3* $2\overline{)500}$ *.4* $3\overline{)39}$ *.5* $3\overline{)8}$

.6 $7\overline{)42}$ *.7* $7\overline{)287}$ *.8* $2\overline{)78}$ *.9* $8\overline{)984}$ *.10* $5\overline{)33}$

.11 $6\overline{)276}$ *.12* $8\overline{)346}$

IIID.13-.22, Division

.13 $7\overline{)903}$ *.14* $16\overline{)64}$ *.15* $23\overline{)74}$ *.16* $13\overline{)324}$ *.17* $26\overline{)962}$

.18 $45\overline{)384}$ *.19* $68\overline{)1782}$ *.20* $27\overline{)8181}$ *.21* $172\overline{)5694}$ *.22* $469\overline{)16,423}$

IV. FRACTIONS

IVA.1-.8, Fractions

Rewrite these fractions in simplest terms:

.1 $18/6=$ *.2* $35/8=$ *.3* $4/6=$

Rewrite these fractions, using the lowest common denominator (LCD):

.4 $3/4=$ $5/12=$ *.7* $6/7=$ $2/5=$ $4/7=$
.5 $4/7=$ $2/3=$ *.8* $3/8=$ $2/5=$ $7/10=$
.6 $5/14=$ $5/6=$

IVB.1-.10, Fractions

.1 $2/8 + 4/8=$ *.2* $5/7 + 2/7=$ *.3* $1/4 + 3/4 + 1/4=$ *.4* $\begin{array}{r} 1/2 \\ +3/8 \\ \hline \end{array}$

..5 $\begin{array}{r} 2/7 \\ +1/2 \\ \hline \end{array}$ *.6* $\begin{array}{r} 5/14 \\ +5/6 \\ \hline \end{array}$ *7* $\begin{array}{r} 2/8 \\ 1/2 \\ +3/8 \\ \hline \end{array}$ *8* $\begin{array}{r} 2/6 \\ 1/3 \\ +5/9 \\ \hline \end{array}$

.9 $3\,2/3 + 4/5=$ *.10* $\begin{array}{r} 8\,4/9 \\ +1\,5/6 \\ \hline \end{array}$

Source: From ENRIGHT® *Diagnostic Inventory of Basic Arithmetic Skills,* © 1983 Curriculum Associates, Inc. Adapted and reprinted by permission.

IV. FRACTIONS *(continued)*

IVC.1-.9, Fractions

.1 $\frac{7}{9}$
$-\frac{4}{9}$

.2 $\frac{3}{4}$
$-\frac{2}{8}$

.3 $\frac{6}{7}$
$-\frac{2}{3}$

.4 $\frac{11}{12}$
$-\frac{3}{8}$

.5 $5\frac{2}{3}$
$-\frac{2}{5}$

.6 $6\frac{3}{4}$
$-\frac{5}{6}$

.7 $5\frac{5}{7}$
$-3\frac{1}{2}$

.8 $11\frac{4}{9}$
$-7\frac{1}{2}$

.9 $6\frac{1}{5}$
$-3\frac{2}{3}$

IVD.1-.6, Fractions

.1 $\frac{2}{8} \times \frac{3}{8} =$

.2 $\frac{1}{3} \times \frac{5}{7} =$

.3 $\frac{3}{5} \times \frac{9}{4} =$

.4 $\frac{4}{9} \times 8 =$

.5 $\frac{3}{4} \times 7\frac{2}{3} =$

.6 $3\frac{1}{5} \times 2\frac{1}{4} =$

IVE.1-.6, Fractions

.1 $\frac{8}{9} \div \frac{2}{9} =$

.2 $\frac{3}{7} \div \frac{5}{6} =$

.3 $\frac{6}{9} \div 3 =$

.4 $4 \div \frac{2}{6} =$

.5 $5\frac{2}{3} \div \frac{4}{6} =$

.6 $4\frac{1}{5} \div 2\frac{1}{4} =$

V. DECIMALS

VA.1-.11, Decimals

.1 .6
+.3

.2 .7
+.8

.3 .33
+.35

.4 .57
+.39

.5 .87
+.48

.6 .48
+.5

.7 .5
+.99

.8 .43 + .8=

.9 6.48
+ .29

.10 3.67
+9.26

.11 6.99 + 3.58=

VB.1-.11, Decimals

.1 .5
-.3

.2 .83
-.31

.3 .74
-.28

.4 .84
-.5

.5 8.8
- .6

.6 6.7
- .9

.7 5.97
- .43

.8 .8
-.56

.9 3.39
- .55

.10 4.88 - .35=

.11 8.86
-3.58

V. DECIMALS *(continued)*

VC.1-.6, Decimals

.1	4 ×.6	*.2*	.5 ×.9	*.3*	.74 ×.8	*.4*	6.47 ×.8	*.5*	3.57 ×.64	*.6*	4.69 ×7.85

VD.1-.6, Decimals

.1 $2\overline{).6}$	*.2* $2\overline{).68}$	*.3* $8\overline{).48}$	*.4* $6\overline{)8.4}$	*.5* $4\overline{)7.56}$
.6 $3\overline{)141}$	*.7* $.78\overline{)25350}$	*.8* $.5\overline{)3.75}$	*.9* $45\overline{)103.05}$	*.10* $7.3\overline{)33.58}$

V. PERCENT

VE.1, Percent

"Convert the following percents to whole numbers:"

200% =   500% =

VE.2-.4, Percent

"Convert these items to decimals:"

.2 89% =   72% =

.3 60% =   40% =

.4 120% =   350% =

VI. PROBLEM SOLVING

First Level:

(a) Bill sees 25 cows. 12 walk away. How many are left?

A.1 Draw a line under the question.

B.1 How many cows did Bill see?

C.1 To find the answer to the question should you add or subtract?

D.1 (See skills in Section III.A and III.B)

E.1 Which answer is right?
   a. $25 - 12 = 13$
   b. $25 + 12 = 37$

(b) There are 14 sail boats. 12 more boats sail up. How many boats are there now?

A.1 Underline the question.

B.1 How many boats sailed up?

C.1 Should you add or subtract to solve this problem?

D.1 (See skills in Section III.A and III.B)

E.1 Which answer is right?
   a. $14 - 12 = 2$
   b. $14 + 12 - 26$

Second Level:

(a) Junior has 325 baseball cards. His friend Sam has 197 cards. How many cards to they have in all?

A.2 Underline the question.

B.2 How many cards did Junior have?

C.2 Should you add or subtract to solve this problem?

D.2 (See skills in Section III.A and III.B)

E.2 Which answer is right?
   a. $325 + 197 = 522$
   b. $325 - 197 = 128$

(b) Ms. Mendez has 256 story books in her second-grade class. She lends 119 story books to another second-grade teacher. How many books are left?

A.2 Underline the question.

B.2 How many books did she lend?

C.2 Should you add or subtract to solve this problem?

D.2 (See skills in Section III.A and III.B)

E.2 Which answer is right?
   a. $256 + 119 = 375$
   b. $256 - 119 = 137$

Third Level:

(a) Morgan saves stamps. He has 250 stamps. He puts them into 5 books. He puts the same number of stamps into each book. How many stamps will he put in each book?

A.3 Underline the question.

B.3 How many books did he have?

C.3 Should you multiply or divide to solve this problem?

D.3 (See skills in Section III.C and III.D)

E.3 Which answer is right?
   a. $250 \times 5 = 1250$
   b. $250 \div 5 = 50$

(b) Katie buys 5 bags of cookies for a party. Each bag has 44 cookies in it. How many cookies does Katie have?

A.3 Underline the question.

B.3 How many cookies in each bag?

C.3 Should you multiply or divide to solve this problem?

D.3 (See skills in Section III.C and III.D)

E.3 Which answer is right?
   a. $44 \times 5 = 220$
   b. $44 \div 5 = 9$

VI. PROBLEM SOLVING

Fourth Level:

(a) The fair at John's school had pony rides for 25 cents each. They collected $18.75 in all for the pony rides. How many children rode the pony?

A.4 What is the question?

B.4 How much did each pony ride cost?

C.4 Should you multiply or divide to solve this problem?

D.4 (See skills in Section III.C and III.D)

E.4 Which answer is right?
  a. $1875 \times 25 = 46875$
  b. $1875 \div 25 = 75$

(b) SuSu's family traveled 350 miles each day on their vacation. They spent 7 days traveling. How many miles did they travel?

A.4 What is the question?

B.4 How many miles did they drive each day?

C.4 Should you multiply or divide to solve this problem?

D.4 (See skills in Section III.C and III.D)

E.4 Which answer is right?

$$\begin{array}{cc} \text{a. } 350 & \text{b. } 350 \\ \underline{\times 7} & \underline{\times 7} \\ 2450 & 2150 \end{array}$$

Fifth Level:

(a) Anna rode her bicycle 12.6 kilometers in the morning. She rode 9.8 kilometers in the afternoon. How far did she ride that day?

A.5 What is the question?

B.5 How many kilometers did she ride in the afternoon?

C.5 Should you multiply or add to solve this problem?

D.5 (See skills in Section V.A)

E.5 Which answer is right?
  a. $12.6 + 9.8 = 22.4$
  b. $12.6 + 9.8 = 224$

(b) Shonda swims 16 lengths of a swimming pool one day. The pool is 25 meters long. How far did she swim?

A.5 What is the question?

B.5 How long is the pool?

C.5 Should you multiply or add to solve this problem?

D.5 (See skills in Section III.C)

E.5 Which answer is right?
  a. $16 \times 25 = 400$
  b. $16 + 25 = 41$

Sixth Level:

(a) Bob makes $3.35 per hour raking leaves after school and on Saturdays. Last week he worked 12 hours. How much did he make raking leaves last week?

A.6 What is the question?

B.6 How much does Bob make per hour?

C.6 Should you multiply or divide to solve this problem?

D.6 (See skills in Section V.C)

E.6 Which answer is right?

$$\begin{array}{cc} \text{a.\$ } 3.35 & \text{b.\$ } 3.35 \\ \underline{\times 12} & \underline{\times 12} \\ \$40.20 & \$39.10 \end{array}$$

(b) Brian is making hamburgers for a cookout. How much meat must he buy in order to make 16 quarter pounders?

A.6 What is the question?

B.6 How many hamburgers does Brian want to make?

C.6 Should you multiply or divide to solve this problem?

D.6 (See skills in Section IV.D)

E.6 Which answer is right?
  a. $16 \times 1/4 = 4$
  b. $16 + 1/4 = 16 \, 1/4$

ANSWER GUIDE TO TESTS FOR BASIC MATHEMATICS

III. Whole Number Computation

A.		B.		C.		D.			
1)	9	1)	3	1)	56	1)	3	16)	24 R12
2)	13	2)	0	2)	69	2)	15	17)	37
3)	8	3)	5	3)	637	3)	250	18)	8 R24
4)	79	4)	6	4)	76	4)	13	19)	26 R14
5)	62	5)	72	5)	522	5)	2R2	20)	303
6)	87	6)	52	6)	916	6)	6	21)	33 R18
7)	96	7)	68	7)	964	7)	41	22)	35 R8
8)	142	8)	17	8)	777	8)	39		
9)	87	9)	232	9)	3546	9)	123		
10)	155	10)	517	10)	403	10)	6R3		
11)	893	11)	367	11)	897	11)	46		
12)	934	12)	467	12)	2405	12)	43R2		
		13)	344	13)	7176	13)	129		
		14)	334	14)	17,136	14)	4		
		15)	243	15)	36,499	15)	3R5		
				16)	93,982				
				17)	347,432				
				18)	19,747				

IV. Fractions

A.		B.		C.		D.		E.	
1)	3	1)	$3/4$	1)	$1/3$	1)	$3/32$	1)	4
2)	$4\,3/8$	2)	1	2)	$1/2$	2)	$5/21$	2)	$18/35$
3)	$2/3$	3)	$1\,1/4$	3)	$4/21$	3)	$1\,7/20$	3)	$2/9$
4)	$9/12\ 5/12$	4)	$7/8$	4)	$13/24$	4)	$3\,5/9$	4)	12
5)	$12/21\ 14/21$	5)	$11/14$	5)	$5\,4/15$	5)	$5\,3/4$	5)	$8\,1/2$
6)	$15/42\ 35/42$	6)	$1\,4/21$	6)	$5\,11/12$	6)	$7\,1/5$	6)	$1\,13/15$
7)	$30/35\ 14/35\ 20/35$	7)	$1\,1/8$	7)	$2\,3/14$				
8)	$15/40\ 16/40\ 28/40$	8)	$1\,2/9$	8)	$3\,17/18$				
		9)	$4\,7/15$	9)	$2\,8/15$				
		10)	$10\,5/18$						

V. Decimals

A.		B.		C.		D.		E.	a.	b.
1)	.9	1)	.2	1)	2.4	1)	.3	1)	2	5
2)	1.5	2)	.52	2)	.45	2)	.34	2)	.89	.72
3)	.68	3)	.46	3)	.592	3)	.06	3)	.6	.4
4)	.96	4)	.34	4)	5.176	4)	1.4	4)	1.2	3.5
5)	1.35	5)	8.2	5)	2.2848	5)	1.89			
6)	.98	6)	5.8	6)	36.8165	6)	470			
7)	1.49	7)	5.54			7)	32500			
8)	1.23	8)	.24			8)	7.5			
9)	6.77	9)	2.84			9)	229			
10)	12.93	10)	4.53			10)	4.6			
11)	10.57	11)	5.28							

VI. Problem Solving

First

(a)
B.1   25 cows
C.1   Subtract
E.1   a. 13

(b)
B.1   12 boats
C.1   Add
E.1   b. 26

Second

(a)
B.2   325 cards
C.2   Add
E.2   a. 522

(b)
B.2   119 books
C.2   Subtract
E.2   b. 137

Third

(a)
B.3   5
C.3   Divide
E.3   b. 50

(b)
B.3   44 cookies
C.3   Multiply
E.3   a. 220

Fourth

(a)
B.4   25 cents
C.4   Divide
E.4   b. 75

(b)
B.4   350 miles
C.4   Multiply
E.4   a. 2450

Fifth

(a)
B.5   9.8 kilometers
C.5   Add
E.5   a. 22.4

(b)
B.5   25 meters
C.5   Multiply
E.5   a. 400

Sixth

(a)
B.6 $3.35
C.6   Multiply
E.6 $40.20

(b)
B.6   16
C.6   Multiply
E.6   a. 4

Content and Study Strategies

Science Skill Objectives

I. Vocabulary

  A. Technical - The student:

    .1–.11 Pronounces technical science terms at the appropriate text level.

    .2–.12 Defines technical science terms at the appropriate text level.

  B. Nontechnical - The student:

    .1–.11 Pronounces nontechnical science terms at the appropriate text level.

    .2–.12 Defines nontechnical science terms at the appropriate text level.

II. Problem Solving

  A. Problem Identification - The student:

    .1 Listens to a passage and orally identifies and explains the problem(s).

    .2 Reads a passage and orally identifies and explains the problem(s).

    .3 Reads a passage and writes the identity and explanation of the problem(s).

  B. Problem Solution - The student:

    .1 Listens to a passage and orally identifies and explains the solution(s).

    .2 Reads a passage and orally identifies and explains the solution(s).

    .3 Reads a passage and writes the identity and explanation of the solution(s).

Social Studies Skill Objectives

I. Vocabulary

  A. Technical - The student:

    .1–.11 Pronounces technical social studies terms at the appropriate text level.

    .2–.12 Defines technical social studies terms at the appropriate text level.

  B. Nontechnical - The student:

    .1–.11 Pronounces nontechnical social studies terms at the appropriate text level.

    .2–.12 Defines nontechnical social studies terms at the appropriate text level.

II. Graphic Aids

  A. Maps - The student:

    .1 Locates specified points on a map of the neighborhood.

    .2 Locates specified points on a map of the state and of the nation.

    .3 Locates specified points on a map of the Western Hemisphere and of the world.

  B. Graphs - The student:

    .1 Reads and explains data from a bar graph.

    .2 Reads and explains data from a circle graph.

    .3 Reads and explains data from a line graph.

Study Strategy Objectives

I. Organization

  A. Categorizing - The student:

    .1   Categorizes objects by size, shape, and color.

    .2   Categorizes pictures by concept.

    .3   Categorizes words by initial, medial, and final letters.

    .4   Categorizes words by concept.

  B. Alphabetizing - The student:

    .1   Alphabetizes words by first letter.

    .2   Alphabetizes words by first and second letters.

    .3   Alphabetizes words by three letters.

    .4   Alphabetizes words by four or more letters.

II. Book Use

  A. Book Handling - The student:

    .1   Maintains proper posture when reading.

    .2   Handles books properly according to teacher standards.

    .3   Keeps place while reading.

  B. Book Parts - The student:

    .1   Locates the title page of a book.

    .2   Points to the title on the title page.

    .3   Locates specified pages throughout.

    .4   Uses the table of contents to locate specific information.

    .5   Uses the index to locate specific information.

III. References

  A. Dictionary - The student:

    .1   Uses guide words to locate specific words in a dictionary.

    .2   Locates specific words in a dictionary.

    .3   Pronounces words as they are marked in the dictionary.

    .4   Locates in the dictionary specific words and reads the correct contextual meaning.

  B. Encyclopedia - The student:

    1   Locates requested information in the encyclopedia.

  C. Card Catalog - The student:

    .1   Uses the card catalog to locate text by author.

    .2   Uses the card catalog to locate text by title.

    .3   Uses the card catalog to locate text by subject.

IV. Study Habits

  A. Outlines from Reading - The student:

    .1   Outlines the main ideas after reading a passage.

    .2   Outlines the key details after reading a passage.

    .3   Constructs a semantic map for a passage.

    .4   Writes a summary paragraph after reading a passage.

  B. Study Strategies - The student:

    .1   Takes notes from reading a passage.

    .2   Takes notes from a lecture or listening activity.

    .3   Demonstrates and applies the steps of a systematic study strategy.

  C. Reading Rate Adjustment - The student:

    .1   Varies reading rate according to reading purpose.

    .2   Skims a passage for the main ideas.

    .3   Scans a passage to locate specific information.

  D. Specific Strategies

    .1–.7   Applies specify strategies to accomplish grade level tasks.

SAMPLE ITEMS FOR TESTS OF CONTENT AND STUDY STRATEGIES

SCIENCE: I VOCABULARY

IA.1-.12 Pronouncing/Defining Technical Vocabulary—*Directions:* Begin on a level you think the student can pronounce the words. Then ask the student to look at each word carefully and say the word orally. When all twenty words on one list have been attempted, go back and request the meanings of each word. (Scoring: 60 percent correct on each list.)

Grade One

dark	___ ___	gases	___ ___	insects	___ ___	plants	___ ___
animals	___ ___	grow	___ ___	young	___ ___	clouds	___ ___
soil	___ ___	food	___ ___	hatch	___ ___	dinosaurs	___ ___
sun	___ ___	living	___ ___	eggs	___ ___	rain	___ ___
earth	___ ___	water	___ ___	fossil	___ ___	seeds	___ ___

Grade Two

space	___ ___	fuel	___ ___	cave	___ ___	desert	___ ___
roots	___ ___	air	___ ___	revolves	___ ___	stems	___ ___
surface	___ ___	energy	___ ___	liquids	___ ___	planet	___ ___
wind	___ ___	shadow	___ ___	forest	___ ___	temperature	___ ___
solids	___ ___	daytime	___ ___	wax	___ ___	electricity	___ ___

Grade Three

filter	___ ___	tadpole	___ ___	orbit	___ ___	generator	___ ___
mammal	___ ___	infect	___ ___	reptile	___ ___	amphibian	___ ___
fungi	___ ___	chemical	___ ___	moon	___ ___	environment	___ ___
pollen	___ ___	seasons	___ ___	crater	___ ___	satellite	___ ___
magnet	___ ___	molecule	___ ___	solar	___ ___	evaporate	___ ___

Grade Four

echo	___ ___	oxygen	___ ___	gravity	___ ___	forecasting	___ ___
conserve	___ ___	compound	___ ___	compound	___ ___	meteorite	___ ___
absorb	___ ___	bacteria	___ ___	lung	___ ___	astronomer	___ ___
migrate	___ ___	spectrum	___ ___	sphere	___ ___	vibration	___ ___
retina	___ ___	magnify	___ ___	smog	___ ___	nerve	___ ___

Grade Five

relic	___ ___	capillary	___ ___	atmosphere	___ ___	scavenger	___ ___
medulla	___ ___	inertia	___ ___	biceps	___ ___	lava	___ ___
artery	___ ___	cerebrum	___ ___	chromosome	___ ___	nutrient	___ ___
weight	___ ___	digestion	___ ___	atmosphere	___ ___	vertebrate	___ ___
enzyme	___ ___	capillary	___ ___	reactor	___ ___	extinct	___ ___

Grade Six

fusion	___ ___	incandescent	___ ___	plaque	___ ___	deciduous	___ ___
convex	___ ___	antibiotic	___ ___	petroleum	___ ___	pistil	___ ___
glucose	___ ___	radioactive	___ ___	hibernate	___ ___	vitamin	___ ___
neutron	___ ___	parasite	___ ___	recessive	___ ___	mucus	___ ___
mucus	___ ___	embryo	___ ___	volume	___ ___	toxin	___ ___

IB.1-.12 Pronouncing/Defining Nontechnical Vocabulary
Directions: Begin on a level you think the student can pronounce the words. Then ask the student to look at each word carefully and say the word orally. After all of the words in each list have been attempted, go back and request the meaning of every word. (Scoring: 60 percent correct on each list.)

Grade One			Grade Two			Grade Three		
move	___	___	star	___	___	cell	___	___
pull	___	___	space	___	___	instrument	___	___
lift	___	___	pupil	___	___	cone	___	___
heat	___	___	heart	___	___	spring	___	___
light	___	___	pit	___	___	matter	___	___

Grade Four			Grade Five			Grade Six		
class	___	___	base	___	___	conductor	___	___
front	___	___	crust	___	___	wave	___	___
model	___	___	organ	___	___	crystal	___	___
cover	___	___	volume	___	___	battery	___	___
pitch	___	___	school	___	___	colony	___	___

SCIENCE: II PROBLEM SOLVING

IIA.1 Identifying Problems—*Directions:* Listen carefully while I read a story about Joel and his family. When I am finished reading I will ask you to tell me about a problem Joel's family had.

> *Story:* Joel and his family had been living in their new, brightly-lighted apartment for only a month. Joel and his two sisters enjoyed the big rooms. They ran in and out all the time from the outside balcony. They had never had a balcony before. For the first time, the refrigerator gave ice and cold water without opening the door. Now the family had two television sets that stayed on most of the time. Joel and his family were happy. In fact, they had just returned from a trip to the store when his dad began to open the mail. "Come in here everyone," he said. "Just look at this electric bill." "Wow," said Joel.

Tell me why you think Joel's dad called everyone in to see the electric bill.

IIB.1 Orally Identifying Solutions—*Directions:* Use the story about Joel and after answering the preceding question, ask: What could Joel and his family do to help solve the problem?

IIA.2 Identifying Problems—*Directions:* Read the following selection about a science fair. After you finish I will ask you about a problem in the story.

> *Story:* The finals of the local science fair were over. Three students from our school won; that was great. Two projects were about plants. The other one was about space. But now there was a reason for concern; the next fair was in a high school. The school was ninety miles away. Their parents worked. The students thought at least one out of their group might win. That is, if they attended the fair.

What problem did the winning students face?

IIB.2 Orally Identifying Solutions—*Directions:* In the preceding story about the science fair, tell me how the students can solve the problem.

IIA.3 Identifying Problems—*Directions:* Read the following story about power and be ready to tell me about a problem involving the author of the story.

> *Story:* It was after school, and a crowd was gathering. As I walked over I could
> hear loud voices; there seemed to be a contest or some kind of disagreement. I
> soon learned about the "challenge." Over the weekend each member of our class was
> to think of sources of energy. The person with the longest list of sources would
> receive the title of "Most Powerful." I said to myself, "Why bother with this?"

Tell me what problem(s) you think the author of this story might have.

IIB.3 Identifying Solutions—*Directions:* After answering the preceding question, write an explanation of how you could solve the problems.

SOCIAL STUDIES: I VOCABULARY

IA.1-.12 Pronouncing/Defining Technical Vocabulary—*Directions:* Begin on a level you think the student can pronounce most of the words. Then ask the student to look at each word carefully and say the word orally. When all twenty words on the list have been attempted, go back and request the meanings for each of the words. (Scoring: 60 percent correct on each list.)

Grade One

share	___ ___	earth	___ ___	holiday	___ ___	family	___ ___
map	___ ___	city	___ ___	neighborhood	___ ___	globe	___ ___
safety	___ ___	school	___ ___	town	___ ___	money	___ ___
work	___ ___	state	___ ___	flag	___ ___	farm	___ ___
group	___ ___	list	___ ___	rule	___ ___	pay	___ ___

Grade Two

laws	___ ___	factory	___ ___	lake	___ ___	holidays	___ ___
factory	___ ___	island	___ ___	community	___ ___	calendar	___ ___
ocean	___ ___	plane	___ ___	equator	___ ___	goods	___ ___
month	___ ___	directions	___ ___	continents	___ ___	river	___ ___
symbol	___ ___	mountain	___ ___	suburb	___ ___	line	___ ___

Grade Three

subway	___ ___	port	___ ___	citizen	___ ___	produce	___ ___
climate	___ ___	volunteer	___ ___	governor	___ ___	government	___ ___
income	___ ___	freedom	___ ___	border	___ ___	fuel	___ ___
crime	___ ___	advertise	___ ___	irrigation	___ ___	canal	___ ___
taxes	___ ___	harvest	___ ___	election	___ ___	valley	___ ___

Grade Four

export	___ ___	tornado	___ ___	altitude	___ ___	volcano	___ ___
opinion	___ ___	century	___ ___	manufacture	___ ___	pioneers	___ ___
atlas	___ ___	import	___ ___	coast	___ ___	fertile	___ ___
profit	___ ___	conserve	___ ___	drought	___ ___	consumer	___ ___
court	___ ___	waterway	___ ___	canyon	___ ___	textiles	___ ___

Grade Five

gulf	___ ___	blockade	___ ___	cavalry	___ ___	decade	___ ___
treaty	___ ___	regulate	___ ___	product	___ ___	surplus	___ ___
invest	___ ___	editorial	___ ___	monopoly	___ ___	labor	___ ___
liberty	___ ___	armistice	___ ___	guarantee	___ ___	prejudice	___ ___
barter	___ ___	inflation	___ ___	technology	___ ___	ratify	___ ___

Grade Six

oasis	___ ___	alliance	___ ___	pollute	___ ___	traditional	___ ___
clergy	___ ___	gaucho	___ ___	scarce	___ ___	population	___ ___
tariff	___ ___	legalize	___ ___	urban	___ ___	artifact	___ ___
plaque	___ ___	descendant	___ ___	judicial	___ ___	migrate	___ ___
myth	___ ___	civilization	___ ___	refugee	___ ___	census	___ ___

IB.1-.12 Pronouncing/Defining Nontechnical Vocabulary—*Directions:* Begin on a level you think the student can pronounce the words. Then ask the student to say each word orally. After all words in a list have been attempted, go back and request a meaning for each word on a list. (Scoring: 60 percent Correct on each list).

Grade One		Grade Two		Grade Three	
watch	___ ___	run	___ ___	party	___ ___
free	___ ___	cold	___ ___	bank	___ ___
time	___ ___	bark	___ ___	raise	___ ___
change	___ ___	turn	___ ___	plot	___ ___
key	___ ___	tank	___ ___	mine	___ ___

Grade Four		Grade Five		Grade Six	
ship	___ ___	forge	___ ___	charter	___ ___
reservations	___ ___	stock	___ ___	services	___ ___
trade	___ ___	rare	___ ___	bullion	___ ___
draft	___ ___	uniform	___ ___	depression	___ ___
draw	___ ___	pass	___ ___	board	___ ___

IIA.1 Interpreting Local Map—*Directions:* Look at the following map and answer these statements. (Teacher: Sketch a map of the school and surrounding area including main streets, buildings, and directions N, E, and W.)

a. Point to the street your school is located on.
b. Which direction is your house from the front of the school?
c. What is the name of the street that borders the school on the west?

IIA.2 Interpreting a Map of the United States—*Directions:* Use a classroom map of the United States and answer these questions.

a. Which ocean touches the most states? (Atlantic)
b. Name the river that runs through Utah and Arizona. (Colorado)
c. Name two southern states.
d. Name two eastern states.
e. What state is bordered by Arizona, Nevada, and Oregon? (California)

IIA.3 Interpreting a Map of the Western Hemisphere—*Directions:* Use a classroom map.

    a. What country is between Canada and Mexico? (United States)
    b. What South American country is larger, Brazil or Argentina? (Brazil)
    c. What is the capitol of Canada? (Ottawa)
    d. Which continent would be most likely to be the warmest? (South America)
    e. Which is closer to Miami; Panama or the Bahamas? (Bahamas)

IIB.1 Interpreting Graphs—*Directions:* Use the following graph and answer these questions.

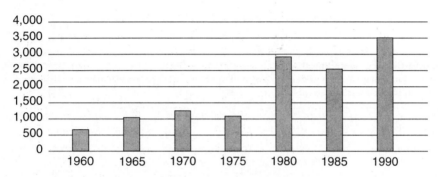

Hospital Patient Enrollment for Valley County

    a. The fewest number of patients is shown for what year? (1960)
    b. In what year did the largest number of patients visit the hospital? (1990)
    c. The largest increase in patients came between which two years? (1975–1980)
    d. How many patients were admitted in 1990? (3,500)

IIB.2 Interpreting Circle Graph—*Directions:* Look at the following graph and tell me the answers to these questions.

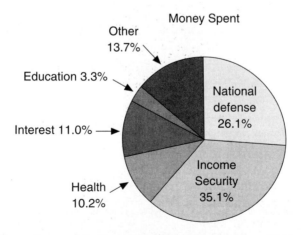

Money Spent

Source: Bureau of the Census, U.S. Office of Management and Budget

    a. In which area of the federal budget is the most money spent?
    b. In which two areas of the budget is the least money spent?
    c. Is more money spent on health or education?

IIB.3 Interpreting a Line Graph—*Directions:* Use the line graph below and answer these questions.

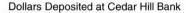

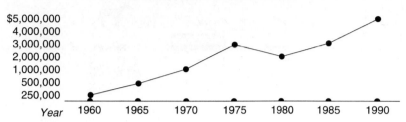

a. Between what years did deposits fall sharply? (1970–1975)
b. Between what years did deposits increase the most? (1980–1985)
c. How would you describe the trend or movement of savings at this bank? (Upward)

STUDY STRATEGIES: I ORGANIZATION

IA.1 Categorizing by size:

Directions:
   Point to the smallest
   item in each row.

Point to two items in each row that are the same shape.

Point to the items across each row that are the same color. (Teacher: Use color markers to shade the symbols before giving the test.)

IA.2 Categorizing by picture:
   Point to the picture that does
   not belong in each row.

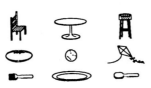

IA.3 Categorizing:
   Directions:

Point to the words in each row that *begin* with the same letter.	at	open	army
	drink	dock	boot
	tool	take	push
	label	dock	leave
Point to the words in each row that *end* with the same letter.	much	name	spice
	dial	head	sand
Point to the words in each row with the same *middle* letter.	tub	cup	top
	pea	fee	got

IA.4 Categorizing by words and concepts
   (See Word Recognition Sample Tests, IIB.11.)

IB.1 Alphabetizing by first letter:
Point to the word that comes first in	sun	for	hand
the dictionary, then second . . .	water	begin	make

IB.2 Categorizing by first and second letters:
Point to the word that comes first in	bag	blue	book
the dictionary, second, . . .	bus	bar	been

IB.3 Categorizing by three letters:
Beginning with number one as shown, number the rest of the words in the order	____ face	____ family	____ fall
they would appear in the dictionary.	____ fault	____ father	____ fast

IB.4 Categorizing by four or more letters:
Beginning with number one as shown, number the rest of the words in the order	____ hair	____ helpful	____ hard
they would appear in the dictionary.	____ heat	____ happen	____ hardly

IC.1 Following oral directions:
Listen carefully and do exactly what I tell you.

"Listen to everything I say before you do anything. Touch your shoe, stand up, wave to me, and sit back down. Now, do what I told you to do,"

IC.2 Following written directions:
Read carefully and then do exactly what it tells you. Here is a pencil and paper.

Write your name somewhere on the top of the paper. Next, circle the first letter of each word in your name. Finally underline your first name.

STUDY STRATEGIES: II BOOK USE

IIA.1-.3 Book Handling—
Directions: Use the following checklist to summarize observational data during several different time intervals.

While reading, the student:	*Usually*	*Sometimes*	*Rarely*
.1 Uses good posture	_____	_____	_____
Keeps both feet on the floor	_____	_____	_____
.2 Handles books carefully	_____	_____	_____
Holds book proper distance	_____	_____	_____
.3 Turns pages easily	_____	_____	_____
Marks place while reading	_____	_____	_____
Other: Reads during free time	_____	_____	_____
Shows an interest in reading	_____	_____	_____

IIB.1-.3 Book Parts—
Directions: Look at the following pages and point out the following information:
.1   Tell me what the first page in a book is called. (title page)
.2   Point to the title page in this book. (Give student a book to use.)
.3   Point to the page that comes after 11; after 17; after 24. (12; 18; 25)
    Point to the page that comes before 5; before 21; before 31. (4; 20; 30)

IIB.4 Uses Table of Contents

Directions: Use this table to answer questions a-c.

Table of Contents

a. Which chapter is about making ice cream? (1)
b. Where would you look to find out about the first ice cream? (II.A.)
c. On what page does the glossary begin? (76)

IIB.5 Uses Index

Directions: Use this simple index to answer the questions a-e.

Backbone, 54-55
Bacteria, 102-107; control of, 109
Balanced diet, 12-15
Baby sitters, 146-147
Beverages, 111
Blood, 58, 60-63; system, 60-78
Bicycle safety, 23-25; rules of, 25-26
Bones, 82, 84-86
Cavity, 122, 124-130; treatment of, 128-129
Cells, 66-69; types of, 67
Checkup, 41-44; physical, 44

a. On what pages would you look to find out abut a tooth ache? (128-129)
b. Under which topic are the most pages written? (blood system)
c. On what page do you find kinds of cells mentioned? (67)
d. Where can you look to find information about eating the right foods? (12-15)
e. Is more information available about cells or baby sitters? (cells)

STUDY STRATEGIES: III REFERENCES

IIIA.1 Uses Guide Words

Directions: Use the following sample dictionary page to answer the questions.

brief   **island**

brief ('bref), **1** short in length. **2** quick.
broadcast ('brod-kast), **1** make public by telling,
   2 tell by television or radio
crate ('krat), **1** wooden box or case. **2** old car
elbow ('el-bo), **1** joint of the arm. **2** to push
fabric ('fab-rik), **1** cloth
igloo ('ig-lu), **1** house made of ice and snow.
   2 house shaped like a dome.

a. Point out the guide words on this page. (brief and island)
b. Would the word "ship" be included in this dictionary page? (no)
c. Could the word "officer" be used as a guide word on this page? (no)

IIIA.2 Locates Words
Directions: Answer the questions by looking at the sample dictionary page in IIIA.1.

    1. Point to the word *crate*.   2. Point to the word *fabric*.

IIIA.3 Pronounces Words—
Directions: Pronounce the words I point to on the page.

           ____ broadcast   ____ fabric   ____ igloo

IIIA.4 Determine Meanings—
Directions: Give a meaning for each word pointed to on the sample dictionary page.

           ____ brief   ____ fabric   ____ elbow

IIIB.1 Encyclopedia—*Directions:* Look at the following encyclopedia drawing and describe which volume will likely contain information about each topic.

a. Where would you look for information about the state bird of Texas? (12)
b. Where could you find information about the city of St. Louis? (10)
c. Which volume might have data about telling one cloud from another? (3-10-13)
d. Where could you find out about how a telephone works? (12)
e. Which volume contains information about the country of Mexico? (10)

IIIC.1 Subject Card—*Directions:* Use the sample card to answer these questions.

> Animal Stories
> F. Franklin, Diris P.
> A Small Animal Kingdom Under the Earth
> Adventure Publisher, Inc., 1986

> Animal Stories
> H. Hall, Martha A.
> The Long and the Brave
> Riverbend Publishers, Inc., 1985

a. Point to the part that tells what these books are about.
b. Which book is probably about one or more small animals?

STUDY STRATEGIES: IV STUDY HABITS

IVA.1-.2 Outlines from Reading (Main Ideas and Details)

Part One—*Directions:* Point to the following symbols in the order they could appear in an outline.

B.   1.   I.   a.   A.   II.   b.   A.   B.

Part Two—*Directions:* Read this passage and make your own outline based on the information. (Teacher: Use a paragraph from a textbook on the student's independent reading level.)

IVA.3 Semantic Mapping—*Directions:* Read this passage and tell me what words you would include if you used two or three main words and three or four other idea words under the main words. (Teacher: Use a paragraph from a textbook on the student's independent reading level.)

IVA.4 Summary Paragraph—*Directions:* Read this passage and then tell me a summary in your own words. You will not be able to look back at the material. (Teacher: Use a paragraph from a textbook on the student's independent reading level.)

IVB.1 Study Techniques (Takes Notes from Reading)
Directions: Read this passage and take notes on ideas you think will help you remember the information. (Teacher: Select 3-5 paragraphs from a textbook on the student's independent reading level.)

IVB.2 Takes Notes from Listening—*Directions:* Listen carefully while I read this passage to you. Take notes that you think will help you remember the information. (Teacher: Select 3-5 paragraphs from a textbook appropriate for the student.)

IVB.3 Uses Study Strategies—*Directions:* Answer each of these questions as I read them to you; listen carefully.

  a. You have been assigned three chapters to read in your history book. By the end of the week you will have a test on the chapters. Tell me how you would prepare for the test.
  b. Do you have a special way of keeping notes in a notebook for the assigned reading you do for homework? If so, explain.
  c. Do you know what a study strategy or study system is? If so, explain.
  d. Describe how you think when you try to figure out a problem.

IVC.1 Adjust Reading Rate for Different Purposes—*Directions:* Answer these questions:

  a. Do you read your mathematics book as fast as you do your history book?
  b. Does any one book take you longer to read?
  c. Would you read the newspaper and your science book about the same speed?

IVC.2 Skimming—*Directions:* Quickly read over the following story and then be ready to tell me what the story is about. (Teacher: Select a 300-400 word story from a book written on the student's independent reading level.)

IVC.3 Scanning—*Directions:* You have 30 seconds to look over the following story and tell me (1) what size airplane is in the story and (2) what was the flight number?

> *Story:* The family gathered at the airport as Cindy left on her first airplane trip. The waiting area was full of people; some rushing here and there. Others were reading or trying to sleep. The flight across country was a long one but we were all impressed to see a huge jet at the gate. It was time to go but Cindy was waiting until the last boarding call. Her excitement was evident. She was about to experience modern transportation in the jet age. As she finally boarded flight 1181, a warm feeling came over me. At last Cindy was on her own. I was sad and at the same time, proud of her.

IVD.1-.7 Specific Strategies: Observational Checklist

Directions: Check each item according to demonstrated student performances.

Student:_____Date:_____Observer:_____

1. Uses a study strategy: Usually   Sometimes   Rarely

    Task   Strategy

    _____   _____   _____   _____
    _____   _____   _____   _____
    _____   _____   _____   _____
    _____   _____   _____   _____

2. Describes a study strategy: Usually   Sometimes   Rarely

    Task   Strategy

    _____   _____   _____   _____
    _____   _____   _____   _____
    _____   _____   _____   _____
    _____   _____   _____   _____

3. Is able to use a study strategy
    after receiving instruction: Usually   Sometimes   Rarely

    Task   Strategy

    _____   _____   _____   _____
    _____   _____   _____   _____
    _____   _____   _____   _____
    _____   _____   _____   _____

4. Strategically utilizes available technology
    to *facilitate* learning: Usually   Sometimes   Rarely

    Task   Strategy

    _____   _____   _____   _____
    _____   _____   _____   _____
    _____   _____   _____   _____
    _____   _____   _____   _____

5. Strategically utilizes available technology
    to *demonstrate* learning: Usually   Sometimes   Rarely

    Task   Strategy

    _____   _____   _____   _____
    _____   _____   _____   _____
    _____   _____   _____   _____
    _____   _____   _____   _____

REFERENCE INDEX

The numbers in brackets refer to the chapters of this book in which each reference is cited.

Abruscato, J. (1993). Early results and tentative implications from the Vermont portfolio project. *Phi Delta Kappan, 74* (6), 474–477. [10]

Aburdene, P., & Naisbitt, J. (1992). *Megatrends for women.* New York: Villard Books. [1]

Adams, A., Carnine, D., & Gersten, R. (1982). Instructional strategies for studying content area texts in the elementary grades. *Reading Research Quarterly, 18,* 27–55. [10]

Adamson, D. R., Matthews, P., & Schuller, J. (1990). Five ways to bridge the resource room-to-regular classroom gap. *Teaching Exceptional Children, 22* (2), 74–77. [4]

Airasian, P. W., & Madaus, G. F. (1972). Criterion-referenced testing in the classroom. *National Council of Measurement in Education, 3* (4). Reprinted in V. R. Martuza (1977), *Applying norm-referenced and criterion-referenced measurement in education* (pp. 330–344). Boston: Allyn and Bacon. [1]

Alberto, P. A., & Troutman, A. C. (1994). *Applied behavior analysis for teachers: Influencing student performance* (4th ed.). New York: Merrill/Macmillan. [3, 4]

Algozzine, B., O'Shea, D. J., Stoddard, K., & Crews, W. G. (1988). Reading and writing competencies of adolescents with learning disabilities. *Journal of Learning Disabilities, 21,* 154–160. [7]

Allen, D. (1989). Periodic and annual reviews and decisions to terminate special education services. In M. R. Shinn (Ed.), *Curriculum-based measurement: Assessing special children* (pp. 182–201). New York: Guilford. [1]

Alley, G., & Deshler, D. (1979). *Teaching the learning disabled adolescent: Strategies and methods.* Denver: Love. [2]

Allred, R. (1984). Spelling trends, content and methods. What research says to the teachers. Washington, DC: National Education Association (ED 248 531). [8]

Alper, S. K., Schloss, P. J., & Schloss, C. N. (1994). *Families of students with disabilities: Consultation and advocacy.* Boston: Allyn and Bacon. [3]

Alvermann, D. E., & Phelps, S. E. (1994). *Content reading and literacy: Succeeding in today's diverse classrooms.* Boston: Allyn and Bacon. [10]

American Psychological Association. (1985). *Standards for educational and psychological testing.* Washington, DC: Author. [1]

Amlund, J. T., Kardash, C. A. M., Kulhavy, R. W. (1986). Repetitive reading and recall of expository text. *Reading Research Quarterly, 21,* 49–58. [6]

Anderson, M. A. (1985). Cooperative group tasks and their relationship to peer acceptance and cooperation. *Journal of Learning Disabilities, 18,* 83–86. [3]

Anderson, R. H., & Pavan, B. N. (1993). *Nongradedness: Helping it happen.* Lancaster, PA: Technomic. [2]

Anderson, S. W. (Ed.) (1993). *Compact classics, Vol II.* Salt Lake City, UT: Compact Classics. [11]

Apple, M. W. (1985). Cooperative group tasks and their relationship to peer acceptance and cooperation. *Journal of Learning Disabilities, 18,* 83–86. [2]

Apple, M. W. (1988). The culture and commerce of the textbook. In W. F. Pinar (Ed.), *Contemporary curriculum discourses.* Scottsdale, AZ: Gorsuch Scarisbrick. [2]

Apple, M. W. (1990). Is there a curriculum voice to reclaim? *Phi Delta Kappan, 71,* 526–530. [2]

Arcavi, A., & Schoenfeld, A. H. (1992). Mathematics tutoring through a constructivist lens: The challenges of sense-making. *Journal of Mathematical Behavior, 11* (4), 321–335. [9]

Archer, A. L., & Gleason, M. (1989). *Skills for school success.* N. Billerica, MA: Curriculum Associates. [1, 4]

Archer, A. L., & Gleason, M. (1990). Skills for school success: Teaching school behaviors, organization skills, and learning strategies. In P. Cegelka & W. H. Berdine, *Effective instructional strategies for low performing students.* Boston: Allyn and Bacon. [1, 7, 10]

Archer, A. L., Isaacson, S., Adams, A., Ellis, E. S., Morehead, M. K., & Schiller, E. P. (1989). *Academy for effective instruction: Working with mildly handicapped students.* Reston, VA: Council for Exceptional Children. [1, 4, 7]

Ariel, A. (1992). *Education of children and adolescents with learning disabilities.* New York: Merrill/Macmillan. [8]

Ashlock, R. B. (1990). *Error patterns in computation: A semi-programmed approach* (5th ed.). Columbus, OH: Charles E. Merrill. [9]

Barbe, W.B (1961). *Educator's guide to personalized reading instruction.* Englewood Cliffs, NJ: Prentice-Hall. [10]

Barbe, W. B., Francis, A. S., & Braun, L. A. (1982). *Spelling: Basic skills for effective communication.* Columbus, OH: Zaner-Bloser. [8]

Barbe, W. B., Lucas, V. H., & Wasylyk, T. M. (Eds.). (1984). *Handwriting: Basic skills for effective communication.* Columbus, OH: Zaner-Bloser. [8]

Barr, R., Sadow, M., & Blachowicz, C. (1995). *Reading diagnosis for teachers: An instructional approach* (3rd ed.). New York: Longman. [5]

Barrett, T., & Smith, R. (1976). *Teaching reading in the middle grades.* Reading, MA: Addison-Wesley. [6]

Bean, T. W. & Pardi, R. A. (1979). Field-test of a guided reading strategy. *Journal of Reading, 23,* 144–147. [10]

Beattie, J. R. (1994). Characteristics of students with disabilities and how teachers can help. In K. D. Wood & B. Algozzine (Eds.), *Teaching reading to high-risk learners: A unified perspective* (pp. 99–121). Boston: Allyn and Bacon. [6]

Beattie, J. R., & Enright, B. E. (1993). Problem-solving: Verify the plan with action. *Teaching Exceptional Children, 25* (2), 60–61. [9]

Beatty, L. S., Madden, R., Gardner, E. F., & Karlsen, B. (1984). *Stanford Diagnostic Mathematics Test* (3rd ed.). San Antonio, TX: Psychological Corp. [1]

Beckman, P., & Weller, C. (1990). Active, independent learning for children with learning disabilities. *Teaching Exceptional Children, 22* (2), 26–29. [4]

Benton, D. A. (1992). *Lions don't need to roar: Using the leadership power of professional presence to stand out, fit in, and move ahead.* New York: Time Warner. [11]

Bereiter, C. (1984). How to keep thinking skills from going the way of all frill. *Educational Leadership, 42,* 75–77. [10]

Berliner, D. C. (1984). The half-full glass: A review of research on teaching. In P. L. Hosford (Ed.), *Using what we know about teaching.* Alexandria, VA: Association for Supervision and Curriculum Development. [2, 3]

Beyer, B. K. (1987). *Practical strategies for the teaching of thinking.* Boston: Allyn and Bacon. [6, 10]

Bjorn, K., Madden, R., & Gardner, E. F. (1983). *Stanford Diagnostic Reading Test.* Orlando: Harcourt Brace Jovanovich. [6]

Blankenship, C. S. (1985). Using curriculum based assessment data to make instructional decisions. *Exceptional Children, 52,* 233–238. [1]

Bloom, B. (1956). *Taxonomy of educational objectives—handbook I: The cognitive domain.* New York: David McKay. [6]

Bloom, B. (1976). *Human characteristics and school learning.* New York: McGraw-Hill. [2, 3]

Bloom, B. (1985). Foreword, In T. R. Guskey, *Implementing mastery learning* (pp. ix–xi). Belmont, CA: Wadsworth. [3]

Bond, G. L., Tinker, M. A., Wasson, B. B., & Wasson, J. B. (1994). *Reading difficulties: Their diagnosis and correction* (7th ed.). Boston: Allyn and Bacon. [5]

Bos, C. S. (1982). Getting past decoding: Assisted and repeated readings as remedial methods for learning disabled students. *Topics in Learning and Learning Disabilities, 1,* 51–57. [6]

Bos, C. S., & Vaughn, S. (1994). *Strategies for teaching students with learning and behavior problems* (3rd ed.). Boston: Allyn and Bacon. [4, 10]

Brandt, R. (1984). *Improving the quality of student thinking.* (Video Tape). Alexandria, VA: Association for Supervision and Curriculum Development. [10]

Brazee, E. (1979). Teaching reading in social studies: Skill-centered versus content-centered. *Colorado Journal of Educational Research, 18,* 23–25. [10]

Brent, R., & Anderson, P. (1993). Developing children's classroom listening strategies. *The Reading Teacher, 47* (2), 122–126. [6]

Brigance, A. (1983). *Brigance Diagnostic Comprehensive Inventory of Basic Skills.* N. Billerica, MA: Curriculum Associates. [3, 5, 8, 9]

Brolin, D. E. (1989). *Life-centered career education: A competency-based approach.* Reston, VA: Council for Exceptional Children. [2]

Brooks, J. G., & Brooks, M. G. (1993). *In search of understanding: The case for constructivist classrooms.* Alexandria, VA: Association for Supervision and Curriculum Development. [2]

Brophy, J. (1992). Probing the subtleties of subject-matter teaching. *Educational Leadership, 49* (7), 4–8. [2, 10]

Brophy, J., & Good, T. (1986). Teacher behavior and student achievement. In M. Wittrock (Ed.), *Handbook of research on teaching* (3rd ed.). (pp. 328–375). New York: Macmillan. [2]

Browder, D. M. (1991). *Assessment of individuals with severe disabilities* (2nd ed.). Baltimore: Paul H. Brookes. [1]

Browder, D. M., & Snell, M. A. (1993). Functional academics. In M. Snell (Ed.), *Instruction of students with severe disabilities* (4th ed.). (pp. 442–479). New York: Merrill/Macmillan. [8]

Brown, A. L., & Palincsar, A. S. (1982). Inducing strategy learning from texts by means of informed, self-control training. *Topics in Learning and Learning Disabilities, 2,* 1–17. [6]

Brown, F. & Snell, M. (1993). Measurement, analysis, and evaluation. In M. Snell (Ed.), *Instruction of students with severe disabilities* (4th ed.). New York: Merrill/Macmillan. [3]

Brown, L., & Hammill, D. D. (1990). *Behavior Rating Profile—2.* Austin, TX: Pro-Ed. [1]

Brown, R. (1989). Testing and thoughtfulness. *Educational Leadership, 46* (7), 31–33. [3]

Brunner, C. E. & Majewski, W.S. (1990). Mildly handicapped students can succeed with learning styles. *Educational Leadership, 48,* 21–23. [10]

Bruno, R. M., & Newman, M. (1985). Modifying content reading to develop comprehension skills in the regular classroom. *Teaching Exceptional Children, 17,* 208–213. [6]

Burns, P. C., & Roe, B. D. (1992). *Burns/Roe informal reading inventory: Preprimer to twelfth grade* (4th ed.). Boston: Houghton Mifflin. [6]

Burns, P. C., Roe, B. D., & Ross, E. P. (1992). *Teaching reading in today's elementary schools* (5th ed.). Boston: Houghton Mifflin. [6, 10]

Burrows, J. (1987). Reading skills: the key to successful study. *Adult Education, 59* (4) 310–316. [9]

Burton, G. M. (1992). Young children's choices of manipulatives and strategies for solving whole number division problems. *Focus on Learning Problems in Mathematics, 14* (2), 2–17. [9]

Buswell, G. T., & John, L. (1925). *Fundamental processes in arithmetic.* Indianapolis: Allen House. [4]

Cain, A. A., & Sund, R. B. (1989). *Teaching science through discovery.* New York: Macmillan. [10]

Calfee, R. C., & Perfumo, P. (1993). Student portfolios: Opportunities for a revolution in assessment. *Journal of Reading, 36* (7), 532–537. [6]

Campbell, B. J., Brady, M. P., & Linehan, S. (1991). Effects of peer-mediated instruction on the acquisition and generalization of written capitalization skills. *Journal of Learning Disabilities, 24,* 6–14. [7]

Canfield, A. A. (1988). *The Learning Styles Inventory.* Los Angeles: Western Psychological Services. [4]

Canfield, J. (1990). Improving students' self-esteem. *Educational Leadership, 48* (1), 48–50. [4]

Canfield, J., & Siccone, F. (1993). *101 ways to develop student self-esteem and responsibility, Volume I: The teacher as coach.* Boston: Allyn and Bacon. [4]

Canfield, J., & Wells, H. C. (1994). *100 ways to enhance self-concept in the classroom,* (2nd ed.). Boston: Allyn and Bacon. [4]

Capps, L. R., & Cox, L. S. (1991). Improving the learning of mathematics in our schools. *Focus on Exceptional Children, 23* (9), 1–8. [9]

Carbo, M. (1990). Igniting the literacy revolution through reading style. *Educational Leadership, 48* (2), 26–29. [10]

Carlisle, J. F. (1989). The use of the sentence verification technique in diagnostic assessment of listening and reading comprehension. *Learning Disabilities Research, 5* (1), 33–44. [6]

Carlisle, J. F. (1993). Selecting approaches to vocabulary instruction for the reading disabled. *Learning Disabilities Research & Practice, 8* (2), 97–105. [5]

Carnine, D. (1989). Teaching complex content to learning disabled students: The role of technology. *Exceptional Children, 55,* 524–633. [3]

Carnine, D., Silbert, J., & Kameenui, E. J. (1990). *Direct instruction reading* (2nd ed.). Columbus, OH: Charles E. Merrill. [5, 6]

Charles, R. I., et al. (1985). *Problem solving experiences in mathematics.* Menlo Park, CA: Addison-Wesley. [9]

Choate, J. S. (1990a). An array of assessment tips: From basics to pragmatics. *Diagnostique, 16* (1), 23–64. [3]

Choate. J. S. (1990b). Problem solving: Study the problem. *Teaching Exceptional Children, 22* (4), 44–46. [9]

Choate, J. S. (1990c). Reading assessment: A checklist of reading problems. *Diagnostique, 16* (1), 32–37. [5]

Choate, J. S., Enright, B. E., Miller, L. J., Poteet, J. A., & Rakes, T. A. (1992). *Curriculum-based assessment and programming* (2nd ed.). Boston: Allyn and Bacon. [1]

Choate, J. S., & Evans, S. S. (1992). Authentic assessment of special learners: Problem or promise? *Preventing School Failure, 37* (1), 6–9. [3]

Choate, J. S., & Rakes, T. A. (1987) The structured listening activity: A model for improving listening comprehension. *Reading Teacher. 41,* 194–200. [6]

Choate, J. S., & Rakes, T. A. (1989). *Reading: Detecting and correcting special needs.* Boston: Allyn and Bacon. [5, 6]

Choate, J. S., & Rakes, T. A. (1993). Recognizing words: The tools for reading comprehension. In J. S. Choate (Ed.), *Successful mainstreaming: Proven ways to detect and correct special needs* (pp. 52–81). Boston: Allyn and Bacon. [5]

Clark, G. M., & Kolstoe, O. P. (1990). *Career development and transition education for adolescents with disabilities.* Boston: Allyn and Bacon. [1, 2]

Clark, J. H. (1990). *Patterns of thinking: Integrating learning skills in content teaching.* Boston: Allyn and Bacon, 13–18. [10]

Clarkson, P. C. (1992). Unknown/careless errors in a mathematical language context: Further investigation. *Focus on Learning Problems in Mathematics, 14* (4), 3–16. [9]

Cleland, D. J. (1981). Highlighting issues in children's literature through semantic webbing. *Reading Teacher, 34,* 642–646. [6]

Cobb, W. D., & Edwards, G. (1907). *School days.* New York: Gus Edwards Music Publishing. [1]

Collins, C. (1987). *Time management for teachers: Techniques and skills that give you more time to teach.* West Nyack, NY: Parker Publishing. [11]

Collins, M. D. (1991). Teaching effective word identification strategies. In B. L. Hayes (Ed.), *Effective strategies for teaching reading* (pp. 13–34). Boston: Allyn and Bacon. [5]

Collins, M. D., & Cheek, E. H. (1993). *Diagnostic-prescriptive reading instruction: A guide for classroom teachers* (4th ed.). Dubuque, IA: Brown/Benchmark. [5, 6, 10]

Congressional Federal Register. (1992). Part II, Department of Education, 34 CFR Parts 300 and 301. Tuesday, 29 September, 1992. Final Rules and Regulations, 44794–44852 (Individuals with Disabilities Education Act). [1]

Connolly, A. J. (1988). *KeyMath Revised: A Diagnostic Inventory of Essential Mathematics.* Circle Pines, MN: American Guidance Services. [1]

Cooper, J. O. (1981). *Measuring behavior* (2nd ed.). Columbus, OH: Charles E. Merrill. [1]

Cooter, R. B. Jr., & Reutzel, D. R. (1994). Instructional techniques for making subject area materials more comprehensible for readers at risk. In K. Wood & B. Algozzine (Eds.), *Teaching reading to high-risk learners: A unified perspective* (pp. 247–267). Boston: Allyn and Bacon. [10]

Council for Educational Diagnostic Services. (1992). Knowledge and skills for beginning special education teachers. *CEDS Communiqué, 19* (3), 1–2. [1]

Council for Educational Diagnostic Services. (1993). Knowledge and skills needed by master teachers in the area of assessment. *CEDS Communiqué, 20* (3), 3. [1]

Council for Educational Diagnostic Services. (Serial editions). *CEDS Communiqué* Newsletter. Reston, VA: Author. [1]

Coutinho, M., & Malouf, D. (1993). Performance assessment and children with disabilities: Issues and possibilities. *Teaching Exceptional Children, 25* (4), 62–67. [3]

Crawford, L. W. (1993). *Language and literacy learning in multicultural classrooms.* Boston: Allyn and Bacon. [6]

CTB/McGraw-Hill (1987). *The California Achievement Tests.* Monterey, CA: Author. [6]

Cuban, L. (1992). Curriculum stability and change. In P. W. Jackson (Ed.), *Handbook of research on curriculum: A project of the American Educational Research Association* (pp. 216–247). New York: Macmillan. [2]

Cunningham, P. M. (1979). A comparison/contrast theory of mediated word identification. *Reading Teacher, 32,* 774–778. [5]

Cunningham, P. M. (1988). When all else fails. . . . *Reading Teacher, 41,* 800–805. [5]

Cunningham, P. M., Moore, S. A., Cunningham, J. W., & Moore, D. W. (1995). *Reading in elementary classrooms: Strategies and observations* (3rd ed.). New York: Longman. [5, 6]

Curry, L. (1990). A critique of the research on learning styles. *Educational Leadership, 48* (2), 50–56. [3]

Danielson, K. E., & LaBonty, J. (1994). *Integrating reading and writing through children's literature.* Boston: Allyn and Bacon. [5]

Darling-Hammond, L. (1993). Reframing the school reform agenda: Developing capacity for school transformation. *Phi Delta Kappan, 74* (10), 753–761. [2]

Davey, B. (1989) Assessing comprehension: Selected interaction of task and reader. *Reading Teacher, 42,* 694–697. [6]

deBono, E. (1985). The CoRT thinking program. In A. L. Costa (Ed.), *Developing minds: A resource book for teaching thinking.* Alexandria, VA: Association for Supervision and Curriculum Development. [6]

Dempster, F. N. (1993). Exposing our students to less should help them learn more. *Phi Delta Kappan, 74* (6), 433–437. [1]

Deno, S. L. (1985). Curriculum-based measurement: The emerging alternative. *Exceptional Children, 52,* 219–232. [1]

Deno, S. L. (1989). Curriculum-based measurement and special education services: A fundamental and direct relationship. In M. R. Shinn (Ed.), *Curriculum-based measurement: Assessing special children* (pp. 1–17). New York: Guilford Press. [1]

Desberg, P. (1994). *Hyper interactive CAI: Using HyperCard™ to develop computer-assisted instruction.* Boston: Allyn and Bacon. [3]

Deshler, D. D. & Schumaker, J. B. (1986). Learning strategies: An instructional alternative for low-achieving adolescents. *Exceptional Children, 52,* 583–590. [10]

Dickerson, D. P. (1982). A study of use of games to reinforce sight vocabulary. *Reading Teacher, 36,* 46–49. [5]

Dolch, E. W. (1942). *Basic Sight Word Test.* Champaign, IL: Garrard Press. [5]

Doll, R. C. (1992). *Curriculum improvement: Decision making and process* (8th ed.). Boston: Allyn and Bacon. [2, 3]

Downing, J., & Perino, D. M. (1992). Functional versus standardized assessment procedures: Implications for educational programming. *Mental Retardation, 30* (5), 289–295. [1]

Doyle, W. (1986). Classroom organization and management. In M. Wittrock (Ed.), *Handbook of re-search on teaching* (3rd ed.) (pp. 392–431). New York: Macmillan. [2]

Doyle, W. (1992). Curriculum and pedagogy. In P. W. Jackson (Ed.), *Handbook of research on curriculum: A project of the American Educational Research Association* (pp. 486–516). New York: Macmillan. [2]

Dudley-Marling, C. (1985). Perceptions of the usefulness of the IEP by teachers of learning disabled and emotionally disturbed children. *Psychology in the Schools, 22,* 65–67. [1]

Duffelmeyer, F. A. & Duffelmeyer, B. B. (1989). Are IRI passages suitable for assessing main idea comprehension? *Reading Teacher, 42,* 358–363. [6]

Duffelmeyer, F. A., Robinson, S. S. & Squier, S. E. (1989). Vocabulary questions on informal reading inventories. *Reading Teacher, 43,* 142–148. [6]

Dunham, M., Baker, E. H., Minder, C., McGuire, L. E., & McCormick, B. (1989). A comparison of academic adjustment between two different kindergarten systems. Paper presented at Louisiana School Psychologist Association Annual Conference, Lafayette, LA. [4]

Dunlap, L. K., Dunlap, G., Koegel, L. K., & Koegel, R. L. (1991). Using self-monitoring to increase independence. *Exceptional Children, 23,* 17–22. [4]

Dunn, L., & Dunn, L. (1981). *Peabody Picture Vocabulary Test—Revised.* Circle Pines, MN: American Guidance Service. [1]

Dunn, R. & Dunn, K. (1992). *Teaching elementary students through their individual learning styles: Practical approaches for grades 3–6.* Boston: Allyn and Bacon. [3]

Dunn, R. & Dunn, K. (1993). *Teaching secondary students through their individual learning styles: Practical approaches for grades 7–12.* Boston: Allyn and Bacon. [3, 8]

Dunn, R., Dunn, K., & Price, G. E. (1989). *Learning style inventory.* Lawrence, KS: Price Systems. [3]

Duran, R. P. (1989). Assessment and instruction of at-risk Hispanic students. *Exceptional Children, 56,* 154–158. [6]

Durkin, D. (1993). *Teaching them to read* (6th ed.). Boston: Allyn and Bacon. [5, 6]

Durrell, D., & Catterson, J. (1980). *Durrell analysis of reading difficulty.* Cleveland, OH: Psychological Corp. [5, 6]

Eanet, M. G. & Manzo, A. V. (1976). REAP-A strategy for improving reading/writing/study skills. *Journal of Reading. 19,* 647–652. [10]

Ebel, R. L., & Frisbie, D. A. (1991). *Essentials of educational measurement* (5th ed.). Englewood Cliffs, NJ: Prentice-Hall. [7]

Edwards, P. (1973). Panorama: A study technique. *Journal of reading, 17,* 132–135. [10]

Ekwall, E. E., & Shanker, J. L. (1993). *Locating and correcting reading difficulties* (6th ed.). New York: Merrill/Macmillan. [5, 6]

Ellis, E. S., & Lenz, B. K. (1987). A component analysis of effective learning strategies for LD students. *Learning Disabilities Focus, 2,* 94–107. [7]

Elmore, R. F., & Fuhrman, S. H. (Eds.) (1994). *The governance of curriculum,* 1994 Yearbook of the Association for Supervision and Curriculum Development. Alexandria, VA: ASCD. [2]

Englert, C. S., & Lichter, A. (1982). Using statement-pie to teach reading and writing skills. *Teaching Exceptional Children, 14,* 164–175. [6]

Enright, B. E. (1983). *ENRIGHT Diagnostic Inventory of Basic Arithmetic Skills.* N. Billerica, MA: Curriculum Associates. [1, 3, 9]

Enright, B. E. (1985). *ENRIGHT computation series* (Books A–D). N. Billerica, MA: Curriculum Associates. [9]

Enright, B. E. (1986). *ENRIGHT computation series* (Books E–M). N. Billerica, MA: Curriculum Associates. [9]

Enright, B. E. (1987). *ENRIGHT S.O.L.V.E.: Action problem solving series.* N. Billerica, MA: Curriculum Associates. [9]

Enright, B. E. (1989). *Basic mathematics: Detecting and correcting special needs.* Boston: Allyn and Bacon. [9]

Enright, B. E. (1990). Mathematics assessment tips: A checklist of common errors. *Diagnostique, 16* (1), 45–48. [9]

Enright, B. E., Hendrickson, J., & Gable, R. A. (1990). How do students get answers like these? *Diagnostique, 13* (2–4), 55–63. [9]

Etscheidt, S. (1991). Reducing aggressive behavior and improving self-control: A cognitive-behavioral training program for behaviorally disordered adolescents. *Behavioral Disorders, 16,* 107–115. [4]

Evans, W. H., Evans, S. S., Gable, R. A., & Schmid, R. E. (1991). *Instructional management for detecting and correcting special problems.* Boston: Allyn and Bacon. [1, 3]

Evans, W. H., Evans S. S., & Schmid, R. E. (1989). *Behavior and instructional management: An ecological approach.* Boston: Allyn and Bacon. [2–4]

Evertson, C. M., Emmer, E. T., Clements, B. S., & Worsham, M. E. (1994). *Classroom management for elementary teachers* (3rd ed.). Boston: Allyn and Bacon. [2–4]

Ezor, E. (1974). *Individualized language arts.* ESEA Title IV-C Project 70-014. Weehawken, NJ: Weehawken School District. [7]

Fagen, S. A., & Long, N. J. (1979). A psychoeducational curriculum approach to teaching self-control. *Behavioral Disorders, 4,* 68–82. [4]

Farr, R. (1973) *Iowa Silent Reading Test.* New York: Psychological Corp. [6]

Fauke, J., Burnett, J., Powers, M., & Sulzer-Azaroff, B. (1973). Improvement of handwriting and letter recognition skills: A behavior modification procedure. *Journal of Learning Disabilities, 6,* 25–29. [8]

Fay, L. (1965). Study skills: Math and science. In J. Allen (Ed.), *Reading and inquiry* (pp. 239–252). Newark: International Reading Association. [10]

Fennell, F. (Ed.) (1992). Ideas. *Arithmetic Teacher, 39* (7), 18–25. [9]

Fernald, G. (1943). *Remedial techniques in basic school subjects.* New York: McGraw-Hill. [3, 5, 8]

Fernald, G. (1988). *Remedial techniques in basic school subjects.* Austin, TX: Pro-Ed. (Original work published 1943). [3, 5, 8]

Fielding, L. G., & Pearson, P. D. (1994). Reading comprehension: What works. *Educational Leadership, 51* (5), 62–68. [6]

Figueroa, R. A. (1989). Psychological testing of linguistic-minority students: Knowledge gaps and regulations. *Exceptional Children, 56,* 145–152. [1]

Fitzgerald, J. A. (1951). *The teaching of spelling.* Milwaukee, WI: Bruce Publishing. [8]

Fitzsimmons, R., & Loomer, B. (1978). *Spelling: Learning and instruction—Research and practice.* Billerica, MA: Curriculum Associates. [8]

Flood, J., & Lapp, D. (1990). Reading comprehension instruction for at-risk students: Research-based practices that can make a difference. *Journal of Reading, 33,* 490–496. [6]

Flood, J. & Lapp, D. (1989). Reporting reading progress: A comparison portfolio for parents. *Reading Teacher, 42,* 508–514. [10]

Ford, M. P., & Ohlhausen, M. M. (1988). Classroom reading incentive programs: Removing the obstacles and hurdles for disabled readers. *Reading Teacher, 41,* 796–798. [6]

Forness, S. R., & Kavale, K. A. (1991). Social skills deficits as primary learning disabilities: A note on problems with the ICLD diagnostic criteria. *Learning Disabilities Research and Practice, 6* (1), 44–49. [4]

Fountain Valley teacher support systems. (1975). Huntington Beach, CA: R. L. Zweig Associates. [1]

Fouse, B., & Brians, S. (1993). *A primer on attention deficit disorder* (FB 354). Bloomington, IN: Phi Delta Kappa Foundation. [4]

Fowler, G. L. (1982). Developing comprehension skills in primary students through the use of story frames. *Reading Teacher, 36,* 176–180. [6]

Fowler, G. L., & Davis, M. (1985). The story frame approach: A tool for improving reading comprehension of EMR children. *Teaching Exceptional Children, 17,* 296–298. [6]

Fox, C. L., & Weaver, F. (1989). Social acceptance of students identified as learning disabled. *Teacher Education and Special Education, 12* (3), 83–90. [4]

Freeman, G., & Reynolds, E. G. (1980). Enriching basal reader lessons with semantic webbing. *Reading Teacher, 33,* 677–684. [6]

Frith, G. H., & Armstrong, S. W. (1986). Self-monitoring for behavior disordered students. *Teaching Exceptional Children, 18* (2), 144–148. [4]

Fry, E. (1980). The new instant word list. *Reading Teacher, 34,* 284–289. [5]

Fuchs, L. S., Deno, S. L., & Marston, D. (1983). Improving the reliability of curriculum-based measures of academic skills for psycho-educational decision making. *Diagnostique, 8* (3), 135–149. [1]

Fuchs, L. S., Deno, S. L., & Mirkin, P. K. (1984). The effects of frequent curriculum-based evaluation on pedagogy, student achievement and student awareness of learning. *American Educational Research Journal, 21,* 449–460. [3]

Fuchs, L. S., & Fuchs, D. (1984a). Criterion-referenced assessment without measurement: How accurate for special education? *Remedial and Special Education, 5* (4), 29–32. [1]

Fuchs, L. S., & Fuchs, D. (1984b). Teaching beginning reading skills: A unique approach. *Teaching Exceptional Children, 17,* 48–54. [5]

Fuchs, L. S., & Fuchs, D. (1990). Traditional academic assessment: An overview. In R. A. Gable & Hendrickson, J. M. (Eds.), *Assessing students with special needs: A sourcebook for analyzing and correcting errors in academics.* New York: Longman. [1, 3]

Fuchs, L. S., Fuchs, D., Hamlett, C. L., & Allinder, R. M. (1991). The contribution of skills analysis to curriculum-based measurement in spelling. *Exceptional Children, 57,* 443–452. [8]

Fuchs, L. S., & Shinn, M. R. (1989). Writing CBM IEP objectives. In M. R. Shinn (Ed.), *Curriculum-based measurement: Assessing special children* (pp. 130–153). New York: Guilford Press. [1]

Fulghum, R. (1988). *All I really need to know I learned in kindergarten: Uncommon thoughts on common things.* New York: Villard Books. [11]

Fullan, M. (1993). Innovation, reform, and restructuring strategies. In G. Cawelti (Ed.), *Challenges and achievements of American education: The 1993 yearbook of the Association for Supervision and Curriculum Development* (pp. 116–133). Alexandria, VA: ASCD. [2]

Furner, B. (1970). An analysis of the effectiveness of a program of instruction emphasizing the perceptual-motor nature of learning in handwriting. *Elementary English, 47,* 61–69. [8]

Gable, R. A., Enright, B. E., & Hendrickson, J. (1991). A practical model for curriculum-based assessment and instruction in arithmetic. *Teaching Exceptional Children, 24* (1), 6–9. [9]

Gable, R. A., Evans, W. H., & Evans, S. S. (1993). It's not over until you examine your answer. *Teaching Exceptional Children, 25* (2), 61–62. [9]

Gable, R. A., & Hendrickson, J. M. (Eds.) (1990a). *Assessing students with special needs: A sourcebook for analyzing and correcting errors in academics.* New York: Longman. [1, 3, 4,9]

Gable, R. A., & Hendrickson, J. M. (1990b). Making error analysis work. In R. A. Gable & J. M. Hendrickson (Eds.), *Assessing students with special needs: A sourcebook for analyzing and correcting errors in academics* (pp. 146–151). New York: Longman. [3]

Gable, R. A., & Hendrickson, J. M. (1990c). Errors in spelling. In R. A. Gable & J. M. Hendrickson (Eds.), *Assessing students with special needs: A sourcebook for analyzing and correcting errors in academics* (pp. 78–88). New York: Longman. [8]

Gaffney, J. S. (1994). Reading Recovery: Widening the scope of prevention for children at risk of reading failure. In K. D. Wood & B. Algozzine (Eds.), *Teaching reading to high-risk learners: A unified perspective* (pp. 231–246). Boston: Allyn and Bacon. [6]

Gajar, A., Goodman, L., & McAfee, J. (1993). *Secondary schools and beyond: Transition of indi-*

viduals with mild disabilities. New York: Macmillan. [1, 3, 8]

Galagan, J. E. (1985). Psychoeducational testing: Turn out the lights, the party's over. *Exceptional Children, 52,* 288–299. [1]

Gall, M. D., Gall, J. P., Jacobsen, D. R., & Bullock, T. L. (1990). *Tools for learning: A guide to teaching study skills.* Alexandria, VA: Association for Supervision and Curriculum Development. [4, 6, 10]

Gambrell, L. B. (1980). Think-time: Implications for Reading instruction. *Reading Teacher, 34,* 143–146. [6]

Gambrell, L. B., & Jawitz, P. B. (1993). Mental imagery, text illustrations, and children's story comprehension and recall. *Reading Research Quarterly, 28* (3), 265–273. [6]

Garcia, E. (1994). *Understanding and meeting the challenge of student cultural diversity.* Boston: Houghton Mifflin. [1, 2, 3]

Gardner, R. L. (1975). Logical connectives in science: A preliminary report. *Research in Science Education, 5,* 161–175. [10]

Gaskins, I., & Elliot, T. (1991). *Implementing cognitive strategy training across the school: The Benchmark manual for teachers.* Cambridge, MA: Brookline Books [11]

Gates, A. I., McKillop, A. S., & Horowitz, R. (1981). *Gates-McKillop-Horowitz Reading Diagnostic Tests,* 2nd ed. New York: Teachers College Press. [5]

Gaustad, M. G., & Messenheimer-Young, T. (1991). Dialogue journals for students with learning disabilities. *Teaching Exceptional Children, 23* (3), 28–32. [7]

George, P. (1986). Teaching handicapped children with attention problems: Teacher verbal strategies make a difference. *Teaching Exceptional Children, 18* (3), 172–175. [4]

Germann, G., & Tindal, G. (1985). An application of curriculum-based assessment: The use of direct and repeated measurement. *Exceptional Children, 52,* 244–265. [11]

Gersten, R., & Woodward, J. (1994). The language-minority students and special education: Issues, trends, and paradoxes. *Exceptional Children, 60* (4), 310 322. [7]

Giangreco, M. F., Cloninger, C. J., & Iverson, V. (1992). *Choosing options and accommodations for children (COACH): A planning guide for inclusive education.* Baltimore: Paul H. Brookes. [2]

Gibson, F. (1991). A new factor in the phonics debate. *Phi Delta Kappan, 72,* 402. [5]

Gickling, E. E., & Thompson, V. P. (1985). A personal view of curriculum-based assessment. *Exceptional Children, 52,* 205–218. [1, 3]

Gillingham, A., & Stillman, B. (1977). *Remedial training for children with specific disability in reading, spelling, and penmanship* (7th ed.). Cambridge, MA: Educators Publishing Service. [3, 8]

Gilstrap, R. (1962). Development of independent spelling skills in the intermediate grades. *Elementary English, 39,* 481–483. [8]

Goldman, M. E. (1993). *Using captioned TV for teaching reading* (FB 359). Bloomington, IN: Phi Delta Kappa Educational Foundation. [6]

Goldstein, A. P., Sprafkin, R. P., Gershaw, N. J., & Klein, P. (1980). *Skillstreaming the adolescent.* Champaign, IL: Research Press. [4]

Goldstein, S., & Goldstein, M. (1990). *Managing attention disorders in children: A guide for practitioners.* New York: Wiley and Sons. [4]

Good, T. L., & Brophy, J. E. (1994). *Looking in classrooms* (6th ed.). New York: Harper Collins. [3, 4, 6]

Graeber, A. Q., & Baker, K. M. (1992). Little in big is the way it always is. *Arithmetic Teacher, 39* (8), 18–21. [9]

Graham, S. (1985). Evaluating spelling programs and materials. *Teaching Exceptional Children, 17,* 299–304. [8]

Graham, S. (1986). A review of handwriting scales and factors that contribute to variability in handwriting scores. *Journal of School Psychology, 24,* 63–71. [8]

Graham, S. (1991). A review of attributional theory in achievement contexts. *Educational Psychology Review, 3,* 5–39. [10]

Graham, S. (1992). Issues in handwriting instruction. *Focus on Exceptional Children, 25,* 1–16. Denver, CO: Love. [8]

Graham, S., & Harris, K. R. (1987). Improving composition skills of inefficient learners with self-instructional strategy training. *Topics in Language Disorders, 7* (4), 66–77. [7]

Graham, S., & Harris, K. R. (1989). Improving learning disabled students' skills at composing essays: Self-instructional strategy training. *Exceptional Children, 56,* 201 214. [7]

Graham, S., Harris, K. R., & Sawyer, R. (1987). Composition instruction with learning disabled students: Self-instructional strategy training. *Focus on Exceptional Children, 20* (4), 1–11. [7]

Graham, S. & Miller, L. J. (1979). Spelling research and practice: A unified approach. *Focus on Exceptional Children, 12,* 1–16. [8]

Graham, S. & Miller, L., J. (1980). Handwriting research and practice: A unified approach. *Focus on Exceptional Children, 13,* 1–16. [8]

Graham, S. & Voth, V. P. (1990). Spelling instruction: Making modifications for students with learning disabilities. *Academic Therapy, 25,* 447–457. [8]

Graves, A., & Hauge, R. (1993). Using cues and prompts to improve story writing. *Exceptional Children, 25* (4), 38–40. [7]

Graves, D. H. (1983). *Writing: Teachers and children at work.* Portsmouth, NH: Heinemann Educational Books. [7]

Graves, D. H. (1985). All children can write. *Learning Disabilities Focus, 1,* 36–43. [7]

Greenbaum, C. R. (1987). *The Spellmaster Assessment and Teaching System.* Austin, TX: Pro-Ed. [8]

Greenspan, S. (1981). Social competence and handicapped individuals: Practical implications and a proposed model. *Advances in special education, 3,* 41–82. [4]

Gregg, N. (1991). Disorders of written expression. In A. M. Bain, L. L. Bailet, & L. C. Moats (Eds), *Written language disorders.* (pp. 65–97). Austin, TX: Pro-Ed. [7]

Gresham, F. M. (1988). Social competence and motivational characteristics of learning disabled students. In M. C. Wang, M. C. Reynolds, & H. J. Walberg (Eds.), *Handbook of special education research and practice, Volume 2, Mildly handicapped conditions.* New York: Pergamon Press. [4]

Griffey, Q. L., Zigmond, N., & Leinhardt, G. (1988). The effects of self-questioning and story structure training on the reading comprehension of poor readers. *Learning Disabilities Research, 4* (1), 45–51. [6]

Gronlund, N. E., & Linn, R. L. (1990). *Measurement and evaluation in teaching* (6th ed.). New York: Macmillan. [3]

Grossman, H. (1995). *Special education in a diverse society.* Boston: Allyn and Bacon. [10]

Guild, P. (1994). The culture/learning style connection. *Educational Leadership, 51* (8), 16–21. [3]

Gunn, V. P., & Elkins, J. (1979). Clozing the reading gap. *Australian Journal of Reading, 56,* 144–151. [6, 10]

Guskey, T. R. (1985). *Implementing mastery learning.* Belmont, CA: Wadsworth. [3]

Guszak, F. (1967). Teacher questioning and reading. *Reading Teacher, 21,* 227–234. [6]

Hall, R. V. (1983). *Behavior modification: The measurement of behavior.* Austin, TX: Pro-Ed. [1]

Haller, E. P., Child, D. A., & Walberg, H. J. (1988). Can comprehension be taught? A quantitative synthesis of metacognitive studies. *Educational Researcher, 17* (9), 5–8. [6]

Hammill, D. D., & Bartel, N. R. (1995). *Teaching students with learning and behavior problems* (6th ed.). Boston: Allyn and Bacon. [3, 8]

Hammill, D. D., Brown, L., & Bryant, B. R. (1992). *A consumer's guide to tests in print* (2nd ed.). Austin, TX: Pro-Ed. [1]

Hammill, D. D., & Larsen, S. (1988). *Test of Written Language–2.* Austin, TX: Pro-Ed. [8]

Hammill, D. D., & Leigh, J. E. (1983). *Basic Schools Skills Inventory—Diagnostic.* Austin, TX: Pro-Ed. [8]

Hanau, L. (1974). *The study game: How to play and win with statement-pie.* New York: Barnes & Noble. [6]

Haney, W., & Madaus, G. (1989). Searching for alternatives to standardized tests: Whys, whats, and whithers. *Phi delta Kappan, 70* (9), 683–687. [3]

Hansen, C. L. (1977). Writing skills. In N. G. Haring, T. C. Lovitt, M. D. Eaton, & C. L. Hansen (Eds.), *The fourth R: Research in the classroom.* Columbus, OH: Charles E. Merrill. [8]

Hansen, J. (1981). The effects of inference training and practice on young children's comprehension. *Reading Research Quarterly, 16,* 391–417. [6]

Hansen, J., & Pearson, P. D. (1983). An instructional study: Improving the inferential comprehension of fourth grade good and poor readers. *Journal of Educational Psychology, 75,* 821–829. [6]

Hargis, C. H. (1982). *Teaching reading to handicapped children.* Denver: Love. [5]

Hargis, C. H., & Gickling, E. E. (1978). The function of imagery in word recognition development. *Reading Teacher, 31,* 870–874. [5]

Hargrove, L. J., & Poteet, J. A. (1984). *Assessment in special education: The educational evaluation.* Englewood Cliffs, NJ: Prentice-Hall. [1, 4]

Harmin, M. (1994). *Inspiring active involvement: A handbook for teachers.* Alexandria, VA: Association for Supervision and Curriculum Development. [3]

Harp, B., & Brewer, J. A. (1991). *Reading and writing: Teaching for the connections.* San Diego, CA: Harcourt Brace Jovanovich. [5]

Harris, K. R., & Graham, S. (1985). Improving learning disabled students' compositions skills: Self-control strategy training. *Learning Disability Quarterly, 8,* 27–36. [7]

Harris, K. R., & Graham, S. (1988). Self-instructional strategy training. *Teaching Exceptional Children, 20* (2), 35–37. [7]

Harris, K. R., & Graham, S. (1992). *Helping young writers master the craft: Strategy instruction and self-regulation in the writing process.* Cambridge, MA: Brookline Books. [7, 10]

Harry, B. (1991). *Cultural diversity, families, and the special education system.* New York: Teachers College Press. [1]

Hasselbring, T. S., & Moore, P. (1990). Computer-based assessment and error analysis. In Gable, R. A. & Hendrickson, J. M. (Eds.), *Assessing students with special needs: A sourcebook for analyzing and correcting errors in academics.* (pp. 102–116). New York: Longman. [3]

Heddens, J. W. (1986). Bridging the gap between the concrete and the abstract. *Arithmetic Teacher, 33* (6), 14–17. [9]

Heddens, J. W., & Speer, W. (1992). *Today's mathematics* (7th ed.). New York: Macmillan. [9]

Heilman, A. W. (1993). *Phonics in proper perspective* (7th ed.). New York: Merrill/Macmillan. [5]

Heilman, A. W., Blair, T. R., & Rupley, W. H. (1994). *Principles and practices of teaching reading* (8th ed.). New York: Merrill/Macmillan. [5, 6, 10]

Heller, M. F. (1991). *Reading-writing connections: From theory to practice.* New York: Longman. [6]

Henderson, E. & Templeton, S. (1986). A developmental perspective of formal spelling instruction through alphabet, pattern, and meaning. *Elementary School Journal, 86,* 305–316. [8]

Henderson, H. (1990). *Teaching spelling* (2nd ed.). Boston: Houghton Mifflin. [8]

Henk, W. A., Helfeldt, J. P., & Platt, J. M. (1986). Developing reading fluency in learning disabled students. *Teaching Exceptional Children, 18,* 202–206. [6]

Hennings, D. G. (1992). *Beyond the read aloud: Learning to read through listening to and reflecting on literature.* Bloomington, IN: Phi Delta Kappa Educational Foundation. [1, 6]

Herber, H. L., & Herber, J. N. (1993). *Teaching in content areas: With reading, writing, and reasoning.* Boston: Allyn and Bacon. [10]

Herber, H. L., & Nelson, J. B. (1975). Questioning is not the answer. *Journal of Reading, 18,* 512–517. [6]

Herman, J. L., Aschbacher, P. R., & Winters, L. (1992). *A practical guide to alternative assessment.* Alexandria, VA: Association for Supervision and Curriculum Development. [10]

Hiebert, E. H., & Taylor, B. M. (Eds.) (1994). *Getting reading right from the start: Effective early literacy interventions.* Boston: Allyn and Bacon. [6]

Hillerich, R. L. (1977). Let's teach spelling—Not phonetic, misspelling. *Language Arts, 54,* 301–307. [8]

Hofmeister, A. (1973). Let's get it write. *Teaching Exceptional Children, 6,* 30–33. [8]

Hofmeister, A. M., & Preston, C. N. (1981). *Curriculum-based assessment and evaluation procedures.* Unpublished monograph, University of Minnesota. [1]

Hopkins, K. D., & Stanley, J. C. (1990). *Educational and psychological measurement and evaluation* (7th ed.). Englewood Cliffs, NJ: Prentice-Hall. [6]

Horn, E. (1919). Principles of methods in teaching spelling as derived from scientific investigation. In *Eighteenth Yearbook, National Society for the Study of Education.* Bloomington;, IL: Public School Publishing. [8]

Horn, E. (1960). Spelling. *Encyclopedia of Educational Research* (3rd ed.). (pp. 1337–1350). New York: Macmillan. [8]

Horn, E. (1954). *Teaching spelling.* Washington, DC: American Educational Research Association. [8]

Horn, T. (1976). Test, then study in spelling. *Instructor, 86,* 81. [8]

Houck, C. K., & Billingsley, B. S. (1989). Written expression of students with and without learning disabilities: Differences across the grades. *Journal of Learning Disabilities, 22,* 561–567, 572. [7]

Howell, K. W. (1991). Curriculum-based evaluation: What you think is what you get. *Diagnostique, 16* (4), 193–202. [3]

Howell, K. W. (1986). Direct assessment of academic performance. *School Psychology Review, 15,* 324–335. [9]

Howell, K. W., Fox, S., L., & Morehead, M. K. (1993). *Curriculum-based evaluation: Teaching and decision making* (2nd ed.). Pacific Grove, CA: Brooks/Cole. [3, 8, 11]

Howell, K. W., & Morehead, M. K. (1987). *Curriculum-based evaluation for special and remedial education.* Columbus, OH: Merrill. [1]

Howell, K. W., Zucker, S. H., & Morehead, M. K. (1982). *Multi-level Academic Skills Inventory.* Columbus, OH: Charles E. Merrill. [9]

Howell, K. W., Zucker, S. H., & Morehead, M. K. (1985). *Multi-level Academic Survey Tests.* Columbus, OH: Charles E. Merrill. [9]

Hudson, F. G., Colson, S. E., Welch, D. L., Banikowski, A. K., & Mehring, T. A. (1989). *Hudson Education Skills Inventory.* Austin, TX: Pro-Ed. [3, 8]

Hull, M. A. (1994). *Phonics for the teachers of reading: Programmed for self-instruction* (6th ed.). New York: Merrill/Macmillan. [5]

Hunt, W. K. (1965). *Grammatical structures written at three grade levels.* (National Council of Teachers of English Research Report No. 3), Champaign, IL: National Council of Teachers of English. [7]

Idol, L. (1987). Group story mapping: A comprehension strategy for both skilled and unskilled readers. *Journal of Learning Disabilities, 20,* 196–205. [6]

Idol, L. Nevin, A., & Paolucci-Whitcomb, P. (1986). *Models of curriculum-based assessment.* Rockville, MD: Aspen. [1, 3]

Jackson, P. W. (1992). Conceptions of curriculum and curriculum specialists. In P. W. Jackson (Ed.), *Handbook of research on curriculum: A project of the American Educational Research Association* (pp. 3–40). New York: Macmillan. [2]

Jacobs, H. H. (1989). The interdisciplinary model: A step-by-step approach for developing integrated units of study. In Jacobs, H. H. (Ed.), *Interdisciplinary curriculum: Design and implementation.* Arlington, VA: Association for Supervision and Curriculum Development. [2]

Jacobs, L. (1991). Assessment concerns: A study of cultural differences, teacher concepts, and inappropriate labeling. *Teacher Education and Special Education, 14* (1), 43–48. [1]

Jacobs, H. H., (1989). The interdisciplinary model: A step-by-step approach for developing integrated units of study. In H. H. Jacobs (Ed.), *Interdisciplinary curriculum: Design and implementation.* Arlington, VA: Association for Supervision and Curriculum Development. [2]

Jensen, R. J. (Ed.) (1993). *Research ideas for the classroom: Early childhood mathematics* (National Council of Teachers of Mathematics Research Interpretation Project). New York: Macmillan. [9]

Johns, J. L. (1988). *Basic reading inventory* (2nd ed.). Dubuque, IA: Wm. C. Brown. [6]

Johns, J. L. (1993). *Informal reading inventories: An annotated reference guide.* DeKalb, IL: Communitech International. [6]

Johnson, D. W. (1993). *Reaching out: Interpersonal effectiveness and self actualization* (5th ed.). Boston: Allyn and Bacon. [11]

Johnson, D. W., & Johnson, R. T. (1986). Mainstreaming and cooperative learning. *Exceptional Children, 52,* 553–561. [4]

Johnson, D. D. & Pearson, P. D. (1984). *Teaching reading vocabulary.* New York: Holt, Rinehart and Winston. [10]

Jongsma, E. (1971). *The cloze procedure as a teaching technique.* Newark, DE: International Reading Association. [10]

Jongsma, K. S. (1989). Portfolio assessment. *Reading Teacher, 43,* 264–265. [10]

Jorm, A. F. (1977). Effect of word imagery on reading performance as a function of reading ability. *Journal of Educational Psychology, 69,* 46–54. [5]

Joyce, B., & Weil, M. (1992). *Models of teaching* (4th ed.). Boston: Allyn and Bacon. [4]

Kameenui, E. J., & Darch, C. B. (1995). *Instructional classroom management: A proactive approach to behavior management.* White Plains, NY: Longman. [4]

Kameenui, E. J., & Simmons, D. C. (1990). *Designing instructional strategies: The prevention of academic learning problems.* Columbus: Merrill. [3]

Kanning, R. G. (1994). What multimedia can do in our classrooms. *Educational Leadership, 51* (7), 40–44. [3]

Karlin, R. & Karlin, A.R. (1987). *Teaching elementary reading: Principles and strategies.* San Diego: Harcourt Brace Jovanovich. [10]

Karlsen, B., & Gardner, E. F. (1984). *Stanford Diagnostic Reading Test* (3rd ed.). San Antonio, TX: Psychological Corp. [1, 3]

Kauffman, J. M. (1993). *Characteristics of behavior disorders of children and youth* (5th ed.). New York: Merrill/Macmillan. [3, 4]

Kay, L., Young, J. L. & Mottley, R. R. (1986). Using Manzo's ReQuest model with delinquent adolescents. *Journal of Reading, 29,* 506–510. [6]

Kazdin, A. E. (1994). *Behavior modification in applied settings* (5th ed.). Pacific Grove, CA: Brooks/Cole. [3, 4]

Keefe, J. W. (1979). Learning style: An overview. In *Student learning styles.* Reston, VA: National Association of Secondary School Principals. [1]

Kerlinger, F. N. (1986). *Foundations of behavioral research* (3rd ed.). New York: Holt, Rinehart & Winston. [1]

Kerr, M. M., & Nelson, C. M. (1983). *Strategies for managing behavior in the classroom.* Columbus, OH: Charles E. Merrill. [1]

Keyser, D. J., & Sweetland, R. C. (Eds.) (Serial editions). *Test critiques.* Austin, TX: Pro-Ed. [1]

Kindsvatter, R., Wilen, W., & Ishler, M. (1988). *Dynamics of effective teaching.* New York: Longman. [3]

King-Sears, M. E. (1994). *Curriculum-based assessment in special education.* San Diego, CA: Singular. [11]

Kletzien, S. B. & Bednar, M. R. (1990). Dynamic assessment for at-risk readers. *Journal of Reading, 33,* 528–533. [6]

Kolker, B., & Terwilliger, P. N. (1981). Sight vocabulary learning of first and second graders. *Reading World, 20,* 251–258. [5]

Koskinen, P. S., Wilson, R. M., Gambrell, L. B., & Neuman, S. B. (1993). Captioned video and vocabulary learning: An innovative practice in literacy instruction. *The Reading Teacher, 47* (1), 36–43. [5]

Kramer, J. J., & Conoley, J. C. (Eds.) (1992). *The eleventh mental measurements yearbook.* Lincoln, NB: University of Nebraska Press. [1]

Krevisky, J., & Linfield, J. (1963). *The bad speller's dictionary.* New York: Random House. [8]

Krupski, A. (1985). Variations in attention as a function of classroom task demands in learning handicapped and CA-matched nonhandicapped children. *Exceptional Children, 52,* 52–56. [4]

Kuhs, T., Porter, A., Floden, R., Freeman, D., Schmidt, W., & Schwill, J. (1983). *Differences among teachers in their use of curriculum-embedded tests.* East Lansing: The Institute for Research on Teaching, Michigan State University. [1]

Lambie, R. A., & Hutchens, P. W. (1986). Adapting elementary school mathematics instruction. *Teaching Exceptional Children, 10,* 185–189. [9]

Langer, J. (1986). Learning through writing: Study skills in the content areas. *Journal of Reading, 29,* 400–406. [10]

Lapp, D., & Flood, J. (1992). *Teach reading to every child* (4th ed.). New York: Macmillan. [6, 10]

Layman, B. G. & Collins, M. D. (1990). Critical reading: A redefinition. *Reading Research and Instruction, 29,* 56–63. [6]

Learning Disability Association (1990). LDA position paper on eligibility for services for persons with specific learning disabilities. *LDA Newsbriefs, 25* (3), 2a. [1]

Lemlech, J. K. (1990). *Curriculum and instructional methods for the elementary school* (2nd ed.). New York: Macmillan. [2]

Lerner, J. W. (1993). *Learning disabilities: Theories, diagnosis, and teaching strategies* (6th ed.). Boston: Houghton Mifflin. [3, 8]

Lerner, J. W., Cousin, P. T., & Richeck, M. (1992). Critical issues in learning disabilities: Whole language learning. *Learning Disabilities Research and Practice, 7* (4), 226–230. [1]

Lewis, A. C. (1993). The administration's education agenda. *Phi Delta Kappan, 75* (3), 196–197.

Lewis, R. (1993). *Special education technology: Classroom applications.* Pacific Grove, CA: Brooks/Cole. [10]

Lewis, R. B., & Doorlag, D. H. (1991). *Teaching special students in the mainstream* (3rd ed.). New York: Merrill/Macmillan. [4]

Lidz, C. S. (1991). *Practitioner's guide to dynamic assessment.* New York: Guilford. [6]

Lindsley, O. R. (1964). Direct measurement and prothesis of retarded behavior. *Journal of Education, 147,* 62–81. [3]

Lindsley, O. R. (1990). Precision teaching: By teachers for children. *Teaching Exceptional Children, 22* (3), 10–15. [3]

Linn, R. J., Algozzine, B., Schwartz, S. E., & Grise, P. (1984). Minimum competency testing and the learning disabled adolescent. *Diagnostique, 9* (2), 63–75. [1]

Lipson, M. Y., & Wickizer, E. A. (1989). Promoting self-control and active reading through dialogues. *Teaching Exceptional Children, 21* (2) 28–32. [6]

Loomer, B. M. (1990). *Spelling research: The most commonly asked questions about* spelling . . . *and what the research says.* Mt. Vernon, IA: Useful Learning. [8]

Loomer, B. M. (1990). *The useful spelling program.* Mt. Vernon, IA: Useful Learning. [8]

Loomer, B. M., & Fitzsimmons, R. F. (1989). *Spelling: Research and practice.* Iowa City, IA: Useful Curriculum Incorporated. [8]

Lovitt, T. C. (1984). *Tactics for teaching.* Columbus, OH: Charles E. Merrill. [4, 6]

Lovitt, T. C. (1993). Recurring issues in special and general education. In J. I. Goodlad & T. C.

Lovitt (Eds.), *Integrating general and special education* (pp. 49–71). New York: Merrill/Macmillan. [2]

Lovitt, T. C., Fister, S., Freston, J. L., Kemp, K., Shroeder, B., & Bauernschmidt, M. (1990). Using precision techniques: Translating research. *Teaching Exceptional Children, 22* (3), 16–19. [3]

Luftig, R. L. (1989). *Assessment of learners with special needs.* Boston: Allyn and Bacon. [1, 7]

Lupi, M. H., & Woo, J. Y. T. (1989). Issues in the assessment of East Asian handicapped students. *Diagnostique, 14,* 146–158. [1]

MacArthur, C. A., & Graham, S. (1987). Learning disabled students' composing under three methods of text production: Handwriting, word processing, and dictation. *The Journal of Special Education, 21,* (3), 22–42. [7]

MacMillan, D. L., Keogh, B. K., & Jones, R. L. (1986). Special educational research on mildly handicapped learners. In M. Wittrock (Ed.), *Handbook of research on teaching* (3rd ed.) (pp. 686–724). New York: Macmillan. [2]

Maheady, L., Mallette, B., Harper, G. F., Sacca, K. C., & Pomerantz, D. (1994). Peer-mediated instruction for high-risk students. In K. D. Wood & B. Algozzine (Eds.), *Teaching reading to high-risk learners: A unified perspective* (pp. 269–290). Boston: Allyn and Bacon. [6]

Mager, R. F. (1962). *Preparing instructional objectives.* Palo Alto, CA: Fearon. [1]

Male, M. (1988). *Special Magic,* Mountain View, CA: Mayfield. [7]

Male, M. (1994). *Technology for inclusion: Meeting the special needs of all students* (2nd ed.). Boston: Allyn and Bacon. [3, 7, 10]

Mangieri, J.N., & Corboy, M. (1992). Reinforcing vocabulary in the content classroom: the why and the how. In E. K. Dishner, T. W. Bean, & J. E. Readence (Eds.), *Reading in the content areas: Improving classroom instruction* (3rd ed.). Dubuque, IA: Kendall/Hunt. [10]

Mann, P. H., Suiter, P. A., & McClung, R. M. (1992). *A guide to educating mainstreamed students* (4th ed.). Boston: Allyn and Bacon. [3, 8]

Manzo, A.V. (1985). Expansion modules for the ReQuest, CAT, GRP, and REAP reading/study procedures. *Journal of Reading, 28,* 498–503. [6]

Manzo, A. V. (1969). The ReQuest procedure. *Journal of Reading, 13,* 123–126. [6]

Manzo, A. V., & Manzo, U. C. (1993). *Literacy disorders: Holistic diagnosis and remediation.* Forth Worth, TX: Holt, Rinehart and Winston. [5, 6]

Marston, D. B., (1989). A curriculum-based measurement approach to assessing academic performance: What it is and why do it. In M. R. Shinn (Ed.), *Curriculum-based measurement: Assessing special children* (pp. 18–78). New York: Guilford Press. [3, 6]

Masters, L. F., Mori, B. A., & Mori, A. A. (1993). *Teaching secondary students with mild learning and behavior problems* (2nd ed.). Austin,TX: Pro-Ed. [8]

Mastropieri, M. A. & Scruggs, T. E. (1988). Increasing content area learning of learning disabled students: Research implications. *Learning Disabilities Research, 4,* 17–25. [10]

Mather, N. (1992). Whole language reading instruction for students with learning disabilities: Caught in the cross fire. *Learning Disabilities Research and Practice, 7* (2), 87–95. [1]

May, F. B. (1994). *Reading as communication* (4th ed.). New York: Merrill/Macmillan. [6, 10]

McBride, W., L. (1992). *The theory and research behind McDougal, Littell's contemporary alphabet system.* Evanston, IL: McDougal, Littell. [8]

McCarthy, M. M. (1993). Challenges to the public school curriculum: New targets and strategies. *Phi Delta Kappan, 75* (1), 55–60. [2]

McCormick, B., Baker, E. H., & Dunham, M. (1991). Factor analysis of the TRSAA, Unpublished study. Monroe, LA: Northeast Louisiana University. [4]

McCoy, K. M., & Prehm, H. J. (1987). *Teaching mainstreamed students: Methods and techniques.* Denver, CO: Love. [8]

McDougal, Littell. (1993). *Handwriting connections.* Evanston, IL: McDougal, Littell. [8]

McEneaney, J. E. (1992). Computer-assisted diagnosis in reading: An expert systems approach. *Journal of Reading, 36* (1), 36–47. [6]

McGinnis, E., & Goldstein, A. P. (1984). *Skillstreaming the elementary school child.* Champaign, IL: Research Press. [24]

McGinnis, E., Goldstein, A. P., Sprafkin, R. P., & Gershaw, N. J. (1984). *Skillstreaming the elementary school child: A guide for teaching prosocial skills.* Champaign, IL: Research Press. [2]

McKenzie, H. S., Egner, A. N., Knight, M. F., Perelman, P. F., Schneider, B. J., & Garvin, J. S. (1970). Training consulting teachers to assist elementary teachers in the management and education of handicapped children. *Exceptional Children, 37,* 137–143. [4]

McKowen, C. (1979). *Get your A out of college.* Los Altos, CA: William Kaufman. [6]

McLoughlin, J. A., & Lewis, R. B. (1994). *Assessing special students* (4th ed.). New York: Merrill/Macmillan. [1, 3, 4]

McNeil, J. D. (1992). *Reading comprehension: New directions for classroom practice* (3rd ed.). New York: HarperCollins. [5, 6]

McWilliams, L. & Rakes, T.A. (1979). *Content reading inventories: English, social studies, science.* Dubuque, IA: Kendall/Hunt. [10]

Meese, R. L., Overton, T., & Whitfield, P. (1994). *Teaching learners with mild disabilities: Integrating research and practice.* Pacific Grove, CA: Brooks/Cole. [8]

Meichenbaum, D. (1986). Cognitive-behavior modification. In F. H. Kanfer & A. P. Goldstein (Eds.), *Helping people change: A textbook of methods* (3rd ed.), (pp. 346–380). New York: Pergamon. [4]

Meltzer, L. J. (Ed.) (1993). *Strategy assessment and instruction for students with learning disabilities: From theory to practice.* Austin, TX: Pro-Ed. [10]

Mercer, C. D. (1992). *Students with learning disabilities* (4th ed.). New York: Merrill/Macmillan. [8]

Mercer, C. D., King-Sears, P., & Mercer, A. R. (1990). Learning disabilities definitions and criteria used by state education departments. *Learning Disability Quarterly, 13* (2), 141–152. [1]

Mercer, C. D. & Mercer, A. R. (1993) *Teaching students with learning problems* (4th ed.). New York: Merrill/Macmillan. [2–4, 6, 8]

Meyer, C. A. (1992). What's the difference between authentic and performance assessment? *Educational Leadership, 49* (8), 39–40. [1]

Michael, R. J., & Trippi, J. A. (1987). Educators' views of procedures for grading mainstreamed handicapped children. *Education, 107,* 276–278. [3]

Miller, L. J. (1990). Tips for analyzing spelling errors. *Diagnostique, 16* (1), 38–40. [8]

Miller, L. J., & Beattie, J. (1992). Problem solving: Line up a plan. *Teaching Exceptional Children, 24* (4), 54–55. [9]

Miller, L. J., Choate, J. S., & Rakes, T. A. (1993). Spelling and handwriting: Tools for written communication. In J. Choate (Ed.), *Successful mainstreaming: Proven ways to detect and correct special needs* (pp. 210–243). Boston: Allyn and Bacon. [8]

Mills, H., O'Keefe, T., & Stephens, D. (1992). *Looking closely: Exploring the role of phonics in one whole language classroom.* Urbana, IL: National Council of Teachers of English. [1]

Milone, M. N., & Wasylyk, T. M. (1981). Handwriting in special education. *Teaching Exceptional Children, 2,* 58–61. [8]

Milone, M. N., & Wasylyk, T. M. (1984). Handwriting in special education. In W. B. Barbe, V. H. Lucas, and T. M. Wasylyk (Eds.), *Handwriting: Basic skills for effective communication.* Columbus, OH: Zaner-Bloser. [8]

Montague, M., & Fonseca, F. (1993). Using computers to improve story writing. *Exceptional Children, 25* (4), 46–49. [7]

Mooney, R. L. (1950). *Mooney problem check list.* New York: Psychological Corp. [1]

Moore, D. W., & Moore, S. A. (1992). Possible sentences: An update. In E. K. Dishner, T. W. Bean, J. E. Readence, & D. W. Moore, *Reading in the content areas: Improving classroom instruction* (3rd ed., pp. 196–202). Dubuque, IO: Kendall/Hunt. [6]

Morsink, C. V. (1989). *Teaching special needs students in regular classrooms* (2nd ed.). Boston: Little Brown. [8, 10]

Morsink, C. V., Thomas, C. C. & Correa, V. I. (1991). *Interactive teaming: Consultation and collaboration in special programs.* New York: Macmillan. [3]

Mosenthal, P.B. (1988). Prescription, description, and prediction in reading research. *Reading Teacher, 42,* 152–153. [10]

Myklebust, H. R. (1981). *The pupil rating scale—Revised.* New York: Grune & Stratton. [1]

Naisbitt, J. (1982). *Megatrends.* New York: Warner Books. [1]

Naisbitt, J., & Aburdene, P. (1990). *Megatrends 2000: Ten new directions for the 1990s.* New York: William Morrow. [1]

National Crisis Prevention Institute (1989). *Nonviolent crisis intervention for the educator* (Vols. I, II, III). Brookfield, WI: Author. [4]

Newcomer, P. L., Barenbaum, E. M., & Nodine, B. F. (1988). Comparison of the story production of LD, normal-achieving, and low-achieving children under two modes of production. *Learning Disability Quarterly, 11,* 82–96. [7]

Newland, E. (1959). *Handwriting demons.* New York: Nobel & Nobel. [8]

NICHCY (1993). Transition summary. *NICHCY (National Information Center for Children and Youth with Disabilities), 3* (1), 1–27. [1]

Nickerson, R.S. (1984). Kinds of thinking taught in current programs. *Educational Leadership, 42,* 26–36. [10]

Niedermeyer, F. (1973). Kindergarteners learn to write. *Elementary School Journal, 74,* 130–135. [8]

Nihira, K., Lambert, N., & Leland, H. (1993). *AAMR Adaptive Behavior Scales—School Edition* (2nd ed.). Austin, TX: Pro-Ed. [1]

Nolet, V. (1992). Classroom-based measurement and portfolio assessment. *Diagnostique, 18* (1), 5–26. [3]

Norton, D. E. (1993). *The effective teaching of language arts* (4th ed.). New York: Merrill/Macmillan. [8]

Nunnally, J. C. (1967). *Psychometric theory.* New York: McGraw-Hill. [1]

O'Connor, N. M., & Rotatori, A. F. (1987). Culturally diverse special education students. In A. Rotatori, M. Banbury, & R. A. Fox (Eds.), *Issues in special education* (pp. 66–77). Mountain View, CA: Mayfield. [1]

O'Neil, J. (1993). Can national standards make a difference? *Educational Leadership, 50* (5), 4–8. [2]

Office of Technology, U. S. Congress (1992). *Testing in American schools: Asking the right questions* (OTA-SET-519). Washington, DC: U.S. Government Printing Office (ED340–770). [3]

Oliva, P. F. (1992). *Developing the curriculum* (3rd ed.). New York: HarperCollins. [2]

Oritz, A. A., & Wilkinson, C. Y. (1991). Assessment and intervention model for the bilingual exceptional student. *Teacher Education and Special Education, 14* (1), 35–42. [1]

Ostrow, A. C. (1992). *Directory of psychological tests in the sport and exercise sciences.* Morgantown, WV: Fitness Information Technology. [1]

Owens, D. T. (Ed.) (1993). *Research ideas for the classroom: Middle grades mathematics* (National Council of Teachers of Mathematics Research Interpretation Project). New York: Macmillan. [9]

Palincsar, A. S., Ransom, K. (1988). From the mystery spot to the thoughtful spot: The instruction of metacognitive strategies. *Reading Teacher, 41,* 784–789. [6]

Palmer, B. C., Hafner, M. L., & Sharp, M. F. (1994). *Developing cultural literacy through the writing process: Empowering all learners.* Boston: Allyn and Bacon. [10]

Panchyshyn, R., & Monroe, E. E. (1986). *Developing key concepts for solving word problems.* Barnell Loft. [9]

Paris, S. G., Calfee, R. C., Filby, N., Hiebert, E. H., Pearson, P. D., Valencia, S. W., & Wolf, K. P. (1992). A framework for authentic literacy assessment. *Reading Teacher, 46* (2), 88–94. [6]

Parker, H. C. (1992). *The ADD hyperactivity handbook for schools.* Plantation, FL: Impact Publications. [4]

Parker, R., Tindal, G., & Hasbrouck, J. (1991). Countable indices of writing quality: Their suitability for screening-eligibility decisions. *Exceptionality, 2,* 1–17. [7]

Patton, J. M. (1992). Assessment and identification of African-American learners with gifts and talents. *Exceptional Children, 59* (2), 150–159. [1]

Pearson, P.D. (1982). A context for instructional research and reading comprehension. Urbana, Ill: University of Illinois Center for the Study of Reading, Technical Report No. 230. [10]

Pearson, P. D., & Dole, J. A. (1987). Explicit comprehension instruction: A review of research and a new conceptualization of instruction. *Elementary School Journal, 88,* 151–166. [6]

Perrin, J. (1990). The learning styles project for potential dropouts. *Educational Leadership, 48,* 23–24. [10]

Phelps J., & Stempel, L. (1987). Revisiting an "R"—news and views of writing. *Reading Improvement.* (ED 292-282) 2–11. [8]

Pierce, L. V., & O'Malley, J. M. (1992). *Performance and portfolio assessment for language minority students.* Washington, DC: National Clearinghouse for Bilingual Education. [10]

Polloway, E. A. & Patton, J. R. (1993). *Strategies for teaching learners with special needs* (5th ed.). New York: Merrill/Macmillan. [2–5, 8, 10]

Polloway, E. A., Patton, J. R., Epstein, M. H., & Smith, T. E. D. (1993). Comprehensive curriculum for students with mild disabilities. In E. L. Meyen, G. A. Vergason, & R. J. Whelan (Eds.), *Educating students with mild disabilities* (pp. 255–272). Denver: Love. [1]

Polloway, E. A., & Smith, T. E. (1992). *Language instruction for students with disabilities* (2nd ed.). Denver, CO: Love. [8]

Polya, G. (1957). *How to solve it.* Englewood Cliffs, NJ: Prentice-Hall. [10]

Popham, W. J. (1985). Measurement-driven instruction: It's on the road. *Phi Delta Kappan, 66,* 628–629. [1]

Poteet, J. A. (1973). *Behavior modification: A practical guide for teachers.* Muncie, IN: Allen House. [4]

Poteet, J. A. (1979). Characteristics of written expression of learning disabled and non-learning disabled elementary school students. *Diagnostique, 4,* 60–74. [7]

Poteet, J. A. (1980). Informal assessment of written expression. *Learning Disability Quarterly, 3,* 88–98. [1, 7]

Poteet, J. A., Choate, J. S., & Stewart, S. C. (1993). Performance assessment and special education: Practices and prospects. *Focus on Exceptional Children, 26* (1), 1–20. [1–3]

Potter, M. L., & Wamre, H. M. (1990). Curriculum-based measurement and developmental reading models: Opportunities for cross-validation. *Exceptional Children, 57,* 16–26. [6]

Pressley, M., Burkell, J., Cariglia-Bull, L., McGoldrick, J. A., Schneider, B., Snyder, B. L., Symons, S., & Woloshyn, V. E. (1990). *Cognitive strategy instruction that really improves children's academic performance.* Cambridge, MA: Brookline Books. [3, 8, 10]

Pressley, M., & Harris, K. R. (1990). What we really know about strategy instruction. *Educational Leadership, 48* (10), 31–34. [6, 10]

Pugach, M. C., & Warger, C. L. (1993). Curriculum considerations. In J. I. Goodlad & T. C. Lovitt (Eds.), *Integrating general and special education* (pp. 125–148). New York: Merrill/Macmillan. [2]

Pugach, M. C., & Wesson, C. (1990). Supporting the participation of exceptional students in today's classrooms. In E. L. Meyen (Ed.), *Exceptional children in today's schools.* (2nd ed.). Denver, CO: Love. [3]

Putnam, Rynders, Johnson, & Johnson (1989). Collaborative skill instruction for promoting positive interactions between mentally handicapped and non-handicapped children. *Exceptional Children, 55,* 550–557. [4]

Radabaugh, M. T., & Yukish, J. F. (1982). *Curriculum and methods for mildly handicapped.* Boston: Allyn and Bacon. [8]

Rainforth, B., York, J., & Macdonald, C. (1992). *Collaborative teams for students with severe disabilities: Integrating therapy and educational services.* Baltimore: Paul H. Brookes. [1]

Rakes, T. A. (1973). Drill me, skill me, but please let me read. *Elementary English, 50,* 451–453. [6]

Rakes, T. A. (1984). Suggested intervention strategies for reading comprehension. *Florida Reading Quarterly, 3,* 36–38. [6]

Rakes, T. A. & Chance, L. H. (1990). A survey of how readers think they remember what they read. *Journal of Reading Improvement, 27,* 122–128. [6]

Rakes, T. A., & Choate, J. S. (1989). *Language arts: Detecting and correcting special needs.* Boston: Allyn and Bacon. [5]

Rakes, T. A. & Choate, J. S. (1990) *Science and health: Detecting and correcting special needs.* Boston: Allyn and Bacon. [10]

Rakes, T. A. & Smith, L. J. (1992) Assessing reading skills in the content areas, In E. K. Dishner, T. W. Bean, J. E. Readence, & D. W. Moore (Eds.), *Reading in the content areas: Improving classroom instruction* (3rd ed.). Dubuque, IA: Kendall/ Hunt. [10]

Raphael, T. E. (1982). Question-answering strategies for children. *Reading Teacher, 36,* 186–190. [6]

Raphael, T. E. (1986). Teaching question-answer relationships, revisited. *Reading Teacher, 39,* 516–522. [6]

Readence, J. E. & Searfoss, L. W. (1992). Teaching strategies for vocabulary development. In E. K. Dishner, T. W. Bean, J. E. Readence, & D. W. Moore (Eds.), *Reading in the content areas: Improving classroom instruction* (3rd ed.). Dubuque, IA: Kendall/Hunt. [10]

Reid, D. K. (1988). *Teaching the learning disabled: A cognitive developmental approach.* Boston: Allyn and Bacon. [8]

Reith, H., Axelrod, S., Anderson, R., Hathaway, R., & Fitzgerald, C. (1974). The influence of distributed practice on weekly spelling tests. *Journal of Educational Research, 68,* 73–77. [8]

Reutzel, D. R. (1986). Clozing in on comprehension: The cloze story map. *Reading Teacher, 39,* 524–528. [6]

Reynolds, M. C. (1990). Educating teachers for special education students. In W. R. Houston (Ed.), *Handbook of research on teacher education* (pp. 423–436). New York: Macmillan. [2, 4]

Richards, J. C. (1993). Using games to help young and at-risk children respond to story characters. *The Reading Teacher, 47* (2), 170–171. [6]

Richek, M. A., List, L. K., & Lerner, J. W. (1989). *Reading problems: Assessment and teaching strategies,* (2nd ed). Englewood Cliffs, NJ: Prentice-Hall. [5]

Rinsky, L. A. (1993). *Teaching word attack skills* (5th ed.). Dubuque, IA: Gorsuch Scarisbrick. [5]

Rivers, D. M., & Bryant, B. R. (1992). Mathematics instruction for students with special needs. *Intervention in School and Clinic, 28* (2), 71–86. [9]

Robinson, F. P. (1961). *Effective study.* New York: Harper & Row. [10]

Roditi, B. (1993). Mathematics assessment and strategy instruction: An applied developmental approach. In L. J. Meltzer (Ed.), *Strategy assessment and instruction for students with learning disabilities: From theory to practice* (pp. 293–320. Austin, TX: Pro-Ed. [10]

Roe, M. F. (1992). Reading strategy instruction: Complexities and possibilities in middle school. *Journal of Reading, 36* (3), 190–196. [10]

Roe, B. D., Stoodt, B. D., & Burns, P. C. (1991). *Secondary school reading instruction: The content areas* (4th. ed.). Boston: Houghton Mifflin. [10]

Rogers, D. B. (1984). Assessing study skills. *Journal of Reading, 26,* 353–354. [10]

Rosenberg, M. S., Wilson, R. J., Maheady, L., & Sindelar, P. T. (1992). *Educating students with behavior disorders.* Boston: Allyn and Bacon. [3]

Royer, J. M., Greene, B. A., & Sinatra, G. M. (1987). The sentence verification technique: A practical procedure for testing comprehension. *Journal of Reading, 30,* 414–422. [6]

Rubin, D. (1994). *A practical approach to teaching reading* (2nd ed.). Boston: Allyn and Bacon. [5]

Rudell, M. R. (1993). *Teaching content reading and writing.* Boston: Allyn and Bacon. [10]

Rupley, W. H., & Blair, T. R. (1989). *Reading diagnosis and remediation* (3rd ed.). Boston: Houghton-Mifflin. [6]

Rusch, F. R., Destefano, L., Chadsey-Rusch, J., Phelps, L. A., & Szymanski, E. (1992). *Transition from school to adult life: Models, linkages, and policy.* Sycamore, IL: Sycamore. [1]

Ryder, R. J., & Graves, M. F. (1994). *Reading and learning in content areas.* New York: Merrill/Macmillan. [10]

Sabornie, E. J., & Beard, G. H. (1990). Teaching social skills to students with mild handicaps. *Teaching Exceptional Children, 23* (1), 35–38. [4]

Sachs, A. (1983). The effects of three prereading activities on learning disabled students' reading comprehension. *Learning Disability Quarterly, 6,* 248–251. [6]

Salend, S. J. (1994). *Effective mainstreaming: Creating inclusive classrooms* (2nd ed.). New York: Macmillan. [3, 8]

Salvia, J., & Hughes, C. (1990). *Curriculum-based assessment: Testing what is taught.* New York: Macmillan. [1, 3, 11]

Salvia, J., & Ysseldyke, J. E. (1995). *Assessment* (6th ed.). Boston: Houghton Mifflin. [1, 3]

Samuels, S. J. (1976). Automatic decoding and reading comprehension. *Language Arts, 53,* 323–325. [5]

Samuels, S. J. (1988). Decoding and automaticity: Helping poor readers become automatic at word recognition. *Reading Teacher, 41,* 756–760. [5]

Sanders, N. M. (1966). *Classroom questions—What kinds?* New York: Harper & Row. [6]

Sawyer, R. J., & Zantal-Wiener, K.(1993). Emerging trends in technology for students with disabilities. *Teaching Exceptional Children, 26,* (1), 70–77. [10]

Schell, L.M. (1988). Dilemmas in assessing reading comprehension. *Reading Teacher, 42,* 12–16. [6]

Schlenger, S., & Roesch, R. (1990). *How to be organized in spite of yourself.* New York: Penguin/Signet. [11]

Schloss, P. J., Smith, M. A., & Schloss, C. N. (1990). *Instructional methods for adolescents with learning and behavior problems.* Boston: Allyn and Bacon. [3]

Schubert, W. H. (1993). Curriculum reform. In G. Cawelti (Ed.), *Challenges and achievements of American education: The 1993 yearbook of the Association for Supervision and Curriculum Development* (pp. 80–115). Alexandria, VA: ASCD. [2]

Schulz, J. B., & Carpenter, C. D. (1995). *Mainstreaming exceptional students: A guide for classroom teachers* (4th ed.). Boston: Allyn and Bacon. [2–4, 10]

Schumaker, J. B. & Deshler, D. D. (1988). Implementing the regular education initiative in secondary schools: A different ball game. *Journal of Learning Disabilities, 21,* 36–42. [10]

Schumaker, J. B., & Hazel, J. S. (1984a). Social skills assessment and training for the learning disabled: Who's on first and what's on second? Part 1. *Journal of Learning Disabilities, 17,* 422–431. [4]

Schumaker, J. B., & Hazel, J. S. (1984b). Social skills assessment and training for the learning disabled:

Who's on first and what's on second? Part II. *Journal of Learning Disabilities, 17,* 492–499. [4]

Schumaker, J. B., Nolan, S. M., & Deshler, D. D. (1985). *The error monitoring strategy.* Lawrence, KS: The University of Kansas. [7]

Schumm, J. S., Vaughn, S., & Leavell, A. G. (1994). Planning pyramid: A framework for planning for diverse student needs during content area instruction. *Reading Teacher, 47* (8), 608–615. [10]

Schworm, R. W. (1988). Look in the middle of the word. *Teaching Exceptional Children, 20* (3), 13–17. [5]

Scruggs, T. E., & Mastropieri, M. A. (1992). *Teaching test-taking skills: Helping students show what they know.* Cambridge, MA: Brookline. [10]

Scruggs, T. E., Mastropieri, M. A., McLoone, B. B. & Levin, J. R. (1987). Mnemonic facilitation of LD students' recall of facts from expository prose. *Journal of Educational Psychology, 79,* 27–34. [10]

Searfoss, L. W., & Readence, J. E. (1994). *Helping children learn to read* (3rd ed.). Boston: Allyn and Bacon. [5, 6]

Shapiro, E. S., & Derr, T. F. (1990). Curriculum-based assessment. In T. B. Gutkin & C. R. Reynolds (Eds.), *The Handbook of school psychology* (pp. 365–386). New York: John Wiley. [1, 3, 11]

Shea, T. M., & Bauer, A. M. (1991). *Parents and teachers of children with exceptionalities: A handbook for collaboration* (2nd ed.). Boston: Allyn and Bacon. [3]

Shepard, L. A., & Smith, M. L. (1990). Synthesis of research on grade retention. *Educational Leadership, 47* (8), 84–88. [3]

Sheridan, M. E. (1981). Theories of reading and implications for teachers. *Reading Horizons, 22,* 66–71. [6]

Shinn, M. R. (1989a). Case study of Ann H.: From referral to annual review. In M. R. Shinn (Ed.), *Curriculum-based measurement: Assessing special children* (pp. 79–89). New York: Guilford. [1]

Shinn, M. R. (1989b). Identifying and defining academic problems. CBM screening and eligibility procedures. In M. R. Shinn (Ed.), *Curriculum-based measurement: Assessing special children* (pp. 90–129). New York: Guilford. [1, 11]

Shinn, M. R. (Ed.) (1989c) *Curriculum-based measurement: Assessing special children.* New York: Guilford. [3, 11]

Shinn, M., & Marston, D. (1985). Differentiating mildly handicapped, low-achieving, and regular education students: A curriculum-based approach. *Remedial and Special Education, 6* (2), 31–38. [1]

Shrag, J., & Burnette, J. (1994). Inclusive schools. *Teaching Exceptional Children, 26* (3), 64–68. [2]

Shriner, J. G., Ysseldyke, J. E., & Thurlow, M. L. (1994). Standards for all American students. *Focus on Exceptional Children, 26* (5), 1–20, [2]

Siccone, F., & Canfield, J. (1993). *101 ways to develop student self-esteem and responsibility, Volume II: The power to succeed in school and beyond.* Boston: Allyn and Bacon. [4]

Silbert, J., Carnine, D., & Stein, M. (1990). *Direct instruction mathematics.* Columbus, OH: Charles E. Merrill. [9]

Silvaroli, N. J. (1994). *Classroom reading inventory* (7th ed.). Dubuque, IA: Brown/Benchmark. [6]

Sinatra, R. C., Berg, D., & Dunn, R. (1985). Semantic mapping improves reading comprehension of learning disabled students. *Teaching Exceptional Children, 17,* 310–314. [6]

Singer, H. & Dolan, D. (1980). *Reading and learning from text.* Boston: Little Brown. [10]

Slavin, R. E. (1991). Synthesis of research on cooperative learning. *Educational Leadership, 48* (5), 71–82. [3, 4]

Slavin, R. E., Madden, N. A., Dolan, L. J., Wasik, B. A., Ross, S. M., & Smith, L. J. (1994). Whenever and wherever we choose: The replication of Success for All. *Phi Delta Kappan, 75* (8), 639–647. [6]

Smey-Richman, B. (1988). *Involvement in learning for low-achieving students.* Philadelphia: Research for Better Schools, 19–23. [10]

Smith, C. R. (1994). *Learning disabilities: The interaction of learner, task, and setting* (3rd ed.). Boston: Allyn and Bacon. [4, 10]

Smith, L. J. & Smith, D. L. (1990) *Social studies: Detecting and correcting special needs.* Boston: Allyn and Bacon. [10]

Smith, T. E., Finn, D. M., & Dowdy, C. A. (1993). *Teaching students with mild disabilities.* New York: Harcourt Brace Jovanovich. [8]

Snider, V. E. (1990). What we know about learning styles from research in special education. *Educational Leadership, 48* (2), 53. [3, 10]

Snider, V. E. (1992). Learning styles and learning to read. *Remedial and Special Education, 13* (1), 6–18. [3]

Sofge, A. (1975). Teacher made tapes provide auditory aids. *Pointer, 20,* 41–45. [8]

Spache, G. (1941). Validity and reliability of the proposed classification of spelling errors. *Journal of Educational Psychology, 31,* 204–214. [8]

Spache, G. D. (1981). *Diagnostic Reading Scales.* Monterey, CA: CTB/McGraw-Hill. [5, 6]

Spache, G. D., & Spache, E. B. (1986). *Reading in the elementary school* (5th ed.). Boston: Allyn and Bacon. [5]

Sparrow, S. S., Balla, D. A., & Cicchetti, D. V. (1985). *Vineland Adaptive Behavior Scales—Interview Edition.* Circle Pines, MN: American Guidance Service. [1]

Sparzo, F. J., & Poteet, J. A. (1989). *Classroom behavior: Detecting and correcting special problems.* Boston: Allyn and Bacon. [1, 3, 4]

Spekman, N. J., Herman, K. L., Vogel, S. A. (1993). Risk and resilience in individuals with learning disabilities: A challenge to the field. *Learning Disabilities Research and Practice, 8* (1), 59–65. [1]

Spikell, M. A. (1993). *Teaching mathematics with manipulatives: A resource of activities for the K–12 teacher.* Boston: Allyn and Bacon. [9]

Stevens, D. D., & Englert, C. S. (1993). Making writing strategies work. *Exceptional Children, 26* (1), 34–39. [7, 10]

Stowitschek, C. E., & Stowitschek, J. J. (1990). Error analysis in handwriting instruction. In R. A. Gable and J. M. Hendrickson (Eds.) *Assessing students with special needs: A sourcebook for analyzing and correcting errors in academics* (pp. 63–77). New York: Longman. [8]

Stowitschek, J. J., Gable, R. A., & Hendrickson, J. M. (1980). *Instructional methods for exceptional children: Selection, management, and adaptations.* Germantown, MD: Aspen. [1]

Stowitschek, J. J., Stowitschek, C. E., Hendrickson, J. M., & Day, R. M. (1984). *Direct teaching tactics for exceptional children: A practice and supervision guide.* Rockville, MD: Aspen. [1]

Sulzer, B., & Mayer, G. R. (1972). *Behavior modification procedures for school personnel.* Hinsdale, IL: Dryden Press. [4]

Swan, W. W., & Sirvis, B. (1992). The CEC common core of knowledge and skills essential for all beginning special education teachers. *Teaching Exceptional Children, 25* (1), 16–20. [1]

Swezey, R. W. (1981). *Individual performance assessment: An approach to criterion-referenced test development.* Reston, VA: Reston Publishing. [1]

Szubinski, G., & Enright, B. E. (1992). Problem solving: Organize the facts. *Teaching Exceptional Children, 24* (3), 58–59. [9]

Taba, H. (1967). *Teacher's handbook for elementary social studies.* Reading, MA: Addison-Wesley. [10]

Tadlock, D.F. (1978). SQ3R—Why it works, based on an information processing theory of learning. *Journal of Reading, 22,* 110–112. [10]

Taylor, R. L. (1993). *Assessment of exceptional students: Educational and psychological procedures* (3rd ed.). Boston: Allyn and Bacon. [1, 3–4, 7]

Taylor, W. (1957). Cloze procedure: A new tool for measuring readability. *Journalism Quarterly, 30,* 415–433. [6]

Test Collection, Educational Testing Service. (Serial dates). *The ETS test collection catalogue.* Phoenix, AZ: Onyx Publications. [1]

Texas Education Agency (1991). *Spelling instruction: A proper perspective.* Austin, TX: author. (ERIC Document Reproduction Service No. ED336752). [8]

Thomas, P. J., & Carmack, F. F. (1990). *Speech and language: Detecting and correcting special needs.* Boston: Allyn and Bacon. [5]

Thousand, J., & McNeil, M. (Eds.) (1990). Teaching teachers to teach strategies [Special issue]. *Teacher Education and Special Education, 13* (2). [1]

Thurber, D. N. (1993). How D'Nealian handwriting meets the needs of all writers. In G. Coon and G. Palmer (Eds.), *Handwriting research and information: An administrator's handbook* (pp. 50–61). Glenview, IL: Scott, Foresman. [8]

Thurber, D. N., & Jordan, D. R. (1991). *D'Nealian Handwriting* (2nd ed.). Glenview, IL: Scott, Foresman. [8]

Tiedt, S., & Tiedt, I. (1987). *Language arts activities for the classroom.* Boston: Allyn and Bacon. [8]

Tierney, R. J., & Pearson, D. P. (1983). Toward a composing model of reading. *Language Arts, 60,* 568–580. [6]

Tierney, R. J., Readence, J. E., & Dishner, E. K. (1990). *Reading strategies and practices: A compendium* (3rd ed.). Boston: Allyn and Bacon. [6, 10]

Tindal, G. A. (1989). Evaluating the effectiveness of educational programs at the systems level using curriculum-based measurement. In M. R. Shinn (Ed.), *Curriculum-based measurement: Assessing special children* (pp. 202–238). New York: Guilford Press. [1]

Tindal, G. A., & Marston, D. B. (1990). *Classroom-based assessment: Evaluating instructional outcomes.* Columbus, OH: Merrill. [1, 8, 10]

Tindal, G., & Parker, R. (1989). Assessment of written expression for students in compensatory and special education programs. *Journal of Special Education, 23,* 169–183. [7]

Trachtenburg, P. (1990). Using children's literature to enhance phonics instruction. *Reading Teacher, 43,* 648–653. [5]

Tucker, J. A. (1985). Curriculum-based assessment: An introduction. *Exceptional Children. 52,* 199–204. [11]

Vacca, R. T., & Vacca, J. L. (1993). *Content area reading* (4th ed.). New York: HarperCollins. [6, 10]

Valencia, S. W., Hiebert, E. H., & Afflerbach, P. O. (Eds.) (1994). *Authentic reading assessment.* Newark, DE: International Reading Association. [6]

Vallecorsa, A. L., Zigmond, N., & Henderson, L. M. (1985). Spelling instruction in special education classrooms: A survey of practices. *Exceptional Children, 52,* 19–24. [8]

Van Acker, R. (1993). Dealing with conflict and aggression in the classroom: What do teachers need? *Teacher Education and Special Education, 16* (1), 23–33. [4]

Vargas, J. S. (1977). *Behavioral psychology for teachers.* New York: Harper & Row. [4]

Venezky, R. L. (1992). Textbooks in school and society. In P. W. Jackson (Ed.), *Handbook of research on curriculum: A project of the American Educational Research Association* (pp. 363–401). New York: Macmillan. [2]

Vergason, G. A., & Anderegg, M. L. (1991). Beyond the regular education initiative and the resource room controversy. *Focus on Exceptional Children, 23* (7), 1–7. [3]

Vineyard, E. E., & Massey, H. W. (1957). The interrelationship of certain linguistic skills and their relationship with scholastic achievement when intelligence is ruled constant. *Journal of Education Psychology, 48,* 279–286. [6]

Viechnicki, K. J., Barbour, N., Shaklee, B., Rohrer, J., & Ambrose, R. (1993–1994). The impact of portfolio assessment on teacher classroom activities. *Journal of Teacher Education, 44* (5), 371–377. [3]

Vygotsky, L. S. (1978). *Mind in society.* (Cole, M., Bteiner, V. J., Scribner, S., & Tauberman, E.) (Trans.) Cambridge, MA: Harvard University Press. [6]

Vygotsky, L. S. (1981). The genesis of higher mental functions. In *The concept of activity in Soviet psychology* (pp. 144–255). Armonk, NY: M. E. Sharpe. [6]

Wade, S. E. (1990). Using think alouds to assess comprehension. *Reading Teacher, 43,* 442–451. [6]

Wade, S. E., Trathen, W. & Schraw, G. (1990). An analysis of spontaneous study strategies. *The Reading Research Quarterly, 25,* 147–166. [10]

Walberg, H. J. (1990). Productive teaching and instruction: Assessing the knowledge base. *Phi Delta Kappan, 7,* 470–478. [3, 8]

Walker, J. E., & Shea, T. M. (1991). *Behavior management: A practical approach for educators* (5th ed.). New York: Merrill/Macmillan. [3, 4]

Walker, S. C., & Bruno, R. M. (1992). Essential skills in diagnosis and assessment for beginning teachers. *Diagnostique, 17* (2), 95–107. [1]

Walmsley, S. A., & Adams, E. L. (1993). Realities of "whole language." *Language Arts, 70* (4), 272–280. [1]

Wang, M. C., Haertel, G. D., & Walberg, H. J. (1993–1994). What helps students learn? *Educational Leadership, 51* (4), 74–79. [3, 4]

Wang, Z. W., & Willoughby, T. L. (1991). An approach to simulate understanding student problem-solving behavior. *Journal of Computers in Mathematics and Science Teaching, 10* (4), 75–87. [9]

Wasylyk, T. M. (1984). The manuscript alphabet. In W. B. Barbe, V. H. Lucas, & T. M. Wasylyk (Eds.). *Handwriting: Basic skills for effective communication* (pp. 86–90). Columbus, OH: Zaner-Bloser. [8]

Weber, A. (1990). Linking ITIP and the writing process. *Educational Leadership, 47* (5), 35–39. [7]

Weinstein, C. E., & Mayer, R. E. (1986). The teaching of learning strategies. In M. Wittrock (Ed.), *Handbook of research on teaching* (3rd ed.) (pp. 315–327). New York: Macmillan. [3]

Wertsch, J. V. (1985). *Vygotsky and the social formation of mind.* New York: Harvard University Press. [6]

West, R. P., Young, K. R., & Spooner, F. (1990). Precision teaching: An introduction. *Teaching Exceptional Children, 22* (3), 4–9. [3]

Westby, C. E. (1993). Whole language and learners with mild handicaps. In E. L. Meyen, G. A. Vergason, & R. J. Whelan (Eds.), *Educating students with mild disabilities* (pp. 273–294). Denver: Love. [1]

Westerman, G. (1971). *Spelling and writing.* San Raefael, CA: Dimensions. [8]

Whimbey, A. (1984). The key to higher order thinking is precise processing. *Educational Leadership, 41,* 66–70. [10]

White, W. J. (1992). The postschool adjustment of persons with learning disabilities: Current status and future projections. *Journal of Learning Disabilities, 25* (7), 448–456. [1]

Whitman, T. L. (1987). Self-instruction, individual differences, and mental retardation. *American Journal of Mental deficiency, 92* (2), 213-223. [4]

Will, M. C. (1986). Educating children with learning problems: A shared responsibility. *Exceptional Children, 52,* 411–415. [1, 3, 11]

Willis, S. (1993a). Are letter grades obsolete? *ASCD Update, 35* (7), 1, 4, 8. [3]

Willis, S. (1993b). Helping students resolve conflict. *ASCD Update, 35* (10), 4–5, 8. [4]

Wilson, R. M., & Cleland, C. J. (1989). *Diagnostic and remedial reading for classroom and clinic* (6th ed.). Columbus, OH: Charles E. Merrill. [5, 6]

Wixson, K. K., Bosky, A. B., Yochum, M. N., & Alverman, D. E. (1984). An interview for assessing student's perceptions of classroom reading tasks. *Reading Teacher, 37,* 346–352. [10]

Wolery, M., Bailey Jr., D. B., & Sugai, G. M. (1988). *Effective teaching: Principles and procedures of applied behavior analysis with exceptional students.* Boston: Allyn and Bacon. [1]

Wong, B. Y. L., Wong, R., & Blenkinsop, J. (1989). Cognitive and metacognitive aspects of learning disabled adolescents' composing problems. *Learning Disability Quarterly, 12,* 300–322. [7]

Wood, J. W. (1992). *Adapting instruction for mainstreamed and at-risk students* (2nd ed.). New York: Merrill/Macmillan [3, 8]

Wood, J. W. (1993). *Mainstreaming: A practical approach for teachers* (2nd ed.). New York: Macmillan. [3, 8]

Woodcock, R. W. (1987). *Woodcock reading mastery tests—Revised.* Circle Pines, MN: American Guidance Service. [5, 6]

Woodcock, R. W., & Johnson, M. B. (1989). *Woodcock-Johnson Psycho-educational Battery—Revised.* Allen, TX: DLM Teaching Resources. [5]

York, J., Doyle, M. B., & Kronberg, R. (1992). A curriculum development process for inclusive classrooms. *Focus on Exceptional Children, 25* (4), 1–16. [2]

Ysseldyke, J. E., & Algozzine, B. (1995). *Introduction to special education* (3rd ed.). Boston: Houghton Mifflin. [3]

Ysseldyke, J. E., & Christenson, S. L. (1993). *The Instructional Environment System—II.* Longmont, CO: Sopris West. [3, 4]

Ysseldyke, J. E., Thurlow, M. L., & Shriner, J. G. (1992). Outcomes are for special educators too. *Teaching Exceptional Children, 25* (1), 36–50. [1–3]

Zabrucky, K. & Moore D. (1989). Children's ability to use three standards to evaluate their comprehension of text. *Reading Research Quarterly, 24,* 336–352. [6]

Zaner-Bloser Evaluation Scales. (1984). Columbus, OH: Zaner-Bloser. [8]

Zaner-Bloser Handwriting: A way to self-expression. (1993). Columbus, OH: Zaner-Bloser. [8]

Zigmond, N., Vallecorsa, A., & Silverman, R. (1983). *Assessment for instructional planning in special education.* Englewood Cliffs, NJ: Prentice-Hall. [3]

Zucker, C. (1993). Using whole language with students who have language and learning disabilities. *The Reading Teacher, 46* (8), 660–670. [6]

INDEX

ABOUT THE AUTHORS

Each member of the author team is active at the national level in the Council for Educational Diagnostic Services; four are past presidents. They have collaborated professionally for the past fifteen years. In addition to their extensive involvement in the field of assessment and programming, each author has researched and written about a specific academic subject area. All the authors are experienced teachers of general and special education classes at the elementary, secondary, and university level.

JOYCE S. CHOATE, Professor of Curriculum and Instruction at Northeast Louisiana University, holds the Ed.D. from Memphis State University. Her teaching experiences have ranged from the preschool to the graduate levels in both general and special education; she also has been an educational diagnostician and reading specialist. She is editor and contributing author of *Successful Mainstreaming: Proven Ways to Detect and Correct Special Needs,* consulting editor for the *Allyn and Bacon Detecting and Correcting Series,* and co-author of the language arts, reading, and science books in that series as well as a reading diagnosis text. Dr. Choate has presented numerous papers on assessment and prescriptive teaching at state and national conferences. Former President of the Council for Educational Diagnostic Services, she is currently Publications Chairperson and serves on the editorial boards of *Teaching Exceptional Children* and *Diagnostique.*

BRIAN E. ENRIGHT holds the Ed.D. from the University of Alabama and is presently Associate Professor of Specialty Studies at the University of North Carolina at Charlotte as well as Director, National Training Network. He has taught a variety of courses in educational assessment, prescriptive teaching, and research design and formerly taught at the elementary, middle, and secondary school levels. He is perhaps best known for his publications in the area of mathematics, which include a test, more than 30 books, and *Basic Mathematics: Detecting and Correcting Special Needs.* A popular consultant, Dr. Enright typically conducts over 50 inservice workshops each year and regularly presents papers at professional conferences. Among his professional activities are service as an associate editor of *Childhood Education, Diagnostique,* and *Behavior Disorders,* and a field editor and special column editor for *Teaching Exceptional Children.* He has also served as an officer of several national education boards and is former President of the Council for Educational Diagnostic Services.

LAMOINE J. MILLER has three decades of experience as an educator, researcher, author, and consultant. He holds the Ed.D. from the University of Kansas in Special Education and is presently Professor and Coordinator of the Special Education Programs at Northeast Louisiana University. His extensive experiences have ranged from elementary to graduate levels in both general and special education. He has also been a school psychologist and learning disabilities teacher. His research and writing have focused primarily on spelling and handwriting, and he has presented numerous papers at state and national conferences in these areas as well as on classroom management, assessment, and prescriptive teaching. Dr. Miller is Editor of *CEDS Communiqué,* an editorial board member for *Diagnostique,* has served on the executive board of the Council for Educational Diagnostic Services in several positions, including Treasurer and President, and is currently CEDS Governor.

JAMES A. POTEET, Professor of Special Education at Ball State University, holds the Ph.D. in Special Education from Purdue University. In addition to teaching assessment and special education courses, he has served as a school psychologist and taught at the elementary level as well as classes for the

499

behavior disordered. A charter member of the Council for Educational Diagnostic Services, he has co-edited a monograph on assessment and has served on the executive board in a variety of roles including Publications Chair, Governor, and President for that organization. Dr. Poteet has published articles on assessment practices, conducted workshops, and served on the editorial board of a number of professional journals, including *Diagnostique.* He is also co-author of *Classroom Behavior: Detecting and Correcting Special Problems,* and author of texts on behavior modification and educational evaluation in special education.

THOMAS A. RAKES has more than two decades of experience as an educator, researcher, author, and consultant. He holds the Ed.D. from the University of Tennessee and is presently Professor of Education and Director of Educational Research and Development at the University of Memphis. In addition to the graduate and undergraduate courses he teaches, his experiences have included directing a university diagnostic center and teaching at the middle school, secondary, and adult education levels. A prolific writer, he is the author of almost 100 professional articles, several book chapters, co-author of *Language Arts: Detecting and Correcting Special Needs, Reading: Detecting and Correcting Special Needs,* and *Science and Health: Detecting and Correcting Special Needs,* two reading diagnosis texts and a series of worktexts. Dr. Rakes is a frequent presenter at national and state conferences and has been a consultant for school districts, colleges, and businesses in 47 states. He has served on the advisory board for a major basal reading series and on the editorial board for several professional journals.